CASES
IN CONSUMER
BEHAVIOR

CASES
IN CONSUMER
BEHAVIOR

F. STEWART DEBRUICKER

University of Pennsylvania

SCOTT WARD

University of Pennsylvania

PRENTICE-HALL, INC., ENGLEWOOD CLIFFS, NEW JERSEY 07632

Library of Congress Cataloging in Publication Data

DeBruicker, F. Stewart.
   Cases in consumer behavior.

   Includes bibliographical references and index.
   1. Consumers—Case studies.   2. Marketing
   research—Case studies.   3. Motivation research
   (Marketing)—Case studies.   I. Ward, Scott, 1942–
   joint author.   II. Title.
HF5415.3.D42   658.8'34   79-17111
ISBN 0-13-118356-7

Editorial/production supervision and interior design
      by Barbara Alexander
Cover design by A Good Thing, Ink.
Manufacturing buyer: John Hall

Printed in the United States of America

10   9   8   7   6   5   4   3   2   1

PRENTICE-HALL INTERNATIONAL, INC., *London*
PRENTICE-HALL OF AUSTRALIA PTY. LIMITED, *Sydney*
PRENTICE-HALL OF CANADA, LTD., *Toronto*
PRENTICE-HALL OF INDIA PRIVATE LIMITED, *New Delhi*
PRENTICE-HALL OF JAPAN, INC., *Tokyo*
PRENTICE-HALL OF SOUTHEAST ASIA PTE. LTD., *Singapore*
WHITEHALL BOOKS LIMITED, *Wellington, New Zealand*

Contents

PART **III**

SPECIAL CONTEXTS FOR CONSUMER BEHAVIOR ANALYSIS

Preface

Ask any marketing manager if a thorough understanding of consumer behavior is a necessary condition for effective marketing strategy, and you will surely get a resounding "Yes." But the manager is probably responding to the generic definition of "consumer behavior," rather than to the *field of study* that attracts so many undergraduate and graduate business students. Careful interviewing probes will undoubtedly reveal that the practicing manager is only dimly aware of the *field* of consumer behavior; the manager might belong to the American Marketing Association but is unlikely to belong to the Association for Consumer Research. In the worst case, the manager may dismiss the whole field as a bunch of ivory tower research, not useful for practical decisions.

What has led to the academic-practitioner schism in this case? It is probably safe to say that growing numbers of practicing managers have been exposed to consumer behavior courses during the undergraduate or MBA study, but it is probably also safe to say that the course is not ranked among the most "relevant" that a manager will recall from his academic preparation.

To a certain extent, business students may expect too much from the consumer behavior field. In marketing—the functional field in which consumer behavior courses are most often located—students can learn the straightforward calculations for breakeven analysis and profit impact, and the functions performed by different types of wholesalers. They come to learn that marketing is some art and some science, but at least there are some firm definitions and guidelines. Consumer behavior, on the other hand, while imbued with some mystique owing to its roots in the promising-sounding "behavioral sciences," often confronts students with theories and concepts which are tediously applied to marketing problems, or a series of complex models which are

similarly difficult to apply. To the physics ma-
jors, the engineers, and the economics-trained
students who make up so many MBA classes,
consumer behavior may be a letdown indeed.

Judging from course outlines and contents
of major consumer behavior textbooks, our
point of view is that consumer behavior courses
are often seen as lacking in relevance because
of the difficulties involved in applying behavioral concepts of theories to specific marketing
problems, and because consumer behavior is
extraordinarily complex and situational in
nature, rendering theories or concepts, or
highly complex models, inadequate to the task
of specific application to specific marketing
problems. Most often, marketing management
decisions are based on analysis of the *interaction*
of factors underlying relevant consumer
behavior. Consequently, sequentially assessing
behavioral phenomena from perception and
motivation, through social and cultural influences, may provide a convenient, discipline-
based way to organize a course or a readings
book, but it is not the most useful way for an
aspiring manager to develop useful decision
skills.

Ray Bauer once said that "the problems of
managers are engineering problems, not behavioral ones." Just as engineers confront
problems inductively, rather than by trying to
deduce solutions from physical theories, we
believe students of marketing can learn more
from consumer behavior if they confront problems rather than simply learning theories and
then trying to apply them to problems. However, we anticipate that this casebook will often
be used with a consumer behavior text and/or
readings book. We urge students to avoid
treating these cases as exercises in identifying
aspects of management problems that can
merely be "labeled" with a concept or theory
from a reader or text. Rather, readers and texts
should help to provide frameworks and notions
of regularities in consumer behavior which can
be used to assess the complex, interacting
behavioral forces that underlie the management problems described in this book.

Cases in Consumer Behavior presents a series
of sixteen cases, each rooted in a practical problem in marketing management—from positioning a new dog food to promotional decisions for
a candidate for public office. The introductory
cases present problems of *Routine Purchasing
Behavior*. While the products are diverse—toys,
soft drinks, pantyhose, etc.—there are similarities in management strategies and behavioral notions pertinent to them. Goods and services that are purchased routinely are generally
lower in price, high in availability and advertising to sales ratios, and purchased relatively frequently and have cost and volume characteristics such that even small shifts in brand share
have strong profit impacts. Behaviorally,
routine purchases normally involve relatively
little prepurchase information seeking, and little economic risk to the consumer. Krugman's
"low involvement" notion would suggest that
these conditions and the mass-communications
environment in which people are exposed to
routinely purchased goods may result in attitude formation *following* purchase and usage.
Moreover, the concept of "evoked" set found
in most consumer behavior models portrays
decision making for routinely purchased goods
as stochastic, and the exact purchase probabilities for single brands within the evoked set
most difficult to assess.

Different sets of management and behavioral considerations characterize the second
grouping of cases in this book. *Extensive Problem-
Solving Purchasing Behavior* characterizes buying
for audio and video equipment, vacations, and
motorcycles. Managers are often dealing with
vastly different types of product lines, distribution characteristics, and promotional considerations. Behaviorally, consumers normally
take longer periods of time in making purchases, involving more word-of-mouth influence, extensive prepurchase information
seeking, and brand comparisons. Often, multiple family members are directly involved, while
they are usually not directly involved in
routinized purchases.

The final section of the book discusses
three cases that represent special contexts for
consumer behavior analysis. In these cases,

consumer behavior analysis is applied to non-profit and public policy contexts.

Three common threads link all the cases in this book. These commonalities reflect our desire to present students with management situations that involve important decisions in actual situations. First, the cases all represent situations in which it is crucial to understand how consumers behave, in order to select optimal marketing strategies. Second, every case contains some type of empirical information, based on data from qualitative research, field surveys, test markets, syndicated research services, or secondary data analysis. Finally, all the cases here are based on actual management situations. While some disguising of situations or data may have been necessary in some cases, these changes do not distort the situations.

Since this book is intended to provide a basis for class discussions, it is useful to review how these cases have been developed, and how students might go about preparing a case.

THE USE OF CASES IN MARKETING AND CONSUMER BEHAVIOR

The first step in case-writing activity is usually initiated by the faculty member, who perceives a need for a particular kind of case to fit into his or her overall conceptualizing in a course. In the Consumer Behavior and the Marketing Research courses that the authors have taught at Harvard and at Wharton, examples would be our development of a case to illustrate psychographics and multivariate analysis techniques for marketing strategy decisions (as in the Ocean Spray cases); another example is the development of a case to provide a basis for discussion of intrafamily consumer decisions, and children's influences on parental buying behavior (as in the Fisher-Price case).

Determining what particular companies or individuals should be contacted to develop cases in order to meet course needs often involves consulting relationships, former students, and ideas gleaned from the trade press. Once initial receptivity is obtained from the company or organization involved, the faculty member and a casewriter visit the personnel involved. Casewriters are normally MBA graduates who are pursuing doctoral degrees. Once a tentative outline of the case is agreed upon, the casewriter discusses the issues in detail with relevant personnel and studies documents, research, and so forth. A draft of the case is developed and is reviewed by management. The purpose of the review is to ensure accuracy and completeness, and to determine if some sensitive information should be disguised. As discussed earlier, disguises may be necessary due to some sensitive issues, but they do not significantly alter the original problem, nor compromise the learning objectives of the case.

While the situations are real, it must be kept in mind that cases present situations that are relatively "neatly packaged." In actual marketing situations, the manager's task is to sift through information that comes to his attention in various forms, in varying degrees of relevance, and, over time. Cases by definition do some of this distillation, but the student's task is still to prioritize the information in a case: What is important, what is less important? How does information interrelate in a way that will be helpful in designing creative solutions to problems? Corey also points out that cases lack reality in one final respect: while students are required in cases to make decisions, they do not have the responsibility for implementing their decisions.[*]

On the other hand, we have found cases to be exciting and effective teaching vehicles. Students are exposed to a great deal more context and detail than can normally be obtained via lectures or readings alone. We believe students come to see various problems of marketing management across the variety of situations in cases, thus developing a professional management skill.

---

[*] E. Raymond Corey, *Industrial Marketing: Cases and Concepts* (Englewood Cliffs, N.J.: Prentice-Hall, 1976).

Perhaps most importantly, the cases in this book are not organized in terms of a series of concepts or theories, as is often found in textbooks and readers in the field. As we have mentioned, we believe it is unrealistic to assume that any single concept, theory, or model in consumer behavior is adequate to the task of designing marketing strategies to solve complex marketing management problems. In each case in this book, students will find a variety of concepts and theories which can be brought to bear in problem analysis. Any one case might easily involve consumer perceptions, motivations, learning, attitudes, interpersonal influence and social class differences, and, perhaps, other concepts. The cases invite the student to explore how these factors interact among themselves and with other aspects of the management situation, and how understanding these interactions is necessary for designing effective solutions to problems.

PREPARING A CASE

While there is no *one* way to prepare a case, some observations based on our experience as case teachers over the last several years may be useful. We suggest that individuals first read briefly through an assigned case, simply to form an initial idea of what the key problems are, and what information is in the case that could be useful in designing recommendations.

A second reading should be much more thorough, underlining key facts and figures, isolating important influences—the basic types of information for analysis. Finally, a specific set of recommendations should be stated, and the student should be able to clearly articulate the analysis and reasoning that has led to these recommendations and, perhaps, not to other recommendations. Over time, students will see

the importance of asking the right questions, for it is only on the basis of adequate understanding of the problems and issues that truly compelling recommendations can be made.

Students should not be surprised to find that all the information one would like to have is not available. Management decisions frequently must be made on the basis of only those facts that are on hand at the time the decision must be made, and frequently these facts are not as complete as might be desired. The ability to make effective decisions in the face of some uncertainty is an essential executive skill. On the other hand, not all of the facts will be useful in every case. Another management skill is the ability to identify and concentrate on significant parts of problems and relevant information.

A final suggestion is to avoid trying to find "the answer" to a case. Because the situations described in the cases are complex and interrelated, there are usually a number of alternative possible solutions, each involving different degrees of risk, cost, and feasibility. The important point is to have as strong as possible a basis for the plan that you propose, and then to listen and evaluate that plan in light of alternative reasoning and plans posed by fellow students.

Finally, cases generate involvement, controversy, and excitement, and we hope the cases in this book will contribute to an enjoyable as well as a rigorous educational experience in consumer behavior.

F. Stewart DeBruicker
Philadelphia, Pennsylvania
Scott Ward
University of Pennsylvania

CASES
IN CONSUMER
BEHAVIOR

Introduction

CONSUMER BEHAVIOR AND MARKETING MANAGEMENT

This book is dedicated to the proposition that a necessary condition for effective marketing management is a good working relationship between the analytic skills of market research and the discipline-based skills of consumer behavior analysis. Marketing managers often have specialist marketing researchers to call upon, and they have at least some experience-based, and often discipline-based, notions of consumer behavior as part of their management skills. The major force that draws together the different bases of knowledge, experience, and theory from the areas of marketing management, marketing research, and consumer behavior is the need to solve problems in the area of marketing.

At its barest and most essential level, we define *marketing management* as the art of designing and delivering consumer satisfactions in ways that maximize the goals and resource allocations of organizations. Depending on whether one holds a public sector or a private industry view, one could add requirements that the process of marketing should deliver fair profits or should operate at an acceptable level of cost efficiency. But the essential element in our definition is that *the consumer* is central to both the design and the delivery responsibilities of marketing managers. Understanding consumers is a complex task, as well as a crucial element of decision making, and those who must make marketing decisions should be aware of the variety of useful analytical tools and problem-solving frameworks that have been developed outside the traditional area of marketing management. Their development has occurred as managers have found the traditional intuitive approach to customer analysis inadequate to the decision-making task.

Marketing researchers are no strangers to the practical considerations forced on them by action-oriented managers. Though a researcher may be well trained in the specialized disciplines of data collection and data analysis, there is still a wide gulf that separates the skilled marketing researcher from the skilled marketing manager, since each approaches a given problem-solving process with very different interests, skills, and experiences. Managers are trained to identify problems and to seek opportunities for their businesses, and to ensure that the problems are solved or the opportunities realized. The researcher, conditioned by the types of training that are typical in the field of marketing research, may see problems only in terms of the procedures that are generally accepted for collecting and for analyzing data. Those procedures usually do not fit problem-solving situations without considerable effort on the part of the manager and the researcher to define all aspects of the problem, to specify how results will be used, and to plan a research process that will respond to management's most strongly perceived information needs. This book describes many situations in which managers and researchers have tried to bring their special skills to bear on a particular strategic problem. Often their results will be judged quite good, at other times they will be found to be quite disappointing. In either event, members of both audiences should draw some lasting conclusions about how to work more effectively together in the future.

Consumer Behavior Analysis

The newest field of study discussed in the cases of this book is that of consumer behavior. Consumer behavior encompasses the study of the processes that consumers undergo when they make purchase decisions, and the field includes a growing number of concepts, models, and theories that are of increasing interest to marketing researchers and managers. While consumer behavior is not a management job in the strictest sense, and while companies do not have managers of consumer behavior in the sense that they have sales managers, product managers, and marketing research managers, the field of consumer behavior involves a set of

ideas and research processes that are as useful, in their place, as the more traditional tools of economics, quantitative methods, and psychology. This book is not intended to advance the cause of any one school of thinking out of the many approaches to consumer research. However, it is intended to describe practical marketing situations in which various concepts, models, and theories in the field of consumer behavior can be examined and applied. Consequently the cases in this volume each require extensive consumer analysis, although a variety of conceptual approaches to that analysis is possible in each case.

The general relationship between consumer behavior, market research, and marketing management is outlined in Figure 1. Since we believe that consumer analysis is basic to the tasks of marketing managers and marketing researchers, it is important to review the perspective from which each of these managers views and uses consumer analysis.

FIGURE 1
Relationship Between Problems and
Disciplines in Consumer Analysis

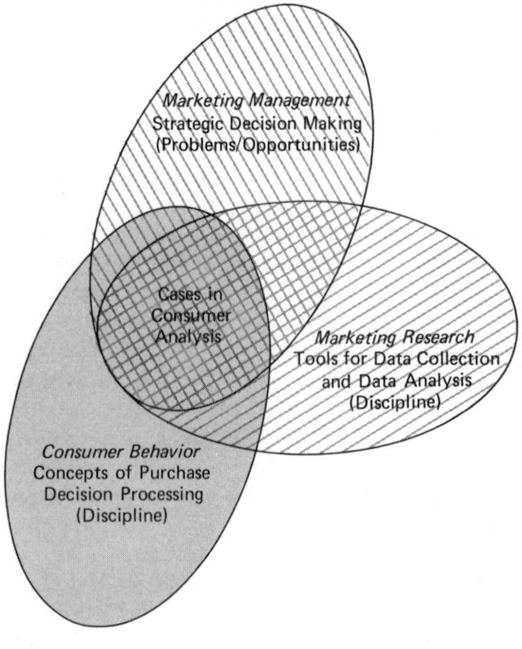

Marketing Management's Perspective on Consumer Analysis

The marketing management perspective on consumer behavior analysis generally stems from a problem-solving orientation. Management's problem-solving process can be described in several ways, but the most widely accepted would be the typical case method of decision making: problem definition, identification of underlying issues, analysis of relevant information, generation of alternative solutions to the problem, and the selection and defense of a most acceptable course of action. Within the field of marketing management, this decision process is used to make strategic choices in areas of choosing basic marketing strategy, and in choosing tactics with the elements of the marketing mix.

At the strategic level, management must make selections of programs of types of products and product line characteristics, and it must identify the specific types of markets for which those products are intended. The selection of implementable programs for product differentiation, market segmentation, and market penetration are among marketing management's most important responsibilities. At the tactical level, management must choose among an infinite variety of alternative programs in the areas of new product development, advertising, personal selling, pricing, channels of distribution, and market research and in marketing control systems. Each of these marketing program areas presents sets of problems with implications for consumer market understanding.

While there are competitive, institutional, and social factors that management must take into account it is axiomatic that marketing management must be founded on knowledge of, or assumptions about, customer needs, wants, and decision-making processes. Without knowledge of consumer decision-making processes, marketing decision makers are likely to fall victim to the temptation of making decisions on the basis of product factors, and assumptions based solely on experience, neither of which may be appropriate or adequate for a given market situation. Furthermore, without explicit consumer behavior information, marketing managers are likely to base their decisions only on their perceptions of consumers in the acts of purchase or consumption. They may therefore ignore prepurchase decision-processing activities that are largely intellectual and are difficult to observe, but which may be crucial in determining optimal strategy. Since consumer choice behaviors can be thought of as outcomes of extended processes of consumers' use of information gathered in a competitive environment, and since marketing managers are responsible for determining the marketing strategy of their business within that same competitive environment, then managers should benefit from knowing how consumers use information and make decisions throughout their entire process of purchase decision making. Concepts in the consumer behavior literature, while not relevant in all situations, can be very helpful in structuring management's perception of a marketing problem, especially by forcing a consumer perspective on management's choices among alternative marketing strategies.

Marketing Research's Perspective on Consumer Analysis

Broadly defined, *marketing research* is a family of techniques for collecting and analyzing data. Given its often rather demanding methodological complexities, the field of marketing research tends to be a rather specialized one, and it is rare that managers will build their careers both on the management and on the research functions of a business. More conventionally, managers and researchers travel different career paths, and though they interact frequently when engaged in problem-solving activities, they tend to have skills and interests that are complementary rather than substitutable. Given these differences between marketing management and marketing research, it would be reasonable to evaluate the marketing research area as a source of structure for an inquiry into the art of consumer analysis.

Marketing research demands analyses of problems that are defined in such a way that they fit the requirements of existing research techniques. Because of the procedural limitations on how data should be collected and the statistical caveats on how data should be analyzed, marketing research practitioners must spend a great deal of their time redefining strategic problems to fit the limitations of their research methods—or worse, spend time searching for a problem that will fit the precise requirements of a favorite methodology. This time invested in matching problems to methodologies is both a blessing and a curse of the marketing research field. The blessing is derived from the visible structure that research techniques force upon problems; the curse is that problems often require rather extensive redefinition in order to be defined in "researchable" terms, and that process of redefinition sometimes diminishes the relevance of the findings when they are presented to management.

There are at least three different ways one can describe the structure marketing research can bring to consumer analysis: techniques employed, analytic methods, and the research process. Various *research techniques* are common to marketing research and its allied fields of operations research, statistics, and social science research. There is a logical hierarchy of complexity within these techniques, and there is a consequently logical sequence in which those techniques are usually studied. The techniques can be ordered from those methods that deal primarily with qualitative issues (e.g., motivation research, focus group interviews) to those that deal with quantitative issues (e.g., surveys and field experiments).

Within the quantitative issues, technical discussions can be ordered with respect to *analytic methods,* and on the underlying assumptions of the methods of analysis.

A third basis for ordering a discussion of marketing research techniques would be to do so in the order in which typical large-scale *research projects are managed,* proceeding from

problem definition, to information need specification, to sample design, measurement development, data collection, data analysis, information presentation, and research follow-up. All of these ways to structure a marketing research course are of merit, and yet each is subject to important limitations when viewed from the perspective of the marketing manager or the consumer behavior analyst.

From the viewpoint of the marketing manager, probably none of these three approaches is very helpful in convincingly describing how and why market research structures consumer analysis. For example, the researcher's instinctive concern for the tidiness of the underlying assumptions about how data analysis should be conducted is often perceived by the manager as arbitrary, and certainly not important to the realistic richness management requires to solve strategic problems.

There may be no way that marketing managers can fully appreciate the requirements of market research for bringing structure and reliability to consumer analysis. Conversely, it is the exception, rather than the rule, for market research managers to appreciate the specific requirements of marketing management. As we have noted, the training, job requirements, and career paths of market researchers and market managers are very different. It may be that the most that can be hoped for is *effective communication* between these two types of managers, so that consumer analysis is most responsive to the marketing manager's practical strategic and tactical decisions. Effective communication depends on the personalities involved, but it also depends on the willingness of both managers to share the objectives of the research, to invest the time and energy to state the objectives in terms amenable to good research, and to appreciate fully how research results will be used. The cases in this book present various problems which invite opportunities for students and practitioners to explore these dimensions of interaction between market and research managers as they grapple with understanding consumer decision-making processes.

Consumer Behavior's Perspective on Consumer Analysis

Compared to its foundation disciplines of sociology, psychology, and statistics, the field of consumer behavior is a very recent addition to the social sciences. While scholars in these foundation disciplines study consumer behavior from their perspectives, many scholars in marketing areas within business schools define their research and teaching interests in the relatively young field of consumer behavior. In spite of these cross-discipline and interdisciplinary perspectives, the resulting field of consumer behavior has yet to develop a generally accepted body of accepted principles that could be used to structure consumer analysis which would be invariably useful to marketing managers. This is not to say that the field of consumer behavior concepts, models, and theories has not been useful in providing managers with a framework for analysis. However, our viewpoint in this book is that actual applications from the field of consumer behavior await more skillful integration of marketing and research management, in their ability to utilize the field in order to structure consumer analysis for practical problem solving. In short, managers need to know what concepts, models, and theories in the field of consumer behavior might usefully be employed in assessment of consumer analysis.

One barrier to effective management utilization of the field of consumer behavior is the fact that the field presents a broad and sometimes confusing array of content. Consumer behavior researchers do not agree on optimal approaches to research, or even on the scope of study.

Probably the earliest models of consumer behavior were derived from hierarchical notions about how decisions are thought to be made (e.g., AIDA, for ''Awareness-Interest-Desire-Action''). These decisions process

models proceed from some early set of predisposing states, through a dynamic, information using, series of (generally unobservable) steps, resulting in some form of consumer choice behavior, and followed by some form of post-choice phenomena.[1] The hierarchies can be relatively simple or they can be very complex, and they can postulate whole hosts of potentially relevant intervening variables and steps in the decision process.[2] The primary utility of the hierarchical notions may be that they provide a basis for consensus among managers and researchers when they try to define researchable strategic problems. As valid models of consumer behavior, however, hierarchical notions have been criticized on various grounds—e.g., not all consumers go through all the posited steps, or stages, and the models propose a very static representation of what may be a very dynamic process.

A second development in the field of consumer behavior was the extensive ''borrowing'' of concepts from the basic disciplines and applying them to marketing phenomena. For example, research in consumer behavior during the late 1950s and early 1960s saw the borrowing of personality concepts from the field of clinical psychology.[3] It was hoped that these concepts—and the extensive and reliable measures of each of them—could be applied to predict a wide range of purchases, from automobiles and cigarettes to one- versus two-ply toilet tissue! Since consumer behavior as a field

---

[1] Russell Colley, *Defining Advertising Goals for Measured Advertising Results* (New York: Association of National Advertisers, 1961).

[2] For an excellent review, see Michael Ray, ''Micro-Theoretical Notions of Behavioral Science and the Problems of Advertising: Present and Potential Linkages and a Proposed System for a Research System,'' (Cambridge: Marketing Science Institute Working Paper, March 1975).

[3] For a review of personality theory applications, see William D. Wells and Arthur D. Beard, ''Personality and Consumer Behavior,'' in *Consumer Behavior: Theoretical Sources*, ed. Scott Ward et al. (Englewood Cliffs, N.J.: Prentice-Hall, 1973).

of study seeks to apply behavioral science notions, some borrowing is inevitable and, in the view of many, desirable and useful. However, much concern has been voiced about "uncritical" borrowing and applying concepts that may not be suited to explain complex consumer choice processes.[4]

Dissatisfaction with borrowing, and growing attention to the field of consumer behavior in its own right, were trends largely responsible for a third development in the field of consumer behavior: the emergence of comprehensive models.[5] These models are typified by the use of extensive process flow diagrams showing paths of decision making, attitude change, information processing, and so on. The models usually permit many complex paths through a single decision process, and most can accommodate variables that are directly related to the marketing strategies of several competing businesses. Most of them are nearly impossible to verify empirically, but they are of value because they suggest overall frameworks within which smaller manageable research projects can be undertaken. They require a rather large investment of time and energy in order for their ramifications to be understood, and their impact on most practicing managers has been rather limited. Though that lack of impact is likely to change in the future, for the present it would be a mistake to use any one of them as the basis for a managerially oriented exploration of cases in consumer market analysis. Students of those models, however, should benefit from exploring the cases in this book and relating them to the relevant sections of the various comprehensive models of consumer choice behavior.

A fourth development in consumer behav-

ior has been the growth of what some authors have called "middle-range" theories.[6] These have evolved from problem specific research streams, and though they usually are not conceptually connected to one another, each represents an existing knowledge base that is often the foundation for a portion of consumer analysis. Important middle-range theories have been developed around the problems of consumer persuasibility,[7] how perceived risk shapes various buying processes,[8] how various forms of communication affect consumer choices,[9] how younger consumers develop consumer skills,[10] how new products diffuse through market segments,[11] and so on.

A fifth—and most recent—approach to the field of consumer behavior stems from interest in relatively complex phenomena which require integration of some middle-range notions, but which are not so complete as to constitute a comprehensive model of consumer behavior. Research in the area of "information processing" illustrates this approach. An early symposium in this area classified research into "initial" and "central" processing.[12] The first deals with such issues as how consumers perceive products and brands, while research in

[4] Thomas S. Robertson and Scott Ward, "Consumer Behavior Research: Promise and Prospects," in *Consumer Behavior: Theoretical Sources,* ed. Scott Ward et al. (Englewood Cliffs, N.J.: Prentice-Hall, 1973).

[5] See J. A. Howard and J. N. Sheth, *The Theory of Buyer Behavior* (New York: John Wiley, 1969); F. M. Nicosia, *Consumer Decision Processes* (Englewood Cliffs, N.J.: Prentice-Hall, 1966); and J. F. Engle, D. T. Kollat, and R. D. Blackwell, *Consumer Behavior* (New York: Holt, Rinehart & Winston, 1968).

[6] The term was coined by R. K. Metton, *Social Theory and Social Structure* (New York: Free Press, 1957). A discussion of middle-range theories in consumer behavior research is in Ward et al., *Consumer Behavior.*

[7] R. A. Bauer, "The Role of the Audience in the Communication Process," in *Proceedings of the American Marketing Association,* ed. S. A. Greyser (Chicago: American Marketing Association, 1963), pp. 73–82.

[8] D. F. Cox, ed., *Risk Taking and Information Handling in Consumer Behavior* (Boston: Division of Research, Harvard Business School, 1967).

[9] R. A. Bauer, "Games People and Audiences Play" (Paper presented at Seminar on Communication in Contemporary Society, University of Texas, 1967).

[10] Scott Ward, Ellen Wartella, and Daniel Wackman, *How Children Learn to Buy: The Development of Consumer Information Processing* (Beverly Hills: Sage Publishing, 1977).

[11] T. S. Robertson, *Innovative Behavior and Communication* (New York: Holt, Rinehart & Winston, 1971).

[12] G. David Hughes and Michael L. Ray, *Buyer/Consumer Information Processing* (Chapel Hill: University of North Carolina Press, 1974).

the second area incorporates such topics as multiattribute models, and cognitive processing during exposure to television commercials. More recently, researchers have continued to define information processing in terms of developing models of how consumers select, store, evaluate, and use product-related information,[13] and in terms of public policy issues.[14]

From a management perspective, the principal advantage of the information-processing approach to the field of consumer behavior is that these notions are not so limited in scope as middle-range theories, nor are they so complex and difficult to operationalize as comprehensive models. Information-processing models and research have only recently emerged, and their utility for practical management decision making has yet to be demonstrated. However, it may be that this conceptualization will prove to be a central organizing framework for the field.[15]

A final approach in consumer behavior that can be useful in consumer analysis for management has to do with the nature of the decision-making unit. Much consumer behavior research focuses on intra-individual processes—i.e., the decision processes of individual consumers. Somewhat less research has been directed toward the buying processes of small groups of persons, such as households or purchasing committees. Beyond descriptive studies of the extent of purchase influence in households,[16] few studies have addressed more complex issues regarding husband-wife decision making or have expanded the scope of inquiry to include offspring as well as couples.[17]

We feel that the ultimate utility of concepts, models, and theories from the field of consumer behavior has been limited to date. As a field of academic research, the perspective is usually based on previous research and theory, rather than from a management viewpoint. Specific conceptualizations of consumer behavior, such as the work on perceived risk, or personality notions, cannot easily be applied to specific marketing management problems, any more than a specific problem can easily be fitted to a particular research method. Just as market and research managers must invest the time and energy to state problems in researchable terms, much work must be done to distill the findings from the field of consumer behavior in such a way that they will prove useful to the marketing manager.

As we suggested in the Preface, we do not feel that the goal of increasing consumer behavior's utility in marketing management is best served by using cases in order to illustrate how behavioral concepts can be applied to describe aspects of management problems. Conversely, we do *not* believe that the goal of case analysis should be to fit strategic marketing problems to particular consumer behavior frameworks. Rather, different frameworks must be examined, and their utility for structuring consumer analysis for practical problem solving assessed. This shifts the pedagogical objectives from applying consumer behavior theories to case problems, to gaining managerial skills through the process of learning. In this case, the latter involves the discipline of eclectic, skillful selection, evaluation, and use of the most pertinent concepts from the diverse field of consumer behavior.

Summary

The cases in this book were written for the purpose of merging the mutual skills and interests of strategic managers, marketing re-

[13] Ward, Wartella, and Wackman, *How Children Learn to Buy: The Development of Consumer Information Processing Skills* (Beverly Hills: Sage Publishing, 1977).

[14] William Wilkie and Paul W. Farris, "Consumer Information Processing: Perspectives and Implications for Advertising" (Cambridge: Marketing Science Institute, Report #76-113, August 1976).

[15] Michael Ray and Scott Ward, "The Relevance of Consumer Information Processing Studies to Communication Research," *Communication Research*, 2, No. 3 (July 1975).

[16] Learner Marketing Research and Development, "New Brand Purchasing Dynamics: An In-Depth Examination of the Critical Incidents and Factors Involved in a New or Different Brand Coming into the Home." Conducted for *Life* magazine, December 1968.

[17] Harry L. David, "Decision Making within the Household," *Journal of Consumer Research*, 2, No. 4 (March 1976).

searchers, and students in the field of consumer behavior. Their mutual interests dictated the need for case studies that emphasized realistic management problem-solving processes, made use of relatively explicit methods of data collection and data analysis, and invited the skillful use of important aspects of current knowledge of consumer behavior. The cases assume that the student has a working familiarity with the concepts and the practices of marketing management, basic quantitative methods for management, and some background in one or more of the social sciences. Strength in any two of those areas is likely to compensate for a relative deficiency in any third area, however.

Given those teaching objectives and the requisite student skills, the following learning objectives are feasible:

1. Develop skill in strategic decision making.
2. Make explicit the ways in which strategic choices are based on consumer decision-making processes.
3. Develop skill in evaluating applications of research methodologies in the area of consumer market analysis.
4. Develop skill in selecting, evaluating, and applying concepts, models, or theories in the field of consumer behavior.

What is intended, ultimately, is not to have the student acquire and retain certain "facts" about how consumers make decisions but to learn an analytical process that can be adapted to a variety of marketing managers' situations.

ROUTINE PURCHASING BEHAVIOR

PART **I**

CHAPTER 1

General Foods:
Opportunities in the Dog Food Market

In March 1970, Mr. Steven Wald was the New Product Manager for the Pet Foods Group of General Foods Corporation's Post Division. After reviewing base line data on consumption, ownership trends and analyses of consumer attitudes about dogs and dog foods, Mr. Wald had to decide what types of dog food concepts should be generated, screened, and committed to a program of formulation and actual use testing. Since subsequent stages in the product development process would be costly, and since there would be a high level of organizational commitment to whatever products that would be developed, he wanted to take advantage of the strategic flexibility that he had at this crucial stage. A wrong choice now might mean much wasted time and expense if later product testing should prove that the conceptual foundations of the new product development program to have been laid in haste and in error.

As background, Mr. Wald had a great deal of information about the competitive environment. He was especially interested in a market segmentation study which had just been completed, which identified segments of demand based on owners' attitudes about their pets, rather than on the traditional measures of demography, socioeconomics and numbers and types of pets owned. A number of product use benefits had been identified that seemed to go beyond the basic nutritional, cost and convenience reasons thought to affect product and

This case was prepared by Edward T. Popper. Research Assistant, under the supervision of Professor Scott Ward, The Wharton School, as a basis for class discussion rather than to illustrate either effective or ineffective handling of an administrative situation.

Revised January 1978 by Assistant Professor F. Stewart DeBruicker, The Wharton School, University of Pennsylvania.

brand choice. Since General Foods had no products participating in the canned dog food category, Mr. Wald wanted to develop product concepts that would give the company a canned brand strategy to complement its entries in the dry and the soft-moist categories of the dog food market. Eleven new product concepts had been generated, and some were quite far-reaching in their implications for the division's marketing directions.

PERSON'S BEST FRIEND

According to studies of pet ownership conducted by a prominent magazine audience research firm, there were approximately twenty-six million dogs owned by households in 1968. This figure represented steady growth at an annual rate of about five percent. About thirty-eight percent of all United States households owned one or more dogs in 1968, and of those households, about one in four owned two or more dogs.

Tabular analysis of the data collected by the magazine audience research firm provided Mr. Wald with a quantitative description of dog-owning households and the feeding patterns that prevailed within them. Exhibit 1 shows that dog ownership was least likely among lower income households, central city dwellers, and households with no children present. Patterns of feeding tabulated by household income and by type of locality are listed in Exhibit 2. There were well-recognized relationships between income, locality and a household's tendency to feed their dog(s) canned, semimoist, or dry commercial dog foods, or table scraps. Heavy users of dry dog food are characterized in Exhibit 3 and heavy users of canned and semimoist products are characterized in Exhibit 4 (only in 1968 was market analysis data first tabulated separately for canned and semimoist products).

Dogs purchased by their owners were less likely to be fed only table scraps than dogs that were received as gifts, as shown in Exhibit 5. The effects of child-companionship, child-surrogate, and utility ownership purposes on feeding patterns are listed in Exhibit 6. Finally, the feeding pattern effects of purebred versus mixed breed, size of dog, and length of pet ownership are listed in Exhibits 7, 8 and 9.

THE CHANGING CANINE ROLE IN SOCIETY

All of these ownership and feeding patterns were expected to change, however, according to some sociological trends that had been identified by Mr. Wald, assisted by the General Foods Marketing Research Department. Both the number of single dog and multiple dog households had increased steadily over the 1960s, and the trend was expected to continue for a number of broad sociological reasons. The General Foods research group reasoned that the trends in popularity of multifamily dwellings, increasing rates of urban growth and crime, decreasing family sizes, increased levels of education and discretionary income, and increases in leisure time all brightened the long range outlook for dog food sales in the United States.

The most significant factor affecting the long-term role of the dog was believed to be the shift from single-unit housing to multiple-family dwellings. This corresponded to a shift from a rural to an urban society and would probably alter the dog's role from worker to companion and protector. United States Department of Commerce figures showed a steady decline in the number of single-family housing starts from 64.5 percent of all starts in 1966 to 53.3 percent in 1969. The long-term effect on dog ownership of this trend was expected to be a relative decline in popularity of larger breeds of dogs in favor of breeds more adaptable to smaller spaces. Among smaller breeds, the more active small hounds, which would be of the appropriate size for apartment living, were expected to also decline in popularity as it might become evident that they required more area to live healthfully. Less active and toy breeds were expected to increase in popularity, however.

Trends in pet ownership by size of dog

were difficult to observe, and were only imperfectly indicated by the number and types of dogs registered with the American Kennel Club (AKC). The AKC registered just over 870,000 dogs in calendar 1968, and compared to the breeds registered in 1967, the largest increases came in the terrier group and the sporting group. Exhibit 10 lists the number of new registrations and Exhibit 11 shows the percentage change in new registrations by types of dogs classified by their normal use. Mr. Wald was not sure of the extent to which, if at all, the AKC figures reflected trends in the ownership patterns for nonregistered purebred dogs and for mixed breed pets.

Concurrent with the growth of multiple dwellings, a coincident growth in the size of cities was expected. While the trend to date appeared to be a migration of the middle class from central cities, the 1970s and 1980s were expected to bring an expansion of the suburbs to a point where the differentiation between them and the central cities would become negligible. The crime rate, historically higher per capita in central cities, was expected to expand at a higher rate in the suburban areas. The impact of this would be an increase in the use of dogs as protectors. The effect of this reuse of dogs in a working capacity would be a greater increase in the dog population than had been experienced in recent years.

One of the primary reasons consumers cited for not currently owning a dog was residence restrictions. Legal challenges to these restrictions had succeeded in recent months, enabling New York apartment dwellers to maintain a dog "for protection." It was assumed that this trend would continue.

Other factors compounded the dwelling and crime effects on the size and character of the dog population. Decreasing family sizes were expected in the 1970s, and though this was not expected to have an effect on the number of dogs owned, it was expected to increase the number of expensive, pedigreed dogs in the population. The effect due to the decreased number of children was somewhat harder to anticipate, given the traditional role

of the family pet either as a child substitute, or as an entertaining companion for children. Since the one-child family was less likely to own a dog than childless households or households with two or more children, an increase in the proportion of "child surrogate" dogs was expected. In that event, there were implications that owners would likely become more concerned and sophisticated in their pet food shopping behaviors.

Trends toward higher levels of education among household heads reinforced the implications drawn from trends of family size. Better-educated household heads would require more apparently rational reasons from dog food advertising than had been necessary in the past. Promises based on taste and convenience would probably have to be supplemented with facts based on physiological needs of the animal as well. Professional sources of information, such as breeders and veterinarians, were likely to increase in importance as information sources in the future.

Finally, as advances in the socioeconomic environment occurred, it was expected that increases in leisure time would occur, and pet ownership would be one area in which household members were likely to invest their newly acquired discretionary time. The total pet market was expected to expand, and since dogs were believed to be among the most symbolic of pets, there would be disproportionate growth among the more specialized breeds of dogs. Recent pet owner surveys had indicated that spending on pets was directly related to income, and as discretionary consumer income increased, the amount spent on pet foods was expected to increase as consumers traded up to better types of pet food.

THE DOG FOOD MARKET

The dog food market had been growing at annual rates that usually exceeded ten percent throughout the middle 1960s. In 1968, the retail value of dog food sales was estimated to be $780 million. Of the four categories of dog foods, canned dog food accounted for nearly half the dollar sales in the industry, and dry dog food accounted for slightly more than a third of the dollar market. The newest category, semimoist varieties of dog food resembling patties of ground raw meat, accounted for thirteen percent of industry dollar sales. The balance of the market was made up of special biscuit and snack products. Exhibit 12 indicates the sales of each category over the years 1965 through 1968.

General Foods brands were well represented in the dry and the semimoist product categories, but General Foods had no brands in competition within the canned category. The company's Gainesburger brand had pioneered in the semimoist category and was still the dominant brand in its category. Three other General Foods semimoist brands helped the company to achieve over a seventy percent share of the category's sales in 1968. The semimoist category's rapid growth appeared to be slowing, however, and it appeared that the category would settle down to between one fifth and one sixth of the total dog food market.

The dry dog food category was dominated by Ralston–Purina, which held nearly forty percent of the $285 million category. General Foods' Gravy Train and Gaines Meal brands led the company to second place with a fifteen percent category share.

Unlike the dry and semimoist categories, in which a few national firms dominated each category's sales, the $360 million canned market was much more fragmented. The economics of production enabled smaller competitors to compete on a price basis, and there were fifteen manufacturers with sales of $4 million or more. In recent years, the number of brands had proliferated, and this trend was expected to continue. The largest brands and manufacturers of canned products are listed in order of 1968 dollar sales in Exhibit 13. The canned product category was headed by Liggett and Myers' Alpo brand, which had overtaken Quaker Oats' Ken-L-Ration as the top canned brand in 1967. Alpo was the most heavily advertised canned product, and at a 1968 media spending level of about $3.6 million, was sec-

ond in industry spending only to Ralston–Purina's $3.9 million in media for Purina Dog Chow, the leading dry product. Market shares for dry and semimoist products are listed in Exhibits 14 and 15, and estimated media spending levels by brand and by manufacturer for all types of products are listed in Exhibit 16.

Mr. Wald concluded that even though the competitive information was over a year old, the implication was clear that to make progress within the canned category, substantial amounts would have to be allocated to media in order to penetrate the information noise barrier created by all the competing campaigns. Dollars alone would not be a guarantee of success, however, especially given the difficulty of differentiating a canned product on dimensions that were likely to have meaning to pet owners. Alpo's all-meat product position appeared to be successful, but it was unlikely that an imitative strategy would be successful, especially when the financial power of Alpo's parent corporation was considered. Mr. Wald knew that he would have to identify product concepts that had communicable features that were important to dog owners. Unfortunately, the research questions aimed at identifying those factors that dog owners considered important, as listed in Exhibit 17, did not suggest unique product features that could be established in a proprietary position for any possible new products. Exhibit 18 indicates that, when asked, most persons who actually fed the household dogs admitted to few reasons that most people gave for switching brands or types of dog food and were equally unilluminating, as listed in Exhibit 19.

MARKET SEGMENTATION STUDIES

To get a different perspective on the dog food market, Mr. Wald asked the General Foods Marketing Research group to conduct an attitude segmentation study of dog food buyers. The purpose of the study was to define households according to the ways that they felt about their pets, and to tie those feelings to the types of food which the household's pets were fed most often. Mr. Wald hoped that the study would help him identify sets of relationships between owners, pets, and the reasons why certain types of dog foods were preferred; given these relationships the major opportunities for new canned product development should be more easily recognized. Mr. Wald asked that the study identify the perceived end use benefits that consumers were seeking from dog food products, and suggest perceived product attributes that operationalized those product use benefits in the pet owner's mind. Mr. Wald recognized that some buyers could be expected to be anthropomorphic—that is, they would project human traits to their pets—while others would hold a more functional set of attitudes about their dogs. It was important to find out the relative size of those attitude groups, and to identify their consumption patterns and the beliefs that affected their choices of types and brands of commercial dog food.

Five attitudinal segments were identified, and seven "bundles" of product attributes were also identified. The attitude segments appeared to have rather realistic differences with respect to the sizes and numbers of dogs owned, the relative level of affection felt for the family pet, and the types of dog food served most often. Mr. Wald inferred that new canned dog food products were not likely to be successful if targeted toward the Functionalist segment, for example, but might have a much better chance of acceptance if targeted toward one or more of the other segments. The major characteristics of the five segments were:

Functionalists relied on canned products for only about nine percent of the feedings their dogs received, but the Baby Substitutes used canned products for nearly half the feedings of their pets. Additional consumption data for canned, soft-moist, dry meal, and biscuit products are tabulated in Exhibit 20. Exhibit 20 also describes each segment in terms of the lifestyle of the pets, the owner's attitudes toward nutrition, the relative selectivity of the pet in choosing or rejecting food, and other dimensions of social settings in which the five segments were found to exist. Some of the members of the General Foods Marketing Research group suggested splitting the Nutritionalist group into two subgroups, the first to be called Caterers, and the second to be called Nutritionalists. The essential difference between the two subgroups was thought to be the owner's willingness to experiment with different types of dog foods for reasons of nutrition versus reasons based on whether the dog apparently "liked" the product.

Mr. Wald believed that the attitude segments were quite useful for identifying different ways to structure the dog food market. He and his colleagues found that it was useful to build series of grids, using data from Exhibit 20, to suggest possible ways to further refine their understanding of the segments. One such grid, based on affection for the dog and most likely size of the dog, is shown on p. 16.

While Mr. Wald believed that the Middle of the Road segment was not particularly interesting because of its "everywhere average" interpretation, the remaining segments were

	Functionalist	Family Mutt	Baby Substitute	Nutritionalist	Middle of the Road
% of Dog Owners	40%	25%	10%	13%	12%
% of Commercial Dog Food Feedings	55%	20%	5%	10%	10%
Pet Attitude	Little attachment to dog	Little interest in dog	Above average attachment to dog	Very personally attached to dog	About average

		Dog Size	
		Larger	Smaller
Attachment to Dog — High	Nutritionalists Caterers		Baby Substitute
		Middle of the Road	
Attachment to Dog — Low	Functionalists		Family Mutt

intriguing because they had relatively distinctive profiles with respect to attitudinal, behavioral and geographic characteristics. He was sure that the study, after further interpretation, would warn him away from areas of low success probability and would suggest the major elements in a positioning strategy for viable new canned product concepts.

The product use benefits study attempted to identify characteristics of products, rather than characteristics of market segments. The product use benefits which dog owners were seeking were identified in greater number and detail than previous research had been able to do, and the supporting product physical attributes were also identified. These data, which are presented in Exhibit 21, suggested ways that product attributes could be designed so that dog owners would infer that the product was in fact delivering the types of benefits that were judged desirable. It was rather difficult to physically blend new products that were perceived as having the intended user benefits, and this task was especially difficult in the area of pet foods where both the pet and the owner were involved in the process of perceiving the product's physical and psychological characteristics.

The benefit-attribute analysis found the following categories of benefits to be of greatest importance to pet owners:

1. Appeal
    Appeal to Dog
    Appeal to People Feeding the Dog
    Fulfillment of Projected Human Preferences
2. Nutrition/Health
    General Health
    Teeth/Mouth
    Dog's Appearance
3. Minimized Doggy Unpleasantness

4. Economy
5. Reliability/Superiority
6. Convenience
    Container
    Product

Product quality, as indicated by high quality of ingredients, high-quality meats, all-beef components, and nonuse of artificial ingredients, was a product attribute that was heavily related to both the Economy and the Reliability/Superiority benefit bundles.

A second example of the way in which product attributes could be related to the perception of a desirable benefit was demonstrated by the finding that one important anthropomorphic benefit was that a desirable dog food was one that "my dog would choose for himself if he could." This benefit was related to the controllable product attributes of a dog food that smelled like meat, had a rich color, did not look stringy, did not form congealed fat on the top of the product, contained only the parts of meat which people would eat, had the right amount of gravy, contained small (or large) chunks of meat, contained no gristle, and was broiled.

Altogether, the analysis had identified forty-four separate benefits which were more or less important to dog owners, and these benefits were manifested in 139 supporting product attributes. Mr. Wald was not sure which of the benefit bundles, and therefore which of the product attributes, was most highly leverageable in a new product development program. He knew that there were always compromises that had to be made between the complexity of a new product's claims and the communicability of those claims, and that such compromises had to be made with some knowledge of the target audience's interest in the product's major benefits.

NEW PRODUCT CONCEPTS

As bases for actionable use of the market segmentation study and the benefit-attribute study, Mr. Wald, working with the Post Division's Research and Development laboratories, had developed eleven new product concepts. Each product concept was technically feasible and each was of the same order of magnitude with respect to development costs if it were decided to commit the concept to a blending and testing program. The product concepts were as follows:

1. *Reveille.* To most users it seemed traditional that when dogs go onto a once-a-day feeding schedule, their *one* meal is served at the dinner hour. Is there a nutritional or physiological advantage in dinner-time feeding? According to veterinarians there is not. In fact, there is evidence to the contrary that if one meal is fed, it would serve the dog better if it were fed at the breakfast hour. Morning feeding supplies the dog with energy throughout the day rather than at an hour when digestion may not be completed before the animal retires for the night. Moreover, food consumed at the breakfast hour is far more likely to be burned off than food consumed at dinner-time. Hence, morning feeding can help the dog to maintain his physical condition without adding the additional pounds that dinner feeding often encourages. Reveille, then, would be designed as the first complete feeding regimen meant to be fed at the breakfast hour. Reveille would incorporate not only cereal but high-meat protein, a complete range of supplementary nutrients, and possibly, cottage cheese solids and egg yolks.

2. *Prime Slices.* This product would be a new form of all-meat dog food. Meat plus other needed nutrients in a digestible casing. Large enough to feed a large dog for two days, medium-sized dog for four days, small dog for a week. The casing is marked with colored lines to indicate proper serving according to dog size . . . blue for large dog, yellow for medium-sized dog, white for small dog. Simply slice with a knife at proper line for a complete serving. Plastic cover slips over exposed area so remaining portion can be stored in refrigerator.

3. *Control.* This new product would be a balanced-nutrition sauce or gravy meant to be added to table scraps. It would do to table scraps what instant breakfast does to a glass of milk. Each serving provides complete balanced nutrition and high-protein energy. Mixed with warm or cold water, and poured over table scraps, it gives the dog every basic and supplementary nutrient and vitamin needed for health and vitality. It can be used with any food. In three delicious gravy flavors (beef, chicken, and liver) that will make any meal more appetizing to the dog. Available in powdered form. In multipacket boxes.

4. *Dog Days.* This product would be the first hot-weather thirst drink for dogs. A pleasant tasting liquid on the order of Gatorade, this product would satisfy a dog's thirst even faster than water. Moreover, it would do what water alone can't. It would replace the natural salts, body sugars and high-protein nutrients a dog loses through perspiration and activity. It would help the dog to safely maintain higher activity levels in hot weather. Available in six-packs of four-ounce cans.

5. *Puppy Prime.* This dog food would be designed as a high-protein, extra-calcium regimen for puppies. Due to their extremely rapid physical growth, puppies require dramatically increased percentages of high-quality protein and calcium. This is doubly true if the mother did not receive a special high-protein diet during the gestation period. While it is true that standard dog foods are high in protein, the protein they supply is of relatively low quality, placing undue stress on the puppy's kidneys, resulting, possibly, in inadequate assimilation of protein. Moreover, most brands tested prove to be insufficient in calcium content for this stage of development. Puppy Prime, then, would be designed to supply both the vital high-quality proteins and the additional calcium so essential for proper bone structure during this critical period. Puppy Prime would take the form of a cereal-based, high-protein product incorporating the probable additives of powdered whole eggs, cod liver oil and dried milk solids.

6. *Prenatum.* This product would be a unique dietary food for the pregnant bitch. Supplies all her normal nutritional requirements, plus her expanded requirements for calcium, iron and complete protein. Metered in calorie structure to control weight. High in appetite and flavor satisfaction. Mild so as not to upset the digestive sensitivities that occur with pregnancy.

7. *Suppertime.* This dog food would be designed as a complete self-sustaining feeding program for the active dog (i.e., the dog with an opportunity for abundant exercise). Formulated of scientifically

metered amounts of complete meat protein, supplementary nutrients and bulk, Suppertime is geared not only to the activity level but also to the maintenance level of the dog. It is designed to satisfy the active adult dog's appetite, maintain his performance level and at the same time regulate his weight—without adding additional pounds.

8. *Weight Watcher.* This dog food would be designed as a complete self-sustaining feeding program for the inactive dog (i.e., the apartment dog, the city dog, the suburban dog who has opportunity for only relatively short, sporadic periods of exercise, the spayed dog, etc.). Weight Watcher would be formulated of scientifically metered amounts of high quality, easily assimilated protein, supplementary nutrients, reduced cereal bulk and noncaloric filler. Weight Watcher is designed to satisfy the dog's complete hunger, answer his total nutritional needs—but provide only half the caloric content of standard dog foods. Weight Watcher may be used as either a maintenance regimen, a pregnancy regimen (in combination with a puppy-type food) or as a reducing diet.

9. *Senior.* This dog food would be designed as a complete feeding program for the older, more mature dog (eight years and over). Roughly fifty percent of dogs in this age group suffer from one or another of a variety of kidney deficiencies, typically revealing themselves as an inefficiency in handling protein. Senior would be formulated with less protein than standard diets, but higher quality protein (much more easily assimilated). Also incorporated would be a complete range of supplementary nutrients, cereal bulk and, probably, powdered eggs. Senior would offer somewhat reduced caloric value.

10. *Gaines Thirty.* This new product would be the first freeze-dried food for dogs. A complete, balanced nutrition, high-protein dog food, this product would offer more fresh meat flavor satisfaction and more natural nutrition than any dog food ever developed. Add water, and the fresh meat flavor, the natural meat texture, and subtlety of diced vegetables and fresh milk all come flooding back. Fresher tasting. More natural tasting. More naturally nutritious than even the most expensive canned or semimoist diets. Moreover, because this product is freeze-dried, it's far more portable, and far easier to carry food from the supermarket. A five-pound bag makes thirty pounds of food. A full month's supply of meals that stores conveniently and compactly right on your pantry shelf. This product would be available in handled boxes. At a premium price.

11. *Max.* This new product would be the first 100 percent fresh dog food. So fresh, it's not even sold in a supermarket. It's delivered to your door with your milk. Formulated of ground fresh meat, fresh milk products and cottage cheese solids, it's better for your dog because it's packed fresh each day for your dog. Unlike canned dog foods that undergo substantial flavor adulterations and nutritional loss as they age on the grocer's shelf, this product assures guaranteed flavor consistency and maximum nutrition. What's more, since this product is delivered with your milk, there are no heavy cans for you to lug home from the supermarket. Packed in one-pound tubs. Priced at slightly premium levels to store-bought dog foods.

EXHIBIT 1

Distribution of Dog Ownership
by Selected Demographics

	Total U.S. Households	Own a Dog
By Locality Type		
Met Central City	31.7%	25.8%
Met Suburban	34.6	36.7
Non-Met	33.7	37.5
By Household Income		
Under $5,000	34.2%	29.7%
$5,000–$7,999	27.4	26.4
$8,000–$9,999	15.5	18.8
$10,000 +	22.9	25.1
By Presence of Children in Household*		
Children under 6 Years	28.1%	28.0%
Children 6–17 Years	42.5	54.2
No Children	46.1	35.7
By Age of Female Head		
18–34	29.0%	27.7%
35–49	31.5	41.3
50 +	38.6	31.0
By Size of Family		
1–2	38.5%	27.8%
3–4	35.6	40.9
5 or More	25.9	31.3

* Percentages add to more than 100% due to the presence of more than one child in some households.

Source: Simmons, 1967.

EXHIBIT 2

Distribution of Users of Dog Food Types by Household Income within Locality

	Dog-Owning Households	Canned Only	Dry Only	Dry and Canned Only	Semimoist*	Other Only**
Total Households						
Under $5,000	29.7%	27.7%	34.6%	20.0%	22.2%	49.2%
$5,000–$7,999	26.4	33.7	28.3	29.2	13.3	27.7
$8,000–$9,999	18.8	16.0	18.4	20.0	27.3	9.2
$10,000 +	25.1	22.6	18.7	30.8	37.1	13.9
Met Central City						
Under $5,000	31.1%	34.3%	33.6%	28.2%	24.3%	43.0%
$5,000–$7,999	25.5	25.9	33.9	29.2	11.6	40.7
$8,000–$9,999	20.4	19.1	15.6	18.5	32.3	3.1
$10,000 +	23.0	20.8	16.9	24.1	31.7	13.2
Met Suburban						
Under $5,000	17.1%	13.3%	22.5%	14.1%	11.2%	37.2%
$5,000–$7,999	27.9	31.3	28.3	32.7	18.3	28.5
$8,000–$9,999	14.6	19.8	24.5	16.8	21.6	11.3
$10,000 +	35.3	35.6	24.7	36.4	48.8	23.1

EXHIBIT 2 (cont.)

	Dog-Owning Households	Canned Only	Dry Only	Dry and Canned Only	Semimoist*	Other Only**
Non-Met						
Under $5,000	40.9%	41.0%	43.2%	22.2%	36.8%	56.0%
$5,000–$7,999	25.6	44.9	25.7	24.6	7.8	23.1
$8,000–$9,999	16.8	7.6	15.6	25.3	29.3	10.4
$10,000 +	16.7	6.5	15.5	27.9	26.1	10.4

* Used alone and in combination with other dog food types.

** Non-commercial feeding.

Source: Simmons, 1967; Life Magazine Cross-Tab.

EXHIBIT 3

Characteristics of Heavy Users of Dry Dog Food, September 1967

	Total Homemakers	Users*	Index
Age of Homemaker			
Under 25 Years	9.9%	7.2%	73
25–34 Years	19.1	23.4	123
35–49 Years	31.7	40.8	129
50–64 Years	24.6	22.7	92
65 Years and Over	14.7	5.9	40
Household Income			
Under $5,000	37.9%	23.5%	62
$5,000–$9,999	39.8	47.2	119
$10,000 and Over	22.3	29.2	131
Education			
Grade School or Less	26.1%	15.9%	61
High School/Not Beyond	51.5	55.8	108
College	22.4	28.3	126
Household Size			
1–2	39.3%	28.0%	71
3–4	36.1	43.8	121
5 and Over	24.6	28.2	115
County Size			
A	38.7%	29.4%	76
B	27.1	29.3	108
C and D	34.2	41.3	121

*Use dry dog food once a day or more.

Source: Brand Rating Index, September 1967.

EXHIBIT 4

Characteristics of Heavy Users of Canned or Semimoist Dog Food, September 1967

	Total Homemakers	Users*	Index
Age of Homemaker			
Under 25 Years	9.9%	8.3%	84
25–34 Years	19.1	19.4	102
35–49 Years	31.7	45.3	143
50–64 Years	24.6	21.1	86
65 Years and Over	14.7	5.9	40
Household Income			
Under $5,000	37.9%	18.7%	49
$5,000–$9,999	39.8	45.4	114
$10,000 and Over	22.3	35.9	161
Education			
Grade School or Less	26.1%	13.4%	51
High School/Not Beyond	51.5	58.1	113
College	22.4	28.5	127
Household Size			
1–2	39.3%	25.3%	64
3–4	36.1	45.5	126
5 and Over	24.6	29.3	119
County Size			
A	38.7%	40.8%	105
B	27.1	30.6	113
C and D	34.2	28.6	84

* Use canned or semimoist dog food once a day or more.

Source: Brand Rating Index, September 1967.

EXHIBIT 5

Type of Feeding by Method of Acquisition

	Bought	Given
Canned Only	21.5%	19.5%
Dry Only	28.2	26.1
Dry and Canned Only	26.5	19.5
Moist and Moist Combinations	18.8	19.8
Other Only	5.0	15.2

Source: Life Sub-Sample of Simmons, 1967.

EXHIBIT 6

Type of Feeding by Reasons of Acquisition

	For Children	For Companionship	For Utility Purposes	Other
Canned Only	16.0%	25.0%	10.6%	28.8%
Dry Only	22.8	22.8	44.2	19.2
Dry and Canned Only	25.3	20.7	25.0	16.4
Moist (Total)	23.5	21.2	10.6	19.2
Other Only	12.3	10.3	9.6	10.4

Source: Life Sub-Sample of Simmons, 1967.

EXHIBIT 7

Type of Feeding by Breed

	Pure	Mixed
Canned Only	20.9%	21.3%
Dry Only	26.9	24.5
Dry and Canned Only	24.8	19.4
Moist and Moist Combinations	20.1	19.4
Other Only	7.2	15.4

Source: Life Sub-Sample of Simmons, 1967.

EXHIBIT 8

Type of Feeding by Size of Dog

	Large	Medium	Small
Canned Only	14.9%	22.7%	25.3%
Dry Only	32.4	24.7	17.6
Dry and Canned Only	25.0	20.4	18.7
Moist and Moist Combinations	15.5	20.8	26.4
Other Only	12.2	11.4	12.1

Note: Large: 30 pounds and over
Medium: 15 to 30 pounds
Small: under 15 pounds

Source: Life Sub-Sample of Simmons, 1967.

EXHIBIT 9

Type of Feeding by Length of Ownership

	1 Year or Less	2–4 Years	5 Years or More
Canned Only	22.9%	17.5%	19.6%
Dry Only	28.2	23.8	26.8
Dry and Canned Only	18.3	27.7	21.1
Moist and Moist Combinations	14.5	19.9	23.7
Other Only	16.0	11.2	8.8

Source: Life Sub-Sample of Simmons, 1967.

EXHIBIT 10

Registrations Processed January 1, 1968 to December 31, 1968

Breed	1968	1967	% Increase/ Decrease
1. Poodle	263,700	255,862	+ 3%
2. German Shepherd	104,127	107,936	(4)
3. Dachshund	57,460	57,133	1
4. Beagle	56,940	61,568	(8)
5. Chihuahua	33,686	37,324	(10)
6. Miniature Schnauzer	30,868	26,000	19
7. Pekingese	26,278	27,242	(4)
8. Collie	24,200	24,325	(1)
9. Labrador Retriever	18,492	16,710	11
10. Cocker Spaniel	18,443	18,525	(.5)
11. Basset Hound	17,452	17,595	(1)
12. Pomeranian	15,047	15,425	(2)
13. St. Bernard	13,490	10,732	26
14. Irish Setter	12,667	10,021	26
15. Shetland Sheepdog	12,537	11,730	7
16. Boston Terrier	12,406	12,579	(1)
17. Doberman Pinscher	11,585	9,512	22
18. Fox Terrier	10,792	10,931	(1)
19. Brittany Spaniel	9,620	9,464	2
20. Boxer	9,450	9,570	(1)
21. German Shorthaired Pointer	9,378	8,616	9
22. Pug	9,181	9,031	2
23. Yorkshire Terrier	9,080	7,580	20
24. Scottish Terrier	8,308	7,519	10
25. Great Dane	7,950	6,777	17
26. Golden Retriever	7,607	6,879	11

EXHIBIT 10 (*cont.*)

Breed	1968	1967	% Increase/Decrease
27. English Springer Spaniel	7,116	6,836	4
28. Weimaraner	5,741	5,767	—
29. Dalmatian	5,104	4,761	7
30. Airedale Terrier	4,972	4,829	3
31. Bulldog	4,903	4,492	9
32. Cairn Terrier	4,532	3,968	14
33. West Highland White Terrier	4,057	3,318	22
34. Samoyed	4,050	3,671	10
35. Norwegian Elkhound	3,850	3,545	9
36. Siberian Huskie	3,833	3,099	24
37. Afghan Hound	3,409	2,660	28
38. Maltese	2,948	2,560	15
39. Basenji	2,901	2,461	18
40. Old English Sheepdog	2,522	1,712	47

Source: American Kennel Club.

EXHIBIT 11

Change in New Registrations, 1967–1968

There are six main classes of dog breeds. Dogs are classified according to their use. The following are the main groups of dogs with some of the breeds that represent each class.

1. *Sporting Group*—hunt by air scent:
   Cocker Spaniel, English Springer Spaniel, Golden Retriever, Irish Setter, Labrador Retriever, Pointer. +9%

2. *Hound Group*—hunt primarily by ground scent:
   Afghan Hound, Basset Hound, Beagle, Bloodhound, Dachshund, Greyhound. −3%

3. *Working Group*—serve as guards, guides and herders:
   Boxer, Collie, Doberman Pinscher, German Shepherd, Great Dane, Mastiff, Old English Sheepdog, St. Bernard, Shetland Sheepdog. +2%

4. *Terrier Group*—hunt by going to earth:
   Airedale Terrier, Bedlington Terrier, Bull Terrier, Kerry Blue Terrier, Miniature Schnauzer, Scottish Terrier, Wire-Haired Fox Terrier. +11%

5. *Toy Group*—serve as companions to man:
   Chihuahua, Italian Greyhound, Maltese, Mexican Hairless, Pekingese, Pomeranian, Yorkshire Terrier. −3%

6. *Nonsporting Group* (miscellaneous)—serve a great variety of uses:
   Boston Terrier, Bulldog, Chow, Dalmatian, Poodle. +3%

Source: American Kennel Club.

EXHIBIT 12

Dollar Sales of Dog Food
(In Millions)

Dog Food	1968	1967	1966	1965
Canned	$360	$315	$285	$250
Dry	285	275	205	185
Semimoist	100	90	80	65
Whole Biscuit, Snacks	35	30	25	25
Total	$780	$710	$595	$525

Source: John C. Maxwell, Jr., Oppenheimer and Company.

EXHIBIT 13

Brand Sales of Canned Dog Food
(In Millions)

Brand	Company	1968	1967	1966	1965
Alpo	Liggett & Myers	$80.0	$63.0	$46.0	$32.5
Ken–L–Ration	Quaker Oats	65.0	57.0	52.0	49.0
Kal Kan	Mars Inc.	41.5	40.0	37.0	35.0
Rival	Associated Products	26.0	24.0	21.0	19.0
Vets	Liggett & Myers	16.0	16.0	16.0	15.0
Laddie Boy	National Can	15.5	15.5	13.0	—
Skippy	National Can	15.0	14.5	13.5	12.5
Friskies	Carnation	13.5	13.0	12.0	11.0
Strongheart	Doric	9.5	9.0	8.0	—
Dash	Armour	8.0	9.0	8.0	—
Calo	Borden	8.0	8.0	8.0	—
Cadillac	U.S. Tobacco Co.	5.0	5.0	4.0	4.0
Red Heart	Morrell	5.0	6.0	6.5	—
Ideal	Wilson	4.5	4.5	5.0	—
Purina Meats	Ralston-Purina	4.5*	—	—	—
Hills	Riviana Fods	4.0	5.0	6.0	—
Pard	Swift	4.0	4.5	5.0	—
All Others		35.0	21.0	24.0	72.0
Total		$360.0	$315.0	$285.0	$250.0

*Regional.

Source: John C. Maxwell, Jr., Oppenheimer and Company.

EXHIBIT 14

Brand Sales of Dry Dog Food
(In Millions)

Brand	Company	1968	1967	1966	1965
Purina	Ralston-Purina	$110.0	$102.0	$96.0	$87.0
Gravy Train	General Foods	25.5	25.5	24.8	24.8
Friskies	Carnation	18.0	16.0	14.0	13.0
Gaines	General Foods	16.4	16.8	16.4	15.3
Jim Dandy	Savannah Sugar	12.5	13.0	13.5	11.4
Hunt Club, Walter Kendall	Standard Brands	11.5	11.0	10.5	10.0
All Others		91.1	90.7	29.8	23.5
Total		$285.0	$275.0	$205.0	$185.0

Source: John C. Maxwell, Jr., Oppenheimer and Company.

EXHIBIT 15

Brand Sales of Semimoist Dog Food
(In Millions)

Brand	Company	1968	1967	1966	1965
Gaines Burgers	General Foods	$34.5	$33.7	$35.5	$34.0
Ken–L–Burger	Quaker Oats	20.0	15.5	6.0	*
Prime	General Foods	17.5	18.7	21.5	21.0
Top Choice	General Foods	11.5	10.5	6.0	—
Gaines Variety	General Foods	8.0	5.0	4.0	—
Ken–L–Ration Special Cuts	Quaker Oats	7.0	4.0	*	—
All Others		1.5	2.6	7.0	10.0
Total		$100.0	$90.0	$80.0	$65.0

* In test.

Source: John C. Maxwell, Jr., Oppenheimer and Company.

EXHIBIT 16

Dog Food Brand Expenditures by Media, 1968

			Newspaper	Television	
	Total	Magazine	Supplements	Network	Spot
General Foods	$10,048,768	$ 32,550	$ 179,718	$4,854,400	$4,982,100
Gaines Burgers	2,924,900	—	—	920,100	2,004,800
Gravy Train	1,861,050	32,550	—	1,241,500	587,000
Prime	1,832,396	—	23,596	346,900	1,461,900
Top Choice	,501,879	—	125,979	749,600	626,300
Prime Variety	1,034,543	—	30,143	1,004,300	100
Gaines Dog Meal	739,600	—	—	592,000	147,600
Gaines Dog Food	99,200	—	—	—	99,200
Gaines Variety	55,200	—	—	—	55,200
Ralston-Purina	$6,889,480	$ 914,651	$ 14,229	$3,822,400	$2,138,200
Purina Dog Chow	3,924,720	212,020	—	3,273,000	439,700
Purina Canned Dog Food	1,143,230	223,101	14,229	—	905,900
Purina Puppy Chow	740,200	—	—	525,700	214,500
Purina Chuck Wagon	716,444	141,544	—	—	574,900
Purina Dog Chow Sweepstakes	241,895	218,195	—	23,700	—
Purina Dog and Puppy Chow Premium Offer	119,791	119,791	—	—	—
Field 'n Farm Dog Chow	3,200	—	—	—	3,200
Quaker Oats	$5,099,588	$ 456,681	$ 95,107	$1,436,500	$3,111,300
Ken–L–Ration Burgers	1,956,094	328,994	—	854,200	772,900
Ken–L–Ration Dog Food	1,689,900	—	—	—	1,689,900
Ken–L–Ration Special Cuts	740,663	75,556	95,107	—	570,000
Ken–L–Ration Canned Dog Food	712,931	52,131	—	582,300	78,500
Ligett & Myers	$4,015,500	—	—	$3,284,000	$ 731,500
Alpo	3,646,800	—	—	3,284,000	362,800
Vets	368,700	—	—	—	368,700
National Biscuit Co.	$1,222,140	$ 10,440		$ 256,100	$ 955,600
Milk Bone Dog Biscuit Biscuits	937,940	10,440	—	256,100	671,400
Flavor Snack Dog Biscuits	284,200	—	—	—	284,200

EXHIBIT 16 (cont.)

	Total	Magazine	Newspaper Supplements	Television Network	Spot
Associated Products	$1,187,100	—	—	—	$1,187,100
Rival	1,187,100	—	—	—	1,187,100
U.S. Tobacco Co.	$ 958,500	—	—	—	$ 958,500
Cadillac	958,500	—	—	—	958,500
Riviana Foods	$ 471,800	—	—	—	$ 471,800
Hills	471,800	—	—	—	471,800
Standard Brands	$ 469,100	—	—	—	$ 469,100
Burger Bits	383,400	—	—	—	383,400
Walter Kendall	85,700	—	—	—	85,700
Savannah Sugar	$ 413,737	$ 181,137	—	—	$ 232,600
Jim Dandy Dog Food	192,000	—	—	—	192,000
Jim Dandy Dog Ration	151,781	151,781	—	—	—
Jim Dandy Chunx Dog Food	40,600	—	—	—	40,600
Jim Dandy Canned Dog Food	29,356	29,356	—	—	—
National Can	$ 385,300	—	—	—	$ 385,300
Laddie Boy	385,300	—	—	—	385,300
Skippy	NOT AVAILABLE				
Carnation	$ 270,917	—	$ 43,317	$ 74,600	$ 153,000
Friskies Canned Dog Food	116,100	—	—	74,600	41,500
Friskies Dry Dog Food	111,500	—	—	—	111,500
Friskies Puppy Food	43,317	—	43,317	—	—
Mars, Inc.	$ 258,800	—	—	$ 214,700	$ 44,100
Kal Kan	258,800	—	—	214,700	44,100
Armour & Co	$ 158,636	—	$ 60,336	—	$ 98,300
Dash	158,636	—	60,336	—	98,300
Borden, Inc.	42,400	—	—	$ 8,700	$ 33,700
Calo	42,400	—	—	8,700	33,700

EXHIBIT 17

Importance of Selected Factors in Choice of Dog Food

	Very Important	Fairly Important	Not Important
Nutritional and Vitamin Content of Food	73.7%	17.8%	8.3%
Your Feeling as to What Your Dog Would like	73.5	19.7	6.6
The Amount of Pure Meat	64.1	24.6	11.0
The Odor the Food Has	55.4	21.4	22.9
Convenience in Serving the Food	48.0	27.6	24.2
Flavors Available	42.3	29.7	27.8
Appearance of the Food	36.1	29.7	34.0
The Brand Name	34.8	22.3	42.7
Cost of Food	29.5	34.8	35.5

Source: Life Sub-Sample of Simmons, 1967.

EXHIBIT 18

Objection to Dog Food Currently Available by Person Doing Most of the Feeding

	Total	Wife	Husband	Both Equally	Someone Else
None	59.8%	59.2%	69.0%	55.4%	57.8%
Packaging	9.8	9.9	5.2	16.1	8.4
Texture/Consistency	6.2	6.6	3.5	3.6	8.4
Not Enough Meat/Too Much					
Additive	6.0	6.3	—	5.4	9.6
Too Expensive	5.1	4.8	10.3	—	6.0
Doesn't Keep Well	2.8	2.9	—	3.6	3.6
Other	20.2	21.0	19.0	30.4	12.1
DK/NA	.4	.4	.6	—	—

Source: Life Sub-Sample of Simmons, 1967.

EXHIBIT 19

Reasons for Changing Brands/Types of Dog Food

	Total		Total
Dog tired of same brand	17.7%	Just wanted to try something new	5.0%
Dog didn't like, would not eat other brand	17.7	Dog is fussy	2.1
Dog likes it	9.2	Miscellaneous master-oriented mentions	23.4
Thought would be better, more nutritional for dog	8.5	Miscellaneous dog-oriented mentions	7.8
Just bought to see if dog liked it	6.4	DK/NA	5.0

EXHIBIT 20

Attitudinal Segmentation Summary Dog Food Market

Name	Functionalist	Family Mutt	Baby Substitute	Nutritionists	Middle of Road
SIZE:					
% of Dog Owners	40%	25%	10%	13%	12%
% of Commercial Dog Food Feedings	55%	20%	5%	10%	10%
DEMOGRAPHY: (Note these are tendencies based upon a given group's profile relative to the other groups)	*Multiple dog ownership;* Children present; lower income/C, D counties	*Own one dog; Average size;* Children present; lower income/C, D counties	Own *one very small,* older dog; Kids not present; higher income, urban	*Multiple dog ownership; largest dogs;* low probability of kids; Eastern, urban, higher income	No distinctive characteristics
ATTITUDES: (Note these are tendencies based upon a given group's profile relative to other groups)	Dogs outdoor/ hearty; eat anything, no bother; Little attachment to dog; Interested in ownership benefits; *Average interest in nutrition;* Housewife not involved with dog.	*Little interest in dog; Dog playful,* no bother; *Below average* menu acceptance; Interest in owner-benefits; *Least interest in nutrition;* Housewife not involved, dog is for kids.	*Dog fragile, indoor animal;* above average *attachment to dog;* Heavily involved in choice of food; Dog finicky eater, great desire to *prepare what dog wants.*	Very personally attached to dog; Dog belongs to housewife; *Most interested in nutrition;* Least interested in cost, food flexibility; Virile dog	
TYPES USED:	Basically meal feeders—very little use of other types	Heavy meal usage but also atypically high use of low priced canned	*High degree of canned use,* relatively *little of meal;* High relative use of soft-moist and biscuits.	*Most feedings meal*—relatively strong *high priced canned* and biscuit use	Feed meal and canned to about same extent; High relative use of soft-moist
% OF TOTAL FEEDINGS GIVEN TO EACH TYPE	Soft-Moist 2.0% Meal 88.2 *Canned* 8.9 High 1.2 Parity 1.8 Economy 5.9 Biscuits 0.9	Soft-Moist 6.4% Meal 63.7 *Canned* 28.4 High 3.2 Parity 8.2 Economy 17.0 Biscuits 1.5	Soft-Moist 7.8% Meal 59.0 *Canned* 27.1 High 10.2 Parity 7.4 Economy 9.5 Biscuits 6.1	Soft-Moist 25.4% Meal 22.7 *Canned* 44.9 High 14.9 Parity 16.9 Economy 13.1 Biscuits 7.0	Soft-Moist 41.0% Meal 43.7 *Canned* 37.7 High 6.7 Parity 12.5 Economy 18.5 Biscuits 4.6
LOCATION: POST REGION	Stronger than average in Central & South; very weak in West.	Stronger than average in East; very weak in West.	Stronger than average in West; relatively weak in East.	Very strong in South & East; very weak in West.	Stronger than average in East and Central; Western South

EXHIBIT 21

Dog Food Product Attributes

CONSUMER GOALS	PERCEIVED PRODUCT ATTRIBUTES
("Perceived End Benefits")	*("Supports")*

APPEAL

Appeal to Dog

1. Dog loves it	1. Has a smell dog likes
2. Deters feeding problems	2. Has a taste dog likes
3. Makes dog's mealtime a pleasure to watch	3. Has been tested with dogs and refined to be sure it has flavor they like best
4. Is completely satisfying to dog	4. Dogs love it right from the first moment it's served
5. Makes dog happy	5. Is liked even by finicky eaters
6. Shows you know how to make your dog happy when you serve it	6. Gets dog excited and happy when it's served
7. Shows your dog you love him when you serve it	7. Is filling
	8. Keeps dog from being hungry until close to his next mealtime
	9. Satisfies even the heartiest appetite
	10. Doesn't make dog a fussy eater, addicted to one kind of food

People Appeal

1. Makes feeding your dog more pleasant	1. Has a pleasant aroma to people
	2. Smells appetizing to people
	3. The smell does not cling to hands if you touch it
	4. The smell does not linger after the food is gone
	5. Is completely odorless
	6. Looks appealing
	7. Looks like people food
	8. Does not splatter when poured from can

Fulfillment of Projected Human Preferences

1. Is the product my dog would choose for himself if he could	1. Smells like meat
	2. Is meaty
	3. Has a rich color
	4. Does not look stringy
	5. Does not form congealed fat on top
	6. Has appetizing-sounding ingredients printed on the label
	7. Does not contain entrails—only the parts of the meat which people would eat
	8. Has just the right texture/consistency
	9. Contains gravy
	10. Has the right amount of gravy
	11. Is moist and juicy
	12. Is not mushy
	13. Stays solid when it comes from the can
	14. Is chunky
	15. Has the right size chunks
	16. Contains small chunk of meat

EXHIBIT 21 (*cont.*)

CONSUMER GOALS (*"Perceived End Benefits"*)	PERCEIVED PRODUCT ATTRIBUTES (*"Supports"*)

Fulfillment of Projected Human Preferences

	17. Contains large chunks of meat
	18. Contains no gristle
	19. Is broiled
	20. Is cooked
1. Offers mealtime variety	1. Can be served a number of different ways
2. Lets you adjust dog's feeding to his special needs which you know best	2. Can be served straight from the can or mixed, as you wish
3. Is a product dog never gets tired of	3. Can be mixed "half and half" with table scraps to provide all the vitamins and nutrients your dog needs
	4. Mixes well with dry dog food
	5. Can be mixed with liquids
	6. Can be served more than once a day
	7. Can be served hot or cold
	8. Is available in a variety of textures and consistencies
	9. Is available in large and small chunks
	10. Is available in a variety of formulas for different types and sizes of dogs
	11. Has different formulas available for long- and short-haired dogs
	12. Has different formulas for large and small dogs
	13. Is available in a variety of flavors
	14. Is available in meatball variety
	15. Contains both large and small chunks of meat
	16. Contains both cooked and raw meats
	17. Contains a varied meal in each can—meat, vegetables, vitamins, and minerals

NUTRITION/HEALTH BENEFITS

Benefits to General Health

1. Is better for dog than other dog foods	1. Provides all the nutrition dog needs for a well-balanced diet.
2. Is a complete, well-balanced meal	2. Contains just the right balance of ingredients
3. Is not too rich to be eaten every day	
4. Minimizes veterinary care dog needs	3. Provides all the vitamins and nutrients your dog needs
5. Keeps dog healthy	
6. Helps dog live longer	4. Contains a vitamin capsule in each can
7. Delays aging	5. Contains iron
8. Keeps dog healthy and active at the peak of his strength for as long as possible	6. Contains minerals
	7. Contains only poly-unsaturated fats
9. Prepares dog for a healthier old age	8. Is low in fat
10. Makes an adult dog feel like a puppy again	9. Is low in carbohydrates
11. Keeps dog robust	10. Is as wholesome as fresh meat, milk, vegetables, and eggs
12. Helps keep dog playful	
13. Helps keep dog active	11. Provides all the protein dog needs
14. Keeps dog from getting fat	12. Contains milk products

EXHIBIT 21 (cont.)

CONSUMER GOALS
("Perceived End Benefits")

PERCEIVED PRODUCT ATTRIBUTES
("Supports")

13. Contains cheese
14. Contains fresh eggs
15. Contains vegetables
16. Is 100% meat
17. Is not 100% meat
18. Contains no cereal products

----

19. Keeps dog's eyes bright and healthy
20. Has special ingredients which are good for dog's eyes
21. Prevents cataracts
22. Has ingredients good for dog's kidneys
23. Has ingredients good for dog's liver
24. Helps keep dog's skin healthy
25. Prevents arthritis
26. Is a high energy dog food
27. Is designed for the metabolism of an adult dog
28. Is used by people who are concerned about their dog's nutrition

Benefits to Teeth/Mouth

1. Keeps dog's bones and teeth strong
2. Keeps dog's mouth in good shape
3. Minimizes dental work dog needs
4. Keeps teeth white

1. Contains all the calcium dog needs
2. Contains some crunchy bits
3. Contains some bone
4. Polishes dog's teeth
5. Is chewy
6. Gives dog chewing exercise

Benefits to Dog's Appearance

1. Keep dog bright and alert
2. Helps you have a dog people love to look at
3. Makes your dog look well cared for

1. Keeps dog trim and in solid muscle tone
2. Helps dog achieve and maintain his proper weight
3. Has special ingredient to give dog a beautiful coat
4. Helps make dog's coat shiny

MINIMIZED DOGGY UNPLEASANTNESS

1. Makes your dog a dog everyone loves to be with
2. Keeps your dog feeling good
3. Makes dog easier and more pleasant to care for
4. Makes taking care of dog's "bathroom" needs less of a chore and easier to schedule
5. Keeps messy clean-up from "accidents" and throwing-up to a minimum

1. Keeps "doggy odor" to a minimum
2. Gives dog an especially pleasant smell
3. Is easy to digest
4. Contains nothing which would trigger a sensitive stomach to throw up
5. Digestible enough to be fed to a dog who isn't feeling well
6. Prevents diarrhea
7. Provides sufficient roughage for dog's digestion
8. Helps assure dog's control and regularity
9. Keeps dog's breath fresh

EXHIBIT 21 (*cont.*)

CONSUMER GOALS (*"Perceived End Benefits"*)	PERCEIVED PRODUCT ATTRIBUTES (*"Supports"*)

ECONOMY

1. Is a good value for the money
2. Is economical in the long run

1. Has frequent specials like coupons, price-off deals, or special offers
2. Contains the vitamins and oils you would otherwise have to buy
3. Is a total care dog food which contains everything your dog needs each day in one can
4. Is not wasteful, dog eats it all
5. Contains only what dog needs—no filler
6. Keeps fresh a long tim after the can has been opened

High Quality

1. Contains high-quality ingredients
2. Contains high-quality meat
3. All of the meat it contains is 100% beef
4. Is low in artificial ingredients

REASSURANCE OF RELIABILITY/SUPERIORITY

1. Is the best food available for your dog
2. Is better than other dog foods

1. Is unique
2. Is the modern way to feed a dog
3. Is especially balanced for your adult dog, not a puppy, and not a senior dog
4. Is not for puppies
5. Contains balancing ingredients to adjust to the normal daily changes in dog's body chemistry
6. Is recommended by veterinarians
7. Is made by a company which has a veterinarian on their staff
8. Has a formula which was developed with the help of a team of veterinarians
9. Is recommended by the American Kennel Club
10. Is recommended by NRC
11. Is fed to racing dogs
12. Is recommended by dog trainers
13. Is government approved
14. Is prepared and canned by people who are themselves dog owners and lovers
15. Contains the foods a dog lover would order if he could custom order dog foods
16. Taste tested by the people who prepare it
17. Is made by a reliable, well-known manufacturer
18. Is made under the strictest sanitary conditions
19. Is made by a company which also makes food for people

EXHIBIT 21 *(cont.)*

CONSUMER GOALS *("Perceived End Benefits")*	*PERCEIVED PRODUCT ATTRIBUTES* *("Supports")*

CONVENIENCE

Convenient Container

1. Has a flip-top lid so that you don't need a can opener
2. Has a flip-top and bottom so that you can open both ends easily and push the food out of the can

Convenient Product

1. Is convenient to use
2. Makes taking care of your dog easier than any other dog food does

1. Is good for all types and sizes of dogs
2. Is a complete meal to be used alone, and does not have to be mixed with anything
3. Is good for everyday use
4. Is easily licked or washed away
5. Does not harden when refrigerated
6. Keeps well after opening without refrigeration

2

Fisher-Price Toys, Inc.

Over the past four decades, the Fisher-Price Toy company had distinguished itself by producing a wide line of quality toys for pre-school children at moderate prices. Jack Asthalter, Fisher-Price's Marketing Vice President, was therefore confronted with a difficult situation in August 1970 when his production staff announced that mold costs on the new ATV Explorer toy would make the intended $12.00 retail price impossible to meet. In fact,

according to the production people, the ATV Explorer could not be profitably distributed at the wholesale level for less than $9.20 per unit, thereby calling for an $18.50 retail price after markups. While concept tests had promised a substantial demand for the new riding vehicle at the $12.00 price, Mr. Asthalter was unsure that these potential consumers would remain interested at the new price. Moreover, because the Fisher-Price product line was generally priced below $5.00 retail, Asthalter believed there would be considerable internal resistance to introducing the ATV Explorer.

---

[1] This section is based on "Note on the Toy Industry," University of Minnesota Graduate School of Business Administration, 1970; 9–514–060, Rev. 11/77.

This case was prepared by Steven L. Diamond, Research Associate, under the supervision of Professor Scott Ward, The Wharton School, as the basis for class discussion rather than to illustrate either effective or ineffective handling of an administrative situation.

INDUSTRY BACKGROUND[1]

Industry sources estimate that toy sales at the retail level in the United States were between two and three billion dollars in 1968. A study by the A. J. Wood Corporation divided total consumption as follows:

	Approximate Percent of Dollar Sales at Retail
Riding toys (including bicycles)	22%
Dolls, doll clothing and accessories	13
Non-riding transportation	12
Sporting goods	12
Games, puzzles, magic sets	6
Educational and scientific	5
Musical	5
Toy guns	5
Handicraft and models	4
Novelty toys	3
Activity toys	3
Stuffed	2
Child-sized furniture	2
Pre-school	2
All others	4
	100%

Approximately one-sixth of the items purchased account for almost two-thirds of the total dollars spent on toys, as the following table shows:

Toy Sales by Retail Price Class

	Percent of Unit Sales	Percent of Dollar Sales
$15.00 and over	4%	33%
$10.00–$15.00	3	13
$ 5.00–$ 9.99	10	20
$ 3.00–$ 4.99	14	16
$ 2.00–$ 2.99	12	8
$ 1.00–$ 1.99	20	6
$ .50–$ .99	16	3
$ Under $ .50	18	1
Not Classified	3	—
Total	100%	100%

The A. J. Wood study showed that parents account for the bulk of toy purchases:

Percent of Unit Sales of Toys, by Purchaser

Parents	72%
Grandparents	11
Uncle/aunt	5
Brother/sister	2
Friends	4
Other (including purchases made by child himself)	6

The toy industry is composed of a few large firms and several hundred small manufacturers. In 1967, there were over 1,000 toy manufacturers in the United States, but the eight largest manufacturers together accounted for 35% of sales, and the 20 largest firms accounted for 58% of sales. Foreign manufacturers supplied only 9% of toy sales in the U.S. (at manufacturer's prices), but foreign imports were growing, particularly for less expensive toys.

The toy industry is highly seasonal in nature. At the retail level, 53% of all dollar sales and 45% of unit sales are made in November and December. Toys are sold through approximately 10,000 retail outlets, distributed as follows:

Percentage Distributions of Sales and Stores

Type of Retail Outlet	Percent of Dollar Sales	Percent of Total Stores
Department	18%	13%
Discount	17	18
Chain discount	11	9
Catalog	9	5
Variety	9	21
Auto supply	7	3
Toy	7	8
Hardware	4	2
Drug	3	5
Hobby	2	2
Supermarket	2	4
Sporting goods	2	1
All others	9	9
Total	100%	100%

Toy retailing had become more concentrated in recent years, and industry sources expected this concentration of more sales through few outlets to continue. For example, the Census of Business indicated that the number of hobby and toy and game shops had declined 18% between 1963 and 1967, although total sales of these shops increased by more than one-fourth. A Stanford Research Institute study predicted that chain stores, particularly discount and variety chains, were likely to continue to be major vendors of toys.

Recently, two major discount chains opened stores which sell only toys. Both managements believed that their chains could do a specialized year-round business in toys because (1) year-round promotion by toy manufacturers and retailers could create a year-round demand, (2) the youth population (ten and under) was growing, with a 27% gain projected until the late 1970s, and (3) American affluence was increasing, with personal income increasing 72% between 1960 and 1968.

Toy industry observers break down the types of toys available into four categories: (1) *prestige items,* most of which are European imports, offering high margins (40%–60% to retailers, with little advertising, but elaborate point-of-sale promotions; (2) *staple nondiscount* toys, including basic items such as clay sets, doctor's kits and building blocks. Many "educational" toys fall into this category. Some advertising is done for these toys, but themes stress quality, and are directed primarily toward women; (3) *semi-discount* items include push-and-pull toys, riding toys, and games. Some national advertising is done, but is essentially "awareness" promotion to keep the name of the product and firm before the consumer; (4) *extreme discount* toys include items which are fads, as well as a few perennial favorites. Most imported toys from the Far East fall into this category, are sold through jobbers to discount, department and toy stores, and offer low (less than 10%) margins.

COMPANY BACKGROUND

Fisher-Price Toys, Inc., was founded in East Aurora, New York, in 1930 with the concept that solid wood blocks with lithographs applied would sell as toys for pre-school children. Herman G. Fisher, President and one of three founders of the firm, believed that "kids not only want toys to play with, but toys to play with them." Accordingly, he saw in wood lithographing the opportunity to make action toys which would walk, crawl, whine and generally "respond" to children.

In order to survive the difficult depression years, Mr. Fisher established as a corporate creed that each Fisher-Price toy must have: (1) intrinsic play value, (2) ingenuity, (3) strong construction, (4) good value for the money, and (5) action. These guidelines for toy-making, still observed today, led to relatively successful operation of the company in its early years. While avoiding head-on competition with the mainstream of the toy business, Fisher-Price continued to make specialty toys of the wood lithograph variety and by 1947 the firm had reached the $1 million sales level.

The next decade was marked by moderate but steady growth under the continuing conservative management of Mr. Fisher. In 1959, however, significant changes in Fisher-Price's product line and pricing policies were instrumental in transforming the firm into a major factor in the toy industry. First, Fisher-Price enjoyed a highly significant breakthrough in the toy industry as the first successful producer of a line of music box toys. While other manufacturers had developed similar toys, they had either been too fragile or prohibitively expensive to attract substantial consumer acceptance. The Fisher-Price line, however, could withstand a good deal of punishment and yet was available at moderate prices. Accordingly, sales of the new line were extremely high, thereby providing the resources and the incentive for further new product introductions.

The changing retail structure of the toy business prompted a second vital decision for Fisher-Price. While Mr. Fisher had always advocated price maintenance, the coming of age of large discounters made such a policy impractical (Exhibit 1). Faced with the threat of losing the growing market share serviced by high volume discount chains, Fisher-Price departed from its stringent pricing policies in 1959.

These fundamental product and pricing strategy changes led Fisher-Price into a decade of substantial growth in the 1960s. During that period Mr. Fisher set aside his policy of promoting solely from within the organization and began hiring professional management from other industries. The impact of the new management team was first evident in the expansion of Fisher-Price's product line with an average net increase of six new toys yearly. Moreover, the purchase mix changed over the decade, reflecting the increased volume in $3 to $5 toys and a relative reduction in the proportion of $1 and $2 toys sold by Fisher-Price. By 1969, Fisher-Price had become a major factor in the toy industry. Sales increased to a respectable $32 million in that year (Exhibit 2) and three-fourths of all toy purchasers recognized Fisher-Price as a leading producer of pre-school toys (Exhibit 3). Nonetheless, under the guidance of Mr. Fisher, the firm continued in its conservative ways in terms of both financial and marketing policies. Accordingly, it was not surprising that the Quaker Oats Company of Chicago saw great potential in Fisher-Price and purchased the firm from Mr. Fisher for $50 million in cash.

While Quaker tended to be a far more aggressive concern than had been Fisher-Price under Mr. Fisher's direction, Quaker's management was hesitant to meddle in the concerns of the toy manufacturer. They recognized Fisher-Price to be a well-run organization and sought to insure continuity of management. At the same time, however, Quaker encouraged Fisher-Price executives to adopt a less conservative posture, specifically in their marketing and advertising programs. Advertising especially took on a dimension of importance with the impersonalization of the retail selling process, creating the need to shift from a push to a pull strategy within the toy business. To accompany this desired change in outlook, Quaker made it clear that it stood ready to provide whatever resources would be necessary to insure a more substantial growth rate.

PRODUCT TESTING AND MARKETING PROGRAMS

Fisher-Price's steady and respectable growth rate was in great measure attributable to the very effective product testing and marketing programs. Unlike other toy manufacturers, Fisher-Price generated virtually all of its new toy ideas internally. While the impetus to such toy introductions had traditionally come from the Research and Development department, marketing executives were increasingly providing the direction for new product design. Accordingly, a review of the Fisher-Price product line and of the pre-school toy market often led to recognition of a potential toy to fill a market niche. This suggestion was then passed on to designers who provided a dozen or so sketches and, given encouragement from top management, would proceed to develop a prototype of the new toy.

Unique within the industry, Fisher-Price operated a licensed on-premise nursery school for local pre-school children at which toy prototypes could be tested. Classes were conducted at two age levels—2 to 3 years and 4 to 5 years—by trained teachers and each met twice weekly for three-hour periods. While classes were in session, corporate engineers and behavioral scientists, the creators of the Fisher-Price toy line, could watch children playing with new toy prototypes as well as already proven toys. By noting children's reactions to toys through such measures as average attention span time and repeat toy usage, these toy designers could effectively pre-test new toys and insure maximum interest, safety, education, durability and the like.

After this pre-test phase, however, Fisher-Price's marketing staff geared its promotions almost exclusively to adult purchasers rather than to child consumers. Because mothers and grandmothers purchase about three-quarters of all pre-school toys (Exhibit 4), corporate advertising was carried in women's magazines such as *Good Housekeeping, Parents' Magazine* and *Woman's Day.* While advertising copy recognized that toys should be enjoyable, parental concerns for safety, durability and quality were always taken into account (Exhibit 5). As Marketing Vice President Jack Asthalter explained, "The real success of this company lies in our ability to think as a mother would."

Fisher-Price also differentiated itself from competitors by promoting an entire product line rather than pushing single items as was customary in the toy industry. While other manufacturers would introduce a variety of new toys each year in the hopes that one or two would become best sellers. Fisher-Price maintained most of its product line year after year adding only a few new toys annually. Advertising and promotional efforts were all designed around this umbrella strategy of selling an entire product line and company image rather than attempting to ride the crest of an occasional fad. Accordingly, each Fisher-Price toy was boxed in a familiar red and blue package and displays were designed to show the toys as a collection of playthings rather than an unrelated group of items (Exhibit 6). To further promote this umbrella strategy, a catalog of all Fisher-Price toys was included with each toy inducing parents and children alike to make further purchases in the Fisher-Price family.

With the attraction of new management to the corporation in the mid-1960s, Fisher-Price's market efforts began to take on a more aggressive dimension. In dealing with the trade, Fisher-Price had traditionally presented its product line and taken orders for each upcoming Christmas season. More aggressive merchandising at trade shows and an increased number of salesmen in the field, however, led to a substantial sales increase in the late 1960s. Also prior to 1969, corporate advertising was confined to the print media and advertising budgets were unrealistically small. Fisher-Price abandoned its no-TV advertising policy in 1969 and (with the added resources and encouragement provided by Quaker) the advertising budget was increased substantially (Exhibit 7). The effect of television advertising in well-supervised test markets indicated the magnitude of its potential impact. While Fisher-Price maintained its insistence on selling a product line rather than individual toys, the line was broadened substantially to accommodate the new demand which television appeared to capture. By 1970 the firm's advertising budget was more than twice the 1968 level with a high proportion of this investment directed to mothers through daytime television talk shows and soap operas. In determining its marketing strategies, corporate executives kept in close touch with relevant public opinion studies (Exhibit 8).

The effect of these new marketing policies became evident in Fisher-Price's sales statistics almost immediately. With a greater number of products and higher volume sales on the already existing product line, it was not long before Fisher-Price's production capacity proved inadequate. In 1970, therefore, a new factory was added in Medina, New York, and a new shipping facility was built in Albion, New York, to accommodate the new sales levels.

PRICING POLICIES AND PRODUCT LINE

While Fisher-Price underwent substantial change as the company grew from a small toy producer to a major factor in the industry, executives who had grown up within the firm continued to cling to one unwritten rule of thumb throughout the company's history: namely, that a toy priced at over $5 retail would not sell in the marketplace. Despite inflationary pressures and increasing levels of disposable income, the old guard at Fisher-Price believed that their success had come from a moderate priced product line in the past and they were hesitant to deviate from this proven track record.

Accordingly, when Mr. Asthalter and Sales Manager Chuck Weinschreider were brought into the firm in the mid-1960s to take over Fisher-Price's market efforts, many of their new ideas met with considerable resistance. Both Asthalter and Weinschreider saw the American toy consumers as being affluent and willing to spend substantial sums on preschool toys if they could be assured of quality and good value for their money. The Fisher-Price image and product line were sufficiently strong, they reasoned, to command higher prices for larger and more intricate toys (Exhibit 9). Clearly, a company which had spent decades earning a reputation unequaled in the toy industry was not going to jeopardize the

Should the ATV be introduced?

If so:
   what price?
   should it be advertised independently of other F-P offerings?
   how should the product be positioned?
   what are the targets of promotion? (mother?, child?)

How do you assess F-P's strengths and weaknesses? How do they impact on the ATV decision?

Required analyses:

   breakeven
   model of the toy purchase process — where does it start? parent? child?

TOTAL MARKET = 2-3 BILLION
RIDING TOYS = 22% = 650 million
$15" & over = 33% = 183 million

PARENTS BUY = 72%
GRANDPARENTS = 11%
                83%

ATV TOOLING 161,000 FOR 500,000 PIECES
Spec tooling 18,000

quality of its products in order to keep prices below the $5 level. At the same time, however, many exciting new product ideas could not be followed through if this imaginary $5 barrier were to be strictly enforced.

Unfortunately, Fisher-Price's single excursion into the over $5 price level in the early 1960s had been a dismal failure. Specifically, in 1962 the company had introduced the Fisher-Price Circus—a snap-together set of circus animals, ladders, rings and the like—at a price of $6.83 to the trade and $13.95 retail (Exhibit 10). The Circus had commanded an average 45 minute attention span time from Fisher-Price's nursery school youngsters as compared with 10 or 15 minute playing times which the children allotted most other toys in the product line. Accordingly, the Circus was introduced into a line of 50 other toys all priced at $5 or less. While initial sales to the trade were reasonable, sales at the retail level were so poor that the toy was eventually dropped from production completely (Exhibit 11).

Against this backdrop, many Fisher-Price executives stood firm on their insistence that toys could not be priced at more than $5. Specifically, they pointed out that Fisher-Price sold a line of products to the trade and that most buyers purchased Fisher-Price toys sight unseen because of the company's reputability and fine track record. Certainly Fisher-Price could not endure more failures such as occurred with the Circus toy, and still command the respect and confidence of the trade.

After considerable controversy within the company, Messrs. Weinschreider and Asthalter did venture forth with another toy in 1964 which broke through the price barrier. This toy, called the Creative Coaster, was the first significant riding toy marketed by Fisher-Price and was priced at a still-modest-by-industry-standards $3.33 cost to the trade and $6.95 retail. Unlike the Circus, the Creative Coaster was a simple, wooden toy, solidly built but lacking a stylish design (Exhibit 12). It was positioned within Fisher-Price's then 72-product line to compete directly with Playskool's similarly constructed pre-school riding toys. Despite the head-on nature of the competition, the Creative Coaster met with great success, selling 226,000 units in 1964 and 332,000 units by 1970 when the price had been raised to $5.25 cost and $10.00 retail (Exhibit 13).

While many corporate officials were convinced that the Creative Coaster experience was a fluke and that the $5 price barrier remained a valid one, Asthalter and Weinschreider continued to pursue attractive toy concepts at a variety of price levels. In 1968 they introduced the Family Farm which pretested well in their nursery school and was expected to hold significant appeal to parents as well as children. Priced at $6.50 cost and $13.00 retail, orders for the Family Farm exceeded production capacity from the start and continued to sell well in the following years. The next higher priced toy, a Play House, was introduced in 1969 at $7 and $14 wholesale and retail respectively, and enjoyed similar success. Nonetheless, a considerable number of executives at Fisher-Price continued in their insistence that the firm should limit its product line to below the magic $5 level.

DEVELOPMENT OF THE ATV EXPLORER

As Fisher-Price continued to meet with success on new toy introductions as well as on their existing product line, Messrs. Asthalter and Weinschreider began seeking new opportunities within the pre-school market. The well-established acceptance of the Creative Coaster by 1969 led them to believe that additional riding toys held considerable promise for Fisher-Price. Discussions with salesmen and with buyers for major retail chains reinforced this belief and accordingly Asthalter requested that the engineering and product design people prepare prototypes of riding toys for product testing.

After considerable experimentation, a product was developed which appeared to hold great promise as an addition to the Fisher-Price line. The toy—called the ATV (All-Terrain Vehicle) Explorer—was a stylish, multicolored plastic vehicle, durable enough to carry as many as 200 pounds. It could be steered, came equipped with a horn, a motor-noise lever, and two small, removable passengers, and provided a storage space to carry additional toys. Designs on the side panels conveyed a moon exploration theme and included an American flag and a model space tracking screen (Exhibit 14).

By early 1970 the ATV Explorer was enjoying substantial success in the Fisher-Price nursery school, commanding a respectable 20-minute average attention span and a high level of repeat usage among youngsters from two to five years old. Furthermore, the toy showed itself to be safe, durable and educational, satisfying all the Fisher-Price guideposts.

Concepts tests among prospective purchasers proved similarly encouraging. In a series of market research sessions, parents of two- to five-year-olds were asked to anticipate their children's reactions to the toy and were then asked to assess the probability that they would purchase the ATV Explorer were it available at a $12 retail price. The direct costs were $4.21 for materials and $.73 for labor. Based upon the results of these interviews, Weinschreider estimated that Fisher-Price could sell about one million units of the toy annually, a volume equaled by only six other products in the Fisher-Price line. At this volume, the ATV would have accounted for higher sales than any other Fisher-Price toy by a wide margin.

While initial reactions were generally quite favorable, the ATV Explorer was not without its drawbacks. Fierce competition in the riding toy area was thought by some Fisher-Price salesmen and executives to justify scrapping the toy. Playskool, a major factor in the pre-school toy industry, had long dominated the riding toy market and was offering six such items in 1970. Industry gossip, however, led Fisher-Price executives to believe that Playskool was losing a substantial share of this market to small, unknown firms which were using new blow

molding processes to produce riding toys for as little as $3 or $4 retail. While these blow molded vehicles could not compare in quality, strength, durability, design and complexity to the Playskool or Fisher-Price entries, their low price apparently held substantial appeal to many toy purchasers. Accordingly, many of the more conservative members of the Fisher-Price staff believed the ATV Explorer far too risky a venture to pursue.

Nonetheless, Asthalter insisted that the gamble was well worth the risk which it carried. He pointed out to other executives that the entire Fisher-Price product line had been enjoying remarkable acceptance both within the trade and among parents (Exhibits 15 and 16). Moreover, Fisher-Price's higher priced entries—with the singular exception of the Circus—were all selling quite well, a factor which Asthalter attributed in great measure to a highly effective television advertising campaign. Finally, while projections of market size showed a decreasing number of children under six years of age in upcoming years (Exhibit 17), there was some reason to believe that the more optimistic forecasts for number of first births (Exhibit 18) was a more relevant market index given Fisher-Price's image as a maker of "hand-me-down" toys which last from one child to the next. For all of these reasons, the decision was made to go ahead with the ATV Explorer and in June 1970, Asthalter directed the Production Department to begin tooling up for the 1971–1972 season.

THE NEW PRICING DILEMMA

Within a month after the Asthalter directive had gone to the Production Department, Fisher-Price's vice president of manufacturing turned up in Asthalter's office with some unfortunate news. He explained that as his manufacturing design people pursued the ATV Explorer a bit more, they discovered that initial costs on the toy would be considerably higher than expected. Specifically, the initial investment in the mold from which the plastic toy would be made was to be $161,000, while special tooling costs would run another $18,000. The company traditionally amortized its investments over a one-year period. Thus, if Fisher-Price were to take its standard markup on cost, the toy would have to sell for $9.20 to the trade (about 17% of which would represent selling and administrative expense) which generally meant an $18.50 retail price. Suddenly, the ATV Explorer, which looked like an attractive investment at $12.00 retail, began to appear increasingly marginal.

Accordingly, Asthalter called in Chuck Weinschreider to discuss their new problem. As Fisher-Price's Sales Manager, Weinschreider suggested that they immediately get in touch with the company's 30-man sales force as well as the six major corporate buyers of Fisher-Price toys. These men were thought to be most sensitive to retail buying habits and were expected to offer much-needed advice on how to proceed with the ATV Explorer.

Contacting the salesmen and buyers, however, proved inconclusive. Many Fisher-Price salesmen, themselves solid believers in the company's product line, felt that customers would recognize value and pay for the new toy accordingly. Still others, generally optimistic, were hesitant to push the toy. While they recognized that a success with the ATV Explorer might mean inroads into a whole series of riding toys, these salesmen focused their concern on relations with the trade. As one of Fisher-Price's leading salesmen summed it up:

> We've spent years building a product line that we know will sell. And we've also spent years establishing a rapport with the trade so that each time Fisher-Price comes out with its annual product line these buyers give us orders with no hesitation. If we come out with this Explorer and it bombs, those retailers will be stuck but good. Stuck with a toy that sells for $18.50, not with a little $3 toy. That could mean a lot of inventory to carry, especially when you do almost all your business at Christmas time [Exhibit 19]. All we need is one failure—all we need to do is to hurt that retailer one time—and he's going to be afraid to take our advice for years to come. I think we should find a way to sell it for $12 or $13 or scrap it for good!

Reactions among major buyers were similarly mixed. Of the six national chains which accounted for a substantial percent of Fisher-Price's volume, two buyers commented that at any price the ATV Explorer would not be a good seller because the moon theme which it conveyed was outdated. Nonetheless, one of these buyers and three of the other four felt that the Fisher-Price name coupled with the attractive design and engineering of the toy would assure reasonable sales at the $18.50 level and accordingly said they would order the toy if Fisher-Price decided to include it in their 1971–1972 product line. Conversely, the remaining two buyers said they would refuse to order the Explorer, pointing to adverse economic conditions and expressing the belief that people will pay only so much for good quality toys.

Asthalter and Weinschreider were confused as to how to proceed. In order to get any definitive reading from the trade or the marketplace they would have to commit themselves to mold and tooling costs. And even at that, a single mold would only be capable of producing 500,000 units of the Explorer. Perhaps the market would be price insensitive and demand would come closer to initial forecasts. If that should happen, Fisher-Price would be unable to meet demand and could accordingly generate substantial ill-will among the trade. At the same time, however, an investment in two molds on a toy which remained a mystery seemed highly risky.

As they continued to discuss their alternatives, Asthalter and Weinschreider recognized still other options. For one, they could cheapen the product a bit, removing a horn or a plastic "passenger" or a secret compartment from the toy. While such an action would be totally inconsistent with the Fisher-Price policy of never sacrificing quality in toys, it would allow the Explorer's price to be brought into line with competitive riding toys.

Still another thought was to depart from corporate advertising policies and push the Explorer on television as a single item. Fisher-Price management has always insisted that they sold a line of toys rather than separate items and their advertising had always reflected this philosophy. Television advertising effectiveness to date, however, indicated that this medium was extremely effective and it could perhaps create a demand for the Explorer, even at the $18.50 level. In giving this idea consideration, Mr. Asthalter even went so far as to have television "storyboard" themes developed and to assess the costs of such a campaign (Exhibit 20).

The final series of options revolved around the price of the toy. Fisher-Price had always taken a fixed markup on direct costs for all of its toys. Possibly reducing its margin in this one instance would begin to bring the whole-sale cost and ultimately the retail price of the Explorer into line with competitive products. At the same time, however, both Weinschreider and Asthalter were reluctant to start a precedent which would permit the production

department to relax its cost cutting efforts with the thought that marketing could always lower its margins if costs got out of line.

On the other side of the fence, there was some consideration of milking the Explorer. Namely, Weinschreider felt that a toy which would sell at $18.50 would also sell at $19.50. Accordingly, he suggested that possibly Fisher-Price should actually increase its price by 50 cents or $1 and use the added revenues to support increased promotion, either to the trade or at the retail level.

With all these possibilities in the air, Asthalter realized that a decision would be necessary almost immediately if Fisher-Price were to have the Explorer in its 1971–1972 line. Because of the seasonal nature and lead times required in the toy business, Fisher-Price had to go into production on its toys by August in order to insure adequate distribution to meet the Christmas rush of the following year.

EXHIBIT 1

Where Toys Are Purchased

Question: How often do you buy pre-school toys in the following places?

	Usually	Sometimes	Never	No Answer
Discount Stores	43.0%	36.8%	7.1%	13.1%
Department Stores	23.6	50.3	12.7	13.5
Variety Stores	8.3	52.5	19.3	19.9
Toy Stores	14.7	38.4	26.5	20.5
Mail-Order Catalog	5.1	25.9	46.2	22.8
Supermarket	1.2	29.5	45.1	24.3
Military Base Store	2.3	1.0	—	—
Drug Store	.6	1.2	—	—
Baby Store	.3	1.	—	—
Other	.6	1.5	—	—

(*n* = 2339)

Note: These results were derived from 2,341 valid returns of a 4-page questionnaire mailed to 6,000 female *Redbook* subscribers, chosen randomly on an "*Nth*" name basis from the complete listing of *Redbook* subscribers.

Source: "*Redbook*'s Baby Products Study," June 1971.

EXHIBIT 2

Sales History of Fisher-Price Toys

Year	Dollar Sales (000)
1960	$ 7,000
1961	9,000
1962	12,000
1963	15,000
1964	16,000
1965	18,000
1966	22,000
1967	26,000
1968	30,000
1969	32,000
1970	52,000 (est.)

EXHIBIT 3

Unaided Brand Awareness Survey

Question: What brands of pre-school toys can you name?

	1962	1969
Fisher-Price	50%	75%
Playskool	85	86
Creative Playthings	N.A.	36
Mattel	78	87

(*n* = 2000)

Source: "*Redbook*'s Baby Products Study," June 1971.

EXHIBIT 4

Who Usually Buys Child's Toys

Question: Who usually buys most of your child's preschool toys?

Wife	63.2%*
Grandparents	30.7
Other Friends or Relatives	12.4
Husband	11.3
No Answer	5.0

(*n* = 2339)

*Note: Table adds to more than 100% because of multiple responses.

Source: "*Redbook*'s Baby Products Study," June 1971.

EXHIBIT 5

Example of Magazine Advertising, 1965

EXHIBIT 6

Retail Toy Display

EXHIBIT 7

Consumer Advertising Budget

1965	$202,000
1966	459,000
1967	365,000
1968	478,000
1969*	643,000
1970	1,100,000 (planned)

* The company began to use television advertising in 1969.

EXHIBIT 8

Attitudes toward Toys

Question: Considering toys in general, please indicate which of the following statements you agree or disagree with.

	Agree	*Disagree*	*No Answer*
Toys are good for children	97.0%	.6%	2.5%
Toys are good value for the money	33.1	60.3	6.5
Toy prices have held the line	12.4	80.2	7.4
There is a wide choice of toys	96.7	1.5	1.9
Toys are more fun than ever	70.5	24.7	4.8
It's difficult to shop for toys	47.1	48.8	4.1
Toys are made better than ever	31.6	62.9	5.5
Toys are safer than ever	44.8	49.0	6.2
You spend too much on toys	54.9	39.7	5.4
Toys last longer than they used to	27.6	65.5	6.8
Toys are more educational than ever	92.4	5.0	2.6

(*n* = 2339)

Source: "*Redbook*'s Baby Products Study," June 1971.

EXHIBIT 9

Best-Known Brand Assessment

Question: Which do you consider the best-known brand of pre-school toys?

Brand	Percentage of Respondents
Fisher-Price	64.7%
Playskool	13.0
Mattel	3.2
Creative Playthings	2.3
Childcraft	.6
Kenner	.4
Tonka	.4
Tupperware	.4
Romper Room	.3
Child Guidance	.3
Hasbro	.1
Kohner	.1
Remco	.1
Other	.7
Don't Know/No Answer	17.4

(*n* = 2339)

Source: "*Redbook*'s Baby Products Study," June 1971.

EXHIBIT 11

Sales History of the Fisher-Price Circus

Year	Unit Sales of Circus
1962	57,000
1963	17,000
1964	13,000
1965	10,000
1966	20,000
1967	27,000
1968	27,500
1969	22,000
1970	Discontinued

EXHIBIT 10

Fisher-Price Circus

EXHIBIT 12

Creative Coaster

EXHIBIT 13

Sales History of the Creative Coaster

Year	Unit Sales of Coaster
1964	226,000
1965	292,000
1966	263,000
1967	254,000
1968	292,000
1969	324,000
1970	332,000 (est.)

EXHIBIT 14

ATV Explorer

EXHIBIT 15

Brand Loyalty Measure

Question: Do you buy one brand of pre-school toys most often?

Response	Percentage of Respondents
Buy one brand most often	60.5%
Do not buy one brand most often	30.1
No answer	9.4

(*n* = 2339)

Source: "*Redbook*'s Baby Products Study," June 1971.

EXHIBIT 16

Brand Purchased Most Often

Question: Which brand of pre-school toys do you buy most often?

Brand	Percentage of Respondents
Fisher-Price	82.7%
Playskool	11.3
Creative Playthings	4.3
Mattel	1.4
Childcraft	.5
Tonka	.5
Child Guidance	.2
Kenner	.2
Remco	.2
Other	1.4
No Answer	.7

(*n* = 1414)

Source: "*Redbook*'s Baby Products Study," June 1971.

EXHIBIT 17

Number of Children under 6 years of age, 1960-1980

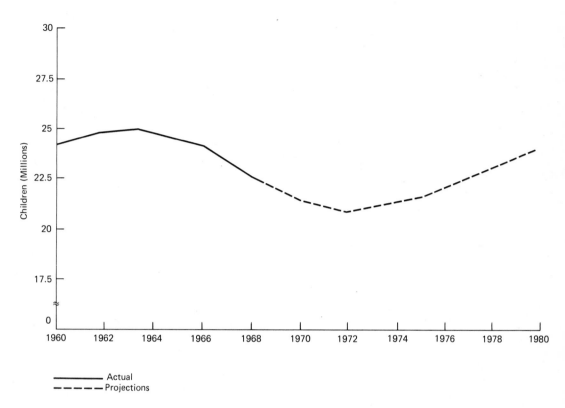

────── Actual

─ ─ ─ ─ Projections

Source: 1960–1969—N.I.C.B./Bureau of the Census.
1970–1980—Bureau of the Census, Series "D" Projections, August 1970—Series P-25—No. 448.

EXHIBIT 18

Number of First Births, 1960-1980

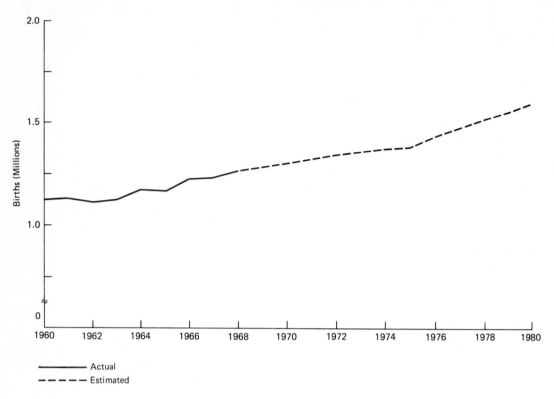

Source: N.I.C.B. Statistical Supplement—The Consumer of the 70s.

EXHIBIT 19

Monthly Sales Percentages

Month	Percent of Sales to Consumer	Percent of Sales to Trade
January	1.8%	3.6%
February	2.6	3.2
March	3.5	8.9
April	3.5	8.2
May	3.3	7.1
June	5.1	8.8
July	4.7	12.0
August	4.1	10.1
September	3.9	12.0
October	5.6	14.5
November	20.6	7.0
December	41.3	4.6

EXHIBIT 20

Proposed Television Storyboard for ATV Explorer

"ATV" Explorer," 30 seconds . . . features our #980 ATV EXplorer but sells the line concept of the quality inherent in all Fisher-Price toys.

Video: ATV Explorer on turntable, slowly revolving to show features.

Anncr.: "Fisher-Price introduces the ATV Explorer."

Anncr.: "This rugged vehicle has six-wheel design, front and back axle maneuverability . . ."

Anncr.: "Flip down cargo space and no motor at all! Its energy source is a remarkable perpetual motion machine."

Anncr.: "Ahh, here it comes now!"

Video: Toddler runs up to car. Flips cargo steps closed.

Video: Jumps on and rides off, beeping horn and working "motor" noise lever.

Super: The Fisher-Price ATV Explorer.

Typical daytime programs utilized will be "Let's Make A Deal," "The Lucy Show," "Where The Heart Is."

Sales-stimulating new commercial "brings them into your store"!

The Adult Toy Buyer: An Exploration of How Parents and Nonparents Buy Toys

TABLE 1

Sources of Toy Ideas
(By Age of Children in Household)

Based on open-end question: "Generally, where do you get ideas for toys to buy for your children?"

	Age of Children			
	6-7	*8-9*	*10-12*	*Over 12*
Sources of Toys Ideas				
Children Themselves	73%	78%	71%	67%
Television	65	56	46	43
Catalogs	35	38	34	29
Newspaper	26	27	31	30
Store Displays	22	23	23	23
Other Adults	13	6	6	6
All Other Sources	4	4	6	6
No Answer	—	—	—	—
Base: Parents	(168)	(97)	(111)	(90)

Sponsored by American Newspaper Publishers Association, 1970.

Reproduced in condensed form by permission of: Bureau of Advertising A.N.P.A.

TABLE 2

"Best" Source of Toy Ideas
(By Presence of Children in Household)

Based on open-end question: "Generally, who or what do you feel is the best source of toy ideas?"

	Total	Parents*	Nonparents**
Best Source			
Children Themselves	40%	40%	42%
Television	21	24	8
Store Displays	13	13	10
Catalogs	11	10	15
Newspaper	4	4	5
Other Adults	4	3	8
All Other Sources	2	1	5
No Answer	5	5	7
Base: All Respondents	(400)	(340)	(60)

 * Have children 12 years old or younger.

** No children 12 years old or younger present.

TABLE 3

Agreement* with Attitudes on Toy Buying
(By Presence of Children in Household)

Based on 4-point scale: Very True, Somewhat True, Somewhat False, Very False.

	Total	Parents**	Nonparents***
Agreement with Attitudes			
Good toys are very important in molding a child.	94%	93%	97%
People spend too much money on toys.	88	89	80
Toys are poorly made and don't last.	74	75	70
Toys keep children occupied and quiet.	74	72	86
When buying toys, I think about those I would have liked when I was a child.	66	65	70
In shopping for toys, I often play with them myself before I buy.	59	59	56
I get confused when choosing from the great variety of toys.	55	56	56
Base: All Respondents	(400)	(340)	(60)

 * Very True, Somewhat True combined.

 ** Have children 12 years old or younger.

*** No children 12 years old or younger present.

TABLE 4

Agreement* with Attitudes on Toy Buying
(By Total Yearly Income)

Based on 4-point scale: Very True, Somewhat True, Somewhat False, Very False.

		Income		
	Total	Under $5,000	$5,000 to $9,000	$10,000 and Over
Agreement with Attitudes				
Good toys are very important in molding a child.	94%	94%	94%	93%
People spend too much money on toys.	88	87	89	86
Toys are poorly made and don't last.	74	60	76	78
Toys keep children occupied and quiet.	74	77	75	72
When buying toys, I think about those I would have liked when I was a child.	66	66	73	56
In shopping for toys, I often play with them myself before I buy.	59	65	63	51
I get confused when choosing from the great variety of toys.	55	54	60	48
Base: All Respondents	(400)	(52)	(218)	(125)

* Very True, Somewhat True combined.

TABLE 5

Type of Toys Vetoed

Based on open-end question: "Thinking back to the last time you vetoed a toy your child asked you to buy: what type of toy was it?"

Type of Toys Vetoed	Total Parents
Dolls, Doll Clothes, etc.	21%
Toy Guns, War Toys, Toys of Violence	20
Nonriding Transportation Toys	17
Activity Toys	10
Games, Puzzles	7
Riding Toys, Accessories	5
Handicrafts, Models	4
Sporting Goods	3
All Others	12
No Answer	1
Base: Respondents who decided not to buy particular toy for a child	(246)

TABLE 6

Last Toy Purchased—Kind of Toy
(By Presence of Children in Household)

Based on open-end question: "What was the last toy you purchased for (your) (a) child?"

Kind of Toy Purchased	Total	Parents**	Nonparents***
Nonriding Transportation Toy	21%	22%	21%
Dolls, Doll Clothing	17	15	27
Games, Puzzles	12	14	8
Toy Guns, Knives, War Toys	7	6	12
Riding Toys and Accessories			
(Excluding Bicycles)	6	6	8
Activity Toys	6	6	5
Musical Toys	5	5	4
Handicraft and Models	5	5	3
Education and Scientific Toys	5	5	2
Preschool Toys	4	4	3
Stuffed Toys	3	3	3
Child's Furniture	3	3	2
Sporting Goods	2	2	2
All Other Toys	4	4	—
Unidentifiable Toys	*	*	—
Base: All Respondents	(400)	(340)	(60)

* Less than 0.5%.

** Have children 12 years old or younger.

*** No children 12 years old or younger present.

TABLE 7

Last Toy Purchased—Assistance in Decision Making
(By Presence of Children in Household)

Based on open-question: "Think of the last time you went to buy a toy but changed your mind and bought another toy. What was the most important thing that made you change your mind?"

	Total	Parents*	Nonparents**
Assisted by:			
Display	52%	52%	60%
Children	22	22	20
Salesperson	5	5	5
All Others***	18	18	15
No Answer	3	3	—
Base: Respondents who changed their mind after start of shopping trip	(118)	(98)	(20)

* Have children 12 years old or younger.

** No children 12 years old or younger present.

*** Includes such things as: "Price of toy purchased cheaper than planned toy," "Didn't have any money," "Just looking for an idea."

TABLE 8

Last Toy* Purchased—Kind of Store
(By Presence of Children in Household)

Based on open-end question: "In what type of store did you buy the most recent toy for (your) (a) child?"

Kind of Store	Total	Parents**	Nonparents***
Department Store	40%	40%	43%
Discount Store	33	35	24
Toy Store	10	9	18
Five & Ten Variety Store	5	4	7
Drug Store	2	3	—
Supermarket	2	2	—
Other Kind of Store	8	7	8
Base: All Respondents	(400)	(340)	(60)

   * Toy over $1.50.

   ** Have children 12 years old or younger.

   *** No children 12 years old or younger present.

TABLE 9

Person Suggesting Last Toy Purchased
(By Presence of Children in Household)

Based on open-end question: "Did either an adult or this child (for whom toy purchased) suggest this toy to you?"

	Total	Parents*	Nonparents**
Suggested by:			
Child Himself	48%	50%	36%
Child's Parent	6	5	8
Other Adult	4	4	5
Other Relative	2	2	3
Not Suggested	40	39	48
Base: All Respondents	(400)	(340)	(60)

   * Have children 12 years old or younger.

   ** No children 12 years old or younger present.

TABLE 10

Planning of Last Toy Purchased
(By Presence of Children in Household)

Based on question: "Thinking back to the last toy you bought, did you buy the toy you planned to buy, did you buy a toy other than the one you'd planned to buy, or did you not have any particular toy in mind?"

	Total	Parents*	Nonparents**
Planned a Toy Purchase	82 = (328)	82 = (280)	80 = (48)
	%	%	%
Bought toy planned to buy	86	86	83
Didn't have particular toy in in mind	12	11	17
Bought toy other than planned toy	2	3	—
Did not plan purchase	*18*	*18*	*20*
Base: All Respondents	(400)	(340)	(60)

* Have children 12 years old or younger.

** No children 12 years old or younger present.

TABLE 11

Who Went on Last Toy Shopping Trip
(By Presence of Children in Household)

Based on open-end question: "Who accompanied you when you went to buy the last toy you bought for (your) (a) child?"

	Total	Parents*	Nonparents**
Accompanied by Other Person	*61%*	*62%*	*60%*
Spouse	38	39	33
Friend or Relative	11	10	20
Child	12	13	7
No one—purchased alone	*39%*	*38%*	*40%*
Base: All Respondents	(400)	(340)	(60)

* Have children 12 years old or younger.

** No children 12 years old or younger present.

TABLE 12

Place of Awareness of Toy Advertising—Past Two Weeks
(By Age of Children in Household)

Based on open-end question: "In the last two weeks, where have you seen toy advertising?"

	Total Parents	Young* Child Only	Old** Child Only	Young and Old Child
Place of Advertising Awareness				
Television	87%	93%	89%	85%
Newspaper	71	71	64	75
Store Displays	32	34	27	35
Mail Circulars	24	20	32	22
Magazines	18	17	16	21
Radio	8	7	7	11
Others	1	2	2	1
Base: All Parents	(400)	(137)	(44)	(116)

* Under 7 years old.

** Over 7 years old.

(Columns add to more than 100% due to multiple mentions.)

TABLE 13

Recall of Advertising—Specific Toy Recalled
(By Presence of Children in Household)

Based on open-end question asked of those who said they recalled toy advertising in past two weeks: "What kind of toy was being advertised?"

	Total	Parents**	Nonparents***
Toy Advertised Recalled	80 = (276)	83 = (245)	65 = (31)
Toys Advertised	%	%	%
Dolls, Doll Accessories	38	37	42
Nonriding Transportation Toy	28	28	26
Games/Puzzles	11	11	13
Activity Toys	7	7	7
Toy Guns, War Toys, Knives	7	7	3
Preschool Toys	3	3	—
Riding Toys & Accessories	3	2	3
Handicrafts/Models	3	2	3
Child-Size Furniture	1	*	7
Stuffed Toys	1	1	—
All Other	5	5	3
Toys Advertised not Recalled	20	17	35
Base: All Respondents	(400)	(340)	(60)

* Less than 0.5%.

** Have children 12 years old or younger.

*** No children 12 years old or younger present.

(Columns add to more than 100% due to multiple mentions.)

TABLE 14

Viewing of Child-Oriented TV Programs
(By Presence of Children in Household)

Based on open-end question: "What child-oriented television programs do you sometimes watch? By child-oriented, I mean shows that (your) (a) child almost always watches and enjoys, like on Saturday mornings and late weekday afternoons."

	Total	Parents*	Nonparents**
Viewing of Child-Oriented Programs			
1–2 Programs	35%	34%	38%
3–4 Programs	18	20	13
5–6 Programs	12	12	12
7–24 Programs	13	14	5
Nonviewers	22	20	32
Base: All Respondents	(400)	(340)	(60)

 * Have children 12 years old or younger.

** No children 12 years old or younger present.

TABLE 15

Agreement* with Statements about TV Commercials
(By Presence of Children in Household)

Based on question: "Here is a list of some things people say about advertising to children. For each of these descriptions, please check one space to indicate if you feel the description is "very true," "somewhat true," "somewhat false," or "very false."

	Total	Parents**	Nonparents***
TV Commercials Are:			
Too "Pushy"	71%	74%	53%
Much too Dramatic	66	70	45
Misleading	65	68	45
Nice for Children	57	54	69
Very Amusing	54	53	57
Generally Truthful	49	48	59
Very Realistic	46	45	45
Annoying to Me	45	49	27
Bad for Children	39	39	35
Base: All Respondents	(400)	(340)	(60)

 * Very True, Somewhat True combined.

 ** Have children 12 years or younger.

*** No children 12 years old or younger present.

APPENDIX

National Toy Advertising Expenditures

	Total	Network[1] Television	Spot[2] Television	Newspapers*[3]	Magazines[4]
Top 10:					
Mattel, Inc.	10,016,442	6,449,000	2,907,920	—	659,522
DeLuxe Topper Corp.	7,874,935	4,849,800	2,799,680	—	225,455
Ideal Toy Corp.	2,912,010	1,959,000	953,010	—	—
Hassenfield Bros.	2,493,680	740,800	1,752,880	—	—
Marx, Louis & Co.	2,468,700	1,313,000	1,155,700	—	—
Remco Industries	2,008,520	1,313,000	695,520	—	—
Bradley, Milton Co.	1,701,227	1,111,800	555,050	9,700	34,280
Kenner Products Co.	1,608,585	826,200	768,960	—	13,425
Multiple Products, Inc.	876,960	651,900	225,060	—	—
Wham-O Manufacturing Co.	758,090	39,200	718,890	—	—
Total Top 10 Toy Advertising Expenditures	$32,719,149	$19,253,700	$12,532,670	$ 9,700	$ 932,682
All Other Toy Advertising Expenditures	$ 8,476,143	$ 1,619,300	$ 5,847,511	$ 95,151	$ 914,181
Grand Total-Toy Advertising Expenditures	$41,204,895	$20,873,000	$18,380,181	$104,851	$1,846,863

* Includes newspaper supplements.

Note: Expenditures do not include retail or co-op advertising expenditures.

Source: [1]TVB/Rorabaugh, [2]LNA–BAR, [3]Media Records, 1965–1966, [4]Publisher's Information Bureau.

CHAPTER 3

Sears, Roebuck & Co.: The Tri-Blend Decision

In January 1971, Mr. Charles Pallino received the last in a series of product feature studies that he had commissioned for a new line of boys' jeans. As Senior Buyer in the Sears Boys' Department, Mr. Pallino had been supervising the so-called Tri-Blend product development program for well over a year. The technical development phase of the program had gone quite well, but a great many marketing strategy decisions had yet to be made. Among the decisions that Mr. Pallino had to

This case was prepared by Edward T. Popper, Research Assistant, under the supervision of Professor Scott Ward, The Wharton School, as a basis for class discussion rather than to illustrate either effective or ineffective handling of an administrative situation.

Distributed by the Intercollegiate Case Clearing House, Soldiers Field, Boston, Mass. 02163. All rights reserved to the contributors. Printed in U.S.A. Revised January 1977 by F. Stewart DeBruicker, Assistant Professor, The Wharton School, University of Pennsylvania.

make were the choice of a product differentiation strategy, a product line pricing policy, and whether to commit the product to a Sears National Brand merchandising program. To assist him in his decision making, Mr. Pallino had drawn together the relevant sections of research studies dating back as far as 1968. The studies provided insights into the matchups between segments and the Sears Children's Store; consumer buying processes within the jeans product category; and consumer perceptions of the Tri-Blend jean.

Mr. Pallino was specifically concerned about whether consumers were prepared to pay a premium price for an exceptionally durable children's jean, especially since a similar durable boys' trousers product marketed by Sears had failed to gain acceptance by consumers.

The Boys' Clothing Department (Department 640) was one of three departments making up the Sears Children's Store, which was headed by Mr. Ira Quint. The Children's

Store also included the Girls' Clothing Department (Department 677) and the Infants' and Children's Wear Department (Department 629). Both of these departments were to receive the product and marketing program developed by Mr. Pallino, though the greatest potential for the program was believed to be in Department 640.

THE INFANTS' AND CHILDREN'S CLOTHING MARKET

Sears had developed a position as one of the nation's leading merchandisers of children's and infants' clothing. A survey conducted in early 1968 in Sears' five sales territories indicated that those consumers buying most of their children's wear at Sears were drawn from all age, income, and occupational groups. The Sears consumer profile showed only minor differences from the consumer profiles of most other stores, though Sears seemed to have a better position with consumers in the 25 to 30 age bracket, with incomes from between $5 thousand and $10 thousand per year, and among the higher paid blue collar worker families. Additional characteristics of the Sears consumer of infants' and children's wear are listed in Exhibits 1 and 2.

Since the Children's Store carried merchandise intended for use by all children from birth through age 17 for boys, and age 14 for girls, Mr. Pallino and his colleagues had to take many different purchasers into account as they planned marketing programs. Exhibit 3 lists store and product characteristics that were important to female household heads in choosing stores, but since, as indicated in Exhibit 4, at least 80 percent of all children over the age of 6 select at least some of their own clothes, Mr. Pallino also had to take into account the interactions between parents and children in making clothing purchase decisions. Most adult shoppers, when asked how they decided whether children's clothing was durable enough to withstand repeated wearings and washings, indicated that they depended on

label information first, and then in descending order on the following factors: materials and workmanship, general quality impressions, past experience, and faith in a store. Brand name reliance, as listed in Exhibit 5, was least important to Sears' shoppers and to those shopping for girls' clothing.

Shoppers for younger boys' slacks demonstrated much less satisfaction with the durability of the products they bought, indicated in Exhibit 6, than shoppers for slacks for older boys. Finally, the 1968 survey indicated that for all shoppers for infants' and children's wear that newspapers were by far the most helpful sources of advertised information. Exhibit 7 lists the perceived helpfulness of a variety of other media.

While the 1968 Infants' and Children's Clothing Market Survey, as excerpted by Mr. Pallino, was helpful in building a broad background picture of the market in which the Tri-Blend program would be introduced, he found it lacking in information pertaining more specifically to the jeans product category. He was assisted by Sears' Market Research Group (Department 733MR) in locating a second study, conducted in July 1968 on a mail panel sample of mothers of boys aged 6 to 12 and a separate sample of boys aged 13 to 17. This provided a somewhat clearer picture of Sears' position within the children's jeans product category.

Sears had always had a strong position in the total jeans market. According to Mr. Pallino, this was due to an evolution of Sears' strength in work clothing for men which transferred to the boys' lines. This interdependency among various lines seemed especially true prior to the change in consumer tastes in the late 1960s when boys' jeans changed from their traditional role as play pants to acceptable school wear. This so-called jeans boom made jeans into a fashion item, much in demand by teenagers. Though the battle for the late teen and young adult jeans market was generally fought and won by nationally branded products sold by manufacturers such as Levi Strauss,

Wrangler and Lee via department stores and specialty stores, the children's and little boys' market was dominated by the major chain retailers.

As indicated in Exhibit 8, only 3 percent of the mothers surveyed had not bought jeans for their children in the previous year, and only 16 percent of the boys between age 13 and 17 had not purchased at least one pair of jeans in the same time period. The jeans phenomenon applied to consumers in small, medium and large population areas, as indicated in Exhibit 9. The study omitted consideration of consumers in very small cities and remote rural areas since they were not likely to be in an area conveniently served by an existing Sears retail outlet. Since catalog sales of jeans accounted for only 1 percent of the most recent purchase events, as indicated in Exhibit 10, Mr. Pallino felt that he was correct in designing his ultimate merchandising program with the retail store buyer in mind, with the catalog buyer remaining a secondary consideration. Exhibit 10 also confirms that Sears led all chain department stores with a 19 percent share of most recent purchase events. Penneys was second with 17 percent. Among other store types, local department stores held 33 percent of most recent purchase events, and discount stores accounted for only 7 percent. Exhibit 11 lists the number of pairs bought and the prices paid tabulated by the purchaser's age and by type of outlet. The loyalty to outlets, when measured by asking whether the most recently purchased pair of jeans was purchased at the same store as the second most recently purchased pair, was indicated as follows:

The family income distributions, tabulated by the type of outlet where jeans were last purchased, were as follows:

	Total	Sears	Penney's Wards
Under $5,000	8%	7%	7%
$5,000-7,999	35	40	35
8,000-9,999	25	23	25
10,000-14,999	24	23	26
15,000 and over	8	7	7
Total	100%	100%	100%
Base	(357)	(70)	(75)

	Local Dept. Stores	Clothing Stores	All Other
Under $5,000	7%	5%	24%
$5,000-$7,999	32	32	38
8,000-9,999	25	35	19
10,000-14,999	28	19	16
15,000 and over	8	9	3
Total	100%	100%	100%
Base	(118)	(57)	(37)

Exhibit 12 indicates the relative degrees of influence used by parents and children in the choices of stores and styles. Mr. Pallino was interested in the fact that even for 16 and 17 year old boys the mother still had a significant influence on the outlet choice decision. Exhibit 13 presents data on those product attributes that influenced the style choice decision. Parents naturally tended to place more importance on issues of durability and ease of washing and ironing, while older boys showed much stronger interest in matters of fashion. Since the Tri-Blend program was mounted to offer

		Respondent		Outlet (Last Purchase)				
	Total	Mothers	Teens	Sears	Penney's Wards	Local Dept. Store	Clothing Store	All Other
Bought jeans last time at								
Same outlet as time before last	63%	59%	68%	69%	77%	58%	55%	51%
Different outlet than time before last	37	41	32	31	23	42	45	49
	100%	100%	100%	100%	100%	100%	100%	100%
Base	(357)	(.95)	(162)	(70)	(75)	(118)	(57)	(37)

consumers greater durability than had traditionally been available in boys' jeans, Mr. Pallino was determined to make the durability issue a major part of his marketing program. Whether consumers would care enough about durability to change their buying habits and pay higher prices was something that was yet to be proved in practice, however.

Exhibit 14 lists likes and dislikes of mothers and wearers about boys' jeans, Exhibit 15 lists color and material preferences, and Exhibit 16 lists the respondents' willingness to pay extra amounts for jeans that featured Perma Press (a feature that eliminated the need for ironing) and non-shrink characteristics. Mr. Pallino was disappointed to find that the 1968 study had not asked questions regarding the price sensitivity of durability attributes, but when asked to indicate the believability of claims of durability based on fabric weight, the responses were as follows:

Q. Would you say this statement is true, false, or you don't know: "The heavier the fabric, the more durable the jeans?"

	Total	Mothers	Teens 13-15	Teens 16-17
True	30%	31%	37%	24%
False	38	43	26	38
Don't Know	32	26	37	38
Total	100%	100%	100%	100%
Base	(398)	(203)	(79)	(114)

Since the knee area was where jeans usually wore out first, the 1968 Jeans Survey asked whether gradual wear, or sudden ripping was of greater concern. The responses were as follows:

Q. Are you most concerned with the gradual wear at the knees because of the normal wear there, or with ripping?

	Total	Mothers	Teens 13-15	Teens 16-17
% concerned with gradual wear of knee	63%	63%	62%	65%

	Total	Mothers	Teens 13-15	Teens 16-17
Ripping at the knee	31	32	33	25
No answer	6	5	5	10
Total	100%	100%	100%	100%
Base	(398)	(203)	(79)	(114)

Finally, respondents were asked their feelings about the types of reinforcement, if any, that the knee area of boys' jeans should have. This question clearly separated the respondents according to mothers vs. teenage boys, and by type of outlet last patronized, as shown on p. 65.

Though the 1968 survey had obviously been conducted before product development had begun on the Tri-Blend program, Mr. Pallino was quite concerned that the durability claims that would very likely be the major part of his merchandising program, would in fact be salient to both mothers and boys alike, and that the claims would be of competitive value in Departments 677 and 629 as well.

THE INDESTRUCTABLES EXPERIENCE

The boys' jeans line covered a range of prices, with the primary price points being $1.98, $2.98 and $3.98. The largest selling item was the top of the line product, the Sears Circle S jean selling at $3.99. Sears traditionally had followed a policy of providing the consumer with the highest possible quality available at any given price. If there was a way to improve the quality and the value the consumer would receive, Mr. Pallino felt that both he and Sears had an obligation to do it.

There were some negative indications as to the opportunities for a higher quality product. Another buyer in the Boys' Department had recently introduced a product called Indestructables and they hadn't been successful. The Indestructables were a corduroy casual jean that was composed of 72 percent nylon and 28 percent cotton (as opposed to 60 percent cotton and 40 percent nylon in Circle S). Laboratory tests demonstrated that the product was

Q. If you were to buy jeans with reinforced knees, which of these types would you prefer? That is, do you prefer a patch of the same material vulcanized to the fabric, inside, at the knee, *or* a tissue-thin polypropylene patch sealed to the fabric, inside, at the knee?

		Respondent Group			Outlet	
Interest in Reinforced Knees	*Total*	*Mothers*	*Teens 13–15*	*Teens 16–17*	*Sears*	*All Others*
Prefer same material vulcanized	20%	32%	18%	3%	23%	20%
Prefer polypropylene patch sealed to fabric	15	20	9	10	23	13
Makes no difference	25	27	24	24	30	24
Do not want reinforced knees	40	21	49	63	24	43
Total	100%	100%	100%	100%	100%	100%
Base	(398)	(203)	(79)	(114)	(70)	(328)

stronger and more durable than any other product on the market and would stand up to heavy wear without needing double knees. They were made in a full range of styles with quality features like Talon Memory Lock® zippers. The product had been targeted for both Department 629 and Department 640 to help defray the high start-up costs. Retail prices were $4.99 for little boys and $5.99 for bigger boys.

To gain consumer support the product was featured in corporate print advertising the month of October 1969, coming directly after the department's major Back to School promotions during August and September. The ads, which appeared in major women's magazines and color newspaper roto sections in major markets, featured the Indestructable's durability story and tied in with the overall promotion themes called the "Sears Cares" campaign. Advertising done by Departments 629, 640 and 677 featured specific products each month as national traffic builders for the Children's Store, and for the entire store as well. Products that were featured in these corporate ads were required to be carried by every Sears store in the country in a full range of sizes, colors and styles. Normally the Sears Retail Division Managers had a great deal of discretion in what they should carry and in what volumes, they could even elect not to carry an item at all.

Traditionally Sears had marketed company branded products rather than nationally branded products. Although Sears was maintaining its no non-Sears brands policy it was modifying it with the introduction of Sears' National Brands. These were products which had a brand which belonged solely to Sears but which received national promotional support similar to that received by manufacturer brands. This was not a new policy for Sears but until recently this national brand status had been reserved for major durables like home appliances (Kenmore) and home electronics (Silvertone). New national promotional campaigns had established the Sears DieHard battery, radial tires and Craftsman tools. In the Children's Store, Winnie the Pooh was being developed as a top of the line brand of clothes. Sears "Circle S" jeans had never been promoted on a national basis.

The Indestructables program was presented to the field store personnel at Territorial Totes. Totes were meetings where the product lines were presented by the buyers from Sears Headquarters so that the divisional managers might decide what items to carry and in what quantities.

The Indestructables were well received by the field, with the exception of the Pacific Southwest where there was some store resistance to corduroy. This regional objection was overcome by showing how well other children's category corduroy items had performed. Unfortunately, consumers did not accept the item. Although they sold well in some areas, sales were very low in the South and Southwest. As inventories built up the product was marked down in price and sold off. Field reorders were low. Eventually, the product was discontinued.

THE TRI-BLEND JEAN

As a Sears buyer, Mr. Pallino's responsibility was to develop sources for his products. This was not merely to find companies that made products he would like to buy. Rather, it was to develop relations with suppliers that would guarantee Sears a source of supply and the manufacturer a profit. In the case of jeans this extended beyond the firm that manufactured the pants themselves to the mill that made the fabric and even the sources of the fiber of which the fabric was made.

Because of the high volumes necessary to supply its vast network of retail outlets, Sears was able to command substantial power among its suppliers. In its typical buying arrangement, the Sears buyer and the supplier operated on a known cost contract with Sears paying a specific percentage over the actual production cost and the supplier getting a fixed profit margin. This volume buying resulted in lower costs for Sears.

The Division Managers in the stores also had pricing authority for the products they sold in their departments. If they bought their products from the Sears parent company at the actual cost paid by the parent they might be tempted to cut prices, increase volume, and increase profits at the store level. Unfortunately, this could have a negative impact on the product planning done by the Sears Parent Merchandising Staff. To control this possibility, products were sold to the stores at a price that would provide a typical profit margin for that department if sold at the suggested retail price. The difference between the price paid by the stores to the parent, and the price paid by the parent company to the supplier, created a pool of funds that could be used for promotional programs to launch a product, pay for national advertising programs, and subsidize the costs of other products under development. In effect,

each Sears buyer acted as a captain in the distribution channel between the manufacturer and the retail outlet.

To make a more durable jean, Mr. Pallino felt he would have to develop a more durable fabric than the one used in the Circle S jean, then the best fabric on the market.

One criteria for durability was whether the knees would rip through. When jeans tore at the knee they almost always tore across the knee from side to side rather than up and down passing over the knee. This meant that the tear occurred when the warp fibers (those fibers going from the top of the leg to the bottom) ruptured rather than the fill (those fibers going from side to side across the leg). A stronger jean would require a stronger warp. DuPont had been working with a new fiber that was a blend of 65 percent dacron and 35 percent nylon. Laboratory tests had proven this fiber to yield an extremely strong fabric. Mr. Pallino decided that this new all synthetic fiber would be the warp for his new jeans. The fill would be part cotton (which would provide absorbency and softness) and part polyester (which provided both strength and allowed the fabric to drape, or fit the body better). The result was a tri-blend fabric, a fabric composed of three different fibers (cotton, polyester and the nylon/ dacron blend) each lending different performance attributes to the product.

A test run of 100 yards of the product was made by DuPont in its Pilot Mill and submitted to the Sears testing laboratories for a performance test. These tests showed that the new Tri-Blend had a greater tensile strength than any other pant on the market, would not fade, and would shrink no more than 1–1½ percent.

The jeans Mr. Pallino designed had heavy duty brass zippers, vulcanized Neoprene double knee patches and the double needle stitching traditionally found on jeans. Double stitching provided two parallel seams for added seam strength. He also used a stronger thread for the stitching (a size 30 strand of polyester sheathed in cotton). The method used to test the strength of the seams was to determine the weight required to break through a seat seam. The minimum acceptable Sears laboratory standard was 50 pounds of force. The Circle S seat seam tested to 65 pounds. The new Tri-Blend tested to 120 pounds.

Having designed what he considered to be an extremely durable jean, Mr. Pallino ordered samples made up for a wear test. Sears conducted this test at a Chicago orphanage. Each of the boys in the orphanage was given two pairs of pants—one pair of the new Tri-Blend jeans and one pair of the Sears Circle S jeans to be worn throughout the day. On Monday the boys would wear the Tri-Blend jeans for the entire day. That evening, Sears technicians would collect all the jeans worn that day and wash them under home laundry conditions. On Tuesday, the boys would wear the Circle S jeans, which would be washed Tuesday night. On Wednesday, the boys would get back their Tri-Blends, on Thursday the Circle S, and so forth until each pair of pants had been worn 100 days and washed 100 times for a total testing cycle of 200 days. At the end of the test not one of the Tri-Blend jeans showed a rupture or tear while the Circle S jean, which Mr. Pallino considered to be the strongest jean in the country, showed product failures after as few as 35, 40 and 50 days.

Mr. Pallino then moved forward to find a source for the fabric itself. He chose West Point Pepperell, maker of the Circle S fabric. Pepperell had experience in working with synthetic warps, which because they had to be woven at high tensions, were extremely difficult to weave. Pepperell developed a dyeing procedure for the Tri-Blend in which the warp fibers were boiled in a pressure chamber for eight hours in order to impregnate the dye into the fiber. Using this process the jeans would be color fast and there would be no washing out or fading of the colors.

There was no question that the Tri-Blend jean he had designed was the most durable on the market. Now Mr. Pallino was faced with deciding how to market the product. It would have to sell for at least $1.00 more than the Circle S, top of the line jean. He had to be sure before going any further that there was a market for the product.

RESEARCH FOR THE TRI-BLEND MARKETING PROGRAM

Mr. Pallino's first problem was to estimate the relationship between the perceived quality of the Tri-Blend product, which had been temporarily named the Tough Jean, and consumers' price sensitivity to a premium pricing strategy. To help him in this matter, he called on Department 733MR to design a study of price and quality issues for boys' jeans. An experimentally designed study was conducted in October 1970. Individual personnel interviews were conducted with 300 mothers at a permanent interviewing location in the Hillside Shopping Center, west of Chicago. Three different jeans were displayed, all unbranded:

1. present $2.99, 75% cotton, 25% nylon blend, Code T.
2. present $3.99, 60% cotton, 40% nylon blend, Code P, Present Sears best.
3. proposed $4.99, dacron, nylon, cotton blend, Code R, New Tough Jean.

To measure the degree to which women could determine, by inspection and handling alone, the relative quality of three jeans, half of those interviewed were initially given no information at all about the jeans. They were asked to rank the three pairs in order of judged quality, and to estimate the selling price of each. They were then presented informative copy for each and asked their likelihood of buying at the regular selling prices, also given.

The other half of the sample were initially shown the jeans and information about each pair, but not the selling price. After they estimated a selling price, the actual prices were given and their likelihood of buying each pair was measured. Exhibit 17 lists the informative copy that was used in the study. The overall relative judgments for the three products are shown in the table on p. 68.

Since Mr. Pallino believed that the price at

	$4.99 Tough Jean	$3.99 Present Top-Line	$2.99 Present Lower-Priced
Judged best quality	80%	13%	7%
Judged middle quality	13	71	16
Judged lowest quality	7	16	77
	100%	100%	100%

(Base: 150) Base equals those shoppers asked to judge quality solely from examination of the three jeans displayed.

which a product should be retailed was the price that consumers expected to pay, he was especially attentive to the findings presented in Exhibit 18 which showed that 46 percent of the respondents who were exposed to the Tough Jean ad copy points expected that the product would be priced above $4.50 in the store. Exhibit 19 lists the stated probabilities that consumers would actually buy each of the test jeans at price points near the five, four and three dollars. Thirty-two percent of the respondents indicated that there was a greater than a ninety percent chance that they would buy the Tough Jean at a price of $4.99. Of all those respondents who indicated that they would "definitely" buy at least one of the jeans at the stated price, the Tough Jean netted 48 percent of the implied net number of purchases, while the Present Top of the Line jean and the Lower Priced jean each netted 26 percent of the implied number of purchases.

Exhibit 20 demonstrates the likely effect of offering the consumer a formally stated one-year guarantee of durability for each of the tested jeans. Mr. Pallino had wondered whether such a guarantee was a significant potential communicator of the durability story that was to be the basis for the Tough Jean product differentiation strategy. Exhibits 21 and 22 list the respective reasons for preferring, and not preferring, the Tough Jean. Finally, since Mr. Pallino was considering using white thread instead of the customary orange seam thread, for reasons of cost efficiency, he had requested that Department 733MR ask for consumer preferences on seam thread color. The findings for this question are listed in Exhibit 23.

As work progressed, Mr. Pallino found that there were questions as to whether the new jean could be a traditional blue jean. The traditional blue jean had a blue warp fiber with a white fill. As the product "washed down" the color changed to a light blue-gray. With the Tri-Blend there would be no washing down. The unfadeable color was going to remain with the fabric and so the exact color that was expected in the jean as it reached the normal wear stage was the same as the original color for the new product. Mr. Pallino requested that 733MR test two different color alternatives, one a true blue, the other a gray/black to determine which color would be more desirable.

The study was conducted in large shopping centers in Chicago and Los Angeles. A total of 200 mothers of boys 6 through 10 and 200 mothers of boys 11 through 15 years of age were shown a display of two identical jeans— one in blue and the other in a gray/black color. Each respondent was asked to compare the two for selected attributes. Sears was not identified as sponsor of the research. As indicated in Exhibit 24, the mothers reported there would be considerable divergence of preference and perception between themselves and their sons, with respect to the blue versus the gray/black color. Since there seemed to be a strong relationship between color and the perceived durability of the jeans, Mr. Pallino faced a difficult decision as to how best communicate the durability benefit to both the parents and younger and older boys.

There were other product features that Mr. Pallino had selected that served to differentiate the Tough Jean. The construction was to be double needle stitching as in traditional jeans, with riveted pockets. A double needle X was to be stitched across each of the rear pockets in the hope that this would become an emblem visible from a distance that could quickly identify the product.

Another identifying feature was a small Sears label sewn into the seam of the right rear pocket. Levis had always used this method for identifying their product. More than twenty years previously, when Levi Strauss was a Sears supplier, Sears had signed an agreement guaranteeing that they would never use a similar tag on a Sears jean. Mr. Pallino felt that a tag of this sort would lend the product substantial credibility and requested that Levi suspend the twenty-year-old agreement. To his surprise, they did.

With respect to color, Mr. Pallino could also offer nonfading red and green in addition to the blue and gray/black.

On the possibility that he might recommend that the Tough Jean received Sears' National Brand treatment when it might be introduced, Mr. Pallino wanted to select a name for the product that would best communicate desirable impressions of ruggedness and high quality. In a name test conducted in late 1970, the name Tough Jeans, which had been used as a kind of in-house favorite over the months of product development, proved to be one of the least effective of the eight names which were evaluated. It scored low in overall rating, low in first choice preference, adequate in communicating ruggedness, and poor in communicating quality. It and the other name candidates were dropped and a second name test was conducted in January 1971 on a set of twelve potential brand names.

Two hundred mothers of children 3 to 15 years old were interviewed. The new jean was displayed, with an information card listing its features. Mothers were asked which would be the best name for "the manufacturer" to use, which name was most descriptive of ruggedness or durability, which one a 5 to 11 year old boy would probably like best, and which name most suggested the highest quality. Sears was not identified with the study.

Exhibit 25 lists the overall rankings of the twelve names. The most preferred name, The Great American Jean, was preferred by only 20 percent of the sample, and preferences were broadly distributed over the remaining names. Patriotic feelings seemed to account most for the preference for The Great American Jean's popularity as shown in Exhibit 26. Mr. Pallino wondered whether patriotism was a sound choice for positioning a boy's apparel item. The ratings of the twelve names with respect to their abilities to communicate ruggedness and quality are listed in Exhibit 27.

SUMMARY

Mr. Pallino felt that it was a smart business decision to try and encourage his customers, to trade up from the present Circle S jean, which sold for $3.99 to a more durable product selling for $4.99. Mr. Quint, the Children's Store Category Manager, was convinced that the Tri-Blend program had potential for not only the Boys' Clothing Department, but also for the Infants' and Children's Department. Together, they had to decide whether the product that had been designed was correctly positioned to be successful within Children's Store's market.

Among their decisions to be made were choices of whether or not to seek a Sears' National Brand program for the product or instead to introduce the product on a limited exposure basis and gain experience with the new marketing program before expanding to larger scales of commitment. Both men were aware of the economies and profits associated with a successful national program, but they were mindful of the failure of the Indestructables program. Further, the research to date had not communicated a way that the price-value-durability-fashion puzzle could be solved for both mothers and their 6 to 16 year old sons. Whatever strategy they selected with respect to introducing the product, tactical decisions would have to be made with respect to promotion targeting, copy points to be communicated, and the colors to be included in the line. The most nagging question seemed to be whether the market was large enough, and whether it was ready for a durable jean at a premium price.

EXHIBIT 1

Infants' and Children's Clothing Market, March 1968

Research Design

A total of 1,800 women were interviewed in their homes to develop the information on which this survey is based. Quotas were set up on the basis of the age and sex of the child shopped for and the store where most of the child's clothing is bought, to give the following sample breakdown:

				Age/Sex of Child			
	Infants/ Toddlers to 36 months	Juveniles age 3–5	Boys 6–11 yrs.	Boys 12–17 yrs.	Girls 6–11 yrs.	Girls 12–14 yrs.	Total
Buy most at Sears	150	150	150	150	150	150	900
Buy most at other stores	150	150	150	150	150	150	900
Total, this age group	300	300	300	300	300	300	1800

The total number of interviews was divided among ten cities, one large city and one medium sized city in each of the five Sears territories, as follows:

Eastern Territory
Pittsburgh
Buffalo

Midwestern Territory
Chicago
Cincinnati

Southern Territory
Atlanta
Birmingham

Pacific Coast Territory
Los Angeles
Seattle

Southwestern Territory
Dallas
Houston

Personal interviews lasting about an hour were conducted in the home by a professional market research agency, using local interviewers. Sears was not identified as the sponsor of the research.

EXHIBIT 2

Demographic Characteristics of Those Shopping Most at Given Stores

			Store Where Shop Most Other Than Sears			
	SEARS	Total	Department	Penney's	Discount	Other Stores*
Total Who Shop Most at This Store	100%	100%	100%	100%	100%	100%
Age of Respondent						
Under 25	9%	10%	7%	10%	22%	9%
25–34	47	41	39	48	50	35
35–44	34	38	44	29	26	40
45 & over	10	11	10	13	2	16
	100%	100%	100%	100%	100%	100%
Family Income						
Under $5000	3%	4%	2%	4%	7%	5%
$5000–$7499	17	16	12	17	29	16
$7500–$9999	32	29	27	37	31	24
$10,000–$14,999	33	33	37	29	25	30
$15,000 or over	11	14	15	12	2	20
Declined to answer	4	4	7	1	6	5
	100%	100%	100%	100%	100%	100%

EXHIBIT 2 (cont.)

| | SEARS | Total | Store Where Shop Most Other Than Sears | | | |
			Department	Penney's	Discount	Other Stores*
Occupation						
Professional/Technical	25%	25%	26%	24%	19%	23%
Managerial	14	19	21	17	9	19
Clerical/Sales	18	19	23	17	11	18
Craftsmen/Foreman	24	21	16	27	29	24
Operatives/Skilled Labor	11	12	8	9	27	14
All Other	8	4	6	6	5	2
	100%	100%	100%	100%	100%	100%
(Base)	(944)	(936)	(481)	(194)	(113)	(148)

*Note: The 16% shopping at other stores breaks down as follows: specialty children's wear—6%; family clothing store—2%; women's and girls' wear—1%; Montgomery Ward—2%; other stores—2%.

Source: March 1968 Infant's and Children's Clothing Market Survey.

EXHIBIT 3

Things Considered Important in Choosing Where to Buy Most by Age of Child Shopped For

Q.7. Now I am going to show you some cards with statements on them that may be used to describe something about stores that sell clothing for (NAME). Please place each card on the board (dart board) at the point that best describes how important or unimportant it is to you when you pick a place at which to shop for (NAME) clothing.

	Total	Infant/Toddler to 36 months	Juvenile 3-5 yrs.	Boys 6-11 yrs.	Boys 12-17 yrs.	Girls 6-11 yrs.	Girls 12-14 yrs.
Quality materials and construction	94%	92%	93%	94%	94%	95%	93%
Good fitting clothes	93	90	92	94	94	94	94
Long lasting clothes	84	84	87	89	86	84	73
Wide variety to choose from	79	81	79	74	79	79	83
Good brand of permanent press	78	71	76	86	87	76	75
Range or quality to select from	75	74	74	72	72	77	80
Friendly, helpful salespeople	74	73	70	76	74	76	75
Nearby location	66	65	64	63	67	68	67
Organized for ease of shopping	66	67	66	64	63	68	67
Good sales	62	61	62	66	59	67	60
Have color coordinated clothing	55	53	54	51	60	54	55
Low prices	53	49	50	57	48	60	54
Latest styles and fashions	49	41	42	46	55	49	63
Well known brands	48	47	49	51	50	47	47
Convenient credit	36	36	35	36	35	35	42
		(Percent describing statement as "Extremely" or "Very" Important)					
(Base)	(1180)	(316)	(297)	(317)	(316)	(331)	(303)

By and large, children's wear shoppers hold the same things to be important in choosing where to shop regardless of the age or sex of the child shopped for. Among minor differences noted, durability and permanent press appear to be more important in shopping for boys, while range of quality seems to be more important in shopping for girls. Also, prices appear to be more of an issue when shopping for children 6-11, while style concepts are more important when shopping for children over 12.

Source: March 1968 Infant's and Children's Clothing Market Survey.

EXHIBIT 4

Extent to Which Child Selects Own Clothes

Q.12. Please look at this card and tell me which statement on it best describes to what extent (NAME) picks (HIS/HER) own clothing?

| | Child Sex and Age Groups | | | | | |
	Infants/Toddlers to 36 months	Juveniles 3-5 yrs.	Boys 6-11 yrs.	Boys 12-17 yrs.	Girls 6-11 yrs.	Girls 12-14 yrs.
Amount of Clothing Selected by Child:						
All	—	2%	1%	21%	4%	18%
Most	—	3	14	35	23	53
Some	5%	37	65	42	66	28
None	95	58	20	2	7	1
	100%	100%	100%	100%	100%	100%
(Base)	(316)	(297)	(317)	(316)	(331)	(303)

Children apparently begin to influence clothing selection before age five. Two-thirds of six to eleven-year-olds pick at least some of their own clothing. Among children age twelve and older, especially girls, over half choose most of their own clothing.

Source: March 1968 Infant's and Children's Clothing Market Survey.

EXHIBIT 5

How Shoppers Judge Durability When Buying Children's Clothing

Q.14a. When you buy clothing for (NAME), how do you decide whether the clothing is durable enough to stand repeated wearings and washings? (PROBE)

| | | Child Shop For | | | Store Where Shop Most | |
	Total	Children Under Age 6	Boys Age 6-17	Girls Age 6-14	Sears	Other Stores
Label Information	67%	67%	70%	67%	65%	69%
Read brand name	26	31	28	19	20	32
Read fabric composition	18	16	18	20	19	17
See if permanent press	18	15	19	19	19	17
Read about washability	12	10	10	15	12	12
Read label	8	6	8	10	8	8
See if color fast	5	6	4	6	5	5
See if pre-shrunk	5	6	5	4	5	4
Look for guarantee	2	1	2	1	2	2
Fabric	40	42	39	41	41	39
Feel the fabric	28	30	27	28	28	29
Weight of material	8	9	9	5	8	7
Have knowledge of materials	5	3	5	6	5	5
Other fabric comments	7	7	5	8	7	7

EXHIBIT 5 (cont.)

	Total	Child Shop For			Store Where Shop Most	
		Children Under Age 6	Boys Age 6-17	Girls Age 6-14	Sears	Other Stores
Workmanship	35	35	29	41	35	34
Examine seams	24	25	17	31	25	24
See how it is made	19	19	14	25	19	20
Look for knee pads	3	3	7	—	3	3
Impression of Quality	14	14	14	14	14	14
Looks durable	6	5	6	6	5	6
Lasts longer if costs more	5	5	5	5	5	5
See if looks like good quality	4	4	4	3	4	4
Misc. Other Comments	—	—	—	—	—	—
Past experience	14	16	16	10	14	14
Faith in store, merchandise	10	10	13	7	11	10
Trial and error	4	4	6	3	5	3
Other comments	3	4	2	3	3	3
(Base) Multiple Response	(1880)	(613)	(633)	(634)	(944)	(936)

Source: March 1968 Infant's and Children's Clothing Market Survey.

EXHIBIT 6

Satisfaction with Durability of Boys' Slacks

Q.14c. Now thinking about the durability of a boy's slacks, please pick the phrase on this card that best describes how you feel about the way that boy's slacks wear.

	Total	Age of Boy Shopped For		Store Where Buy Most Boy's Clothes	
		6-11 yrs.	12-17 yrs.	Sears	Other Stores
Extremely satisfied	15% ⎫	9% ⎫	20% ⎫	15% ⎫	15% ⎫
	⎬ 64%	⎬ 54%	⎬ 73%	⎬ 68%	⎬ 61%
Very satisfied	49 ⎭	45 ⎭	53 ⎭	53 ⎭	46 ⎭
Somewhat satisfied	27	33	22	25	29
Slightly satisfied	6	9	3	5	7
Not at all satisfied	3	4	2	2	3
	100%	100%	100%	100%	100%
(Base)	(633)	(317)	(316)	(318)	(315)

Source: March 1968 Infant's and Children's Clothing Market Survey.

EXHIBIT 7

Sources of Advertising Found Helpful by Children's Wear Shoppers

Q.20a. What sources of advertising do you find most helpful and informative with regard to clothing for (NAME)? (DO NOT READ LIST)

		Child Shop For			Store Where Shop Most				
	Total	Children Under 6 yrs.	Boys 6-11 yrs.	Girls 6-14 yrs.	Sears	Department	Penney's	Discount	Other Stores
Newspapers	73%	71%	74%	75%	72%	80%	73%	65%	60%
Catalogs	20	21	19	20	29	8	16	12	17
Mail Circulars	11	11	11	12	13	9	6	20	11
Magazines	9	11	6	10	8	11	11	5	11
Television	5	6	4	4	5	3	7	6	3
Word of Mouth	2	3	3	1	2	2	6	2	2
Point of Purchase	2	2	2	1	1	2	1	2	2
Other (Radio, Yellow Pages, etc.)	1	2	1	1	1	2	2	3	1
None, Don't Notice Advertising	4	3	5	4	3	5	2	5	11
(Base)	(1880)	(613)	(633)	(634)	(944)	(481)	(194)	(113)	(148)
Multiple Response									

Source: March 1968 Infant's and Children's Clothing Market Survey.

EXHIBIT 8

Incidence of Jeans Purchases

Q. Have *you* bought any boys' jeans in the past year?

	Bought During Past 12 Mo.	Not Bought During Past 12 Mo.	Total	(Base)
Total	91%	9%	100%	(398)
Respondent Group:				
Mothers of Boys 6-12	97	3	100	(203)
Boys 13-17	84	16	100	(195)
City Size:				
50,000-499,999	92	8	100	(133)
500,000-1,999,999	90	10	100	(158)
2,000,000 or more	90	10	100	(107)
Region:				
East	86	14	100	(79)
Central	93	7	100	(149)
South	92	8	100	(96)
West	89	11	100	(74)

Source: July 1968 Jeans Panel Survey.

Usage Group, According to Central City and Suburban Residences

	Total	Heavy Users	Medium Users	Light Users
50,000–499,999 Population				
Central City	15%	21%	15%	11%
Suburban	18	20	17	17
500,000–1,999,999 Population				
Central City	17	15	20	13
Suburban	23	19	24	25
2,000,000 and Over Population				
Central City	7	5	7	10
Suburban	20	20	17	24
Total	100%	100%	100%	100%
Summary All Markets				
Central City	39%	41%	42%	34%
Suburban	61	59	58	66
Total	100%	100%	100%	100%
Base	(398)	(123)	(179)	(88)

Source: July 1968 Jeans Panel Survey.

EXHIBIT 10

Outlet Where Jeans Purchased Last

Q. (If jeans bought in past year) The last time you bought boys' jeans, from what type of store were they purchased?

		Respondent Group				User Group**			Region			
	Total	Mothers	Total Teens	Teens 13-15	Teens 16-17	Heavy	Medium	Light	East	Central	South	West
Local Department Store	33%	34%	31%	33%	31%	33%	33%	35%	45%	27%	38%	27%
Sears	19	27	11	13	8	24	19	15	19	19	19	21
Penney's	17	19	15	19	13	19	17	13	8	20	16	21
Clothing Store	16	6	28	16	36	13	16	20	15	20	12	15
Discount Store	7	6	9	9	8	4	7	12	7	6	8	8
Wards	4	5	2	6	–	4	4	3	–	6	3	5
Variety Store	2	2	2	2	2	1	2	1	5	–	3	–
Mail Order House*	1	1	1	2	–	2	1	1	1	1	–	2
Other	1	–	1	–	2	–	1	–	–	1	1	1
Total	100%	100%	100%	100%	100%	100%	100%	100%	100%	100%	100%	100%
Base	(357)	(195)	(162)	(63)	(97)	(114)	(165)	(75)	(67)	(136)	(88)	(66)

* Spiegel, Aldens, etc.

** Heavy users bought 7 or more pairs of jeans during past 12 months, medium users 4 to 6 pairs, light users 1 to 3 pairs.

Source: July 1968 Jeans Panel Survey.

EXHIBIT 11

Number and Price of Jeans Last Purchased (By Respondent and Outlet)

Q. The *last time* you purchased jeans, how many did you buy?

	Respondent					Outlet				
	Total	Mothers	Total Teens	Teens 13–15	Teens 16–17	Sears	Penney's Wards	Local Dept. Store	Clothing Store	All Other
One	25%	17%	33%	29%	36%	11%	25%	29%	42%	8%
Two	41	42	39	43	38	40	36	41	32	62
Three	18	20	17	16	18	19	20	19	17	16
Four	10	13	7	6	7	14	12	10	7	6
Five or More	6	8	4	6	1	16	7	1	2	8
Total	100%	100%	100%	100%	100%	100%	100%	100%	100%	100%
Average	2.4	2.6	2.1	2.3	2.0	3.0	3.4	2.1	2.0	2.5
Base	(357)	(195)	(162)	(63)	(97)	(70)	(75)	(118)	(57)	(37)

Q. For each pair of jeans you purchased last time, what price did you pay for each pair of jeans excluding tax?

	Respondent					Outlet				
	Total	Mothers	Total Teens	Teens 13–15	Teens 16–17	Sears	Penney's Wards	Local Dept. Store	Clothing Store	All Other
Under $2.75	11%	15%	5%	8%	1%	17%	14%	8%	—	15%
$2.75–3.24 ($3.00)*	21	28	10	13	8	20	34	14	13	24
$3.25–3.74 ($3.50)	10	12	9	16	4	10	10	14	5	10
$3.75–4.24 ($4.00)	22	23	22	27	19	28	24	20	3	39
$4.25–4.74 ($4.50)	5	6	3	3	4	7	2	4	7	1
$4.75–5.24 ($5.00)	13	9	18	10	24	10	9	16	20	8
$5.25–5.74 ($5.50)	6	2	11	7	14	2	2	8	17	1
$5.75–6.24 ($6.00)	6	2	10	8	12	3	2	6	20	—
$6.25 and over	5	1	11	8	13	—	3	8	15	1
Don't know/no answer	1	2	1	—	1	3	—	2	—	1
Total	100%	100%	100%	100%	100%	100%	100%	100%	100%	100%
Median	$3.95	$3.24	$4.75	$3.98	$5.03	$3.76	$3.30	$4.07	$5.30	$3.76
Base**	(808)	(477)	(331)	(134)	(192)	(187)	(174)	(250)	(110)	(87)

* Midpoints of each range in parentheses.

** Pairs of jeans bought last time.

Source: July 1968 Jeans Panel Survey.

EXHIBIT 12

Decision Makers for Outlet and Style

Q. Thinking of the *last time* you bought jeans, who made the decision as to which *store* to buy from?

Q. Who made the decision as to which *styles(s)* you bought?

	For 6–12	For All Teens	For Teens 13–15	For Teens 16–17
*Outlet***				
Mother	93%	37%	47%	31%
Son	3*	60	51	66
Father	3	—	—	—
Brother	—	3	2	3
Other	1	—	—	—
Total	100%	100%	100%	100%
*Style of Jeans****				
Mother	66%	6%	8%	5%
Son	29*	88	85	91
Father	3	1	—	1
Brother	—	4	5	3
Other	2	1	2	—
Total	100%	100%	100%	100%
Base	(195)	(162)	(63)	(97)

* Includes brothers

** In 78% of the cases, the respondent made the outlet decision.

*** In 76% of the cases, the respondent made the style decision.

Source: July 1968 Jeans Panel Survey.

EXHIBIT 13

Reasons for Buying a Particular Pair of Jeans

Q. Why did you buy the particular jeans you purchased instead of some other style in the store?

	Total	Mothers	Total Teens	Teens 13–15	Teens 16–17
Style	33%	27%	39%	52%	31%
Fit	21	16	28	24	31
Quality	19	29	7	6	8
Durability	13	20	5	3	6
Quality	4	5	3	3	2
Reinforced knees	3	6	–	—	—
Price	19	27	8	11	6
Price/Economical/Reasonable	10	15	5	6	4
Sale	8	12	3	5	1
Personal preference/Just liked	11	8	14	11	16
Permanent Press/Easy to clean/No ironing, wash and wear	7	10	4	5	3

EXHIBIT 13 *(cont.)*

	Total	Mothers	Total Teens	Teens 13–15	Teens 16–17
Appearance/Neat	7	7	7	—	12
Selection/Availability	6	7	5	5	4
Color	4	5	4	5	3
Weight of material	3	4	2	—	3
Base	(357)	(195)	(162)	(63)	(97)

Note: All reasons mentioned by at least 3% of all respondents.

Source: July 1968 Jeans Panel Survey.

EXHIBIT 14

Particular Likes and Dislikes about Jeans Bought

Q. What do you like particularly about the jeans you bought?

	Total	Mothers	Total Teens	Teens 13–15	Teens 16–17
Likes					
Permanent press/no ironing wash and wear/ease of cleaning	39%	59%	14%	16%	11%
Fit	33	19	50	51	50
Quality	32	41	22	18	25
Durability	24	26	22	16	25
Reinforced Knees	8	15	—	—	—
Quality	2	3	1	2	—
Style*	17	7	28	25	30
Appearance	15	19	12	8	14
Color	11	9	12	13	12
Price	5	6	3	3	3
Weight of Material	5	6	3	5	2
Type of Fabric	4	5	4	3	4

All reasons mentioned by at least 3% of all respondents.

*Includes popular style 8%, slim legs 3%, loops for belt 1%, type pockets 1%, liked style 1%, etc.

Q. What, if anything, do you dislike about the jeans you bought?

	Total	Mothers	Total Teens	Teens 13–15	Teens 16–17
Dislikes					
Nothing disliked	58%	51%	66%	73%	61%
Fit	8	8	9	8	10
Too Loose	6	4	7	8	6
Too tight	1	1	1	—	2
Too long	1	2	1	—	1
Doesn't wear well/not sewn well	7	8	6	2	9
No reinforcement/double knees	6	10	1	—	1
Type of fabric	5	5	4	5	4
Not permanent press	5	7	3	—	4
Style	4	3	6	3	7
Base	(357)	(195)	(162)	(63)	(97)

All reasons mentioned by at least 3% of all respondents; other reasons include price 2%, material stain/fade 2%, color 2%, shrinks 1%.

Source: July 1968 Jeans Panel Survey.

EXHIBIT 15

Color and Material Preferences

Q. What is your favorite color of jeans?

| | | Outlet | | Respondent Group | | | | Usage Group | |
| | | Sears | Other | Mothers | Teens 13-15 | Teens 16-17 | Heavy | Medium | Light |
Favorite Color	Total	Sears	Other	Mothers	13-15	16-17	Heavy	Medium	Light
Blue	39%	30%	41%	36%	39%	46%	29%	44%	43%
Olive	17	27	15	24	5	13	21	17	11
Black	11	9	11	11	8	13	13	10	9
Wheat	8	10	7	8	13	4	7	7	10
Green	8	11	7	8	13	3	13	6	3
Brown	7	9	6	7	9	5	5	10	2
Tan	5	6	5	5	3	6	4	5	6
Blue Grey	4	1	4	6	3	1	3	2	8
White	3	3	3	1	4	6	2	2	8
Gold	2	1	2	1	4	4	3	1	1
Other	1	–	1	–	1	1	–	1	–
No Answer	4	6	4	3	5	6	5	4	3
Total	109%	113%	106%	110%	107%	108%	105%	109%	104%
Base	(398)	(70)	(328)	(203)	(79)	(114)	(123)	(179)	(88)

Adds to more than 100% because of multiple responses.

Qa. Which type of material do you prefer for your jeans?

Favorite Material

Cotton/Polyester	20%	24%	20%	26%	19%	12%	21%	26%	9%
Cotton/Fortrel	19	23	19	25	10	16	27	16	17
All Cotton	16	3	18	8	15	29	11	15	24
Cotton/Dacron	15	23	14	17	23	6	14	18	13
Cotton/Nylon	13	20	12	17	11	7	10	13	17
Other	3	1	3	2	–	5	2	2	6
No Preference	16	7	17	9	20	24	17	15	16
No Answer	4	6	4	3	4	5	2	3	6
Total	106%	107%	107%	107%	102%	104%	104%	108%	108%
Base	(298)	(70)	(328)	(203)	(79)	(114)	(123)	(179)	(88)

Adds to more than 100% because of multiple responses.

Source: July 1968 Jeans Panel Survey.

EXHIBIT 16

Willingness to Pay Extra for Perma Press, Non-Shrink and Soil Release/Stain Resistance

Q. Suppose you were able to buy jeans with just the features you wanted to pay for, and a "basic" pair of jeans cost $3.00. How much extra would you be willing to pay for them with permanent press?

		Outlet		Respondent Group		
	Total	Sears	All Others	Mothers	Teens 13–15	Teens 16–17
Perma Press						
Nothing Extra	9%	–	10%	6%	10%	18%
$ .10 extra	3	7	2	3	2	3
.25 extra	5	3	5	4	5	5
.50 extra	27	25	28	31	25	20
.75 extra	13	13	12	12	18	11
1.00 extra	43	52	43	44	40	43
Total	100%	100%	100%	100%	100%	100%
Cumulative						
$ .10 or more	91%	100%	90%	94%	90%	82%
.25 or more	88	93	88	91	88	79
.50 or more	83	90	83	89	83	74
.75 or more	56	65	55	56	58	54
1.00	43	52	43	44	40	43
Base	(398)	(70)	(328)	(203)	(79)	(114)

Q. Suppose you were able to buy jeans with just the features you wanted to pay for, and that a "basic" pair of jeans cost $3.00. Would you buy them with a non-shrink feature for:

Non-Shrink						
Nothing Extra	11%	7%	12%	9%	13%	15%
$ .10 extra	9	12	8	11	5	9
.25 extra	15	12	15	18	12	10
.50 extra	33	32	33	35	34	27
.75 extra	12	10	13	7	22	15
1.00 extra	20	27	19	20	14	24
Total	100%	100%	100%	100%	100%	100%
Cumulative						
$ .10 or more	89%	93%	88%	91%	87%	85%
.25 or more	80	81	80	80	82	76
.50 or more	65	69	65	62	70	66
.75 or more	32	37	32	27	36	39
1.00	20	27	19	20	14	24
Base	(398)	(70)	(328)	(203)	(79)	(114)

Source: July 1968 Jeans Panel Survey.

EXHIBIT 17

Informative Copy Used in Study

Code "P"	Code "R"		Code "T"
(Present "Sears Best") ($3.99)	(New Tough Jean) ($4.99)		($2.99)
	Copy R_A Without Guarantee	Copy R_B With Guarantee	

60% cotton blended with 40% nylon—wears twice as long as an all cotton jean	The strongest jean ever made	The strongest jean ever made	75% cotton blended with 25% nylon for 70% longer wear than all cotton jeans
	Exclusive blend of dacron for durability, nylon for strength, cotton for wearability—wears four times longer than all cotton jeans	Exclusive blend of dacron for durability, nylon for strength, cotton for wearability—wears four times longer than all cotton jeans	Permanent Press—needs no ironing
Permanent Press—needs no ironing			
			Less than 1% shrinkage*
Less than 1% shrinkage*	Permanent Press—needs no ironing	Permanent Press—needs no ironing	
			Double knee guaranteed to outlast the jean
Double knee guaranteed to outlast the jean	Less than 1% shrinkage	Less than 1% shrinkage	
	Will not fade	Will not fade	
	Double knee guaranteed to outlast the jean	Double knee guaranteed to outlast the jean	
		Entire jean guaranteed for one full year's normal wear	

* This line should not have appeared for Jeans "P" and "T." However, because its inclusion could be expected only to enhance the appeal of "P" and "T," and because "R" was preferred in any event, this should not affect the study results.

Source: October 1970 Hillside Price Quality Study.

EXHIBIT 18

Price Expected to Pay

Q. Here are three pairs of boys' jeans with some information about each of them. Please feel free to examine the jeans and read the information. About what price, in dollars and cents, do you think pair "P" would sell for in the store? "Pair "R"? Pair "T"?

	Jeans Style					
	($4.99) Tough Jean		($3.99) Present Top-Line Jean		($2.99) Present Lower-Priced Jean	
	Informed	Uninformed	Informed	Uninformed	Informed	Uninformed
$2.50 or less	2%	4%	13%	13%	19%	29%
$2.51 to $3.50	13	19	45	35	44	48
$3.51 to $4.50	39	39	33	40	26	17
$4.51 or more	46	38	9	12	11	6
	100%	100%	100%	100%	100%	100%
Median Price Estimate	$4.12	$3.94	$2.97	$3.74	$2.93	$2.76
(Base)	(150)	(150)	(150)	(150)	(150)	(150)

Note: "Informed" are those who were shown sign copy for all jeans before price estimates were requested. The "Uninformed" were shown no sign copy, but estimated prices based solely upon examination of the garments.

Source: October 1970 Hillside Price Quality Study.

EXHIBIT 19

Rated Likelihood of Buying

Q. Suppose you saw these three pairs of jeans in a store, priced as shown. If you were to buy jeans for your 5 to 11 year old boy, how likely would you be to buy Pair "P" at the price indicated. Please look at this card and tell me which one of those numbers best describes how likely you would be to buy "P." As you see, the more likely you are to buy it, the higher the number you give it. The less likely, the lower the number. How likely would you be to buy pair "R" at the price shown? And Pair "T"?

	Jeans Style		
	$4.99 Tough Jean	$3.99 Present Top-Line	$2.99 Present Lower-Priced
100–90 Definitely would buy	32%	13%	10%
80–70 Probably would buy	22	35	21
60–40 Might or might not buy	17	31	23
30–20 Probably would not buy	12	13	19
10–0 Definitely would not buy	17	8	27
	100%	100%	100%
Median Buying Likelihood	59	57	43
(Base: 300)			

Source: October 1970 Hillside Price Quality Study.

EXHIBIT 21

Reasons for Preferring the Tough Jean

Q. For what reasons would you be more likely to purchase pair "R" rather than one of the others?

	Respondents Preferring Tough Jean
Quality/Durability	93%
Will last longer	59%
Guaranteed for 1 year	28*
Reinforced/Double knee	17
Stronger fabric	16
Feels stronger	11
Sewed stronger	10
Will take a lot of abuse	10
Good quality (unspec.)	3
Material	36
Heavier fabric	17
Nylon-Dacron/blend of material	10
Feels good	3
Softer	3
Closer weave	3
Maintenance	33
Permanent press/no ironing	17
No fading	9
Washes well	7
No shrinkage	6
Appearance	18
Looks good (unspec.)	11
Dressy look	6
Like appearance of stitching	4
All other appearance	2
Price/Value	10
Good value for the money	8
Higher price means better quality	4
(Base)**	(145)
(Multiple Response)	

* The base for this figure *only* is 69—the number of respondents preferring the Tough Jean who were informed of the 1-year guarantee.

** Base equals those who indicated a greater likelihood of buying the Tough Jean than either of the other two jeans displayed.

Source: October 1970 Hillside Price Quality Study.

EXHIBIT 20

Most Likely Jeans Purchase

Q. (HALF OF THOSE INTERVIEWED WERE SHOWN TOUGH JEAN COPY INCLUDING A ONE-YEAR GUARANTEE. HALF WITHOUT THE GUARANTEE.) Here is some (further) information about each of the three jeans, like you might see in a store. Please read each card (ALLOW TIME FOR READING). If you were to buy jeans for your 5 to 11 year old boy, how likely would you be to buy "P" at the price shown? (EXPLAIN RATING SCALE.) "R"? "T"?

	Tough Jean with 1-Year Guarantee	Tough Jean without 1-Year Guarantee
$4.99 Tough Jean	46%	51%
$3.99 Present Top-Line	29	24
$2.99 Present Lower Priced	25	25
	100%	100%
(Base)	(150)	(150)

Source: October 1970 Hillside Price Quality Study.

EXHIBIT 22

Reasons for Not Preferring the Tough Jean

Q. For what reasons would you be less likely to purchase Pair "R" than "___" (INSERT LETTER OF MOST LIKELY PURCHASE.)

	Respondents Not Preferring Tough Jean
Price	78%
Higher price	23%
Too high a price for jeans	17
Higher price for same quality	14
Child outgrows too fast to pay this much	14
Too much for play clothes	10
Price (unspec.)	4
Other price comments	2
Material	27
Too stiff	21
Not comfortable	5
Would irritate skin	2
Doesn't feel good	2
Other material comments	6
Quality/Durability	23
Won't wear better	12
Will still wear out at knee	7
Not better quality	3
Other quality comments	2
Appearance—Don't like style, color, stitching	7
(Base)*	(155)
(Multiple Response)	

---

* Base equals those who did *not* select the Tough Jean as their most likely purchase.

Source: October 1970 Hillside Price Quality Study.

EXHIBIT 23

Thread Color Preference

Q. You may have noticed that jeans like these may be sewn with orange thread, or with white thread. Which phrase on this card best describes your preference for thread color?

	Total Respondents
Very much prefer orange thread	7%
Somewhat prefer orange thread	10
Don't really care whether the thread is orange or white	38
Somewhat prefer white thread	17
Very much prefer white thread	28
	100%
(Base)	(300)

Source: October 1970 Hillside Price Quality Study.

EXHIBIT 24

Color Perception Test

Q. Which pair looks the most durable?

	Total	Mothers of Boys	
		6–11	12–15
Gray/Black Jeans Considered More Durable	79%	77%	81%
Blue Jeans Considered More Durable	20	20	19
Both Jeans Equally Durable	1	3	—
Total	100%	100%	100%
Base	(200)	(101)	(99)

Q. Which pair looks the most expensive?

	Total	Mothers of Boys	
		6–11	12–15
Gray/Black Jeans More Expensive	71%	68%	74%
Blue Jeans More Expensive	28	30	25
Both Jeans Equally Expensive	1	2	1
Total	100%	100%	100%
Base	(200)	(101)	(99)

Q. Which pair looks like the pair my son would like best?

	Total	Mothers of Boys	
		6–11	12–15
Gray/Black	54%	53%	55%
Blue	46	47	45
Total	100%	100%	100%
Base	(200)	(101)	(99)

Q. Overall, which do you like the best?

	Total	Mothers of Boys	
		6–11	12–15
Gray/Black Jean Preferred	65%	61%	70%
Blue Jeans Preferred	34	38	30
Both Colors Preferred Equally	1	1	—
Total	100%	100%	100%
Base	(200)	(101)	(99)

EXHIBIT 25

January 1971 Hillside Name Test

Q. On each of these cards is one possible name. We would like you to give us your opinion of this name by using this thermometer scale. As you can see, the scale ranges from 100 or like very much, to 0 or dislike very much. Which point of this scale best describes your reaction to this name?

	Average Ratings of Alternative Names			Most Preferred Name		
	Total	Sears Charge Owners	Mothers of 5 to 12 Year Old Boys	Total Sample	Sears Charge Owners	Mothers of 5 to 12 Year Old Boys
Toughskins	59	59	56	15%	13%	10%
Rawhide Jean	57	56	57	13	13	13
The Great American Jean	56	56	53	20	22	15
Die Hard Jean	49	48	50	10	10	12
The Brute Jean	49	51	49	7	7	7
Challenge Jean	47	48	46	4	4	3
Hardwear Jean	46	46	48	7	5	10
Thickskins	46	45	48	3	3	4
The Hand-Me-Down Jean	44	43	45	10	12	11
The Long-Time Jean	44	44	46	4	4	5
Bruted Blend Jean	44	47	46	4	5	6
T Jean	29	29	31	3	2	4
				100%	100%	100%
(Base)	(200)	(125)	(134)	(200)	(125)	(134)

EXHIBIT 26

Reasons for Preferring Each of the Five Most Popular Names

Q. Why did you rate _____ highest?

	Preferred Name				
	The Great American Jean	Toughskins	Rawhide Jean	Hand-Me-Down Jeans	Die Hard Jean
Tough, durable, stronger	20%	50%	60%	14%	50%
Long-wearing, can be handed down	5	13	12	81	25
Western rugged, cowboy	—	3	44	—	—
Describes the jeans/ fitting name	5	13	24	5	15
All-American, patriotic	56	—	—	—	—
Masculine name/for boys	10	16	8	5	10
Different/catchy/clever/ short/easy to remember	8	45	12	33	35
(Base = Number Preferring) (Multiple Response)	(39)	(31)	(25)	(21)	(20)

Source: January 1971 Hillside Name Test.

EXHIBIT 27

Attribute Communication Results

Q. Which *one* of these names do you think best suggests ruggedness or *durability* of the new jeans?

Q. Which *one* name do you think suggests the highest quality?

	Total Sample	Sears Charge Owners	Mothers of 5 to 12 Year Old Boys	Total Sample	Sears Charge Owners	Mothers of 5 to 12 Year Old Boys
Toughskins	21%	19%	16%	6%	8%	5%
Rawhide Jean	19	18	22	7	9	10
The Great American Jean	4	2	4	28	26	25
Die Hard Jean	9	9	10	6	8	6
The Brute Jean	7	9	7	6	7	6
Challenge Jean	3	2	1	7	9	7
Hardwear Jean	12	11	13	10	8	11
Thickskins	2	2	2	3	2	2
The Hand-Me-Down Jean	11	14	12	13	12	14
The Long-Time Jean	6	8	7	8	6	7
Brute Blend Jean	6	6	6	6	5	7
T Jean	—	—	—	—	—	—
	100%	100%	100%	100%	100%	100%
(Base)	(200)	(125)	(134)	(200)	(125)	(134)

Source: January 1971 Hillside Name Test.

Chapter **4**

Grey Advertising: Canada Dry Account

The main topic on the agenda of the weekly management board meeting of Grey Advertising on December 12, 1968, was the agency's Canada Dry Mixers account. Canada Dry had assigned the multimillion dollar advertising account for its mixers product line two years ago to Grey, one of the ten largest U.S. agencies in terms of client billings. Grey subsequently developed a new advertising campaign for the account, "America's Going Dry," that was built around a prohibition-era theme. By

1968, Canada Dry Ginger Ale (its primary mixer product) sales had grown by over 8%. Yet this growth had been necessary just to keep pace with the expanding mixer and soft drink market—Canada Dry Ginger Ale's share of market had remained stable, but both actual volume and share of market for other Canada Dry mixers had declined (see Exhibit 1).

At the meeting it was agreed that Canada Dry had three basic alternatives for the future marketing and advertising strategies of its mixer line:

1. To position its product line as a quality line of mixers, expand its mixer line, and continue the "America's Going Dry" campaign.

2. To position Canada Dry Ginger Ale as a soft drink and compete head to head with the major soft drink producers, such as Coca-Cola, Pepsi-Cola, and Seven-Up.

3. To remain a major mixer producer, but to also expand its position to include some soft drink orientation.

This case was prepared by Craig E. Cline, Research Assistant, under the supervision of Professor Scott Ward, The Wharton School, as the basis for class discussion rather than to illustrate either effective or ineffective handling of an administrative situation. It is a revised and condensed version of the Grey Advertising: Canada Dry (A) and (B) cases, originally prepared by Edward T. Popper, Research Assistant.

Whichever alternative was chosen would be launched by a series of advertising spots on national television over a four-week period, costing $2 million. But it was generally agreed among the members of the board that both the agency and its client lacked sufficient information to decide how to reposition Canada Dry's mixer line. Sales data, it was felt, were not sufficient to support repositioning decisions.

Consequently, the management board decided to delegate the responsibility of evaluating Canada Dry's market position, and providing the agency with a research base necessary for helping the client to develop effective marketing campaigns, to one of its members—Ms. Jessica Swann, Executive Vice President and Director of Research Studies. When the meeting ended, Mr. Edward Pointsman, Executive Vice President and Director of Client Services, pulled Ms. Swann aside as the others left the room and said:

As you may know, Canada Dry's previous advertising agency was dropped not because it was doing a bad job for them—it just hadn't done well enough. We got their account, I'm told, because our president personally staked his reputation on the effectiveness of our research services delivering good data to our account executives and the client. He wants the new TV campaign to be a success, and your research should help to point the way. To be forewarned is to be forearmed.

CANADA DRY CORPORATION

Canada Dry was a nationwide marketer of a premium line of mixers and soft drinks, with sales of 127 million cases (24 eight-ounce bottles each) in 1968. The company was one of 9 major national carbonated beverage producers, but also competed against 23 regional, local, and private label competitors. Together, these 32 carbonated beverage producers sold more than 3.8 billion cases (24 eight-ounce bottles each) in 1968.[1] (See Exhibit 1.)

Of this 3.8 billion case total, 140 million

cases were classified in the trade as "mixers," including ginger ale, tonic water, and soda water; some definitions included flavored beverages such as bitter lemon, grapefruit, etc., as "mixers," although these could be classified as either mixers or soft drinks. Ginger ale was the largest in sales volume, roughly equal the combined volume for tonic and soda water. Unlike soft drinks, which were marketed on a national basis by Coca-Cola, Pepsi-Cola and several other companies, mixers had only one national brand—Canada Dry (although Schweppe's was making a bid for national distribution and consumer recognition).

Canada Dry's mixer line[2] included Ginger Ale, Soda Water, Tonic (Quinine Water), and Bitter Lemon. Wink (a grapefruit-flavored drink) was considered to be both a mixer and a soft drink. Plans were under way for expanding the mixer line to include Bitter Orange, Collins Mix, and other "pre-mixed" cocktail mixers. Of Canada Dry's existing mixer products, Canada Dry's 1968 share of mixer market (based on volume) for its three major mixer products—Ginger Ale, Tonic Water, and Soda Water—were 34.7%, 43.5%, and 52.9%, respectively.[3] A Diet Ginger Ale was also marketed.

In 1968, Canada Dry had 170 franchised bottlers in the United States as well as eight company-owned and operated bottling plants, each with exclusive geographic marketing areas. Bottlers were responsible for the production and distribution of their products. More than two-thirds of all soft drinks were sold through food outlets, such as supermarkets and other grocery stores. The remaining one-third was sold in nonfood outlets, such as vending machines, hotels, bars, liquor stores, and restaurants. Canada Dry's sales were equally divided between grocery stores and liquor stores. Canada Dry's bottlers therefore had had

---

[1] Nationally, two-thirds of the soft drink volume generally were colas.

[2] Canada Dry also marketed soft drinks, including a cola product (Jamaica Cola) and other fruit-flavored soft drinks.

[3] Ginger Ale accounted for approximately 3.17% of total U.S. carbonated beverage volume; soda and tonic water for about 1.41% combined.

to develop sales contacts in the liquor stores as well as establish more frequent deliveries, since liquor stores (typically) were not large enough to inventory large supplies of mixers.

Because of the large volume involved, it was difficult for Canada Dry's marketing management to obtain accurate sales data on liquor store mixer sales. The normal retail store sales monitoring services could not account for sales through liquor stores, and the data that were obtained for these outlets were largely estimates made by the local bottlers. Furthermore, since mixers were not high margin items for liquor stores (compared with liquor), point-of-sales promotions were primarily dependent on the efforts of the bottler's sales and distribution personnel.

Conversely, supermarket sales data were easily obtainable. Since soft drinks and mixers were a highly profitable category for supermarkets in spite of their large shelf-space requirements (see Exhibit 2), supermarkets were prone to using these products in price promotions. Mixers were especially useful for this purpose since soda and tonic water, as well as ginger ale had seasonal fluctuations, with holidays sparking high sales periods. Consequently, mixer price promotions drew people into the store on occasions when they were likely to be making larger than average grocery purchases.

COMPETITIVE ENVIRONMENT

Canada Dry competed not only against other mixers and soft drinks, but beverages such as milk, juice, coffee, beer, and tea, as well. And because Canada Dry's mixers were used as a mixer, its mixer sales were directly related to liquor sales.

The carbonated beverage industry was a beneficiary of a life style and eating habit change that had shifted beverage consumption patterns. Carbonated beverage consumption had increased dramatically since the turn of the century, especially during the 1960s, when per capita consumption increased by over 50%:

Gallons Per Capita Consumption in U.S., 1960 and 1968

	1960	1968
Carbonated Beverages	17.5	28.5
Coffee	40.0	36.5
Milk	28.5	24.0
Beer	15.0	16.5
Distilled Spirits	1.2	1.8

Canada Dry, however, did not benefit from these increases as much as had other beverages. It owed a substantial portion of its usage to the mixer market, and thus was tied to the distilled spirit market, which remained relatively stable.

The tie to liquor consumption had a significant impact on Canada Dry sales, making them seasonal and dependent on consumer drinking habits. A large portion of mixer sales occurred during the Christmas holiday period, reflecting the surge in holiday parties. Moreover, tonic tended to be tied to clear spirits consumption (gin, vodka, rum), which was higher during the summer. While total consumption of distilled spirits had been increasing gradually, changes in the composition of liquor sales volumes had also affected Canada Dry mixer sales. The decrease in the volume of blended and bonded whiskey sold had reduced the consumption of ginger ale (which, as a mixer, was primarily mixed with whiskey). The effects of this trend were somewhat offset, however, by an increase in scotch, gin, and vodka sales, which had led to increased club soda and tonic usage (Exhibit 3).

The Mixer Market

According to Mr. Pointsman, the mixer market was highly competitive. Canada Dry had to compete nationally, regionally, and locally. Mixer usage varied geographically, with the Northeast, for example, using more than the Midwest. But he felt the largest single factor complicating the competitive environment in the mixer market was the consumer's perception of the product. In his opinion, the consumer in many instances could not see or taste a difference between competing mixer brands. Tonic and soda water resembled "water," and all mixers had their tastes diluted by the liquor added to them. The consumer, therefore, tended to consider mixers as a "commodity," and consequently bought national, regional, local, or private brands interchangeably. The consumer, he said, was also "very responsive" to price promotions.

Mr. Pointsman went on to cite several additional factors that in his view correlated with, and in many ways enhanced, the consumer's perception of mixers as a commodity product. Since both bottler and dealer margins were high (especially for food outlets), and bottlers used little or no extract in the manufacture of mixers, they were frequently the target of severe price competition. And because of the ease of manufacture, more local bottlers prepared mixers—especially for commercial bar use where the brand name was rarely seen. Furthermore, the increased use of carbonated beverage dispensing units behind the bar reduced commercial sales of nationally-branded mixers.

In spite of these factors, Mr. Pointsman felt that there was a position in the marketplace for premium quality mixers. He pointed to the success of Schweppes mixers as an indication of the public's willingness to demand quality mixers as a symbol of taste and quality when entertaining in the home and as an assurance of quality when ordering mixed beverages away from home. He also thought that Canada Dry's mixers could be positioned in the market as soft drinks:

Even though mixers are brought into a consumer's house as a mixer initially, they frequently get used as soft drinks. When people are thirsty, they will drink everything they have on hand. Canada Dry's mixers have a very small piece of a large pie. So it might be possible to position ginger ale as a soft drink without hurting its image as a quality mixer.

ADVERTISING AND PROMOTION

In addition to supplying extract and packaging materials to its bottlers, Canada Dry was responsible for generating a demand for its product. This was accomplished through a major national and local advertising program, which was administered by Canada Dry and funded jointly by the company and its bottlers. Each year, Canada Dry executives met with their bottlers individually and presented the national advertising and promotion campaign. Each bottler was then assessed a portion of the national advertising and promotional costs (which were prorated for the bottler's marketing area on the basis of share of national population). This cost was evenly divided between Canada Dry and the bottler. Canada Dry also presented a recommendation for local advertising and promotion that was shared equally by the bottler and the company. The dealer had the option of increasing or decreasing the local program. The company shared the cost of any local program as long as the bottler's program was an extension of the national program (each bottler was provided with an extensive selection of fully prepared advertisements and commercials to choose from). Canada Dry's national agency, Grey Advertising, was responsible for placing the ads. However, if the bottler chose to run materials other than the national campaign, it had to bear all costs of its campaign.

Brand selection of beverages was highly sensitive to advertising, and so major investments in advertising and promotion were necessary simply to remain competitive in the marketplace. With the high volume of advertising and promotion being sustained by all factions of the beverage industry in 1968 (Exhibit 4), establishing a distinct brand image was essential for cutting through commercial clutter. For Canada Dry, the problem was even more difficult. Clearly, it would be difficult to compete directly for visibility as a soft drink against Coca-Cola, which outspent Canada Dry by a rate of four to one. Establishing a brand identity as a mixer was a far easier task that Canada Dry had been successfully doing since its inception. Yet, in 1965 and 1966 its position as the quality premium brand was being challenged nationally by Schweppes and regionally by White Rock for the first time.

As the largest of the mixer companies,

Canada Dry might benefit substantially from a campaign to generate primary demand. Yet even that course was fraught with problems. Creating primary demand would also benefit competitors, especially local and private-label brands that could compete on the basis of price and lure the customer away from Canada Dry at the point of sale.

The "America's Going Dry" Ad Campaign

The uncertainty surrounding the positioning of its mixer line had been largely responsible for Canada Dry having assigned its mixer account to Grey Advertising in early 1966. After evaluating the products and their competitive environment, Grey decided to strengthen the company's premium image. Grey's objectives were to convince consumers that they were not getting the best product if they were not being served Canada Dry mixers; that serving mixers other than Canada Dry was not socially acceptable; and that Canada Dry was the highest quality line of mixers on the market.

The vehicles for communicating this message were ads and commercials built around the theme "America's Going Dry." By using models dressed in styles reminiscent of B-movie versions of prohibition mobsters and molls, Canada Dry's ads and commercials were able to describe a product that was designed to be mixed with alcoholic beverages without ever mentioning the latter directly. This was pivotal to the strategy, since commercials were specifically prohibited from explicitly mentioning alcoholic beverages or their consumption. Although this requirement did not apply to print advertising, the campaign was used in all media for the sake of consistency.

Grey tested this campaign, as it tested all campaigns, to determine how successful it was in accomplishing a number of basic tasks. The agency measured a variety of responses to test commercials that were exposed to samples of respondents under clinical conditions. These responses included attention (measured by unobtrusively observing respondents' eye move-

ments during exposure); recall and comprehension of copy points; and attitude change. The last variable was obtained by comparing respondent attitudes toward Canada Dry products before exposure to the commercial with the same attitudes after exposure. The "America's Going Dry" campaign performed extremely well against all of these criteria.

Ms. Swann's Research Project

While Canada Dry Ginger Ale sales were stable relative to the rest of the market, the sales of their other products were eroding. As she reviewed the sales and competitive situation, Ms. Swann wondered how changing liquor consumption patterns would affect future mixer sales. In fact, what impact would the changes in life style, eating habits and general beverage consumption have on Canada Dry's mixer line?

What was needed, Ms. Swann decided, was a full picture of the Canada Dry and soft drink consumers—what they thought about Canada Dry and its products, what they thought about soft drinks and mixers, and, most important, what motivated them to purchase each. Were there different groups of soft drink consumers? How did they differ? And, how could their differences be turned into opportunities for Canada Dry?

The executives at Canada Dry agreed with Ms. Swann's assessment of their needs for consumer research data, and so authorized her to proceed with a major study of the carbonated beverage market. The project was designed to help Canada Dry answer the following questions:

What should Canada Dry's corporate strategy be, in terms of:
  Product emphasis within the existing product line—
    What is the relative potential for each of the existing Canada Dry brands?
What should Canada Dry's brand strategy be?
  Positioning—
    Should Ginger Ale be positioned as a soft drink only, or as a mixer as well?
    Should Ginger Ale compete against other

ginger ale brands only, or should it seek expansion from other beverage types?

Can Ginger Ale compete against all types of beverages, or only against selected ones?

Should mixers be promoted independently or within the same framework as Ginger Ale?

Target Market—
What group of consumers represents the best target market for each brand?

Buying incentive—
What appeals should be used in advertising to appeal to the target market?

Advertising impression—
What impression and "flavor" should advertising strive for? How does current advertising fit in with the desired direction?

The study was designed in two stages—the first a group of in-depth interviews to develop the ideas, directions, question wording, etc., to be used in the second stage, a national survey of consumers' attitudes, perceptions, and motivations. This national survey was based on a probability sample so that results could be generalized for the entire United States.

In the first stage, 20 "depth interviews" were conducted with men, women, and teenagers in the metropolitan New York area. In "depth" interviews, a trained interviewer meets individually with a consumer, and determines the consumer's range of feelings about a product by using a relatively unstructured interview format that could last for 2–3 hours. The objective was to develop a "phrase list" of product associations applicable to ginger ale and other soft drink consumption that could then be reduced to a series of scale questionnaire items for use in the national survey. Over 130 individual phrases were generated by individuals in the depth interviews, and these were reduced to 22 clusters of phrases by means of a statistical technique known as "factor analysis." This technique was used to cluster highly correlated phrases into a single evaluative dimension consumers used to judge a product—in this case, a carbonated beverage. Each of these single evaluative dimensions, or "factors," had a meaning independent from

other factors. (See Appendix 1 for an outline of Ms. Swann's study as well as a listing of the factors involved and several representative phrases that make up each of them.)

The second stage of the study involved a nationally projectable survey (using personal, in-home interviews) with 1,970 adults and teenagers. The survey gathered four types of information: (1) demographic data on consumers, such as age, income, education, etc.; (2) consumption patterns and brand ratings—that is, information on incidence of use and consumption volume concerning the types of carbonated beverages consumed; (3) attitudinal information, concerning consumer perceptions of "ideal" beverages, and Canada Dry products in particular; and (4) "psychographic" data. The latter was a general term referring to information on consumer attitudes, interests, and opinions (both general and product-related), which was used as a basis for market segmentation. "Psychographic" data were often used in cases in which demographics do not provide clear-cut and actionable differentiation among consumer subgroups, and/or when rather detailed and subtle information was required about consumers (for example, for use in advertising appeal and product-positioning decisions). Such detailed and "subtle" information was often required for products in markets characterized by intense brand competition among competitive products that were functionally relatively similar.

Key results from phase 2 of Ms. Swann's study are in Appendix 2. Tables 1–7 in that appendix present demographic, consumption patterns, and brand-rating results. Tables 8–11 concern the psychographic results. For this part of the study consumers completed a section of the questionnaire that asked carefully worded questions designed to measure 12 general psychological attributes.[4] Additional questions were asked to measure considerably more

---

[4] The twelve psychological attributes were Abasement, Activeness, Cheerfulness, Conscientiousness, Dominance, Exhibitionism, Impulsiveness, Masculinity, Playfulness, Sociability, Succorance and Trust.

product-specific attributes, such as the consumer's desire for carbonated taste and concern about calories. Again using the technique of factor analysis, results from the psychographic portion of the questionnaire were reduced to a set of factors that grouped consumers who responded in similar ways to the psychographic items and who were relatively distinct from individuals in the other segments. Here five segments of consumers were identified. These were judgmentally labeled as follows (Information in Appendix 2 describes each factor, or segment, in detail):

		Share of Population
Segment A	Adult—Morally concerned	35%
Segment B	Adult—Socially concerned	19
Segment C	Adult—Pleasure oriented	24
Segment D	Adult and Teen— Low-calorie concerned	14
Segment E	Other Teens	8
		100%

Each segment was then analyzed in terms of demographics (Table 8), beverage consumption patterns (Table 9), key attitudes concerning carbonated-beverage attributes (Table 10), and patterns of carbonated-beverage usage, ginger ale consumption, and Canada Dry awareness and usage (Table 11).

Current Situation. Ms. Swann received the results of the study in mid-March 1969. A quick reading of the results clearly showed that areas of opportunity for mixer-line repositioning existed. But Ms. Swann also knew that her tasks of analyzing the data and making recommendations would be carefully scrutinized within the agency and by the client. A "management summary" would not suffice since the stakes were high, and both Grey's and Canada Dry's management groups would want to know explicitly the results on which recommendations were based.

As she tried to determine what recommendations she would make to Grey's management board concerning mixer-line positioning strategy when it met the last week of the month, she hoped that the study had fully addressed the questions raised initially. She vividly recalled Mr. Pointsman's advice at the end of the December 12 meeting, and had heard that the president of the agency was anxious to present a "winning" advertising campaign to Canada Dry when he met with its executives in mid-April.

EXHIBIT 1

Carbonated-Beverage Consumption

National	1966 Million Cases*	1966 SOM**	1967 Million Cases*	1967 SOM**	1968 (Estimated) Million Cases*	1968 (Estimated) SOM**
Canada Dry Corporation						
Ginger Ale	35.0	1.1%	37.0	1.0%	40.0	1.1%
Wink	20.0	0.6	20.0	0.6	15.0	0.4
Soda Water	18.0	0.5	16.0	0.5	15.0	0.4
Tonic and Bitter Lemon	12.0	0.4	10.0	0.3	10.0	0.3
Other***	45.0	1.3	45.0	1.3	47.0	1.2
Total	130.0	3.9	128.0	3.7	127.0	3.4
Coca-Cola Company	1,240.0	37.6	1,380.0	39.4	1,558.0	40.7
Pepsi Company, Inc.	595.0	18.0	620.0	17.7	672.0	17.5
Royal Crown Cola Company	262.0	7.9	270.0	7.7	290.0	7.6
Seven-Up Company	200.0	6.1	200.0	5.7	226.0	5.9
Dr Pepper Company	97.0	7.6	100.0	2.9	117.0	3.1
Beverages International	80.0	2.4	96.0	2.7	115.0	3.0
Cott Corporation	61.0	1.9	68.9	2.0	83.1	2.2
Schweppes	10.0	0.3	11.0	0.3	11.0	0.3
Regional & Local						
Nesbitt Food Corporation	50.0	1.5	64.0	1.8	70.0	1.8
Moxie-Monarch-NuGrade Company	43.0	1.3	49.0	1.4	53.2	1.4
Shasta	27.0	0.8	31.0	0.9	38.4	1.0
Dad's Root Beer Company	13.5	0.4	19.0	0.5	23.8	0.6
Frank's Beverages	14.0	0.4	19.0	0.5	21.0	0.5
Mason & Mason	18.5	0.6	19.2	0.6	21.4	0.5
White Rock Corporation	17.5	0.5	19.5	0.6	21.5	0.6
Big K (Kroger)			11.9	0.3	18.0	0.5
Double Cola					20.0	0.5
Grape He Company	18.0	0.5	19.0	0.5	19.0	0.5
Yukon (A&P)			9.2	0.3	13.0	0.3
Cragmont (Safeway)			7.0	0.2	10.0	0.3
11 Others	404.5	12.2	354.3	10.2	294.6	7.8
Grand Total	3,300.0	100.0%	3,500.0	100.0%	3,830.0	100.0%

* Case = 1 case of twenty-four 8 ounce bottles.

** Share of total carbonated-beverage market.

*** Includes all Canada Dry soft drinks, such as Jamaica Cola, root beer, etc.

EXHIBIT 2

Soft Drinks & Mixers: National Supermarket Performance, 1968

	Sales		Profit		Assortment	Gross Margin
	% of Dept. Sales	Dollar Volume (Millions)	% of Dept. Gross Profit	Gross Profit Dollar (Millions)	Items/Brands Sizes at Warehouse	Ave. Gross Margin (% of Retail)
Carbonated Soft Drinks						
Regular Bottled	68.0%	$620.1	64.9%	$143.2	N.A.	23.1%
Regular Cans	14.7	134.1	15.2	33.6	17	25.0
Low Calorie	9.7	88.4	9.8	21.6	17	24.5
Carbonated Mixers						
Powders, Presweetened	4.6	41.9	6.2	13.8	11	32.6
Powders, Regular	1.7	15.5	2.0	4.4	17	28.5
Ice Bar Mixers	0.3	2.8	0.5	1.1	4	40.3
Syrups	0.2	1.8	0.2	0.4	4	24.2
Tablets	0.2	1.8	0.2	0.4	4	24.2
Nonalcoholic Cocktail Mixers						
Liquid	0.5	4.6	0.9	2.0	7	43.6
Powdered	0.1	0.9	0.1	0.2	1	24.2
Total	100.0%	$911.9	100.0%	$220.7		24.2%

% of Total Store Volume 1.69%
% of Gross Profit 1.92%
N.A. = not ascertainable.

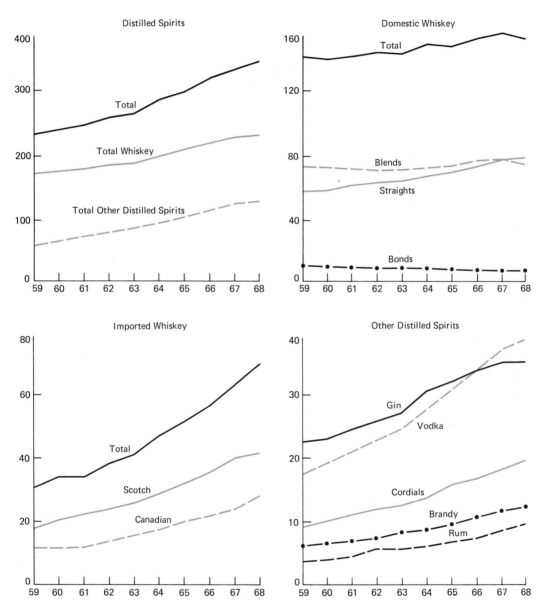

EXHIBIT 3

**Distilled Spirits Entering Trade Channels
in Millions of Wine Gallons**

97

EXHIBIT 4

1968 Consumer Media Expenditure Analysis*
Selected Soft Drink, Beer, and Liquor Companies

	Total	Newspaper		General Magazine		Spot T.V.	
	Advertising $	$	% of Total	$	% of Total	$	% of Total
Soft Drinks							
Coca-Cola Co.	55,992,564	2,631,651	4.7%	3,527,532	6.3%	29,900,029	53.4%
PepsiCo.	38,940,890	1,557,636	4.0	1,635,517	4.2	12,850,493	33.0
Canada Dry Corp.	13,000,000	2,080,000	16.0	4,056,000	31.2	3,068,000	23.6
Seven-Up Co.	15,808,951	727,212	4.6	189,707	1.2	8,758,159	55.4
Royal Crown Cola Co.	12,988,426	246,780	1.9	25,977	0.2	5,909,734	45.5
Beer							
Jos. Schlitz Brewing Co.	17,707,628	212,492	1.2	726,013	4.1	8,127,801	45.9
Anheuser-Busch, Inc.	15,785,072	426,197	2.7	3,078,089	19.5	2,572,967	16.3
Falstaff Brewing Co.	9,287,061	371,482	4.0	1,263,040	13.6	4,615,669	49.7
Pabst Brewing Co.	9,070,908	54,425	0.6			5,687,459	62.7
Liquor							
Distillers Corp.—							
Seagrams, Ltd.	46,353,367	12,608,115	27.2	25,077,171	54.1	1,019,774	2.2
Heublein, Inc.	18,330,533	2,382,969	13.0	5,865,771	32.0	3,079,530	16.8
National Distillers	16,504,682	4,340,731	26.3	8,516,416	51.6	49,514	0.3
Hiram Walker	14,536,530	5,858,403	40.3	6,788,560	46.7		

	National T.V.		Spot Radio		Outdoor		Business		Other	
	$	% of Total	$	% of Total	$	% of Total	$	% of Total	$	% of Total
Soft Drink										
Coca-Cola, Co.	8,342,892	14.9%	9,686,714	17.3%	1,343,822	2.4%	559,926	1.0%	38,941	0.1%
PepsiCo.	12,149,557	31.2	8,995,346	23.1	1,285,049	3.3	428,350	1.1		
Canada Dry Corp.			2,496,000	19.2	1,144,000	8.8	169,000	1.3		
Seven-Up Co.	2,150,017	13.6	3,272,453	20.7	553,313	3.5	158,090	1.0		
Royal Crown Cola Co.	2,104,125	16.2	4,065,377	31.3	597,468	4.6	51,954	0.4		
Beer										
Jos. Schlitz Brewing Co.	4,179,000	23.6	4,302,954	24.3	159,369	0.9				
Anheuser-Busch, Inc.	3,267,510	20.7	4,840,728	31.3	1,168,095	7.4	331,487	2.1		
Falstaff Brewing Co.	92,871	1.0	2,126,737	22.9	817,261	8.8				
Pabst Brewing Co.	1,886,749	20.8	8,898,020	9.9	544,254	6.0				
Liquor										
Distillers Corp.—										
Seagrams Ltd.	3,061,199	16.7	1,778,062	9.7	6,767,592	14.6	834,361	1.8		
Heublein, Inc.					2,071,350	11.3	91,653	0.5		
National Distillers					2,574,730	15.6	1,023,290	6.2		
Hiram Walker					1,642,628	11.3	247,121	1.7		

* Measured media only.

APPENDIX 1

The Canada Dry Study, the Methods Employed, and Its Execution and Analysis

Method

Phase I: Exploratory Interviews (to develop phrase list for attitude measurements)
20 depth interviews with men, women, teens
Metropolitan New York
August 1968

Phase II: National Study
1970 personal interviews
1422 adults (19 years and older)
548 teenagers (13–18)
National probability sample of the United States, based on 145 Primary Sampling Units

Procedure Used in Determining What Consumers Look for in Carbonated Beverages

To determine the important attitude factors in judging beverages, four steps were taken:

1. The Basic Phrase List
A list was compiled of 125 phrases typically used by consumers to describe what they are looking for in carbonated beverages. These were generated by individual consumers in the depth interviews.

2. Desirability Ratings
Consumers then rated the desirability of these phrases (or product associations) in carbonated beverages using a six-point scale ranging from "extremely desirable" to "not at all desirable."

3. Factor Analysis of Phrases
Consumers' ratings on the 125 phrases were analyzed on a computer to *objectively* group those phrases which are highly correlated by consumers. Grouping of phrases into an attitude factor means:
    that these phrases together represent a single evaluative dimension for judging a carbonated beverage.
    that this attitude factor has an independent meaning from other factors.

4. Naming Each Factor
Each attitude factor was judgmentally given a name which we felt best summarized the phrases in that factor.

General Description of Factors	*Factor #*	*The 22 Attitude Factors by Which Adults and Teens Evaluate Carbonated Beverages with Representative "Basic Phrases" Composing Each*
Subjective Taste:	1	*Fresh satisfying taste*
		Has a clean taste
		Has a crisp taste
	2	*Natural flavor (adults only)*
		Has real fruit flavor
		Has a "true" flavor
Specific taste:	3	*Grapefruit/lemon taste*
	4	*Strong/bitter/sour taste*
		Tickles your tongue (adults)
		Has a strong taste (teens)
	5	*Subtle/dry taste with no aftertaste*
		Has a light taste (adults)
		Has no aftertaste (teens)
	6	*Sweet taste (teens only)*

General Description of Factors	Factor #	*The 22 Attitude Factors by Which Adults and Teens Evaluate Carbonated Beverages with Representative "Basic Phrases" Composing Each*
Taste as a Mixer:	7	*Masks the taste of liquor* Makes the liquor drinks less strong (adults) Helps keep you from getting high (teens)
	8	*Good mixer/adds to the taste of liquor (adults only)* Mixes well with the kind of liquor I like
Physical Effects:	9	*Gives you a lift* Is relaxing (adults) Gives you a kick
	10	*Thirst quenching without bloating or filling you* Doesn't bloat you Not syrupy
	11	*Low in calories*
	12	*Medicinal values*
Product Attributes:	13	*Highly carbonated/long-lasting carbonation* It sparkles It tingles Has high carbonation
	14	*Low carbonation (teens only)*
	15	*Variety of bottle sizes*
	16	*Easy to use cans*
	17	*Has sugar (teens only)*
Associations with Product:	18	*Drunk by modern/sociable people* Drunk by modern people Drunk by well-educated people Drunk by mature people
	19	*Liked by children*
Miscellaneous:	20	*Good to drink any time* Good for picnics Good with meals Good by itself Good in hot weather
	21	*Good company reputation* Made by leading soft drink company Made by company with lively ideas
Judgmentally Added:	22	*Good value*

APPENDIX 2

Phase 2 Results
Market Target/Buying Incentive Study of Carbonated Beverages

TABLE 1

Importance of Demographic Groups in Total Soft Drink Consumption
Adults and Teens*

	Population	Share of Soft Drink Volume	Canada Dry Users** in Past Two Weeks
Sex			
Males	49%	54%	53%
Females	51	46	47
Age			
Teens (13–18)	15	17	13
19–34	28	38	30
35–49	25	23	26
50 & Over	32	22	31
Income			
Under $5,000	25	22	14
$5,000–$9,999	47	52	54
$10,000–Over	28	26	32
Occupation of Head of Household			
White Collar			
Professional	26	26	27
Clerical/Sales	14	11	16
Blue Collar	41	52	43
Retired & Other	19	11	14
Geographic Region			
West	19	18	11
South	25	31	12
Central	29	28	22
East	27	23	55
City Size			
1,000,000 or more	39	45	66
50,000–1,000,000	27	23	16
Nonurban	34	32	18

* This and all subsequent tables are based on the 85% of adult and 69% of teen consumers in the study who indicated they had consumed carbonated beverages in the past two weeks.

** Any Canada Dry product (except Wink).

TABLE 2

Brand Awareness: Unaided*
(% of Total Sample)

Coca-Cola	88%	Canada Dry**	24
Pepsi-Cola	80	Sprite	24
7-Up	60	Diet Rite	23
Royal Crown	35	Diet Pepsi	22
Fresca	34	Wink	22
Dr Pepper	31	Squirt	17
Tab	27		

* Based on question: "What carbonated-beverage brand names can you think of?"

** Does not include Wink.

TABLE 3

Awareness of Canada Dry Products: Aided*

Ginger Ale	91%	Cherry	26%
Club Soda	69	Cola	23
Tonic Water	51	Strawberry	23
Orange	47	Tahitian Treat	15
Cream Soda	36	Raspberry	15
Grape	34	Wink	N.A.
Root Beer	32	Bitter Lemon	N.A.

* Based on question: "What Canada Dry brand beverages can you think of?"

TABLE 4

Brand and Type of Carbonated Beverages Used in Past Two Weeks

	% of Sample Using Product in last 2 weeks	% (Volume)* of Carbonated Beverages Consumed in Past 2 Weeks by Those in Sample Saying They Used Each Type during Past 2 Weeks	
		Total Sample	Children 5–12**
Colas			
Regular Colas	34%	51%	50%
Diet Colas	9	12	10
Total	43%	63%	60%
Green-Bottle Items			
Lemon-Lime	14	11	5
Grapefruit	9	7	4
Ginger Ale	6	4	6
Total	30%	22%	15%
Flavors			
Root Beer	9	5	8
Orange	7	4	9
Grape	3	2	5
Cherry, Strawberry	2	1	3
Raspberry	N.A.	N.A.	N.A.
Total	20%	12%	25%
Club Soda	4	2	
Summer Mixers	3	1	
	100%	100%	100%

N.A. = Not ascertainable.

 * In the study, volume estimates were based on questions concerning the amounts of various beverages purchased during various time periods.

** As reported by parents.

TABLE 5

Share of Soft Drink Volume by Use & Location of Consumption
(% of Total Volume per Type)

	Total	Colas	Ginger Ale	Lemon-Lime	Grape fruit	All Green Bottle Items	Summer Mixers**	Club Soda	Flavors
						Green Bottle Items			
Typical use as soft drink vs. mixer									
Mixer	7%	1%	38%	18%	14%	23%	73%	64%	
Soft drink	93	99	62	82	86	77	27	36	100%
At home vs. away from home (typically)									
Away from home	36	35	23	42	29	31	N.B.	N.B.	43
At home	64	65	77	58	71	68	N.B.	N.B.	57
Per-capita consumption (# of glasses)—past two weeks*	13	12.3	3.9	4.9	5.0	4.6	N.B.	N.B.	1.7

N.B. = Base too small for percentage.

  * % of total adults & teens who indicated they had consumed carbonated beverages in past two weeks.

** Includes quinine water, bitter lemon, and bitter orange.

TABLE 6

Types of Substitute Carbonated Beverages Used by Carbonated Beverage Consumers
Who Indicate a Generally Preferred Carbonated Beverage*

	Coca-Cola Drinkers	Pepsi-Cola Drinkers	7-Up Drinkers	Ginger Ale Drinkers	Wink Drinkers	Fresca Drinkers	Orange Drinkers	Root Beer Drinkers
				Preferred Carbonated Beverages				
Substitute Type								
Colas	72%**	83%	19%	18%	12%	13%	26%	61%
Green-Bottle Items***								
Lemon-Lime	12	6	27	50	45	45	10	7
Ginger Ale	3	2	20	8	27	23	4	2
Grapefruit	2	1	20	5	6	7	4	3
Flavors	11	7	12	12	8	10	55	26
Club Soda/Summer Mixers	****	1	2	7	2	2	1	1
	100%	100%	100%	100%	100%	100%	100%	100%

  * % of total sample of adult and teen drinkers of each brand who gave a substitute based on question: "You said that ——— was your favorite kind of soft drink. Supposing you had to pick a substitute for it. What kind of soft drink would you substitute?"

  ** Should be read: "72% of Coca-Cola preferrers say they prefer another cola as a substitute for Coca-Cola."

  *** Should be read: "17% of Coca-Cola preferrers say they prefer green-bottle items (lemon-lime, ginger ale, or grapefruit) as a substitute for Coca-Cola."

  **** Less than .5%.

TABLE 7

Ideal Beverage Attributes vs. Canada Dry

The 22 Attitude Factors Reduced from "Basic Phrase" List	% of Adults Rating Extremely Desirable in Ideal Carbonated Beverages	% of Adults Rating Canada Dry Excellent		% of Teens Rating Extremely Desirable in Ideal Carbonated Beverages	% of Teens Rating Canada Dry Excellent	% Difference between Ideal & Canada Dry	
		(All Adults)	Users*			All Adults**	All Teens**
Good value	39%	20%	25%	41%	20%	−19%	−21%
Fresh satisfying taste	47	34	52	45	31	−13	−13
Thirst quenching without filling or bloating you	40	25	38	41	29	−15	−12
Good to drink at any time	38	27	37	55	35	−11	−20
Liked by children	38	24	27	30	20	−14	−10
Medicinal values	37	26	30	36	26	−11	−10
Gives you a lift	33	22	28	29	20	−11	−14
Natural flavor	31	21	31	—	—	−10	—
Low in calories	25	13	15	23	18	−12	−7
Easy to use cans	25	18	36	33	27	−7	−6
Variety of bottle sizes	23	—	—	32	—	—	—
Good mixer/adds to the taste of liquor	22	24	40	—	—	+2	—
Has sugar	—	—	—	22	17	—	−5
Sweet taste	—	—	—	20	16	—	−4
Drunk by modern sociable people	19	21	31	19	18	+2	−1
Highly carbonated/long lasting carb.	19	20	28	25	25	+3	0
Good company reputation	18	26	38	25	27	+8	+2
Subtle/dry taste with no aftertaste	15	14	18	27	15	−1	−4
Low carbonation	—	—	—	15	8	—	−7
Masks the taste of liquor	14	12	17	16	14	−2	−2
Grapefruit/lemon taste	10	—	—	11	—	—	—
Strong/bitter/sour taste	7	8	13	11	8	+1	−3

* Adults who drank a Canada Dry carbonated beverage during the past 6 months.

** Calculated: (% rating Canada Dry Excellent)—(% rating factor extremely desirable): (−) sign means ideal rated higher than Canada Dry; (+) sign means Canada Dry rated higher.

DEFINITIONS OF PSYCHOGRAPHIC PROFILES

Segment A:
Adult—Morally Concerned

Segment A adults are characterized by a puritanical and conservative personality. They are humble, compliant people who conscientiously fulfill their duties. They see themselves as moral, unpretentious and content with their work, their families and what they consider to be the pleasures of a simple life.

Segment A drinkers disapprove of self-seeking people and those who live for pleasure alone. They are likely to disapprove of liquor drinking.

Soft drinks represent a mild pleasure that is consistent with their simple way of life. They would be likely to favor beverages that possess the old-fashioned virtue they seek. Thus, well-established brands that are made with natural ingredients would be in keeping with their personality.

Segment B:
Adult—Socially Concerned

Segment B adults are motivated primarily by a need to be liked by their peers. They want to be seen as easy to get along with, part of the gang, and an asset in social situations. Actually socially uneasy and insecure people, they are anxious to conform, to do what is expected of them, and to fit in with what is considered to be fun and pleasurable by normal, well-rounded people.

Socializing and the pursuit of good times are very important to these consumers. They value most the feeling that they belong, that they are accepted. The purpose of the occasion, whether bowling, informal home entertainment, breaks at work, etc., is less important than a shared feeling of being part of a lively group who are unmistakably enjoying themselves. Essentially unsophisticated, they would be likely to seek out the most conventionally popular pursuits.

The Segment B drinkers are more likely to look favorably upon brands or types of beverages that are "in"—not exotic or unconventional, but popular and well thought of as they themselves would like to be.

Segment C:
Adult—Pleasure Oriented

Segment C adults are pleasure seekers. Confident, assertive people, they see themselves as being able to achieve whatever they want. Intent on living life to the fullest, they lay great emphasis on self-gratification and on their image as leading pleasure-filled lives.

Both men and women in Segment C display an earthy, robust approach to life, particularly when it comes to pleasure. In contrast to Segment B, they care little about what others think and what is socially accepted. They harbor an ideal fantasy of unfettered freedom to enjoy all pleasures as they desire them.

Carbonated beverages fit well into the amusement and diversion-seeking orientation of Segment C individuals, as does liquor. They are likely to be heavy consumers of both. Their preferences in carbonated beverages would tend to reflect little concern for health or weight, but great concern with physical gratification.

Segment D:
Adult and Teen—
Low-calorie Concerned

Results from adults and teens were highly similar, so these groups were combined for analysis. Segment D adults and teens are a self-controlled people with cheerful and altruistic outlooks on life. They tend to subordinate the material aspects of life and are motivated by the desire to engage in unselfish and constructive activity. Teens are well adjusted, desire individuality, and are "planners" for the future.

Even in their pleasures, Segment D drinkers remain in control; they have little capacity for indulging their lustier impulses or physical appetites. Their pleasures would tend to be wholesome, temperate, and refined.

To Segment D adults and teens, soft

drinks are acceptable but not relished. Typically, they would like to suggest that they can take them or leave them. They are likely to look favorably upon brands or types that denote refinement, are not perceived as too gratifying, and are suggestive of control rather than indulgence.

Segment E: Other Teens

Segment E teens are primarily motivated by their desire to pursue fun and pleasure as a way of life. They are characterized by physical, fast-paced and extroverted behavior. However, much of the activity that they engage in is a means of compensating for their underlying insecurities. Continuous distractions enable them to avoid self-confrontation with their own shortcomings.

Their groups of friends are very important to fulfilling their need for social acceptance and approval. They are less likely to seek out individual friendships than to want to be part of a group.

Carbonated beverages fit in with these teenagers' concept of good times within a group, and the act of drinking fulfills their need for immediate impulse gratification. They would be most likely to seek the carbonated beverage that offers the greatest amount of acceptance by the group.

TABLE 8

Demographic Summary by all Psychographic Segments

Psychographic Segments	Sex		Age					Presence of Children			Income		
	Male	Female	19–24	25–34	35–44	45–54	55+	No Children	1–2	3+	Under $5,000	$5,000–$9,999	$10,000 plus
Segment A (Adult—morally concerned)	41%	59%	11%	14%	19%	20%	36%	51%	28%	21%	34%	46%	20%
Segment B (Adult—socially concerned)	49	51	16	22	20	20	22	43	26	31	20	50	30
Segment C (Adult—pleasure concerned)	59	41	18	26	23	19	14	39	37	24	13	50	37
Segment D (Adult & Teen—low-calorie concerned)	35	65	20*	21	20	13	26	43	31	26	23	33	44

	Age of Teen		Education of Teen		
	13–15	16–18	6–8 Grade	9–12 Grade	College/Not in School
Segment E (Other Teen)	66%	34%	25%	66%	3%

*Age category is 13–24.

	Education of Household Head				Occupation of Household Head				Region				City Size		
	Grade School or Less	Some H.S.	Completed H.S.	Some College or More	White Collar Prof./Mgr.	Clerical Sales	Blue Collar	Retired & Other	West	South	Central	East	Non Urban	50,000 1,000,000	1,000 or More
	24%	25%	30%	21%	19%	12%	39%	30%	14%	38%	29%	19%	39%	30%	31%
	13	25	35	27	24	10	46	20	17	19	31	33	27	23	50

107

TABLE 8 (cont.)

| | Education of Household Head | | | | Occupation of Household Head | | | | Region | | | | City Size | | |
| | Grade School or Less | Some H.S. | Completed H.S. | Some College or More | White Collar | | Blue Collar | Retired & Other | West | South | Central | East | Non Urban | 50,000 1,000,000 | 1,000 or More |
					Prof./Mgr.	Clerical Sales									
	9	12	37	42	35	15	35	15	25	15	28	32	28	27	45
	11	18	32	39	28	19	28	25	30	12	28	30	39	22	39
	14	23	35	28	25	21	47	7	15	24	30	31	35	21	44

TABLE 9

Segment Summary

	Share of Population	Share of Soft Drink Volume	Share of Mixer Volume	Share of Total Ginger Ale Volume	Share of Ginger Ale Soft Drink Volume	Share of Ginger Ale Mixer Volume	Share of Cola Volume	Share of Club Soda Volume	Share of Tonic Volume	Share of Diet Soda Volume
Segment A (Adult—morally concerned)	35%	35%	7%	17%	23%	7%	36%	8%	8%	37%
Segment B (Adult—socially concerned)	19%	20%	39%	42%	30%	60%	19%	32%	27%	17%
Segment C (Adult—pleasure concerned)	24%	22%	44%	28%	26%	30%	23%	49%	45%	22%
Segment D (Adult & Teen—low-calorie concerned)	14%	13%	10%	7%	13%	3%	13%	10%	18%	18%
Segment E (Other Teens)	8%	10%	—	6%	8%	—	9%	1%	2%	6%
	100%	100%	100%	100%	100%	100%	100%	100%	100%	100%

TABLE 10

Differentiating Attitudes regarding Ideal Carbonated Beverage Relative* to Other Segments Averages

	Segment A Adult— Morally Concerned	Segment B Adult— Socially Concerned	Segment C Adult— Pleasure Concerned	Segment D Adult & Teen— Low-Calorie Concerned	Segment E Other Teens
General Factors					
Fresh/satisfying taste	+ 6%*			− 20%	
Drunk by modern/sociable people		+23%	− 18%	− 24	+ 22
Liked by children	+ 6	+ 14	− 14	− 21	
Good value			− 12	+ 11	
Natural flavors	+ 5			− 14	
Easy to use cans				+ 11	+ 15
Good to drink any time	+ 5	+ 11		− 17	
Gives you a lift				− 17	
Good company reputation	+ 4	+ 16	− 13		+ 15
Low in calories		+ 10	− 14	+ 27	− 20
Low carbonation					+ 13
Variety of bottle sizes		+ 10			
Highly carbonated/long-lasting carbonation					+ 21
Has sugar					+ 17
Sweet taste				− 12	+ 14
Mixer Factor					
Masks the taste of liquor	− 11**	+ 33	− 4		
Good mixer/adds to taste of liquor	− 31	+ 25	+ 8		

* To be read "Segment A is 6% more concerned about fresh/satisfying taste than the average of the other segments."

** To be read "Segment A is 11% less concerned about masking the taste of liquor."

(+) means more concerned about than average.

(−) means less concerned about than average.

TABLE 11

Carbonated Beverage Consumption by Psychographic Segment & Relative to Average of Remaining Segments
(As Percentage of Total Sample)

	Segment A Adult— Morally Concerned	Segment B Adult— Socially Concerned	Segment C Adult— Pleasure Concerned	Segment D Adult & Teen— Low-Calorie Concerned	Segment E Other Teens
Use of Carbonated Bev. Drink	85%*	86%	92%	84%	
As a Soft Drink Only	78	57	65	58	
Both	6	26	24	22	
As a Mixer Only	1	3	3	4	
Drank Alcohol in Past 2 Wks.	13	42	48	42	
With Mixer Only	4	21	19	21	
Both	3	8	9	5	
Without Mixer Only	6	13	20	16	

TABLE 11 (cont.)

	Segment A Adult— Morally Concerned	Segment B Adult— Socially Concerned	Segment C Adult— Pleasure Concerned	Segment D Adult & Teen— Low-Calorie Concerned	Segment E Other Teens
Type Soft Drink Used in Past 2 Weeks					
Cola Incidence (volume)	69 (70)	67 (62)	74 (66)	60 (64)	89% (68)
Lemon/Lime Incidence (volume)	24 (10)	33 (11)	29 (9)	20 (8)	34 (11)
Grapefruit Incidence (volume)	15 (6)	21 (8)	18 (7)	24 (12)	20 (4)
Ginger Ale Incidence (volume)	8 (2)	16 (4)	11 (3)	12 (3)	11 (2)
Flavors Incidence (volume)	28 (12)	31 (13)	37 (13)	26 (10)	49 (10)
Club Soda or Mixer Incidence (volume)	1 (1)	2 (3)	3 (4)	5 (6)	1 (1)
Ginger Ale Usage					
Total Incidence ("Recently")	8.6	20.6	14.2	15.4	10.9
As a Mixer Only	1.0	10.0	10.0	11.0	
Both	0.8	5.6	1.5	0.6	
As a Soft Drink Only	6.8	5.0	2.7	3.8	
Canada Dry Penetration					
Unaided Awareness	19	24	33	25	16
Knowledge of Canada Dry Label Products (# of Brands Known)	# 3.5	# 4.3	# 4.7	# 4.9	# 4.4
Overall Attitude (% Rating Excellent)	17%	26%	22%	27%	12%
Incidence of Drinking Any Canada Dry ("Recently")	3	11	7	12	5

* To be read: "85% of Segment A consumers used a carbonated beverage during last two weeks."

CHAPTER 5

L'eggs Products, Inc. (A)

Jack Ward sat down at his desk one day in early 1973 to resolve a problem which would soon require a decision. As Group Product Manager of L'eggs Products, Inc., he had to decide what specific alternative—or what combination of specific alternatives—to employ for L'eggs Pantyhose's first national promotion during the coming fall season.

L'eggs Products, Inc., was a subsidiary of the Hanes Corporation, producers of hosiery, knitwear, and foundation garments. L'eggs Pantyhose was the first major nationally

branded and advertised hosiery product distributed through food and drug outlets. It had been remarkably successful since its first test market introduction in 1970, through market-by-market rollout, and now was distributed through grocery and drug stores in 90% of the country. By mid-1973 it accounted for over 25% of the hosiery volume done by food and drug outlets. These outlets represented between 20% to 25% of total U.S. hosiery sales. The resulting 5% to 6% over-all market share made L'eggs Pantyhose the largest selling single brand in the hosiery industry.

With success, however, had come increased competitive efforts from other major manufacturers and from private label brands. In response, and in keeping with the L'eggs philosophy of aggressive marketing utilizing packaged goods techniques to reinforce consumer purchase behavior, L'eggs was planning its fall promotional activities. These would coincide with the back-to-school season and the advent of cooler weather, both traditional stimuli to hosiery sales. The focus of these activities was to be some form of packaging and/or or "cents-off" promotional deal to consumers on a national basis.

The prime objective for the promotion was to generate, profitably, the largest number of incremental sales over the next six months. However, there were two other important objectives. In many markets the trial rate for L'eggs Pantyhose had peaked at a level considered satisfactory, and the product group felt that promotional vehicles to increase trial would not be necessary or effective. The aim in these markets, therefore, was to find the best promotional alternative to stimulate the repeat rate and to load the consumer with product, thereby reducing her motivation to purchase from competitors. In other markets, however, the trial rate was considerably lower and was judged unsatisfactory. In these markets, the strategy was to utilize the fall promotion for the objective of increasing trial. Absorbing short-term promotional costs would be tolerated here for the purpose of generating increased trial, greater market share, and, hopefully, sustained long-run volume.

Four alternative promotional vehicles had been developed and screened. Some of the alternatives appeared to be more effective, on a sales basis, in achieving one of the objectives—trial among nonusers. Others seemed to be more effective in generating repeat and loading among current users. In addition, the alternatives had different costs associated with their use. Finally, there were nonquantifiable factors arguing for or against the implementation of each.

Mr. Ward knew he would have to analyze the results and decide whether just one alternative could be utilized—and which one it should be—or whether the efficiency and ease of implementation of having just one promotional vehicle on a national basis should be sacrificed to the effectiveness of using a combination of alternatives targeted to specific areas.

DEVELOPING THE L'EGGS STRATEGY 1969-1972[1]

L'eggs was the first brand in the hosiery industry to utilize a "packaged goods" marketing program to advertise, promote, display, and sell hosiery to the consumer through food and drug outlets. This represented a departure from the traditional methods used to merchandise hosiery through any retail outlet.

Before introduction of L'eggs, branded hosiery sales by major industry producers (including Hanes) were made exclusively through department and specialty stores. Starting in 1965, however, sales of private label hosiery through supermarkets and drugstores had grown dramatically and by 1969 represented a significant share—6% for drugstores and 12% for supermarkets—of the $1.5 billion retail hosiery market.

Noting these trends, Hanes investigated entry into these mass merchandising outlets on a branded basis. Extensive market, consumer, and product research studies were made to determine: (a) the actual size, composition, and nature of the market; (b) consumer attitudes and behavior toward hosiery in general and supermarket hosiery in particular; (c) by means of in-home concept and product use tests, whether new products developed by Hanes would fulfill planned advertising promises and consumer expectations generated.

Market information received from the A. C. Nielsen Co. store audits in 1969 verified the existence of a substantial market, but indicated problems to be overcome if food and drug hosiery sales were to reach full potential (as compared with health and beauty aids prod-

---

[1] Material in this section is taken from a speech made to the A.M.A. in November 1972 by David E. Harrold, the original marketing director of L'eggs Products, Inc., and now president of Hanes Knitwear Division.

ucts, for example, where mass outlets accounted for 50% of industry volume). Further channel research isolated these problems:

1. A very fragmented market. Over 600 different hosiery brands were sold in mass outlets, and no brand had more than a 4% share.
2. Advertising and promotion to stimulate sales was based on price only—not informing the consumer about product qualities or why she should consider buying in a particular outlet.
3. Stock-outs ran as high as 25%—manufacturers did not anticipate needs and keep stocks in balance, and did not provide necessary service.
4. Retail turnover lagged behind the average of all food and drug products—the retailer's return on investment was unattractive.

Consumer research provided answers on what had to be done to establish a permanent branded franchise:

1. The consumer felt that supermarket and drugstore hosiery had a low quality image.
2. There was no brand loyalty.
3. Products lacked consistency from package to package.
4. Frequent stock-outs diluted her confidence in product availability and drove her back to traditional hosiery outlets where such problems did not exist.

Despite these problems, the research indicated a strong consumer desire to purchase hosiery regularly in convenience outlets if she could develop a lasting confidence in the product.

Hanes concluded that the trade and consumer needed a completely new hosiery product and marketing program for these outlets, which would build consumer loyalty by virtue of unique product benefits: a distinctive name, package, and display; heavy advertising to build awarensss of the product, benefits, outlet of availability, and product consistency; and promotional techniques to stimulate trial and repeat, to build the habit of purchasing and repurchasing the product.

The company had developed a new and superior product (preferred over any product tested against it, including the consumer's own brand). It was a one-size, super-stretch pantyhose which had no shape until placed on the woman's leg, and then shaped itself to conform to her leg structure, thereby providing excellent fit for 70% of all wearers. This product was more expensive to manufacture than conventional pantyhose. However, with one size needed, Hanes could drastically reduce the inventory and display space required at retail, and could consider major innovations in packaging and display.

Hanes started to develop an integrated food and drug hosiery program where all elements including name, package design, display configuration, advertising, and promotion would complement each other. The name, package, and display had to focus retail consumer attention in the store. Other objectives were: (a) a modular package to distinguish the package from other brands (and minimize pilferage, of major concern to the trade); (b) a package to make both the consumer selection process as well as replenishing the display convenient; (c) a display of use only to Hanes, to ensure separation from other brands; (d) the display had to provide service and education to the consumer via information panels, literature racks, etc., to duplicate in these self-service outlets the personalized service available in department stores; (e) a display using a minimum of costly square footage and a maximum of free vertical space; (f) a display capable of holding sufficient inventory to minimize stock-outs.

Working with a package design consultant, the Hanes new product group developed the brand name "L'eggs." Within the name was the answer to the package—an actual plastic egg held in color-coded cylinders (for various colors and styles) that was modular and distinctive from competition. They developed a plastic display (called the L'eggs Boutique) that carried through the egg concept. It had only a two-foot diameter, carried 24 dozen pairs, lent itself to island locations in high traffic locations of the store where consumer exposure was great, and proved to be a most effective point-of-purchase device. Exhibit 1 illustrates the L'eggs Boutique.

The L'eggs program was supported by advertising and promotion spending equal to that of a new cigarette or detergent introduction. Introductory advertising was at the rate of $10 million nationally, using day and night TV, magazines, Sunday supplements, and local newspaper media. Harrold reviewed L'eggs advertising and promotion objectives:

Given the unstructured market, the nonexistent brand awareness of food and drug hosiery, and the need to reinforce brand permanency to the consumer and the trade, we wished to: (a) build strong brand awareness and recognition of our logo and package; (b) let the consumer know where L'eggs was available, that it was new and different, and that it would become a permanent grocery and drugstore fixture; (c) stress our major product attribute, that L'eggs fit better than any other hosiery product—our theme was "Our L'eggs fit your legs;" (d) show the display and package in all advertising to make them synonymous with the L'eggs program.

The company launched the largest advertising campaign for any hosiery product. Spending was double the amount previously used by the entire hosiery industry for name brands. In L'eggs test market cities, two out of three hosiery commercials seen by consumers were for L'eggs—a brand available only in supermarkets and drugstores.

In addition, a $5 million market-by-market consumer promotion plan was tested, using introductory direct-mail coupons worth 25¢ or 35¢ off the purchase of one pair, as the products were introduced in each test market. This was the hosiery industry's first use of heavy couponing as a strategic trial generating device to increase consumer awareness and product experience.

The L'eggs marketing strategy also in-cluded a major innovation in the distribution system offered to the trade. L'eggs hosiery was delivered through the front door of the store directly to the retail display by L'eggs sales personnel in their own L'eggs trucks. These salespersons saw that styles and colors were always in stock. They ensured attractiveness and cleanliness of the display. They rotated and balanced inventory for each store's display rack to maximize sales velocity at each location. Accordingly, the displays had excellent turnover. The company estimated that L'eggs dollar sales per square foot were more than seven times the retailer's average for all goods and—since the products were consigned—the retailer had no investment. The sales route force also acted as a detail force to implement promotions and other merchandising events at store level.

Another innovation was a computerized, on-line marketing and sales information network to support the distribution system. It tracked product movement for each display, and through its reports L'eggs could assure balanced product availability on every route van, in every warehouse, and along the pipeline from factory to each market. An outside management consulting firm was hired to design and implement this information and control system. In use, it coordinated manufacturing, warehouse distribution, retail inventory balancing, sales and market analysis, and billing and accounts receivable. Each sales call to a display unit provided a body of inventory and sales information to the system. This information was then assembled by display, by account, by route, by market, and by branch warehouse on a weekly basis, and provided an excellent and timely data source for analysis of sales performance. In addition, extensive marketing information was routinely gathered in all markets via store audits and diary panels purchased from syndicated information sources. Special field survey research in specific markets conducted by outside research contractors, and concept tests and focus group interviews conducted by the company's own market research personnel, supplemented the routine syndicated information.

SALES RESULTS THROUGH 1972

Test marketing was conducted from March to October of 1970. After the first six months of test market, 40% of all potential women users had tried L'eggs at least once. Over two-thirds of those triers repeated with one or more subsequent purchases. Brand awareness and advertising awareness exceeded 80% after only seven weeks of advertising in the test markets. L'eggs became the leading brand of pantyhose through any outlet in the test markets. At the end of six months, almost 25% of all women listed L'eggs as their regular brand.

Market-by-market rollout commenced in the fall of 1970. At its introduction into each geographical market, L'eggs was accompanied by high levels of advertising, demonstration, introductory coupons, and cents-off deals to induce initial trial. This introductory program was often continued for 13 weeks or more, until the product group felt that the introductory objectives had been met. Additional coupon promotions in specific markets were generally repeated several times per year. The L'eggs brand quickly became the dominant factor influencing the entire industry's approach to consumer marketing of hosiery products. L'eggs quickly established a consumer franchise among a significant proportion of all women.

In 1970, L'eggs retail sales were $9 million, representing only nine months' sales experience in test markets accounting for 3½% of the United States and two months' sales in the first rollout market. In 1971, retail sales were over $54 million. L'eggs became firmly established as the best selling hosiery brand in the country, regardless of outlet, with over a 3% share of the total $1.6 billion market. This level was reached with average 1971 distribution in only 33% of the United States.

The L'eggs program dramatically expanded hosiery sales through food and drug outlets. Prior to the introduction of L'eggs, only one out of four women had purchased hosiery in these outlets. After six months in test markets, over 40% of all women had tried L'eggs which was available only through food and drug outlets. Nielsen data confirmed that total hosiery sales through convenience outlets had expanded substantially, and so L'eggs sales were primarily "add-on" sales. Trade acceptance and distribution levels in all market areas equalled the penetration that an established marketing company such as Procter & Gamble or General Foods would expect to achieve on a major new product introduction—even though this was Hanes' first exposure to mass merchandising channels.

By the end of 1972, the program had expanded into 75% of all retail markets. Fifty major markets had been opened in the span of 18 months. About 45,000 stores were under contract to display the L'eggs Boutique in prominent, high traffic locations.

1973: MARKETING ORGANIZATION AND STRATEGY

As of mid-1973, L'eggs' success continued. As market-by-market rollout proceeded, and L'eggs attained deeper penetration of each successive market, retail sales climbed to over $110 million in 1972 and were projected to top $150 million for the fiscal year ending December 31, 1973. By mid-1973, L'eggs had achieved distribution in over 90% of the United States and was represented in every major market except New York City. The company's goal was to become fully national by late 1973.

The marketing organization had expanded from an in-house group that in 1969 consisted only of a marketing director, one product manager, an assistant and one merchandising manager. The present structure included product managers for each of L'eggs' major product extensions; assistants and merchandising managers for each; a new product and a market development manager; and a marketing research group. This was in addition to some 700 sales and administrative personnel. An organization chart is shown in Exhibit 2.

Since introducing the original L'eggs Pantyhose and stockings, the company introduced several successful product extensions under the L'eggs brand: Sheer From Tummy to Toes pantyhose, Queensize pantyhose, Sheer Energy (a support hosiery product positioned toward nonsupport hose wearers), and L'eggs Knee Highs. All of these product extensions cannibalized the original L'eggs brand to some extent, but the majority of sales were true incremental sales—coming at the expense of competitors in the market place and expanding the total unit and dollar sales of L'eggs Products, Inc.

The use of packaged goods marketing techniques received the same emphasis of 1973 as it did during the original test market period. Now that L'eggs was approaching 100% national distribution, the initial test market advertising and promotion spending of $15 million on an equivalent national basis had evolved to an actual spending level of nearly $20 million for advertising, promotion, market research and new product development.

The sales effectiveness of this strategy was readily apparent, as detailed in the following table:

L'eggs Share of Total Hosiery Sold through Food and Drug Outlets—Unit Basis (pair)

	Jan.- Feb.	Mar.- Apr.	May- June	July- Aug.	Sept.- Oct.	Nov. Dec.
1972	20%	22%	25%	27%	27%	27%
1973	29%	30%	31%	29%		

Source: Nationally syndicated retail audit service.

THE INDUSTRY

L'eggs was introduced into a mature, stable industry. After some expansion in the 1960s with the widespread introduction of pantyhose, the industry had stabilized at a dollar volume of about $1.5 billion and was not expected to increase. Unit sales had increased moderately over the last few years but this increased demand had not expanded dollar volume, since the increased sales had only come in the wake of decreased prices. Many purchases had merely shifted from name brand department store hosiery at an average price of around $3.00 to discount hosiery sold in food and drug outlets at prices typically ranging from $0.99 to $1.39. Trade publications had estimated that up to 50% of food and drug private label hosiery pairs sold at prices as low as $0.39.

Grocery and drugstore outlets represented the fastest growing hosiery channel. Estimates in the trade were that these outlets had accounted for only 5% of the units (pairs) sold in 1968. They accounted for 22.1% of unit sales in 1972 and were expected to account for as much as 50% of unit sales by 1976. L'eggs Products, Inc., had prepared its own estimates of distribution channel changes which are described in Exhibit 3.

The major companies in the industry appeared to be hastening this trend with huge amounts of marketing spending to advertise and promote food and drug hosiery. Estimates of industry spending ran as high as $33 million in each of 1972 and 1973 by three companies alone, although this was probably based on announced intentions and not actual spending.

COMPETITION

Although there were almost 600 different brands of hosiery competing in food and drug outlets, many were private label and house brands and the large majority of these were distributed only locally or in a grocery chain's own outlets. L'eggs' only identifiable branded competition in 1972 and 1973 were those products marketed by the Hanes Corporation's major competitors in the hosiery industry: Kayser-Roth Corporation and Burlington Industries. These companies, like Hanes, witnessed the stagnation in department store outlets, and soon after L'eggs appeared brought out their own heavily advertised and promoted brands for food and drug outlet distribution. Kayser-Roth's entry was called No Nonsense Pantyhose, and Burlington called its product Activ pantyhose.

These competitors were companies with considerable financial resources in comparison to the Hanes Corp. Hanes' 1972 sales were $245 million, of which women's hosiery accounted for about $140 million. Hanes' other divisions manufactured and marketed men's and women's knit and outerwear and underwear, foundation garments, and swimwear. Kayser-Roth had sales of $519 million in 1972, of which women's hosiery was estimated to account for less than 20% of sales. Kayser-Roth also manufactured men's sportswear and clothing, women's sportswear and swim suits, textiles, and Supphose, the industry's leading support hosiery brand. Burlington Industries was even larger, with 1972 sales of $1.8 billion, of which women's hosiery sales were $101 million. Burlington also manufactured many other products, such as fabrics, yarns, hosiery for private label marketers, carpets, furniture, sheets and pillowcases, and industrial textiles. Additional financial information for the three companies is given in Exhibit 4.

These competitors each utilized a somewhat different marketing strategy for hosiery products sold to food and drug channels. Kayser-Roth marketed its No Nonsense brand through supermarket warehouse distributors, who delivered to the back door inventory area of the store—a system typical of packaged goods products. To compensate the store or chain for stocking and cleaning retail displays, No Nonsense offered a retail margin of 42% versus L'eggs' 35%. The No Nonsense retail prices started at $0.99 versus L'eggs from $1.39.

Burlington distributed its Activ brand like L'eggs, using Activ salespersons and vans to deliver via the "front door" to the Activ display in food and drug outlets. In addition, Burlington distributed Activ through the General Cigar Corp., which placed the product in cigar stores and newsstands to achieve a retail base beyond food and drug outlets. Like No Nonsense, Activ's suggested retail price of $1.00 was substantially below that of L'eggs.

L'eggs responded to this price competition neither by direct price-cutting policies of its own, nor by permitting the retailers to reduce normal L'eggs prices at the store level. L'eggs was a Fair-Traded item, and indeed the maintenance of the Fair Trade policy was strictly enforced by the company. Management had not hesitated to drop individual stores or even chains from the retail network when they became aware of discounting and abuse of suggested prices for L'eggs products (via information gathered by the route salespersons during store visits). Retail price maintenance was an important part of L'eggs' over-all marketing strategy.

The L'eggs response to competitive price differences was to continue the original strategy of competing in food and drug channels on bases other than price, particulary superior fit. L'eggs management believed that higher prices were necessary and justified because their product was more expensive to produce, due to specially developed high quality yarn and 100% inspection. L'eggs management preferred over the long run to pursue a strategy of maintaining prices and using the resulting margins toward product improvements and advertising to the consumer. In 1973, L'eggs' gross margin was about $5.00 per dozen pairs. However, L'eggs often built its business in specific geographical markets via promotions, temporary price deals, and special packages.

An additional reaction to branded price competition came in 1971 when L'eggs Products, Inc., test marketed its own 99¢ brand, First To Last. The First To Last marketing strategy did not utilize price as the primary sales quality differentiating the product— because there were numerous house brands and private label pantyhose in all retail outlets that sold at prices considerably below 99¢. Rather, the durability and long-lasting qualities of the product were stressed. Advertising and promotion for First To Last made a conscious effort to minimize any linkage in the consumer's mind between First To Last and L'eggs brands, thereby reducing the degree of cannibalization. The First To Last rollout proceeded cautiously, with the objective of profitable penetration before further expansion, and in mid-1973 First To Last was distributed in less than 10% of the United States. The 1973 fall national promotion was concerned only with the L'eggs brand.

Although Activ and No Nonsense each announced, at their respective introductions, planned advertising and promotion spending levels of $10 million nationally, the actual figures were much less. Industry estimates were that No Nonsense would spend not more than $3 million and Activ no more than $1.5 million in 1973. This was partially due to a slower distribution growth than originally planned. While Kayser-Roth announced that No Nonsense would be distributed in 60% of the United States by the end of 1973 and 100% by 1974, Mr. Ward estimated that actual distribution had reached less than 15% of the country by mid-1973 and would be no more than 40% by the end of the year.

While Burlington planned for Activ to be distributed in 35% of the United States by the end of 1973 and 50% by 1974 or 1975, Mr. Ward estimated that actual distribution had reached less than 10% of the country by summer of 1973, and would be no more than 30% by late fall. Market shares for No Nonsense and Activ reflected this lack of national distribution and penetration in comparison to L'eggs: in late summer 1973, national market shares were 1% for both No Nonsense and Activ, compared to 29% for L'eggs Pantyhose. Mr. Ward noted, however, that actual spending levels indicated that these competitors could be major factors in geographical markets where they had achieved distribution.

PLANNING THE 1973 FALL
NATIONAL PROMOTION

Now that L'eggs had almost completed national rollout, the planning had begun for a national promotion to impact on all markets. The evolution of the desires of major competitors for increased penetration and profitability dic-

tated further marketing efforts at this stage of L'eggs life cycle. In particular, the product group was looking for a single, high-impact promotional vehicle. They preferred the promotion to be run as an in-store promotion, although the alternative of a coupon mailed to consumers' homes was being considered.

Management's preferences for in-store promotions in this case were due to their feeling that such vehicles were more likely to result in multiple purchases per customer. Experience with coupon promotions during market introductions had shown that coupons rarely led to multiple purchases. In addition, an in-store effort would help to cement relations with the retailers, since L'eggs planned to feature the promotional event in its media advertising that fall and thus would demonstrate their considerable effort to draw customers into retail outlets for other purchases as well.

The goal of having one national promotion across all markets was complicated by the fact that L'eggs seemed to have at least two distinct types of markets in terms of responsiveness to its product. Like many mass marketers, L'eggs used as a measure of this responsiveness a quantity called the BDI (Brand Development Index). For L'eggs, BDI was defined for each geographical market as: number of L'eggs pairs sold per thousand target women per week divided by the national average number of L'eggs pairs sold per thousand target women per week, then multiplied by 100. An area with BDI below 100 was an area where L'eggs lagged in penetration versus its national average. Exhibit 5 presents a listing of markets, their BDIs, and share of L'eggs sales accounted for by each.

In certain regions of the country, BDIs were consistently less than 80. Mr. Ward's rationale was that these areas had longer warm seasons that might explain lower pantyhose sales. Consumer surveys and panels conducted frequently by L'eggs market research group, by the advertising agency, and by hired outside research organizations had shown that these low BDI markets almost uniformly had low—and unsatisfactory—

L'eggs trial rates. Typical comparisons between markets are shown in Exhibits 5 and 6. Thus, a major objective in low BDI areas was to increase trial rates.

In other areas of the country trial rates had peaked at around 50% in 6 to 12 months after markets were opened. The brand group did not feel that trial rates in these areas could be increased profitably, or at least would not sustain increases long enough to generate profitable long-run sales. The major problem in high BDI areas, therefore, was to increase the repurchase rate of L'eggs purchasers.

From different sources of research data, Mr. Ward inferred that much brand switching was taking place: in consumer market surveys, typically 20% to 30% of consumers would *say* that L'eggs was their usual brand. However, actual sales figures taken from the company's sales tracking system and from syndicated store audits indicated that L'eggs had achieved around a 10% share of market in these high BDI areas. Therefore, the most important objectives of the promotion in these areas were to change users (even repeaters) from casual users to loyal users, to increase their repurchase rate, and to load users with product to decrease the probability they would switch to competitive brands. Both Activ and No Nonsense were running introductory promotions as part of their rollouts in many market areas that fall.

To summarize, the objective of the fall promotion in poor, or low BDI markets, was offensive—to increase trial. The product group was willing to absorb a certain level of promotional costs in order to raise trial rates on the theory that this would lead to greater penetration, more market share, and sustained profitable long-run sales increases. In contrast, the objectives of the promotion in high BDI markets were both offensive (increase repeat rates and product loyalty) and defensive (short-run loading). Mr. Ward's problem was to decide which one specific promotion, of the alternatives that were now before him, would be most effective against these differing objectives and differing market conditions.

THE ALTERNATIVES

Four alternative promotional vehicles were being evaluated. Each alternative had, in some form, been used with moderate success in specific markets during L'eggs rollouts over the past two years.

The national promotion alternatives in the summer of 1973 were:

1. A 40¢-off twin-pack offer (see Exhibit 7).
2. A 25¢-off twin-pack offer.
3. A coupon mailed to homes worth 25¢ off one package (pair) of L'eggs.
4. A 20¢-off single-pack offer (see Exhibit 8).

In choosing these alternatives the product group had reasoned as follows about their likely effects: the 40¢ twin-pack probably would achieve the objective of loading the consumer in high BDI areas best (for her next pair, the consumer would have the second pair of L'eggs in the twin-pack already and would have no need to go out and purchase, perhaps, a competitive brand). Hopefully, more product use and experience with two pairs rather than one would predispose the consumer more to repurchase L'eggs the next time she needed hosiery. However, Mr. Ward thought the twin-pack might not be effective in low BDI areas because with low trial and low market share in these areas, sufficient numbers of consumers might not purchase the twin-pack often enough to make the promotion effective. Besides, the consumer, not a L'eggs user anyway, might balk at having to purchase two pairs in order to try L'eggs.

The 25¢-off twin-pack would presumably produce the same behavior against those objectives, and would improve unit contributions considerably. The question in Mr. Ward's mind was whether the offer would be effective enough—whether 25¢ off on two pairs would induce sufficient incremental purchases—to produce desirable results.

The mailed coupon worth 25¢-off on one pair was included as an alternative even though the brand group preferred the fall promotion vehicle to be an in-store offer. The 25¢ mailed coupon had been reasonably effective when used in many rollout markets during introduction. It was expected to induce trial among nonusers. It was to be mailed to all homes, thus coming to the attention of women who were nonusers or who may not have noted an in-store offer because they would not look for, or at, a L'eggs display. The coupon was not expected to be effective in inducing consumer loading or repurchase, however, because it could only be used to purchase one pair.

The 20¢ single-pack seemed to be somewhat effective against both objectives. In low BDI areas, consumer takeaway for the promotion (the number of consumers purchasing) would presumably be higher because the new trier would not be forced to purchase two pairs. So the single-pack might be more effective in raising trial rates. In high BDI areas the consumer might buy two or more single packs, satisfying the objective of consumer loading and raising repeat rates. On the other hand, there was nothing to encourage the consumer (or force the consumer, as was the case of the twin-pack) to purchase more than one pair. Mr. Ward judged the single-pack somewhat less effective as a means of consumer loading and increasing the total number of pairs purchased under the promotion.

For each alternative except the coupon, L'eggs would bear 65% of the cost of the promotion and the retailer would bear 35% of the cost, the same ratio as the retailer's gross margin. For example, for the 20¢-off single-pack, the retailer would absorb 7¢ (35% of 20¢) and L'eggs would absorb 13¢ (65% of 20¢). For the coupon, L'eggs would absorb the full cost and reimburse the retailer upon receipt of the coupon.

IMPLEMENTATION ISSUES
IN SELECTING THE PROMOTION

Since L'eggs was a Fair-Traded item, Mr. Ward knew that it could not appear in any store under a cents-off deal unless for a limited time only, and could not appear in any store

under two different prices for the same quantity (such as a regular-priced boutique pair and a 20¢-off promotional single-pack simultaneously). This meant that to implement the single-pack offer, L'eggs would have to move all existing inventory out of stores at the beginning of the promotion, replace them with special 20¢-off single-packs, remove all special packs at the promotion's end, and move all regular inventory back in.

A possible solution was for L'eggs to make the special single-pack a simple variation of the regular pack. At the promotion's start all existing store packs could have a flag inserted, then removed at the promotion's end. Exhibit 8 actually shows a flag inserted into a regular L'eggs pack. Because the over 600 L'eggs route persons were fully occupied by their normal stocking, accounting, and boutique cleaning operations in over 70,000 outlets, a temporary work force would have to be hired to travel with the route persons to insert flags. Mr. Ward estimated each of the 600 L'eggs route persons would need a temporary assistant for one 3-week cycle. These temporaries could be hired from well-known agencies at the rate of $30 per day per person. After the promotion was begun, the temporary labor would be replaced by factory labor because flags would be inserted in boutique-destined replacement packs at the factory. For unflagging boutique packs at the promotion's end, it was decided that they could do without the temporaries and use the efforts of route persons only, even though their route schedules could be delayed considerably by the extra work.

To supplement the boutique in the stores during the promotion, the factory would also make up special "shippers"—self-contained cardboard floor displays packed at the factory to minimize setup time at the retail store, but which (if accepted by the retailer) would require allocating additional floor space to L'eggs (see Exhibit 9). Mr. Ward estimated the cost of the single-pack shippers, freight, point-of-sale material, etc., would average out to 35¢ per dozen pairs. These shippers could simply be removed at the promotion's conclusion.

The twin-pack required no such expensive field labor to implement. Because the quantity in the twin-pack promotional packs would differ from regular boutique packs (1 pair each), the twin-pack shipper display could be utilized to implement the promotion (see Exhibit 10 for a mock-up of the twin-pack shipper) without boutique flagging. The shipper and promotional packs for it could be completely factory-made and placed in the store to co-exist with regular-priced boutique packs, then simply removed at the promotion's conclusion. Fair Trade laws would not be violated, since the cents-off promotional twin-packs would hold different quantities than the regular-priced boutique packs. Mr. Ward estimated the cost of making up these shippers, freight, point-of-sale material, and twin-packs at 38¢ per dozen hosiery pairs.

He anticipated a bit of increased trade resistance for the twin-pack alternatives since the shippers were absolutely necessary in the case of the twin-packs—and thus the retailer would have to devote roughly six more square feet of selling space to L'eggs during the promotion. In contrast, the 20¢ single-pack alternative could be accomplished solely via flagged boutique packs if the retailer refused the additional single-pack shippers. However, Mr. Ward expected this resistance to be minimal because of L'eggs' outstanding sales velocity. In addition, retailer acceptance for the twin-pack alternatives might be greater: the retailer could be shown that because the boutique packs at regular prices (and margins) were still in his store, consumers could still elect to purchase a single-pack at normal prices and margins instead of the twin-pack with its commensurately lower margins per pair.

ESTIMATING SALES RESPONSE TO PROMOTION

Relying on his personal judgment, and his experience gained during the national rollouts, Mr. Ward estimated some of the sales response effects of the 20¢ single-pack and the 40¢ twin-pack promotions. For the 20¢ single-pack, he reasoned that during the four weeks the promotional packs were actually in the stores, about 80% of what would be L'eggs purchases at normal prices would be made instead at the reduced price. The other 20% would represent stores that did not accept the promotion, lost flags, and similar factors. Since normal L'eggs volume was running at 150,000 dozens per week, or 600,000 dozens per four weeks, Mr. Ward estimated that normal purchases at reduced prices would thus total 80% of 600,000, or 480,000 dozen.

The hardest factor to estimate was, of course, the effect of the promotion itself on incremental business. Mr. Ward made the working assumption that the single-pack promotion would generate a 10% to 11% net cumulative sales increase over an immediate period of 20 weeks during and following the promotion, plus a 10% long-term (sustained) sales increase.

For the 40¢ twin-pack alternative, Mr. Ward judged that during the four weeks the packs were actually in the stores, about 60% of what would be L'eggs purchases at normal prices would be made instead at the reduced price. This estimate was lower than the 20¢ single-pack figure because:

1. Single pairs at regular prices would be coexisting in the stores with promotional packs, and women—even L'eggs users—who did not want two pairs would still have the opportunity to purchase at regular prices.

2. Mr. Ward fully expected the twin-pack alternative to have less effect with nonloyal L'eggs users who might resist buying two pairs at a time, but might pick up one pair, even at regular price.

3. Some stores might not accept the promotion.

Finally, Mr. Ward assumed that the twin-pack alternative would generate a 10% net cumulative sales increase over the immediate 20-week period during and following the promotion, but would produce no long-term increase in sales. The 25¢ twin-pack was expected to show the same general sales response pattern as the 40¢ twin-pack, although the magnitude of the expected responses was likely to be considerably smaller. Historical coupon redemption rates had never exceeded 8% and often were much lower.

A MIXED PROMOTION STRATEGIC ALTERNATIVE

Mr. Ward did have the option, of course, to select a combination of two (or more) of the alternatives for implementation during the fall promotion, rather than just one. One alternative would be chosen which best met the objectives of high BDI markets, while a second alternative would be used for low BDI markets. He wanted to resist that option, because L'eggs planned to support the promotion with a heavy schedule of TV and local newspaper advertising. If separate alternatives were used in selected market areas, all national media would have to be switched to local spot media at considerable additional cost. This advertising support was not included in analyzing costs of the promotion because the advertising would substitute for, not supplement, L'eggs' normal advertising over the weeks of the promotion.

In addition, the mechanics of implementing two or more promotions would cause headaches for L'eggs production and warehouse personnel in producing and shipping several different types of point-of-sale materials, special packages, and shipper displays of merchandise. Life would also be more difficult for L'eggs sales account managers trying to explain (and sell) the mechanics of the promotion to national accounts (chain store operators). Mr. Ward's example was, "How do you convince Safeway's national buyer to take the promotion when you also have to tell him why Los Angeles stores must take single-packs and Little Rock stores must take twin-packs?"

EXHIBIT 1

L'eggs Products, Inc.

The classic L'EGGS Boutique.

—A traffic-stopping showpiece.
—Easy to shop.
—Displays 288 of the most attractive packages ever seen in the hosiery industry.
—Stands on a 2-foot circle of floor space.

EXHIBIT 3

Women's Hosiery Unit Sales
1971–1973 Estimated, 1974 Forecast
Units: Millions of Dozens of Pairs

	All Hosiery				Pantyhose			
	Total Volume	% Change	In Food & Drug	% Change	Total Volume	% Change	In Food & Drug	% Change
1971	123		28		82		20.8	
1972	121	−2%	29.5	+5%	92	+12%	24.4	+17%
1973	114	−6	29.9	+2	85	−8	25.6	+5
1974	110	−4	30.5	+2	79	−7	25.0	−2

Source: Company estimates.

EXHIBIT 2

Organization Chart

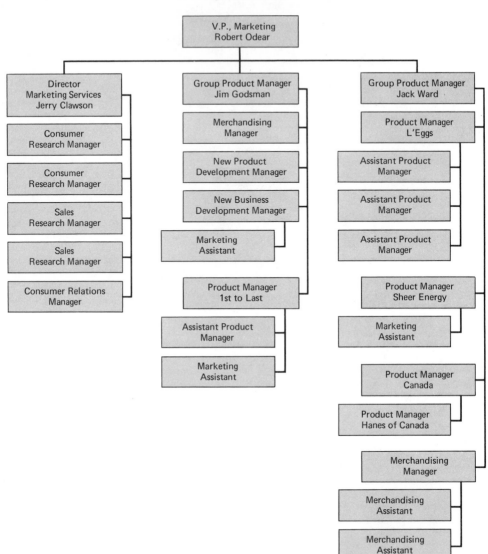

EXHIBIT 4

Company Financial Data
(All Figures in Millions)

	Hanes	Kayser Roth	Burlington
1972 Total Sales	$245	$579	$1,816
1972 Women's Hosiery Sales (est.)	142	80–100	101
1972 Total Net Income	8.2	11.9	49.6
1971 Total Sales	$176	$467	$1,727
1971 Women's Hosiery Sales (est.)	88	70–95	115
1971 Total Net Income	3.5	12.3	40

Source: Annual Reports; Corporate 10–K forms filed with the Securities and Exchange Commission.

EXHIBIT 5

1972 Performance in Markets Opened during 1971 and Earlier

Markets	BDI	Share of Sales	Markets	BDI	Share of Sales
Portland	80	1%	Binghamton	110	1%
Sacramento	60	1	Springfield	140	1
Milwaukee	90	2	Hartford/New Haven	90	2
Kansas City	70	1	Erie	160	*
Chicago	110	6	Buffalo	100	2
Los Angeles	120	7	Rochester	110	1
Eugene	80	*	Syracuse	150	2
Medford	60	*	Utica	50	*
Klamath Falls	80	*	Columbia/Jefferson City	90	*
St. Joseph	80	*	Macon	60	*
Topeka	60	*	Chattanooga	70	1
Madison	40	*	Grand Junction	170	*
Rockford	70	*	South Bend/Elkhart	100	1
Santa Barbara	70	*	Cincinnati	120	2
Philadelphia	130	9	Dayton	100	2
Reno	80	*	Indianapolis	110	2
Chico/Redding	90	*	Harrisburg/York	120	2
San Francisco	90	6	Green Bay	60	1
Salinas/Monterey	120	1	Terre Haute	60	*
San Diego	90	1	Eureka	130	*
Detroit	140	6	Las Vegas	130	*
Flint/Saginaw	150	2	Grand Rapids/Kalamazoo	150	2
Lansing	180	1	Fort Wayne	100	1
Boston	130	8	Boise	100	*
Providence	100	2	Twin Falls	110	*
Cleveland	110	5	Idaho Falls/Pocatello	130	*
Youngstown	90	1	Fresno	80	1
Atlanta	90	2	Phoenix	100	1
Denver	150	2	Tucson	60	*
Colorado Springs	100	1	Salt Lake City	80	1
Cheyenne	200	*	Miami	50	1
Toledo	90	1	Tampa	80	1
Columbus	150	2	West Palm Beach	60	*
Lima	110	*	Fort Myers	60	*
Zanesville	120	*	Pittsburgh	100	2
					100%

* Less than 0.5%.

EXHIBIT 6

Penetration Measures in High and Low BDI Areas

Market:	Kansas City (Low BDI)			Philadelphia (High BDI)		
Time after Introduction:	13 Weeks	6 Months	12 Months	13 Weeks	6 Months	12 Months
	%	%	%	%	%	%
Brand Awareness	90	90	90	100	100	100
Advertising Awareness	60	60	60	80	70	70
Trial	20	20	30	30	40	50
Repurchase Rate*	60	70	70	60	70	80
Product Satisfaction	70	70	70	90	90	90
L'eggs Is Usual Pantyhose Brand	10	10	10	10	20	20

* Defined as % triers who bought more than once in last three months.
Source: Company data.

EXHIBIT 7

L'eggs Products, Inc.

L'eggs Products, Inc. (B)

Near the end of 1972, L'eggs Products, Inc., a subsidiary of the Hanes Corporation, had achieved distribution for its line of L'eggs branded hosiery products in over 75% of the United States. In looking forward to achieving fully national distribution late in 1973, Mr. Jack Ward, Group Product Manager for L'eggs, had begun to plan for the product's first national promotion campaign which was scheduled for the Fall 1973 selling season. Four alternative promotions involving different combinations of cents-off price discounting and special packaging were being considered. Because the national promotion would have to meet criteria of acceptability imposed by differing levels of market development, differing levels of L'eggs market penetration, and increasing levels of competitive activity, the choice among the four possibilities was not an easy one. Furthermore, the promotion finally selected would have to be implemented in a way that encouraged the support of drug and grocery chains. Finally, the promotion would have to encourage the desired balance of trial and repurchase behaviors among consumers.

The alternatives were a 25¢ coupon which would be mailed to prospective user households and redeemed for a discount at the time of purchase of one pair of pantyhose, a 25¢ price-off twin pack, a 40¢ off twin pack and a 20¢ off single pack. The latter three promotions would be implemented in point-of-purchase displays placed in high foot traffic locations in drug stores and supermarkets. Although Mr. Ward had con-

This case was prepared by Harvey N. Singer, Instructor, The American University, under the direction of Assistant Professor F. Stewart DeBruicker, The Wharton School, as a basis for class discussion rather than to illustrate either effective or ineffective handling of an administrative situation.

See L'eggs Products, Inc. (A) for additional discussions of company and industry background.

siderable experience gained by managing the promotions of L'eggs products as they were rolled out into individual new market territories, he had very few objective bases for judging between the alternatives for the planned national promotion.

In choosing these alternatives to be tested, the product group had reasoned as follows about their likely effects: the 40¢ twin-pack probably would achieve the objective of loading the consumer in high L'eggs penetration areas best (for her next pair, the consumer would *have* the second pair of L'eggs in the twin-pack already and would have no need to go out and purchase, perhaps, a competitive brand). Hopefully, more product use and experience with the two pairs rather than one would predispose the consumer more to purchase L'eggs again the next time she did need hosiery. However, Mr. Ward thought the twin-pack might not be effective in low L'eggs penetration areas because with low trial and low market share in these areas, sufficient numbers of consumers may not purchase the twin-pack often enough to make the promotion effective. Besides, the objective here was to increase trial and the twin-pack might inhibit trial—the consumer, not a L'eggs user anyway, might balk at having to purchase two pairs in order to try L'eggs.

The 25¢-off twin-pack would presumably produce the same behavior against those objectives, and would improve unit contributions considerably. The question in Ward's mind was whether the offer would be effective enough—whether 25¢ off on 2 pairs would induce sufficient incremental purchases to produce any results at all.

The mailed coupon worth 25¢ off on one pair was included as an alternative to be tested for comparative effectiveness, even though the brand group really wanted the fall promotion vehicle to be an in-store offer. The 25¢ mailed coupon had been reasonably effective when used in many rollout markets during introduction, and should aid in inducing trial among nonusers because it was to be mailed to all

homes (thus coming to the attention of women who were nonusers, whereas these women may not have noted an in-store offer because they would not look for, or at, a L'eggs display). The coupon was not expected to be effective in inducing consumer loading or repurchase, however, because it could only be used to purchase one pair.

The 20¢ single-pack seemed to be somewhat effective against both objectives. In low penetration areas, consumer takeaway for the promotion (the number of consumers purchasing) would presumably be higher because the new trier would not be forced to purchase two pairs. So the single-pack was assumed more effective in raising trial rates. In high penetration areas, there was certainly nothing to prevent the consumer from buying two or more single-packs, so the objective of consumer loading and thus raising repeat rates might just be satisfied. On the other hand, there was nothing to encourage the consumer (or force the consumer, as was the case of the twin-pack) to purchase more than one pair—and so the single-pack was judged somewhat less effective against consumer loading and increasing the total *number of pairs* purchased under the promotion. In addition, the single-pack was significantly more expensive to implement.

With considerable uncertainty, then, about the effectiveness of each of the alternatives against each of the objectives in each type of market, Mr. Ward turned to the L'eggs marketing research group to test the alternatives. Hopefully, these tests would provide information useful in resolving the problem.

MARKET RESEARCH AT L'EGGS

Just as L'eggs Products, Inc., differed considerably from the rest of the hosiery industry in its marketing and distribution strategies, it also took a radically different approach to marketing research. The original research policy adopted in 1970 has been continued and strengthened by Paul Fulton, L'eggs' President, and Bob Odear, L'eggs' Marketing Vice

President. This policy, in effect, said: any marketing decision, whether major or minor, must have justification based on marketing research data. Evidence that that policy was in effect could be taken from the marketing research budgets. From the original $400,000 that was spent through 1970 on consumer and channel research, funding had grown to include over $1 million for the development of L'eggs on-line computer system for marketing information and sales tracking. In addition, over 1% of sales was spent for ongoing product and market research activity each year—an amount expected to exceed $1 million in 1973. This was considered very high for a company of L'eggs' size and was even more dramatic in comparison to the traditional hosiery industry approach to research which was described by Ward as ". . . just have salesmen find out what the trade buyer wants."

The director of marketing research at L'eggs, Jerry Clawson, had a staff of two consumer research managers and two sales research managers working under him. Exhibit 1 describes the organization of the marketing and marketing research groups at L'eggs in the summer of 1973. The sales research group did all the analysis of the data supplied by the on-line sales tracking system.

The sales research managers' specific duties included:

1. Routine sales tracking using the internal marketing information system.
2. Competitive sales tracking using syndicated Nielsen and MRCA data.
3. Forecasting using Nielsen, MRCA, and L'eggs' own data.
4. Tracking the sales effects of special advertising and promotional tests.

For consumer behavior research, the usual practice was to have the L'eggs market research personnel do all planning and research design themselves, make use of the advertising agency or independent outside suppliers to execute the research and make a preliminary

analysis, then the consumer research analysts did their own data analysis and prepared conclusions for brand management.

The consumer researchers' specific duties included:

1. Product tests—the company ran roughly 10 major performance tests for each year on existing and new products.
2. Advertising research—concept tests, "ad labs," testing consumers for quantitative and qualitative impact of recognition and recall of advertising.
3. Consumer surveys—to measure cannibalization, proportions of sales purchased "on deal" versus regular price in a market.
4. "ATU" studies—the group ran frequent studies titled "Attitude, Trial, and Usage" in L'eggs markets to develop measures of brand awareness, product satisfaction, trial and repeat rates.

The market research group had access to many techniques and data sources for information to support marketing decisions: product tests, concept tests, focus group interviews, Nielsen store audits, consumer surveys, trade research, and sales tracking data from L'eggs' own on-line marketing information system. But despite the large budget allocation and many sources of information, the market research function at L'eggs had to cope with some severe problems in carrying out meaningful research. Primary among these was the short and complicated history of hosiery products in food and drug channels. Research projects were frequently disrupted by such events as the introduction of new product extensions, new advertising and promotion activities, and competitors' product introductions and promotions. Competitive events in markets could of course not be controlled.

THE MARKET TESTS

Using procedures developed as the research group had gained experience with the L'eggs product information system, Mr. Clawson developed a strategy for testing the four promotion alternatives. Each of the promotions would be implemented in a carefully chosen test market, and the results of each test market would be compared with similar data observed in an equally carefully selected control market. Sales data would be obtained from the on-line product information system, and consumer attitude and behavior data would be obtained via special consumer surveys to be conducted in each of the test markets.

Specially made up promotion packs in shipper displays were put into stores in the test markets as follows:

Denver—20¢ single-pack (in Denver, flags were also put into regular boutique packs)[1]

Syracuse—40¢ twin-pack

Columbus—25¢ twin-pack

In the fourth test market, Cincinnati, coupons worth 25¢ off one pack were mailed to 50% of the households. The control market, which received no cents-off promotion and only normal L'eggs advertising, was Boise/Twin Falls/Pocatello (hereafter referred to as Boise). The testing period was set at four weeks, the same time period to be used for the impending Fall promotion. In addition to the special packages and retail prices, each promotion was supported by point-of-sale and local newspaper advertising to simulate the national support program. No special attention was given to adjusting the use of spot television advertising and, of course, it was impossible to simulate the effects of network television advertising.

---

[1] Wherever the 20¢ single-pack promotion was implemented, field labor was required to change all existing L'eggs packs in the store to 20¢ off also to comply with Fair Trade laws. This was to be done by inserting flags specifying 20¢ off into all existing promotional packs. For the other alternatives, the price-off promotional twin-packs could coexist in the stores with regular-priced single-packs without violating Fair Trade (because different quantity packages were involved). Thus, no field labor or flags were necessary for the twin-pack alternatives or for the 25¢ mailed coupon.

In earlier market tests, the technique most often used to evaluate sales performance in test markets was an experimental design which separated markets into test markets (which received the "treatments" consisting of different strategies or alternatives) and control markets which were given no such treatment. Control markets were chosen to approximate closely the behavior of test markets before the treatments were given. Test market sales were compared with control market sales before, during, and after the testing period. This technique had been used with satisfactory results, but Jerry Clawson commented that good control markets were becoming harder to identify, and that he was actively searching for better research methods.

In general, Clawson preferred control markets that had high measures of statistical correlation in pretest sales trends with the test markets; that roughly matched the test markets on the length of time L'eggs had been in distribution; that had minimal exogenous activities due to competitors' and L'eggs other marketing developments; and that were roughly equivalent in seasonality effects of sales. For this test, the Boise ADI was the only candidate that met Mr. Clawson's criteria.

At weekly intervals, sales results in each test market were to be obtained from the on-line information system. For each test market, the research group would measure both absolute sales results, and the variance or change in sales results over time from a "norm." This norm was defined as the expected sales in the test market if the test market had behaved in relation to the control market as it had before the alternatives were introduced. For example, if Denver sales were uniformly 1.45 times Boise sales before the test, then the Denver norm over the test period would be 1.45 times actual Boise results. Of course, the product group hoped for sustained sales increases over the expected norm in the winning test market, or at least a sales increase sufficient to cover increased costs of the promotion.

Concurrent with sales tracking in each of

the test markets, surveys were to be undertaken in each test market to determine consumer reactions and response to the promotional alternatives. The surveys would be used to break the sales figures down into estimates of new trials versus repurchases, which sales figures alone would not reveal. Given these two kinds of data, the brand group could then project test market results onto the national population and determine which promotion strategy best met the objectives of a national promotion program. Jerry Clawson sent a proposal to Jack Ward and to Bob Odear, L'eggs Marketing Vice President, which described the consumer survey project that the Market research department proposed to undertake. That proposal is included as Exhibit 2.

As in previous promotional tests, the market research group expected a pattern in each test market as follows: First, a period of sales increase, designated the "bump" period, was expected in the weeks immediately following introduction of the promotion. This would represent consumers purchasing their normal amount of purchases plus increased purchasing due to the promotion. Then, there would be several weeks of decreased purchases relative to the norm, designated the "loading" period, which would come about because regular pur-

chasers had presumably "loaded up" on promotional packs during the bump period and would have no need to make their regular purchases. After the bump and loading periods, a period of sustained increase was hoped for which would be due to regular purchasers, new triers, and new repeaters making regular purchases after the promotion ended.

Mr. Clawson's proposal was accepted and the test market program was implemented during the spring of 1973.

MARKET TEST RESULTS— SALES ANALYSIS[2]

The actual sales results from the market tests led the Sales Research group to conclude that each of the four promotions was somewhat effective in generating a short-term sales increase, but that none of the alternatives were likely to result in significant long-term sales increases. They arrived at these conclusions by

---

[2] Reported sales volume does not equal consumer (retail) sales exactly, but is rather a total of retail sales plus new inventory shipped into stores—this method of reporting was common at L'eggs and usually served as a reliable surrogate measure of consumer sales. Sales units are in dozens of pairs.

Syracuse: Two for 40¢ Price Off

	(Units-Dozens)	Cumulative
1. Increase (Bump) Period: Weeks 1–4		
Expected Sales	10,000	10,000
Actual Sales	19,000	19,000
Increase	9,000	9,000
% of Increase	90%	90%
2. Loading Period: Weeks 5–6	(Units-Dozens)	Cumulative
Expected Sales	5,000	15,000
Actual Sales	4,000	23,000
Increase (Decrease)	(1,000)	8,000
% of Increase (Decrease)	(20%)	53%
3. Post-Promotion Period: Weeks 7–16	(Units-Dozens)	Cumulative
Expected Sales	23,000	38,000
Actual Sales	21,850	44,850
Increase (Decrease)	(1,150)	6,850
% of Increase (Decrease)	(5%)	18%

comparing sales results during and after the test in each test market with the expected norms for each market, derived from Boise control market sales. Results of the Syracuse test are presented on p. 132. Comparisons for each market were made in the same manner.

In analyzing the unit sales for the 4 promotions, the sales research group noted that the sales increases or decreases might not be directly comparable between markets because of differing time periods for the bump and loading effects in each market. With this warning, they presented the following table summarizing the effects of the four alternatives:

The 25¢ coupon promotion (Cincinnati) was the least effective promotion with a 3% short-term increase in sales felt over 8 weeks. From the eighth week forward, sales have fluctuated (which may be partially due to a wide swing in number of sales calls by the L'eggs sales personnel). The net effect has been an overall 6% cumulative decrease in sales over 16 weeks.''

MARKET TEST RESULTS— CONSUMER SURVEY RESEARCH

The consumer survey research was supervised by the Market Research Department at the L'eggs advertising agency, Dancer-

	2 for 40¢ Off	20¢ Price Off	2 for 25¢ Off	25¢ Coupon
Market	Syracuse	Denver	Columbus	Cincinnati
Initial Bump— Increased Sales	90%	30%	82%	3%
Loading Period— Decreased Sales	−20%	−10%	−33%	−15%
Total Cumulative Short-Term Sales Effect	53%	20%	−12%	−6%
Cumulative Long-Term Sales Effect	18% dropping	7% dropping	−12%	−6%
Number of Weeks of Promotional Effect:				
Bump	4	6	3	8
Loading	2	2	13	8
Long-term	10	8	0	0
Total	16	16	16	16

Based on these findings, the sales research group concluded:

"The 2 for 40¢-off promotion (Syracuse) was the most effective, with a net short-term cumulative increase in sales of 53% felt over 6 weeks. The 20¢ price-off promotion (Denver) was the second most effective, with a net cumulative short-term increase of 20% felt over 8 weeks.

The 2 for 25¢ price-off promotion (Columbus) had as high an initial increase in sales as the 2 for 40¢ price-off, but the market has not recovered from the loading period for 13 weeks afterward. Ten weeks after the start of the promotion, sales had returned to within the expected range of the norm. However, for the 6 weeks following that, the L'eggs sales group has reduced their sales calls to Columbus stores and therefore the possibility of ascertaining the exact loading period, all other things being equal, has been obscured.

Fitzgerald-Sample (DFS) and carried out by Burke Marketing Research, Inc., an independent research company. After receiving the data from Burke, DFS personnel examined it and sent their report to the L'eggs consumer research group. Following that, L'eggs consumer research personnel examined the data and presented Mr. Ward with a report of their findings. Excerpts from the DFS report are included in Exhibit 3.

The L'eggs market research group interpreted the findings from the survey data. They reported:

The 25¢ coupon and 40¢ twin-pack created more awareness (respondents who remembered the promotion) among competitive brand users than did either of the other alternatives. Promotional awareness among L'eggs' usual branders was highest for the coupon and lowest for the 25¢ twin-pack. The 25¢ coupon was most successful in obtaining involvement—i.e., purchase of L'eggs on promotion—among competitive branders. The price-offs did not show great differences, but the 25¢ twin-pack was the weakest. The 20¢ single-pack involved the greatest percentage of L'eggs usual branders. These data are summarized in Exhibit 4.

The promotions having the greatest retail value produced the greatest immediate sales effect. Very high percentages of those sales, however, were to customers who already considered L'eggs their usual brand. The coupon was the only one of the 4 promotions which sold more goods in total to competitive usual branders than to L'eggs usual branders—and it sold about as many total pairs, per thousand women exposed, as did the 25¢ twin-pack.

The following table illustrates this:

It is recommended that the 25¢ coupon be considered the most viable of the promotions tested for use in an *offensive* strategy designed to obtain involvement of competitive usual branders while holding to a minimum the promotional sale of L'eggs to women who already consider it their usual brand. The 20¢ single-pack and 40¢ twin-pack are recommended as defensive promotions when the strategy is to load L'eggs customers with product and have them less responsive to competitive promotions. It is recommended that the 25¢ twin-pack be dropped from further consideration at this time.

Mr. Ward requested the market research group to estimate how many of the pairs sold on promotion in each instance would not have been sold if there had been no promotions.

Pairs of L'eggs Sold on Promotion, per Thousand Wearers Exposed to Promotion	40¢ Twin		20¢ Single		25¢ Twin		25¢ Coupon	
	#	%	#	%	#	%	#	%
All Respondents	338	100	382	100	201	100	199	100
L'eggs Usual Branders	238	70	322	84	151	75	63	32
Competitive Usual Branders	100	30	60	16	50	25	136	68

The 25¢ coupon was most successful in generating first-time trial among competitive usual branders. There was little difference among the price-offs on that measure, with the 20¢ single-pack having whatever edge did exist, as shown below:

Clawson's group attempted to determine this from the survey data. They reported:

None of these attempts produced results which seemed judgmentally reasonable. The basic difficulty

Promotion Purchase Was the First Time L'eggs Ever Purchased	40¢ Twin	20¢ Single	25¢ Twin	25¢ Coupon
% of Competitive Usual Branders	1%	2%	1%	6%

The 25¢ coupon was the most successful of the 4 promotions tested in involving numbers of competitive branders, inducing purchase by them, and obtaining first time trial. It minimized the number of pairs sold on promotion to women who already considered L'eggs their usual brand. The price-off promotions generally produced more activity among L'eggs usual branders than among users of competitive brands. The 20¢ single-pack was most popular with L'eggs women. While the 40¢ twin-pack was also heavily weighted toward L'eggs users, it sold proportionally more units to competitive users than did the 20¢-off one promotion. The 25¢ twin-pack was the weakest promotion tested.

is in obtaining a sound measure of the long-term effects of loading. For example, it is quite easy to see that many L'eggs usual branders loaded up on L'eggs when they saw the price-off promotions, and thereby purchased considerably more pairs than they otherwise would have during that period. But the question of how that affects the total number of pairs they buy over a longer period of time remains unanswerable from this particular research. Sales tracking of these promotion markets is being done, and hopefully will provide insight into this question.

The market research group had included questions in the survey designed to enable them to gauge switching from competitive brands to L'eggs in the consumer interviews, but found that "in these surveys, participation in the promotions by competitive usual branders was too low to provide usable basis for switching analyses."

CONFLICTING RESULTS

Given the results from the sales analysis and the consumer research in the test markets, Mr. Ward was still not sure of the implications of the marketing research for his decision. First, the results obtained seemed to disprove some of the pre-research reasoning (i.e., that the 20¢ single-pack would be more effective in inducing trial or purchase among competitive users, that the 40¢ twin-pack would be a more effective consumer loading vehicle among L'eggs usual branders, that the 25¢ coupon would not have as high an impact on either objective as the in-store alternatives, and that the winning alternative, at least, would generate significant long-term volume after the promotion).

In addition, some of the results of the consumer research were in direct conflict with the results of the sales tracking analysis. The most glaring example of this conflict was the 25¢ coupon's apparent effectiveness in the consumer survey versus its poor performance in the sales analysis.

Mr. Ward tried to sort out the effects of the research findings upon his analysis of each alternative. The 25¢ twin-pack might be dropped from consideration because of its poor showing on both tests (subject to perhaps a quick re-examination to see if the apparent poor showing was more than compensated for by its minimum margin loss, thereby looking more attractive on a cost-effectiveness basis).

The 25¢ coupon's poor showing in actual sales results might be partially due to the differences in test versus control markets. In the consumer research it received top awareness scores, top impact on number of competitive branders it influenced, fair results in terms of

the number of pairs purchased, and the best effect on inducing new trial.

The real conflict came in evaluating the 40¢ twin-pack and 20¢ single-pack alternatives. Both seemed to be reasonably strong promotions in generating incremental sales through trial by nonusers and loading among users. The 20¢ single-pack involved more total people in the promotion. The sales analysis showed that it did seem to increase the permanent franchise slightly. Many users did indeed buy two or more promotion packs, so that alternative accomplished the loading objectives, in part. However the results showed that the 20¢ single-pack seemed to be even more effective against L'eggs users than the 40¢ twin-pack. Given that it would be the most expensive promotion to implement and in terms of reducing margins by 20¢ on every purchase, not only incremental purchases, he wondered whether to recommend its implementation.

The 40¢ twin-pack alternative also appeared to be a reasonably strong promotion. It involved L'eggs users heavily and sold more pairs to each L'eggs user who did purchase under promotion, thus accomplishing the loading objective. By substituting the second incremental pair in the pack for a possible other brand purchase, it would help to ensure users being repeaters. The sales tracking analysis confirmed that the twin-pack was most effective in terms of total actual sales gains. The alternative, however, was not quite as effective as the single-pack in generating purchase among numbers of competitive users (although it loaded them more when they did purchase) and in generating new trial.

MORE TESTS

Due to new style introductions, the promotion was not needed immediately. Therefore, Mr. Ward made the decision to do some further testing. He was especially concerned about learning the effects of the 40¢ twin-pack and the 20¢ single-pack more clearly, since they were the two in-store promotions which had given the best indication of producing sustained sales increases. However, since the two differed considerably in costs and problems to implement, he wished to determine more clearly which one gave better results and he wanted to ensure that the better alternative did in fact build long-run volume.

As a means of determining this information, he called on the market research group to retest these two alternatives in several additional markets and to perform sales tracking analyses on the results. The methodology was to be the same as in the original market tests (each promotion to run for 4 weeks with ad and point-of-sales support), except that only the 40¢ twin-pack and the 20¢ single-pack alternatives were tested. Each of these was to be tested in high and low penetration markets. Sales results were to be measured but no consumer awareness surveys were planned for the retest.

The 40¢ twin-pack promotion was tested in Salt Lake City, Santa Barbara, Las Vegas, and Salinas, California, and the results were analyzed each week for 20 weeks after the start of the promotion. The respective control markets were Fresno, Green Bay, and Colorado Springs. The pre-test sales correlation between each pair of promotion and control markets was .98.

The 20¢ single-pack promotion was tested in Houston (low penetration) and Albany (high penetration). Again, sales tracking analysis was done each week for 20 weeks. The Dallas market was matched as a control market against Houston, and Davenport was matched as a control market against Albany.

RETEST RESULTS—40¢ TWIN-PACK

Figures for all four test markets in which the twin-pack was placed were reported in aggregate, rather than individually. The market research group summarized their findings:

During the first 5 weeks of the promotion, L'eggs sales increased 105% in these markets. During the next 5 weeks, it appears that only 10% of the sales gained in the first 5 weeks were lost because of consumer loading. During the most recent 10 weeks,

L'eggs sales have increased relative to the control markets by 20%. This indicates that the promotion had a long-term positive effect on L'eggs sales in these markets.

It appears that the promotion generated long-term incremental volume in these markets and increased the size of the L'eggs franchise. Long-term incremental cumulative volume has increased by 30% and is holding at that level.

Although test results were not broken out by individual markets, the market research group informed Mr. Ward that the 40¢-off twin-pack had apparently performed better in high penetration areas (Salinas and Las Vegas) than in low penetration areas (Santa Barbara and Salt Lake).

RETEST RESULTS—20¢ SINGLE-PACK

The market research group analyzed this re-test by looking at sales results separately for each of the two markets which received the 20¢ single-pack in the re-test. They reported to Mr. Ward:

In Houston, the promotion appears to have generated a sizeable amount of long-term volume. After 23 weeks, L'eggs sales increased 11% relative to the control market—an incremental volume of 5,000 dozen. The 23 weeks following the start of the promotion are grouped into 3 periods:

1. First 6 weeks—During and immediately following the actual promotion, L'eggs sales increased 38% relative to the control market (increase of 4,200 dozen).

2. Next 8 weeks—During this period, L'eggs sales declined 5% (800 dozen) relative to the control market, indicating that 20% (800 divided by 4,200) of L'eggs incremental sales in the promotion period was lost because of the negative effect of consumer loading during the next 8 weeks.

3. Final 9 weeks—During this period, L'eggs sales increased 9% (1,600 dozen) relative to the control market. This suggests that the promotion has increased the size of the L'eggs franchise in Houston, although 9 weeks may not be long enough to tell exactly how much it has been increased.

In this market test, no intervening factors on the scale of the sales call pattern switching in the original tests occurred. Within limits, the test proceeded as smoothly as could be expected in a generally volatile marketing environment.

For the Albany test, the following results were reported.

For the 16-week period following the start of the 20¢-off promotion in Albany, L'eggs sales increased 4% relative to the control market. The 20¢ single-pack appears to have gained volume for L'eggs for a 10-week period (the large decline during this initial period appears to be function of the L'eggs Easter packages being placed earlier in the control market than in Albany). During this 10-week period, L'eggs volume still increased 14% (3,200 dozen) relative to the control market.

During the most recent 6 weeks, L'eggs sales in Albany declined 14% (1,700 dozen) relative to the control. At this time 53% (1,700 divided by 3200) of the volume gained in the first 10 weeks have been lost due to consumer loading.

We conclude that in Houston, for the 23-week period following the start of the promotion, the promotion appears to have increased L'eggs share of market among L'eggs users during the promotion period and/or attracted new or infrequent L'eggs buyers. The promotion did not seem *only* to load up L'eggs customers with our goods and thus remove them from the market for awhile.

In Albany, for the 16-week period following the start of the promotion, the 20¢ single-pack also appears to have achieved at least the objective of loading up L'eggs customers with our goods. It is too early to tell if the promotion will generate any incremental long-run volume in this market. If the Houston and Albany tests can be validly compared, it appears that the 20¢-off single-pack alternative performed better in a low penetration area (Houston) than in the high penetration area (Albany).

PAYOUT ANALYSIS
ON A NATIONAL BASIS

Despite the fact that these additional tests of the 20¢ single-pack and 40¢ twin-pack alternatives still did not resolve all the issues surrounding the research, Mr. Ward knew that he must soon come to a final decision. Since the fall season was rapidly approaching and there was much work needed to implement the chosen alternative, he felt that there was no time to perform any more market tests and that the decision would have to be based on analysis of the information he had at that point. As part of that analysis, Ward decided to structure payout projections for the single-pack and twin-pack promotions on a national basis, based on the costs of the alternatives and their assumed effectiveness shown in the market tests previously performed.

Some of the factors were known with relative certainty. Costs of packaging, sales materials, flags, and additional freight for shippers averaged out to 35¢ per dozen for the 20¢ single pack and 38¢ per dozen for the 40¢ twin pack. The 20¢ single pack would require a temporary labor force to put flags on the existing L'eggs boutiques, and the cost of that would be approximately $270 thousand. No temporary labor force would be required for the 40¢ twin pack alternative.

Another factor which Ward could estimate, though with less precision, was the percentage of routine L'eggs purchases at normal prices that would be diverted to promotional priced merchandise with a resulting loss in gross margin. From the market tests, he believed that 80% and 60%, respectively, of the 20¢ single and 40¢ twin-pack promotions would represent diverted sales.[3] Since normal sales were running at the rate of about 3 million dozens of pairs over a 20-week period (the short-run payout analysis to be performed was done on the basis of a 20-week period, consistent with the market tests, even though the promotional packs would only be in the stores for 4 weeks), the losses in margin due to diversion could be estimated using these assumptions in the payout calculation.

---

[3] 80% for the 20¢ single-pack because of some stores not taking the promotion, lost flags, etc.; 60% for the 40¢ twin-pack because single pairs at regular prices would coexist in stores with twin-pack promotions, and women who did not want 2 pairs might still buy a regular pack at normal prices.

The hardest factor to estimate was, of course, the effect of the promotion alternatives on incremental business. Based on his first interpretations of the test market results, Ward guessed that incremental sales of about 10% or more could be achieved through either promotion, at least for the 20-week period beginning with the start of the promotion.

Finally, there was the question of to what extent, if any, either promotion would foster incremental sales growth beyond the 20-week period used in the national payout projections. Ward estimated a step increase of 10% under the 20¢ single-pack promotion, but using the Syracuse results from the earlier test market, he assumed no long-term sales increase for the 40¢ twin-pack. He wondered whether other assumptions were better supported by the test market findings.

The above assumptions resulted in the national payout projections listed in Exhibit 5. Over the 20-week period used in the near term analysis, the 40¢ twin-pack appeared to be superior with a net payout of $216 thousand versus a net loss of $198 thousand for the 20¢ single-pack. The 20¢ single-pack, however, was expected to show a much better long-run payout. There were differences in implementation issues between the two promotions, but those seemed secondary to the question of which promotion met the objectives of the proposed national promotion, and which was likely to show the best return for the funds to be employed.

IMPLEMENTATION OF THE PROMOTIONS

In addition to the possible payouts for each alternative, Mr. Ward's decision would also be influenced by the non-quantifiable factors involved for each alternative. For example, there were the problems of trade resistance to promotions in general, and specific trade resistance to devoting additional floor space necessary for the promotional shippers. Mr. Ward wanted to choose the alternative which maximized the potential effect of sales and profit gains while minimizing trade resistance, in order that the alternative would actually be implemented in as many stores as possible.

A related question was whether L'eggs should advertise the promotion via national and local media. Given some trade resistance, advertising the deal would almost force all retailers to take the promotion, and would ensure more promotional awareness, thus increasing the chances of overall success. On the other hand, arguments could be made for using this advertising time and cost for other purposes and messages, and for improving trade relations by giving retailers more flexibility to refuse the promotion. Again, the key seemed to be in choosing an alternative which would be palatable to the trade.

Mr. Ward reviewed the earlier implementation arguments. The 20¢ single-pack alternative could conceivably be accomplished solely via flagged boutique packs without the need for shippers and extra store floor space. However, because of the Fair Trade laws, virtually every pair sold during the promotion would be at reduced price (and reduced margin for the retailer). Thus L'eggs must convince the retailer, perhaps via the use of test market results, that the promotion would lead to significant numbers of increased purchases—or else the retailer would see his total dollar markup eroding. Such persuasion was crucial here, because in low penetration markets where the 20¢ single-pack had shown the best results, L'eggs wanted *all* retailers to accept the promotion in order to get the increased trial effect and thus long-term sustained volume increases predicted by the test markets.

The 40¢ twin-pack alternative required shippers (and thus extra floor space) to implement. On the other hand, the retailer could not only be shown test market indications of higher volume, but also would be allowed to retain regular single boutique packs at regular prices (and margins) during the promotional period and thus could be shown that purchases made under the promotion were more likely to represent incremental volume rather than substitute volume. Again, the product group was anxious to get full cooperation for the twin-pack alternative. This was especially true in high penetration areas and stores with heavy L'eggs sales volume, since market testing had shown that the twin-pack was a successful loading vehicle in high penetration areas.

Finally, he had to consider implementation problems involved should a mixed strategy be chosen—with each alternative being implemented in specific markets, instead of using one national promotion vehicle across all markets. He thought he should give hard consideration to the mixed strategy because the market research studies did in fact seem to show that the 20¢ single-pack might lead to increased trial and some increased sustained volume in low penetration markets, while the 40¢ twin-pack led to loading of customers in high penetration markets and perhaps some increased sustained volume. Those were important factors when Mr. Ward considered the planned introductions of Activ and No Nonsense products into L'eggs markets that fall

with a potentially unfavorable effect upon the L'eggs franchise in those markets.

However, implementing two alternatives rather than one posed serious problems, some of which were referred to earlier. Local rather than national network media would have to be used to advertise the promotion, at additional cost. Two sets of point-of-sale materials, packages, and shipper displays complicated production and distribution logistics. The mechanics of persuading retailers (especially national chains) to accept two different promotions would be difficult for the L'eggs sales force to implement. Nevertheless, the option of two alternatives must be considered if choosing just one alternative did not seem to meet the promotional objectives in both types of markets— the long-run benefits of going with both might just be sufficient to offset the considerable difficulty and cost of doing so.

With all the information before him, Mr. Ward sat down to look once more at the results of the test markets and surveys. He would go through further analysis of the information presented by his market research department, and come to a decision.

EXHIBIT 1

Organization Chart

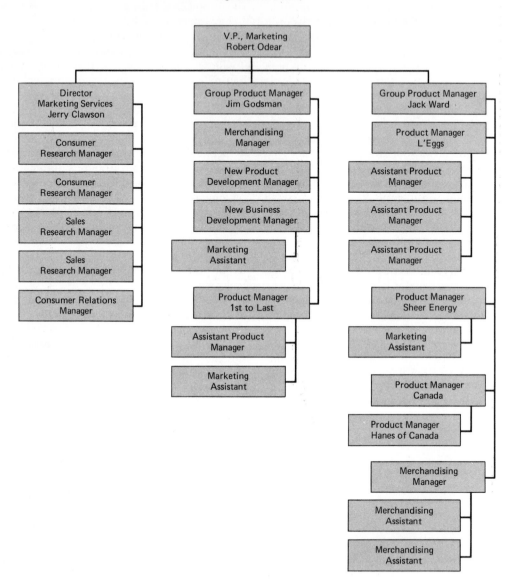

EXHIBIT 2

TITLE: L'eggs 25¢ Coupon and Price-Off Promotions Evaluation

PURPOSE: To determine the effectiveness of a 25¢ direct mail coupon and three "price-off" promotions in inducing trial of and conversion to L'eggs among competitive brand users.

BACKGROUND: These are several promotional techniques being tested for possible national use in the fall of '73. Alternatives to be market tested are a 20¢-off single unit price pack, Twin-Pack price pack (Buy 2—Save 40¢), Twin-pack price pack (Buy 2—Save 25¢), and a 25¢-off one pack coupon mailed to about 200,000 households. Each alternative will be placed in a different test market. Each test will involve the full pantyhose line. Point of purchase and newspaper advertising will support the promotion. The price packs will be on the boutiques for about four weeks, while the coupon mailings will be implemented in three mailing "flights" with approximately one week's time between each flight. Sales tracking will be done to monitor the effect on sales. This project is to help determine the types of consumer reactions which generate the sales.

EXPECTED USE OF RESULTS: Results will be used in helping to decide which, if any, of the promotions would be most promising for national program utilization.

METHODOLOGY: Five weeks after price packs are placed in stores, and five weeks after the second mailing flight of coupons, telephone interviewing will be done among pantyhose users. Data will be collected on usual pantyhose brand, awareness of the L'eggs coupon or price pack promotion, degree of participation in the promotion, any recent switching in usual pantyhose brand, and usual brand before switching.

NUMBER, LOCATION, AND DESCRIPTION OF RESPONDENTS:

	Pantyhose Users in General
Denver (20¢-Off Single Unit)	400
Syracuse (40¢-Off 2-Pack)	400
Columbus (25¢-Off 2-Pack)	400
Cincinnati (25¢ Mailed Coupon)	300

TIMING: Implementation—As soon as approval given to this proposal and promotional materials made up (Approx. 6 weeks)
Interviewing—Approx. 5 weeks after implementation
Report—Approx. 6 weeks after interviews

ESTIMATED COST: $10,000—3 price pack alternatives
                              6,000—Coupon alternative

Note: This cost includes interviewing and report preparation. It does not include cost of promotional materials or margin loss from the promotional deals.

Submitted by Jerry Clawson

EXHIBIT 3

**Consumer Survey Research Findings from the Spring 1973
Test Markets—Excerpts from the DFS Report**

I. Coupon Awareness and Purchase—Cincinnati*

44% of respondents report awareness (remember receiving the coupon).

16% of respondents purchased under the promotion (redeemed coupon).

25% of coupon redeemers were new L'eggs customers.

	Aware (Remembered Receiving Coupon)	Purchase (Redeemed Coupon)	Coupon Purchase Was First L'eggs Purchase
All Respondents:*			
(Sample Size = 300)	44%	16%	4%
Respondents Who Were			
L'eggs Usual Branders	68%	34%	—
Respondents Not L'eggs			
Usual Branders	40%	13%	6%

The large majority of those who redeemed the coupon (82%) purchased a single pair.

* Figures for "All Respondents" in both reports should be interpreted as: "figures for all respondents who were non-support pantyhose wearers."

In reporting results of the 25¢ coupon, all actual figures obtained were doubled to obtain the figures used in the reports. This was because only about half of the households in Cincinnati actually were sent the coupon. Therefore, when figures were obtained from the 300 interviews, they were treated as if those same figures were obtained from a base population of 150. For example, among all 300 consumers interviewed, 22% or 66 reported awareness of the promotion. Since only half the households in Cincinnati received the coupon, the base was cut to an estimated 150 and the percentage was therefore reported as 66/150 or 44%.

II. Price-Off Deals Awareness and Purchase—Denver, Syracuse, Columbus

More women responded to the 20¢-off single-pack (Denver) than to the other two promotions.

The 40¢-off twin-pack (Syracuse) ranked second and the 25¢-off twin-pack (Columbus) ranked a poor third.

Awareness	Denver (20¢ Single)	Syracuse (40¢ Twin)	Columbus (25¢ Twin)
All Respondents:	22%	27%	20%
Respondents Who Were			
L'eggs Usual Branders:	53%	50%	43%
Respondents Not L'eggs			
Usual Branders:	13%	22%	14%
Sample Size	400	400	400

The largest number of women who purchased L'eggs during the promotion were in Denver (20¢ single). Syracuse (40¢ twin) was second and Columbus (25¢ twin) was third.

Promotion buyers were much more likely to be L'eggs regular branders than non-L'eggs in all cases.

In both Columbus (25¢ twin) and Syracuse (40¢ twin), over 50% of purchasers bought two promotion packs (i.e., 4 pairs). In Denver, 30% bought a single-pack (pair) and 30% bought 2 packs (pairs).

Purchase:	Denver (20¢ Single) Bought on Promotion	Denver (20¢ Single) First L'Eggs Purchase	Syracuse (40¢ Twin) Bought on Promotion	Syracuse (40¢ Twin) First L'Eggs Purchase	Columbus (25¢ Twin) Bought on Promotion	Columbus (25¢ Twin) First L'Eggs Purchase
All Respondents	13%	2%	10%	1%	6%	1%
Respondents Who Were L'eggs						
Usual Branders	43%	—	33%	—	23%	—
Respondents Not L'eggs Usual						
Branders	4%	2%	5%	1%	2%	1%

EXHIBIT 4

Consumer Survey Results Presented by L'eggs Market Research

I. PROMOTION AWARENESS (Respondents who remembered the promotion)

	40¢ Twin-Pack	20¢ Single	25¢ Twin-Pack	25¢ Coupon
Awareness				
All Respondents	27%	22%	22%	44%
L'eggs Usual Branders	50	53	43	68
Competitive Usual Branders	22	13	14	39

II. PURCHASE OF L'EGGS ON PROMOTION

	40¢ Twin-Pack	20¢ Single	25¢ Twin-Pack	25¢ Coupon
% respondents purchasing on promotion				
All Respondents	10%	13%	6%	16%
L'eggs Usual Branders	33	43	23	34
Competitive Usual Branders	5	4	2	13
Average # pairs purchased by respondents who did purchase				
All Respondents	3.4	2.9	3.2	1.2
L'eggs Usual Branders	4.0	3.4	3.4	1.1
Competitive Usual Branders	2.4	1.7	2.5	1.3

EXHIBIT 5

Comparison of National Payout Projections

Item	20¢ Single-Pack	40¢ Twin-Pack
1) Normal Sales Expected Over 20 Weeks, (Dozens of Pairs)	3,000,000	3,000,000
2) Sales Increase Over 20 Weeks (Percent)	10%–11%	10%
3) Sales Increase Over 20 Weeks (Dozens) [line 1 times line 2]	320,000	300,000
4) Incremental Gross Margin @ $5.00 per Dozen	$1,600,000	$1,500,000
5) Normal Sales Over 4 Weeks That Promotional Packs Are in Stores (Dozens)	600,000	600,000
6) Normal Purchases Made at Reduced Prices (Percent)	80%	60%
7) "Regular" Pairs Bought on Deal (Dozens) [line 6 times line 7]	480,000	360,000
8) Total Pairs on Which Margin Loss Absorbed (Dozens) [line 3 plus line 7]	800,000	660,000
9) Dollar Margin Loss ($.13/pair) (12 pair/dozen) times [line 8] For the 20¢ off each pair, L'eggs would absorb 13¢ and the retailer would absorb 7¢.	($1,243,000)	($1,030,000)
10) Costs of Packaging, Sales Materials, Freight, Flags, Etc. (Per Dozen)	$.350	$.385
11) Total Costs of Packaging, Sales Materials, Freight, Flags, Etc. [line 8 times line 10]	($280,000)	($254,000)
12) Cost of Temporary Labor to Flag Boutique Packs	($270,000)	0
13) Total Costs of Promotion Over 20 Weeks [Lines 9 + 10 + 12]	($1,798,000)	($1,284,000)
14) Total Payout Over 20 Weeks [line 4 minus line 13]	($198,000)	$216,000
15) Expected Long Run Weekly Volume Increase (Percent)	10%	0
16) Expected Weekly Long Run Gain @ $5.00/Dozen Gross Margin	$75,000	0

CHAPTER 6

Ocean Spray Cranberries, Inc. (A): The Fruit Positioning Study

In December, 1971, the research team from Appel, Haley, and Fouriezos, Inc., under the direction of Mr. Russell Haley presented the results of a survey among 200 cranberry sauce users to Mr. Jerry Melvin, Brand Manager of Ocean Spray's cranberry sauce products, and Mr. Ken Witham, Manager of Marketing Research at Ocean Spray. Brand management had requested the study to find ways of repositioning its cranberry sauce, which had experienced no sales growth in the latter 1960's and had actually registered a six percent sales decline in fiscal year 1970. The research team had completed a pilot study which was to be the basis for an expanded survey of consumers' product attitudes, personality patterns and life style characteristics relevant to canned cranberry sauce and cranberry jelly. The management group had requested the presentation as an interim review of the project, which had resulted in expenditures of about one-third of its alloted budget.

THE COMPANY AND THE CRANBERRY INDUSTRY

Practically all processing and marketing of cranberries[1] have in recent years been made by various cooperatives. The sales of fresh cranberries were lower than in the 1950's and

This case was prepared by Jan-Erik Modig, Instructor, the Swedish Institute of Management, under the direction of Assistant Professor F. Stewart DeBruicker, The Wharton School, as the basis for class discussion rather than to illustrate either effective or ineffective handling of an administrative situation.

[1] Cranberry is according to Webster's *New World Dictionary* "a firm, sour, edible red berry, the fruit of any of several trailing evergreen shrubs of the heath family."

early 1960's, while the processed products had almost doubled their sales. However, the yield per acre increased faster than the amount which could profitably be marketed, so the industry became confronted with a significant surplus problem. The surplus was by 1968 serious enough to cause growers to resort to the Agriculture Marketing Agreement Act of 1937.[2] The Cranberry Marketing Act of 1968 stipulated that no new acreage was to be developed over the next six years. 87% of all growers voted in favor of the order making it binding on all cranberry growers.

In the early 1970's 99 per cent of the industry's sales of cranberries had been made by various cooperatives. In 1970 production was slightly above two million barrels. Around 370,000 barrels went to fresh sales and 1,400,000 barrels to processing. The difference between production and utilization represents economic abandonment. The "set aside" amounted in 1970 to more than 40 million pounds. Between 1965 and 1971, the production and utilization (i.e., fresh sales and processed) of cranberries developed as follows:

U.S. Industry:	1965	1966	1967
Production, 1000 barrels*	1,437	1,599	1,404
Utilized, 1000 barrels	1,423	1,578	1,313
Average price received by growers, $/barrel**	$15.60	$15.60	$15.50

	1968	1969	1970
Production, 1000 barrels*	1,468	1,823	2,037
Utilized, 1000 barrels	1,413	1,760	1,845
Average price received by growers, $/barrel**	$16.50	$16.30	$12.90

* 1 barrel = 100 lbs.

** Price per barrel is based on utilized cranberries.

Source: Annual reports of Crop Reporting Board, Statistical Reporting Service, USDA.

---

[2] Under this act growers can regulate and control the size of an agricultural crop if the Federal Government and more than two-thirds of the growers by number and tonnage agree to a plan for restriction.

The cooperatively owned Ocean Spray Cranberries, Inc., of South Hanson, Massachusetts (OSC), dominated the cranberry growing, processing, and distribution in the United States. Its sales volume had developed as follows:

	Fiscal Years Ending in August		
	1965	1966	1967
OSC Sales, 1000 Barrels	967	1,036	1,054
OSC Sales, $ Millions	$44.4	$ 50.9	$ 55.4

	1968	1969	1970
OSC Sales, 1000 Barrels	1,145	1,265	1,197
OSC Sales, $ Millions	$ 62.5	$ 70.8	$ 71.4

Source: Company annual reports.

As a growers' cooperative, OSC was tax exempted as long as 95% or more of its business was cranberry-based. Year-end operating profits were determined by deducting from sales all manufacturing, marketing, administrative and other expenses, advances on berries delivered by the growers, and any retained earnings. Total net proceeds (equivalent to operating profits (before taxes) were then divided by the number of barrels of cranberries received by OSC, and the resulting average pool price was used to pay each member-grower on the basis of cranberries delivered to OSC. Operating figures from 1963 through 1970 are listed in Exhibit 1.

OSC was the largest cooperative and had operations in all the principal growing areas of North America: Massachusetts, New Jersey, Wisconsin, Washington, Oregon, British Columbia, and Nova Scotia. Over 800 growers were members of the OSC cooperative in 1971, and there was very little year-to-year change in that number.

The "Ocean Spray" brand name had been is use since the 1920's for canned cranberry products. Product development activities over the years expanded the retail line of Ocean Spray cranberry products to include the following as of late 1970:

Fresh cranberries
Jellied cranberry sauce
Whole berry cranberry sauce
Deluxe cranberry-raspberry sauce
Cranberry juice cocktail
Cranberry-orange relish
Cranapple drink
Cranprune juice drink
Grape-berry juice drink
Low calorie cranberry products
Institutional cranberry products
Industrial cranberry products

Operations were divided among four divisions: Food Service, Government and Industrial, International, and Retail. The retail operations accounted for the major part of OSC's total sales. Brand managers were responsible for retail marketing. Exhibit 2 shows the marketing organization.

Many of the OSC products enjoyed good retail distribution. The company used 85 food brokers to contact the retailers. These brokers were assigned all OSC retail products in their areas, which could be quite large. There was, for example, only one broker for New England. Twelve OSC field salesmen functioned mainly as regional managers, supervising the activities of the brokers.

OSC spent substantial monies in the advertising and sales promotion of its products. The promotional budget included "early shipping allowances" well in advance of Thanksgiving, in-store display allowances, couponing and special price-margin features for all products, and local food store advertising programs. OSC's own advertising for all brands exceeded $5 million annually between 1968 and 1970. Well above 75 per cent of this advertising supported Cranberry Juice Cocktail, and Cranapple Juice Drink. Most consumer advertising was directed through network television.

OSC products sold at significantly higher prices than those of competitive brands at both retail and wholesale level. A price differential of 10 to 15 per cent was quite common. Competition was mainly from private labels. The OSC president had the view that the "competitive pressure at the retail level being generated by private store-label merchandise is steadily increasing and represents a serious challenge in all of our current marketing strategies."

New product opportunities in old or new product categories were actively pursued by OSC. During fiscal 1970 two new sauce products (cranberry-raspberry sauce and a deluxe cranberry sauce) were being tested as well as a jellied form of applesauce. The number of tested but rejected product ideas from earlier decades was considerable.

OSC had a strong position in the Canadian market and its products were also sold in the United Kingdom and West Germany. Plans were being made to penetrate the Swedish and Dutch export markets.

MARKETING RESEARCH AT OSC

The marketing research department consisted of one manager, Mr. Ken Witham, and one secretarial assistant. Mr. Witham spent a considerable amount of time supervising or monitoring field tests of new marketing programs. These tests mostly dealt with new products, but sometimes special research projects were undertaken to measure the effectiveness of new advertising or promotional vehicles and messages for mature products. Usually, new product tests required most of Mr. Witham's attention. The department was also involved in preparing sales analyses and quarterly forecasts for financial planning and budgeting.

Mr. Witham could suggest new marketing research projects but normally the brand managers took such initiatives. They also had to seek the approval for the research budget. In the definition and planning stages of a project, Mr. Witham's role was mainly an advisory one. He would make comments on how the new project related to previous research, and the costs and benefits of different research approaches and techniques. He would also be in charge of establishing and maintaining contacts with outside suppliers of marketing research. Outside firms were used in the data collection and analytical phases of special projects, and Mr. Witham participated in the interpretation phases of each study with the brand managers and representatives of the research supplier.

In a typical year there were 5 to 10 projects with a total budget of around $150,000. This sum did not include salaries, which amounted to around $30,000. The advertising agencies responsible for various product groups would occasionally undertake marketing research in connection with their handling of OSC accounts.

Apart from these research efforts OSC also bought syndicated marketing information. OSC management received Nielsen Index reports bimonthly on all retailed cranberry products. These reports contained information gathered by retail store audits about price, shelf position, in-store promotion, and estimated sales volume of OSC and competing brands. Monthly SAMI reports on warehouse withdrawals were purchased for the sauce products during the main selling season. For beverage products only, a third syndicated data base was purchased from the operators of the MRCA National Consumer Panel, a diary-based service reporting within household purchasing activities over continuous time periods for a variety of consumer products. Occasionally, OSC would buy other syndicated information, like the MRCA National Household Menu Census. In a typical year, OSC spent approximately $200,000 for syndicated marketing information.

MARKETING OF OSC CRANBERRY SAUCE

Industry sales of cranberry sauce totaled about 6 million cases (1 case = 24 lbs) annually. It had been learned from previous research that more than 90 per cent of all U.S. households consumed some cranberry sauce during a year. A large consumer segment with very high usage consisted of relatively old people. For most consumers cranberry sauce was purchased and used a couple of times a year. The four months from October to January accounted for 60 per cent of retail sales.

OSC's sauce was sold in two forms—whole berry and jellied. A cranberry-raspberry sauce

and a deluxe sauce were in test markets during the fall of 1970. Retail sales and marketing expenditures for the OSC jelly and whole-berry sauce were as follows (year ending August 31):

	1965	1966	1967
Million Cases			
Retail Sales (Sauce)*	4.25	4.53	4.54
($1000)			
Advertising (Sauce)**	$ 240	$ 226	$ 214
Promotion (Sauce)	446	473	312
Total	$ 686	$ 699	$ 526

	1968	1969	1970
Million Cases			
Retail Sales (Sauce)*	4.64	4.55	4.25
($1,000)			
Advertising (Sauce)**	$.	$.	$ 72
Promotion (Sauce)	182	344	605
	$ 182	$ 344	$ 677

* A. C. Nielsen.
** Company Records.

The overall marketing strategy for sauce during the latter half of the 1960's was characterized as a milking strategy. Marketing support was sharply curtailed in 1964 for two reasons. First, the brand had not responded to previous advertising, and second, cutbacks were necessary in order to fund introduction of the juice product and still maintain grower returns. The only noticeable advertising efforts for sauce during this period were an outdoor campaign in 1965–1967 and newspaper supplement ads at Easter in 1970.

OSC retailed 8-ounce and 1-pound packages at a higher price than competitors. A retail price of around 27 cents was common for the one pound can. Other brands, if any, were usually sold at 3 to 7 cents less per can. It was difficult to estimate the retail mark-up on sauce, because retailers set price drastically different dependent on whether or not it was in-season or off-season. During off-season, a common retail mark-up was 18 per cent. However, many retailers used sauce as a "loss leader" during the peak season. One New York retailer had sold the OSC sauce for one cent to those customers who made more than $5 worth of other purchases.

The brand manager for sauce worked with the sales division in planning in-store promotion activities. Broker commissions varied between 3% and 5% based on OSC factory prices, depending on volume generated in the broker's market. Management was satisfied with the results obtained by the brokers during the major season, but less so regarding off-season activities.

Limited couponing was used before or after the main fall season, but brand management could not find economic justification for using coupons in connection with peak selling seasons. However, some food retailers included coupons for OSC sauce in their newspaper ads during the major selling season.

Despite some losses to private labels, OSC still had a dominant position in cranberry sauce. Its brand name was truly a household word. No other manufacturer of sauce had a national market. The competitors relied almost entirely on selling their cranberry sauce under private labels. Many fruit or vegetable cooperatives as well as other manufacturers having a canning operation were active during the main season. On an annual basis, the private labels accounted for around 26 per cent of the sauce volume in 1970–71 and this share had been increasing very slowly.

OSC did participate in cranberry private-label business to a very limited extent in the 1960's. No concerted effort was made to gain such business. In fiscal year 1970, OSC sold around 100,000 cases of sauce under private labels, which represented an addition to regular sauce sales of around two per cent. OSC usually received 2–4 cents less for the one-pound can of sauce when sold as private label. This was offset by savings in distribution and production costs (another sauce formula was used). The private-label business was not the responsibility of the OSC sauce brand manager although he was kept informed about it.

OSC sold three times more jelly than whole berry sauce. This ratio had been very stable

during the 1960's. However, the ratio was about 4 to 1 in New England and 2 to 1 in California. The brand manager had so far not found any good explanation for the regional differences. He knew, however, that the whole berry sauce was relatively more often used as an ingredient in preparing a meal. The two products were always jointly advertised and promoted. It was felt that management did not have a clear indication as to how the marketing of the two variants could be beneficially differentiated.

PREVIOUS MARKET RESEARCH FOR SAUCE

While handling the OSC sauce and drink accounts the McCann-Erickson advertising agency undertook in 1962 an ''Exploratory Motivation Survey of Consumer Attitudes toward Cranberries.'' This study followed a general format which McCann-Erickson called ''MARPLAN '62.'' The study had a great impact on OSC management and it was often referred to or reviewed in the following years.

The MARPLAN study found that cranberry sauce was tradition-bound, almost synonymous with Thanksgiving and turkey. It indicated that this aspect of the image was not likely to change. The rejection of cranberry sauce by nonusers who have tried it seemed to be a fairly permanent factor. Close analysis of the verbatims and ratings suggested that rejection was primarily based on taste.

It seemed unlikely that nonusers could be taught to like cranberries by advertising. The study concluded that if advertising were to be used, the effort would have to be substantial. Advertising should be aimed at overcoming the force of habits and traditional views among year-round users and in-season-only users rather than persuading rejecters to become triers again. However, OSC management opted for the implicit alternative of minimal advertising and promotional expenditures.

In 1967 OSC had purchased information from the MRCA National Household Menu Census. The survey gave demographic data on sauce users and nonusers. When the results of the 1967 study were compared with those of MARPLAN '62, a shift in the age distribution of the sauce franchise to a reduction in the annual usage in younger age groups was apparent.

Incidence of Cranberry Sauce Usage in Preceding 12-Month Period

Age of Female Head of Household	1962 MARPLAN* N = 2027	1967 MRCA** N = 4000
Under 25	68%	59%
25–34	85	75
35–44	91	99
45–54	88	95
55 +	83	81
Average	85	85

* Based on claimed usage.

** Special survey conducted among members of the MRCA National Consumer Panel.

MARPLAN '62 and the Menu Census also revealed that even though many householders used sauce with chicken servings, sauce was only used in connection with 6 percent of all chicken servings. In the brand manager's eyes this was an opportunity for growth. Another possibility for growth read from these reports was the fact that if the "seasonal" users could be stimulated to buy one additional can, this would represent around 25 per cent increase in total volume.

Apart from reports from the sales organization, the brand manager received Nielsen retail audit reports and SAMI warehouse shipment figures during the peak sales season. These standardized reports were helpful for short-term marketing planning and control. However, it was equally clear that they were not particularly designed to be used in analyzing and developing long-term strategy for OSC's cranberry sauce.

DEVELOPMENTS DURING 1969–1971

Before joining OSC as a brand manager in 1969, Mr. Jack Walsh worked with the General Foods Company. He had there been witness to many attempts to increase sales and/or market share of commodity-like food products. These attempts centered primarily around advertising, positioning and occasionally around product quality since changing other marketing variables like price or distribution were deemed unprofitable. According to Mr. Walsh, the management and marketing process dealt with trying to identify large consumer groups which seemed to be similar to medium or heavy user groups. If one group of consumers only differed markedly as to the amount consumed of a certain product when compared with another group, then it ought to be possible to "convert" this group of lighter users to a group of heavier users.

A central question in these studies was choosing which specific consumer characteristics to measure. In addition to traditional measures of product usage, demographic and socioeconomic characteristics, some market segmentation studies had begun experimentation with newer measures of consumers' life styles, their attitudes toward a product class, and their beliefs about the kinds of benefits a product should provide. Though studies of consumers' attitudes and product usage patterns were not new, it became fashionable to refer to the more recent research efforts as psychographic studies. Whereas demographics referred to the characteristics of an individual or a population in terms of its age, sex, and location, psychographics included any of a range of more-or-less systematic measures of a consumer's (or a group's) personality as it related to the scenarios of purchase and consumption of a given product category.

Mr. Walsh's first task was brand management of the cranberry cocktail and sauce business. He saw three ways to increase sauce sales and profits: (1) gain in market share by selling part of production under private label; (2) by more aggressive pricing and merchandising of the OSC sauce; or (3) expansion of sauce demand by stimulating heavier usage among various consumer segments. Various opinions were held by the members of the OSC management as to which was the best way to go and, above all, whether or not any offensive marketing action was likely to help OSC's position in the market for cranberry sauce. Mr.

Walsh himself argued that there were opportunities to expand the sauce market. "We have a premium brand of an inexpensive food product which two out of every three U.S. households buy once or twice a year. The marketing challenge is to raise this to twice or three times a year."

Possible reasons for infrequent usage of sauce came easily to mind, and the following explanations were popular among OSC managers: "Many consumers consider cranberry sauce as a tradition strictly connected with the Thanksgiving and Christmas holidays and the turkey meal;" "many find it inconvenient to serve;" and "many housewives don't buy it more often because some family members don't like the taste."

Management's thinking about the role of consumer advertising was affected by the experiences from the substantial effort made in the early 1960's. The objective at that time had been to promote sauce consumption year-round. Cranberry sauce as an accompaniment to a variety of meals was featured in the advertising copy. The advertising program was stopped because little consumer reaction was observed. Measurements of advertising results showed the early 1960's program had failed to make consumers more aware of sauce advertising in out-of-season periods.

Mr. Walsh thought the sauce market was ripe for an application of psychographic research along the lines he had experienced while at General Foods. The sauce business was very important for OSC, because it accounted for around 40 per cent of growers' returns. Top management, on the other hand, was not convinced that advertising would be a sound investment for these reasons:

The "milking" strategy seemed to be successful.

Past advertising efforts had not succeeded in generating sufficient sales growth to "pay-out."

Marketing funds would have to be diverted from OSC drinks which were growing rapidly.

Lack of any OSC exclusivity in previous creative submissions made it likely that growth resulting from successful advertising would be disproportionately shared with price brands, whose cranberries were supplied by growers who were not members of the Ocean Spray cooperative.

For these reasons it had been reluctant to spend money on the advertising of OSC sauce, or for that matter, invest substantial sums in sauce marketing research.

When the sales of OSC sauce products decreased by nearly 7 per cent in fiscal year 1970, management became more willing to take action. The decline was due to a combination of a 3 per cent drop in total sauce sales and the inroads of low-priced private-label products in selected major markets.

Management abandoned the milking strategy of 1965–1969 and implemented a merchandising and promotion program in 1970 that was credited with stabilizing a declining situation. While advertising spending in fiscal 1970 was limited to a $72,000 Easter campaign, $605,000 was spent on promotion and merchandising activities. Brand management's plan for the 1971 fiscal year, approved late in the summer of 1970, called for an increase of over $500,000 in spending for sauce to be divided approximately equally between advertising and promotion, and some of those funds could be diverted for research studies if properly justified with top management.

In this situation, just after the selling season of fall 1970, Mr. Walsh outlined a marketing research project which could give management information about how the apparent market expansion opportunity should best be seized. His memorandum to key personnel at OSC and the advertising agency, Young & Rubicam (who had obtained the sauce account late in the 1960's), stated that the project would:

(a) observe the psychodemographic characteristics of heavy sauce users; (b) generate hypotheses for their high service frequency; and (c) develop selling propositions which, delivered against similarly profiled light/nonusers, will position regular sauce as complementary to their life style.

The ultimate objective was to "turn on" some segment of light and/or nonusers of sauce.

As Mr. Walsh saw it, the direction for development of communication approaches would come from observation and analysis of heavy user subgroups. He gave the following simplified example of how this would be done:

One segment of heavy users may be characterized by a "Family Centered" orientation, where meals are a medium for expressing affection for family and where it can be concluded that the role of sauce is to communicate affection at common, easily-prepared, or otherwise "unspecial" meals.

Next, this segment would be viewed against normative data to determine potential (that is, incidence in the total consumer universe) and reachability (in terms of media habits).

Were the above completed and were "Family Centered" concluded to be the optimal target, the Agency would go to work. Advertising would be produced which communicated the life style of the target audience and positioned cranberry sauce service as complementary to or supportive of that style. The desired end result would be target prospects "self-selecting" ("Hey, that's me"), perceiving sauce service out-of-season as desirable and commencing to buy the product. For the heavy users necessarily reached, the advertising would reinforce and, hopefully, stimulate their already profitable behavior pattern.

Mr. Walsh foresaw the need to work with "an agency trained in psychodemographics who would provide the formal game plan," in the meantime, he indicated that the following research activities would take place:

Screen for a statistically reliable sample of heavy users.

Segment sample through psychological testing and analysis by a research firm (include demographic and media habit data by segment).

Generate hypotheses for the sauce usage of each segment in context of their now available psychographic profiles or life styles.

Select the most promising segment.

Develop and test the selling platform for that segment.

Late in December of 1970, Walsh's superiors agreed to a marketing research project for sauce, mainly to help management better evaluate and plan the increased marketing spending on sauce.

Having set out research objectives, guidelines for the methods to be used, and organization of the project, Mr. Walsh initiated and participated in a series of meetings with agency and OSC marketing managers and research specialists. Late in the spring of 1971, OSC invited the agency and two other marketing research firms to submit proposals and bid for the project. These two firms were Daniel Yankelovich, Incorporated, and Appel, Haley, Fouriezos, Incorporated. The latter came out as the winner. An important factor was that Mr. Russell Haley of AHF had successfully completed similar consulting assignments for General Foods. Mr. Walsh was familiar with this work.

In the spring of 1971, Mr. Walsh was promoted to Group Product Manager and Mr. Jerry Melvin became Brand Product Manager for sauce. Mr. Melvin was earlier an assistant to Mr. Walsh.

THE FRUIT POSITIONING STUDY

By the end of the summer 1971, the research project was a major concern of Messrs. Walsh, Melvin and Witham. Mr. Haley's proposal had called for "a benchmark study of the market for cranberry sauce." The overall proposed study was to be the development of an understanding of cranberry sauce users—their behavior, attitudes, opinions, and beliefs. Mr. Walsh decided the study would focus only on the sauce product category and would not investigate other OSC products in any depth.

The research objectives were formulated as follows:

To identify and describe the kinds of women who use cranberry sauce;

To provide an understanding of what consumers are seeking in choosing between complementary products for use—in salads, and with main food courses;

To look into the consumption of various food types as sources and potential sources of cranberry sauce usage;

To describe consumer usage patterns with regard to cranberry sauce;

To identify broad media types for OSC sauce in getting across its message to consumers; and

To investigate new product or line extension possibilities.

It was argued that guidance for formulation of three basic components of the marketing strategy would result from a fulfillment of the above research objectives. The three components were in the words of the AHF proposal as follows:

1. *Positioning*: Where are additional sales most likely to originate? Should the product or its image be modified, to maximize its long-term sales appeal, and if so, how?

2. *Market Target*: Who are the best prospects for cranberry sauce?

3. *Buying Incentives*: What should be said about OSC's cranberry sauce to make it most attractive to its market target?

At the meeting between the brand group, OSC research and Mr. Haley, it was agreed that the project should have three phases with a final report in early spring 1972. The cost of the three phases would be about $45,000 with a plus or minus 10% contingency for unforeseen costs or savings. The three phases were to cover (1) exploration of areas to be covered, (2) development of measurement tools, and (3) measurement of the market on a national basis.

PHASE ONE—EXPLORATION OF AREAS TO BE COVERED

The immediate purpose of the first phase was to define the competitive environment and to compile lists of product attributes, consumer beliefs, and personality and life style characteristics of special relevance for cranberry sauce consumption. Past research on the cranberry

sauce market consisted mainly, as has been mentioned above, of the MRCA study from 1967 and the so-called MARPLAN study from 1962. These studies were reviewed in search of areas to be measured. Mr. Witham put down a one-page list of hypotheses concerning the activities, opinions, life styles and demographics of heavy users of cranberry sauce.

Heavy Sauce Users

1. Use cranberry sauce with a variety of meats and numerous preparations—i.e., fried, broiled, cold meats, as well as baked;

2. Perceive sauce as a part of the meal rather than a garnish or a symbol of tradition;

3. Have sauce in their kitchen as a staple year-round;

4. Often make their own sauce or relish when fresh cranberries are available;

5. Feel sauce has a food value as well as an attractive appearance and good taste;

6. Often use sauce as an ingredient in cooking;

7. Consider sauce a convenient, inexpensive food item;

8. Have (demographics):

   larger families
   several children living at home
   better education
   a 30–45 year old female head-of-house
   a higher family income
   up-scale socio-economic characteristics; and

9. Have a life style which includes:

   a wife/mother who enjoys cooking
   active participation in community affairs
   being concerned with nutrition of the family, quality of environment
   preference for natural foods versus synthetics
   a planned food budget and shopping from a shopping list
   strong family ties.

Mr. Melvin, the sauce brand manager, gave the AHF team a list of 41 cranberry sauce usage hypotheses, for example, "since sauce is perceived as appropriate for formal meals, the difference between heavy and light users has to do with the number of formal meals served," and "new products like Shake 'n Bake are cutting into the sauce business."

To supplement management's judgment, two focused group sessions were conducted among women who used cranberry sauce. The first group session was conducted in Boston among ten heavy users. The light user group was gathered in Kansas City. A light user had to have used only one can of cranberry sauce within the past year, and not served any within the past month.

One finding was that several of the women were concerned about serving a colorful meal. A difference between the two groups was the food items chosen to make a meal more colorful. The heavy users primarily chose cranberries while the light users specified a combination of green and yellow vegetables, salads and beets. Cranberry sauce was not mentioned by this group particularly because they considered it to be strictly a traditional food.

Twenty women were also the subjects for a perceptual mapping exercise. Each respondent was asked to make judgments about which two out of a set of three food items were most alike in terms of use. Twenty-four food accompaniments, including cranberries, were considered in this way. Figure 1 was developed using the perceived similarities data, and suggests how the 20 respondents positioned cranberries

relative to other foods. In discussing this map with OSC managers, Mr. Haley suggested that the two dimensions could be interpreted as "spicy-nonspicy" and "condiment–side dish." Cranberries were perceived as average of the first scale and more of a side dish or fruit than a condiment on the second scale.

PHASE TWO—DEVELOPMENT OF MEASUREMENT TOOLS

The qualitative results from Phase 1 were used to design a questionnaire. Marketing management made several extensions and modifications of the questions which the research team first suggested, and the list of questions became quite lengthy. Management and the AHF staff came up with 75 questions dealing with attributes of ideal canned fruit products, 103 questions on overall opinions and feelings about cranberry sauce, and 55 on personality and life style. The 75 questions on attributes were to be replicated for jellied and for whole cranberry sauce, respectively. Traditional questions on product usage and on various demographical variables were also to be included.

A pilot test was conducted in fall 1971 to try to determine which of the many items best

FIGURE 1

Perceptual Map of Various Food Accompaniments

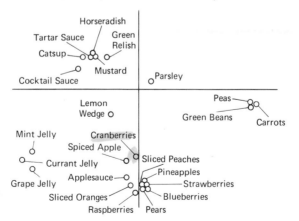

reflected strong, underlying consumer dimensions in the cranberry sauce market. That such dimensions of attitudinal or other character existed was believed by both OSC marketing management and the AHF research team.

Two hundred females living in ten different market areas were personally interviewed in their homes. The procedure to select the sample was thought to acceptably approximate a national probability sample. Potential respondents were personally screened to determine if they had purchased canned cranberry sauce in the past year. Around 220 females had to be contacted to yield a sample of 200 qualified respondents.

The, personal interview lasted around 30 minutes. It covered purchasing and usage of cranberry sauce, brands, frequency of serving various foods, and demographical and socioeconomic variables. A self-administered questionnaire containing questions about the subjective areas mentioned previously (overall opinions and feelings about cranberry sauce) was given to the respondent at the end of the personal interview. The interviewer picked up the completed questionnaire later the same day. A promised gift was delivered in return for the completed questionnaire.

ANALYSIS OF PILOT TEST DATA

A major objective of the pilot test was to investigate the extent to which consumers in fact exhibited the characteristics that management had hypothesized. The self-administered portion of the pilot survey questionnaire contained 383 separate items covering five separate areas of inquiry:

The pilot questionnaire had been constructed to cover as many different characteristics of consumers and the product category as could conceivably be relevant to the purchase and use decision process of important market segments. The research strategy involved letting the data and subsequent analysis determine which subsets of all the original items were of more or less analytical and managerial interest, rather than strictly relying on "expert judgment" as a basis for building a more succinct list of final items. Whatever redundancy might be present in the original items would thus be identified and could be eliminated, and furthermore, if certain items seemed to be tapping a fundamental consumer or product characteristic not explicitly measured, that characteristic could be inductively identified. The pilot questionnaire, then, was thought of as a preliminary and exploratory vehicle that would shape the form and content of a smaller, final set of questions to be employed in Phase 3 of the project.

The five data sets were analyzed one at a time—however, always in combination with a sixth group of variables. This sixth group consisted of the following variables:

1. Cranberry sauce usage—heavy or light;
2. Age—young or old;
3. Meat consumption—heavy or light;
4. Fruit (and vegetable) consumption—heavy or light; and
5. Education—high school or further.

Respondents were given the values "1" or "0" in the coding of these variables. It was hoped that by including these basic marketing

Area	Type of Data	No. of Items
1	Attributes of an Ideal Canned Fruit	75
2	Perceived Attributes of Jellied Cranberry Sauce	75
3	Perceived Attributes of Whole Berry Cranberry Sauce	75
4	Overall Attitudes and Feelings about Cranberry Sauce	103
5	Self-Description of Personality and Life Style	55
	Total Number of Self-administered Items	383

variables, the analyses would give results, which were easier to understand.

The computerized data analysis was done in 5 steps and repeated for each of the five sets of data. The steps for the analysis of "Description of personalities and life styles" were as follows:

Step Analysis

1. Calculation of means and standard deviations of the responses to each item (Exhibit 3).

2. Preparation of a matrix of the pairwise correlations between these items. (A portion of the fifty-six × fifty-six correlation matrix is shown in Exhibit 4.)

3. The use of a computerized data analysis technique called principal components analysis to identify which sets of variables tended to be scored by respondents according to a consistent pattern. The output of the principal components analysis was a series of factors.

4. Each factor consisted of a set of weights (called loadings) which showed the degree of association between each variable and an underlying theoretical pattern of responses. Loadings could range between -1.0 and 1.0, and loadings that were near zero indicated there was no association between a variable and a particular factor. Exhibit 5 lists the loadings of the fifty-six Personality and Life Style variables on the first of the 13 factors.

5. The theoretical response pattern represented by a given factor was then identified using the following procedure: a list of highly loaded variables was compiled for each of the 13 factors. Exhibit 6 is such a list as prepared by the Factor Analysis program for Factor One. The list was then inspected and the research team made a judgment regarding what underlying phenomena seemed to best explain the factor. Factor One was judged to be a measure of cooking enthusiasm and was so labeled. This process was repeated for the remaining twelve personality and life style factors, resulting in the labels listed in Exhibit 7.

The use of the principal components analysis had suggested the possible underlying dimensions of consumers' attitudes toward the product category, and had identified a rela-tively small subset of important variables in each of the five types of measurements. The research team then began construction of a revised questionnaire—with no redundant or irrelevant items—to be used in a full-scale survey.

The revision of the pilot questionnaire resulted in changes so that instead of the 75 original questions on attributes of ideal canned fruit products, jellied and whole berry cran-berry sauce, the research team now wanted to use 33 questions; 43 of the original 75 had been dropped and one added. Furthermore, of the 103 questions on overall attitudes and feelings about cranberry sauce, only two were retained. An additional set of 20 question items would be included. Finally, of the 51 statements regarding personality and life style, 17 were dropped. This part would consist of the remaining 34 plus one additional item.

PREPARATION FOR A FULL–SCALE SURVEY

A meeting was held between the research team and the marketing research and brand managers from OSC to report on the results of the pilot test. In discussing the planned full-scale consumer survey, the research team reiterated the earlier objectives for Phase 3 of the project. A larger sample would result in more reliable estimates of the attitudes and behaviors of cranberry sauce users. Furthermore, the pilot test had enabled the research team to develop a better version of the questionnaire.

Mr. Haley's brief to the OSC managers contained the following question areas suggested for Phase 3:

In the personal interview:

Usage of main dishes with which cranberry sauce may be eaten

Usage of and overall attitudes toward competitive complementary products

Occasions of use

Brand awareness and trial

Brand loyalty

Demographic characteristics

In the self-administered questionnaire:

Attitude ratings of whole berry and jellied cranberry sauce

Desirability of product attributes and benefits

Images of branded and private label cranberry sauce

Perceived compatibility with various main dishes

Beliefs

Personality and life style characteristics

Exposure patterns to different types of media

It was suggested that personal interviews should be conducted regarding consumer usage of cranberry sauce and the demographic profile of the respondent. Live questions would ask about the frequency of serving various meats and complementary products (like cranberry sauce) with these meats, cranberry sauce purchases, etc.

The other items discussed above would be measured by a self-administered questionnaire. The questionnaire would include some questions on television, radio and newspaper exposure patterns as well as questions regarding readership of 24 general or female audience magazines. This magazine list was, according to the account manager at Young & Rubicam, "totally representative of the books which would be considered for a magazine effort for

sauce." In the communication to the AHF team he had, however, added that it was "highly improbable that all of the magazines would ever be used."

In order to obtain around 1000 qualified respondents (purchased one or more cans in the last year), it seemed likely that around 1200 women would have to be contacted in their homes. If standard estimates for the costs of this kind of field work were used, the OSC managers figured that the additional expenditure for Phase 3 would amount to around $30,000. About $12,000 had been spent through the completion of Phase 2. Phase 3 costs would include the data collection, analysis and reporting to OSC management. The research team promised delivery of a report in March 1972. The field interviews would be made in late January and early Febraury. Mr. Melvin was concerned about the timing because he had to prepare the marketing plan well before the new fiscal year started in September 1972.

Preliminary reports for the 1971 fall selling season indicated that OSC cranberry sauce sales were up by around five per cent compared to the previous year. Mr. Melvin attributed the increase to the fact he had mustered an almost 80 per cent higher marketing expenditure budget in fiscal 1971 than in fiscal 1970. He certainly hoped that the AHF study would give indications about how the marketing effort should be directed to give even better results in 1972.

EXHIBIT 1

Financial Review, 1963–1970
(Thousands)

Fiscal Year Ended August 31	1963	1964	1965	1966	1967	1968	1969	1970
Net Sales ($000)	32,294	37,430	44,401	50,909	55,429	62,513	70,815	71,365
Barrels Sold (000)	938	978	967	1,036	1,054	1,145	1,265	1,197
Per 1,000 Barrels ($)	34.4	38.3	45.9	49.1	52.6	54.6	56.0	59.6
Selling, Marketing and Administrative Expenses ($000)	6,314	7,441	9,264	10,590	11,774	11,512	12,983	12,896
Per 1,000 Barrels ($)	6.73	7.61	9.58	10.2	11.2	10.1	10.3	10.8
Net Proceeds ($000)	11,369	13,607	15,788	17,584	17,534	18,652	20,298	20,536
Net Proceeds as Per Cent of Net Sales (%)	35.2	36.4	35.6	34.5	31.6	29.8	28.7	28.8
Total Capital Employed ($000)	7,190	7,198	6,597	6,858	7,201	9,781	11,628	13,699

Source: Annual reports.

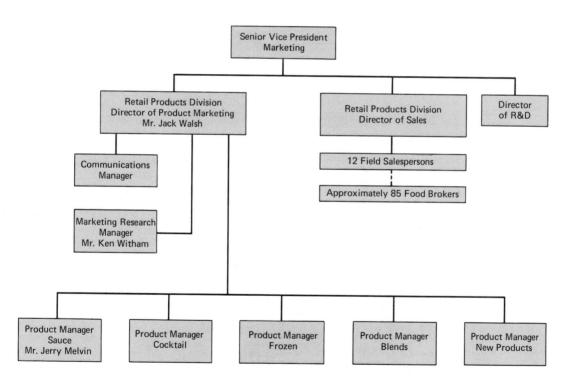

I agree
5 disagree

EXHIBIT 3

Analysis of "Descriptions of Personalities and Lifestyles" Data

TABLE A-1

Means and Standard Deviations of "Descriptions of Personalities and Lifestyles"

Variable No.	Label	Mean	Standard Deviation
1.	I like to have friends over for dinner	2.04	1.02
2.	I prefer fresh vegetables to canned or frozen products	2.23	1.15
3.	I watch my calories carefully	3.17	1.31
4.	I like to rough it and live simply	3.22	1.17
5.	I'm not a good cook	3.60	1.29
6.	I believe in things my parents believed in	2.68	.91
7.	I'm a nervous sort of person	3.09	1.28
8.	I usually get together with the family for holiday meals	1.73	1.04
9.	When I see something I like, I buy it	2.65	1.02
10.	I prefer natural foods to ones with artificial ingredients	1.95	1.06
11.	I really enjoy eating	1.63	.88
12.	I don't feel well, but don't know what is wrong	4.30	1.03
13.	I enjoy having lots of people around	2.43	1.07
14.	I tend to be good to myself	2.44	.97
15.	I like to cook new dishes	2.08	1.05
16.	I usually serve several relishes and other extras at holiday meals	1.70	.87
17.	I try to serve my children the things they like to eat	2.01	1.00
18.	I like to have my meals planned and organized in advance	2.16	1.10
19.	I often buy store brands instead of national brands	2.91	1.17
20.	I like to look for sales in the grocery store	1.92	1.10
21.	I am frequently on a diet	3.25	1.35
22.	I think Sunday is a traditional day	2.38	1.24
23.	I have few pains	3.20	1.40
24.	I enjoy cookouts	2.19	1.16
25.	My family appreciates the work I put into a meal	2.05	.97
26.	I like to prepare fancy dishes even if they take a long time	2.70	1.30
27.	I am in better health than most of my friends	2.67	1.15
28.	The foods I serve reflect my moods	2.86	1.14
29.	I like to keep busy in leisure time	2.03	1.06
30.	I usually get to cook things for my husband	1.88	1.19
31.	I plan my life carefully	2.79	1.10
32.	I enjoy cooking more for guests than for the family	3.47	1.25
33.	I like to balance my meals carefully to make sure they're nutritious	1.84	.87
34.	I like to prepare colorful salads	2.15	1.04
35.	In running my home—I think how mother would do things	3.50	1.19
36.	I enjoy entertaining at home	2.10	1.04
37.	I wish I were not so shy	3.57	1.33
38.	I try to get color and taste contrast in my main meals	2.00	.97
39.	I rarely serve leftover foods	3.32	1.25
40.	Food advertising interests me	2.56	1.22
41.	I enjoy taking time to prepare meals	2.28	1.03
42.	I serve quite a few casseroles	2.90	1.05
43.	I always keep some fruit around for the family	1.51	.75
44.	We prefer plain and simple foods	2.19	.90
45.	I believe we are on earth to enjoy ourselves	2.23	.95
46.	I like to cook	1.84	1.01
47.	I think the meat is the most important part of the meal	1.78	.85
48.	I enjoy being active	1.63	.73
49.	I enjoy serving spicy dishes	2.89	1.11
50.	Meals are a way to express affection for the family	2.11	1.05
51.	I feel guilty about wasting food	1.84	1.12
52.	Sauce: heavy/light user	.52	.50

158

Variable No.	Label	Mean	Standard Deviation
53.	Age: younger/older	.39	.49
54.	Meat: heavy/light user	.43	.50
55.	Fruit: heavy/light user	.51	.50
56.	Education: high school/ +	.65	.48

Keys to variable number:

1-51. Respondents answered along a five-point scale—ranging from "describes me completely" (1) to "describes me not at all" (5);

52. Respondents who stated that they had purchased ≥7 cans of cranberry sauce in the past year were considered to be heavy users. Heavy users were given the value "1" and light users "0" on this variable;

53. Respondents in the age ≤34 years were given the value "1;"

54. Heavy users were those who reported a total score ≥31 on questions regarding the frequency of eating meats during an average month. Nine different meats were mentioned and a seven-point scale was used. Heavy users were given the value "1;"

55. Heavy users ("1") were those who reported a total score ≥56 on sixteen fruits and vegetables;

56. Respondents with high school as highest grade were given the value "1."

EXHIBIT 4

Sample from Matrix of Pairwise Correlations of "Descriptions of Personalities and Lifestyles"

Column headers:
1. I like to have friends over for dinner
2. I prefer to canned or frozen products
3. I watch my calories carefully / I prefer fresh vegetables
4. I like to rough it and live simply
5. I'm not a good cook
6. I believe in things my parents believed in
7. I'm a nervous sort of person
8. When I see something I like, I buy it / I usually get together with the family for holiday meals
9. I prefer natural foods to ones with artificial ingredients
10. (continuation)

		1	2	3	4	5	6	7	8	9	10
Food advertising interests me	40	.197	−.002	.172	.166	.108	.230	.144	.122	.081	.106
I enjoy taking time to prepare meals	41	.362	.145	.179	.193	−.234	.205	.005	.080	.090	.216
I serve quite a few casseroles	42	−.083	.172	.105	−.023	.027	.056	−.054	−.067	−.053	.102
I always keep some fruit around for the family	43	.184	.123	.132	.077	−.076	.056	.143	.111	.127	.162
We prefer plain and simple foods	44	−.046	.070	.060	.086	.126	.180	.078	.027	−.009	.136
I believe we are on earth to enjoy ourselves	45	.213	.166	.166	.171	.070	.091	.078	−.010	.184	.354
I like to cook	46	.328	.084	.182	.137	−.248	.149	.011	.018	.068	.147
I think meat is the most important part of the meal	47	.191	.052	.087	−.039	−.056	.163	.004	.111	.131	−.004
I enjoy being active	48	.225	.153	.108	.041	−.021	.179	−.111	.016	.080	.172
I enjoy serving spicy dishes	49	.161	.082	.120	.072	−.106	−.063	−.043	−.024	.142	.104
Meals are a way to express affection for the family	50	.207	.161	.085	.166	−.095	.218	.081	.031	.008	.248
I feel guilty about wasting food	51	−.026	.072	.074	.189	.031	.229	.145	−.076	−.259	.266
Sauce: heavy/light user	52	−.065	−.005	.024	.086	.102	−.047	.160	−.203	−.031	.054
Age: younger/older	53	−.038	.045	.143	−.025	.019	.046	−.013	−.042	−.066	.162
Meat: heavy/light user	54	−.020	−.101	−.054	−.001	.109	−.011	.031	.033	.005	−.157
Fruit: heavy/light user	55	−.015	−.091	−.052	−.033	.114	.028	−.005	.028	−.123	−.109
Education: high school/ +	56	.129	.002	.037	−.198	−.132	−.076	−.091	−.180	.004	−.052

EXHIBIT 5

Detailed Listing of Factor No. 1*

Variable No.	Loading	Variable No.	Loading
1	.3181	29	.0059
2	-.0005	30	.1188
3	.0222	31	.0052
4	.1522	32	-.0747
5	-.4790	33	.0713
6	.0026	34	.1572
7	-.0962	35	.0830
8	-.0224	36	.2865
9	.0163	37	-.0482
10	-.0274	38	.1051
11	.3798	39	.0970
12	.0591	40	-.0651
13	.0576	41	.6165
14	-.0359	42	.0987
15	.5778	43	.0274
16	.2069	44	-.3540
17	.0666	45	-.0569
18	.1351	46	.7470
19	-.0125	47	.1416
20	-.0444	48	.0265
21	.0629	49	.4987
22	-.0020	50	.4555
23	.0866	51	.1326
24	.2609	52	-.1613
25	.3921	53	-.0679
26	.5584	54	-.0393
27	.0945	55	-.0539
28	.1781	56	.0460

* Loadings determined by Equimax rotation of the 13 factor principal components solution.

EXHIBIT 6

Factor Analysis of "Descriptions of Personalities and Lifestyles:" Managerial Summary
Factor One
(5.9 Percent Variance Explained)

Assigned* Variable No.	Loading	Label
46	.7470	I like to cook
41	.6165	I enjoy taking time to prepare meals
15	.5778	I like to cook new dishes
26	.5584	I like to prepare fancy dishes even if they take a long time
49	.4987	I enjoy serving spicy dishes
5	-.4790	I'm not a good cook
50*	.4555	Meals are a way to express affection for the family
25*	.3921	My family appreciates the work I put into a meal
11*	.3798	I really enjoy eating
44*	-.3540	We prefer plain and simple foods
24*	.2609	I enjoy cookouts
16*	.2069	I usually serve several relishes and other extras at holiday meals

Interpretive label: "Cooking enthusiast"

* A variable was assigned to Factor No. 1 if the absolute value of the largest loading of that variable on any of the 13 factors was equal to or greater than .30 and the absolute value of the loading of the variable on Factor 1 was within .15 of the absolute value of the maximum loading. An * indicated that the variable had been assigned to more than one factor.

160

EXHIBIT 7

**Summary of Interpreted Factors for the
"Descriptions of Personalities and Lifestyles"**

Factor Number	Interpretive Label	Percent of Total Variance	Cumulative Percentage
1	Cooking Enthusiast	5.9	5.9
2	Sociable	5.8	11.7
3	Conscious Meal Planner	4.9	16.6
4	Traditional Values	4.4	21.0
5	Active	4.2	25.2
6	Husband/Family Oriented	4.1	29.3
7	Dreamer	3.9	33.2
8	Weight Watcher	3.9	37.1
9	Self-Indulgent	3.7	40.8
10	Economically Minded	3.7	44.5
11	Youth Orientation	3.7	48.2
12	Light Users	3.4	51.6
13	Healthy	3.1	54.7

EXHIBIT 8

Labels Given to Factors Extracted from Five Types of Data

First Ten Factors in Order of Extraction	Attributes of Ideal Canned Fruit Products	Attributes of Jellied Cranberry Sauce	Attributes of Whole Berry Cranberry Sauce	Overall Attitudes and Feelings about Cranberry Sauce	Self-Description of Personality and Life Style
1	Convenience orientation	Appropriate for all meats	Appropriate for trad./formal meals	Rejection of frequent use	Cooking enthusiast
2	Attractive appearance	Attractive Color	Easy accessibility	Family usage and interest	Sociable
3	Used with a variety of meats	Nourishing	Brings out variety of meat flavors	Perfect for special occasion meals	Conscious meal planner
4	Nutritive value	Traditional yet formal	Consistency	Appropriate for all meats	Traditional values
5	Fancy/special meals	Easy accessibility	Appetizer/snack	Elegant/fancy food	Active
6	Unique taste	Snack food	Wholesome	Tastes good/good for you	Husband/family oriented
7	Less frequent uses	Sharp taste	Sharp taste	Jellied form preferred	Dreamer
8	Adaptable	Every day food	Heavy users of meat/fruit	Unique taste	Weight watcher
9	Relish association	Sweet/unusual taste		Negative taste aspects	Self-indulgent
10	Heavy users of meat/fruit	Smooth		Because of mom	Economically minded

161

Ocean Spray Cranberries, Inc. (B):
Findings of the Fruit Positioning Study

Mr. Russell Haley of Appel, Haley, Fouriezos, Incorporated, presented in March 1972 the conclusions of the Fruit Positioning Study to the managers of marketing and marketing research at Ocean Spray Cranberries, Inc. (OSC) and the advertising agency personnel involved with OSC sauce products.[1] A 305-page report and additional computer printouts were also handed over by Mr. Haley.

---

[1] For details of the exploration and pilot test phases of this research and for additional industry and company background, see Ocean Spray Cranberries, Incorporated (A).

This case was prepared by Jan-Erik Modig, Instructor, the Swedish Institute of Management, under the direction of Assistant Professor F. Stewart DeBruicker, The Wharton School, as the basis for class discussion rather than to illustrate either effective or ineffective handling of an administrative situation.

The study was generally given a favorable reception by the OSC managers. They noted that some findings confirmed those of a study undertaken in 1961–1962 by McCann-Erickson.

According to Mr. Haley, the central marketing problems for cranberry sauce were (1) relatively low per capita use and (2) an aging franchise. He suggested the following as five promising ways of increasing consumption:

1. Promoting cranberry sauce as a versatile poultry and meat accompaniment;
2. Changing people's perceptions of cranberry sauce;
3. Reminding people to use it;
4. Focusing communications efforts more sharply on potentially productive market segments; and
5. New product introductions.

The AHF research team stated in its 305-page report that ''four clearcut attitudinal segments were found in the cranberry sauce market.'' These were labeled as follows:

Segment 1: Convenience oriented

Segment 2: Enthusiastic cooks

Segment 3: Disinterested

Segment 4: Decorators

Each consumer segment was described in a variety of ways. For instance, when compared with all consumers, the convenience-oriented segment was said to have ''a higher preference for jellied form of cranberry sauce relative to whole berry,'' and ''a higher share of people 45 years or older.''

BACKGROUND

At the invitation of OSC management, the marketing research firm Appel, Haley, Fouriezos, Inc., had conducted the final phase of a three-phased consumer research study about cranberry sauce. The overall purpose of the study was to develop a better understanding of cranberry sauce users—their behavior, attitudes, opinions, and beliefs. This would be accomplished by achieving the following research objectives:

1. Identify and describe the kinds of persons who use cranberry sauce
2. Provide an understanding of what consumers are seeking in choosing between complementary products for use such as in salads or with the main course
3. Look into the consumption of various food types as sources and potential sources of cranberry sauce usage
4. Describe consumer usage patterns with regard to cranberry sauce
5. Identify broad media types for OSC sauce for getting across its message to consumers
6. Investigate new product or line extension possibilities.

The cost of the whole project would be $44,500 ± 10 percent contingency for unforeseen costs or savings. The project was proposed

in three phases which covered (1) exploration of areas to be covered, (2) development of measurement tools, and (3) measurement of the market on a national basis.

The purpose of the first phase was to define the competitive environment and to compile lists of product attributes, consumer beliefs, and personality and lifestyle characteristics of special relevance for cranberry sauce consumption. To this end, two focused group sessions were conducted among 20 women who were either heavy or light users of sauce in the past year. The results from Phase 1 were used in designing a questionnaire. The tentative list of questions was quite lengthy. The purpose of Phase 2 was to determine which of the many questions best reflected underlying consumer dimensions in the cranberry sauce market. Data for Phase 2 was collected by a pilot survey undertaken in the fall of 1971, in which a sample of 200 females living in ten market areas was personally interviewed.

Analysis of the pilot test data resulted in substantial revisions of the questionnaire. Between 30 to 98 percent of the items were dropped or exchanged within parts of the questionnaire. The structure of the questionnaire was, however, basically retained for later use in a national survey. Thus, most of the questions dealt with the following five areas:

1. Opinions about attributes of ideal canned fruit products;
2. Opinions about attributes of jellied cranberry sauce;
3. Opinions about attributes of whole berry cranberry sauce;
4. Overall attitudes and feelings about cranberry sauce; and
5. Descriptions of personalities and lifestyles.

The new questionnaire also included some questions on exposure patterns to broadcast and newspaper media as well as questions regarding readership of 24 national magazines for general or female audiences. At a meeting with Mr. Haley late in 1971, OSC management agreed to proceed with Phase 3.

PHASE 3

The purpose of the third phase—a national survey—was to provide a better understanding of the attitudes and behavior of cranberry sauce users and to suggest potentially innovative ways of segmenting the existing demand for sauce. The respondents were sampled from 47 areas, 37 of which were Standard Metropolitan Statistical Areas, and the remaining 10 were nonmetropolitan counties. Quotas of persons to be interviewed were then established for each area, for example, 12 for Larimer County (Ft. Collins), Colorado, and 100 for New York. Blocks or roads were randomly selected from maps of the sampling areas. A list with names of blocks or roads was given to each interviewer, who was directed to personally contact and screen a given number of females according to a specific procedure for choosing households within a block or road. The interviewers made daily reports through their supervisors to AHF of the number of completed interviews with eligible respondents. As in the pilot survey, potential respondents were personally screened to determine if they had purchased canned cranberry sauce in the past year. Around 1,300 women were contacted and 1,004 of them qualified as respondents and participated in the interviews.

ANALYSIS OF THE SAMPLE IN THE AGGREGATE

Before seeking the identity of potentially interesting homogeneous subgroups within the sample, the AHF research team examined the characteristics of the entire sample of 1,004 respondents. Frequency counts of the total sample on various demographic and socioeconomic characteristics, compared to available national distributions, are shown in the table at the top of p. 165.

The most commonly accepted opinions or beliefs about cranberry sauce reflected its traditional nature, food value, and integration as part of a meal rather than a garnish. The percentage of all respondents strongly agreeing or disagreeing with different belief statements is shown in Exhibit 1.

When consumers were asked about their inventory of cranberry sauce, 48% of them said they had at least one can at home. Of the 48%, 85% reported they had OSC cans. Since more than half of the respondents strongly agreed with the statement that "I probably would serve more cranberry sauce if I thought of it, but I don't," Mr. Haley suggested that promotions be directed toward building increased in-home inventories and stimulation of product usage.

It was found that "nutritious" and "has vitamins" were said to be "extremely important" characteristics of an ideal canned food product by 46% and 37%, respectively, of all interviewed cranberry sauce users. However, only 22% and 19%, respectively, "agreed completely" that jellied cranberry sauce had these characteristics. The research team concluded that a fortified product would help to provide reassurance in these areas.

The researchers thought that a second new cranberry sauce product might be one with "a consistency more similar to that of applesauce." They argued that "one principal reason for the popularity of cranberry sauce is its convenience in use. If it were made even more convenient (so that it could be easily spooned out of the can or stored in refrigerator dishes) it might provide a worthwhile stimulus to sales."

The research team found grounds for the statement that cranberry sauce is sold "in a somewhat ambiguous competitive environment, being perceived as something of a cross between a fruit and a garnish." A perceptual map developed as part of the Phase 1 research was put forward in support of this statement. Of the various food accompaniments, cranberry sauce products were perceived to be "closer" to applesauce than to catsup. This map was based on data collected from twenty women who had participated in the Phase 1 focused group interviews.

When the research team examined the ways in which cranberry sauce and jelly were served,

	AHF Sample N = 1004	1970 U.S. Population Census
Age		
18–39	42%	44%
40–64	47	40
65 +	11	16
	100%	100%
Education		
High school or less	66%	79%
Some college or more	34	21
	100%	100%
Employment		
Full- or part-time employed	22%	42%
Children		
Have children 18 years or under living at home	63%	55%

they discovered the following reported usage patterns:

Application	Percent of Cranberry Serving Occasions
Accompaniment to Meats	84%
As a Vegetable Substitute	3
In Plain or Molded Salads	9
In Cooking (Glaze or Topping)	1
In Baking	1
In Desserts or Dessert Toppings	1
Other	1
	100%

By combining information on consumers' frequency of use of the sauce with various meats and the frequency of eating these meats, it was found that chicken, roast beef and pork were worth special consideration for future advertising copy and package label. The method and data which led the research team to this conclusion were the following:

Each respondent was given a score based on her frequency of use of cranberry sauce with an individual meat—5 for "always," 4 for "frequently," 3 for "sometimes," 2 for "seldom," and 1 for "never." The average score for light users was subtracted from the average score for heavy users. (25% of all users were classified as heavy users, and 28% as light users.) The results were multiplied by the frequency of eating an individual meat and this figure in turn was multiplied by 100. In other words, the numbers in the following table are indicative of the relative amounts of volume which would result if light users were to behave like heavy users.

Management observed that the aggregated sample analyses were not inconsistent with the findings of the MARPLAN '62 study which they had received in 1962. One of the major differences between the 1962 study and the AHF study, however, was AHF's determination to identify subsets of the entire sauce market in psychographic terms and to suggest

Jellied	Index		Whole Berry	Index
Fried Chicken	187		Baked or Roast Chicken	180
Baked or Roast Chicken	180		Fried Chicken	119
Leftover Chicken	130		Pork/Pork Chops/Pork Roast	105
Roast Beef	125		Leftover Chicken	104
Broiled Chicken	120		Baked or Roast Turkey	102
Pork/Pork Chops/Pork Roast	105		Broiled Chicken	96
Hamburger	86		Hamburger	86
Ham	80		Roast Beef	75
Leftover Beef	76		Leftover Turkey	72
Leftover Turkey	60		Steak	68

variations in OSC's strategy based on the resulting market segments.

DETERMINING PSYCHOGRAPHIC MARKET SEGMENTS

The method used by AHF to determine a segmentation strategy and structure for the cranberry sauce and jelly market was described to the casewriter by Mr. Tibor Weiss, Senior Vice President of AHF. The data collection phase of Phase 3 had produced three separate categories of information dealing respectively with lifestyles, personality, and product attribute judgments.

These data were eventually input to a cluster analysis program, but first the original data sets were reduced to a smaller number of important variables. Instead of using individual items of the questionnaire as possible bases for clustering, a small number of summed scales were constructed. For example, four scales of various belief items were constructed as follows. Using judgment supported by factor analysis, a few items were selected and their responses were added together to form a new scale, thus creating a new variable or item.[2] The four resulting belief scales and the tentative labels attached by the AHF research team were:

Scale 1 = 6 - ("I usually keep a can of
"Traditional"   cranberry sauce in the cupboard year round") + "I don't like to serve cranberry sauce too often because it loses its significance." [Note $(6 - x)$ reverses the polarity of item x, thus $S_1 = (6 - x_4) + x_{15}$]

Scale 2 = "I often use jellied cranberry
"Cook and Bake"   sauce as an ingredient in cooking and baking" + "I use whole cranberry sauce as a

---

[2] This new scale is sometimes called a cumulative or Guttman scale.

cooking or baking ingredient." [$S_2 = x_{13} = x_{11}$]

Scale 3 = "Cranberry sauce is served
"Serving   with pork because it cuts the
Interest"   grease" + "Cranberry sauce should be served only on Thanksgiving and Christmas" + "I serve cranberry sauce to cool hot food" + "A firmer jellied sauce is a higher quality cranberry sauce."

[$S_3 = x_8 + x_{21} + x_{20} + x_7$]

Scale 4 = "Cranberry sauce is part of
"Food Value"   the meal rather than a garnish" + "Cranberry sauce has food value as well as an attractive appearance and good taste." [$S_4 = x_3 + x_2$]

Similarly, six summed scales of personality items, and six summed scales of benefit items, were also constructed. The full list of belief variables is included in Exhibit 1.

The belief scales, personality scales and benefit scales then were compared for their potential as bases for defining market segments. Each set of scales was used in the cluster analysis program separately producing 3 possible interpretations of market structure.

The cluster analysis program assigned individual members of the sample into groups such that all members of a given group were relatively similar in terms of the belief, personality or benefit characteristics input to the program, and such that each successive group would be relatively dissimilar when compared to all other groups. A more explicit description of the cluster analysis is included as Appendix A. The research team at AHF decided that the beliefs data provided the best of the three bases or clustering, and that there were four clusters that were of managerial consequence. Those clusters were named "Convenience Oriented," "Enthusiastic Cook," "Disinterested," and "Decorator."

When the four segments were compared on some standard marketing variables, the results were as follows:

| Segment | Convenience Oriented | Enthusiastic Cook | Disinterested | Decorator | Total |
Size	299	257	270	178	1004
Percent of all respondents	30	25	27	18	100
Percent of total volume purchased	34	32	16	18	100
Percent of jellied	35	29	17	19	100
Percent of whole berry	30	40	14	16	100
Percent heavy users (19 or more cans per year)	27	38	13	25	25
Percent medium users (7 to 18 cans per year)	48	45	40	54	46
Percent light users (6 or less cans per year)	25	18	47	21	28
Total	100	100	100	100	100
Percent who noticed price difference between OSC and other brands	34	37	30	36	34
Percent who purchased 10 OSC cans of last 10	75	74	76	74	75
Age distribution: 18–39	36	35	58	37	42
40–64	53	56	35	44	47
65+	11	9	6	17	10
	100*	100	100	100	100

* All columns may not add up to 100% due to rounding.

To enrich the understanding of the four clusters, a variety of psychographic and traditional marketing variables were cross-tabulated against cluster membership patterns. The resulting tabulations were presented by Mr. Haley as a means of making the clusters more lifelike, more humanistic and more realistic potential targets for the OSC marketing strategy. In turn, the clusters were described according to their central tendencies as indicated by the following types of measurements:

1. Key benefits of ideal fruit products
2. Key beliefs about cranberry sauce products
3. Key food related lifestyle characteristics
4. Key attitudes toward cranberry sauce products
5. Product usage behavioral tendencies
6. Demographics
7. Media exposure patterns

Exhibit 2 lists the between cluster comparisons for each of the above characteristics, and also compares the individual clusters to the population means on many individual items.

PRESENTATION TO MANAGEMENT

In his presentation to OSC management, Mr. Haley said the four clusters were "four clearcut attitudinal segments." He went on to say that "three of the four segments just described are attractive targets and, based on the information now available to us, tailormade campaigns can be designed for each segment." He described these campaigns in terms of buying incentives, copy visuals, copy tonality, promotions, and media, as shown in the table on p. 168.

Comparisons of the clusters, which differed in volume consumed and in types of cranberry products used, led the research team to talk about "a cycle running through the market." The lightest sauce users seemed to strongly favor the jellied form. At the next heavier usage level people became somewhat more frequent

Copy

| | Target Clusters | | |
	"Convenience Oriented"	"Enthusiastic Cook"	Decorator
Buying Incentives	Position as a convenient, versatile meat accompaniment rather than as a special-purpose product. A natural food.	Both jellied and whole berry can be promoted for this segment. Color, versatility, and usefulness as a cooking/baking ingredient are desirable claims.	A good way of dressing up your meats, and leftovers. A way of interjecting a festive note at mealtimes.
Copy Visuals	Informal settings, family meals, baked/roast chicken particularly good.	Larger family scenes or scenes with guests. Big eaters.	Mature models, slight accent permissible, leftovers particularly good.
Copy Tonality	Brisk, matter of fact. These women are not involved in cooking.	Friendly, sociable reflecting interest in people and in cooking.	Reassuring reinforcing. Emphasis on color. These people already love cranberry sauce.
Promotions	Tie-ins with chickens, and meats.	Recipes, cookbooks, salads, not price conscious.	Price promotions are apt to be especially effective.
Media	Small-space reminders in newspapers. *Ladies' Home Journal, Reader's Digest, TV Guide, Good Housekeeping.*	*Family Circle, Woman's Day, Better Homes & Gardens, Good Housekeeping, McCall's, Ladies' Home Journal.*	*True Story, True Romance, Reader's Digest.*

users of the jellied form. As a still higher level were heavier users who used both whole berry and jellied sauce, favoring whole berry because of its usefulness in cooking and baking. Finally, there was the real cranberry enthusiast who employed fresh berries in making her own sauce.

The researchers did not think that efforts to attract nonusers held large promise. This had also been the conclusion of a similar though nonsegmented study undertaken in 1962 by McCann-Erickson. Moreover, only 23% of the households originally contacted were nonusing households. Some researchers thought that light users might be difficult to motivate because of their relatively low interest in cooking. Their general advice was that the best

point of emphasis seemed to be somewhere in the middle of the usage cycle. "People at this point have shown their acceptance of cranberries. However, by the standard of heavy cranberry users or average applesauce users, their volume of consumption is still low. Thus we believe that a huge potential lies in this intermediate group. Moreover, we believe that a marketing strategy aimed at increasing the consumption of this group will, at the same time, draw new users into the market."

Mr. Haley also offered suggestions regarding pricing of jellied and whole berry sauce. "Since the jellied form has the greatest expansion potential, its price should be kept as low as is economically feasible. However, people who consume whole berry are less price conscious.

Therefore, it should be possible to allow the price to float a little upward without damage to unit sales volume. Thus it appears that whole berry can safely be established as a higher profit margin item.''

Shortly after OSC management had received the study, Mr. Melvin, brand manager for sauce, requested his advertising agency to develop advertising campaign proposals in light of the findings regarding market segmentation. Mr. Melvin's first reactions were that the study certainly was a needed updated version of the old 1962 study, and furthermore, that it would give him information to propose a more efficient advertising and promotion program. The right segmentation of the franchise should produce a much higher efficiency. There were, however, different opinions as to which of the four segments ought to be the prime target. Mr. Melvin felt the ''convenience-oriented'' group would be best, but Mr. Walsh, director of product marketing, argued for the ''enthusiastic (or creative) cooks.'' The discussion about selecting a segment dealt also with the practical problems of identifying and reaching a particular consumer segment.

Mr. Melvin thought also that the broad approaches to advertising used in the previous two seasons had not worked too well and should be reevaluated in light of some of the new findings. He noticed that the respondents generally overstated their volume of sauce consumption. It seemed that OSC had a huge potential in just bringing actual volume up to claimed volume of consumption.

EXHIBIT 1

Consumer Opinions or Beliefs (Overall Attitudes and Feelings) regarding Cranberry Sauce

Variable Number	Belief Statement	Agree Completely/ Strongly	Disagree Completely/ Strongly	Difference
1	Cranberry Sauce Is a Traditional Food	92%	3%	89%
2	Cranberry Sauce Has Food Value as Well as an Attractive Appearance and Good Taste	87	4	83
3	Cranberry Sauce Is Part of the Meal Rather Than a Garnish	72	17	55
4	I Usually Keep a Can of Cranberry Sauce in the Cupboard Year Round	65	26	39
5	I Probably Would Serve More Cranberry Sauce if I thought of It, but I Don't	57	31	26
6	I Serve Cranberry Sauce with Turkey to Add Moistness	43	39	4
7	A Firmer Jellied Sauce Is a Higher Quality Cranberry Sauce	29	34	−5
8	Cranberry Sauce Is Served with Pork because It Cuts the Grease	26	37	−11
9	Cranberry Sauce Is Too Tart to Serve with Spicy Foreign Foods	16	56	−40
10	I Often Make My Own Cranberry Sauce When Fresh Cranberries Are Available	26	68	−42
11	I Use Whole Cranberry Sauce as a Cooking or Baking Ingredient	20	69	−49
12	Cranberry Sauce is Appropriate for Roast Whole Chicken but Not for Broiled or Fried Chicken	16	67	−51
13	I Often Use Jellied Cranberry Sauce as an Ingredient in Cooking and Baking	16	74	−58
14	I Feel Almost Patriotic When I Serve Cranberry Sauce	10	71	−61
15	I Don't Like to Serve Cranberry Sauce Too Often because It Loses Its Significance	9	77	−68
16	I'll Eat Cranberry Sauce in a Restaurant, But I Don't Serve It Very Often at Home	12	80	−68
17	Cranberry Sauce Dries Up in the Can Before It Is Used Up	8	79	−71
18	All Brands of Cranberry Sauce Are Made by Ocean Spray	5	80	−75
19	Eating Cranberries Can Cause Health Problems	3	78	−75
20	I Serve Cranberry Sauce to Cool Hot Food	6	81	−75
21	Cranberry Sauce Should Be Served Only on Thanksgiving and Christmas	5	87	−82

Sample Size = 1004

EXHIBIT 2

Characterization of Four Consumer Segments

Note: The % number to the right of each item shows the difference between the frequency count (%) for the segment and the frequency count for the total sample on the item.

Type of Measurement	Segment 1 "Convenience Oriented" $N_1 = 299$	%	Segment 2 "Enthusiastic Cook" $N_2 = 257$	%	Segment 3 "Disinterested" $N_3 = 270$	%	Segment 4 "Decorator" $N_4 = 178$	%
	Benefit		**Benefit**		**Benefit**		**Benefit**	
Key Benefits of Ideal Food Products Rated "Very Important"	Quick	4	Appropriate for holidays	4	Different taste	−1	Easy availability	12
	Goes well with turkey	4	Goes well in salads	3	Festive	−1	Appropriate for formal meals	11
	Easy to serve	3	Colorful	3			Acceptable to everyone	10
	Smooth consistency	3					Appropriate for holidays	9
							Variety of uses	9
							Available year round	9
							Festive	8
							Quick	8
							Has vitamins	8
							Sweet taste	8
	Belief	%	**Belief**	%	**Belief**	%	**Belief**	%
Key Beliefs, Rated "Agree Very Much"	Part of meal rather than garnish	20	Use whole cranberry sauce as a cooking/baking ingredient	21	Would serve more cranberry sauce if I thought of it, but I don't	1	Firmer jellied sauce is higher quality	23
	Has food value as well as attractive appearance	15	Usually keep can year round	14			Cranberry sauce is served with pork because it cuts the grease	17
	Usually keep can year round	13	Often makes own cranberry sauce when fresh berries are available	10			Usually keep can year round	17
	Traditional food	5	Often use jellied cranberry sauce as a cooking/baking ingredient	9			I serve cranberry sauce with turkey to add moistness	15
			Cranberry sauce is one of favorite foods	7			Cranberry sauce is one of favorite foods	8
							Should be served only on Thanksgiving and Christmas	5

171

EXHIBIT 2 (cont.)

Type of Measurement	Segment 1 "Convenience Oriented" $N_1 = 299$	Segment 2 "Enthusiastic Cook" $N_2 = 257$	Segment 3 "Disinterested" $N_3 = 270$	Segment 4 "Decorator" $N_4 = 178$
	Characteristic — %	*Characteristic* — %	*Characteristic* — %	*Characteristic* — %
Key Life Styles Rated "Describes Me Completely"	Prefer natural foods to ones with artificial ingredients — 1	Enjoy being active — 9; Like to cook — 8; Like to cook new dishes — 7; Enjoy taking time to prepare meals — 7; Like to prepare fancy dishes — 6; Like to prepare colorful salads — 6; Sociable — 6; Like beef on the rare side — 6	Prefer fresh vegetables to canned or frozen products — 0	I believe we are on earth to enjoy ourselves — 14; Nutrition conscious — 11; Believe in things parents believed in — 10; Interested in food advertising — 10; Gets together with family for holidays — 8; Prefer natural foods to ones with artificial ingredients — 8; Serve children with things they like to eat — 7; Like to look for sales in the grocery store — 7; Enjoy taking time to prepare meals — 7
Attitudes / Main Attitude	See cranberry sauce as a convenient staple. High preference of jellied form relative to whole berry	High in seeing cranberry sauce as a cooking/baking ingredient	See cranberry sauce as a change of pace	See cranberry sauce as a means of sprucing up meals
	Attitude — %	*Attitude* — %	*Attitude* — %	*Attitude* — %
Supporting Attitudes Rated "Agree Very Much"	High rejection of whole berry — 6; High brand awareness — 4; High regular brand OSC — 2; High future OSC purchase intention — 2; High in seeing OSC as costing more — 2	Low on rejection of whole berry — -16; Low on rejection of jellied — -4; Low on preference of jellied over whole berry — -3	High rejection of whole berry by adults and children — 9; High rejection of jellied by adults and children — 7; High on preference of jellied relative to whole berry — -3; Low on brand awareness — -3; Low on regular brand OSC — -2	Low on rejection of whole berry — -3; Low on rejection of jellied — -1; High on preference of jellied form relative to whole berry; Low on future OSC purchase intentions — -3

	Behavior	%
Behavior Rated to do Frequently"	High on eating baked/roast chicken	9
	High on eating leftover chicken	3
	High on eating applesauce as accompaniment	-2 + 4
	High on use of cranberry sauce as meat accompaniment	-5 + 2
	High on serving cranberry sauce on all occasions, espec. informal meals	3-6

	Characteristic	%
Key Demographics	45 and older	5
	Low on college	-3
	High on U.S. as parents' country	2

	Media	%
Media	Buy newspapers	2
	Above average readership of:	
	Ladies' Home Journal	3
	Reader's Digest	2
	TV Guide	2
	Good Housekeeping	2

Behavior	%
High use of whole berry with turkey	13
High on consumption of all meat, poultry, and fish	-1 + 6
High on use of 16 oz. cans	8
High on serving cranberry sauce on all occasions	10

Characteristic	%
40 to 64	6
High on college or more	2
High on U.K. as parents' country or origin	7
High on upscale occupation of household head	3

Media	%
Buy newspapers	3
Above average readership of:	
Family Circle	8
Woman's Day	8
Better Homes & G.	6
Good Housekeeping	5
McCall's	5
Ladies' Home J.	5

Behavior	%
High consumption of pork, and fried chicken	5
Low on accompaniments, including cranberries	
Low on use of 16 oz. cans	-7
High on use of cranberry sauce as a meat accompaniment only Low on serving cranberry sauce on all occasions	– 11
Serve cranberry sauce at Thanksgiving and Christmas	

Characteristic	%
18 to 39	10
High on some college	3
High on children living at home	11
High on U.S. as parents' country of origin	5
High on middle occupation of household head	4

Media	%
Buy newspapers	-5
Low on magazines	

Behavior	%
Favors jellied and applesauce as accompaniments	
Low on jellied with chicken	-7
High on consumption of leftover beef, leftover chicken, and broiled chicken	4-7
Low on use of 16 oz. cans	-3
Low on using cranberry sauce on all occasions	-4

Characteristic	%
65 and older	7
High on some high school or less	8
Low on children living at home	-8
High on Germany/ Austria, Italy, and Russia as parents' country of origin	3

Media	%
Buy newspapers	-1
Above average readership of:	
True Story	4
True Romance	2
Reader's Digest	2

APPENDIX A

Construction and Interpretation of Belief Clusters

The Appel, Haley, and Fouriezos, Inc., research team used two complementary data analysis techniques to form the four belief clusters presented to the Ocean Spray Company brand management team. The two techniques require the use of large digital computers and have many specific forms depending upon how they are programmed, but generically they are known as cluster analysis and multiple discriminant analysis. While both methods have been applied to impersonal objects and to variables observed over classes of objects, it is most illustrative to think of the two methods as they are routinely applied to samples of individual consumers. Cluster analysis is a procedure for forming an arbitrary number of relatively homogeneous subgroups of individuals within a larger, heterogeneous sample of respondents. Multiple discriminant analysis is a procedure for interpreting the differences between a number of existing groups of respondents.

CLUSTER ANALYSIS

Cluster analysis can be performed in a variety of ways and many statistical algorithms have been written that have essentially the same objective: to form homogeneous groups of respondents drawn from a heterogeneous population. Procedures are either aggregative (proceeding by combining individuals into groups, and smaller groups with individuals or other smaller groups to form larger groups) or disaggregative (proceeding by taking the entire sample—the largest possible group—and breaking it into successively smaller groups of increasing homogeneity). Both aggregative and disaggregative procedures have been written that allow for an individual respondent to be reassigned from an existing subgroup to a newer subgroup that better matches the characteristics of that respondent.

Users of cluster analysis are not required to know in advance how many, or what kind of, clusters they eventually will choose. The purpose of the analysis is to suggest several alternative clustering arrangements from which analysts must select one that best meets their particular information needs. The analyst, perhaps in consultation with management, must decide how many clusters will make up the "solution" to the grouping problem being addressed. The analyst has the additional burden of interpreting the solution, first in terms of descriptions of the central tendencies of the resulting clusters, and eventually in terms of what the clusters imply for purposes of marketing decision making.

MULTIPLE DISCRIMINANT ANALYSIS

Cluster analysis is used to form groups, and multiple discriminant analysis is used to interpret the statistical differences between a given number of existing groups. Given a set of existing groups, multiple discriminant analysis can also be used to predict into which existing group a new individual, not presently a member of any of the existing groups, is more likely to be classified. Thus multiple discriminant analysis, working with an existing set of groups, is used to perform tasks of interpretation and classification. Because it works with grouped data, it is a good counterpart technique to cluster analysis. Together, the two methods give the analyst a series of procedures that can be used to form groups from survey observations, interpret some of the underlying differences between those groups, and develop a classification scheme for predicting the group membership of individuals not represented in the original sample.

THE AHF SEGMENT BUILDING PROCESS—CLUSTER ANALYSIS

The sample was split in two halves of 502 respondents each and separate cluster analysis solutions were determined for each sample. This split-half technique was used to give the researchers an opportunity to judge the stability of the cluster solutions. The two subsamples consisted of individuals with even and

Number of Clusters		2		3		4		5		6	
Sample Halves		Even	Odd	Even	Odd	Even	Odd	Even	Odd	Even	Odd
	Beliefs	238	231	175	194	159	153	123	124	79	85
Items:	Personality	143	146	82	81	66	71	50	46	44	44
	Benefits	112	119	101	101	59	66	57	51	36	51

odd identification numbers, thus there would be reason to expect strong similarities between the two cluster solutions except in the event that the relationships between the beliefs variables and homogeneous population subsets were spurious. A series of cluster analyses were performed using a top-down, hierarchical, disaggregative algorithm. Briefly, this computer program worked in the following way:

1. All respondents were first assigned to a single group.

2. The respondent farthest from the cluster mean or centroid was then selected as the centroid for a second cluster.

3. All respondents were sequentially tested to determine if a reassignment to the second cluster would reduce the within group sum-squared error, a statistical measure of within group homogeneity.

4. When it was no longer possible to reduce the within group sum-squared error by reassigning any single respondent to the second cluster, then that individual farthest from either of the two centroids became the centroid for a third cluster and the reassignment process was repeated.

5. The number of clusters was allowed to increase to some maximum number of clusters, set by the researcher. This number was set at six.

6. When this limit was reached, the program automatically terminated.

After constructing 4 product belief scales, 6 personality scales and 6 product use benefit scales, each set of scales was used as the basis for two cluster analyses—one for the 502 respondents with even numbers and the second for the 502 with odd numbers. The clustering solution derived from the 4 belief scales lead to the highest ratio of between group variation to within group average variation as calculated for all solutions. The computer printouts contained the following values for this ratio, as shown at the top of this page. The belief clusters were therefore selected as the basis for deriving the market segments eventually presented to OSC management. Mr. Haley considered the belief items to have the most direct implications for marketing.

Looking at the cluster solutions for the belief items, it seemed clear that the samples should be divided into no less than 4 clusters. With only 2 or 3 clusters, the third belief scale, Serving Interest, appeared not to be a basis for between-cluster differentiation as indicated in the Table of F ratios shown below. On the other hand, it seemed that little was gained by using more than 4 clusters. (See table at the bottom of this page.)

The similarities between the "even" and "odd" halves of the sample were judged quite acceptable and gave the research team con-

Number of Clusters:	2		3		4		5		6	
Sample Halves	Even	Odd	Even	Odd	Even	Odd	Even	Odd	Even	Odd
Univariate F Ratios										
Scale 1, "Traditional"	1214	1117	337	413	340	377	392	347	358	289
Scale 2, "Cook and Bake"	101	53	452	600	275	307	380	283	330	294
Scale 3, "Serving Interest"	5	4	19	20	198	186	169	194	193	247
Scale 4, "Food Value"	228	318	407	320	273	255	248	345	268	295
Average within Group Sums of Squares (W)	2.02	2.05	1.51	1.48	1.14	1.13	.92	.91	.78	.79
Between Group Sums of Squares (B)	484	474	263	287	182	174	114	112	66	62
B/W Ratio	238	231	175	194	159	153	124	123	85	79

fidence that there were systematic relationships between the belief measurements and stable consumer subgroups. One of the two 4-cluster solutions was chosen as the basis for a complete classification of the 1004 respondents. The "odd" solution was chosen because of apparently cleaner delineations, as measured by generally larger F ratios, of the 4 clusters on the 4 scales.

CLASSIFYING THE REMAINING RESPONDENTS—MULTIPLE DISCRIMINANT ANALYSIS

Having accepted a cluster solution, the AHF team used the structure of the "odd" groups to define a strategy for classifying the entire sample. The classification strategy employed multiple discriminant analysis (MDA). The means and standard deviations of the scale values for each of the 4 clusters were:

Science Computing Facility of the University of California, Los Angeles. The program calculated a discriminant function for each cluster with coefficients similar to those in regression analysis. The classification rule based on this set of discriminant functions was that a respondent should be assigned to cluster 1 if the value of L_1 was higher than the values of L_2, L_3 and L_4, which were obtained by plugging the respondent's values on each of the four X's into the functions. The following four functions were obtained, as shown at the bottom of this page.

As we see in the table at the top of p. 177, this classification of the "odd" sample using that rule led to a near perfect (92 percent correct) classification of the 502 respondents.

The same set of discriminant functions was then used to classify the remaining 502 respondents from the "even" sample into one of the four clusters. A probabilistic estimate

Means and Standard Deviations

Group	Size	"Traditional" X_1	"Cook and Bake" X_2	"Serving Interest" X_3	"Food Value" X_4
Cluster 1	134	3.15	2.51	7.60	9.40
		(1.30)	(0.80)	(1.83)	(0.81)
Cluster 2	123	3.24	6.55	7.64	8.27
		(1.38)	(1.82)	(2.04)	(1.45)
Cluster 3	148	6.51	2.90	8.33	6.99
		(1.56)	(1.36)	(2.20)	(1.80)
Cluster 4	97	3.32	3.18	11.61	7.97
		(1.48)	(1.71)	(2.44)	(1.65)
Total "Odd Half"	502	4.19	3.74	8.60	8.13

The computer program used was a stepwise discriminant analysis program called BMDO7M selected from the Biomedical Computer Programs library written at the Health

that the respondent belonged to a certain cluster was computed. The discriminant function coefficients were used to compute the four L-values for each respondent. The resulting

Discriminant Functions

	Constant	"Traditional"	"Cook and Bake"	"Serving Interest"	"Food Value"
$L_1 =$	−24.66	$+ 0.2505\ X_1$	$-0.0915\ X_2$	$+ 1.128\ X_3$	$+ 3.984\ X_4$
$L_2 =$	−24.87	$+ 0.3488\ X_1$	$+ 2.123\ X_2$	$+ 0.8438\ X_3$	$+ 3.082\ X_4$
$L_3 =$	−21.73	$+ 2.187\ X_1$	$+ 0.2419\ X_2$	$+ 0.9776\ X_3$	$+ 2.521\ X_4$
$L_4 =$	−26.29	$-0.0481\ X_1$	$+ 0.0572\ X_2$	$+ 2.182\ X_3$	$+ 3.067\ X_4$

Classified by Cluster Analysis	Number of Respondents Classified by MDA				
	Cluster 1	Cluster 2	Cluster 3	Cluster 4	Total
Cluster 1	127	0	1	6	134
Cluster 2	11	111	1	0	123
Cluster 3	2	4	141	1	148
Cluster 4	8	4	1	84	97
Total	148	119	144	91	502

L-values were then considered to be normally distributed around the L-values of the four cluster means and using the assumptions of the normal distribution, probabilities of group membership were computed. Respondent 256, for example, was found to have a .94 probability of being a member of cluster 2. The group membership probabilities for a few members of the odd sample are as follows:

The discriminant functions were also useful in interpreting the obtained clusters, for example, since cluster 2 was strongly associated with high scores on scales 2 and 4, the interpretive label "enthusiastic cook" seemed appropriate. Additional interpretations of the clusters were made using cross-tabulations such as those presented in Exhibit 2.

Respondent No.	Probabilities of Group Membership				Group Assignment
	Group 1	Group 2	Group 3	Group 4	
255	.52440	.31081	.00028	.16449	1
256	.04790	.93954	.00127	.01127	2
257	.00280	.99135	.00100	.00484	2
258	.00021	.78391	.21548	.00037	2
259	.49128	.13987	.32159	.04724	1
260	.24562	.00029	.00109	.75299	4

The respondent was allocated to the cluster she was most likely to belong to. The AHF analysts had by these procedures obtained the following four clusters:

Cluster	Number of Respondents
1	299
2	257
3	270
4	178
Total	1004

7

General Foods Corporation: Tang Instant Breakfast Drink (A)

One day late in 1972, Mr. Dick Jackson, product manager of General Foods' Tang Instant Breakfast Drink,[1] sat down to resolve a problem which had both strategic and tactical consequences. In preparation for the next year's Annual Business Plan, he had to decide what total budget amount to recommend for Tang advertising and promotional (cents-off

[1] Tang is a concentrated instant beverage formulation. A small amount (2/3 cup) is added to a larger amount of water (1 quart) to make over one quart of beverage. Tang was described by its package label as "A natural tasting orange flavor breakfast drink. It contains more Vitamin C and A than like amounts of orange, grapefruit, or tomato juice. Tang is not a juice, juice product, or a soft drink mix. Tang is a nutritious instant breakfast drink."

This case was prepared by Harvey N. Singer, Instructor, The American University, under the direction of Assistant Professor F. Stewart DeBruicker, The Wharton School, as a basis for class discussion rather than to illustrate either effective or ineffective handling of an administrative situation.

Copyright © 1974 by the President and Fellows of Harvard College.

deals, coupons, etc.) activities.[2] Within that total budget amount, he also had to recommend what proportion to allocate to advertising, and what proportion to promotion.

Mr. Jackson's decision was made more difficult because all members of his product group were not yet in complete agreement about the strategic thrust of the brand's activities. Some believed that Tang was still viable after 14 years as a long-run growth vehicle. This would justify investment spending on marketing activities like advertising and promotion to build future sales, while meeting some satisfactory profitability goals for next year. Others were of the belief that Tang business was peaking and could not support further marketing investment in the long run, which would dictate a strategy which concentrated primarily on short-term profits. Mr. Jackson felt that he must present a spending

[2] Dollar and unit figures used in this case are disguised.

plan which delivered substantial profitability next year and assured sufficient long-run sales volume for Tang.

As inputs to his decision, Mr. Jackson had before him the results and recommendations generated by two mathematical models developed to help analyze the advertising and promotion spending decision. One was built in-house by the division's Operations Research Group. The other was developed by the Management Science Department at Young & Rubicam, the brand's advertising agency. The output of each model was in slightly different form. The conclusions from the two models were also somewhat in conflict. Mr. Jackson thought this was due to the differing structure and assumptions upon which each model was built. However, the direction of the conclusions was the same: both models seemed to recommend spending levels which were a good deal higher than Tang was presently employing, and both seemed to recommend an advertising/promotion balance weighted more heavily toward advertising than Tang had used.

BACKGROUND

General Foods Corporation (GF) was a leading manufacturer and marketer of grocery products, chiefly convenience foods. Its brands were among the best-selling products nationally in a variety of categories: coffee, frozen foods, gelatin desserts, puddings, soft drink mixes, syrups, semi-moist and dry dog food, and cereals. Going into the last quarter of fiscal 1973, sales were expected to be over $2.5 billion and net profit over $100 million for the year.[3] The company's long-term strength was built on large consumer franchises for its 400 products and some 30 of the food industry's best-known brand names, including Maxwell House coffee, Birds Eye frozen foods, Post cereals, Jell-O desserts, Gaines pet foods, and Tang instant breakfast drink.

In the early 1970s, the company experi-

enced some pressure on sales and profits. In 1970 the company's net income dropped for the first time in 20 years due to an after-tax extraordinary loss of $11 million resulting from the U.S. Government's decision that year to restrict sales of food and beverage products containing the artificial sweetener cyclamate. Although some of GF's and its competitors' products suffered from this decision, the Tang business was not adversely affected because its sweetening agent was sugar.[4]

In 1972 General Foods' net income dropped again due primarily to a $47 million after-tax write-off resulting from the firm's decision to dramatically write down its fast food restaurant operations.

In terms of General Foods' marketing organization, a product manager worked within a product group, which in turn worked within a Strategic Business Unit, designated an SBU. Until very recently the company's marketing activities had been organized by products produced by similar technologies or by products that had developed as line extensions of a single brand. In the early 1970s, when the company was experiencing pressure upon sales and profits in the highly competitive convenience food markets, a major reorganization took place in the marketing structure.

Individual products and brands were placed into groups according to the SBU concept. This meant that all products, regardless of brand name or technology, which would be viewed in the same competitive framework by the consumer in the marketplace, were grouped and managed together, so that General Foods could concentrate on strategic markets as well as individual products. For example, all dessert products, whether Birds Eye frozen desserts or Jell-O gelatins, were placed in the Dessert SBU. All main meal dishes, whether Birds Eye

---

[3] Fiscal years began April 1; fiscal 1973, for example, began April 1972 and ended March 1973.

[4] Other ingredients in descending order of weights, were: citric acid (for tartness), calcium phosphates (to regulate tartness and prevent caking), gum arabic (vegetable gum to provide body), natural flavor, potassium citrate (to regulate tartness), vitamin C, cellulose gum (vegetable gum), hydrogenated coconut oil, artificial flavor, artificial color, vitamin A, and B.H.A. (a preservative).

frozen vegetables or Minute Rice or Shake & Bake seasoned coating mixes, were placed in the Main Meal SBU. Tang was included in the Beverage SBU, along with frozen beverage products (frozen orange juice concentrate and Orange Plus), other breakfast beverages (Start and Postum), and refreshment beverages (Kool-Aid products).

The SBU managers reported to the president of one of the company's major divisions. Tang belonged to the Beverage and Breakfast Division. In addition, there were other divisions which marketed pet foods, grocery products (Dessert and Main Meal SBUs), coffee and institutional food products. Each division also had support staff personnel (staffs for finance, production, technical R&D, and a field sales force) to service its SBUs. Division presidents then reported to General Foods' top corporate management, which included the president, executive and group vice presidents, and support staffs at that level which provided service to all of the divisions—chief among them a financial staff and the corporation's Market Research Group.

An organization chart sketching these relationships is shown in Exhibit 1.

Each product manager at GF acted as both a marketing and business manager for his brand. On the marketing side, he had the mission of planning and executing all advertising, promotion, pricing and merchandising strategies for the brand. More generally, he had to compete for and coordinate all of his division's functional resources as they impinged upon his product: technical inputs, marketing research, sales force activities, processing, packaging, etc. On the operations side, he was responsible for the brand's financial contribution through volume attainment, marketing spending, and pricing decisions. On the planning side, he worked with GF top management in the development of current fiscal year objectives and longer range objectives.

Dick Jackson, Tang's product manager, was assisted by an associate product manager (as were the product managers of other major brands in the SBU). They were supported by product development personnel and promotional (merchandising) personnel within the SBU. Mr. Jackson reported to Mr. Bill King, the product group manager with responsibility for Tang, Start, and Postum breakfast beverages. Mr. King in turn reported to the Beverage SBU manager.

TANG HISTORY

Tang powdered instant breakfast drink was introduced nationally in 1958. After its introduction, Tang volume grew slowly but steadily. Volume seemed to plateau as the product matured about 1962, so marketing spending was stepped up and new copy devised. Mr. Jackson indicated this gave the product a "shot-in-the-arm," and sales improved through 1968, when stagnation began again. Accordingly, marketing efforts again intensified in fiscal 1969. The product was significantly improved, and sampling efforts, advertising, and promotional spending were increased. The brand's media copy program, which tied the product to America's space exploration efforts, was effective as the Apollo program became very active, providing frequent opportunities for media saturation during the televised Apollo flights. Tang sales were up 29% for fiscal 1969 over fiscal 1968.

In fiscal 1970, this approach continued and sales gained. Even when its price was raised, instead of depressing sales, volume continued strong due in part to the government's ban on cyclamates and Tang's immediate response with advertising noting that it used no artificial sweeteners. Sales were up 31% for the year.

In fiscal 1971, the Apollo program became less active, and a new Tang copy theme was presented. Sales continued to rise but at a slower rate, up only 19% for the year. In fiscal 1972, sales growth continued to slow. Tang prices had been increased to maintain profit margins close to historical levels, although some margin erosion had occurred as additional advertising and promotion funds were invested in the business. A flavor extension,

Grape Tang, was introduced and advertising and promotion funds to support it were diverted from the original Orange Tang. Another flavor extension, Grapefruit Tang, was introduced, with further diversion of funds. Finally, competitive powdered breakfast drinks began to appear. One firm introduced a product which offered more ounces in a package with the same price as Tang. Store private label brands appeared with packages the same size as Tang, but costing 40% less. Estimates of competitive prices versus Tang and competitive advertising are listed in Exhibit 2. Orange Tang sales for fiscal 1972 were up only 3%.

At about this time, General Foods began implementing a portfolio approach to its many businesses modeled after the Boston Consulting Group's terminology. Products were classified as "stars" which justified investment spending with the objective of high volume and market share growth; "cash cows" which had less growth potential but could provide positive cash flow which could be channeled to the stars, and should be managed for the objective of market share stability and positive cash flow; and "dogs" which should be dropped.

Early in fiscal 1973 (spring, summer and fall of calendar 1972) sales began to fall precipitously—as much as a 13% drop in some bimonthly periods versus previous year figures—and the product group became increasingly concerned over the issues of advertising copy and marketing spending. Exhibit 3 shows Orange Tang sales and marketing spending figures from fiscal 1968 through mid-fiscal 1973, as well as competing powdered orange beverage product sales and price differences between Tang and frozen orange juice concentrate (FOJC).

Mr. Jackson felt that a serious reassessment of Tang's marketing plans was necessary if Tang were to continue to justify its star classification in the GF portfolio. Early in fiscal 1973 he could see volume shrinking and could see that Tang would not meet its goal set in the company's 1973 Annual Business Plan of $7 million contribution after marketing costs.

Tang's gross margin was approximately $3.15 per 10½ lb. unit; marketing costs were primarily the amounts spent on advertising and promotion.

Mr. Jackson felt that a further price increase to deliver profits was infeasible. Product line extension (new flavors) to increase volume was no longer favored by the product group. No copy alternatives to the NASA theme had been developed and tested. The primary area of leverage seemed to be marketing spending, but where spending levels should be set to deliver sufficient profits next year *and* assure sustained sales growth was not clear to Mr. Jackson. Also, the proportions of funds that should be spent for advertising and for promotion were equally unclear. Historically, the spending balance for Tang had been roughly 50%–60% for advertising, 40%–50% for promotions in prior years. But there was uncertainty that these historical spending patterns were best, given the current status of the brand.

In order to meet fiscal 1973's financial goals while the regrouping was taking place, planned advertising spending was reduced to a yearly rate below $3.0 million, whereas $4.0 to $4.5 million had been planned and current advertising themes were pulled off the air. Promotional spending for immediate sales impact was increased by $800,000. Media choices were examined and revised. Development and testing started on new advertising copy based on authority identity figures; for example, a female with a Ph.D. in nutrition, who was also a mother, who fed her family Tang. Product improvement programs were started.

Finally, the product group accelerated two related research projects which were begun late in fiscal 1972 to determine via statistical methods how Tang's marketing budget should be determined and allocated.

THE PLANNING MODELS—BACKGROUND

Early in 1972 at the request of Mr. King, two models had been put into development. The purpose of these models was to aid the product group in analyzing the problem and in making decisions regarding optimal total marketing spending and advertising/promotion split. Although not initiated expressly because of the present sales slump, the impetus for hastening development of these models came directly from the brand's depressed performance. In particular, Mr. King wanted both present diagnostic analysis and future planning put on a more quantitative basis. He felt sure that his market research support staff could help in finding relationships between advertising and promotional spending on the one hand, and both short-run and long-run sales and profitability on the other. Messrs. King and Jackson wanted the models to answer some specific questions:

1. What would sales and profit response be to varying levels of total advertising and promotional spending?

2. Within those levels, what advertising/promotion split would be most efficient?

3. Building up to the above, what is more efficient in each of Tang's geographical sales districts:[5] allocating all TV advertising dollars to national network TV, or putting varying amounts into each district via the use of (more expensive) spot TV?

4. Again building up to the above, what were the optimal amounts of advertising and promotion to allocate to each district—the amounts that would lead to the most sales and profits in each district?

The last two questions were important in their own right. General Foods had moved from the allocation of total funds to sales districts based on only the district BDI (Brand Development Index, or the ratio of sales per household in that district to sales per household nationally), thereby spending more where

penetration was better, to an allocation that took into account not only BDI but the media costs in each district. But Messrs. King and Jackson reasoned that each district could have a unique responsiveness to spending in the form of increased sales per ad dollar or increased sales per promotion dollar. If they could estimate these district response levels, they could allocate funds based on responsiveness, as well as cost and BDI, and achieve even greater spending efficiency. They could also make a major contribution to the corporation if this method of analysis could be applied to other products.

To aid in analyzing and making these decisions, Mr. Jackson decided that two separate and distinct models should be built and their results compared. One was to be built in-house by Mr. Mike Goldberg, who was a marketing information services' operations research specialist assigned to work with the Tang and other product groups. Mr. Goldberg was a recent MBA graduate who had joined the company late that spring as a marketing research analyst. Although he had had limited quantitative experience prior to his MBA training, he was interested in operations research and his assignment upon joining General Foods was to aid in applying quantitative methods to brand management functions. The Tang model was the first major assignment that he undertook as a member of the marketing research staff. The second model would be developed by the management science group of Tang's advertising agency, Young & Rubicam.

Mr. Jackson gave several reasons for the parallel research efforts. He said he had full confidence in the in-house OR Group, but the OR Group had had to take on assignments for many other products as well. Mr. Jackson, therefore, wanted a cross-check on the group's work. He also wanted the agency group to participate in the study so that the agency would be tied into at least some of the conclusions and thus work better with the product group to implement those conclusions. The cost of each model was minimal—the in-house model was charged to Tang's existing research budget,

---

[5] The field sales force handling Tang and the division's other products was organized, at that time, into 21 geographical districts which roughly corresponded to television media ADIs (areas of dominant influence). Thus the sales reporting and control systems, as well as advertising and promotional execution, were done in terms of these geographic sales districts.

and the agency model cost less than $15,000. Mr. Jackson said he truly desired alternate views so as to make the best possible decisions about spending recommendations. Finally, Mr. Jackson knew that the backing of two models to justify his recommendation would carry more weight. His hope, of course, was that the two models developed independently would generate parallel results and reach the same conclusions.

In commissioning the models to be developed, Mr. Jackson wanted the models to incorporate both short-run and long-run time frames so that the brand group could answer the larger question of investment spending (star status) versus short-run profitability (cash cow status) for the brand, and so could justify its recommendations on that issue to GF's top management.

Prime data sources were in-house shipment and spending information, Nielsen store-audit data on Tang and competitive retail sales, and advertising agency data on costs of network and spot TV for each district. Putting this data in usable form presented some problems. TV advertising dollars, both network and spot, had to be compiled from past years' data. Because of different TV delivery costs in different areas, any attempt to relate sales to advertising would not only have to input advertising dollars spent, but also a measure of how much consumer impact these dollars had. Thus advertising dollars were converted to Gross Rating Points or GRPs (100 gross rating points equalled one impression per TV household per time period). Promotional dollars spent in past years had to be compiled for consumer promotion and trade promotion categories. Sales of competitive products in aggregate and by brand had to be compiled from sparse data. All this data for the geographical districts had to be rearranged into consistent time frames and consistent geographical areas.

Examples of national data used as input to the models are found in Exhibit 3. Examples of geographical data by district used as input are found in Exhibit 4.

Once the data were in hand, the agency and in-house model building efforts proceeded independently, and though the research strategies chosen by each group were similar in their overview of the problem, they differed substantially in the execution of their respective analyses. The two groups' approaches were similar in that both framed the problem in two parts, the first part being an estimation of sales response to advertising expenditures, and a second part being a resource allocation procedure that used the response estimates to suggest how marketing budgets should be set and apportioned among advertising, promotion and geographic areas. In the response estimation phase, the research approaches diverged with respect to how they attempted to account for a variety of intervening market variables and in their treatment of temporal and geographic effects. In the resource allocation phase, the research approaches used conventional marginal cost-benefit analysis methods and differed only with respect to the underlying estimated response functions.

ESTIMATING SALES RESPONSES TO ADVERTISING AND PROMOTION

The in-house response estimation procedure was the more straightforward of the two and was based on a regression equation of the following form:

$$S_{i,t} = a_{0,i} + a_{1,i} A_{i,t} + a_{2,i} P_{i,t} + a_{3,i} D_{i,t} \quad (1)$$

where

$S_{i,t}$ is the estimated sales in the ith territory in time period t;

$A_{i/t}$ is the number of GRPs impacting in territory i in time period t;

$P_{i/t}$ is the number of promotion dollars impacting in territory i in time period t'

$D_{i/t}$ is the percentage of retail outlets carrying Orange Tang in all package sizes in territory i in time period t;

$a_{0i}, a_{1i}, a_{2/i}, a_{3/i}$ are response coefficients estimated by the regression analysis.

Mr. Goldberg had decided to include the distribution variable, $D_{i,t}$, when he found it improved the equation's "fit" with the data summarized in Exhibit 4 for any particular territory. In an attempt to adjust the equation to show the diminishing effects of advertising over time, Mr. Goldberg modified the variable $A_{i,t}$ so that it would reflect the cumulative effects of both present and past period's advertising. The modification he made was of the form:

$$A_{i,t} = A_{i,t} + \sum_{m=1}^{M} R^m A_{i,t-m}$$

where R was a number less than one which indicated what proportion of a given period's advertising was thought to have impact in the succeeding period, and M was the number of prior periods for which these carryover effects were to be accounted. The NASA-based message strategy, in an independent prior study, had indicted that R, when defined as a form of advertising retention rate, was found to be 0.80. This was assumed to be a practical maximum and the message quality of other Tang campaigns would be adjusted in the model by judgmentally lowering the value of R. Since only three years of quarterly data were available, Mr. Goldberg let $M = 12$ throughout the response estimation part of the study. As an example, using these assumptions, the carryover effect from one prior period was $(.8)^1 (A_{t-1})$, and from three prior periods would be $(.8^1) A_{i,t-1} + (.8^2) (A_{i,t-2}) + (.8^3) (A_{i,t-3})$. Obviously, higher powers of R approached zero, thus estimated carryover effects diminished relatively quickly.

Since the response coefficient $a_{1,i}$ described an upwardly sloped straight line, it implied that increased values of $A_{i,t}$ would yield sales returns without limit at the same rate as long as adver-

tising expenditures were increased. Though this was known to be unrealistic, the linear model fit the data better than any curvilinear models that Mr. Goldberg had tried. The model was made to conform to expected practice by assuming that the true response curves were really S shaped and that the values of $a_{i,1}$ described Tang's recent responses along the linear portion of the curve. Mr. Goldberg and the product group worked together to determine judgmentally where the upper and lower tails of the assumed response curves should be set on one hand so that increased spending would indicate no further sales increases and, on the other hand, so that threshold spending levels necessary to have any effect on sales would also be specified. Figure 1 illustrates the in-house model's relationship between sales and advertising.

The response coefficients of the in-house model were estimated on a territory-by-territory basis using the 12 quarterly observations of sales, advertising GRPs, promotion dollars, and distribution percentages from fiscal 1970, 1971 and 1972. When the territorial response coefficients had been determined and when they were applied to the actual data from

FIGURE 1

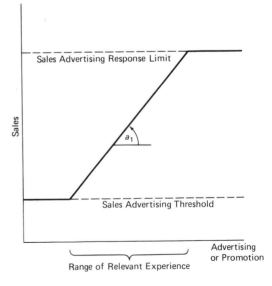

fiscal 1973 spending plan for each of the 26 territories, they predicted 1973 nation-wide sales of 4.5 million units. Taking into account results through late fall of calendar 1972 (almost three quarters into fiscal 1973), the brand group's best estimate of full fiscal year 1973 volume was about 4.3 million units. Considering that the model's inputs took into account little or no competitive experience, the model's prediction appeared to be quite accurate. The model's 26 separate advertising response coefficients and 26 promotion response coefficients, along with the judgmentally determined thresholds and upper response limits, were the essential inputs to a resource allocation model.

The Young & Rubicam response estimation model used the same information required by the in-house model and also utilized demographic data from each territory. Probably the most significant difference was in the structure of the regression analysis used by the agency model, which used regression analysis rather than judgment to estimate curvilinear responses to advertising and promotion. The agency model used a different procedure for accounting for territorial differences. Finally, the agency model treated the entire country as a single universe, rather than treating each sales territory independently. This last point was important, since the data were broken down into 26 territories and 12 quarters. The data base for the agency regression analyses was 312 observations instead of the 12 observations for an industrial district. As a result, the agency model could handle more independent variables with greater statistical reliability.

The agency response estimation model was built in two steps. The first step was to show how *changes* in sales occurred as functions of advertising GRPs and promotion dollars. The second step was to determine and demonstrate how the direct sales-advertising-promotion relationships should be modified due to interactions with distribution by package size, price differentials with competition, existing sales levels, demographic factors and seasonality. (For example, if improved distribution tended to increase sales, what effect, if any, would improved distribution have on the ability of advertising to generate sales?)

The agency model's structure was evolved from the following regression equation:

$$S_t - S_{t-1} = a_0 + a_1 A_t + a_2 P_t \qquad (2)$$

where S_t and S_{t-1} are the sales (per capita) of a given district at periods t and $t-1$ respectively

A is the (per capita) advertising in time period t,

P_t is the (per capita) promotion in time period t,

a_0, a_1, a_2 are coefficients estimated by regression analysis.

The agency Director of Management Sciences described the next steps in the model building procedure as follows:

We hypothesized that the sales response to advertising would display a pattern of diminishing marginal return. To test that hypothesis, the advertising variable was expressed as a quadratic function. In other words, in addition to regressing S_t against A_t and P_t, we also regressed S_t against a quadratic function of S_t *and* A_t and against a lagged sales variable, S_{t-1}, forming a measure of sales retention. The resulting equation had the following form:

$$S_t = a_0 + a_1 A_t + a_2 A_t^2 \\ + a_3 P_t + a_4 P_t^2 + a_1 S_{t-1} \qquad (3)$$

When this was done, the signs of a_1 and a_3 were positive and the signs of a_2 and a_4 were negative, which meant, of course, that the partial derivative of S_t with respect to A_t (the sales increase with an increase in advertising) was smaller as A_t grew larger. In other words, the sales relation to advertising exhibited a diminishing marginal return.

At this point an exponential fitting program was used to build a new equation for purposes of extrapolation since equation 3 when used for purposes of extrapolation resulted in sales values that approached minus infinity when carried forward over many time periods. The extrapolation equation, which was consistent with the diminishing, curvilinear marginal returns concept supported by equation 3, was of the following form:

$$S_t = a_0 + a_1 [1 - e^{-bA}t] + a_2 P_t + a_3 S_{t-1} \quad (4)$$

Equation 4 recast the advertising variable, A_t, into an exponential form of e, the base of natural logarithms; b was a coefficient estimated by means of a least squares exponential fitting program. Structuring the advertising variable in this manner resulted in a relationship between S_t and A_t that was curvilinear, with a size and rate of change that are indicated by a_1 and b as illustrated in Figure 2, and showed diminishing returns from larger expenditures. Equation 4 also permitted the estimation of the sales asymptote with increased advertising, which was interpreted as the maximum "advertising leverage."

The second step of the agency's response

FIGURE 2

General Form of Agency Model's Advertising Response Function

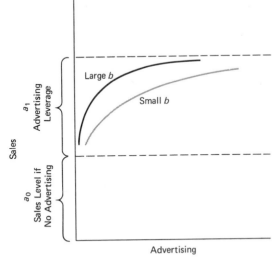

Notes: Under conditions where all other factors are constant, a_1, the coefficient of $(1e^{-bAt})$, denotes the sales difference between no advertising and unlimited advertising, a quantity called "advertising leverage"; b, the coefficient of A_t, indicates the rate at which incremental advertising taps the remaining sales potential due to advertising leverage.

model building was to determine whether certain potentially interactive factors should explicitly be accounted for in the model of equation 4. The procedure involved searching via some rather complex estimation procedures for values to include in L, a modifier of the coefficient a_1, which altered equation 4 as follows:

$$S_t = a_0 + a_1 L [1 - e^{-bA}t] + a_2 P_t + a_3 S_{t-1} \quad (5)$$

As the value of L changed, the estimate of advertising leverage would also change, in response to whatever variables were included in the definition of L. For example, Figure 3 shows the type of relationship that was found to exist between sales and the level of distribution at various advertising spending levels. At any level of advertising, higher levels of distribution were associated with higher estimated sales. Furthermore, the incremental sales growth between \$2 million and \$3 million advertising spending was everywhere greater than the incremental sales growth estimated between \$3 million and \$4 million advertising spending, as was earlier suggested in Figure 2. Finally, the difference in sales between any two levels of spending was greater as the level of distribution became larger. In short, advertising leverage was found to be related to the level of distribution.

In this situation, L was set equal to D^{c_1}, where D was the distribution level in a territory and c_1 was a coefficient estimated via exponential least squares estimation procedures. L eventually came to be defined as:

$$L = D^{c_1} M^{c_2} S^{c_3}$$

where M was a demographic measure of the population in a sales territory, S was measure of the existing sales level, and c_1, c_2 and c_3 were coefficients found by the analysis. L was thus a composite coefficient that adjusted advertising leverage according to distribution, demographics, and existing sales levels in a territory. An examination of the advertising interactive effects of seasonality, package size distribu-

FIGURE 3

**Estimated Orange Tang Sales Growth
under Different Levels of Distribution
and Advertising Spending**

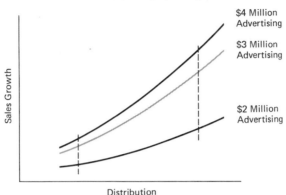

tions, promotion, and price differentials with competition were found *not* to be sufficiently significant to retain in the computation of L. One measure of the improvement that L contributed to equation 5 was that it improved the t value of a_1 from about 8.0 to about 20.0, indicating a large increase in the association between advertising and sales when interactively weighted by intervening market and marketing factors. L became the measure of a sales territory's advertising leverage and hence advertising effectiveness. The range of sales territory advertising effectiveness figures were found to range between 0.8 to 1.5 times the national average by the agency model.

To estimate the long-term effects of advertising and promotion, the agency used a model which showed the extent to which cumulative advertising or promotion expenditures were related to a present period's sales level. The model was of the form:

$$S_t = a_0 + a_1 (A_t + A_{t-1} \ldots + A_{t-n}) \qquad (6)$$

where n was the number of preceding periods for which the estimated cumulative advertising effects were desired. The value of a_1, which was determined by the regression analysis, was an indicator of the effects of the sum of each

previous period's advertising on current sales, for any number of time periods for which data existed. A similar model was constructed using prior periods' promotional expenditures as the independent variable, and b as the estimate of long-term carryover effects of promotion:

$$S_t = b_0 + b_1 (P_t + P_{t-1} + \ldots + P_{t-n}) \qquad (7)$$

Using equations 6 and 7, it was possible to estimate the long-term carryover effects of both advertising and promotion up to n time periods. The agency found that the carryover effects for promotion expenditures were substantially lower than those for advertising. The agency later applied the carryover estimates to alternative advertising plans and showed the expected future incremental sales over n periods from a present advertising schedule. The incremental contributions resulting from those sales were then evaluated in terms of their net present value to the advertiser using a 15% cost of capital.

ALLOCATING MARKETING RESOURCES

With the results of their respective procedures for estimating how sales responded to advertising and promotion in hand, the in-

187

house group and the agency group followed similar procedures for evaluating alternative spending strategies. For decisions that involved choosing between competing sales territories and for choosing between advertising and promotion programs, the allocation procedure employed a marginal cost-marginal revenue framework. For example, assuming a fixed media budget and two sales territories with different sales response curves, the allocation procedure divided funds between the groups, such that the total budget was consumed and each territory's budget was set at that point on the sales response curve where the respective slopes were equal. District A, below, would receive $A and District B would receive $B, and both districts would show the same marginal rate of return, although their budgets might differ significantly.

In the case of the linear in-house models, funds were allocated only up to the judgmentally determined upper limit of territory responsiveness or to the equivalent of 2,250 GRPs, depending on which was lower.

Since each group had 26 advertising response functions and 26 promotion response functions, both the agency and the in-house allocation procedures could either apportion a fixed budget, or show an optimal budget, given relaxation of budget constraints. Furthermore, by using estimated carryover effects, each group could adopt either long-run or short-run planning horizons and demonstrate the temporal implications of a given spending strategy.

The expected contributions from a given media program were expressed by both alloca-

tion methods net of media costs, and this led to a different interpretation of implications for media scheduling between the in-house and agency groups. The in-house sales response model showed response curves of apparently sufficient slope to justify use of more expensive spot TV. Spot TV costs per GRP were roughly 60% higher than network in many areas. The agency sales response model did not justify the use of spot TV, and the agency recommended the use of spot TV only in the event competition in the powdered orange beverage category increased in certain districts.

With respect to competitive factors, the agency allocation model modified its Tang sales and profit projections based on assumed competing sales of 1.0 million, 1.5 million and 2.0 million annual units. The model assumed only 40% of competitive sales would come from market expansion, while the rest would come from taking sales away from Tang. The in-house model made no explicit adjustment for anticipated competitive sales.

RESULTS OF THE MODELING PROCESS

The GF operations group used the findings of the response estimation research and the allocation model to write a computer simulation program that facilitated trial of many alternative advertising strategies.

The user of the program could specify the advertising retention rate, the number of periods in the planning horizon, the product's estimated VGP or Variable Gross Profit per

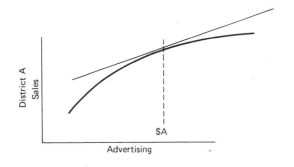

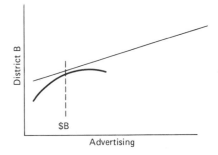

unit, and the program option desired: program calculates optimal budget, or program allocates given budget. The program then produced sales and profit forecasts and recommended budget allocations to network TV, spot TV and promotions by sales territory.

After running the model many times using varying budgets and examining the resulting sales and profit projections, the operations research group presented a report on the model's implications to Tang brand management. The report contained the following conclusions:

1. A minimum of $4 million per year in advertising expenditure is necessary to maintain volume at current levels. Any expenditures above this amount will lead to volume growth. Expenditures below this amount will result in erosion of the franchise. For maximum long-term sales growth and profitability, advertising levels in excess of $6 to $7 million per year seem necessary.

2. Promotional spending does not affect long-term growth, only short-run sales volume. However, some minimal level of promotions probably has become part of the cost of doing business because of the expectations of the user franchise.

3. Tang definitely appears to be a star brand today because of its responsiveness to marketing spending and resultant profitability. The amount of advertising support that it receives in the near future will in large part determine how long it remains a star.

The model's results for several proposed budget allocations with corresponding sales and profit forecasts are listed in Exhibit 5. Most of the in-house media allocations recommended about one-fifth of the media budget be placed in spot TV.

The agency's Management Science Department's report presented its conclusions in terms of short-term and long-term implications. Because of the significant advertising carryover effects which the agency found in its research, adopting a long-term time frame argued for higher advertising spending levels than if a one-year time frame were assumed. Assuming either a four-year or a six-year time horizon, the agency model suggested that a sus-

tained media spending level of $6.9 million was most profitable; assuming a one-year time frame media spending level of $4.0 million was suggested with the caveat that it would not sustain long-term sales volume. The one-year forecasts under 10 alternative advertising and promotion budgets are listed in Exhibit 6. Long-term forecasts for sales and profits at the ends of two, four and six years, assuming competitive sales increases of 0.5 million units per year of which 25% are claimed from Tang's franchise, are listed in Exhibit 7. The agency's media recommendations included no spot TV allocations, except for the Denver territory where spot TV was relatively low cost and for other territories only as competing products might exhibit rapid growth.

USING THE MODELS

Although Mr. Jackson had not reached a final evaluation of the models, and had not concluded whether the in-house model or the agency model might be the superior candidate for use and further development, he had used the models on three separate occasions in late calendar 1972. First, with the approval of the Beverage SBU manager, he used the models to show that Tang had advertising response rates that were historically higher than several other beverage products, justifying shifts in marketing funds to Tang.

Second, as the final quarter of fiscal 1973 approached, he found the models were helpful in supporting divisional requests for an additional marketing spending infusion of $260,000 in the last quarter of fiscal 1973 to help Tang achieve its fiscal 1973 sales and profit targets. The targets were in grave danger of not being met due to large advertising and promotion reductions midway through the year. In his request, Mr. Jackson had written:

The incremental $260,000 advertising and promotion spending should generate an incremental 18,700 units, or $60,000 variable gross profit for the quarter. Additionally, the $260,000 should pay back within one year. These conclusions are based upon mathematical analyses by both GF Operations Research and Young & Rubicam of the past three years of the Tang business. In brief, both analyses indicate that at current spending levels, Orange Tang marketing spending is generating approximately a 180% + return on advertising and promotional dollars within one year. Projections from the models are:

1974 projections, Mr. Jackson used corporate average advertising retention rates of .7 per quarter rather than the NASA .8 per quarter campaign retention rates; assumed a competitive cannibalization of 50% of projected Tang growth, and assumed a competitive volume of 2.5 million units in fiscal 1974.

		Time Period	
Incremental Funds: $260,000 in next quarter		Next Quarter	Next 4 Quarters
Y & R Analysis:	Incremental volume*	45 K units	130 K units
	Adjusted volume**	22 K units	65 K units
	Net contribution	$70,000	$205,000
In-House Analysis:	Incremental volume*	33 K units	140 K units
	Adjusted volume**	16 K units	70 K units
	Net contribution	$50,500	$220,000

* Incremental volume is the increase versus latest estimate of volumes under the current spending plan.

** Adjusted volumes assume: (a) Advertising retention rate is average, not the high rate used in the models; (b) Competitive developments reduce incremental volume impact by 50%.

Finally, in December 1972, Mr. Jackson was considering using the models to renegotiate the volume objectives of the fiscal 1974 Annual Business Plan. Midway through the 1973 fiscal year and before the models were available, Mr. Jackson had submitted a preliminary business plan for fiscal 1974. Management had responded by asking Mr. Jackson to try to find ways to increase fiscal 1974 target volumes by 225,000 units and target profits by $270,000, by increasing marketing funds only slightly. When the models became available, he prepared projections that showed that his original plan was consistent with the models' forecasts, but that the revised targets proposed by corporate management were infeasible according to the models. In making these fiscal

As he prepared his final draft of his proposed 1974 Annual Business Plan he summarized the situation, as shown in the table at the bottom of this page.

Mr. Jackson knew that the long-term recommendations of the models called for advertising spending to be increased from the present annual rate of about $4 million to about $7 million, while reducing the promotional spending from about $3.5 million to less than $2 million. He wondered whether this was the time to initiate a major change in advertising and promotion strategy for Tang, and, if so, how he should justify those changes to division and corporate management.

	Jackson's Initial Proposal for Fiscal 1974 ABP	Management's Counter Proposal for Fiscal 1974 ABP
Advertising and Promotion Budget	$7.9 million	$8.4 million
Judgmental Volume, Target, Units	3,900 K	4,125 K
Agency Model, Projected Volume, Units	3,800 K	3,860 K
In-House Model, Projected Volume, Units	3,924 K	3,990 K

EXHIBIT 1

General Foods Marketing Organization

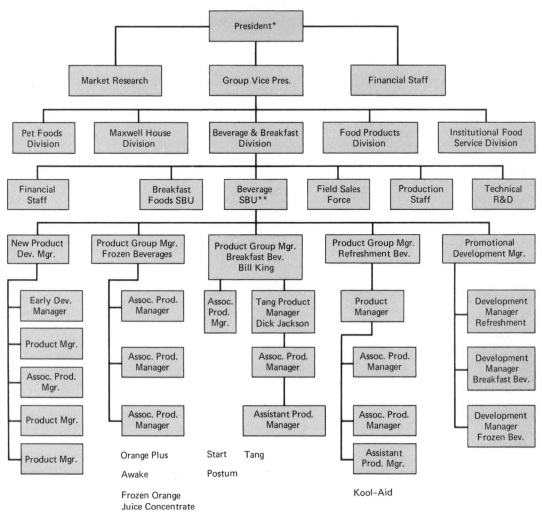

* Also attached to the President's office were support staffs for legal, purchasing, etc.

** The SBU Manager also had a staff supporting him with functions similar to the Divisional Staffs.

EXHIBIT 2

Recent Competitive Efforts

1. Tang price/unit over time (10½ lb. units)

Retail

Fiscal 1967	$8.42
Fiscal 1968	8.41
Fiscal 1969	8.38
Fiscal 1970	8.71
Fiscal 1971	8.70
Fiscal 1972	9.03
Fiscal 1973 (first half)	9.08

2. Competitive price estimates (10½ lb. units)

Retail

Fiscal 1972	$7.49
Fiscal 1973 (first half)	7.53

3. Competitive advertising ($000)

	Borden	*Lipton*
Fiscal 1972	59	—
Fiscal 1973 (first half)	278	630

EXHIBIT 3

National Data Available to Modelers

Period		Orange Tang Sales (1000s of 10½ lb. units)	Advertising ($1,000)	Promotion ($1,000)	Competitive Sales (1000s of 10½ lb. units)	Price Difference: FOJC—Tang (cents per 24 ounces)
Fiscal Year	*Quarter*					
1968	1	530	365	289	0	−0.5
	2	511	435	338	0	0.1
	3	514	303	330	0	1.4
	4	545	188	190	0	2.2
	Total	2,100	1,291	1,147	0	
1969	1	579	437	1,006	0	3.3
	2	615	331	51	0	3.8
	3	664	570	129	0	4.7
	4	850	1,176	471	0	6.0
	Total	2,708	2,514	1,657	0	
1970	1	801	992	254	0	6.3
	2	853	771	356	0	5.1
	3	872	802	128	0	4.8
	4	1,029	988	448	0	4.0
	Total	3,555	3,553	1,186	0	
1971	1	1,019	1,400	710	0	3.4
	2	1,002	806	549	0	3.2
	3	1,024	843	1,011	0	2.5
	4	1,197	1,110	684	0	2.1
	Total	4,242	4,159	2,954	0	
1972	1	1,088	883	339	0	3.4
	2	1,070	769	1,070	22	4.8
	3	1,052	864	1,006	50	5.1
	4	1,142	430	763	89	8.0
	Total	4,352	2,946	3,178	161	
1973	1	1,044	884	576	200	7.9
	2	965	363	851	271	7.9

EXHIBIT 4

Orange Tang Annual Sales, Advertising and Promotion Data by Sales District

District	Fiscal Year	Orange Tang Sales 10½ lb. Units per 1,000 Persons	Orange Tang Advertising 1,000's of Gross Ratings Points	Orange Tang Promotions Dollars per 1,000 Households	Spot Media TV Costs Dollars per 1,000 Household Impressions
1. Boston	1970	38.38	3.64	17.31	
	1971	43.58	6.92	35.10	
	1972	46.75	2.56	34.62	3.02
2. New York	1970	39.52	3.99	19.45	
	1971	46.92	5.21	37.22	
	1972	46.98	2.35	50.50	1.63
3. Syracuse	1970	55.31	3.58	21.74	
	1971	69.70	7.23	50.72	
	1972	69.25	3.11	54.73	3.26
4. Philadelphia	1970	62.46	3.79	24.78	
	1971	75.95	5.51	53.55	
	1972	72.27	2.69	69.21	2.59
5. Youngstown	1970	72.80	4.01	21.54	
	1971	88.27	6.71	49.12	
	1972	88.84	3.42	83.27	1.87
6. Washington, D.C.	1970	54.68	3.92	15.12	
	1971	63.74	6.26	43.95	
	1972	65.98	2.83	48.23	2.71
7. Charlotte	1970	55.80	3.51	13.29	
	1971	69.65	5.86	37.36	
	1972	73.06	3.03	31.65	2.52
8. Jacksonville	1970	34.38	3.15	9.07	
	1971	43.73	4.56	26.54	
	1972	47.32	2.73	21.27	2.76
9. Atlanta	1970	50.97	3.59	10.84	
	1971	55.11	6.32	27.63	
	1972	50.38	2.83	27.63	2.43
10. Memphis	1970	56.57	3.89	14.62	
	1971	57.84	6.57	37.73	
	1972	58.63	2.97	29.50	1.78
11. Detroit	1970	73.66	4.23	19.37	
	1971	91.35	7.18	62.19	
	1972	95.87	2.98	66.56	2.15
12. Indianapolis	1970	89.41	3.66	23.10	
	1971	92.43	5.75	65.71	
	1972	85.12	3.05	71.86	1.99
13. Cincinnati	1970	71.29	3.48	27.68	
	1971	91.75	5.93	56.21	
	1972	86.93	3.07	62.43	2.15
14. Chicago	1970	62.95	3.37	19.65	
	1971	81.58	6.09	57.69	
	1972	82.30	2.74	71.55	1.63

EXHIBIT 4 (cont.)

District	Fiscal Year	Orange Tang Sales 10½ lb. Units per 1,000 Persons	Orange Tang Advertising 1,000's of Gross Ratings Points	Orange Tang Promotions Dollars per 1,000 Households	Spot Media TV Costs Dollars per 1,000 Household Impressions
15. Milwaukee	1970	85.05	3.40	16.78	
	1971	97.58	7.53	57.44	
	1972	107.10	3.32	23.88	2.46
16. Minneapolis	1970	80.88	3.59	36.04	
	1971	95.60	5.52	78.60	
	1972	96.84	3.24	80.10	2.46
17. Omaha	1970	67.61	2.72	34.63	
	1971	97.16	4.27	71.93	
	1972	97.93	3.22	53.95	2.24
18. St. Louis	1970	65.48	3.99	24.61	
	1971	71.45	5.39	52.30	
	1972	72.95	3.07	53.52	2.20
19. Kansas City	1970	59.18	3.52	27.22	
	1971	68.41	5.05	58.23	
	1972	69.44	2.70	52.35	2.20
20. Dallas	1970	57.06	3.63	21.45	
	1971	62.85	6.45	49.41	
	1972	65.26	2.80	44.21	1.77
21. Houston	1970	47.35	3.69	16.88	
	1971	53.52	5.67	46.78	
	1972	58.14	2.93	32.79	1.77
22. Phoenix	1970	90.11	3.54	22.62	
	1971	114.24	5.12	80.82	
	1972	118.46	3.11	87.28	2.52
23. Denver	1970	85.11	3.61	24.57	
	1971	114.33	5.50	78.62	
	1972	128.70	2.81	69.71	1.52
24. Portland	1970	72.22	3.29	18.52	
	1971	86.06	5.98	70.63	
	1972	96.11	2.87	59.44	1.98
25. San Francisco	1970	55.14	3.59	21.11	
	1971	68.72	5.35	45.50	
	1972	61.25	2.36	52.04	3.40
26. Los Angeles	1970	56.06	3.98	16.32	
	1971	63.24	5.88	48.40	
	1972	71.42	2.39	56.93	2.45
National	1970	59.16	3.68	19.78	
	1971	70.58	5.96	49.16	(Network)
	1972	72.41	2.81	52.88	1.41

EXHIBIT 5

Findings of the In-House Model

This table summarizes the results of running the Resource Allocation System on the Tang Model

Yearly Budget	Advertising/ Promotion Split	First Year Volume (units)	First Year* Net Contribution	Years to** Peak	Peak Year Volume (units)	Peak Year Net Contribution
$ 7,000,000	$5,000,000 Ad 2,000,000 Promo	4,763,000	$ 8.0 million	3	5,152,000	$ 9.2 million
7,000,000	4,000,000 Ad 3,000,000 Promo	4,502,000	7.2 million	1	4,502,000	7.2 million
7,000,000	3,000,000 Ad 4,000,000 Promo	4,291,000	6.5 million	0	Will not Sustain Current Volume	—
7,000,000	6,500,000 Ad 500,000 Promo	4,806,000	8.1 million	4	5,381,000	9.9 million
8,000,000	7,000,000 Ad 1,000,000 Promo	5,409,000	9.0 million	3	5,790,000	10.2 million
5,000,000	4,750,000 Ad 250,000 Promo	4,203,000	8.2 million	4	4,500,000	9.2 million
10,000,000	8,000,000 Ad 2,000,000 Promo	5,816,000	8.3 million	2	6,092,000	9.2 million

* Net Contribution = Sales in units times Variable Gross Profit of $3.15 per unit minus Ad and Promo Costs.

** Peak year is the year in which Tang volume fails to grow significantly (starting with the given budget level and repeating it each year thereafter).

EXHIBIT 6

Tang One-Year Forecasts Estimated by Agency Model*

Yearly Budget ($ million)	Ad/Promotion Split ($ million)	If Competition Sells 1.0 Million Units		If Competition Sells 1.5 Million Units		If Competition Sells 2.0 Million Units	
		Tang Sales (million units)	Tang Net** ($ million)	Tang Sales (million units)	Tang Net ($ million)	Tang Sales (million units)	Tang Net ($ million)
$ 5.0	$2.5 A 2.5 P	3.68	$6.60	3.46	$5.90	3.23	$5.18
5.5	2.5 A 3.0 P	3.72	6.22	3.50	5.52	3.27	4.79
6.25	3.75 A 2.5 P	4.28	7.23	4.06	6.54	3.83	5.81
6.5	3.75 A 2.75 P	4.31	7.07	4.08	6.35	3.86	5.65
7.0	4.5 A 2.5 P	4.39	6.61	4.17	6.13	3.94	5.41

* Assumes 40% of competitive sales come from market expansion, 60% from Tang's franchise.

EXHIBIT 6 (cont.)

Yearly Budget ($ million)	Ad/Promotion Split ($ million)	If Competition Sells 1.0 Million Units		If Competition Sells 1.5 Million Units		If Competition Sells 2.0 Million Units	
		Tang Sales (million units)	Tang Net** ($ million)	Tang Sales (million units)	Tang Net ($ million)	Tang Sales (million units)	Tang Net ($ million)
7.5	4.5 A 3.0 P	4.42	6.42	4.20	5.73	3.97	5.01
8.0	5.5 A 2.5 P	4.48	6.11	4.25	5.23	4.03	4.69
8.5	5.5 A 3.0 P	4.50	5.67	4.27	4.95	4.05	4.26
9.5	7.0 A 2.5 P	4.57	4.89	4.34	4.17	4.12	3.47
10.0	7.0 A 3.0 P	4.59	4.45	4.36	3.73	4.14	3.04

** Net equals unit sales times unit contribution of $3.15 minus advertising and promotion costs.

EXHIBIT 7

Tang Long-Term Forecasts Estimated by Agency Model*

Yearly Budget ($ millions)	Ad/Promotion Split ($ millions)	Year 2		Year 4		Year 6	
		Tang Sales (million units)	Tang Net** ($ millions)	Tang Sales (million units)	Tang Net ($ millions)	Tang Sales (million units)	Tang Net ($ millions)
$ 6.5	$4.5 Ad 2.0 Promo	5.58	$11.1	5.68	$11.4	5.71	$11.5
$ 7.0	$4.5 Ad 2.5 Promo	5.63	$10.7	5.76	$11.1	5.79	$11.2
$ 7.5	$4.5 Ad 3.0 Promo	5.70	$10.5	5.83	$10.9	5.85	$10.9
$ 8.0	$6.0 Ad 2.0 Promo	5.75	$10.1	6.48	$12.4	6.55	$12.6
$ 8.5	$6.0 Ad 2.5 Promo	5.83	$ 9.9	6.56	$12.2	6.62	$12.3
$ 9.0	$6.0 Ad 3.0 Promo	5.89	$ 9.6	6.62	$11.9	6.69	$12.1
$ 9.5	$7.5 Ad 2.0 Promo	5.86	$8.9	6.91	$12.3	7.00	$12.6
$10.0	$7.5 Ad 2.5 Promo	5.94	$ 8.7	6.99	$12.0	7.08	$12.3
$10.5	$7.5 Ad 3.0 Promo	6.01	$ 8.4	7.06	$11.7	7.15	$12.1

* Assumes competitive sales increases of 500,000 units per year and 75% of competitive sales come from market expansion, 25% from Tang's franchise.

** Tang net equals sales in units times unit contribution of $3.15 minus advertising and promotion costs.

General Foods Corporation: Tang Instant Breakfast Drink (B)

In September 1972, Mr. Bill King, Product Group Manager of the Breakfast Beverage Product Group at General Foods, was faced with a most pressing and difficult decision. Sales of Orange Tang Instant Breakfast Drink[1] had been dropping precipitously and this decline was attributed to the wearing out of the

effectiveness of the brand's present advertising theme.

In order to reverse the downward sales trend, the brand's product group management and its advertising agency, Young & Rubicam, had prepared new advertising approaches. The new approaches, which had been prepared over the summer of 1972, took the form of four 30 second television commercials. Young & Rubicam (Y&R) had just completed the final phase of testing for the four commercials, and Mr. Frank Thomas, Y&R's Account Executive for Tang, had just completed his presentation of the findings. Mr. Thomas and Ms. Sharon Wolf, the Assistant Product Manager for Tang, had argued for the selection of one of the alternatives on the basis of qualitative research findings, but Mr. Dick Jackson, the Tang

---

[1] Tang is a trademark of the General Foods Corporation. A small amount of Tang, a dry crystalline powder, added to a larger quantity of water made a beverage described by the Tang package label as, "A natural tasting orange flavor breakfast drink. It contains more Vitamin C and A than like amounts of orange, grapefruit or tomato juice. Tang is not a juice, juice product, or soft drink mix. Tang is a nutritious instant breakfast drink."

This case was prepared by Harvey N. Singer, Instructor, The American University, and Mr. Gary R. Garrasi, Research Assistant, The Wharton School, under the supervision of Assistant Professor F. Stewart DeBruicker, The Wharton School. This case is to be used as the basis for class discussion and not to illustrate either the effective or the ineffective handling of a marketing administrative situation. Revised September, 1978.

Product Manager, disagreed with their choice on the basis of quantitative measures of brand related recall. Mr. Jackson argued instead for the selection of a different alternative, based on his interpretation of the research results.

Having had the benefit of hearing Messrs. Thomas and Jackson and Ms. Wolf defend their choices, Mr. King had to make the final selection and defend it to his Strategic Business Unit manager and division president.[2] It seemed that further copy development work was inadvisable, given the deteriorating sales record of Tang over the recent weeks.

BACKGROUND

General Foods Corporation (GF) was a leading manufacturer and marketer of grocery products, chiefly convenience foods. Its brands were among the best-selling products nationally in a variety of categories: coffee, frozen foods, gelatin desserts, puddings, soft drink mixes, syrups, semi-moist and dry dog food, and cereals. Going into the last quarter of fiscal 1973, sales were expected to be over $2.5 billion and net profit over $100 million for the year.[3] The company's long-term strength was built on large consumer franchises for its 400 products and some 30 of the food industry's best-known brand names, including Maxwell House coffee, Birds Eye frozen foods, Post cereals, Jell-O desserts, Gaines pet foods, and Tang instant breakfast drink.[4]

---

[2] Dollar and unit figures in this case are disguised.

[3] Fiscal years began on April 1. Fiscal 1973, for example, began on April 1, 1972 and ended March 31, 1973. Operating quarters were named for the month in which they ended: June, September, December and March.

[4] Tang's ingredients, in descending order of weight were: sugar, citric acid (for tartness), calcium phosphates (to regulate tartness and prevent caking), gum arabic (vegetable gum to provide body), natural flavor, potassium citrate (to regulate tartness), Vitamin C, cellulose gum (vegetable gum), hydrogenated coconut oil, artificial flavor, artificial color, Vitamin A, and BHA, a preservative.

In terms of General Foods' marketing organization, a Product Manager worked within a Product Group, which in turn worked within a Strategic Business Unit, or SBU. Until very recently the company's marketing activities had been organized by products produced by similar technologies or by products that had developed as line extensions of a single brand. In the early 1970s, when the company was experiencing pressure upon sales and profits in highly competitive convenience food and fast food restaurant markets, a major reorganization took place in the marketing structure.

Individual products and brands were placed into groups according to the SBU concept. This meant that all products, regardless of brand name or technology, which would be viewed in the same competitive framework by the consumer in the marketplace, were grouped and managed together, so that General Foods could concentrate on strategic markets as well as individual products. For example, all dessert products, whether Birds Eye frozen desserts or Jell-O gelatins, were place in the Dessert SBU. All main meal dishes, whether Birds Eye frozen vegetables or Minute Rice or Shake & Bake seasoned coating mixes, were placed in the Main Meal SBU. Tang was included in the Beverage SBU, along with frozen beverage products (frozen orange juice concentrate and Orange Plus), other breakfast beverages (Start and Postum), and refreshment beverages (Kool-Aid products).

The SBU managers reported to the president of one of the company's major divisions. Tang belonged to the Beverage and Breakfast Division. In addition, there were other divisions which marketed pet foods, grocery products (Dessert and Main Meal SBUs), coffee and institutional food products. Each division also had support staff personnel (staffs for finance, production, technical R&D, and a field sales force) to service its SBUs. Division presidents then reported to General Foods' top corporate management, which included the president, executive and group vice presidents, and support staffs at that level which provided service to all of the divisions—chief among them a financial staff and the corporation's Market Research Group.

An organization chart sketching these relationships is shown in Exhibit 1.

Product Managers at GF acted as both a marketing and business manager for their brands. On the marketing side, they had the mission of planning and executing all advertising, promotion, pricing and merchandising strategies for the brand. More generally, they had to compete for and coordinate all of their division's functional resources for their respective brands, which included technical inputs, marketing research, sales force activities, processing, and packaging. On the operations side, they were responsible for the brand's financial contribution through volume attainment, marketing spending, and pricing decisions. On the planning side, they worked with GF top management in the development of current fiscal year objectives and 5-year strategic plans.

Dick Jackson, Tang Product Manager, was assisted by an Associate Product Manager and an Assistant Product Manager, Ms. Sharon Wolf. They were supported by product development personnel and promotional merchandising personnel within the SBU. Mr. Jackson reported to Mr. Bill King, the Product Group Manager with the responsibility for Tang, Start, and Postum breakfast beverages. Mr. King in turn reported to the beverage SBU Manager.

TANG HISTORY

Tang powdered instant breakfast drink was introduced nationally in 1958. After its introduction, Tang volume grew slowly but steadily. Volume seemed to plateau as the product matured about 1962, so marketing spending was stepped up and new copy devised. Mr. Jackson indicated this gave the product a "shot-in-the-arm," and sales improved through 1968, when stagnation began

again. Accordingly, marketing efforts were intensified in fiscal 1969. The product was significantly improved, and sampling efforts, advertising, and promotional spending were increased. The brand's media copy program, which associated the product with America's space exploration efforts, was effective as the Apollo program became very active.

The Apollo launches and flight coverage provided frequent opportunities for media saturation and Tang sales were up 29% for fiscal 1969 over fiscal 1968.

In fiscal 1970, this approach continued and sales gained. Even when its price was raised, instead of depressing sales, volume continued strong due in part to the government's ban on cyclamates and Tang's immediate response with advertising noting that it used no artificial sweeteners. Sales were up 31% for the year.

In fiscal 1971 the Apollo program became less active so a new Tang campaign was introduced which was designed to enlighten and excite consumers about the "future" in space. This continued the Tang overall strategy of being associated with NASA and space, but shifted the campaign from actual space flights to potential space programs made feasible by the Apollo program. Sales continued to rise but at a slower rate, up only 19% for the year. In fiscal 1972, sales growth slowed. Tang prices had been increased to maintain profit margins close to historical levels, although some margin erosion had occurred as additional advertising and promotion funds were invested in the business. A flavor extension, Grape Tang, was introduced and advertising and promotion funds to support it were diverted from the original Orange Tang. Another flavor extension, Grapefruit Tang, was introduced, with further diversion of funds. Finally, competitive powdered breakfast drinks began to appear. One firm introduced a product which offered more ounces in a package with the same price as Tang. Store private label brands appeared with packages the same size as Tang, but costing 40% less. Estimates of competitive prices versus Tang and competitive advertising are listed in Exhibit 2. Orange Tang sales for fiscal 1972 were up only 3%.

It was about this time that Sharon Wolf began to question the efficacy of the Apollo copy theme. Ms. Wolf contended that both the client and the agency might be putting too much faith in the campaigns which were so closely associated with the hardware and mechanics of the space program. Though the overall strategy of space and NASA support were never in question, she felt that the brand group should consider alternative or backup strategies and campaigns in the event that something were to go awry with the space-associated themes.

Also about this time, General Foods began implementing a portfolio approach to its many businesses modeled after the Boston Consulting Group's terminology. Products were classified as "stars" which justified investment spending with the objective of high volume and market share growth; "cash cows" which had less growth potential but could provide positive cash flow which could be channeled to the stars, and should be managed for the objective of market share stability and positive cash flow; and "dogs" which should be dropped.

Early in fiscal 1973 (spring and summer of calendar 1972) sales began to drop precipitously—as much as a 13% drop in some bimonthly periods versus previous year figures—and the product group became increasingly concerned over the issues of advertising copy and marketing spending. Exhibit 3 shows Orange Tang sales and marketing spending figures from fiscal 1968 through mid-fiscal 1973, as well as competing powdered orange beverage product sales and price differences between Tang and frozen orange juice concentrate (FOJC).

Mr. Jackson felt that a serious reassessment of Tang's marketing plans was necessary if Tang were to continue to justify its star classification in the GF portfolio. Early in fiscal 1973 he could see volume shrinking and could see that Tang would not meet its goal set in the company's 1973 Annual Business Plan of $7 million contribution after marketing costs.

Tang's gross margin was approximately $3.15 per 10½ lb. unit; marketing costs were primarily the amounts spent on advertising and promotion.

Mr. Jackson felt that a further price increase to deliver profits was infeasible. Product line extention (new flavors) to increase volume was no longer favored by the product group. No copy alternatives to the NASA theme had been developed and tested.

THE CLIENT–AGENCY RELATIONSHIP

There was a corresponding management hierarchy for the Tang account at Y&R. Mr. Walter Roberts was the Senior Management Supervisor on the Tang account, and for a variety of other accounts handled by Y&R. Reporting to him were Mr. Jack Kelso, Account Supervisor, and Mr. Frank Thomas, Account Executive. Mr. Thomas was responsible for planning and directing the Y&R support staffs for creative, media and research, and for supervising the activities of two assistant account executives. Mr. Thomas and his staff were in regular contact with the members of the Tang product management group; it was not unusual for the agency and client management teams to meet daily when engaged in strategic planning activities. During these meetings, the agency and client managers functioned as a team, with the agency personnel often taking strong advocacy positions for points of view with which the client might disagree. Final responsibility for decision making rested with the client, however. At meetings between the agency and client, it was customary for the most junior members of the agency and client staffs to offer their analyses and recommendations first, with other participants joining the discussion in order of increasing management responsibility.

The relationship between the GF product management group and the agency group was unusually strong. Since Tang was one of Y&R's largest clients in terms of billings, both the agency and the product group viewed themselves as partners in the Tang business. In this regard, the agency's responsibilities encompassed not only developing advertising strategies and creating and producing copy executions, but providing marketing research and merchandising consulting services too.

A number of people from the agency's account management group and creative department had worked on the Tang account for several years. Some had become very successful as a result of Tang performance. In fact, one of the agency's Executive Vice Presidents had risen to his present position as a result of Tang successes. Additionally, members of the agency groups and the GF product group had had continuous professional contact with each other over the years on accounts other than Tang. This continuity of service on the part of both groups was considered to be one of the Tang marketing program's major strengths.

ORANGE TANG POSITIONING AND MESSAGE STRATEGY

Since its introduction in 1958, Tang had always been treated in a serious vein. The product group and agency had gone to great lengths to design strategy and copy that would portray Tang as a highly nutritional and flavorful breakfast drink substitute for fresh frozen orange juice concentrate. Over the years the product had been upgraded by increasing its vitamin content and improving its flavor. The issue of Tang's legitimacy as a substitute for frozen orange juice concentrate had been of continuous concern to both the product group and the agency.

The NASA testimonials used in the Tang media strategy throughout the late 1960s had provided a strong sense of legitimacy to the product, differentiating it from children's beverage mixes. Studies conducted by both GF and Y&R had confirmed that Tang consumers felt that if the product were nutritional enough to be selected by NASA to be included in the Apollo astronauts' diets when they traveled to the moon, then it must be nutritional enough

to serve to their families as a substitute for frozen orange juice concentrate or fresh orange juice.

Though sales in the fourth quarter of fiscal 1972 had declined compared to the same period one year earlier, Tang's basic message strategy was confirmed in an April 1972 meeting of the brand management team and members of the account team from Y&R. The product would continue to be positioned against fresh and concentrated frozen orange juice; private label and "me-too" competition would not be discussed in any way; and the target audience would continue to be married women between the ages of 18 and 44, with two or more children, and with at least a high school education. The copy development guidelines were that the nutritional story would continue to receive the major emphasis, and that emphasis upon flavor and the brand's NASA connection would be continued.

There was to be one noteworthy change in the copy strategy. Whereas the NASA themes had always associated the brand with the space program, the management group felt that the space theme was too "sterile" an environment to be realistic for many present users of the product. Therefore, the agency was instructed to develop thematic approaches that placed the product in more conventional consumption environments. Until satisfactory new copy approaches were developed, Mr. Jackson decided, with the approval of both Mr. King and the SBU Manager, that the planned annual media spending on Tang would be reduced for the remainder of fiscal 1973 from $4.5 million to only $3.0 million, and that consumer promotional expenditures would be increased by $800 thousand.

Sales in the first quarter of fiscal 1973 declined slightly from the level of the same period in 1972, but as the second quarter began, sales declines of over 10 percent from the previous year's levels were becoming evident nationwide, and an atmosphere of crisis descended on the product management group. In order to hasten new advertising copy development, some of the normal procedures were suspended, and a major econometric analysis of the historic sales effects of advertising and promotion spending was begun. The agency forwarded a Creative Work Plan to Mr. Jackson which described a so-called ''Authority Strategy'' aimed at further legitimatizing Tang as a substitute for frozen orange juice concentrate. Mr. Jackson approved the work plan, which is presented in Exhibit 4. In late June, Mr. Jackson decided to cancel the September quarter's planned advertising until more effective copy strategies could be developed, thus vividly demonstrating to the agency the product group's dissatisfaction with the performance of the then available advertising copy. This cancellation was approved by the SBU Manager.

THE SEARCH FOR
NEW COPY EXECUTIONS

Ordinarily, the typical advertising creative process involved the creation of a large number of copy executions by the agency's creative teams, with the executions then being reviewed by the agency's Creative Supervisor. After being reviewed, the executions would then be forwarded to Y&R's Associate Agency Creative Director. The Associate Agency Creative Director would either send the copy back to the creative supervisor for reworking by the creative teams or, if he was satisfied with the executions, would present them to Ms. Carol Alexander, the agency Creative Director, for inspection. If Ms. Alexander approved of the copy, she would authorize the Associate Creative Director to forward the executions to the Account Executive, Frank Thomas. Mr. Thomas would closely examine the copy executions for consistency with the product's strategy and, if the executions were satisfactory to him, would present them to Dick Jackson at GF.

The Product Manager would examine the copy executions with the Account Executive and, more often than not, would request that the copy be reworked according to his suggestions. When the revisions had been made by

the creative teams, the copy would then find its way back to the Product Manager via the account executive. If the Product Manager was satisfied with the revised copy, he would present it to Bill King, the Product Group Manager, who usually requested further revisions. When the Product Group Manager was satisfied with the executions, he would present them to the SBU Manager for his approval. Normally six to eight executions, in rough story board form, survived at this point in process.

After the SBU Manager was satisfied with the copy executions, the agency and product management group would meet and decide which executions should be rough produced on 16mm film. Once filmed, the commercials would be tested for their intrusiveness, i.e., their recall or memorability, and sales point communication. On the basis of these test results and the agency's recommendation, the product group management would select one or more of the commercials for 35mm production. Spot and/or network television time would then be purchased and the commercial would be televised nationally.

Both the agency and client viewed this process as an opportunity to provide the more junior members of their organizations with a valuable learning experience regarding the preparation of a product for market and the mechanics and intricacies of the agency/client relationship.

The severity of the present crisis did not permit the luxury of the normal procedures, however. To speed up the preparation of fresh advertising messages and new television commercials, the agency and the client agreed to reduce the number of formal copy presentations and to condense the decision making process accordingly.

The client group decided that the agency should make the initial presentation of the copy executions directly to Dick Jackson and Sharon Wolf, so that the Product Manager and his assistant could suggest copy revisions and begin winnowing out some of the weaker executions immediately. In the summer of 1972 the Tang

Associate Product Manager was on special assignment elsewhere at GF and was not a part of the decision making process.

By the end of June 1972, the agency had produced 16 storyboard executions for the product manager's consideration. At the initial presentation of the copy executions at the agency, the product manager and his assistant made several suggestions regarding copy content. The agency quickly revised the copy according to the client's suggestions and made a second presentation at the agency to Mr. Jackson and Ms. Wolf. This time only 8 of the executions were selected for further development. A third screening was convened, this time at General Foods in White Plains during the first week of July. This presentation was attended by the entire product management group as well as the agency account management group. The agency presented 6 copy executions to the product group (2 others had been eliminated since the second presentation) and recommended that the product group produce executions entitled ''Andromeda'' (the agency Creative Director's favorite), ''Food Selection,'' and ''Packing.''

After some discussion of the agency's copy analyses and recommendations, the product group management authorized the agency to produce those three executions. The client group also requested that the agency produce ''Lady Ph.D.'' as well. Sharon Wolf argued for this inclusion rather persuasively, even though no research had yet been conducted on any of the executions. Ms. Wolf contended that there was something about a real mother with an authentic scientific background serving her children Orange Tang for breakfast that seemed to overcome the legitimacy obstacle while depicting a situation to which the target audience could readily relate.

At the conclusion of this meeting, the client authorized the agency to go directly to 35mm production. This was a rather expensive procedure since the services of both professional production crews and professional actors and actresses had to be contracted. The cost of 35mm production was charged directly to the client. Due to the urgency of the present situation, Dick Jackson considered the cost of 35mm production of all four executions to be a necessary and unavoidable expense. Filming of the four commercials was contracted out to independent production companies and was completed at the end of July. Photoscripts of the completed commercials are presented in Exhibits 5 through 8.

COPY STRATEGY RESEARCH

The commercials were immediately put into a program of research designed to develop data to help management choose the most effective execution for use in the Fall media period, and to use as a basis for developing more refined executions of the winning concept later in the fall. The commercials were tested using focus group interviews and sample surveys of television recall. The focus group interviews were conducted by the agency in several shopping malls in early August. In the interviews, small groups of women typical of the target audience were invited to an informal screening of several commercials, then interviewed in groups to determine their feelings as to the commercials' intent and effectiveness. The results of the interviews provided qualitative guidance but due to their subjective nature they were considered only one ingredient in the mix of data and judgments used to make the final decisions on a set of executions. Mr. Thomas, the Account Executive, noted that most of the respondents seemed not to like the spokesperson used in the ''Lady Ph.D.'' commercial, but they did seem to respect her judgment in matters of choosing nutritious foods for her family. He believed, however, that unless that element of respect could be demonstrated in the sample surveys used in the TV recall testing procedures, he would have a difficult time selling the ''Lady Ph.D.'' execution to management. Interview summaries for ''Lady Ph.D.'' and ''Food Selection'' are presented in Exhibits 9 and 10.

The television recall tests were designed to

develop data of a more quantitative nature on large samples of viewers of the four commercials in a more realistic, in-home setting. The TV recall tests were conducted by GF's corporate marketing research group using standardized procedures that had been used to test past Tang advertisements. The procedures involved the "cutting in" of each of the four candidate commercials into the normal network commercial period on a nationally televised program. Next-day telephone interviews were then conducted in the respective market areas within 24 hours of the airing of the test commercials and questions were asked to determine their memorability and copy point playback performance. That commercial which achieved the highest level of memorability in excess of the historic Tang norm, and which best communicated the strategic copy points, would be selected for airing. Arrangements were made for the commercials to be inserted into the 9:24 P.M. slot in the CBS Thursday Night Movie, "Night Gallery," on September 7, 1972, in the following cities:

Execution	Cities
"Andromeda": 30	Atlanta, Hartford, Sacramento
"Food Selection": 30	Buffalo, Indianapolis, San Diego
"Lady Ph.D": 30	Cincinnati, Denver, Omaha, Syracuse
"Packing": 30	Minneapolis, Phoenix, Portland, Youngstown

The cost of the TV recall studies was approximately $14 thousand in out-of-pocket charges to the Tang budget.

The recall measurement procedure was a standard GF methodology which involved asking a hierarchy of questions to determine whether or not the respondent had in fact seen the commercial being tested, and if so, what level of awareness the commercial had generated for the respondent. There were two measures, not necessarily independent of one another, which were used to classify respondents into a hierarchical order that was roughly equivalent to the commercial's ability to pro-

mote accurate retention of intended copy points. The first measure was related to the level of cueing, or prompting, that was necessary in order to stimulate the respondent's memory of having seen (or not seen) the commercial.

As described in Exhibit 11 which is a flow diagram of the questionning procedure, three levels of prompting were employed: the first level was the category prompt, in which only the product category—orange breakfast drink—was used as a memory cue. The second level was the brand prompt, in which the respondent was asked directly whether or not she saw a Tang commercial last night on TV. The final level was the commercial prompt, in which the respondent who claimed to have seen the program in which the commercial was shown, but couldn't recall the commercial, was cued by prompts drawn from the dramatic storyline of the program before and after the airing of the Tang commercial. This was called the commercial prompt. The hierarchy of cues then, was:

Level of Prompting	Type of Prompt
Unaided	Category: "Did you see a commercial for a brand of orange breakfast drink?"
Aided	Brand: "Do you remember seeing a commercial for Tang last night?"
Prompted	Commercial: "Right after this scene, there was a commercial for Tang. Do you recall seeing this commercial?"

The second measure of the quality of awareness which each commercial promoted was based on the verbatim responses of the respondents when directly questioned about the commercials which they claimed they had seen. Seven questions, listed in Exhibit 12, were asked of each person claiming to have seen the commercial being tested. Based on whether or not the verbatim responses described the actual content of the commercial, respondents were classified as falling into one of the three categories: Proven recallers, Related recallers, or Incorrect recallers. Proven recallers had the highest levels of recall with respect to the message and format of presentation of the commercial. Related recallers showed a grasp of the basic content of the commercial though they were often less certain of the details of presentation. Incorrect recallers were those respondents who claimed to have seen the commercial, but whose verbatim descriptions of the commercial's content were highly inaccurate. Incorrect recallers were usually eliminated from the tabulations of results prepared in management summary form by the GF marketing research department, while Proven and Related recallers were reported both separately and in the aggregate.

The verbatim responses to the seven questions regarding the test commercial's content were coded by specific copy points and reported in the quantitative summary of the test. Finally, the verbatim responses were reported in a qualitative supplement to each test commercial's research report, and were often used by management to enrich their insight into the commercial's audience impact.

The GF marketing research department summarized the results of the TV recall tests in a brief memo that accompanied the four separate reports, each numbering about 18 pages of tabulated findings and about a like number of pages of verbatim transcripts. In the management summary, the research department concluded: "The total proven and related recall was above the Tang norm for Food Selection and Packing, at the norm for Lady Ph.D., and below the norm for Andromeda:"

to report: "Playback of all major copy points were below norm for Andromeda. Food Selection had superior playback on taste/flavor and convenience. Lady Ph.D. had superior playback on space association, vitamins and taste/flavor. Packing had superior playback on vitamins and convenience and average playback on nutrition." See the table at the top of page 206.

The research department's summary concluded: "Responses to special questions directed to recallers of Lady Ph.D. to elicit attitudes toward the presenter were generally positive and indicated that she was believable, convincing and seemed to lend an air of authority to the message. Responses to special questions to recallers of Andromeda to elicit attitudes toward the unique execution were generally negative."

The copy testing studies were completed in about half the normal time, and by mid-September the findings had been reported to both the brand group and the agency. Mr. Thomas, as the head of the administrative center for the copy development program, had prepared an analysis of the findings and with his colleagues from the creative and account groups, journeyed to what was to be the final decision making meeting in White Plains in late September.

At this meeting the agency group first presented and discussed the results of the TV Recall scores and verbatims, followed by a qualitative analysis of the strengths and weaknesses of each of the four commercial copy ex-

Percent of Commercial Audience (Unaided + Aided)

Measure	Tang Norm	Andromeda	Food Selection	Lady Ph.D.	Packing
Proven Recall	11	7	19	7	18
Related Recall	8	3	9	12	3
Proven and Related Combined	19	10	28	19	21

Additional recall tabulations are reported in Exhibit 13.

The marketing research summary went on

ecutions. Frank Thomas concluded his presentation with a recommendation that the client use the "Lady Ph.D." commercial to launch

Percent of Commercial Audience (Unaided + Aided + Prompted)

Copy Point	Tang Norm	Andromeda	Food Selection	Lady Ph.D.	Packing
Space Association	63%	46%	59%	66%	55%
Vitamins	53	23	43	66	74
Nutrition	29	8	20	24	29
Taste/Flavor	49	23	70	55	23
Convenience	37	15	48	34	45

the new advertising campaign. Mr. Thomas explained that although Food Selection scored highest on the TV recall tests, Lady Ph.D. seemed to be communicating the sales message better as indicated by the quality of verbatim responses associated with this particular commercial. The verbatim reports of the individual telephone interviews for "Lady Ph.D." and "Food Selection" covered over 54 pages of material and are not reproduced here for reasons of length. The subjective content of the verbatims is imperfectly, but adequately, conveyed by the focus group interview summaries listed in Exhibits 9 and 10. Sharon Wolf, assistant product manager, supported Mr. Thomas' position.

Dick Jackson, the Product Manager, however, disagreed with their line of reasoning. He contended that the quality of the verbatim responses should not be given so much weight in this particular instance as it normally would because of the rather large margin in recall scores in favor of "Food Selection." The product manager argued that although the "Lady Ph.D." verbatims were indeed richer qualitatively than those of "Food Selection," the latter's recall scores were nearly one and a half times greater than those of "Lady Ph.D." Further, Mr. Jackson stated that the quality of the "Lady Ph.D." verbatims would mean very little if consumers were unable to recall that "Lady Ph.D." was specifically associated with Orange Tang.

At that point of apparent impasse between the Assistant Product Manager and the Account Executive on one hand, and the Product Manager on the other, Mr. Bill King, the Product Group Manager, began his review of the situation. Everyone in the meeting was well aware that the shipments of Tang in the second quarter of fiscal 1973 had dropped well below the previous year's level, and further declines seemed likely in the absence of effective, fresh advertising copy.

EXHIBIT 1

General Foods Marketing Organization

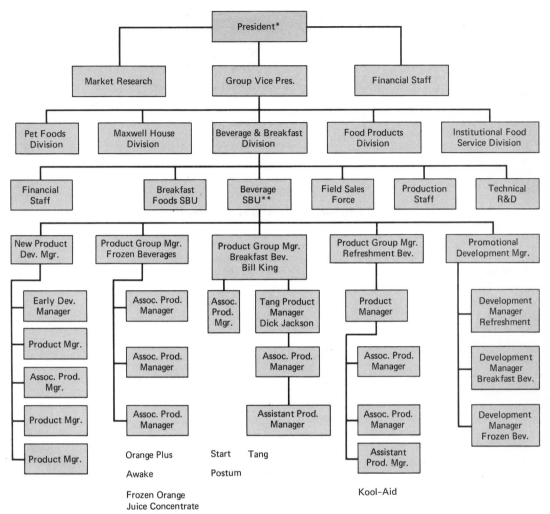

* Also attached to the President's office were support staffs for legal, purchasing, etc.

** The SBU Manager also had a staff supporting him with functions similar to the Divisional Staffs.

EXHIBIT 2

Recent Competitive Efforts

1. Tang price/unit over time (10½ lb. units)

	Retail
Fiscal 1967	$8.42
Fiscal 1968	8.41
Fiscal 1969	8.38
Fiscal 1970	8.71
Fiscal 1971	8.70
Fiscal 1972	9.03
Fiscal 1973 (first half)	9.08

2. Competitive price estimates (10½ lb. units)

	Retail
Fiscal 1972	$7.49
Fiscal 1973 (first half)	7.53

3. Competitive advertising ($000)

	Borden	Lipton
Fiscal 1972	59	—
Fiscal 1973 (first half)	278	630

EXHIBIT 3

Tang Sales and Marketing Spending History

Period		Orange Tang Sales (1000s of 10½ lb. units)	Advertising ($1,000)	Promotion ($1,000)	Competitive Sales (1000s of 10½ lb. units)	Price Difference: FOJC–Tang (cents per 24 ounces)
Fiscal Year	Quarter					
1968	1	530	365	289	0	−0.5
	2	511	435	338	0	0.1
	3	514	303	330	0	1.4
	4	545	188	190	0	2.2
	Total	2,100	1,291	1,147	0	
1969	1	579	437	1,006	0	3.3
	2	615	331	51	0	3.8
	3	664	570	129	0	4.7
	4	850	1,176	471	0	6.0
	Total	2,708	2,514	1,657	0	
1970	1	801	992	254	0	6.3
	2	853	771	356	0	5.1
	3	872	802	128	0	4.8
	4	1,029	988	448	0	4.0
	Total	3,555	3,553	1,186	0	
1971	1	1,019	1,400	710	0	3.4
	2	1,002	806	549	0	3.2
	3	1,024	843	1,011	0	2.5
	4	1,197	1,110	684	0	2.1
	Total	4,242	4,159	2,954	0	
1972	1	1,088	883	339	0	3.4
	2	1,070	769	1,070	22	4.8
	3	1,052	864	1,006	50	5.1
	4	1,142	430	763	89	8.0
	Total	4,352	2,946	3,178	161	
1973	1	1,044	884	576	200	7.9
	2	965	363	851	271	7.9

EXHIBIT 4

Key Fact

Orange Tang prime prospects, both regular and infrequent users, reflect a positive interest in the brand, yet are concerned about its legitimacy as a food product due to its powdered form.

Problems Advertising Must Solve

Due to OT's artificial form, most people do not believe it to be a legitimate substitute for FOJC at breakfast and, therefore, not as "healthy" and "good" for their families.

Advertising Objective

To reassure current users and convince infrequent users that OT is a legitimate substitute for FOJC and, consequently, is good for their families at breakfast.

Prospect Definition

Women who are characterized as mothers ages 18–44 with two plus children under 12 years of age with incomes of $10,000 plus living in A&B counties and users of FOJC and/or IBD. Attitudinally, these women are somewhat self-indulgent and have respect for authority. They are concerned with the well-being of their families and try to provide (not necessarily feed) them with a nutritionally adequate diet.

Principal Competition

FOJC is considered OT's primary competition and major source of volume. Lower priced IBD's are OT's secondary competition.

Promise

OT is a good-tasting, legitimate food product that helps you fulfill your role as the supplier of nutrition and health to your family by serving it at breakfast.

Reasons Why

1. Nutritious OT has a full day's supply of Vitamin C plus Vitamin A.
2. OT has a taste that can be enjoyed by the entire family and is especially liked by kids.
3. OT has been selected for use by the NASA astronauts.

Tone and Manner

The advertising must establish a sense of authority in support of the posture that Tang is a legitimate, serious food product. It must be consistent with the stature relationship between Tang and NASA.

Constraint Agreement

A consent agreement between GF and FTC prohibits statements "disparaging" to any natural fruit juices.

EXHIBIT 5

Andromeda Photoscript

YOUNG & RUBICAM INTERNATIONAL, INC.

CLIENT: GENERAL FOODS CORP.   LENGTH: 30 SECONDS
PRODUCT: ORANGE TANG   COMM. NO. GFOT2518
TITLE: "ANDROMEDA"

   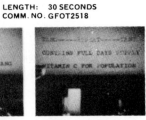

1. (SFX: TYPEWRITER)   2. (SFX: TYPEWRITER)   3. (SFX: TYPEWRITER)   4. (SFX: TYPEWRITER)

5. (SFX: TYPEWRITER)   6. (SFX: TYPEWRITER)   7. (SFX: TYPEWRITER)   8. (SFX: TYPEWRITER)

9. (SFX: TYPEWRITER)   10. (SFX: TYPEWRITER)

EXHIBIT 6

Food Selection Photoscript

YOUNG & RUBICAM INTERNATIONAL, INC.

CLIENT: GENERAL FOODS CORP.
PRODUCT: ORANGE TANG
TITLE: "FOOD SELECTION"

LENGTH: 30 SECONDS
COMM. NO: GFOT2517

1. (MUSIC THROUGH-OUT)

2. ANNCR: (VO) The Nutrition Team at the NASA Space Center

3. worked long and hard to come up with breakfast for outer space.

4. They looked at 28 versions of the scrambled egg ...

5. Spent months getting bacon crispy ...

6. Then they decided on an orange-flavored instant breakfast drink

7. straight from the super-market...

8. Tang. With a full day's supply of Vitamin C.

9. Good, nutritious Tang.

10. It passed the test.

EXHIBIT 7

Packing Photoscript

YOUNG & RUBICAM INTERNATIONAL, INC.

CLIENT: GENERAL FOODS CORP.
PRODUCT: ORANGE TANG
TITLE: "PACKING"

LENGTH: 30 SECONDS
COMM. NO. GFOT2516

1. (MUSIC THROUGH-OUT) WOMAN: (VO) If you were leaving for a day on the moon,

2. you'd have to pack a little differently.

3. You'd need a helmet, so you could breathe...

4. an extra-vehicular suit...

5. something special in the way of footwear...

6. and protective gloves.

7. But there's one scientific miracle that you could pack right from your kitchen table...

8. Tang. The orange-flavored instant breakfast drink

9. with a full day's supply of Vitamin C.

10. Tang. Good no matter where you're having breakfast.

EXHIBIT 8

Lady Ph.D. Photoscript

YOUNG & RUBICAM INTERNATIONAL, INC.

CLIENT: GENERAL FOODS CORP.
PRODUCT: ORANGE TANG
TITLE: "LADY P.H.D."

LENGTH: 30 SECONDS
COMM. NO: GFOT2520

1. MARY ETHIMION: I'm a mother of two children.

2. And I have a PHD in biological science.

3. You know a woman involved with science

4. wants to be sure her family gets their breakfast vitamins.

5. I know the astronauts use Tang,

6. and I am sure NASA took a lot of time and trouble to find good things for them.

7. Things that would maintain

8. their vitamin supply.

9. And Tang is a good source of Vitamin C and A.

10. We drink it all the time.

11. Mm. It really tastes

12. great.

EXHIBIT 9

Lady Ph.D. Group Interview Summary

COMMUNICATION OF PRODUCT MESSAGES

In both sessions, it was quite clear that virtually all of the respondents seemed to understand what was being said in the "PhD" commercial and all of the women played back the messages that Tang is "good for you" because of its vitamin content. In addition to pointing out that Tang is rich in vitamins C and A, the women came away with the impression that Tang is a "well researched product" that is scientifically accepted as being nutritious. The NASA reference seemed to be picked up by many of the women too, and the women seemed to realize that if Tang is being sent to the moon with the astronauts, it must be a nutritionally superior product. Consequently, the NASA reference, plus the presence of a Ph.D. endorsing the product, seemed to convey the intended claim that Tang is a "good product" for spacemen and earth families.

REACTIONS TO THE COMMERCIAL

In reaction to the commercials and its messages, there was a mixed response, with users of Tang, interestingly enough, being particularly inclined to react favorably to the Ph.D. theme and to the idea that this knowledgeable "authority" was endorsing the product (which, incidentally, is a product they themselves use). These women seemed to accept the commercial as being both believable and convincing in conveying the idea that Tang is nutritionally "good for you." Spontaneously, several volunteered that Tang has apparently been well researched by scientists and many of the women seemed to be impressed with the idea that a "mother with her doctorate in science" believed in the product enough to integrate it into her family's diet. It is important to note that, in the course of discussing this commercial, several of the women latched on to the "mother/scientist" role of the presenter and the respondents reacted positively to the fact that this woman thinks enough of Tang, from a professional vantage point, to use the product in her home. As one woman remarked, "my children are first in my mind and I want to take good care of them." Virtually all of the users in the session, as well as several nonusers of the product, spontaneously commented that a scientist obviously has more "authority" and "knowledge" about the product than the average housewife and yet, at the same time, she is a mother of two children who naturally wants the best for her family. In a sense, the women seemed to feel that the commercial combined "the business and home life together."

A number of these women went on to describe "Lady Ph.D." as being a "capable" woman whose first concern is her children's health and well-being. The respondents seemed to feel that this spokesman was "happy and healthy" looking, "neat and attractive" and "realistic" in that she isn't the typical model type but rather an ordinary housewife who is the mother of two children. A few of the respondents volunteered that they could "relate to her" on a personal level because of her age and her appearance. In total, it should be recognized that the differences in the reactions of users and nonusers can possibly be attributed to the fact that the Ph.D. mother, as the spokesman for the product, seemed to reinforce for the users the idea that they are "good mothers" in that they are concerned about their children's health and diet and, at the same time, to offer them additional rebuttal for the reservations they themselves might have had about the product.

EXHIBIT 9 (cont.)

Among the nonusers, however, the reactions to the commercial were somewhat different. While some of the women seemed to respect the opinion of a "mother/scientist" as being an authority on nutrition, others in the session, upon being directly probed, indicated that they couldn't really relate to or identify with "Ph.D." in spite of the fact that they respect her educational background. On a more personal level, they seemed to perceive the woman as being "cold," "stiff" and somewhat "distant." One or two of the respondents commented that she didn't seem like a "homey" person, but rather, like an "efficient" person who is more "executive" than motherly.

Yet, despite their tendency to disassociate themselves from the presenter, the nonusers also agreed that her education makes her a qualified person to speak about the nutritious elements of Tang and, at least on an intellectual level, they too were able to take away the essential "nutrition" message of the commercial.

EXHIBIT 10

Food Selection Group Interview Summary

COMMUNICATION OF PRODUCT MESSAGES

In both the sessions with users and nonusers, there seemed to be some confusion on the part of the respondents as to what the "Food Selection" commercial was saying about the product. Those who seemed to understand the commercial played back the idea that the astronauts' menu is carefully planned and selected and that Orange Tang has been chosen over other orange drink products because of the superior taste and nutritional value. The women, who seemed to grasp the idea that selectivity has gone into making Tang the drink of the astronauts, pointed out that nutritionists have sampled and evaluated many foods and came up with Tang as the best in the orange drink category. The nutritional quality of the product, rich in Vitamin C, was played back frequently by these respondents and the astronaut association seemed to confirm the fact that Tang must be nutritious. Several of the women seemed to say, "If it is good enough for the spacemen, then it should be good enough for us."

Others in the session were baffled as to what point the commercial was trying to make. Some of the women were confused as to why the eggs and bacon were being rejected. Interestingly enough, because of their lack of understanding, they played back the message that Tang is a complete breakfast drink . . . "a product that can replace bacon and eggs." These respondents failed to understand the intended idea that NASA is highly selective in choosing food that is suitable for the astronauts and, consequently, they got the impression that Tang will take the place of a full course breakfast.

Interestingly enough, some of the respondents found the commercial confusing because they could not understand the purpose of showing bacon and eggs. A few of the women added that Tang contains vitamins whereas bacon and eggs are protein foods and they could not see the connection or purpose for showing both kinds of foods. Thus, it was apparent that a number of the women were confused about what the commercial was trying to say about Tang.

EXHIBIT 10 (cont.)

REACTIONS TO THE COMMERCIAL

On the whole, the respondents in both Denver as well as St. Louis seemed to react negatively to the way in which this commercial was presented. In fact, it appeared that the "Food Selection" commercial seemed to antagonize many of the consumers interviewed, which in effect, caused many of the respondents to disbelieve the product claims.

A number of the respondents specifically commented that they were "turned off" by the actors in the commercial who were portraying the researchers. As one woman put it, "I would expect my little boy to react this way over eggs but not an adult." Others also seemed to disapprove of the way in which NASA was represented in the commercial, and here too, the women commented that "researchers would never look or act like the people in the film." Furthermore, because the women seemed to perceive the commercial as being "cartoon-like" and "spoofish," it was difficult for them to relate to the product messages as being real and credulous. In a sense, science and research seem to be a matter taken more seriously by the respondents and they seemed to resent the way it was portrayed in the commercial. By parodying NASA in a "Mickey Mouse" way, many of the women immediately seemed to discredit what was being said.

In light of this objection to the commercial, the respondents went on to object to the hard sell approach of the commercial. These consumers from the midwestern states complained that the pace of the commercial was "too fast" and "pushy." One woman in particular objected to the "driving tempo" that was constant throughout the commercial. Several women in each of the sessions mentioned that they resent being told to use a product because "the astronauts use it" and these women went on to say that they feel quite qualified to judge for themselves whether a product is good or not. In a sense, they seemed to feel "put down" by the commercial and tended to feel that it was "stupid" and "insulting."

Consequently, in spite of the fact that some of the women were getting the message that Tang is a nutritious orange drink, the claim itself seemed to be ignored in light of the presentation. Surprisingly, even those women who were using Tang commented that a commercial like "Food Selection" would never motivate them to buy the product.

EXHIBIT 11

Flow of Questions to Determine Level of Prompting Required to Stimulate Recall

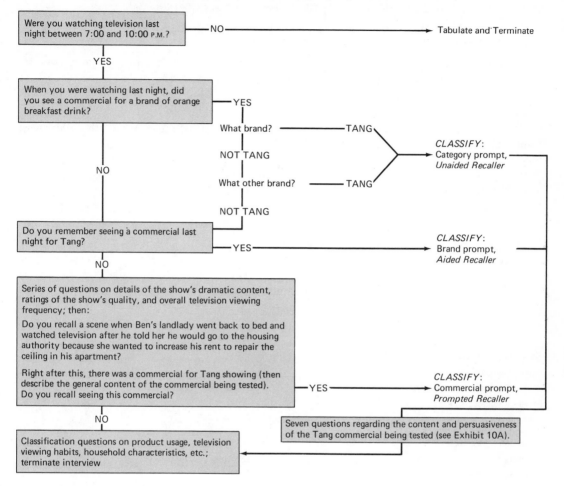

EXHIBIT 12

Open Ended Questions Used to Determine Whether
Proven Recaller, Related Recaller, or Inaccurate Recaller

1. Please tell me anything at all you remember about the Tang commercial you saw last night? (PROBE FOR DETAIL, RECORD VERBATIM)

2. In addition to what you already told me, what did the commercial look like? What did you see in the Tang commercial last night? (PROBE, RECORD VERBATIM)

3. What (else) did they say about Tang in last night's commercial? (PROBE, RECORD VERBATIM)

4. What ideas about Tang were brought out in the commercial last night? What other ideas were brought out? (PROBE, RECORD VERBATIM)

5. Advertising generally tries to tell you what is good about a product and tries to convince you to buy it. What did the advertising for Tang tell you in order to convince you that it is good or that you should buy it? (PROBE, RECORD VERBATIM)

6. Did the commercial make Tang seem different from other brands? (If yes, in what ways did it make it seem different?) (PROBE, RECORD VERBATIM)

7. Have you ever seen this very same commercial before?

EXHIBIT 13

Results of Recall Test*

Commercial	Andromeda		Food Selection		Lady Ph.D.		Packing	
Number of Contacts	2266		4048		3745		3470	
Number of Program Viewers	170		249		206		214	
Size of Commercial Audience	128		160		148		146	
Proven Recallers	N	%	N	%	N	%	N	%
Unaided (Category Prompt)	9	7%	34	15%	6	4%	11	8%
Aided (Brand Prompt)	2	2%	7	4%	1	1%	15	10%
Prompted (Commercial Prompt)	0	0%	1	1%	3	2%	8	5%
Total	11	9%	32	20%	10	7%	34	23%
Related Recallers								
Unaided (Category Prompt)	3	2%	5	3%	3	2%	2	1%
Aided (Brand Prompt)	1	1%	8	5%	16	11%	3	2%
Prompted (Commercial Prompt)	1	1%	6	4%	7	5%	5	3%
Total	5	4%	19	12%	26	18%	10	7%
Incorrect Recallers								
Unaided (Category Prompt)	5	4%	7	4%	5	3%	2	1%
Aided (Brand Prompt)	4	3%	8	5%	6	4%	4	3%
Prompted (Commercial Prompt)	3	2%	3	2%	2	1%	1	1%
Total	12	9%	18	11%	13	8%	7	5%
No Claimed Recall	100	78%	91	57%	99	67%	95	65%
Grand Total	128	100%	160	100%	148	100%	146	100%

* Percentages may not add due to rounding.

CHAPTER 8

Pennsylvania Pen Company

In the late spring of 1971, John Holt, the Marketing Manager of the Pennsylvania Pen Company, was evaluating test market results for a new product: the "Pilot" pen. This was a throwaway plastic ball-point pen which had been test-marketed by Pennsylvania Pen in Boston during March and April of 1971. One objective of the test market was to evaluate the impact of pricing the pen at 15¢, as opposed to 19¢ (retail).

The Pilot pen was in direct competition with Waterman Bic Corporation's 19¢ line of ball-point pens. Pennsylvania Pen had not previously marketed ball-point pens in this price range. However, it did market some pens in the 25¢ to 50¢ range. It also held a strong position in the mechanical *pencil* market,[1] with items in the 85¢ to $5.00 retail price range. Finally, it was a dominant firm in the butane cigarette lighter industry. These products were distributed through the same channels as ball-point pens.

This case was prepared by Ralph G. M. Sultan, Chief Economist, Royal Bank of Canada, and revised by Assistant Professor F. Stewart DeBruicker, The Wharton School, as the basis for class discussion rather than to illustrate either effective or ineffective handling of an administrative situation.

THE WRITING INSTRUMENT MARKET

Following World War II, the advent of disposable pens had greatly changed the industry. What used to be a low-volume, high-

[1] A mechanical pencil is a metal or plastic writing device in which the refillable lead is advanced by twisting the barrel of the pencil, as needed.

dollar-margin business had become a high-volume, low-dollar-margin business.

In 1970, United States manufacturers shipped 1.89 billion units of writing instruments of all types, valued at $279 million at factory prices. Of these, ball-point pens constituted 1.39 billion units, valued at $152 million. Nonrefillable, or "throwaway," ball-point pens accounted for 0.7 billion units, valued at $59 million.

Over 1950–1970, volume growth averaged about 14% per year. However, in 1970 there was a decrease in industry unit volume and a leveling off of factory sales dollars (see Exhibits 1 and 2). Some sources attributed the decline to a filling of the channels of distribution. Continued growth was exhibited by fiber-tip pens and nonrefillable ball-point pens. Nevertheless, even their growth was leveling off:

Annual Volume Percentage Increase

	Porous Tip Writing Markers	Nonrefillable Ball-Point Pens
1968	30%	8%
1969	20%	10%
1970	10%	2%

In 1971, the fine-line porous pen (or felt-tip pen) market was estimated to be $70 million at retail. The major competitors in this market were the Paper Mate Division of Gillette Company, and the Parker Pen Company.

Some industry observers questioned whether the low-priced ball-pen market (less than 49¢) was still growing. Bic had created a mass market for low-priced ball-point pens. As the idea of a disposable pen took hold, the average number of pens purchased per person per year rose from 14.3 in 1951 to 20.5 in 1967. At some point, it seemed, the consumer might fill his (or her) "pipeline" and industry growth would decline.

Demand for ball-pens was highly seasonal. The "Back-to-School" period, late August through September, accounted for about 50% of yearly sales at the retail level. Market research in March 1971 indicated that many retailers were still selling off their "Back-to-School" specials from the previous September.

DISTRIBUTION

The industry relied upon stationery and office supply jobbers (distributors) to provide local warehousing. These middlemen carried thousands of different items and were not captive of any one manufacturer. Their function was usually confined to showing off manufacturers' *promotional* items, to order-taking, and to carrying inventory stocks. A distributor received about 15% margin. Distributors and retailers were generally interested only in a manufacturer's volume items. They did not desire complete product lines from a single source.

Manufacturers used jobbers to move their products into retail channels. Many supplemented the jobbers' efforts with their own detail salesmen working at retail. Primary sales contacts were regional and local distributors, and certain chain-store accounts. Detail salesmen spent much of their time writing orders, which were then executed through the distributors.

Concerning retail distribution, Mr. Robert Adler, President of Waterman-Bic, had observed, "Disposable pens are like candy bars and razor blades." Independent retail stores were serviced by distributors. Chain outlets were serviced through regional warehouses. Chains were sold by calling on the national buying offices. Salesmen attempted to have their products placed in the catalogue of products available to the local chain-store manager. Detail men frequently were not allowed in the chain retail outlets.

Some retail outlets (e.g., variety and discount stores, and college bookstores) carried a vast variety of writing instruments, often duplicating items with different brands. Other stores were characterized by a narrow product line, with little or no item duplication. Such stores usually carried the dominant brand only, and only the largest volume products. Characteristic of this second type were the

"Mom-and-Pop" grocery stores, and the chain health and beauty aid stores, such as RIX (Boston) and CVS (Boston), which constituted a large and growing outlet for low-priced writing instruments. In high-volume outlets, the ball-pen display was frequently large (see Exhibit 3).

Writing instruments purchased by office and other commercial buyers, and writing instruments purchased for use as promotional items, amounted to about 40% of manufacturers' sales dollars in 1970.

WATERMAN-BIC

The low-priced pen market was dominated by one pen manufacturer, Waterman-Bic. Complete information on the strategy and performance of Waterman-Bic was difficult for PPC managers to assemble, due to the secretive nature of its owner, Marcel Bich, and his privately held French company. However, it was known that (see Exhibit 4) Waterman-Bic had a United States sales volume of $37 million in 1970, up from approximately $17 million in 1966. In 1967 Bic earned an estimated $10 million on $60 million in worldwide sales. Bic's U.S. market share was estimated to be 50% to 60% of all retail units sold. Bic manufactured and sold ball-point pens priced from 19¢ to 98¢. In 1970, Bic sold over 430 million pens in the United States and Canada.

Bic had paid $1 million in cash for 60% of the stock of Waterman Pen Company. According to press accounts, it required seven years and $10 million of additional investment to make the company profitable. Bich applied to Waterman the formula that had been successful for him in Europe: mass advertising of an improved, cheap product. His United States managers are reported to have advised him to concentrate on making a more expensive pen, with a metal clip and an opaque body, but Bich chose a different approach, with great success.

The company's clear plastic nonrefillable, nonretractable pen had been selling at the suggested retail price of 19¢ since 1962. After introduction of the clear barrel pen, the company broadened its line of nonretractable pens by introducing other models with different barrel colors, styling and different point sizes for specific uses, including an accountant's fine-point pen and a pen designed for use in photocopy work. These pens were available at suggested retail prices ranging from 19¢ to 49¢.

Mr. Robert Adler, President of Waterman-Bic, explained the original strategy: "We came into the industry when it was beginning to change over to a mass business and we had the good fortune to come in not knowing anything. So we tried the unconventional."[2] Doing the unconventional meant passing up big department stores for a time in favor of "Mom-and-Pop" stores, especially those located near schools. While other pen companies concentrated upon the top 30% of retail outlets in terms of sales per outlet, Bic discovered that certain of the "Mom-and-Pop" stores could perform equally as well as a large department store.

Bic products were sold by approximately 120 company salesmen to about 9,000 accounts, which include tobacco, drug and stationery wholesalers, as well as variety, drug and food retail chains. The wholesale accounts in turn distributed the company's products to retail outlets. In 1970 no single account contributed as much as 2% of the company's sales, and the ten largest accounts together contributed approximately 10% of such sales. Sales to industrial and commercial customers for their own use were generated principally by the company's own sales force. Pens carrying the purchaser's name, trademark, corporate symbol or other such imprint were sold for advertising specialty purposes, through outside agencies and by specialized company salesmen.

In 1968, the company introduced a retractable and refillable ball-point pen, the "Bic Clic," at a suggested retail price of 49¢ and its refill at 25¢. In the spring of 1971 the company

---

[2] "Waterman-Bic—On the Ball with the Ball Point," *Nation's Business,* December 1970.

commenced distribution of a 98¢ four-color retractable pen manufactured by Société Bic in France.

In 1967, Waterman-Bic produced about 480 million pens in the United States. In 1968, production was reported to have dropped to 325 million units. In 1969, Bic's volume was approximately 330 million units. In 1970, it moved up to 400 million units. One observer believed the drop in production may have been a result of competition from new fiber-tip pens which entered the market strongly in 1968. During 1970, nonretractable pens accounted for 93% of the company's unit sales, retractable pens for 6%, and refills for 1%.

Bic pens were advertised on national television networks and in national publications with broad circulation. Consumer advertising was concentrated in two major campaigns of three months each, starting in January and August in order to have the greatest impact during back-to-school periods. In addition, the company maintained a cooperative advertising program whereby it shared the cost of certain advertising done by retailers. It also provided a wide variety of product displays, seasonal sales promotion material and other advertising and merchandising aids to retail outlets.

In 1971, Bic was placing emphasis on selling through food stores. *Advertising Age* related: "A promotion aimed at shaking up supermarket people so that they come to realize the 'profit power of ball pens' has been launched by [Bic], which does 15% of its retail volume in food stores, and wants to increase that figure at least 10%. . . . The drive began with a mailing to 1,600 headquarters buyers influencing the purchasing for 90,000 food chain stores. The mailing included an eight-page brochure which put ball-pen annual volume at $150 million, with a profit margin of 50%." About 7% of total ball-pen sales were going through food outlets.[3]

There were trade rumors that late in 1971 Bic would enter the porous (felt-tip) pen market

with a $3 million advertising campaign to be handled by Wells, Rich, Greene, Inc. It was also reported that Bic was planning to introduce a 29¢ retractable ball-point pen, with a youth-oriented $1.5 million advertising campaign to be handled by N. W. Ayer.

In the spring of 1971, in Boston area markets, Bic appeared to be emphasizing "trading up" to the 25¢-and-above priced pens. In many stores the 19¢ pens were not even available.

PENNSYLVANIA PEN COMPANY

The Pennsylvania Pen Company (PPC) had traditionally been one of the major writing instrument manufacturers in the United States. In recent years its prominence had been whittled away by the inroads of new companies (e.g., Waterman-Bic) and new products (e.g., felt-tip pens). Currently, the mechanical pencil and butane lighter were PPC items which the trade accepted unequivocally. From this base, Pennsylvania had followed a policy of introducing new products regularly, in the hope of generating "excitement" in the trade.

In 1970, PPC had an operating loss of $1 million on sales of $32 million (see Exhibit 5).

Because of financial pressures, the company had recently spent relatively little on consumer or trade advertising. As an alternative, Pennsylvania relied on three factors: First, marketing a full line of writing instruments, merchandised as a unit. The PPC display cabinet was designed to offer strong point-of-purchase appeal, tying the movement of other Pennsylvania products to the successful mechanical pencils and lighters. Second, the long-established and respected Pennsylvania name was used to gain trade acceptance. Third, Pennsylvania relied on its skilled sales force to gain and maintain distribution. Pennsylvania's support of its salesmen came in two forms: through giving them prepackaged deals (2 for 1, etc.) to take to the trade, and through having a regular introduction of new products. The salesmen called on distributors and, occasionally, retailers.

---

[3] "10% Increase in Supermarket Sales Is Aim of Bic Push," *Advertising Age,* June 23, 1969.

It was estimated that Pennsylvania's market share in writing instruments had declined from 25% (in 1958) to 6% (in 1968). PPC managers estimated that between 125,000 and 150,000 retail outlets carried PPC products. Pennsylvania was largely a "retail" marketer. Only a small portion of its sales were to commercial outlets.

PPC's sales force was organized under 5 division managers who managed 32 district managers. Most district managers had one factory representative who "detailed" the independent retailers and who wrote "turnover orders" which were given to the distributor. These salespeople sold other PPC products as well as writing instruments.

THE PILOT PEN

The success of Bic seemed to indicate that the market for ball pens was price-sensitive. New automation techniques at PPC made it possible to offer a stick pen at 15¢ retail. The quality and writing characteristics of the new 15¢ ball-pen were judged to be superior to the Bic pen. Displays had been set up in several college bookstores in Philadelphia and consumer acceptance of the product appeared to be good. PPC believed that it was selling one pen to every three Bic pens in those outlets. Bookstore managers were enthusiastic about the product. Pennsylvania's initial marketing mix thinking for the new pen consisted of the following elements:

1. Packaging: *Bulk* 4- and 8-dozen bulk displays; with only limited use of blister packs.[4]

2. Branding: Pennsylvania's name would differentiate the product.

3. Channels of distribution: Normal channels and specific outlets such as college bookstores.

4. Price and margins: 15¢ retail price, and normal margins to retailer (40%).

---

[4] A blister pack is a transparent, plastic-enclosed cardboard package in which one pen would be encased. The cardboard backing provided some means for hanging the blister pack on a rack, provided space for a printed advertising message, and discouraged pilferage.

5. Advertising: None.

6. Promotion: Introductory free goods.

7. Product: Blue ink only, initially.

THE MARKETING PLAN

The following working assumptions were made:

Price: Consumers are highly price-sensitive as demonstrated by the success of the 19¢ Bic. The 4¢ price differential (between 19¢ and 15¢) will be the strongest element in the marketing mix and will be significant enough to induce initial purchase. Some blister packs would be provided at 19¢, but emphasis would be upon the 15¢ pen sold in bulk.

Brand Image: The Pennsylvania name connotes quality in the consumer's mind. It will have appeal to both trade and consumer.

Quality: Mass production quality will equal or exceed that of prototype models. Quality and writing characteristics will be superior to that of the 19¢ Bic. Quality will certainly influence repurchase. Ink quantity will be double Bic's, giving twice the writing distance. This has been proven in tests by an independent testing ageny.

Packaging: Initial packaging would be concentrated upon the bulk display in order to permit a low retail price. Some blister packs (one pen per blister pack) would be available, according to trade demand. Bulk retail displays will be central to the over-all marketing plan for the Pilot pen.

Typical pricing would be as follows:

	Bulk	Blister Pack
Consumer pays (per pen)	15.00¢	19.00¢
Retailer margin (40%)	6.00	7.00
Price to retailer	9.00¢	12.00¢
Distributor margin (15%)	1.35	1.80
Manufacturer price	7.65¢	10.20¢
Shipping and delivery cost	1.00	1.00
Net manufacturer revenue	6.65¢	9.20¢

Direct costs were expected to be as follows:

In bulk:	Direct cost: 3.5¢ per pen
In blister packs:	Direct cost: 5.0¢ to 5.5¢ per pen

(Direct costs encompass prime manufacturing costs, plus a modest assessment for manufacturing, general, and administrative overhead. There is no allowance for marketing expenditures or profit.)

Bulk Display: The plan involved marketing the Pilot pen in "bulk displays." These would present the consumer with a loose collection of Pilot pens, in a plastic bin, from which to choose. In-store display stands for the pens in bulk could be provided for the following cost:

Large Bulk Display Cost	35¢ each
Small Bulk Display Cost	25¢ each

The display would be in the form of an open plastic cup in which the pens would stand (on end), attached to a cardboard placard which could be placed on a counter top in the store.

To achieve planned distribution, 70,000 large display units and 70,000 small display units seemed to be an appropriate mix. These would contain the following number of pens, in an initial stock:

Total Bulk Distribution	=	140,000 outlets
70,000 (Large Bulk Display)	=	6.72 million pens
70,000 (Small Bulk Display)	=	3.36 million pens
Total		10.08 million pens

Blister-Pack Display: Each blister pack would contain one pen. The plan was initially to achieve distribution of one million blister packs (i.e., one million pens) in this form, supplementing the bulk displays.

Introductory Offer: For the introductory offer, PPC would offer one free unit of merchandise (blister pack or bulk) with each unit of merchandise purchased, to aid in achieving distribution. A possible budget for the introductory offer was:

Costs	
Cost of Goods (Bulk) 10 million @ 3.5¢	$350,000
Cost of Goods (Blister) 1 million @ 5.5¢	55,000
Cost of Displays (Large and Small)	42,000
Total Introductory Expense	$447,000
Revenues	
Bulk: 5 million @ 6.65¢	$332,500
Blister: 1/2 million @ 9.20¢	46,000
Displays (Large and Small)	42,000
Total Introductory Revenues	$420,500
Net Introductory Gain (Loss)	($ 26,500)

THE BOSTON MARKET TEST

In the spring of 1971, John Holt authorized a market test of the Pilot pen. Pennsylvania marketing managers were uncertain as to the best retail price. Also, they were not sure of the sales impact of the blister pack versus the bulk display. To provide answers, a market test was conducted in Boston.

The market test was formulated to measure the impact of retail price and whether the Pilot pen display was located near the check-out register or in the "pen department" of the retail outlet. Ancillary data was obtained on the relative uniqueness of the Pilot pen display (whether other brands shared the same display space) and on the degree to which the competing Bic line of stick pens was available in each retail outlet. The major measure of consumer response was the sales volume of Pilot pens vs. the total sales of Pilot pens and the competing brands of similarly priced stick pens, although some attempt was made to gather data on the attitudes of the trade and of consumers of throwaway pens. The market test was organized according to the following design:

	Retail Price	
Display Location	19¢	15¢
Check-Out Register		
Pen Department		

COMPARABLE MARKETS

The test markets would be confined to eastern Massachusetts, to conserve time and money. Comparable markets were identified from *Sales Management* magazine. Markets were matched in terms of total retail sales, range of services offered, purchasing power, newspaper circulation, population, and other relevant criteria.

The markets ultimately selected were: Framingham, Malden, Medford, and Waltham.

The validity of selecting these four markets was then tested by referring to the *1970 Survey of Buying Power,* published by *Sales Management* magazine (see Exhibit 6). Comparisons of the four cities on their respective figures for Effective Buying Income (generally equivalent to "disposable personal income"), Net Cash Income (money income remaining after taxes) and the Buying Power Index (a weighted index converting three basic elements—population, Effective Buying Income and retail sales—into a measure of a market's ability to buy, expressed as a percentage of the U.S. total potential) showed that they were reasonably well *matched,* for the purpose of the test. The reason for omitting such obvious trade areas as Boston and Cambridge was that no other comparable areas could be found in eastern Massachusetts, for matching.

MARKET OUTLETS

Within these four markets, retail outlets were chosen in relation to their current participation in the sale of writing instruments.[5] The original test plan called for ten outlets per market, or a total of forty. However, due to a shortage of pens during the first half of the test, and also the predominance of large chain stores in the markets, the number of eventual outlets was limited to nineteen.

The selection of retail outlets was accomplished on a non-random basis due to their

---

[5] Food stores were not listed due to Pennsylvania's insignificant distribution through these outlets.

limited number, and by the practical problems of gaining store cooperation. Some high-volume discount stores were not fully represented.

Department stores were not selected because of their extremely small participation in disposable ball-pen sales in the four areas. Other outlets, such as some discount stores, (Zayre, CVS), were unreceptive to placement of open *bulk* displays, due to pilferage problems. Blister packs were unavailable until very late in the test—too late to obtain placement in these outlets.

The test was run for six weeks. Bulk displays were replaced with blister packs in three outlets only for the remaining two weeks of the test.

In order to obtain cooperation from the local store managers and purchasing personnel in chain organizations, the cooperating merchants were not charged for the merchandise.

Actual pen movement was audited weekly at each outlet. A physical inventory of the Pilot disposable pen, along with competitors—primarily Bic—was taken by the researchers each week. This information, plus purchase tickets, permitted a calculation of the number of pens sold to consumers each week.

In the various outlets, the retail price was varied—some being at 19¢ (for bulk display) and some being at 15¢. The blister packs, when they became available, were priced at 19¢. The 19¢ blister pack was put only into outlets where the Pilot pen was already priced at 19¢.

One key variable was whether the Pilot pen display was in the "pen department" or at the cash register checkout counter. In two outlets, bulk displays were placed at *all* of the cash registers.

Another key variable was whether or not the display location for the Pilot pen was "unique," or whether the display was located within the display area of other pens. The idea was to assess the degree of special in-store position which the Pilot pen received.

The calibre of the competitive display, and breadth of the competitive product line showing, were also assessed. This ranged all the way from very comprehensive Bic pen displays, including all products, to very narrow product selections for the competing ball-pen products. The rating of competition was:

"Excellent:" Good to excellent Bic line.

"Fair:" Majority of Bic pens displayed were not the normal 19¢ or 25¢ but were broken out of a blister-pack dozen.

"Poor:" Bad Bic representation.

Throughout the test, there was no indication that the competition had changed their pricing or displays at any of the test outlets.

One complication was a religious holiday during the week ending April 10. Although stores were not closed on that day, some students were not in school. And students were not in the public schools the following week (Easter vacation).

TRADE AND CONSUMER ATTITUDES

Following the test, additional qualitative data were collected by interviewing chain buying managers, distributors, and store managers. (See Appendix A.) As a separate part of the testing program, 45 college students in Boston were given the Pilot pen. Four to six weeks later they were interviewed regarding their attitudes toward the pen (see Appendix B).

RESULTS

Store-by-store tabulations of the results of the market test are presented in Exhibits 7 through 11.

EXHIBIT 1

Writing Instrument Market Statistics: 1951–1969

	1951 Estimated Number of Units Shipped	1951 Estimated Total $ Value at Factory Prices (Exclusive of Tax)	1952 Estimated Number of Units Shipped	1952 Estimated Total $ Value at Factory Prices (Exclusive of Tax)	1953 Estimated Number of Units Shipped	1953 Estimated Total $ Value at Factory Prices (Exclusive of Tax)	1954 Estimated Number of Units Shipped	1954 Estimated Total $ Value at Factory Prices (Exclusive of Tax)
Fountain Pens	41,033,972	$ 45,127,081	37,378,744	$ 42,253,086	40,133,581	$ 42,162,936	40,303,465	$ 41,692,878
Ball Point Pens	52,831,167	13,496,605	68,192,148	18,204,989	122,516,826	38,050,624	162,003,879	48,892,059
Mechanical Pencils	70,559,080	27,042,691	63,801,600	24,427,062	60,966,228	22,725,246	57,634,371	21,973,372
Desk & Dip Pen Sets	2,063,859	4,568,966	2,211,942	5,139,576	1,822,924	4,720,744	1,787,677	4,500,395
	166,488,078	$ 90,235,343	171,584,434	$ 90,024,713	225,439,559	$107,659,550	261,729,392	$117,058,704

	1955 Estimated Number of Units Shipped	1955 Estimated Total $ Value at Factory Prices (Exclusive of Tax)	1956 Estimated Number of Units Shipped	1956 Estimated Total $ Value at Factory Prices (Exclusive of Tax)	1957 Estimated Number of Units Shipped	1957 Estimated Total $ Value at Factory Prices (Exclusive of Tax)	1958 Estimated Number of Units Shipped	1958 Estimated Total $ Value at Factory Prices (Exclusive of Tax)
Fountain Pens	40,817,881	$ 40,212,341	42,814,844	$ 41,453,432	40,852,416	$ 38,237,624	44,873,330	$ 35,003,706
Ball Point Pens	210,708,038	50,603,066	265,875,544	63,513,939	300,532,798	67,691,183	485,635,116	64,993,847
Mechanical Pencils	55,804,613	22,502,279	64,021,959	21,808,904	67,753,819	20,679,697	64,619,769	18,942,272
Desk & Dip Pen Sets	2,283,060	4,776,359	3,214,628	6,243,663	2,909,175	6,504,021	2,480,784	4,123,030
	309,613,592	$118,094,045	375,926,975	$133,019,938	412,048,208	$133,112,525	597,608,999	$123,062,855

	1959 Estimated Number of Units Shipped	1959 Estimated Total $ Value at Factory Prices (Exclusive of Tax)	1960 Estimated Number of Units Shipped	1960 Estimated Total $ Value at Factory Prices (Exclusive of Tax)	1961 Estimated Number of Units Shipped	1961 Estimated Total $ Value at Factory Prices (Exclusive of Tax)	1962 Estimated Number of Units Shipped	1962 Estimated Total $ Value at Factory Prices (Exclusive of Tax)
Fountain Pens	44,332,377	$ 33,493,472	48,715,222	$ 35,109,563	43,848,409	$ 28,091,799	46,403,059	$ 29,558,868
Ball Point Pens	657,216,402	70,981,036	761,942,521	81,628,191	775,240,610	86,080,560	779,295,793	85,749,857
Mechanical Pencils	63,800,793	18,829,913	60,078,084	18,687,711	45,130,949	15,060,506	45,073,636	15,023,977
Desk & Dip Pen Sets	8,124,358	4,969,321	4,083,561	3,683,354	3,166,460	2,628,884	2,952,001	2,991,023
	773,473,930	$128,273,742	874,819,388	$139,108,819	867,386,428	$131,861,749	873,724,489	$133,323,725

	1963 Estimated Number of Units Shipped	1963 Estimated Total $ Value at Factory Prices (Exclusive of Tax)	1964 Estimated Number of Units Shipped	1964 Estimated Total $ Value at Factory Prices (Exclusive of Tax)	1965 Estimated Number of Units Shipped	1965 Estimated Total $ Value at Factory Prices (Exclusive of Tax)	1966 Estimated Number of Units Shipped	1966 Estimated Total $ Value at Factory Prices (Exclusive of Tax)
Fountain Pens	37,732,054	$ 27,759,732	33,126,236	$ 25,413,432	27,753,770	$ 24,252,740	29,665,201	$ 24,221,601
Ball Point Pens	846,182,336	97,754,836	914,694,939	100,681,560	1,051,533,535	106,786,598	1,217,209,672	126,382,915
Markers	54,950,032	21,714,245	86,490,168	22,780,768				
Marking Instrs.					75,178,680*	22,114,380*	79,625,174	24,221,656
Writing Instrs.					82,472,722	15,165,708	169,633,744	28,837,736
Mechanical Pencils	50,723,836	15,549,816	47,210,544	15,992,837	64,009,160	18,916,852	61,342,289	18,168,868
Desk & Dip Pen Sets	1,264,905	2,804,497	2,187,132	3,327,254	10,703,699	5,000,596	3,021,853	4,585,827
	990,853,163	$165,583,226	1,083,709,019	$168,195,851	1,311,651,616	$192,236,874	1,560,497,933	$226,418,603

* Adjusted.

Source: Writing Instrument Manufacturers' Association, Inc.

EXHIBIT 1 (cont.)

	1967		1968		1969	
	Estimated Number of Units Shipped	Estimated Total $ Value at Factory Prices (Exclusive of Tax)	Estimated Number of Units Shipped	Estimated Total $ Value at Factory Prices (Exclusive of Tax)	Estimated Number of Units Shipped	Estimated Total $ Value at Factory Prices (Exclusive of Tax)
Fountain Pens	25,667,000	$ 22,909,000	17,591,000	$ 17,399,000	12,350,000	$ 16,043,000
Ball Point Pens						
Refillable	662,221,000	80,584,000	725,006,000	89,605,000	761,256,000	94,085,000
Non-Refillable	577,388,000	52,034,000	623,635,000	53,399,000	686,270,000	58,738,000
Markers:						
Marking Instrs.	102,976,000	26,227,000	123,471,000	28,831,000	116,767,000	26,820,000
Writing Instrs.	194,926,000	34,870,000	253,404,000	41,876,000	304,084,000	50,251,000
Mechanical Pencils	56,395,000	20,386,000	55,873,000	20,091,000	65,510,000	22,314,000
Desk & Dip Pen Sets	3,330,000	4,442,000	6,065,000	9,743,000	7,234,000	10,247,000
	1,622,903,000	$241,452,000	1,805,045,000	$260,944,000	1,953,471,000	$278,498,000

EXHIBIT 2

Total Industry Factory Sales

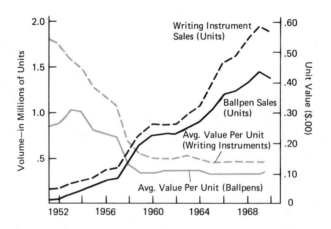

EXHIBIT 3

Typical Displays of Ball-Pens in Harvard Square Area

OPEN BINS, HARVARD SQUARE COOP

OPEN BINS, BUSINESS SCHOOL COOP

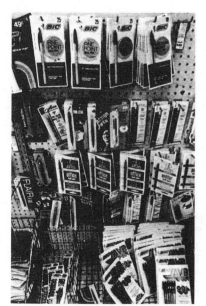

BLISTER PACKS, WOOLWORTH

BLISTER PACKS, RIX

EXHIBIT 4

Income Statements
Bic Pen Corporation
(1,000's)

	Year Ended December 31		
	1970	1969	1966
Net sales	$37,689	$36,587	$17,822
Cost of goods	15,857	15,560	6,544
Gross profit	$21,832	$21,027	$11,278
Selling, advertising and general administrative expense	13,057	11,653	6,302
Profit from operations	$ 8,775	$ 9,374	$ 4,976
Other income	142	191	31
Total income	$ 8,917	$ 9,565	$ 5,007
Taxes	4,298	4,628	2,302
Income after tax	$ 4,619	$ 4,937	$ 2,705

EXHIBIT 5

Statement of Consolidated Income
Pennsylvania Pen Company
(1,000's)

	Year Ended December 31	
	1970	1969
Net sales	$31,929	$31,229
Cost of sales	21,764	21,416
Gross profit	$10,165	$ 9,813
Selling and administrative expense	10,179	10,266
Depreciation	911	1,099
Interest expense	402	248
Other expense	3	70
Total expenses	$11,495	$11,683
Profit (loss) before tax	(1,330)	(1,870
Current credit for income tax	78	687
Deferred credit for income tax	177	—
Total income tax credits	$ 255	$ 687
Net profit (loss) after tax	($1,075)	($1,183)

EXHIBIT 6

Boston Test Market Criteria

Measurement	City			
	Framingham	Malden	Medford	Waltham
Population Estimates, 12/31/69				
Total (000)	60.6	58.2	57.6	59.7
Per cent of U.S.	.0298	.0286	.0283	.0293
Households (000)	17.6	18.7	17.0	16.6
Effective Buying Income, 1969				
Net $ (000,000)	232.4	202.4	205.9	211.8
Per cent of U.S.	.0371	.0323	.0329	.0338
$ per household	13,206	10,821	12,112	12,762
Per Cent Households by Cash Income				
$0–2,999	4.8	6.6	5.2	4.9
3,000–4,999	6.0	9.6	7.6	7.2
5,000–7,999	18.7	27.2	25.4	24.4
8,000–9,999	19.9	20.8	19.9	20.7
$10,000 and over	50.6	35.8	41.9	42.8
Retail Sales Estimates—1969 ($000,000)				
Total retail sales	172.4	92.3	127.8	147.0
Per cent of U.S.	.0496	.0265	.0367	.0423
Food	31.5	14.4	33.8	32.7
General merchandise	50.7	15.0	24.8	33.4
Drug	4.6	3.5	9.9	9.9
Buying power index	.0394	.0298	.0331	.0355

Source: 1970 Survey of Buying Power, *Sales Management,* June 10, 1970.

EXHIBIT 7

Market Retail Outlets, by Category

Category/Market	15¢ (Malden/Medford)	19¢ (Framingham/Waltham)
General Merchandise/ Variety	W. T. Grant—Medford Sq. W. T. Grant—Malden Woolworth's—Fellsway Woolworth's—Medford Sq. Woolworth's—Malden	McDaniel's—Shoppers' World Woolworth's—Framingham Woolworth's—Natick Mall Woolworth's—Waltham
Discount	Rix—Malden	Rix-Framingham Rix—Shoppers' World
Drug	Crandell's—Medford	Lighthall Drugs—Waltham
Mom-and-Pop	Cramer's Smoke	Hanson's Pharmacy*
Office Supply/ Stationery		ABC Typewriter Laramie Supply Mil's Card Shop

* Hanson's Pharmacy fit two descriptions, Drug and Mom-and-Pop, but the latter seemed more fitting.

EXHIBIT 7 (cont.)

Definitions of categories *as used in this test:*

General Merchandising/Variety: retailer operating a full-line store differing in two respects from conventional department stores:

They are national chains, and

Their buying organizations are centralized.

Discount: retailer merchandising an assortment of notions, toiletries, stationery, etc., at margins lower than those of traditional outlets.

Drug: retail outlet operating prescription department and featuring proprietaries, cosmetics, toiletries, and sundries.

Mom-and-Pop: general category of proprietorship characterized by low sales volume, relatively unsophisticated merchandising, and strong local sales appeal.

Office Supply/Stationery: retailer offering specialized line of commercial office supplies and/or retail stationery items and sundries.

EXHIBIT 8
Unit Sales during Test Market
(Units per Week, Purchased by Consumers)

Name of Store	Unit Sales: Pilot Pens Week Ending						Total Units: Bic & Pilot Pens (in the 15¢ to 25¢ range) Week Ending					
	3/6	3/13	3/20	3/27	4/3	4/10	3/6	3/13	3/20	3/27	4/3	4/10
Variety Stores												
1. Woolworth's	42	93	29	28	19	22	53	103	39	30	34	27
2. Woolworth's	25	25	21	32	23	12	50	37	43	56	49	38
3. Woolworth's	24	29	31	12	23	8	32	35	37	17	48	23
4. Woolworth's	33	26	29	38	33	12	95	96	114	95	100	63
5. Woolworth's	12	10	12	14	14	6	50	44	60	74	59	40
6. Woolworth's	50	56	32	53	54	33	59	68	41	64	64	38
7. W. T. Grant	4	15	18	6	6	6	5	17	27	9	9	10
8. W. T. Grant	38	52	34	37	19	15	63	70	51	77	40	35
9. McDaniel	40	74	50	41	22*	3*	68	107	85	70	49	8
Discount Stores												
10. RIX	15	13	15	19	9	1	20	19	19	24	19	4
11. RIX	11	6	20	15	3*	2*	18	12	26	20	8	2
12. RIX	24	24	14	17	0*	1*	30	36	22	23	7	7
Drug Stores												
13. Crandell's	11	12	10	9	11	9	27	27	25	21	33	12
14. Lighthall	1	0	1	6	6	7	19	14	16	31	26	32
"Mom-and-Pop" Stores												
15. Cramer's Smokes	5	9	4	11	6	13	11	20	12	25	18	23
16. Hanson's Pharmacy	9	10	4	3	3	3	28	31	33	19	23	27
Office Supply & Stationery												
17. ABC Typewriter	10	11	6	5	5	14	31	27	29	15	13	39
18. Laramie Supply	29	39	34	26	24	17	75	89	60	104	92	81
19. Mil's Card Shop	8	8	8	2	0	2	9	10	10	8	6	2

* Blister packs substituted for bulk display placards.

EXHIBIT 9

Point-of-Sale Conditions during Test Market

Name of Store	Location of Pilot Pen Display	Uniqueness of Pilot Display Location	Degree to Which the Full Bic Pen Product Line Is Represented
Variety Stores			
1. Woolworth's	Single register	Unique location	Poor
2. Woolworth's	Pen department	Unique location	Excellent
3. Woolworth's	Single register	Unique location	Fair
4. Woolworth's	Single register	Comparable location to Bic	Excellent
5. Woolworth's	Single register	Comparable location to Bic	Excellent
6. Woolworth's	Multiple registers	Unique location	Poor
7. W. T. Grant	Pen department	Comparable location to Bic	Excellent
8. W. T. Grant	Single register	Unique location	Excellent
9. McDaniel	Multiple registers	Unique location	Excellent
Discount Stores			
10. RIX	Pen department	Comparable location to Bic	Excellent
11. RIX	Single register	Unique location	Excellent
12. RIX	Single register	Unique location	Poor
Drug Stores			
13. Crandell's	Pen department	Unique location	Fair
14. Lighthall	Pen department	Unique location	Excellent
"Mom and Pop" Stores			
15. Cramer's Smokes	Single register	Comparable location to Bic	Excellent
16. Hanson's Pharmacy	Pen department	Unique location	Excellent
Office Supply & Stationery			
17. ABC Typewriter	Pen department	Unique location	Excellent
18. Laramie Supply	Single register	Comparable location to Bic	Excellent
19. Mil's Card Shop	Single register	Comparable location to Bic	Poor

EXHIBIT 10
Results of Test Market: % Market Share

Name of Store	Location	Town	Pilot Pen Price	Pilot % Share of Total Pilot Plus Bic Unit Sales in the 15¢ to 25¢ Range — Week Ending					
				3/6	3/13	3/20	3/27	4/3	4/10
Variety Stores:									
1. Woolworth's	Medford Sq.	Medford	15¢	80%	90%	74%	93%	56%	81%
2. Woolworth's	Fellsway	Medford	15	50	67	49	57	47	31
3. Woolworth's	Pleasant St.	Malden	15	75	83	84	70	48	35
4. Woolworth's	Framingham Ctr.	Framingham	19	35	27	25	40	33	19
5. Woolworth's	Natick Mall	Framingham	19	25	23	20	19	24	15
6. Woolworth's	Moody St.	Waltham	19	85	82	78	82	85	87
7. W. T. Grant	Pleasant St.	Malden	15	80	88	67	67	67	60
8. W. T. Grant	Medford Sq.	Medford	15	60	75	67	68	47	43
9. McDaniel	Shoppers' World	Framingham	19	59	71	59	59	45*	38*
Discount Stores:									
10. RIX	Pleasant St.	Malden	15	75	68	79	79	47	25
11. RIX	Framingham Ctr.	Framingham	19	60	50	77	75	38*	100*
12. RIX	Shoppers' World	Framingham	19	80	67	64	74	0*	14*

* Blister packs substituted for bulk display placards.

EXHIBIT 10 *(cont.)*

Name of Store	Location	Town	Pilot Pen Price	Pilot % Share of Total Pilot Plus Bic Unit Sales in the 15¢ to 25¢ Range					
				Week Ending					
				3/6	3/13	3/20	3/27	4/3	4/10
Drug Stores:									
13. Crandell's	High St.	Medford	15	41	45	40	43	33	75
14. Lighthall	Moody St.	Waltham	19	5	0	6	19	23	22
"Mom-and-Pop" Stores:									
15. Cramer's Smokes	Main St.	Malden	15	45	45	33	44	33	56
16. Hanson's Pharmacy	Main St.	Waltham	19	32	32	12	16	13	11
Office Supply & Stationery:									
17. ABC Typewriter	Main Street	Waltham	19	32	40	20	33	38	36
18. Laramie Supply	Shoppers' World	Framingham	19	39	44	57	25	26	21
19. Mil's Card Shop	Framingham Ctr.	Framingham	19	89	80	80	25	0	100

EXHIBIT 11
Summary of Pilot Pen Test Market Results

Store #	City	PPC Share of Market %*	Price, ¢	Display Location	Display Uniqueness**	Bic Repre- sentation***
1	Medford	79	15	Register	PP Only	Poor
2	Medford	50	15	Pen Dept.	PP Only	Exc
3	Malden	66	15	Register	PP Only	Fair
4	Framingham	30	19	Register	PP — Bic	Exc
5	Framingham	21	19	Register	PP — Bic	Exc
6	Waltham	83	19	Register	PP Only	Poor
7	Malden	72	15	Pen Dept.	PP — Bic	Exc
8	Medford	60	15	Register	PP Only	Exc
9	Framingham	55	19	Register	PP Only	Exc
10	Malden	62	15	Pen Dept.	PP — Bic	Exc
11	Framingham	67	19	Register	PP Only	Exc
12	Framingham	50	19	Register	PP Only	Poor
13	Medford	46	15	Pen Dept.	PP Only	Fair
14	Waltham	13	19	Pen Dept.	PP Only	Exc
15	Malden	43	15	Register	PP — Bic	Exc
16	Waltham	19	19	Pen Dept.	PP Only	Exc
17	Waltham	33	19	Pen Dept.	PP Only	Exc
18	Framingham	35	19	Register	PP — Bic	Exc
19	Framingham	62	19	Register	PP — Bic	Poor

* Six-week store mean share, Pilot vs. total Bic plus Pilot.

** PPC Only: Pilot displayed separately. PPC — Bic: Pilot and Bic share same display.

*** Degree to which Bic Pen product line is represented.

APPENDIX A

Distributor and Retailer Comments

Distributor and retailer attitude data were collected in interviews with Boston area retailers and distributors between January and April 1971. Selected comments were:

In my opinion there are far too many pens and writing instruments being offered to the public today. At one point, the 39¢–49¢ pen was a strong seller. Now the manufacturers are glutting the market with 19¢ pens. This not only lowers the profit picture, but leaves a doubt in the consumer's mind as to the real quality of the merchandise. . . . It's a shame to ruin this market with a lower quality pen such as some manufacturers are offering

. . . . .

It seems as though everyone wants to get into this market. We have way too many lines in stock. . . . Yes, I think customers are confused and I know darn well we are.

. . . . .

There are simply too many different writing instruments on the market.

. . . . .

It is impractical for even a large dealer like ourselves to carry everything. It seems manufacturers could save themselves a lot of money and make the dealer more effective if there weren't so many choices.

One trade source felt no motivation to buy other products besides the 39¢ pencil. "39¢ pencil is a good mover; a proven product."

15¢ is too cheap for the consumer.

. . . . .

I can buy a 19¢ pen for 4¢ from a loft manufacturer, so why should I buy these pens if I don't have to?

. . . . .

15¢ price might make a difference to the commercial market.

Pricing delusion. Volume and packaging savings give fictitious impression of profit. Some merchandise will come back and ill-will will build up in trade and at retail.

. . . . .

Pennsylvania has a good pencil; I'm not pushing anything else.

. . . . .

Pennsylvania name is not strong enough to pull anything through.

. . . . .

Display (placard merchandiser) is horrible.

. . . . .

I will carry (this pen) if people ask for it.

. . . . .

Jordan Marsh prefers to let jobbers finance and control writing instrument inventory rather than buying direct.

. . . . .

There is a predominantly depressed attitude among retailers. There is a lack of movement through retail stores and merchandise is backed up in the outlets.

. . . . .

Want national advertising.

. . . . .

Zayre has a policy of carrying only nationally advertised writing instruments (Bic, Flair, Wearever).

. . . . .

Prices to the trade are a real jungle because of PMs, deals, promotions, and returns.

. . . . .

Distributors have the power. I want the manufacturer to pull—this is not a push market. With the 15¢ pen I need more volume to make the same profit. The key is to motivate the public—can't get distributor to move—don't control outlets—have to sell them what they want.

. . . . .

I will carry it if people ask for it.

College Student Survey

Approximately 45 college students were given, more or less at random, samples of the Pilot pen during January and February 1971. In April 1971, 38 interviews regarding the pen were collected from these individuals. Each question is listed, with the responses following in order of frequency. Multiple answers were possible.

1. What does the name "Pennsylvania" mean to you?

	%	Number of Responses
Pen company	32.3	18
Mechanical pencil	19.8	11
Quality	14.5	8
Low-priced pen	10.5	6
Ball-point pen	10.5	6
Nothing	8.8	5
Medium-priced pen	3.5	2
		56

2a. What did you like most about the Pilot pen?

	%	Number of Responses
Smooth writing	43.3	26
Doesn't clot	10.0	6
Flexible	10.0	6
See ink supply	8.3	5
Good point	8.3	5
Low (anticipated) price	6.7	4
Good "feel"	5.0	3
Nothing	5.0	3
Doesn't skip	1.7	1
Removable clip	1.7	1
		60

2b. What did you like least?

	%	Number of Responses
Clotting/Smearing	28.3	15
Uncomfortable "feel"	15.1	8
Flexibility	13.2	7
Clip	11.3	6
Nothing	11.3	6
Skips	9.4	5
Cap falls off	7.5	4
Cap sticks	3.8	2
		53

2c. Do you have any other general comments?

"If you're left-handed it smears. Why can't Pennsylvania develop and use a non-smearing ink?"

"Liked it, but the tip dropped off after about 2 months."

"The Bic 25¢ pen looks more expensive."

"Always looks like it is going to leak around the tip."

3. Where do you normally buy pens?

	%	Number of Responses
College bookstore	45.6	26
Someone else buys	29.8	17
Stationery store	7.0	4
Drug store	7.0	4
Department store	3.5	2
Supermarket	3.5	2
Discount store	3.5	2
		57

4. What type do you normally buy? (How often?)

	%	Number of Responses
Bic (Avg. one per month)	34.0	17
Fiber-tip pen (Avg. one per month)	24.0	12
Parker (all received as gifts)	12.0	6
Cross (" " " ")	12.0	6
Lindy (Avg. one per two months)	8.0	4
Any cheap pen (Avg. one per month)	6.0	3
Mechanical pencil	4.0	2
		50

5. What do you like best about pens you use?

	%	Number of Responses
Writes well	33.8	22
Low price	23.1	15
Distinctive appearance		11
"Feel" of the pen	16.9	6

5. (cont.)

	%	Number of Responses
Ink	6.2	4
Point	6.2	4
Quality	3.1	2
Looks like a pen should	1.5	1
		65

7. Do you still have our pen?

	%	Number of Responses
Yes	57.8	22
No	42.2	16
		38

6. Will you buy, or have you bought, the Pilot pen? (The pen was available at the local college bookstore for 15¢.)

	%	Number of Responses
No	37.0	14
Yes	31.5	12
Might	31.5	12
		38

EXTENSIVE PROBLEM-SOLVING PURCHASING BEHAVIOR

PART

CHAPTER 9

Zenith Radio Corporation: Allegro

Mr. Robert Bowen, Vice-President–Marketing of Zenith Radio Corporation, and Mr. Robert Pierce, Director of Audio Planning for Zenith, were reevaluating product strategy for Zenith in the field of modular stereo equipment. They were particularly interested in strategic planning for the Zenith Allegro line, which had been introduced the previous summer.

Zenith Radio Corporation was a major producer of television receivers in the United States. Zenith had dominated the black and white television market since 1959, and became the leader in sales of color television sets in 1972. Sales for 1973 were expected to exceed $1 billion, with almost all of these sales coming from television products.

Zenith had a reputation for quality in the console market (see glossary of terms, Exhibit 1), in which its major competitors were Magnavox and RCA. This market was in decline due in large part to recent consumer trends: differences in life styles, size of living quarters, etc. Zenith management hoped to penetrate the market to smaller sound systems and to build on its reputation for quality sound systems with the introduction of Allegro modular units.

The Allegro line consisted of a series of modular stereo "packages" made up of an AM–FM tuner/amplifier, plus some combination of a phonograph and/or tape deck, and separate speakers. The main feature of the new line was a unique tuned-port speaker which had been designed with the aid of a computer.

This case was prepared by Edward Popper, Research Assistant, under the supervision of Professor Scott Ward, The Wharton School, as the basis for class discussion rather than to illustrate either effective or ineffective handling of an administrative situation.

The tuned-port speaker design gave twice the acoustic efficiency of air suspension speakers of comparable size, found in competitive sound systems. (See Exhibit 2 for a product brochure, and advertising used in 1973.)

Zenith's product strategy was to market a higher quality line of modular systems. While Allegro is higher priced than most other modular lines, the characteristics of the line closely parallel the industry in many respects. Zenith offers five models with 8-track; six models are full-featured (i.e., containing tuner, amplifier, phonograph and tape player); and the entire line is either matrix adaptable or quadraphonic. The Allegro line is shorter (only 13 models) than that of most other manufacturers, an aspect viewed as desirable by many retailers.

THE HOME ENTERTAINMENT SYSTEM MARKET

The home stereo equipment market is a significant part of the consumer electronics industry. Total 1973 retail sales approached $12 billion for the industry with sales of approximately $2.1 billion, or 18% of the total for the home stereo equipment market (see Exhibit 3).

From 1960 to 1972, the consumer electronics industry grew at an average compound rate of between 10% and 11% per annum, including inflation effects. The average "real" (i.e., excluding inflation) compound growth rate of 6% to 8% was expected to continue through the decade of the 1970s, although no real growth was expected for the industry as a whole in 1974. As one of the mature segments of the consumer electronics industry, the home stereo equipment market was expected to grow at a slightly lower average real growth rate of 5% to 7% per annum. The largest market in this industry was for color television sets, which accounted for approximately 45% of industry dollar sales in 1972. A downturn was seen for 1974 dollar sales, owing to maturity in the black and white color television markets.

The remainder of the industry (grouped together as "other" in Exhibit 3) included the small but rapidly growing markets for personal electronic devices such as calculators. This segment of the industry was expected to grow more rapidly than the other segments.

I. Industry Structure

Zenith executives were interested in four segments of the home stereo equipment market: audio component, console, modular and component system.

Audio Component. The audio component segment of the home stereo equipment market was both the largest, in terms of dollar volume, and also the most rapidly growing segment of the market. Retail sales in this segment were estimated to have been approximately $950 million in 1973, or 46% of total home stereo market sales. This was the only segment for which a sales increase was predicted in 1974. Most industry experts expected continued strong growth.

This segment was characterized by a high degree of fragmentation at the manufacturer level. Most manufacturers competing in this segment were small, privately held firms tending to specialize in certain functional classes of components (i.e., speakers, receivers, etc.). In addition, many of these manufacturers marketed their product only within a limited geographic area, contributing to the fragmentation cited above. Audio component systems generally ranged in price from $300 to $900, with most volume falling in the $400–$600 price range.

Console. With an estimated retail sales level of $400 million in 1973, the console segment of the home stereo market was the second largest, accounting for 19% of this market's sales. In 1974, sales were expected to decline approximately 5%, as popularity of consoles continued to wane, and as prices continued to soften.

This was the one segment of the home stereo market which, while fragmented, was still dominated by three large U.S. consumer electronics firms: Magnavox, Zenith, and

RCA. Console prices ranged from $100 to $720 retail, with most sales in the $300–$400 range.

Modular. The modular, or compact system, segment of the market was approximately the same dollar size as the console market. Retail sales in 1973 were estimated to have been approximately $390 million, or 19% of the home stereo market. Sales were expected to be slightly lower in 1974. Sixty-five percent of modular stereo purchases were under $200, and 75% were under $250.

This segment was also fragmented, although not to the extent of the audio component segment. In 1973, the top five manufacturers accounted for only 39% of total unit purchases. Modular retail prices ranged from $50 to over $500, with the bulk of sales in the $15–$250 range.

Component System. Retail sales in this segment of the market were estimated to have been approximately $330 million in 1973, or 16% of total home stereo market sales. This segment, falling somewhere between the audio component and the modular segments in terms of product and price points, also fell between the two in terms of forecast sales. The segment was expected to achieve the same dollar sales volume in 1974 as in 1973. Component system stereos ranged from approximately $100 to $550, with most sales in the $200 to $300 range.

This segment rated second highest in terms of fragmentation, falling between audio components and modular systems. In 1973, the top five manufacturers together accounted for only 21% of total unit purchases.

II. Distribution and Retail Trends

Distribution systems in the home stereo market are varied and complex (see Figure 1).

Generally, audio component manufacturers sell to retail via manufacturers' agents; console, modular, and components are sold either directly to retailers or via company-owned or independent distributors. For example, Zenith sells via eighty independently owned, and five wholly owned, distributors. Each has an average of twenty years of association with Zenith, and approximately 30% operate exclusively with Zenith. Distributor operating expenses average 12% of revenues with a range of 7–14%. (See Exhibit 4 for Zenith sales organization.)

In Zenith's case, 600 distributor salesmen sell the entire product line (including televisions) to about 17,500 retail accounts. Many are small independent dealerships, and the salesmen have excellent relations with them. Retailer margins for the Allegro line vary by geographic location and type of outlet, with 28–32% margins prevailing.

Although television sales predominate for Zenith distributor salesmen (e.g., 13:1 ratio of sales of color television to each modular or console system sold), salesmen are motivated to sell

FIGURE 1

Distribution Systems in the Home Stereo Market

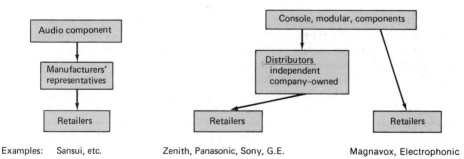

Examples: Sansui, etc.   Zenith, Panasonic, Sony, G.E.   Magnavox, Electrophonic

stereo equipment by significant bonuses, in addition to already high commissions. Additionally, Zenith, together with some distributors, had experimented with hiring audio specialist salesmen, and results had been good. However, specialist salesmen had not significantly outsold regular Zenith salesmen who had participated in the company's sales training program for Allegro.

Zenith's distribution pattern for modular equipment was somewhat different from other modular manufacturers, since the company had built its strength early in the home electronics industry with televisions, and stereo consoles, and had utilized retail outlets whose functions had changed over the years. For example, modular sales for Zenith were concentrated in appliance and radio–TV stores, versus concentration in department and discount stores for the company's major modular competitors (see Exhibit 5).

Messrs. Bowen and Pierce conducted some qualitative research (group interviews) with distributors and retailers in various areas of the country. Their purpose in conducting the research was to ascertain distributor and retailer attitudes toward Allegro specifically, and stereo sales generally. The information could be useful in marketing programs for the current line, and for stimulating ideas about line extensions and new products. The results showed that department and discount store buyers felt that the modular equipment market would be the fastest growing segment of the market by far. Most expressed the view that audio components would decline in importance, owing to lack of customer sophistication and high equipment cost.

Discount store buyers were primarily concerned with finding manufacturers who provide good quality, consistent supply, and advertising support. Often, discounters look for equipment "dumps" by nonregular suppliers, in which equipment may be purchased for promotional use, while maintaining gross margins. The research results strongly suggested that discount buyers were attempting to reduce the number of lines carried. Most now carry from five to seven lines and want to carry fewer lines in order to reduce inventory risk, as well as minimize customer confusion.

Department store buyers were generally pleased with Allegro, particularly sales training aids made available by Zenith. These buyers had relatively focused ideas about the consumer behavior for stereo equipment in department stores. Most felt that the "typical" consumer is upscale, doesn't shop around, is influenced by his confidence in the outlet as well as service considerations, and is often presold on a configuration when he comes to the store. For all these reasons, Mr. Bowen felt, the department store buyer (and the hardgoods store buyer) buys a wide range of equipment, is interested in service and sales training programs, and, since he competes less on price and more on service, is less influenced by purchasing economics than the discount buyer.

While few of Zenith's sales were through audio specialty stores, management reasoned that the trend for some manufacturers of audio components to market through department stores might produce a reverse trend in which companies like Zenith, with strength in department and hardgoods stores, might be able to promote sales via audio specialty stores. Consequently, Zenith conducted some research among audio component store buyers.

These buyers indicated their perceptions of the consumer: ranging from the audiophile to the individual who is merely seeking information. Most are younger and relatively intrigued by the intricacies of audio equipment. Since these outlets are the only ones in which audio component manufacturers sell their equipment, they are critically important to them. Conversely, audio speciality stores differentiate themselves from other stereo retailers with such equipment. There was some indication among these buyers that they would be fearful of large manufacturers, such as Zenith, attempting to market audio components through their outlets, and then "giving over" the line to department and discount stores once an image of quality and sophistication had been established.

Audio component system price points overlap modular system price points at the upper end of the modular price spectrum. A minimum expenditure for an audio component system would be approximately $300. For the same expenditure, the consumer could also choose one of the more expensive modular units.

The sale of audio component equipment requires certain skills that are not required for modular sales. For example, the time required to make a component sale is much longer than for a modular sale due to the options available, the complexity of the equipment, and the tendency of audio component purchasers to shop around. It is very important to have a "sound room" where equipment can be carefully evaluated and compared with other equipment. Also, there is a tremendous mix problem in trying to provide enough manufacturers' lines to allow the consumer an adequate selection of products.

Finally, it is difficult to hire and/or train an adequate sales force. Audio component salesmen need to have considerable familiarity with a large number of specific brands, and with audio technology, so that they can help the consumer "mix and match," or at least appear knowledgeable enough to provide the confidence a consumer is looking for. Manufacturers and retailers are attempting to alleviate the problems caused by customer system building by prepackaging some systems and offering them at a special (i.e., "below retail") price.

In looking over the data from all the distributors and retailers, there were some shared perceptions. There was consensus that the majority of modular sales would remain around the $200 price point, and that the consumer would continue to prefer full featured models, e.g., with 8-track tape capability, which had become popular. Most interviewed felt that acceptance of a four-channel system was a long way off, and there was skepticism of manufacturers moving too quickly into qua-

draphonic sound systems. Finally, there was general agreement that fewer lines and models were desirable, to cut down consumer confusion.

III. Advertising and Promotion

Zenith spent $1 million for Allegro advertising in 1973, stressing quality sound, and the Allegro and Zenith names, in print advertising. The target market was defined as 18–34 year-old men, who had attended or graduated from college, with incomes over $10,000. Media vehicles were quality, male-slanted magazines.

Advertising and promotion in the home stereo equipment market range from no advertising and little promotion by some manufacturers, such as Capehart, to very high advertising expenditures by others, such as Panasonic and Magnavox. Zenith's audio advertising effort falls somewhere in the middle, but near the low end among well known brands.

The audio component manufacturers do little advertising, but tend to rely on "word-of-mouth" and retail push to realize sales. The ads which do appear are usually in audio specialty magazines or prestigious men's magazines.

In the console, modular, and component system segments of the market, the amount of preselling that goes on seems to be directly proportional to the manufacturers' effort to sell an image, be it "quality" (Magnavox), or "quality/innovator" (Sony and Panasonic). Zenith seems to be somewhat of an exception to this rule, for although the Zenith brand is highly associated with quality,[1] Zenith's audio advertising expenditures were less than one-third of Panasonic's in 1972. (See Exhibit 6.) While Sony's audio advertising expenditures nearly doubled between 1970 and 1972, Zenith's advertising expenditures were approximately

---

[1] According to a study done by Louis Harris and Associates in May 1973, Zenith had a reputation second to none, among consumers, as a manufacturer of high quality televisions, and high quality radios.

10% less in 1972 than in 1970. Finally, the overall trend of Zenith's audio advertising expenditures seemed to be downward, while leading competitors seemed to be steadily increasing their advertising budgets.

According to the consumer studies, Zenith's outstanding reputation for quality among consumers closely paralleled the company's relative market position in both television and console stereo. In the case of high quality "component"[2] stereo equipment, however, Zenith's reputation seemed to be at a much higher level than market performance would indicate reflecting the omnipotent nature of the Zenith brand name in the consumer electronics market and a "spill-over" from previous Zenith advertising. Other significant findings from consumer research were:

The Zenith name was more often associated with quality in stereo "components" than were the Panasonic and Sony names—brands which seemed to have achieved an image of quality by means of aggressive advertising programs;

Owners of Zenith TV and radio products were less frequently dissatisfied with these products than the owners of any other major brand; and

Despite higher average sales prices, Zenith TVs, of all brands mentioned, were most often associated with the statement: "They are the best value for the money."

IV. Competitive Trends and Strategies

The company's primary competition in the modular and console markets were: Panasonic, RCA, Sony, Magnavox, General Electric and Electrophonic. The analysis gave an overview of trends and strategies in the audio component market. (See Exhibit 7 for breakdown of competitors and prices and Exhibit 8 for share comparison.)

Panasonic. Panasonic offered 33 models, of which 11 were matrix adaptable and 11 were quad. Twenty-six models were under $300,

---

[2] The precise meaning of "component," as used in the consumer studies, is unknown, but probably had a broad meaning which would include modular systems, as well as component systems.

and 86% of the company's sales were in this range. As in the case with the industry averages, Panasonic's largest modular volume fell between $176–$200. Nine Panasonic models were full-featured (two with cassettes), and seven additional models had 8-track.

The new "Technics" line was an effort by Panasonic to become a major force in the audio component market. Although no definite statement could be made about the line's success, several retailers and distributors expressed doubts as to whether the line would be successful.

Although slightly lower than Sony, Panasonic offered competitive retail margin: approximately 28%. Although using a two step distribution system, Panasonic had an unusually small number of distributors (a combination of company owned and independent). Unlike Zenith, Panasonic by-passed distributors when dealing with national accounts. On the other hand, "Technics" was handled by separate one-step distribution.

According to Trendex data, the largest percentage of Panasonic's compact models (27%) were sold in department stores, with the second most important outlet being discount stores (21%). This pattern (i.e., strength in both department and discount stores) was atypical and had resulted in consternation on the part of numerous retailers. Many of them were disturbed by their perception that Panasonic's models were "sold everywhere" at "a wide range of prices." A positive factor, in the eyes of the retailer, was that Panasonic was viewed as an innovator. This characteristic was extremely important to a dealer because by carrying Panasonic he was virtually assured of having the latest innovations in his product line.

The Panasonic consumer (in comparison to the industry average and Zenith) was more urban, less often female, younger, and in a higher income bracket. Panasonic was the leader in industry audio advertising expenditures. The company had steadily increased its commitment to consumer advertising each year, and this was viewed as an important factor in influencing the consumer's perception of Panasonic as being of higher quality than most popularly priced lines. Further, it was viewed as a positive factor by the retailer as it helped to stimulate demand.

Sony. Sony's strategy was to market a quality product at a premium price. Dealer exclusivity, superior service, and delivery were stressed to retail accounts. Recent Trendex data showed that 68% of Sony's modular sales occurred above the $200 price point, with 45% occurring above $300. In keeping with its premium priced strategy, Sony referred to its systems as "integrated component music systems," not "modular systems."

The product line consisted of sixteen different models, and was one of the shortest in the industry. Seven models were full-featured. Sony was unique in offering an inordinate number of models (4) with cassette players, while only two models featured four-channel. In addition to these modular systems, Sony offered an extensive line of audio components.

Sony used a two-step distribution system, allowing retailers margins of 33–35%. According to recent Trendex data, the majority of Sony's sales occurred in department stores (32%) and radio–TV stores (20%)—with only a small percentage (12%) occurring in discount outlets.

In the eyes of retailers (and Zenith distributors), Sony was a major force in the market. The short, simple line was a boon; yielding little consumer confusion. Further, Sony was viewed as a high quality line, and one which retailers saw as being prestigious. This image, combined with above-average dealer margins on the Sony line, probably resulted in exceptional support or "push" on the part of the retailers that carried the line. In line with its prestige image, Sony trailed only Panasonic and Magnavox in audio dollar expenditures.

RCA. Magnavox's product strategy was to offer a modular line which covered the spectrum of price points. The result was that the majority (53%) of Magnavox's sales occurred below the $200 price point. Further, in line with industry characteristics, the company had a higher modular volume (21%) in the $176–$200 price range than in any other price range.

The Magnavox line, featuring twenty-one models, was one of the longest in the industry (second only to Panasonic). Twelve models were priced above $300, six models were full-featured, and three others featured a tape system. (Magnavox marketed only one model with a cassette player.) The product line contained four quadraphonic models, each containing a tuner, phonograph and amplifier, selling in the $300–$400 price range.

EXHIBIT 1

DEFINITION OF TERMS

Audio Component: a stereo component which is manufactured and packaged to be sold as a separate unit. These units are incomplete sound system components which are typically married to other units at the retail level to form a complete system.

Modular or Compact System: a stereo system which contains one main power source unit and two or more separate enclosed speaker systems. The main source unit may also include tape recording and/or playing devices, and AM/FM radio, a record player, or a combination of these.

Component System: a stereo system which contains four or more units packaged to sell as one sound reproduction system. At least two of these must be units other than speakers. The system may include an AM/FM radio, a turntable, or a combination of components. The system may include more than two separate enclosed speaker systems.

Console: a stereo system which includes a central power unit and at least two speakers in a single cabinet which is also designed to serve as a furniture piece. The central unit may include an AM/FM radio, a television receiver, tape recording and/or playing devices, a turntable, or any combination of these. The system may also include additional separate enclosed speaker systems.

Four-Channel: also quadraphonic, or "quad." A sound system capable of producing a four-dimensional stereophonic aural effect, and including the following systems: speaker matrix, matrix and discrete. Also the software designed for quadraphonic systems.

Software: a prerecorded program material in the form of magnetic tapes or phonographic discs.

Stereo: a sound system capable of reproducing a multi-dimensional aural effect from a broadcast or prerecorded signal. Four-channel sound is a special subcategory of stereo.

EXHIBIT 2

Zenith Radio Corporation: Allegro

New Zenith Allegro brings deeper, richer sound to 4-channel.

THE QUADRILLE—Model F736W

Here's how:

You're looking at the Zenith Allegro tuned port.* It's part of an innovative speaker system designed to reproduce more faithfully the finest sound on your records and tapes. You see, with a lot of speakers (even air-suspension speakers), you never hear some of the deep, rich bass. It gets trapped inside the speaker cabinets. But this tuned port channels out more of that sound so you do hear it. (In fact, if you put your hand over the port, you can even feel it).

In conjunction with this tuned port, Allegro has a specially-designed woofer which also produces solid middle-range sound. And with a horn-type tweeter to deliver the high notes, you end up hearing virtually the full range and all the exciting sound of the original performance. You also get a more efficient sound system. In fact, other systems with comparable size air-suspension speakers need twice the wattage to match Allegro's overall sound performance.

But as remarkable as the Allegro speaker is, it's not the whole story. There's equally good audio componentry behind it. Most important, a precision, solid-state tuner/amplifier specifically designed to work with the Allegro speakers.

Finally, Allegro offers versatility. AM, FM and 4-channel matrix FM broadcasts. A 4-channel discrete 8-track tape player. A precision record changer that plays 4-channel matrix records. Plus the ability to play (and greatly enhance) present forms of stereo.

Zenith Allegro 4-channel. Once you hear it, you'll know how 4-channel sound should sound.   *patent pending

The surprising sound of Zenith.®   **ZENITH** *Allegro*

The quality goes in before the name goes on*

EXHIBIT 2 (cont.)

Client: Zenith Radio Corporation
Product: Allegro Stereo
Title: "Blueprint"

SPECIFICATIONS	ALLEGRO 3000	ALLEGRO 2000	ALLEGRO 1000
Enclosure:	Tuned Port	Tuned Port	Tuned Port
Speakers:	Woofer: 10" diameter, 5 lb. Alnico magnet structure	Woofer: 8" diameter, 3 lb. Ferrite magnet structure	Woofer: 6½" diameter, 2 lb. Ferrite magnet structure
	Tweeter: 3½" horn	Tweeter: 3½" horn	Tweeter: 3½" horn
Crossover:	Inductance Capacitance (LC)	Inductance Capacitance (LC)	Inductance Capacitance (LC)
Crossover Frequency:	2500 Hz	2500 Hz	2500 Hz
Impedance:	16 ohms	16 ohms	8 ohms
Frequency Range:	40–15,000 Hz	50–15,000 Hz	60–15,000 Hz
Dimensions:	22¾" (H) x 14½" (W) x 8½" (D)	18½" (H) x 12¾" (W) x 7¾" (D)	16½" (H) x 10½" (W) x 7½" (D)
Cable Length:	15 ft.	15 ft.	15 ft.
Weight:	28 lb.	21 lb.	14 lb.

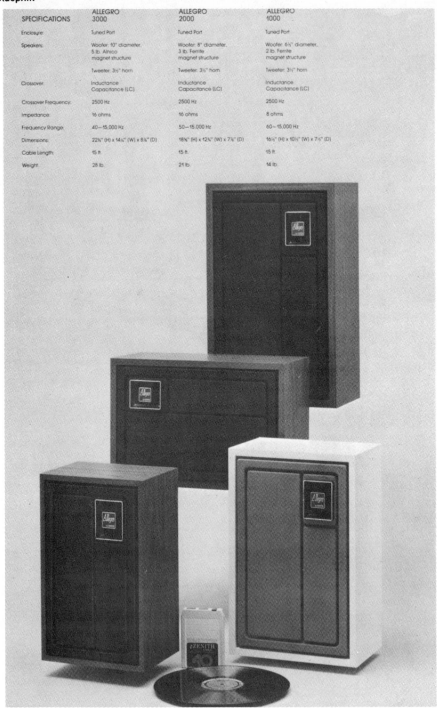

EXHIBIT 2 (*cont.*)

The Search for Concert Hall Realism in a Home Sound System

In a well-designed concert hall, all the sound of the live performance; from the deepest tones of the organ to the tinkling of triangles, is accurately presented to the listener.

But in an ordinary gymnasium, even the world's greatest symphony orchestra doesn't sound like a great orchestra. Poor acoustic surroundings, tonal hangover, reverberations and cancellation distort and color the sound.

Ideally, the speakers in a fine home entertainment system should respond accurately to the entire spectrum of musical sound. But playing records or tapes through some speakers can be like the orchestra's performance in the gymnasium—important sound quality is lost, distorted or colored because of poor acoustic design or speakers improperly matched to other components. Even in matched sound systems, some of the deeper, richer sounds can get trapped inside certain speaker enclosures so it is never heard.

Zenith Allegro speakers were designed to virtually recreate the live performance sound you enjoy in a well-designed concert hall. The Allegro speakers were developed on the basis of a thorough analysis of the advantages and disadvantages of the various speaker enclosure design alternatives. Zenith engineers computer-programmed the characteristics and performance variables for each of the respective speaker enclosure types: open back, closed back, air-suspension and tuned port or bass-reflex. From this analysis, it was concluded that the tuned port enclosure offered the greatest potential for refinement into an outstanding home sound system speaker.

EXHIBIT 2 *(cont.)*

Inside Zenith Allegro

The Woofer (A). The Allegro system's woofer, or low-frequency loudspeaker, is specially designed—unlike typical loudspeakers found in open back, closed back, air-suspension or other tuned port systems, it has a massive magnet structure, larger than those used on most other systems, which is an efficient energy converter. This serves to improve the Allegro woofer's transient response (the loudspeaker's ability to respond accurately to a sudden change in electrical input signals without unwanted tonal hangover). It transforms electronic power input into acoustic power output, putting the high air pressure within the cabinet to use to increase the system's efficiency at low bass frequencies. The woofer also reproduces clear midrange frequencies for a more complete sound reproduction.

The Horn Tweeter (B). The horn tweeter, or high-frequency loudspeaker, is capable of producing crisp high frequencies up to 15,000 Hz. A special construction combines wide-angle, wide-range response found in dome-type tweeters with the higher efficiency of a horn, creating an optimum match with the high-efficiency woofer. The circular mouth of the tweeter horn uniformly disperses equal amounts of high frequencies along horizontal and vertical planes, a feature impossible to achieve with rectangular horns found in some speaker enclosures.

The Tuned Port (C). The function of Allegro's tuned port, unlike that of conventional small ported speakers, is not solely to lower distortion. While Allegro's sealed cabinet prevents air pressure from the back of the woofer from escaping through the back of the enclosure (as in open back systems), the tuned port puts this pressure to use as another sound source. The port also acts as a filter, allowing only bass frequencies to pass through it. (Allegro 3000 systems reproduce frequencies down to 40 Hz., Allegro 2000 systems down to 50 Hz., and Allegro 1000 systems down to 60 Hz.). By means of a physical time delay, these waves from the port are in phase with the waves produced from the front of the speaker cone within the system's operating range (at and above the tuned frequency), thus enhancing the reproduction of bass tones. (Bass frequencies below 100 Hz. are the tones most speaker systems lose; frequencies below 40 Hz. seldom occur in music.)

The Crossover Network (D). Allegro's frequency crossover system helps provide clear, distortion-free sound by feeding high tones only to the horn tweeter and lower tones only to the woofer. The construction of the woofer itself acoustically and electrically performs the crossover function—preventing high tones from emitting from the woofer and eliminating the need for any additional electrical network of the type found on some speaker systems. The horn tweeter has a quality inductance capacitance (LC) crossover network which prevents low tones from reaching the tweeter.

The Enclosure (E). The Allegro cabinet is a solid construction which prevents back wave escape. Every joint is glued in a continuous pattern to eliminate gaps or free resonant points which can cause distortion. A specially-selected sound-dampening material used inside the enclosure in carefully determined amounts, causes the air inside the cabinet to actually change its operating characteristics. As a result, the Allegro system performs as if the internal proportions were equal to an unfilled cabinet 25 percent larger than Allegro's enclosure. This ability to simulate a larger enclosure size allows the use of a popular-sized cabinet while retaining the recognized performance characteristics of a larger enclosure.

EXHIBIT 2 *(cont.)*

A Choice of Systems—Versatile and Distinctive

Modular Sound Systems. Allegro modular systems are available in both 2-channel stereo and 4-channel models. Systems include combinations of AM/FM/Stereo FM tuner/amplifier, record changer and 8-track cartridge tape player or tape player/recorder, with either two or four Allegro speakers. (Most Zenith modular stereos feature "speaker matrix" circuitry for enhanced 4-dimensional effect with the addition of two extra Allegro speakers.) All components in Allegro modular systems are matched with the speakers for optimum efficiency and sound performance.

Console Sound Systems. Most Zenith 2-channel stereo consoles and all 4-channel consoles feature Allegro speakers. All models have record changer and AM/FM/Stereo FM tuner/amplifier. All 2-channel stereo models also feature built-in 8-Track cartridge tape player or player/recorder; 4-channel units feature 2/4 channel 8-Track cartridge tape players. And cabinets are available in a choice of fine furniture styles: Early American, Mediterranean and Contemporary, or complement a variety of room decors. Some 4-channel units also offer separate free-standing Allegro speakers in matching fine furniture cabinets.

Allegro Bookshelf Speakers. Available in three sizes, Allegro 1000, Allegro 2000, and Allegro 3000 (see specifications on facing page), Allegro speakers offer design as distinctive and exciting as their sound. Enclosures are available in two color combinations—wood-grained Walnut color with a handsomely sculptured black grille of special stretch-knit acetate, or in contemporary white color with a sculptured blue grille of knit polyester (Allegro 2000 and 3000 only). All materials used in Zenith grilles must be colorfast and pass rigid environmental testing requirements to assure uniform performance in a variety of climates. And Allegro speakers perform equally well in either an upright or horizontal position—matching preference for style and space requirements. The Allegro nameplate on the tuned port opening rotates to match speaker positioning.

These speakers are not only unique in design, they are unique as part of home sound systems. An outstanding performer, Allegro is a welcome innovation in home musical enjoyment, bringing the exciting realism and presence of the concert-hall, from symphonies to rock bands, into the home.

Zenith Quality

More than 50 years ago, Zenith introduced its first product manufactured to the highest standards of quality. This was the beginning of a philosophy which was to become a Zenith tradition . . . a tradition that has made Zenith first choice of millions who want and demand the finest.

When you select a Zenith, you know you have a product built to provide years of dependable performance because it was manufactured by people with a dedication to the tradition of Quality Without Compromise.

EXHIBIT 3

The Consumer Electronics Market
(millions retail dollars)

	1973	Percent	Est. 1974	Percent
Television				
Color	5,250	45.0	5,050	43.5
Black and white	1,050	9.0	900	8.0
SUBTOTAL	6,300	54.0	5,950	51.5
Home Stereo Equipment				
Audio Component	950	8.0	1,050	9.0
Console	400	3.5	380	3.25
Modular	390	3.5	380	3.25
Component System	330	3.0	330	3.0
SUBTOTAL	2,070	18.0	2,140	18.5
Other (approximate)				
Radios	900	8.0	N/A	
Calculators	700	6.0	N/A	
Car Radios	600	5.0	N/A	
Electronic Musical Instruments	350	3.0	N/A	
Other (under $100 MM @)*	750	6.0	N/A	
SUBTOTAL	3,300	28.0	3,500	30.0
TOTAL	11,670	100.0%	11,590	100.0%

* Other includes electronic kits, hearing aids, personal communications, security systems, etc.

Source: Published industry data and CMS Group estimates

EXHIBIT 4

Zenith Sales Company Organization

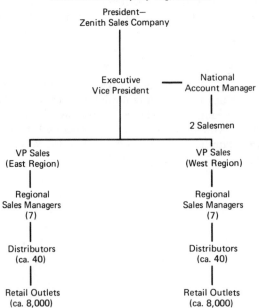

President—
Zenith Sales Company

Executive
Vice President

National
Account Manager

2 Salesmen

VP Sales
(East Region)

VP Sales
(West Region)

Regional
Sales Managers
(7)

Regional
Sales Managers
(7)

Distributors
(ca. 40)

Distributors
(ca. 40)

Retail Outlets
(ca. 8,000)

Retail Outlets
(ca. 8,000)

EXHIBIT 5

Modular Sales Volume by Outlet Type

	GE	RCA	Panasonic	Zenith	Elect/M.	Magnavox	Sony	Total
Department	20.5	16.7	27.2	3.3	38.0	11.8	32.0	30.6
Radio/TV	0	4.2	10.4	23.3	2.5	25.5	20.0	10.0
Discount	27.3	12.5	20.8	3.3	21.5	0	12.0	27.3
Furniture	6.8	25.0	0.8	10.0	10.1	19.6	4.0	5.5
Direct from Mfr	0	0	0.8	3.3	0	0	0	0.2
Music store	2.3	0	3.2	3.3	5.1	9.8	8.0	3.8
PX/BX	0	0	5.6	0	1.3	2.0	0	2.5
Appliance	15.9	37.5	7.2	36.7	8.9	21.6	4.0	9.7
Audio Specialty	2.3	0	5.6	3.3	2.5	5.9	12.0	5.2
Other	25.0	4.2	16.8	13.3	8.9	2.0	8.0	11.0
Mail Order/Catalogue	0	0	1.6	0	1.3	2.0	0	4.2
TOTALS	100	100	100	100	100	100	100	100

Source: Trendex, Inc.

EXHIBIT 6

Competitive Audio Advertising Expenditures
(Total Audio)

$(000)	1969	1970	1971	1972	1973*	1974*	1969–74 Trend
Industry	15,215	13,394	11,786	12,742	15,500	15,000	–
Zenith	2,314	1,349	1,709	1,224	1,599	1,428	–
Magnavox	2,233	2,873	3,234	3,172	4,019	4,000	+
Panasonic	2,527	3,282	3,280	3,733	4,277	4,200	+
Sony	565	954	1,472	1,600	1,859	1,800	+
G.E.	782	570	360	1,177	1,414	1,400	+
RCA	3,041	2,350	405	444	713	700	–
Sylvania	836	1,392	494	497	550	550	–
Hitachi	248	307	386	436	564	550	+

* Zenith 1973 and 1974 expenditures are actual and proposed. Competitors' 1973 and 1974 expenditures are projections based on reported data for first half 1973 and trends 1969–1973.

Source: FCB Research Department.

EXHIBIT 7

Modular Stereo Sales and Model Distribution by Price Range for Leading Manufacturers

Price Range (dollars)	A*	Panasonic Models No.	Panasonic Models %	Panasonic Sales %	Sony Models No.	Sony Models %	Sony Sales %	Magnavox Models No.	Magnavox Models %	Magnavox Sales %	Zenith Models No.	Zenith Models %	Zenith Sales %	RCA Models No.	RCA Models %	RCA Sales %	GE Models No.	GE Models %	GE Sales %
<100	10.9	3	9.1	5.8	—	—	4.5	1	5	—	—	—	—	1	5.3	8.7	—	—	35.7
100–150	23.9	3	9.1	19.8	—	—	9.0	1	5	26.3	—	—	15.4	—	—	17.3	2	16.7	21.4
150–200	29.6	9	27.3	33.9	2	12.5	18.1	4	19	26.4	1	7.7	19.2	5	26.3	13.0	3	25.0	31.0
200–250	9.8	3	9.1	7.4	5	31.3	9.1	3	14	7.9	2	15.4	15.4	5	26.3	4.3	2	16.7	7.1
250–300	11.7	8	24.2	19.0	3	18.8	13.6	—	—	5.3	4	30.8	26.9	5	26.3	26.1	1	8.3	2.4
300–350	3.8	1	3.0	5.8	2	12.5	13.6	4	19	7.9	3	23.1	3.8	1	5.3	—	2	16.7	—
350–400	5.2	3	9.1	5.0	3	18.8	18.2	4	19	15.8	2	15.4	7.7	2	10.5	8.7	—	—	2.4
450–500	2.7	3	9.1	1.7	1	6.3	—**	2	10	5.3	1	7.7	11.5	—	—	—	2	16.7	—
>500	3.3	—	—	1.7	—	—	13.6**	1	5	5.3	—	—	—	—	—	21.7	—	—	—
Total Models		33			16			20			13			19			12		

* A refers to Trendex Retail Sales Volume (% of units)

** Phenomena such as these may occur due to consumer confusion over the definitions of compact systems and component systems.

Sources: Trendex, Inc., and Manufacturers' Price and Model Sheets.

EXHIBIT 8

Brand Share, Compact and Component Systems—1970 to 1973
(Percent)

I. COMPACT SYSTEMS

Jun–Dec 1970		Jan–Jun 1972		Jun–Dec 1972		Jan–Jun 1973		Jun–Dec 1973	
Panasonic	19.1	Pan.	14.8	Pan.	13.9	Pan.	14.6	Pan.	13.8
Electroph.	6.1	Elec.	10.0	Elec.	9.9	Elec.	10.0	Elec.	8.8
RCA	5.7	Magn.	6.8	GE	5.3	Magn.	5.5	Sears	6.1
Magnavox	4.7	RCA	4.5	Magn.	4.9	Sears	4.6	Magn.	5.6
Sears	3.9	GE	4.0	Sony	4.3	Sony	4.0	GE	5.1
GE	3.7	Sony	3.2	Sears	4.0	Zenith	3.7	M. Ward	5.0
Zenith	3.5	Lloyd's	2.8	M. Ward	4.0	RCA	3.1	Lloyd's	4.1
Philco	2.4	Penny	2.8	S'design	3.5	GE	2.8	S'design	3.5
Sony	2.4	Zenith	1.9	Zenith	3.3	M. Ward	2.7	Zenith	3.1
TOTAL	51.5		50.8		53.1		51.0		55.1

II. COMPONENT SYSTEMS

June–Dec 1970		Jan–Jun 1972		Jun–Dec 1972		Jan–Jun 1973		Jun–Dec 1973	
Panasonic	11.7	Pan.	9.0	Pan.	10.1	Pan.	7.4	Pan.	8.2
RCA	6.0	Magn.	4.0	Elec.	7.4	Elec.	5.3	Elec.	4.2
Realistic	5.2	M'work	3.5	Sears	4.0	Magn.	2.6	Sony	4.2
GE	4.4	GE	3.0	Sony	3.7	Real.	2.4	Real.	2.8
Electroph.	4.0	Elec.	3.0	Real.	3.4	S'design	2.4	Magn.	2.5
Magnavox	4.0	Sansui	3.0	Zenith	3.0	Sony	2.1	S'design	2.5
Zenith	3.6	Fisher	3.0	RCA	2.7	RCA	1.8	Zenith	2.5
Masterwork	2.8	Zenith	1.0	Fisher	2.7	Zenith	1.2	Sears	2.3
TOTAL	41.7		29.5		37.0		25.2		29.2

Notes: This exhibit includes the first six months of Zenith Allegro market exposure. This is probably too early to allow conclusions to be drawn regarding market reaction to the new product.

Due to confusion, on the part of consumer, over the "compact"–"component system" distinction, brand shares in each category may be distorted for certain brands (including Zenith).

Source: Trendex, Inc.

CHAPTER 10

Zenith Radio Corporation: Videodisc

In June 1977, Robert Bowen, Senior Vice President for Marketing at Zenith Radio Corporation, was reviewing the situation in the videodisc market. Competitive products were being introduced and Zenith faced decisions about extending its consumer electronics leadership into this new market.

Mr. Bowen faced a number of difficult questions. Is the videodisc destined to become an established durable good, or is it just a fad for the wealthy? Should Zenith consider producing a tape or a disc system? Finally, Mr. Bowen recognized that it is difficult to use traditional market and consumer research as a basis for forecasting videodisc sales, but he needed some estimates of demand in order to make decisions about when and how to enter the market. He was skeptical of trying to do consumer surveys, however, since it's one thing to ask consumer attitudes and preferences for a new food product, but it would be difficult to attribute much reliability to consumer attitudes about buying a high ticket durable good, such as a videoplayer (VP).[1] Nonetheless, Mr. Bowen had data from group depth interviews, as well as data on trends which might reflect on VP sales. He wondered how best to use these sources of information for his multiple decisions.

THE PRODUCT CONCEPT

Videoplayers represent an extension of videotape recording (VTR) technology from professional to in-home use. Videoplayer hard-

---

This case was prepared by Professor Scott Ward, The Wharton School, as a basis for class discussion.

---

[1] The term "videoplayer," or "VP," will be used throughout this case to refer to systems which employ

ware and software available now—or soon to be available—would have some combination of the following functions:

1. Record television programs off-air. A timer can be used to automatically turn the recorder on and off when the owner is not home. Thus, a favorite show could be watched at a later time. Another feature would permit recording from one channel while the set was actually tuned to another channel. Thus, if two desirable programs were scheduled for the same time slot, one could be viewed at that time, and the other recorded and viewed later. These features characterize the market-pioneering Sony Betamax (see Appendix A).

2. Optional camera and microphone equipment could be used in much the same way as traditional 8 millimeter home movies. However, videorecordings can be played back immediately since no film development is involved.

3. In-home libraries of movies and television specials could be developed in much the same way as many Americans now have stereophonic record collections. Movie studios and television production houses could package and sell copies of software (e.g., movies) but some fear pirating will occur as people record films off-air, in possible violation of copyright laws.

Mr. Bowen knew that different companies were developing one of two principal non-compatible videoplayer systems: tape or disc. The two systems are similar in a number of ways. Both can be designed as stand-alone systems to be used with standard TV sets. Programming can be played through a television by attaching appropriate cables to the receiver antenna terminals, and both systems provide visual and audio quality better than normal TV reception. The physical similarities between the systems, however, go no further. With the tape system, consumers can record a program, immediately play it back, erase the program, and reuse the tape, all without intermediate processing. Standard videoplayer tape can record about 60 minutes of programming (though

some do record up to 112 minutes) and, for exceptionally durable cartridge tape systems, will last up to about 1,000 passes.

There are two basic disc system approaches, both of which are playback only, and, therefore, must employ prerecorded software. A mechanized pressure scanning system—commonly called a "capacitive" system—reproduces signals embedded in grooves on a plastic disc's surface through a mechanism similar to a phonograph arm and stylus. The laser reproduction system—employs a low power laser beam to "read" images embedded within the disc's surface. The discs for both systems resemble phonograph records, although they vary in size, rigidity, and transluscence.

The capacitive disc has a limited life (about 400 plays) due to the direct contact with the player stylus. The optical disc, on the other hand, has an unlimited life. Not only is there no mechanical contact with the player arm to wear down the disc, but a metallic coating over the embedded image layer protects the disc's program from elements such as dust, finger prints, and superficial scratches. This makes the optical disc more durable and less sensitive to handling.

The effective playing time for a disc has not yet been fully determined. A capacitive disc capable of playing 30 minutes has been developed, and one was rumored to have a 60-minute disc ready for production in the near future. An automatic disc changer which can stack discs and increase nonstop playing time does not seem economically feasible.

The tape system, while well suited for home-recorded programs, is expensive for mass prerecorded programs. The disc cannot be used for home-recorded programming but allows prerecorded programs to be sold relatively inexpensively.

One difficulty in determining the future retail price of the discs with any exactitude is the uncertainty as to just how many discs will be sold. Two factors affecting this figure might be the development of disc leasing versus the development of a mass market for discs. Since the variable cost of pressing a disc is so low

either disc or tape technology. These systems are described later in the case.

(about $1.00 per hour of programming) relative to the fixed cost of mastering (perhaps $1 million of fixed costs per capacity of 9,600 units per shift and $100 per minute of mastering per disc), high volume production favors the disc and lower disc prices. On the other hand, tape duplication is a high variable-cost, low fixed-cost means of transmitting programming, with a cost advantage relative to discs over a small volume of production. The tape-disc cost indifference is approximately 1,000 units, with discs having total unit cost advantage above this figure.

COMPETITION

Although Zenith was leaning toward introduction of a disc system, Mr. Bowen knew that three companies would form the major competition for Zenith in the Videodisc market: Sony, which introduced its Betamax (tape) system in 1976–77 and was estimated to have sold about 25,000 units in the U.S. during the first year of sales; RCA, which was committed to a capacitive system; and Philips/MCA, which was planning an optical system. Philips had purchased Magnavox in order to gain access to an established distribution network. An arrangement with MCA assured a supply of software, since MCA was the leading developer of entertainment programming in the U.S. For example, MCA produced such movies as *Earthquake*, and in one recent year, 12 hours per week of prime time TV programming.

Mr. Bowen felt that RCA believed videodiscs would become a major home entertainment medium over the next decade. They were committed to the capacitive system since it is most consistent with RCA's production, manufacturing and repair strengths, and since the system would be the least expensive—at least initially—and easiest for consumers to operate, since capacitive systems were much like record player turntables. Apparently, Mr. Bowen felt, RCA did not aim to go into programming production, but would arrange

licensing agreements. According to industry sources, RCA believed consumers would buy 10 hours of programming in the first year, and about 7 hours in successive years, at prices ranging from $10 to $15 for feature movies. RCA was also believed to project penetration of these movies at from 5 to 30%, and project player and programming sales of the total videodisc market as follows:

	Player Sales	Programming Sales	Total
1980–1982	$0.8 billion	$0.4 billion	$1.2 billion
1982–1984	$1.0 billion	$1.0 billion	$2.0 billion
1987	$1.0 billion	$1.8 billion	$2.8 billion

The other future competitor for Zenith was Philips/MCA, which was ready to introduce an optical system. Philips was one of the world's largest manufacturers of televisions, with worldwide annual sales in excess of $10 billion. Along with other manufacturers, Philips perceived potential consumer demand for videodisc among affluent Europeans since programming variety was very limited due to government control in most countries.

Philips' U.S. subsidiary, North American Philips, paved the way for introduction of the videodisc in the U.S. by purchasing Magnavox, thus gaining access to a distribution system of 2,600 dealers (4,500 total outlets), and by the licensing agreement with MCA. The latter company owns Spencer Gifts, which sells merchandise through 211 stores and via 90 million catalogues sent to 25 million homes. Initial distribution of over 500 titles (movies, television series) would be via the Spencer network, as well as through Magnavox dealers where the hardware would be sold, and, perhaps, via "tape clubs," similar to book-of-the-month clubs.

It was generally known that MCA felt that much market potential existed for educational as well as entertainment materials. However, they apparently planned a kind of test market, to carefully monitor the kinds of discs consumers buy in various markets which achieve some minimum level (about 1,000) sales of their optical system. In this way, MCA would be able to project consumer tastes for software as the market continues to expand. Table 1 summarizes the competition.

The Sony Betamax was the product pioneer. A tape system, Betamax had been introduced in late 1975 and early 1976, selling for about $1,300. In just over a year, the typical retail price was about $800–1,000. MCA had initiated a lawsuit against Sony in an attempt to stop the distribution and sale of Betamax. Essentially, the suit charged that consumers would record off-air, thus scrambling audience compositions and making it impossible to accurately describe audiences at particular times. Additionally, it was charged that off-air recording would violate copyright laws. The suit was still pending as Mr. Bowen contemplated the situation.

PROGRAMMING

Companies like Warner Communications, Columbia Pictures, and Twentieth Century-Fox derive a substantial percentage of their

TABLE 1

Summary of Zenith's Competitors in the Videoplayer Market

	RCA	Philips/MCA	Sony
System Commitments	Capacitive 30 mins. per side	Optical	Tape
Key Reasons	Consistent with production, manufacturing, and repair capabilities. Least expensive to consumer, but easiest to understand.	Superior audio quality. MCA has software.	Consistent with existing production and manufacturing capabilities.
Key Product Concept	Home entertainment; extensive options not needed.	Home entertainment *and* education.	Off-air recording in anticipation of software development market pioneer.
Distribution	Selective through high traffic retail locations.	Direct—2,600 Magnavox dealers (4,500 total outlets) using Magnavox brand name; MCA will distribute programming via dealers and catalogues.	Sony outlets. Already in discount stores.
Issues	Software development.	Weak distribution. May license.	
Price (Approximate)	Est. $400	Est. $550–640	$1300 in 1975–76. $800 in 1977.
Est. Disc Prices	$12–15 per program, lowering to $10.	$2–10 per program.	$10 per 30 min. tape.

revenues and profits from motion pictures, have substantial libraries of proven "classics" and contemporary feature films, and stand to profit considerably from disc and tape royalties, distribution, and conceivably, manufacture. Yet none of the three are ready to take an active role in the introduction of the videoplayer and its software. They are cautiously watching the development of the videoplayer from the sidelines.

These filmmakers want to make sure that VPs will be reliable, and easy to operate, in order to insure quality of reproduction. Second, filmmakers want long playing time per disc or tape so viewing will be easy and uninterrupted. Finally, they want strict guards against unauthorized duplication and distribution of software programming.

Original programming for VPs would, of course, depend on future demand. For now, licensing for a movie, for example, would proceed in the following order:

1. Theatre: first-run
2. Theatre: second-run
3. Airlines, hotels with their own channels; Pay TV
4. Colleges
5. Networks
6. Syndications sales to local non-network stations
7. Videoplayer software

DIFFERENT BASES FOR FORECASTING VIDEOPLAYER SALES

Mr. Bowen reviewed several sources of information which he hoped would be useful in forecasting demand for videoplayers. He was not only interested in estimating the rate of market penetration, but he hoped to gain some understanding of what market segments would be innovators and which would be followers. Clearly, Zenith would follow Sony and possibly Philips/MCA and RCA into the market. What market strategies would be required when Zenith did enter the market? He reviewed the literature on opinion leadership and new prod-

uct adoption,[2] and gathered kinds of secondary and primary information. First, Mr. Bowen reasoned that certain demographic trends, such as leisure time patterns, would be indirectly related to VP demand. He also felt that attitudes and variables such as satisfaction with television programming would be related. And he commissioned a small scale survey among entertainment industry leaders to gauge their opinions about the future of VPs. Finally, he felt that some qualitative data explicitly concerning consumer reactions to VPs could be useful. Consequently, he commissioned group depth interviews with various segments of potential consumers. From these direct and indirect sources of information, Mr. Bowen hoped to have a reasonably valid basis for predicting VP sales and for beginning the task of planning Zenith's market strategy in the developing market.

1. DEMOGRAPHIC TRENDS

1. Recreational and Leisure Time Trends. Mr. Bowen examined data on changes in recent decades in recreation and leisure time expenditures. He noted that total personal consumption for recreation had increased 104% from 1960 to 1970 (Exhibit 1). Individuals were estimated to spend 46% of their passive leisure time watching television, as opposed to less than 1% reading books (Exhibit 2). A Gallup poll reported that almost half of those questioned said "watching TV" was a "favorite way of spending an evening" (Ex-

---

[2] See, for example, Elihu Katz and Paul Lazarsfeld, *Personal Influence* (New York: Free Press, 1955); Elihu Katz, "The Two-Step Flow of Communication: An Up to Date Report on an Hypothesis," *Public Opinion Quarterly,* 21 (Spring 1957), 61–78; and John G. Myers, "Patterns of Interpersonal Influence in the Adoption of New Products," *Proceedings of the American Marketing Association,* ed. R. A. Hass, AMA, 1966, pp. 750–57. The most recent and extensive review is Thomas S. Robertson, *Innovative Behavior and Communication* (New York: Holt, Rinehart & Winston, 1971).

hibit 3). Various leisure time activities were also analyzed by various demographic groupings (Exhibit 4).

While there has been an upward trend in such at-home forms of recreation as those listed above, certain away from home leisure activities have experienced a decline, most notably motion picture attendance. Not only is television viewing the most dominant form of leisure time activity, but it is also widespread across all income and educational classes. Other, miscellaneous data on leisure time activities among Americans is summarized in Appendix B.

2. Satisfaction with Broadcast Television. Public opinion polls offer the most useful source of data on current levels of satisfaction with TV. As indicated in Exhibit 3, television viewing is a favorite way of spending an evening for 46% of Americans. Most Americans across all income brackets and geographical areas believe that there are enough shows on television which interest or entertain them, although there is a sizable minority which disagrees (see Exhibit 5).

Exhibit 6 shows the relative satisfaction/dissatisfaction with the programs available on broadcast television. News specials and dramas are the program categories with the highest level of unfilled viewer demand. Nevertheless, the overall responses seem to indicate that most television watchers want "more of the same." The same study mentions that 35–50% of television viewers watch TV only when there is nothing better to do and 50–60% read while watching TV (see Exhibit 7).

II. INTERVIEWS WITH ENTERTAINMENT INDUSTRY LEADERS AND RESEARCHERS

Executives of companies interested in the development of the videoplayer emphasized the difficulty in defining which consumers would emerge as purchasers of the videoplayer. Some felt a mass market would develop quickly, while others saw a much slower take off.

Warren Lieberfarb of Twentieth Century-Fox offered the only explicit definition of the consumer: affluent, middle-aged, highly educated, purchasing for status and desirous of building a library of his own discs. While not explicitly stating the same criteria, Robert Sarnoff of RCA echoed these sentiments by indicating that the consumer will buy the player primarily for the satisfaction of owning and building a collection of programs. Sarnoff believed firmly that both frequent and infrequent TV viewers would be attracted to the product as would all kinds of movie-goers. He indicated that RCA market research had found high levels of consumer acceptance across wide demographic ranges.

A less optimistic view of the market was expressed at CBS. Research analysts there found no mass market, but did estimate that the small potential demand that would emerge would be extremely price sensitive and entirely entertainment oriented. People who will buy the player will be those who are ready to pay a high cost per hour of entertainment, those who are not satisfied with present TV programming, and possibly those who want a continuous source of education or information.

Conflicting views arose concerning the type of programming that would be demanded. Alan Adler of Columbia Pictures and Tom McDermott of RCA saw the purchasers as only being interested in movies, whereas officials of WGBH, a Boston public broadcasting company, saw culture orientation existing which is partially served by the public TV sector. In summary, it seems that the industry leaders and observers view the market as those people with higher than average income and education who are primarily entertainment oriented. The vast majority of industry analysts minimized the degree to which an educational market would develop at the outset. Only WGBH, with a vested interest in the area of educational programming, saw demand moving away from an entertainment orientation.

III. GROUP DEPTH INTERVIEWS

To probe potential consumer demand, selected consumer panels with varying interests were chosen to participate in focus group interviews to discuss the product concept and its fit with differing life-styles.

Panels for the focus group session were chosen based both upon a consideration of the above trends and an analysis of the characteristics of individuals who might be interested in the product concept. Appendix B provides the characteristics of several groupings which were thought to be target markets.

Six groups were chosen for analysis:

#1. General, (Upper-middle Class)

#2. Innovators

#3. Innovators

#4. Educationally-Oriented Parents

#5. Heavy TV Viewers

#6. Young Couples with High Disposable Income—
Selective TV Watchers

Analysis centered upon assessing the response of these groups, both as regards parallels and differences, in attempting to gain an understanding of the consumer.

The results are presented below in the form of an analysis of the common trends in the sessions.

A. The Product Concept

Every member of the focus groups after being given the description of the product and a picture of the product, very quickly grasped the concepts of videoplayers and saw the potential of such systems. No one was overwhelmed with the technological aspects of the player but saw the systems as merely another means of delivering programming to the TV screen. This illustrates a key finding, which was summed up by a member of the sixth—Young Professional—group who said:

If the hardware companies try to appeal to a mass audience by having popular, mass appeal soft-

ware available in a limited catalogue (old movies and sports) then people will see this as only another TV. People really are indifferent to *how* the picture gets on their tube; they are more concerned with the type and variety of available programs.

None of the interview groups, from the blue collar housewives who watched seven hours of TV per day (Group 5) to the young professionals group (Group 6) with high disposable income, were enthusiastic about the concept, even *before* price was discussed.

In general, estimates of the price of the videoplayer varied, but surprisingly, many members of each group predicted that such a player might cost between $300 and $500. When confronted with the probable cost of the two technologies ($600–1200 figures were used in the groups) many people said they would be interested. Later in many of the group interviews, the opinion was expressed that VP prices would decline over time.

The young professionals group was less sensitive to the $600 price. However, most of this group were unwilling to pay more than $2 for a full two hours of entertainment. Their reasoning was, as one participant pointed out, "I have a limited amount of time available for leisure, and I quite frankly would rather get out of the house and do something."

For a relatively affluent couple with no children (the type of group which Mr. Bowen felt would easily spend $200 for a Nikon camera), paying $10 for a disc was viewed as too expensive since the two of them have the mobility to go to a movie or a play. The upscale groups also reflected a definite stigma associated with mass oriented television entertainment. They watch television for the news or specials, so the video player would have to compete against outside interests. As for those who are more accepting of broadcasting fare, they are relatively willing to spend $10 for each album or tape, but the initial outlay is seen as too much and there is not sufficient dissatisfaction with broadcast TV to justify buying the videoplayer.

Although they would not purchase at the

given price levels of $600–1200, all groups identified similar positive attributes about the player:

1. The viewer can see what he wants to see when he wants to see it.
2. There are no commercial interruptions.
3. The viewer can see something as often as possible.
4. Videoplayers offer the opportunity to watch programming not generally available on TV. The types of programs desired were:
    Old movies (most of the group expected to see the newer movies on TV)
    Old sports
    Children's programming
    Theater, drama
    Children's films
    Educational programming (Jacques Cousteau)
    Pornography
    Travel films
    Biographies
    Lectures
    Documentaries

There might be a status value to the videoplayer, especially since the groups could envision inviting a neighbor over to watch a new disc, swapping discs, etc.

All groups found the physical appearance of videoplayers attractive, an item they would like in their living rooms. Some suggested that a wood casing would be appropriate to match the cabinet television sets.

Many group members had difficulty in justifying purchasing a disc since they felt a disc would be viewed at the most two times. Unlike an audio record, which can serve as background music for a variety of activities, this would require the same amount of attention as current broadcast TV, which does not generally serve as background noise.

B. Technological Issues and Features of the Player

Focusing on disc technology, there was little importance attached to the issue of capacitance versus optical systems. They were merely viewed as different ways of getting a picture on the TV tube. The features were not significant in themselves but were required for a product with such a price. All groups made quick analogies—even if not exactly accurate—with the features of a record player for the capacitance system. However, one housewife in the fifth group pointed out that her washing machine had many buttons for the various cycles that she never used, so that she could not see using some of the features on the videoplayer, namely the fast forward, reverse, slow motion, and freeze frame.

Each group spontaneously mentioned their fears of technological obsolescence. The eight mm and Super-8 home movie cameras were mentioned specifically as an illustration. One member of the group recounted a tale of buying a home movie camera only to discover that the Super-8 film would not fit the camera, with the consequence that he had to purchase a new camera for the film. All were quite reluctant to purchase a system which might be superseded in a few years by a more advanced one.

The members of the focus groups felt that with two competing systems on the market they would be reluctant to purchase any system. They found the prospects of serving as guinea pigs for a manufacturer of a new system even more disturbing. Their inclination was to wait until the technology had been improved. Even the "innovators" were inclined to delay purchases until one system had established a reputation for reliability. All were somewhat reluctant to purchase a new system unless they were assured that it could be easily repaired and could perform as well as current electronic equipment. The optical system enjoyed the distinct advantage, in the minds of the interviewees, of being on the leading edge of technology. It was felt that the capacitance system, a familiar technology, was more susceptible to obsolescence.

There was some reluctance to allow a laser system into the home, not because of irrational fear of the "laser" but because of recent announcements of radiation leakage from television sets, a technology which has existed for at least 25 years.

While some viewed the videoplayer as akin to a stereo system that the children would be forbidden to touch, most parents felt that the children would be using the player. Concerns were expressed about safety in product design, and ease of use for children.

C. The Purchase Decision

It was strongly felt by many that they would only buy the player if there were a large variety of different discs available. Members of the groups felt that the selection of programs offered would have to include much more than just old movies. In fact, there would have to be sufficient variety of discs available to target the videoplayer to each small group's special interest.

Participants viewed themselves as being "locked into" an expensive medium if they purchased the videoplayer. More specifically, they realized that they would have to pay a great deal to build up a library of the variety required, or be prepared to rent discs they only wished to use once. They were acutely aware that the entire system would be expensive.

It was a common expectation that the programs available on the videoplayer would not be similar to broadcast television. If, in fact, the first programming were similar to broadcast TV, then the videoplayer would be perceived as being akin to that medium. There was a wide range of program interest so that most people would, at some time, be willing to see almost anything that was available on the videoplayer. However, they would not purchase the videoplayer just to see one type of program.

The participants would be willing to purchase only those discs which they would want to see repeatedly. Old movies and other TV type entertainment would not be watched more than once. Cultural events, such as opera and ballet, and children's programs were mentioned as being the types of programs which would be watched more than once.

The durability of the discs was not important, except that the discs should be able to be handled by children. Most members of the groups felt that they would not want to watch a disc more than two or three times; even children's programs would not need to last more than 200 times. However, a later point was developed which built upon the durability of the optical system: "If discs are to be rented out, they had better not wear out rapidly."

Most participants felt that they would purchase relatively few discs per year, primarily because of the disc's cost. Most estimated that they would buy eight to ten discs per year if the player were available at what they perceived to be a reasonable price.

D. Software Pricing

The first five interview groups felt that $5 to $10, or even $12, for two hours of programming was reasonable. They were, however, unwilling to invest any money in *purchasing* programs unless those programs were ones which would be watched repeatedly. Although most heads of households were quick to point out that paying $10 to see a movie at home was significantly cheaper than taking the family out to a movie, all felt considerable psychological reluctance to pay $10 for a disc which would be viewed only once or twice at the most. Many felt that the video disc was more akin to a television program and less like an investment in a book. All pointed out that the disc was not like a record, which one could listen to as background for a variety of activities.

Many parents were quite willing to purchase educational or children's programming. The reasons for this emerged strongly in the interviews with the women who were heavy TV watchers and with the group of parents of school age children. Parents are relatively price insensitive for children's programming because they see the potential of VPs as a babysitter, particularly at times when there is nothing on broadcast television that children might want to watch. Additionally, since pre-teen children watch an average of six hours of television per day parents expressed a desire to have greater control over the quality of programs their children watched. Since the children want to watch TV anyway, they might as well watch a story on *David Copperfield,* so that they can learn about the "classics" while being entertained.

Finally, mothers of younger children noted that children up to the age of 12 actually prefer repetition, so that the discs could be easily used 20 to 30 times during the year.

Virtually all groups were quite reluctant to purchase programming for adults unless it would be watched repeatedly. Some group members suggested renting discs from a library; or a lending library, either free or with an annual subscription fee; or a "disc of the month" club selection system whereby a commitment to purchase some discs brought about a reduction in the cost of each disc purchased.

Finally, during each of the group discussions, it was mentioned that the videoplayer had an ability to combine audio performance to existing records or tapes with the optical system's indestructibility. During the last focus group it was suggested that the group might be interested in purchasing the optical system primarily for use as a high class audio component. The practically indestructible records and the fact that each disc could have up to 17 1/2 hours of audio listening appealed to the group. The video viewing would be a complete option, an extra. The young professionals were very enthusiastic about this option. All were then quite receptive to paying $400 to $600 for a turntable. Immediately, the members perceived that the issue of programming was solved since there already existed a wide catalogue of audio records which could be made available.

FORECASTING VIDEOPLAYER SALES

Mr. Bowen hoped that he could use elements of his analysis to date as a basis for estimating future sales of videoplayers. He made three types of forecasts. First, he estimated hardware sales based on hunches and combinations of findings from analysis of the consumer behavior data; second, he made hardware demand estimates based on various levels of market penetration of potential buyers. Finally, he made some assumptions about sales of hardware and software under three different hardware pricing scenarios, for tentative forecasts of 1983–87 sales.

A. Estimates Using Consumer Behavior Findings

Mr. Bowen reasoned that the target consumer for videoplayers during the first several years of sales will be "upscale"—having an annual household income in excess of $15,000. Other evidence for the "upscale" market definition was the opinion of focus group respondents that most entertainment and "how to do" oriented programs would be viewed only once or twice. There was a decided inclination to rent this type of programming, an option which will probably not be available until the product gains acceptance. Since both RCA and MCA intend to emphasize these kinds of programs in their advertising and in their disc libraries, the consumer will have to be willing to build a library of discs in order to get frequent usage from the player. Therefore, the high cost of programs reinforces the contention that, in the early years at least, income will be a prime determinant of consumer acceptance.

Mr. Bowen also reasoned that prospects would be color television set owners, so he added this second factor—color TV penetration figures among lower and upper income groups—into his demand forecast assumptions.

A third characteristic of the potential consumer was thought to be that he (or she) *not* be prone to lengthy prepurchase deliberation. He (or she) must be willing to take a risk, to put his money "on the line." Focus group respondents associated considerable risk of obsolescence with the video disc player due to perceived product improvements and technological standardization. Consequently, it is assumed that the potential consumer will not be a "planner," that is, a person who generally plans ahead and deliberates extensively before buying expensive items. The psychographic characteristic of relative inclination to plan and deliberate is more characteristic of the middle than either the lower or upper income group. This is because the perceived risk for the middle income group is higher and because they have a greater investment in career, reputation and accumulated property than the lower group, and less disposable income than the upper group. Of course, the perceived risk will decline with long-term exposure and falling prices for the product, so this factor will gradually become less important.

Finally, the consumer research strongly indicated that the potential VP consumer will be a medium to heavy TV viewer. Light and non-TV watchers indicated an aversion to the medium of TV with its mass audience programming orientation. For these people there is a stigma associated with excessive television watching, which in turn attaches to the video disc player, which was perceived as an adjunct to TV.

Exhibit 8 shows how these 4 characteristics were combined into a market forecast for 1977-87.

Based on this forecast, Mr. Bowen made some further calculations about the effects of a regional "roll-out" strategy, assuming the video disc system would be made available for purchase to 10%, 25%, 60% and 100% of U.S. households over the 1977-80 years.

B. Estimates Based on Different Levels of Market Penetration

Mr. Bowen also asked a group of economists at a leading western business school to forecast demand based on different levels of penetration of the potential market. These economists assumed wide distribution, and an average unit price of $450 at retail over the 1977-1982 period. Their forecasts ranged from a worst case penetration of 28,500 units ($12.7 million sales) to a best case of 281,200 units ($126.6 million sales), as their results in Exhibit 9 show.

C. Forecasts for 1983-1987

Finally, Mr. Bowen made some tentative market forecasts for 1983-87. He assumed high, medium and low pricing structures (over $400, between $325-375, and under $250, respectively), and he assumed that some players will be sold to consumers with less than $15,000 annual household income (adjusted for inflation). Specifically, under the medium price scenario, 25% of sales will come from households of less than $15,000 income by 1987. Under the low price scenario, households below $15,000 in income will be the source of 50% of sales by 1987. The forecasts contained in Exhibit 10 indicate a range in mean annual sales by 1987 of approximately 270,000 units under

Effect of Regional "Roll-Out" Strategies on Size of Potential Market by Year
(Based on Market Forecast in Exhibit 8)

	Potential Market (millions)	% Distribution Attained	Millions of Households Potential Buyers
1977	5.96	10	.596
1978	6.6	25	1.65
1979	7.2	60	4.32
1980	7.9	100	7.9
1981	8.7	100	9.6
1982	9.6	100	9.6
1983	10.4	100	10.4
1984	11.41	100	11.41
1985	12.41	100	12.41
1986	13.52	100	13.52
1987	14.57	100	14.57

high price assumptions to 3,400,000 under low price assumptions.

The 1983–87 projections also factored in software sales projections, based on findings in the focus group interviews. Consumers had indicated a willingness to purchase six to eight discs per year, which is assumed to be equivalent to an annual dollar expenditure of $65. Most interviewees stated that they purchase only four or five audio records in a year, but that a higher number of video discs would be purchased in order to achieve a satisfactory level of player usage.

The projections are based upon a $10 price for two hours of programming and a $5 price for one thirty-minute disc. Mr. Bowen knew that, should the actual price vary significantly from this estimate, it would dramatically affect the demand for software and could affect the demand for hardware.

THE TASKS AHEAD

Mr. Bowen set aside the various materials he had been reviewing, and pondered some difficult questions. Since demand forecasts were of such crucial importance, should he consider pursuing other sources of data, and design new forecasts? Recognizing the radically new technology of videoplayers, he wondered if he really had a valid understanding of the consumer behavior involved for videoplayer sales. Should other consumer research be done?

Then there were the hard strategic decisions. Zenith had been leaning toward a disc system, but had flexibility. Which system would the market eventually prefer? When and how should Zenith enter the market? Mr. Bowen felt he had a reasonable basis for suggesting market segmentation, product positioning, pricing, and other strategic alternatives to top management, but he recognized the necessity of proposing and evaluating various market strategies, based on different assumptions. These assumptions would relate to the competitive environment, growth of software support, and market demand, and, perhaps, other factors.

EXHIBIT 1

Percent Changes in Recreational Expenditures, 1950 to 1960 and 1960 to 1970

	1950 to 1960 % change	1960 to 1970 % change
Total Personal Consumption	70	104
Passive		
Admittance to Theatres, Operas ...	99	101
Books, Magazines	93	185
Magazines, Newspapers, Sheet Music	47	106
Radio, T.V., Records, Musical Instruments	41	186
Active		
Foreign Travel	157	153

Source: Conference Board, Roadmap to Industry #1712, April 15, 1973.

EXHIBIT 2

Passive Leisure Time Activities by Hours and Dollars Spent

	1950	1971			
	% of Total Expenditures	Total Expenditures		Hours/Year/Capita	
		Billion $	%	Hours	%
Newspapers	33	9.9	33	218	8
Television	9	7.5	25	1200	46
Radio	20	2.4	8	900	35
Magazines	10	3.0	10	170	7
Records/Phonograph	5	2.7	9	68	3
Books	2	1.2	4	10	.4
Motion Picture	14	1.2	4	9	.4
Cultural & Sports Events	2.5	.75	2.5	3	.1
Other	4.5	1.35	4.5	3	.1
TOTAL	100.0	30.0	100.0	2581	100.0

Source: CBS Study, 1970.

EXHIBIT 3

Favorite Evening Activities

Question: What is your favorite way of spending an evening? (base: all respondents)

	1960** % of respondents	1974** % of respondents
PASSIVE ACTIVITIES		
Watching T.V.	28	46
Reading	10	14
Staying at home with family	17	10
Movies/theatre	6	9
Resting/relaxing	*	8
Listening to radio/records	0	5
ACTIVE ACTIVITIES		
Entertaining friends	*	8
Playing adult games (cards)	6	8
Participating in sports	*	5
Dining out	*	12
Visiting friends	8	10

* Not covered in 1960 study.

** Figures do not add to 100% due to multiple responses.

Source: Gallup Poll mentioned in *N.Y. Times*, March 7, 1974.

EXHIBIT 4

Percent of Population Engaging in Various Leisure Activities by Personal Characteristics*

	T.V.**	Visits with Friends***	Yardwork***	Mags.**	Books**	Pleasure Drives***	Records**	Meetings***	Hobbies***
Percent of all respondents	57	38	33	27	18	17	14	11	10
Age									
15–19	56	46	20	31	21	25	35	11	11
20–29	57	41	24	29	19	21	16	9	9
30–39	56	40	33	25	17	18	14	10	10
40–49	61	36	39	25	15	14	10	11	10
50–59	56	33	38	23	15	11	6	11	12
60 & over	53	37	42	27	21	11	6	12	11
Sex & Employ.									
Men	56	32	36	25	17	15	9	10	8
Women									
All	57	42	34	27	18	16	13	11	12
Employ.	56	42	27	26	16	16	15	11	9
Unemploy.	58	43	38	28	19	16	11	11	14
Rural-Urban									
Rural	56	40	43	27	18	15	11	11	9
Urban									
Below 100,000	56	42	34	31	18	20	13	12	11
100,000–999,999	59	37	31	28	18	17	15	11	13
1,000,000 & over	56	35	23	22	18	15	17	9	9
Education (over 20 yrs.)									
Below 8th grade	51	38	35	12	12	10	8	11	9
8th grade	56	35	36	19	15	11	8	8	9
Some high school	59	40	34	24	15	17	11	9	11
High school	61	38	35	29	15	18	11	11	11
College	55	36	37	40	30	18	13	14	11
Annual Family Income									
Under $3,000	47	39	35	23	20	13	13	11	8
$3,000–4,999	60	38	30	25	16	17	12	10	12
$5,000–6,999	59	38	33	27	18	18	14	10	11
$7,000 & over	59	39	34	33	20	17	15	11	11

* Activities in decreasing order of participation.

** Passive leisure activities.

*** Active leisure activities.

Source: Opinion Research Corporation: A Survey for Motion Picture Association of America, Inc.

EXHIBIT 5

Interest in Television Programming

Question: On most evenings are there enough shows on T.V. that interest or entertain you? (base: Total)

	Enough	Are Not Enough	Varies (vol.)	Not Sure
	%	%	%	%
Total	58	31	10	1
East	59	28	12	1
South	63	28	8	1
Midwest	52	35	12	1
West	57	35	7	1
Cities	59	29	11	1
Suburbs	55	33	11	1
Towns	59	31	9	1
Rural	59	32	8	1
Age 18–29	59	29	11	1
Age 30–49	57	32	10	1
Age 50 and over	57	33	9	1
Under $5,000 income	61	27	11	1
$5,000–$9,999 income	60	29	9	2
$10,000–$14,999 income	60	31	9	—
$15,000 and over	52	35	12	1
Single	51	34	12	3
Married	58	32	10	—
Married, with children	59	30	10	1
Male	56	33	10	1
Female	61	28	10	1
White	56	32	10	2
Non-white	69	22	7	2
Owns black & white set(s) only	58	30	11	1
Owns color set(s)	58	32	9	1

Source: Louis Harris Study made in 1971 for Zenith.

EXHIBIT 6

TV Viewing Preferences

	No. of Shows	% Households Watching	Avg. % Wanting		% Affluent Wanting	
			More	Less	More	Less
Variety-Entertain. Special	20	82	23–37	19–10	18–39	24–11
Situation Comedies	15	81	21	27	16	39
Network News	21	73	22	5	23	4
Crime & Spy Shows*	9	67	19	30	15	35
Plays & Drama Series*	9	59	30	18	47	12
Local News	21	54	26	4	26	6
Westerns*	5	53	24	30	16	37
Talk Shows	19	52	14	33	16	32
Live Sports*	7	50	32	18	34	17
Quiz Shows	11	42	14	35	11	45
Child. Shows & Cartoons	25	48	36	6	39	6
Soap Operas	17	41	8	52	4	63
Movies	7	39	45	11	46	12
News Specials	9	30	38	10	48	8
Serious Discussion Shows	15	26	29	16	39	13

* High % viewing with limited program availability.
Source: Louis Harris Study made in 1971 for Zenith.

EXHIBIT 6 *(cont.)*

Wanting More (Over 30%)

Average	Affluent
New & TV Movies—45%	New Specials—48%
News Specials—38%	Plays & Dramatic Series—47%
Entertainment Specials—37%	New & TV Movies—46%
Children's Shows—36%	Children's Shows—39%
Live Sports—32%	Entertainment Specials—39%
Plays & Dramatic Series—30%	Serious Discussion Shows—39%
	Live Sports—34%

EXHIBIT 7

Positive and Negative Attitudes towards Television
(Base: All TV Viewers)

Positive Attitudes

80%–95% of all TV viewers feel that the immediacy and movement of TV coverage of major events is important.

83%–88% feel that the low cost aspect of TV is critical.

More people see all things that interest them (except art shows) on TV than see them live.

Negative Attitudes

35%–50% of all the viewers watch TV only when there is nothing better to do.

50%–60% read newspapers or magazines while watching TV.

83% feel that TV has too many commercials.

Source: Louis Harris Study made for Zenith in 1971.

EXHIBIT 8

Potential Market for the Video Player, 1977-1987: Assumptions and Calculations

ASSUMPTIONS

1. Forecast of Color Penetration Rates as % of Total U.S. Households, 1975-1985

1975	1976	1977	1978	1979	1980	1981	1982	1983	1984	1985
72	75	78	80	85	90	92	93	94	95	95

Source: Zenith

2. %Very Heavy, Heavy and Medium TV viewing households by income (1975)

	% Very Heavy	% Heavy	% Medium	Total
$15–24,299	15.2	21.6	23.2	60.0
$25,000 +	13.0	15.7	27.0	55.7

Source: Target Group Index

EXHIBIT 8 (cont.)

3. Percent of "Planners" by Income, 1977–1987

According to the Target Group Index, 44% and 41% of those people in the $15–24,999 and $25,000+ income groupings, respectively, may be classified as "planners" (defined as those who "generally plan far ahead to buy expensive items such as automobiles"). These figures are used here as an indication of risk aversion and proclivity to deliberate before purchasing. They are assumed to decline in importance over time with respect to purchasing the video disc player.

% Assumed to be "Planners" by Income, 1977–1987

	1977	1978	1979	1980	1981	1982	1983	1984	1985	1986	1987
$15–24,999	44	44	44	42	40	38	36	34	32	30	28
$25,000+	41	41	41	38	36	33	30	28	26	24	22

CALCULATIONS

Year/Income	1 # of Households (millions)	2 Color TV Penetration (%)	3 # Color TV Households (millions) (1) · (2) = (3)	4 Very Heavy- Medium Viewers (%)	5 Non- Planners (%)	6 Potential Market (millions) (3) · (4) · (5) = (6)
1977						
$15–24,999	15.9	86	13.7	60.0	56	4.60
$25,000+	4.6	90	4.1	55.7	59	1.36
						5.96
1979						
$15–24,999	17.7	92	16.3	60.0	56	5.6
$25,000+	5.2	95	4.9	55.7	59	1.6
						7.2
1981						
$15–24,999	19.5	94	18.3	60.0	60	6.6
$25,000+	6.0	97	5.8	55.7	64	2.1
						8.7
1983						
$15–24,999	21.3	96	20.4	60.0	64	7.8
$25,000+	6.7	99	6.6	55.7	70	2.6
						10.4
1985						
$15–24,999	23.4	98	22.9	60.0	68	9.3
$25,000+	7.6	99	7.5	55.7	74	3.11
						12.41
1987						
$15–24,999	25.6	98	25.1	60.0	72	10.9
$25,000+	8.6	99	8.5	55.7	78	3.67
						14.57

EXHIBIT 9

Cumulative Sales Forecast of Videoplayers, 1977-1982, Based on Different Penetration Rates

Year	High Penetration Rate (%)	Unit Sales (000)	Unit Sales (millions $)	Mean Penetration Rate (%)	Unit Sales (000)	Unit Sales (millions $)	Low Penetration Rate (%)	Unit Sales (000)	Unit Sales (millions $)
1977	.5	3.3	$ 1.5	.3	2.1	$ .9	.2	1.5	$ .7
1978	.5	9.1	4.1	.3	5.8	2.6	.1	2.0	.9
1979	.5	21.8	9.8	.3	12.6	5.7	.09	4.0	1.8
1980	.6	46.0	20.7	.3	27.6	12.4	.07	7.0	3.1
1981	.8	80.0	36.0	.4	40.0	18.0	.07	7.0	3.1
1982	1.1	121.0	54.5	.5	55.0	24.8	.06	7.0	3.1
		281.2	$126.6		143.1	$64.4		28.5	$12.7

Note: Assumes an average player price of $450.00.

EXHIBIT 10

Forecast of 1983-1987 Sales under Different Pricing Scenarios

Year	Penetration Rate (%)	Hardware % of Sales from Potential Market	Unit Sales (000)	Dollar Sales (millions)	Software**** Unit Sales (millions)	Dollar Sales (millions)	Total Dollar Sales (millions)	Hardware Sales as % to Total
I. High Price Scenario (>$400):								
1983	.7	—	72.6	30.9*	1.51	14.0	44.9	69
1984	.9	—	104.0	44.2	2.24	20.8	65.0	68
1985	1.1	—	140.0	59.5	3.22	29.9	89.4	67
1986	1.4	—	195.0	82.9	4.58	42.6	125.5	66
1987	1.8	—	272.0	115.6	6.49	60.2	175.8	66
II. Medium Price Scenario ($325-$375):								
1983	.8	95	90.0	31.5**	1.63	15.2	46.7	67
1984	1.1	90	140.0	49.0	2.61	24.3	73.3	67
1985	1.5	85	215.0	75.2	4.12	38.2	113.4	66
1986	2.0	80	340.0	119.0	6.50	60.3	179.3	66
1987	2.6	75	510.0	178.5	10.10	93.5	272.0	66
III. Low Price Scenario (<$250):								
1983	1.7	90	200.0	40.0***	2.40	22.3	62.3	64
1984	2.5	80	360.0	72.0	4.92	45.7	117.7	61
1985	3.9	70	700.0	140.0	9.82	91.2	231.2	61
1986	6.6	60	1500.0	300.0	20.32	188.7	488.7	61
1987	11.7	50	3400.0	680.0	44.12	409.7	1089.7	62

* Assumes an average price/unit of $425.

** Assumes an average price/unit of $350.

*** Assumes an average price/unit of $200.

**** Three assumptions affect the forecasts of software sales:

a. That an average of 7 discs are sold annually per player in use.

b. That the average annual expenditure for discs is $65 per player in use.

c. That there are 143,100 video disc players in use by 1982 (Refer to forecast of mean sales of hardware 1977-1982).

SONY PRESENTS THE NEXT THING.

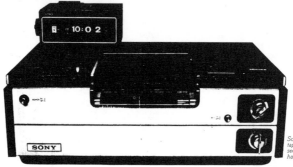

Sony's Betamax Video-tape Deck. It lets you see shows you would have missed.

You're looking at Betamax, a revolutionary new product from Sony that plugs into any TV and enables you to see programs you would have otherwise missed. We'll explain.

First off, let's take a situation where there are two shows on opposite each other and you'd like to watch both of them. Well, believe it or not, now you can. Because Sony's Betamax deck can actually <u>videotape something off one channel while you're watching another channel.</u> Then, when you're finished watching one show, all you do is push some buttons and you can play back a tape of the show that you would have missed.

Pretty incredible, huh? Well, listen to something else

Reuse the tape cassettes or, if you prefer, build a library.

TV PICTURE SIMULATED

Betamax does that's equally incredible.

Let's say you have to go somewhere, or do something, at a time when there's something on TV you want to see. Well, Sony's Betamax is equipped with a timer that can be set to <u>automatically videotape that program while you're not there.</u> Then, whenever you want, you just play back the tape—and again you see what you would have missed.

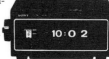

Set the timer and automatically video-tape something while you're doing something else.

(Our one-hour tapes, by the way, are reusable—just record over them and use them over and over again. Or, if you prefer, don't record over them and build a library of your favorite shows.)

Imagine. With Sony's Betamax, you'll never again miss a program you want to see. Ah, progress!

Betamax plugs into any TV, even if it's not a Sony (though you'll be missing a lot if it's not).

BETAMAX®
"IT'S A SONY."

APPENDIX B

Selected Potential Markets

This exhibit contains demographic and psychographic information concerning the consumer's use of his leisure time. The activities selected were chosen because of their potential substitutability with the videoplayer as alternate uses of passive leisure time.

1. Frequent Movie-Goer

50% of the frequent viewers are under 24.

The younger the person, the more likely he is to be a frequent viewer.

The frequent viewer is more educated than the non-viewer: 74% of the frequent viewers have graduated from high school, whereas only 48% of non-viewers did not graduate from high school.

Because of the age characteristics, only 65% of the frequent viewers are employed.

50% of frequent viewers come from families with household income between $10–$25,000.

Black and other minorities tend to go more often to the movies than whites.

Singles as a group are also disproportionate movie viewers.

60% of frequent viewers are married. Couples with younger children tend to go more often to the movies than the population as a whole.

There is a strong correlation between the frequency of TV-viewing and the frequency of movie-going, particularly in the 25–34 age group.

2. Frequent Television Viewers

60% of frequent viewers are women, most of them in the less than $10,000 income group.

Younger people (18–26) as a group tend to watch TV more than the general population. Conversely older people, especially over 50, watch much less than the general population.

There are more college graduates in the non-viewer population (12%) than in the frequent viewer population (8%).

63% of frequent viewers have an income between $5 and $15,000.

3. Book Club Members

The majority (62%) of members are between 25 and 49.

Members have a significantly higher education: 45% have at least some college education. Those who graduated from college are much more likely to be members than the general population.

As a group, professionals are much more likely to be members than the general population.

Two-thirds of members earn between $10,000 and $25,000, and wealthier people show a higher propensity to be book club members than the general population.

There is a high correlation between book club membership and magazine readership.

4. Frequent Book Buyers

60% of books are bought by men.

There is a higher concentration of frequent buyers in the younger age group and among college educated and professional people.

The over $25,000 income group shows the highest percentage of frequent book buyers.

Book buyers tend to be infrequent TV watchers.

5. $400 Encyclopedia Buyers

A startling number of buyers are under 34 (80%).

Two-thirds of these buyers are high school graduates or people with some college attendance.

Professionals and managers show the highest inclination to purchase encyclopedias.

A majority of buyers have children under 6, are heavy TV watchers and don't buy newspapers.

6. Record Club Members

Two-thirds of the members are under 26.

College graduates, managers and professionals, as well as people with incomes over $25,000, form a disproportionately large segment of record club members.

7. Buyers of Expensive Stereo Systems

74% of buyers are under 34.

42% of the buyers graduated from high school.

Singles show the highest percentage of buyers.

44% of the buyers have no children.

People frequently exposed to radio and magazines show a higher percentage of stereo ownership than the population as a whole.

8. Frequent Record Buyers

55% of the buyers are under 24.

46% of frequent purchasers are single.

41% of frequent purchasers listen to radio often.

9. Frequent Buyers of Prerecorded Tapes and Cassettes

70% of prerecorded material is bought by men.

53% of the frequent buyers are under 24.

Singles show the highest tendency for being frequent purchasers.

CHAPTER **11**

Club Mediterranee

In the summer of 1977, Jean Lallement, President of Club Mediterranee, North America, was evaluating the Club's marketing approach to the U.S. market. He had just received the results of interviews conducted among the GMs[1] at the Club's Caribbean villages during the peak holiday season. He wondered if there would be any reason to modify the Club's Strategy.

BACKGROUND

Club Mediterranee was founded as a sports association in France in 1950 by Gerard Blitz, a former member of the Belgian Olympic

Team, along with a group of his friends. The initial Club Med venture was a "vacation village" (Alcudia in Majorca, Spain) opened to an initial membership of 2,500. This first venture consisted of a tent village in which members slept in sleeping bags and took turns helping to cook meals and wash dishes. At that time, the staff numbered five sports instructors.

Today, the Club operates a total of 77 villages in 24 countries, 19 of which are ski villages; 35 summer villages; 26 all year villages; and 2 winter seaside villages with a combined total of 53,865 beds. These resorts are located throughout the Mediterranean countries, in the Caribbean, Middle East, Africa, Mexico, the Bahamas and the South Pacific. With 1,102 sports instructors, 11,000 village staff members (or GOs[2]), and an active membership of over one million, Club Mediterranee is the largest vacation organization of its kind. Last year, the Club provided

---

[1] Guests are referred to as "GMs" or "nice members."

This case was prepared by Michael Chevalier, Assistant Professor, INSEAD, and revised by Professor Scott Ward, The Wharton School, strictly as the basis for class discussion rather than to illustrate either effective or ineffective handling of administrative situation.

---

[2] GOs translates as "nice organizers."

vacations for 510,000 people. Out of this number 47.3% were French, 17.9% were from North and Central America, with 26.5 from other Western European countries, and 8.5% miscellaneous.

The Club launched its Western Hemisphere operation in 1966 and currently has six offices located in New York; Scottsdale, Arizona; Mexico City; Caracas, Venezuela; Toronto and Montreal. In addition, there are sales representatives in Los Angeles, San Francisco, Chicago, Miami, Houston and Vancouver. Today, Club Mediterranee numbers approximately 100,000 U.S. and Canadian members, of which 83,000 vacationed with the Club over the past year. The Club's Western Hemisphere villages are located on Guadeloupe and Martinique in the Caribbean, Moorea near the island of Tahiti, Bora Bora, Hawaii's Kauai Island, Mexico's Yucatan and West Coasts, Paradise Island, Nassau, and the Bahamian island of Eleuthera.

Total sales for Club Med, Inc., the North American sales representative responsible for marketing the Club in the Western Hemisphere, totaled $47 million for the fiscal year ending October, 1977. It was projected that sales for fiscal year 1978 would climb to $56 million, with $127 million in total revenues to be reached by 1980. Worldwide, Club Med revenues for 1977 totaled $241 million.

THE CLUB PHILOSOPHY

Mr. Lallement felt that the success of the Club was largely the result of its unique approach to the concept of vacationing. This concept arises from the belief that what urban people need and seek on vacation is a society and environment radically different from that of their daily lives, a society in which there are no barriers, rules or restraints, and in which human contacts are made sincerely. All facilities for full enjoyment of the vacation must be easily and freely available, and problems of financial risk should be reduced to the absolute minimum. Dress at Club Med villages is always casual—a bikini and pareo (a colorful length of cloth worn sarong style) is the order of the day. There are no telephones, radios or newspapers, for the Club believes that a vacation is truly a time to escape the cares of everyday life. Mr. Lallement proudly cited a book by Victor Franco on the early days of Club Med, which he believed still captured the Club's spirit (see Exhibit 1).

Mr. Lallement strongly believed that the Club staff (GOs) were not hotel employees in the traditional sense. They are usually well-educated young men and women who regard their service in the Club as an extended working vacation. When they are not serving members as sports instructors, hostesses, entertainers, administrators, etc., the GOs live and eat with the members, participate in all activities, and generally enjoy all the privileges of the GMs. Their participation on a basis of equality and as friends is an important element in the free society and special character of the Club. They are not permitted to accept tips which are considered a token of the master-servant relationship.

CLUB OPERATIONS

Mr. Lallement described Club Med's operation as substantially different from conventional vacation hotels. Club resorts (called villages) are usually located away from large centers on more isolated sites selected for their natural beauty and for the recreational facilities they offer. They are completely self-contained communities with all the facilities needed for a vacation. Certain villages emphasize particular sporting activities (see Exhibit 2).

Club Mediterranee offers package prices which include roundtrip transportation on specified charters or group flights with airport-village transfers, accommodations in hotel rooms or bungalows, all meals (including free table wine with lunch and dinner), use of sports facilities and expert instruction in all sports activities. Members check their wallets in the bank upon arrival and sign for any optional purchases, settling their account prior to departing the village. (For example, drinks are paid for with a string of multicolored poppet beads that can be worn as a necklace, as a wristband, as a belt, and so on.)

CLUB MEDITERRANEE MARKETING

Since its inception in France, Club Med had relied on heavy print advertising, repeat "members" and word-of-mouth influence to promote Club vacations. Prices had always been comparable to package tour vacations, but Club Mediterranee attempted to offer a consistent but unique vacation experience. Mr. Lallement felt that many people, worldwide, are confused by the number and variety of "package tours" available, and feel that quality is not predictable (hotels may be bad, charter air tours have a bad reputation, etc.).

Just as the "Club Village" concept attempts to distinguish Club Med from packaged vacations, the concept of the "Gentile Membre" promoted the uniqueness of Club Med. "Membership" information is used to create a direct mail list which Mr. Lallement thought was largely responsible for Club Med's high rate of return vacationers. While he felt Caribbean resorts attracted fewer repeaters than other Club Med facilities, the worldwide figure was 70%, i.e., at any given Club Med facility, about 70% of the GMs had been on a Club Med vacation before. He felt this indicated a high degree of satisfaction, and was undoubtedly associated with effective word-of-mouth advertising about Club Med.

Mr. Lallement had no exact data on Club Med's market segments, but he felt that most were between 20 and 40 years old, upscale, and estimated about one-third were single. Most, he felt, were from larger urban areas in the U.S. He felt that Club Med was unusual in drawing from all socio-economic strata, except for the very top and the very bottom.

Club Med was its own tour operator for its company-owned resorts. In the U.S., travel agents book the majority of Club Med vacations, but Mr. Lallement felt that Club Med had a "brand identity" as opposed to package tours, making Club Med less dependent on travel agents to suggest Club Med vs. other types of vacations to prospective customers. Travel agent margins are provided by a percentage of the air fare or total booked tour retail price. While these are comparable within given classes of vacations, Mr. Lallement felt

that some tour operators of competitive package vacations gave kickbacks and other considerations to some large travel agencies, a practice that Club Med totally avoided. Nonetheless, Club Med did make a 50-page booklet describing Club Med's villages and vacation packages available to virtually all major travel agencies in large U.S. cities, and these were distributed in large quantities so that many agencies had spare copies for customers. An average price for a week-long Club Med vacation at a Caribbean resort was about $350, including everything but liquor and air fare (per person, per week, at peak season). The average number of beds at a Club Med village was approximately 300, although the Caravelle Village, on Guadeloupe, was a converted luxury hotel, recently expanded to accommodate over 800 guests.

Occupancy for Caribbean-area Caravelle and Buccaneer's Creek villages averaged over 90% during the winter season. Fort Royale averaged around 75% during the same periods. Fort Royale seemed to attract more families than the other Club Med Caribbean villages.

The Club continued to believe that the most effective communications medium was word-of-mouth advertising by satisfied GMs. This was supported by a public relations program directed at securing press coverage for the Club in the New England/New York/ Washington corridor and by advertising running in magazines like the *New Yorker* and *New York* (see Exhibit 3).

The primary method for evaluating Club performance was through comment cards that were distributed to departing GMs.[3] Lallement felt that the results of the comment-card tabulations (Exhibit 4) showed that GMs were overwhelmingly impressed by the Club.

To further probe GM reaction to the Club, especially by American GMs, Lallement sent a

---

[3] The Club had each guest deposit his or her passport and return ticket with the cashier upon arrival. They were returned when the customer had paid any outstanding bills prior to departure. The ticket were returned in a Club Mediterranee ticket folder. The inside of that folder was a detachable, pre-addressed (but not postage paid) reply card (Exhibit 4).

consultant to interview GMs at the Caribbean villages. The consultant detected a number of items that he felt could represent potential problems to the Club (Exhibit 5). Upon review of these, however, Lallement was easily able to discount all of them (Exhibit 6).

THE TASK AHEAD

Mr. Lallement contemplated Club Med's future in the North American market. He felt that Club Med had only begun to tap the American market, but he was uncertain what the future emphasis of Club Med's marketing efforts should be. Should he push for expansion through acquisition or building new hotels in the Caribbean, or elsewhere? Should he try to orient American consumers toward Club Med vacations in other parts of the world? Finally, there remained the question of how best to sell the American market. Was there a more effective way to market or was the Club's accumulated investment in GM goodwill going to pay off through word-of-mouth selling?

EXHIBIT 1

Description of Club Mediterranee Vacation*

"We've made a lot of fun of the 'rituals' of the Club—the sarong, for example. 'A ridiculous fashion,' wrote one of my fellow journalists. 'Mock Polynesian,' quipped another, without realizing that this rather childish folklore was only a symbol. In the village, as in the army, city clothes are exchanged for the vacation 'uniform'—swimsuit or sarong—and at the same time the 'civilian' mentality and way of life are abandoned in favor of becoming a simple 'Gentil Membre' [Club member]." Whether seamstress or movie star, sales girl or corporate president, famous writer or obscure ministerial clerk, you forget your identity, your age, your duties, and your past and sometimes discover your true personality. I know a director of a Paris department store whose office is full of sophisticated telephones, dictaphones and strange lights blinking on and off. For years, he had spent his vacations in places along the French or Italian Riviera. 'I found the same old people as in Paris,' he told me. 'You vow not to talk business, but you do anyway . . . I spent my days like an idiot on the beach in the middle of a mass of bodies doing the same stupid thing. To avoid boredom, I went to the casino every night . . . Back at the hotel, I was furious. An army of doormen, valets, and chamber maids, hands held out, but hearts in their pockets, watching my every gesture, endlessly calling me 'Mr. President,' but in reality, treating me like a money machine. In the elevator, if I happened to greet people I saw ten times a day, I got strange looks. As a result, I went back to my office without having rested, as tense as I was when I left.'

The money machine wound up showing "Tilt." An actress, as celebrated for her talents as for her obsession with peace and quiet, advised him one day to try the Club: he went to Agadir: 'The first impression frankly bothered me, this insipid, boyscout aspect. Then, I let myself go. I made new friends: they didn't know my name or my job, but they knew *me* . . . If I went to breakfast barefoot—and why not, on vacation!—nobody would be thinking things like, 'all the same, considering his age and position! . . . 'It's stupid to say, but it's true: for a month I rediscovered a simpler, a more pure part of myself' . . .''

---

* From *La grande aventure du Club Mediterranee*, by Victor Franco.

EXHIBIT 2

Sports Centers

All Year and Summer Villages

Sailing	49 centers	Tennis	59 centers
	385 sailing instructors		370 courts
	1,215 sail boats		107 instructors
Water Skiing	20 centers	Riding	16 centers
	112 instructors		57 instructors
Scuba Diving	9 centers		520 horses
	89 instructors	Windsurfing	3 centers (Caravelle, Guadeloupe; Cancun, Mexico; and Paradise Island, Nassau)

In addition, swimming, snorkeling, yoga, and calisthenics with instruction are available at most villages.

Winter Villages

| Skiing | 19 centers | Cross-Country Skiing | 1 center (Pontresina, outside |
| | 600 instructors | | St. Moritz, Switzerland) |

Source: Club Mediterranee, Inc.

EXHIBIT 3

Club Mediterranee

EXHIBIT 4

Customer Comment Card

	OVER ALL IMPRESSION / L'IMPRESSION D'ENSEMBLE	GENERAL ORGANIZATION / L'ORGANISATION GENERALE	THE TEAM OF ORGANIZERS / L'EQUIPE DES G.O.	ACCOMMODATIONS / LE CONFORT	FOOD / LA TABLE	BAR / LE BAR	EXCURSIONS / EXCURSIONS	SPORTS / LES SPORTS	ORCHESTRA / L'ORCHESTRE	ENTERTAINMENT / LES SOIREES	JOURNEY / LE VOYAGE
OUTSTANDING EXTRAORDINAIRE											
GOOD BIEN											
SATISFACTORY PASSABLE											
BAD MAUVAIS											
VERY BAD TRES MAUVAIS											

YOUR COMMENTS
VOS REMARQUES _____

VILLAGE VISITED
VOTRE VILLAGE _____

DATES—FROM _____ TO
DE _____ A _____

NAME—NOM _____

ADDRESS—ADRESSE _____

_____ ZIP _____

MEMBER NO.
ADHERENT NO. _____

I first learned about the Club through (check one)
J'ai entendu parler du Club par (indiquer ci–dessous)

Advertisement ☐   Editorial article ☐
Publicité   Editorial

A friend ☐   A travel agent ☐
Un ami   Agence de voyage

American Express ☐

Summary: Evaluation of Vacation by Resort
(Averages—Scale = 1–20, Negative to Positive)

	Caravelle	Martinique	Fort Royale
Overall impression	19	20	17
General organization	18	18	17
GOs (team of organizers)	18	16	17
Accommodations	17	16	16
Food	18	16	17
Bar	14	14	15
Excursions	17	16	16
Sports	18	19	18
Bands	14	15	14
Entertainment	16	16	17
Travel to club	14	10	15
(n = 461)			

Note: Averages in each column are the weighted averages of all respondents arrived at in the following manner: responses were assigned point values: outstanding, 20 points; good, 15 points; satisfactory, 11 points; bad, 5 points; very bad, 3 points. Response points were totaled and divided by the number of responses to the question to arrive at a question average rating.

Summary: Sources of Information about Club Med by Resort

	Caravelle	Martinique	Fort Royale
Advertisement	17%	24%	12%
A friend	65	66	63
Editorial article	-	3	4
Travel agency	15	4	17
American Express	3	3	4
	100%	100%	100%
(n = 461)			

EXHIBIT 5

PRE-TRIP PROBLEMS

1. Matching Customers to Clubs: These three Caribbean Clubs each have a very distinct personality which is oriented towards a specific (and different) type of customer. Many GMs aren't aware of these differences before they get to the Club and their travel agent has not matched their needs to the personality of the Club (by and large neither does the Club's literature). A number of people clearly were not at the Club best suited to their needs and therefore were having a less than pleasant stay. Many said that they would not return to the Club (any location) nor would they recommend it to their friends.

2. Inadequate Understanding of the Club Concept: Many Americans are not used to the type of service and facilities offered by the Club. This, in itself, represents no problem since it is the very reason many come to the Club (and, indeed, the Caribbean Clubs are nowhere near as spartan as some of Club Med's other facilities). Yet, it must be made plain, in advance, to first-time customers, that this is what they will encounter. Apparently this is not made sufficiently clear in either your brochures or advertising because many GMs were expecting something quite different and were disappointed by the Club.

3. Misimpressions of Arrangements: Many GMs who took Air France "charters" out of Miami had been under the impression that this would be an all-Club, non-stop, charter flight. In fact, it's a four-stop flight, eight hours, with the majority of passengers not coming to the Club. Many GMs felt that they had been lied to—or at least misled and described the plane as the filthiest they'd been in.

4. Overbooking: Upon arrival on Guadeloupe GMs were told that although they had reservations for the Caravelle, it was overbooked and they would have to go to Fort Royal instead. The reason for this overbooking was that GMs already at the Club had decided to extend their stays and the Club's Chef D'Village had allowed them to, disregarding the incoming GM loads. The next morning GMs were told they could transfer over the Caravelle but might have to stay "four or five to a room."

ON-SITE PROBLEMS

1. Anti-Americanism Among GOs: American GMs detected anti-American attitudes among many of the GOs. GOs said that they felt that American GMs were spoiling the Club and if the Club continued to expand its American clientele it would become an unpleasant place to work and visit. American GMs felt this attitude was clearly evident in the way many of them were treated.

2. Language Barriers: Although the Caribbean Clubs were supposed to be bilingual, many of the GOs were either unable or unwilling to speak English.

3. GO Apathy: At the Caravelle, GMs felt that many of the GOs had no time to interact with the GMs and on those occasions when they did interact they were cold and harsh. Interestingly, this situation was very different at the Fort Royal. Two possible reasons for this were mentioned. First, there is the size of the Caravelle (it was described by one Fort Royal GO as a factory). When the Caravelle was enlarged, although the number of GOs may have increased, it did not increase proportionally to the number of rooms, and therefore, GM capacity added. The result was a lower GM/GO ratio. Secondly, there is the attitude of the Chef D'Village who seems to set the pattern for the way the GOs act. At the Fort Royal Ringo was pleasant and involved with the GMs and his GOs followed his example. Bernard, at the Caravelle, by contrast, seemed

EXHIBIT 5 (cont.)

to be far more concerned with performing in the evening show* and had little time for GMs. Once again, the GOs followed their example.

Bernard did not even have time for explaining the Club and its facilities to incoming guests even though we were given a card at registration and said he would be meeting with us to do this (in fact, this introduction to the Club was never given by anyone).
A Caravelle GM

4. *Hours of Operation:* The difference between the expectation of the European GM and the American GM were apparent in their reactions to the hours of the Club's various services (boutiques, planning, cashier). European GMs expected offices and shops to be closed in the afternoon; the American does not. The American GM cannot understand why he is unable to buy suntan lotion (or anything else, except drinks) during an afternoon.

It seems that the hours of various services and activities are set up for the convenience of the GOs rather than the GMs.

5. *Negative Attitudes:* Americans have been brought up with the attitude "the customer is always right." Perhaps this is a basic flaw in our society (it probably is). None the less, this is the way they are. Many of the GOs, however, took just the opposite attitude. For example.

A GM wanted to go on a sailing picnic and went to the activities booth to sign up. The girl at the booth said that the list had already been sent up to the main building but that he *would* be able to sign up there. At the main building he was told, "That girl did not say that to you!" It isn't important whether or not the individual was allowed to go on the picnic. What is important is that the GO, in effect, was calling the GM a liar when in fact the GM was telling the truth.

6. *Theft:* Two examples of theft at the Club were mentioned. The first occurred when someone discovered that Traveler's Checks had been removed from an envelope that had been checked with the Club's cashier where all valuables are to be checked. It was clear that a theft had occurred. The amount that had been signed over to the cashier (and countersigned by the cashier) was definitely higher than the amount the individual was given back and the difference was in checks that had been removed from the checkbook out of sequence. Clearly they had been removed since the checks were accepted by the cashier for safekeeping yet the attitude of the cashier and everyone behind the counter was that *the customer had made a mistake* and that the Club was blameless.

The second occasion of theft consisted in three bungalows being burglarized the night before the departure of a group of GMs. In two cases the rooms were broken into while the occupants were in them. Departures had been publicly posted announcing who was to be leaving early the next morning and that they were to clear their bills and get valuables the evening before. The Club not only had made sure that valuables would be left, that evening, in a room that could be locked only from the inside (and still easily broken into) but had announced that fact.

POST-TRIP PROBLEMS

1. *Management Reaction to Theft:* When one of the GMs who was burgled made his reaction known to the Club's New York office, his call was passed along down the line to a customer service agent who finally told the GM that it was his own fault that he had been burglarized. Further, although the GM gave the customer service agent the names of other couples who had been robbed, the employee didn't even bother to contact them.

---

* At all Club Med villages entertainment is provided by GOs.

EXHIBIT 6

Reaction to GM Interview Summary

PRE-TRIP PROBLEMS

1. Matching Customers to Clubs: It is quite true that each of our villages has its own special ambiance and we attempt to keep it that way. Some members would tend to prefer one Club over another. Each Club is briefly described in our brochure called "Trident." Since we sell to the public only through travel agencies, we give travel agents, from time to time, a familiarization trip to the villages. We feel that it is part of their function to send their clients to a particular Club most suited to them.

2. Inadequate Understanding of the Club Concept: This is also the function of the travel agent. In most cases, we have no contact with the GMs until they arrive at the airport or Club.

3. Misimpression of Arrangements: As a courtesy to American GMs, we provide reservation service on regular airlines. Members arrive and depart with regular flight tickets. Since our operation is run on a week-to-week basis, many people arrive on the same plane and are met at the airport. Members may arrive/depart on their own, the only difference being that they are not met and transferred from/to airport. Due to the energy shortage there are fewer flights available. We have no control over our airline schedules or maintenance. Any passengers' complaints should be addressed to the airline in question.

4. Overbooking: During certain weeks, we may be faced with over-capacity situations. This is in the nature of the hotel and travel business. If this situation were to happen, we would supply equivalent facilities. In some cases, allowances are made to the GMs for any discomfort.

ON-SITE PROBLEMS

1. Anti-Americanism among GOs: We know that most GOs like Americans because of their far more easy-going attitude. A slight annoyance can be translated by an American into evidence of an anti-Americanism. This is not peculiar only to the Club. If a cab driver in New York or elsewhere is rude you wouldn't consider him to be anti-American. A tourist in France would consider this to be anti-Americanism in action.

2. Language Barriers: The recruiting of GOs is done in our Paris office. We attempt to hire GOs who are bi-lingual, specially for the Western Hemisphere, and a greater percentage every year will have this ability. Our policy is to rotate our GOs every season (6 months). At that time, we eliminate those who have not met our standards. This also renews the vigor and youthfulness of our organization.

3. GO Apathy: The GOs are not full-time professional entertainers. Their main function is to assist and instruct in the various sports (tennis, water-skiing, scuba diving, etc.) Any lack of these skills in the field should be reported and will be dealt with by our management.

Bernard is considered to be one of our best Chefs D'Village. Therefore, I'm surprised that the GMs interviewed did not find it to be so. His team is among the best in our Clubs. Those who do not get any attention from a GO may consider this to be "apathy." Many GMs perfer to be left alone to enjoy the natural surroundings we provide for them.

4. Hours of Operation: The shops and services are set up to supply only the basic needs of our members. Therefore, opening hours must be limited.

5. Negative Attitudes: You may always find some incidents of a negative attitude. Specially when dealing with a large number of people. Generally speaking, this is not a major factor.

EXHIBIT 6 (*cont.*)

6. Theft: Insurance is available at a very small premium ($5.00) up to $500.00 coverage. The informality of the Club does not encourage GMs to bring valuables of any kind. There is no tipping and practically no need for cash. Bar beads and services can be obtained by signing for them. Theft is a problem in any part of the world and an unwary person is apt to suffer.

POST—TRIP PROBLEMS

1. Management Reaction to Theft: I'm sure no one likes to hear about a robbery. Perhaps the customer service people should be more sympathetic. However, the fact that there is no lock on the door should convince the GMs not to leave any valuables in their room. This advice is not only confined to our Clubs but should be followed universally.

In summary, I would like to submit that many of the points mentioned—apathy, language barriers, negative attitudes, theft, anti-Americanism, etc.—are problems of our entire society.

Supplemental Market Data

EXHIBIT 1

Foreign Travel by U.S. Residents 1972-1971-1970

	People in Thousands			Expenditures in Millions		
	1972	1971	1970	1972	1971	1970
Estimated Total	22,925	22,317	20,868	$7,716	$6,633	$6,173
Transportation	—	—	—	2,860	2,355	2,200
Expenditures Abroad	—	—	—	4,856	4,278	3,973
Foreign-Flag Carriers	—	—	—	1,580	1,290	1,215
U.S. Flag Carriers	—	—	—	1,280	1,065	985
Total Overseas Areas	6,790	5,667	5,260	2,870	2,335	2,184
By Sea	73	95	120	—	—	—
By Air	7,717	5,572	5,140	—	—	—
Canada[1]	13,583*	14,450	13,648	1,036	1,111	1,049
Mexico[2]	2,552*	2,200	1,960	950	832	740
Europe & Mediterranean	3,843	3,202	2,898	1,853	1,540	1,425
Western Europe	3,666	3,030	2,783	1,645	1,373	1,310
United Kingdom	1,492	1,358	1,365	342	324	293
France	1,115	975	996	200	169	160
Italy	976	817	873	215	178	172
Switzerland	811	696	794	119	99	108
Germany	964	805	922	163	126	148
Austria	537	432	538	64	52	54
Denmark	361	279	317	46	38	39
Sweden	212	170	177	32	22	24
Norway	196	148	160	39	25	31
Netherlands	587	461	520	57	44	44
Belgium-Luxembourg	365	310	292	31	22	22

* Foreign government sources

[1] Visitor staying 24 hours

[2] Visitors to interior, however, expenditures include border traffic

EXHIBIT 1 *(cont.)*

	People in Thousands			Expenditures in Millions		
	1972	1971	1970	1972	1971	1970
Spain	639	481	439	152	105	85
Portugal	267	208	226	37	31	29
Ireland	190	232	230	36	52	42
Greece	324	260	203	84	63	40
Other Western Europe	349	274	—	28	23	19
Other Europe and Mediterranean	—	—	—	208	167	115
USSR	60*	45*	—	—	—	—
Yugoslavia	—	250*	207*	—	—	—
Israel	319	300	198	124	110	62
West Indies & Central America	1,992	1,736	1,663	504	408	390
Bermuda	291*	273*	256*	69	62	63
Bahamas[3]	1,245*	1,225*	1,129*	144	120	127
Jamaica	317*	287*	247*	105	90	95
Other British West Indies	—	—	—	60	56	44
Netherlands West Indies	—	—	—	40	28	18
Other West Indies and Central America	—	—	—	86	52	43
South America	338	254	249	113	92	90
Venezuela	—	115*	94	—	—	—
Colombia	—	57*	47*	—	—	—
Other Overseas Areas	617	475	450	400	295	279
Japan	326*	314*	359*	121	88	97
Hong Kong	213*	218*	252*	70	50	53
Thailand	—	147*	158*	—	—	—
India	59*	55*	59*	—	12*	13*
Lebanon	92*	72*	53*	—	—	—
Egypt	35*	24*	21*	—	—	—
Turkey	77*	66*	55*	—	—	—
Australia & New Zéaland	—	—	—	50	47	34
Cruise (85% Caribbean)	655	629	557	—	—	—

* Foreign government sources
(3) Includes cruise passengers

Sources: Official U.S. Figures except when noted by asterisk.

EXHIBIT 2

Estimated Air Departures from the U.S. for 1972

Cal. Year	From	To	Flag of Carrier	Total	%	U.S. Citizens	%	Non-U.S. Citizens	%
1971	All Ports	Africa	All Flags	28,178	100.00	21,663	76.9	6,515	23.1
1972				44,000	100.00	33,400	75.9	10,600	24.1
% ±				+56.2	—	+54.2		+62.7	
1971	All Ports	Bahamas, Bermuda, Non-U.S. Car.Is.	All Flags	2,091,657	100.00	1,538,884	73.6	552,773	26.4
1972				2,435,000	100.00	1,776,000	72.9	659,000	27.1
% ±				+16.4	—	+15.4		+19.2	
1971	All Ports	Central America	All Flags	164,335	100.00	69,188	42.1	95,147	57.9
1972				200,000	100.00	92,000	46.0	108,000	54.0
% ±				+21.7	—	+33.0		+13.5	
1971	All Ports	Europe	All Flags	4,315,030	100.00	2,957,958	68.6	1,357,072	31.4
1972				5,200,000	100.00	3,570,000	68.7	1,630,000	31.3
% ±				+20.5	—	+20.7		+20.1	
1971	All Ports	Far East	All Flags	726,743	100.00	340,637	46.9	386,106	53.1
1972				885,000	100.00	368,000	41.6	517,000	58.4
% ±				+21.8	—	+8.0		+33.9	
1971	All Ports	India	All Flags	11,303	100.00	4,910	43.4	6,393	56.6
1972				33,500	100.00	11,100	33.1	22,400	66.9
% ±				+196.3	—	+126.1		+250.4	
1971	All Ports	Israel	All Flags	122,852	100.00	103,077	83.9	19,775	16.1
1972				150,000	100.00	129,500	86.3	20,500	13.7
% ±				+22.1	—	+25.6		+3.7	

EXHIBIT 2 (cont.)

Cal. Year	From	To	Flag of Carrier	Total	%	U.S. Citizens	%	Non-U.S. Citizens	%
1971	All Ports	Mexico	All Flags	972,276	100.00	653,542	67.2	318,734	32.8
1972				1,235,000	100.00	852,000	69.0	383,000	31.0
% ±				+27.0	—	+30.4		+20.2	
1971	All Ports	Panama/ Canal Zone	All Flags	91,303	100.00	54,427	59.6	36,876	40.4
1972				105,100	100.00	62,000	59.4	43,000	40.6
% ±				+14.4	—	+13.9		+16.6	
1971	All Ports	South America	All Flags	518,709	100.00	204,791	39.5	313,918	60.5
1972				636,000	100.00	275,000	43.2	361,000	56.8
% ±				+22.6	—	+34.3		+15.0	
1971	All Ports	South Pacific	All Flags	208,059	100.00	111,997	53.8	96,062	46.2
1972				235,000	100.00	123,500	52.6	111,500	47.4
% ±				+12.9	—	+10.3		+16.1	
1971	All Ports	U.S. Trust Islands	All Flags	53,638	100.00	27,856	51.9	25,782	48.1
1972				68,500	100.00	31,000	45.2	37,500	54.8
% ±				+27.7	—	+11.3		+45.5	
1971	All Ports	Other Dests.	All Flags	83,574	100.00	51,812	62.0	31,762	38.0
1972				113,000	100.00	71,500	63.3	41,500	36.7
% ±				+35.2	—	+38.0		+30.7	
1971	All Ports	All Dests.	All Flags	9,387,657	100.00	6,140,742	65.4	3,246,915	34.6
1972				11,340,000	100.00	7,395,000	65.2	3,945,000	34.8
% ±				20.8	—	20.4		+21.5	

Source: Nettleton-Travel Research Center based on projections of first 9 months 1972. Travel Agent Magazine.

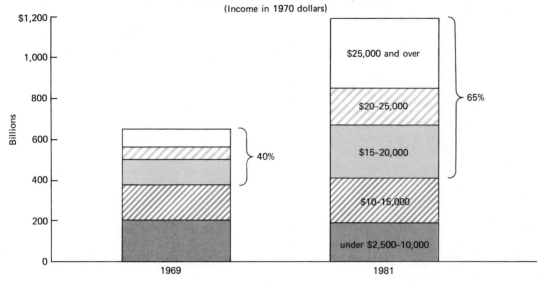

EXHIBIT 3

Total Income of Consumer Units in United States

(Income in 1970 dollars)

Source: Dept. of Commerce, Fortune, Corporate Planning.

Consumer Units in United States

(Income in 1970 dollars)

Source: Dept. of Commerce, Fortune, Corporate Planning.

EXHIBIT 4

First Destinations
of U.S. Citizens Departing by Air

	1972	1971	1970
Total	7,577,342	6,329,129	5,818,499
Europe	3,693,631	3,047,944	2,769,142
United Kingdom	1,039,195	880,868	805,523
Mexico	835,431	656,725	568,796
Bahamas	690,194	654,996	661,981
Germany	512,761	447,190	405,436
Italy	358,974	300,399	239,328
France	338,473	271,201	272,576
Jamaica	310,160	274,594	239,507
Spain	294,200	210,785	165,772
Japan	279,676	253,923	273,323
Bermuda	255,062	232,756	235,138
Netherlands	212,313	190,463	167,419
Switzerland	156,768	118,705	97,393
Scandinavia	144,730	115,567	111,071
Ireland	140,370	142,953	125,789
Netherlands Antilles	136,077	114,457	102,241
Greece	134,975	84,010	64,388
Portugal	128,411	103,649	120,344
Israel	122,831	103,077	80,659
Dominican Republic	118,620	84,151	59,939

Source: U.S. Immigration Dept.—Travel Weekly

EXHIBIT 5

Citizen Departures by Air by Port

	1972	1971	1970
Total	7,577,342	6,329,129	5,818,499
New York	3,152,233	2,680,030	2,572,869
Miami	892,489	758,927	755,723
Los Angeles	411,957	323,969	282,031
Chicago	407,699	306,828	248,436
Boston	361,848	292,556	257,514
Honolulu	285,076	264,724	252,901
San Juan	224,912	166,834	137,935
Philadelphia	176,998	115,294	92,306
Agana	132,854	103,634	83,883
Anchorage	118,256	87,862	100,493
San Antonio	116,116	101,157	96,693
Bangor	110,952	118,762	86,243
Washington	104,001	88,460	68,641

Source: U.S. Immigration Dept.—Travel Weekly

EXHIBIT 6

U.S. Airline Border Traffic
(Scheduled Service)
1972 vs. 1971

	1972 Revenue pass.-miles (000)	% Chg.	Load factor 1972	Load factor 1971	% share of the market* 1972	% share of the market* 1971
MAINLAND–BAHAMAS						
Delta	164,475	13.0	50.5	51.9	13.23	12.28
Eastern	133,510	(5.9)	58.4	63.6	49.83	48.95
Pan Am	215,861	(11.4)	64.5	62.2	36.94	38.77
TOTAL	513,846	(3.3)	57.8	59.3	100.00	100.00
MAINLAND–BERMUDA						
Delta	64,802	5.3	63.9	64.1	15.76	15.50
Eastern	201,261	1.4	63.3	59.0	46.97	49.19
Pan Am	152,108	12.2	55.5	60.1	37.27	35.31
TOTAL	418,171	5.7	60.3	60.1	100.00	100.00
MAINLAND–MEXICO						
Airwest	26,856	46.0	50.9	46.1	2.77	1.93
American	387,160	12.1	56.1	56.0	23.09	25.35
Braniff	151,794	32.1	52.1	49.3	14.85	13.18
Eastern	409,877	15.8	55.3	47.8	17.85	18.07
Pan Am	140,936	(0.8)	59.2	58.2	13.85	14.37
Texas Intl.	15,209	24.1	40.3	39.8	3.73	4.39
Western	488,833	20.1	69.8	59.3	23.86	22.71
TOTAL	1,620,665	16.3	58.9	53.8	100.00	100.00
MAINLAND–PUERTO RICO						
American	1,314,819	56.2	65.9	55.5	25.05	18.18
Caribbean	6,782	76.2	3.5	4.4	.15	.10
Delta	118,420	74.4	63.7	59.3	44.17	51.12
Eastern	2,204,700	(1.8)	63.7	59.3	44.17	51.12
Pan Am	1,389,643	2.2	60.3	56.8	28.97	29.23
TOTAL	5,034,364	13.9	61.4	57.2	100.00	100.00

* Based on revenue passengers.

EXHIBIT 7

TRAVEL AGENTS TOUR OPERATIONS

Among the wide range of U.S. businesses classified as "retail enterprises" it is difficult to find any group with a record of growth equaling that of travel agencies. A recent national survey conducted by Louis Harris and Associates for *Travel Weekly* documented the fact that in the U.S. 8,000 conference-appointed travel agencies produced $7.7 billion in sales in 1972. A similar study conducted in 1970 showed sales of $5 billion produced by the 6,700 conference-appointed agencies in existence at that time.

This 54 percent growth in sales during a two-year period was indicative of great future potential for a business that responds directly to the rapid increase in the number of consumer units moving into the higher income brackets.

The prominent position that the travel agent now holds in America's retailing structure was documented in a penetrating editorial by *Travel Weekly's* Irwin Robinson, who pointed out that

EXHIBIT 7 (cont.)

travel agency sales have reached a point where they are:

Greater than the combined volume of all retail shoe and hardware stores;

50 percent greater than all men's and boys' wear stores;

a third greater than tire, battery and accessory stores;

25 percent more than household appliance, radio and TV stores;

10 percent greater than all variety stores;

slightly above all U.S. retail women's apparel and accessories stores.

The *Travel Weekly* survey shows that the number of agencies doing a dollar volume of business of $1.5 million-and-over increased from 940 in 1970 to 1,440 in 1972, while at the other end of the scale the number of agencies with a volume less than $500,000 decreased from 2,680 in 1970 to 2,640 in 1972. The median average agency's gross sales has increased from $626,000 in 1970 to $750,000 in 1972.

While the study disclosed that larger-volume agencies were increasing their share of the total business done by all agencies, it reconfirmed the conclusion from the previous study that it takes a majority of agents (some 4,200 out of the 8,000) to produce 80 percent of overall bookings.

Domestic travel, defined as including mainland U.S., Hawaii, Alaska, Puerto Rico and the U.S. Virgin Islands, accounted for 55 percent of all agency business with international travel accounting for the remaining 45 percent.

Air travel arrangements accounted for 66 percent of domestic and 50 percent of the international volume. Overall, the sale of air tickets provided 59 percent of total agency sales. Steamship travel (mostly cruises) accounts for 12 percent of sales, hotels 12 percent, rail travel 2 percent, bus travel 1 percent, and the remaining 14 percent comes from car rentals and miscellaneous ground arrangements.

The average agency in the United States had 5.4 full-time employees and 1.8 part-time workers.

Unlike many other types of retail businesses, increased sales do not necessarily mean increased profits. Handling the many differing requirements of clients means that this is a business where productivity in terms of profit per employee is difficult to increase. Dollar volume per employee does increase as gross dollar volume increases. Small agencies with gross volume under $500,000 show gross volume per employee at $81,000, while the largest agencies with $1.5 million-and-over in volume show gross sales of $201,000 per employee.

In the United States and Europe increase in volume of business did not assure increase in profits for the large travel agencies and tour operators. Costs continued to rise, competition increased, the complexity of airline fares reached a point where firm advance quotations were impossible, and experienced employees were in short supply. As a result, profit margins were low despite highly satisfactory increases in volume of business.

A top official at Thos. Cook and Son in New York pointed up the problem in his comment: "Despite every possible economy, costs of staying in business continue to spiral. Despite a healthy growth in volume of travel sales, the static status of basic commission strutures simply did not bring in sufficient revenue to offset rising costs."

The year 1972 was a year of change for Thos. Cook and Son. Early in the year, the British

EXHIBIT 7 *(cont.)*

government announced the final guidelines for the return of the Cook organization to the private sector after a long stewardship under the aegis of the British Transport Holding Company. Apparently the historic name of Cook, together with its worldwide chain of agencies and its various financial services, was considered a property of considerable value. A consortium of three—The Midland Bank, Trust Houses Forte and the Automobile Association of Great Britain—paid $58 million to become the new owners of the oldest travel agency in the world.

AMERICAN EXPRESS REPORTS GROWTH IN WESTERN HEMISPHERE AND DOMESTIC TOURS

Despite difficulties in keeping pace with rapid increases in the cost of doing business, American Express continued to expand its travel operations and exhibited an enthusiastic, upbeat outlook in keeping with its leadership position in the agency and tour operator field.

For the fourth straight year, consolidated travel sales for American Express worldwide established record highs. It reported that greatest interest was in tours to Europe. More than 3,000 escorted and hosted group tours departures were conducted on 85 itineraries in 1972.

A development of major importance was the lengthening of the international travel season. A dramatic example of this trend was seen on Labor Day weekend when close to 9,000 participants in American Express tours departed for Europe from U.S. airports.

Sales of domestic and Western Hemisphere tours registered one of the largest increases (up 70 percent over 1971). Greatest interest was shown in escorted tours to Hawaii, Mexico and the Caribbean. There was also important growth in South American tours.

Progress was also made in the development of sales by subsidiaries and representative offices outside the U.S. Most notable were the more than 1,000 European-tour bookings form Australia. There were also marked increases in travel sales to residents of Italy and Mexico.

The American Express "Visit U.S.A." program was intensified with promotions in eight languages and the introduction of nine new tour programs. These activities, combined with favorable economic factors, resulted in almost doubling the number of foreign visitors brought to the United States.

The pilot ITC (Inclusive Tour Charter) program operated last year in conjunction with World Airways, providing low-cost travel between the West Coast and Europe, proved to be a solid success. At the same time American Express tour bookings, on scheduled airlines on the same routes, set new records.

In 1973 European tours showed a substantial weakening but Western Hemisphere tours continued strong growth.

THE VULNERABLE POSITION OF THE INDEPENDENT TOUR OPERATOR

For a number of years in Europe and Japan there has been a growing development of self-contained complexes of travel services and travel plant. These vertical integrations of retailer, tour operator, carrier, hotel and sightseeing services in various combinations have been slow to penetrate the U.S. travel market. In 1972 there were a number of developments in the U.S. which seemed to presage fundamental changes in the structure of the American travel business in ways that would weaken the position of the independent tour operator.

EXHIBIT 7 (cont.)

There will, of course, always be a place for the small tour operator who performs some specialized services for areas where traffic is too limited to capture the attention of the major travel organizations. But for those origin-destination pathways through which the world's heaviest tourist traffic flows (Europe to Mediterranean, U.S. to Europe, Japan to Hawaii, U.S. to Caribbean or Mexico), it seems inevitable that new vertical combinations will appear that will absorb or eliminate a number of the functions of some of the medium-sized tour operators.

In the United States the entry of national retail organizations such as mail order houses, publishers such as *Holiday* and *Time*, Inc., and others outside of the travel agency field, have not proved to be successful. Exceptions, of course, are the well-established American Automobile Association and a number of banks which, in many instances, have been in business as long as most of the travel agencies. Even the banks, in 1972, were having trouble in the courts in maintaining their right to sell travel.

With the advent of the TGCs (Travel Group Charters) there was another flurry of companies outside the travel industry seeking to gain a foothold. Grand Union supermarkets began promotion TGCs in 450 markets throughout the country. And recently Sperry and Hutchinson, the "green stamp" organization, entered the travel field. Fotomat, which bills itself as the world's largest photographic developing service, has also entered the tour operating field with the creation of Fotomat Travel Services. And *Reader's Digest* has recently entered the travel field with the purchase of the Foreign Study League, reportedly the largest organizer of foreign study programs.

The airlines, eager to capture a greater share of the pleasure travel field, have been expanding their hotel ownership or management of hotels, have been accepting commissions for selling hotel rooms and rental cars and have been providing such large promotional subsidies to certain tour operators that the tour operator has become, in effect, an in-house company.

For 1973, the business of tour operating was in a state of flux, with changes taking place so rapidly that the future shape of the industry was hard to foresee. Much would depend on how the air carriers solved the problem of selling bulk travel at economy prices. Whether the TGC, or some revised version of this charter concept, would prove viable was a question that has yet to be answered. In the meantime, travel is growing and those with experience in the field are finding profitable ways to adjust to the new conditions.

EXHIBIT 8

Caribbean

The year 1973 in the Caribbean was a year of self-appraisal. Island governments were busy trying to overcome a condition of tourism indigestion caused by a rapid influx of visitors during the 1960s, with accompanying real estate speculation, the building of hundreds of luxury hotels and finally a backlash of local political and social forces that have severely injured the image of the Caribbean in the eyes of many prospective visitors.

Tourism is a new economic force in the Caribbean, barely 20 years old. It arrived so rapidly that neither governments nor local populations have been able to adjust from their previous agricultural-based way of life to an economy requiring skills in providing recreational services and entertainment to vacationing North Americans. With limited natural resources, many islands have no choice other than to capitalize on their very real tourism potential if they are to provide a satisfactory standard of living for their growing populations.

EXHIBIT 8 (cont.)

Yet, unless the tourism product can be properly maintained, and unless the images of these beautiful, peaceful tropical playgrounds with touches of British, French, Spanish, Danish and Dutch cultures, can be preserved and enhanced, then the future well-being of these island peoples seems very bleak indeed.

Perhaps tourism has come too quickly to the Caribbean. Tourism, unlike any other industry, depends on presenting an image of hospitality. Without a cheerful, hospitable labor force that enjoys serving the visitor, there can be no long-term success in this industry. The creation of this needed labor force is a selective process that requires identifying those individuals who enjoy this kind of work and then providing them with the necessary education.

This fundamental fact has now been recognized by many of the local governments. What is now taking place, is a serious attempt to assure the local populations that tourism is an honorable and enjoyable profession; that the jobs in the banks, insurance companies, post offices, shops, civil service departments and other places of employment that owe their growth to tourism's contribution to the economy, will in the future depend on the quality of service provided by the front-line troops of waiters, taxi drivers, maids and others in direct contact with the visiting tourists.

The slowing down of the growth of tourism, in some of the major resort areas, where small local populations have been unable to provide enough qualified workers needed to staff the tourism plant, is quite likely a disguised blessing. Time is needed to upgrade the skills of those employed in the tourist industry as well as to educate the general public to understand the role of tourism in improving the overall economy. Time is also needed for the local governing bodies to educate themselves in the art of administering to populations oriented to tourism rather than to agriculture.

There is also growing recognition of the need for modest-priced accommodations, smaller hotels and condominium apartments to supplement the high-priced luxury hotels. In the first great surge of tourism in the 1960s, the tendency was to try to imitate Miami Beach with luxury hotels designed to cater to the New York market. Now it is recognized that there is a vast North American market that prefers smaller, simpler accommodations designed to be more in keeping with the local culture and historic background of the particular island.

One subject that must soon be addressed by all Caribbean nations is that of creating some long-range planning mechanism to forecast tourism needs and resources over the next 20 years. This cannot be the task of a single government but must be a joint undertaking by all countries within the area, including Central America and the northern coast of South America. It must be recognized that at any given point in time there can be too many resort areas, just as there can be too many aircraft seats or too many hotel rooms. Growth must take place in step with market capacity to supply tourists in sufficient numbers. Moving forward in balance is still the key to success in the world of tourism.

Recent fear that Europe is the Caribbean's principal competitor seems unfounded. Only a tiny fraction of the North American public visits Europe to relax on beaches or engage in recreational activities. Europe is visited for sightseeing, education, business, or seeing friends or relatives. The Caribbean is visited for rest and recreation.

What is happening in the Caribbean is a general dispersal of visitors from a few major resort areas to a growing number of new destinations. Originally Cuba was the major destination of most North American visitors to the Caribbean. With the coming of Castro, Cuban tourism disappeared. The rapid increase in demand for vacations in the Caribbean and recognition by

EXHIBIT 8 (cont.)

island govenments of the power of advertising and public relations to attract visitors, enabled the Bahamas, Puerto Rico and the Virgin Islands to develop rapidly as major resort areas. Now many smaller islands are attracting increasing numbers of visitors. At the same time Mexico, Venezuela, Colombia, the Dominican Republic, Haiti and other Caribbean countries are launching plans to introduce resort areas. Cuba, eventually, is bound to take its place again as an important vacation playground. The competition in the future will not be with Europe but will be from newly developed areas within the Caribbean basin. Although there is certain to be a vast expansion in the potential market, it is quite possible to create new resort areas at a faster pace than the market can supply visitors. Obviously there is need to examine all of the projected developments throughout the area and place against these the probable number of visitors available over the next ten to 20 years.

At the same time island governments will discover that traffic will rearrange itself in patterns that follow price levels and degrees of hospitality. Large investments in accommodation facilities and in promotional campaigns are not feasible in the long run unless accompanied by a hospitable labor force and a reasonable price structure. Consumerism will continue to be a powerful force in the highly competitive tourism market place.

BAHAMAS CELEBRATES INDEPENDENCE

On July 10, 1973, the Bahamas officially severed its ties with Great Britain and celebrated its first Independence Day. This nation, which owes much of its tourism charm to its ability to offer a British Colonial atmosphere within easy reach of major U.S. population centers, will now stand on its own after 244 years of British rule.

With tourism accounting for 73 percent of Bahamas gross revenues, the Bahamian government is not likely to become so intoxicated by independence as to neglect the business that has produced the highest per-capita income among all the Caribbean nations. Yet its problems, at the present, are serious and may require a number of years to correct. Nature has provided an ample supply of beautiful islands, beaches and climate, but unfortunately its population of 185,000 is so small that it has difficulty in staffing its hotels, restaurants and other service industries. A number of years may be required to create a labor force skilled in the art of presenting a feeling of genuine hospitality. In the meantime tourist traffic and earnings seem to have reached a point of high-level stagnation.

During the late 1960s tourism grew at a rapid rate, averaging about 22 percent annually. In 1970 the islands suffered their first setback with a drop in traffic of 2.6 percent. There was a recovery in 1971, with an increase of 12.7 percent. Growth of traffic in 1972 slowed to 3.3 percent. During the first half of 1973 traffic fell below the same period in 1972, showing a decrease of about 3 percent.

For 1972, total visitor arrivals numbered 1,511,858 (up 3.3 percent). Air stopovers were 976,516 (up 8 percent). Sea stopovers were 59,594 (up 5 percent). Cruise visitors numbered 407,191 (decreased 7 percent). There were also 68,457 transit passengers included in the overall total.

EXHIBIT 8 *(cont.)*

VIRGIN ISLANDS SUFFERS FROM PAST SUCCESS

Like the Bahamas, the Virgin Islands has suffered from too much tourism too soon. The U.S. Virgin Islands, with a land area of only 132 square miles, has a population of about 80,000, and of these some 20,000 are aliens imported from other islands to work in the hundreds of hotels and restaurants. Visitors in 1972 numbered 1.2 million with 25 percent arriving from cruise ships and 75 percent by air. Earnings from tourism amounted to about $100 million. It is doubtful whether earnings in 1973 will show any gain over 1972.

Unlike the Bahamas, the Virgin Islands have tried to meet the service needs of the tourist industry by importing alien workers. As a rule the native islanders shun the menial hotel jobs and seek employment in white collar positions. As a result the population is dependent on the government as a major source of employment opportunities.

The social upheaval caused by the influx of tourists, the large numbers of outside owners who arrived to operate the tourist-related businesses and the employment of the thousands of alien workers has injured the image of these once peaceful and slow-paced resort communities. The lesson to be learned is that there is a limit to the speed with which tourism can be introduced into small islands with tiny populations. The Bahamas have limited the importation of alien workers and have gained a reputation for indifferent service and lack of hospitality. The Virgin Islands have imported the needed workers and have caused such local unrest as to bring about an increase in crime, and a degree of inhospitality to visitors that has been reflected in the North American press, to the detriment of the tourist trade. In both cases the speed with which tourism was introduced was too great to permit the orderly preparation of the local governments and the local populations to adjust to a switch from small agricultural-based economies to the sophisticated needs of the modern tourism trade.

Because the standard of living of the inhabitants of these islands is for the most part dependent on maintaining the large tourism industry and the bureaucracy it supports, the size of the annual promotional budget allocated by the islands' Senate Finance Committee is a matter of great political importance. For the fiscal year 1974 a budget of $1.2 million was approved. This represented a reduction of about $150,000 as compared to the previous year and fell short of the needs expressed by industry spokesmen.

EXHIBIT 8 (cont.)

Total Caribbean Visitors by Country and Method of Arrival—1972

	Air	Sea	Total	Cruise Ships	Grand Total	
					1972	1971
Antigua, W.I.	70,140	2,188	72,328	64,099	136,427	105,754
Aruba, N.A.	88,078	574	88,652	45,358	134,010	113,229
Barbados, W.I.	208,995	1,354	210,349	100,093	310,442	268,234*
Bonaire, N.A.	8,067	—	8,067	1,196	9,263	10,387
British V.I.	22,000	22,800	44,800	NR	44,800	38,600*
Cayman Islands, W.I.	30,646	—	30,646	1,014	31,660	25,262
Colombia, S.A. (includes San Andres)	171,183	2,471	173,654	NA	229,111**	197,503
Curacao, N.A.	126,683	NR	126,683	119,204	245,887	207,032
Dominica, W.I.	14,737	557	15,294	1,509	16,803	14,429
Dominican Republic	91,451	NR	91,451	18,443	109,894	106,468
Grenada, W.I.	35,081	2,852	37,933	94,060	131,993	84,278
Guadeloupe, F.W.I.	45,000	NR	45,000	22,738	67,738	66,531
Haiti	67,625	NR	67,625	92,329	159,954	87,438
Jamaica, W.I.	404,704	17,334	422,038	71,450	493,488	448,564
Martinique, F.W.I.	68,947	—	68,947	179,325	248,272	164,236
Montserrat, W.I.	10,449	1,014	11,463	1,066	12,529	9,073
Puerto Rico	1,172,885	—	1,172,885	261,159	1,434,044	1,245,389
St. Kitts Nevis Anguilla, W.I.	15,991	254	16,245	2,862	19,107	16,827
St. Lucia, W. I.	41,586	813	42,399	37,267	79,666	76,057
St. Marten Saba St. Eustatius, N.A.	121,139	1,041	122,180	111,398	233,578	192,640
St. Vincent, W.I.	15,701	1,201	16,902	11,418	28,320	29,734
Surinam, S.A.	NA	NA	NA	NA	NA	18,028*
Trinidad & Tobago	112,350	2,200	114,550	NR	114,550	111,330
Turks & Caicos Islands	4,390	280	4,670	NR	4,670	2,742
U.S. Virgin Islands	774,474	76,431	850,905	364,645	1,215,550	983,209
Total	3,722,302	133,364	3,855,666	1,600,633	5,511,356	4,622,974*

* Adjusted Figure   ** Includes 55,457 visitors by land.   NA—Not Available at time of printing.   NR—Not Reported.

Source: Caribbean Travel Association.

EXHIBIT 9

TABLE 1

Estimated Expenditures for Tourism in the U.S.A.
Household Consumers, Business, and Foreign Visitors, 1980, in Current and in 1970 Dollars
(Millions of Dollars)

Expenditure Item	Expenditures in 1980 Dollars				Expenditures in 1970 Dollars			
	Household Consumers	Business	Foreign Visitors	Total	Household Consumers	Business	Foreign Visitors	Total
Food, out of home city	12,458.7	7,011.3	2,381.3	21,851.4	8,385.6	4,719.1	1,602.8	14,707.5
Lodging, out of home city	17,615.8	7,199.2	2,303.9	27,118.6	11,547.2	4,719.1	1,510.2	17,776.5
Public transporataion, out of home city	9,196.4	10,038.1	565.8	19,800.4	7,107.3	7,757.7	437.3	15,302.2
Recreation, out of home city, business entertainment	3,180.4	134.2	901.0	4,215.9	2,138.7	90.2	605.8	2,834.7
Other incidentals	8,597.5	3,886.9	901.0	13,385.5	6,155.2	3,296.4	645.0	10,096.6
Owned vacation home, cabin, etc.	2,308.1	—	—	2,308.1	1,523.9	—	—	1,523.9
Non-auto expenditure Sub-total	53,357.3	28,269.7	7,053.0	88,680.1	36,857.7	20,582.5	4,801.1	62,241.4
Auto expenditures (allocated):								
Gas, oil, tolls	6,308.1	1,908.1	155.0	8,371.1	5,349.5	1,618.2	131.4	7,099.1
Other operating expenditures	11,867.2	3,249.9	—	15,117.1	9,011.8	2,354.4	—	11,366.2
Purchase cost	11,769.0	2,946.9	—	14,715.9	10,686.0	2,675.8	—	13,361.8
Auto expenditure Sub-total	29,944.1	8,105.0	155.0	38,204.1	25,047.3	6,648.3	131.4	31,827.1
Grand Total	83,301.5	36,374.7	7,208.0	126,884.1	61,905.1	27,230.8	4,932.6	94,068.4

Note: Details may not add up to totals shown because of independent rounding.

EXHIBIT 9 (cont.)

TABLE 2

Summary of Estimated Tourism Expenditures 1960-61, 1970, and 1980
(Millions of Dollars)

By Expenditure Item	Constant (1970) Dollars			Current Dollars		
	1960-61	1970	1980	1960-61	1970	1980
Food	$ 4,854	$ 7,536	$14,708	$ 3,331	$ 7,536	$ 21,851
Lodging	5,381	8,635	17,777	3,602	8,635	27,119
Public Transportation	4,039	7,469	15,302	3,161	7,469	19,800
Recreation	731	1,271	2,835	506	1,271	4,216
Other incidentals	3,440	5,269	10,097	2,428	5,269	13,386
Owned Vacation Home	398	718	1,524	268	718	2,308
Gas, Oil, Tolls	3,009	4,535	7,099	2,577	4,535	8,371
Other Auto Operating Expenditures	3,922	6,691	11,366	2,887	6,691	15,117
Auto Purchase Cost	4,623	7,604	13,362	4,219	7,604	14,716
Total	$30,397	$49,729	$94,068	$22,980	$49,729	$126,884
By Tourist Category						
Households	18,463	31,266	61,905	14,162	31,266	83,302
Business	10,674	16,301	27,231	7,946	16,301	36,375
Foreign Visitors	1,261	2,162	4,933	873	2,162	7,208
Total	$30,397	$49,729	$94,068	$22,980	$49,729	$126,884

Source: National Tourism Resources Review Commission.

EXHIBIT 10

Passports Issued and Renewed 1969-1972

	1972 Number	% Change over 71	1971	1970	1969
Calendar Year	2,728,021	+ 13.7	2,398,968	2,219,159	1,820,192
Jan–Mar	711,574	+ 19.9	593,707	523,139	392,732
Apr–June	967,585	+ 10.3	877,048	854,986	725,722
July–Sept	658,049	+ 11.9	588,272	543,385	438,129
Oct–Dec	390,813	+ 15.0	339,941	297,649	263,609

Passport Distribution by Geographical Area

Geographical Area	100 Passport Recipients 1972	100 Passport Recipients 1971	Increase or Decrease
Northeastern	34	42	− 8
North Central	21	21	0
Pacific	17	15	+ 2
South Atlantic	15	12	+ 3
South Central	9	7	+ 2
Mountain	4	3	+ 11

EXHIBIT 10 (cont.)

Citizenship of Passport Recipients
January Thru December

CITIZENSHIP

	Total Passports Issued 1972	1971	Percentage Change 1972 over 1971
TOTAL	2,728,021	2,398,968	+ 14
Native Born	2,553,750	2,270,610	+ 12
Naturalized	174,271	125,358	+ 39

AGE OF PASSPORT RECIPIENTS

TOTAL	2,728,021	2,398,968	+ 14
Under 20	469,580	392,130	+ 20
Under 5	61,960	46,200	+ 34
5–9	55,550	44,140	+ 26
10–14	89,010	75,190	+ 18
15–19	263,060	226,600	+ 16
20–29	584,880	554,460	+ 5
20–24	330,690	330,150	—
25–29	254,190	224,310	+ 13
30–39	369,450	305,260	+ 21
30–34	191,650	157,390	+ 22
35–39	177,780	147,870	+ 20
40–49	434,320	377,610	+ 15
40–44	199,180	174,360	+ 14
45–49	235,140	203,250	+ 16
50–59	437,300	377,860	+ 16
50–54	238,550	202,230	+ 18
55–59	198,750	175,630	+ 13
60–74	375,730	340,880	+ 10
60–64	164,310	151,960	+ 8
65–69	137,130	117,870	+ 16
70–74	74,290	71,050	+ 5
75 and over	56,781	50,768	+ 12

Object of Travel
January thru December

	Total Passports Issued 1972	1971	Percentage Change 1972 over 1971
TOTAL	2,728,021	2,398,968	+ 14
NON-GOVT. TRAVEL	2,591,120	2,300,030	+ 13
Personal Reasons	2,042,560	2,156,640	– 5
Pleasure	441,010	109,210	+ 304
Business	68,700	15,570	+ 341
Education	33,290	16,040	+ 108
Religion	3,980	1,380	+ 188
Health	800	130	+ 515
Scientific	780	1,060	– 26
GOVT. TRAVEL	136,901	98,938	+ 38
Military Dependent	80,331	50,568	+ 59
Military Travel	33,100	31,500	+ 5
Civ. Govt. Travel	23,470	16,870	+ 39

EXHIBIT 10 *(cont.)*

Passports Issued by Occupation
January thru December

OCCUPATION	Total Passports Issued		Percentage Change 1972 over 1971
	1972	*1971*	
TOTAL	2,728,021	2,398,968	+ 14
Housewife	467,340	390,170	+ 20
Student	548,010	505,600	+ 8
Retired	157,230	134,970	+ 16
Clerk-Secretary	127,400	115,850	+ 10
Teacher	146,820	136,600	+ 7
Independent Business or Profession	818,580	810,790	+ 1
Skilled Technical or Sales Worker	143,060	47,880	+ 199
Military	56,930	55,700	+ 2
Civilian Government	56,840	51,150	+ 11
Transportation and Travel	27,800	21,880	+ 27
Religious	18,520	16,800	+ 10
Entertainment	10,260	9,470	+ 8
Journalism	8,350	6,470	+ 29
Unskilled Workers	4,560	700	+ 551
Sports	2,330	880	+ 165
None Stated	133,991	94,058	+ 42

Sex of Passport Applicants

	Sample Distribution	Share of Market	Total Dollar Volume Production (All Agencies)
	January thru December Total Persons Included in Passports		
	1972		*1971*
TOTAL	3,013,570		2,661,480
Male	1,400,190		1,298,570
Female	1,613,380		1,362,910

Domestic Passports Issued and Renewed
Fiscal Years 1950-1974
(Fiscal Years end June 30 of Calendar Year)

1950—306,871	1960— 828,512	1970—2,079,863
1951—254,332	1961— 842,243	1971—2,311,789
1952—373,729	1962— 867,378	1972—2,605,321
1953—416,563	1963—1,018,488	1973—2,900,000 Est.
1954—434,644	1964—1,088,958	1974—3,275,000 Est.
1955—499,941	1965—1,267,750	
1956—546,470	1966—1,454,923	
1957—580,946	1967—1,624,940	
1958—652,253	1968—1,753,606	
1959—699,042	1969—1,759,286	

EXHIBIT 10 (cont.)

Passports Issued by State
January thru December

STATE OF RESIDENCE	Total Passports Issued		Percentage Change 1972 over 1971
	1972	1971	
TOTAL	2,728,021	2,398,968	+ 14
NORTHEAST	982,641	929,598	+ 6
New York	451,051	429,178	+ 5
New Jersey	159,940	158,340	+ 1
Pennsylvania	140,060	132,730	+ 6
Massachusetts	121,570	120,630	+ 1
Connecticut	66,920	51,150	+ 31
Rhode Island	16,640	15,480	+ 7
New Hampshire	11,480	9,930	+ 16
Maine	9,100	6,930	+ 31
Vermont	5,880	5,230	+ 12
NORTH CENTRAL	585,030	498,650	+ 17
Illinois	149,810	137,640	+ 9
Ohio	103,820	86,370	+ 20
Michigan	97,250	78,150	+ 24
Indiana	44,670	34,050	+ 31
Minnesota	47,880	38,880	+ 23
Wisconsin	44,230	37,740	+ 17
Missouri	37,230	32,600	+ 14
Kansas	17,720	16,720	+ 6
Iowa	23,100	21,170	+ 9
Nebraska	10,190	8,790	+ 16
South Dakota	5,800	4,120	+ 41
North Dakota	3,300	2,420	+ 38
PACIFIC	494,400	406,120	+ 22
California	395,950	315,600	+ 25
Washington	44,290	39,820	+ 11
Hawaii	27,380	26,920	+ 2
Oregon	21,440	20,640	+ 4
Alaska	5,340	3,140	
SOUTH ATLANTIC	351,120	307,810	+ 14
Florida	100,610	96,540	+ 4
Virginia	68,170	53,700	+ 27
Maryland	69,020	56,470	+ 22
Georgia	28,290	24,670	+ 15
North Carolina	31,880	28,860	+ 10
South Carolina	14,450	12,310	+ 17
Washington, D.C.	22,740	19,780	+ 15
Delaware	6,840	9,160	- 25
West Virginia	9,120	6,320	+ 44
SOUTH CENTRAL	223,780	184,480	+ 21
Texas	103,220	81,350	+ 27
Tennessee	25,860	19,480	+ 33
Louisiana	25,720	21,920	+ 17
Alabama	18,750	15,840	+ 18
Kentucky	14,760	13,930	+ 6
Oklahoma	17,470	16,280	+ 7
Mississippi	8,410	7,470	+ 13
Arkansas	9,590	8,210	+ 17

EXHIBIT 10 (cont.)

STATE OF RESIDENCE

	Total Passports Issued		Percentage Change 1972 over 1971
	1972	1971	
MOUNTAIN	89,530	71,280	+ 26
Colorado	27,950	26,900	+ 4
Arizona	21,810	14,540	+ 50
Utah	11,690	10,710	+ 9
New Mexico	8,290	5,250	+ 58
Nevada	7,180	4,410	+ 63
Idaho	5,120	2,570	+ 99
Wyoming	3,140	2,010	+ 56
Montana	4,350	4,890	− 11
OTHER	1,520	1,030	48

Passport Distribution
January thru December

METROPOLITAN AREA OF RESIDENCE

	Total Passports Issued		Percentage Change 1972 over 1971
	1972	1971	
TOTAL	2,728,021	2,398,968	+ 14
New York Area			
New York City	337,460	367,730	− 8
Newark	17,320	29,780	− 42
Paterson-Clifton-Passaic	8,790	7,120	+ 23
Los Angeles Area			
LA-Long Beach	189,640	163,920	+ 16
Anaheim-Santa Ana-Garden Grove	5,540	960	+ 477
Chicago	142,070	132,390	+ 7
Washington, D.C.	111,650	99,920	+ 12
SF-Oakland	73,910	98,520	− 25
Boston	103,730	111,750	− 7
Detroit	81,840	69,170	+ 18
Philadelphia	38,750	34,870	+ 11
Minneapolis-St. Paul	43,690	37,470	+ 17
Seattle	39,510	31,860	+ 24
Pittsburgh	21,610	28,060	− 23
Denver	20,300	23,300	− 13
Baltimore	18,600	14,260	+ 30
Miami	27,770	34,010	− 18
San Diego	16,300	7,820	+ 108
Houston	20,850	12,830	+ 63
Milwaukee	28,900	33,420	− 14
Atlanta	8,330	8,500	− 2
Dallas	13,970	14,610	− 4
Cleveland	15,530	12,960	+ 20
St. Louis	11,110	10,570	+ 5
Indianapolis	12,370	9,060	+ 36
San Jose	8,900	6,300	+ 41
New Orleans	8,580	7,310	+ 17
Kansas City	8,600	9,690	− 11
Cincinnati	9,370	8,390	+ 12
San Bernardino	4,140	1,400	+ 196
Buffalo	6,240	5,330	+ 17

Total Residing in the Metropolitan Areas   202,000

12

Yamaha Motor Corporation: U.S.A.

Bill Wilkie, Vice President of Marketing for Yamaha Motor Corporation, was preparing his annual marketing plan for the Board of Directors meeting in 1976. In the past, his marketing plans were simply an extension of plans from previous years, with minor modifications. Since 1974, however, industry sales had been under considerable pressure, resulting in intense competition among the major motorcycle manufacturers to establish market position and increase their share of market. In response to these competitive pressures, Wilkie had recently commissioned a major survey of motorcycle owners and their motorcycle purchase decision process (PDP). With this new research input, he planned to reassess Yamaha's market position and to develop a marketing strategy for the future.

This case was prepared by Professor Scott Ward, The Wharton School, as a basis for class discussion rather than to illustrate either effective or ineffective handling of an administrative situation. Some data and dates are disguised.

Yamaha Motor Corporation, like many motorcycle manufacturing firms, is a Japanese-owned company. Yamaha's North American manufacturing and sales operations are headquartered in Southern California. The company manufactures a full line of motorcycles, but is noted for its strength in the "off-road" and "combination bike" markets.[1] These models are used primarily for enjoyment (e.g., racing and exploring trails), although combination motorcycles can be used for "cruising" (i.e., recreational riding on highways and back roads) and transportation as well. In 1975, Yamaha's best selling motorcycles included the

----

[1] "Off-road" motorcycles are constructed with heavier-duty materials than street bikes. They are used primarily for riding over dirt trails, open areas and deserts, and other areas which are not easily accessible by foot or car. "Street bikes," in contrast, are designed for traveling on roads and highways and are frequently used for transportation as well as enjoyment. "Combination bikes" can be used for both off-road and street riding.

175 cc., 250 cc., and 360 cc. "off-road" line and the 175 cc. and 250 cc. "combination bike" models.[2] These models retail for between $750 and $1650. (Prices tend to increase with engine size as shown in Exhibit 1.) The entire Yamaha line was composed of almost twenty models which ranged in price from $500 to $2500. These prices were competitive with similar models marketed by other manufacturers.

Yamaha sold its motorcycles through a network of about 1,600 franchised dealers throughout the country. Most dealers carried one or two major brands (e.g., BMW, Harley-Davidson, Honda, Kawasaki, Suzuki and Yamaha). Dealers carried at least a basic stock of Yamaha parts, and received sales assistance, technical point-of-sale materials, and cooperative advertising support from Yamaha. Most of the major motorcycle manufacturers followed similar distribution procedures.

Dealers were compensated approximately 17 percent of the manufacturer's suggested retail price on most major brands, including Yamaha. Price discounting was common in some of the larger, competitive markets, but dealers rarely sold motorcycles for more than $50 off the sticker price. Most dealers believed that customers were not especially sensitive to price differences of up to 10 percent between similar models. However, some premium models such as BMW were able to command a significantly higher price, while models with less attractive features sold poorly even at lower prices.

In 1975, Yamaha spent approximately $1.5 million on media advertising. About 55 percent of this budget was devoted to network prime time advertising, usually on movies, sports events and adventure series. Another 45 percent was spent on print advertising in motorcycle magazines such as *Cycle, Cycle World* and *Cycle Guide*; automotive magazines including *Car and Driver* and *Hot Rod*; general interest magazines such as *Playboy* and *Field and Stream,* and on cooperative newspaper advertising with dealers. Yamaha spent an additional $550,000 on dealer promotions, and on point-of-sale literature—especially on technically oriented specifications brochures, which were distributed to dealers at no cost. In addition to these materials, Yamaha distributed a full line of parts and repair instructions to its factory authorized dealers. Virtually all of the advertising and promotion budget was spent during the spring months.

Among motorcycle owners, Yamaha was known for its two-stroke engine,[3] its heavy, durable motorcycles, and for its "off-road" and "combination" bikes which lent themselves to racing. Suzuki had a similar image, though it did not enjoy the racing appeal of Yamaha's products. Honda, the market leader, had built its reputation on a large, efficient dealer network and on its dependable, smooth riding, four-stroke "street bikes." These motorcycles were especially well suited for personal transportation and for long distance riding. Kawasaki was also known for its four-stroke engine. Kawasaki's strength was in larger motorcycles, however, which offered speed and high performance beyond that required for street transportation alone.

While each of these manufacturers offered a range of products, their advertising generally focused on their areas of competitive strength. As a result, producers tended to enjoy very large market shares in some product categories and small shares in other categories (Exhibit 3).

According to Mr. Wilkie, the years between 1968 and 1973 were marked by rapid growth of sales in the motorcycle industry. The number of registered bikes doubled over this period to 1.6 million. (Motorcycle sales data by cycle type and engine size are shown in Exhibit

---

[2] Motorcycles are generally named by their engine size, as measured in cubic centimeters displacement (i.e., "cc's").

[3] Two-stroke engines have no valves and require that gas and oil be mixed separately. They are designed for smaller engine (i.e., cc.) sizes and provide power at lower riding speeds. Four-stroke engines are used in larger motorcycles and perform best at faster speeds. These engines operate with valves (like automobile engines) and employ a crank case for oil. They tend to produce fewer polluting byproducts and generally last longer than two-stroke engines.

2.) Because of this growth, most motorcycle companies were forced to concentrate on manufacturing, rather than marketing issues. Over this period, for example, Kawasaki built its first manufacturing facility in the United States and many other manufacturers expanded their facilities.

With the introduction of larger manufacturing facilities, each of the four major motorcycle manufacturers began extending its product line. This move toward full product lines was intended to increase total sales volume for each company and therefore to spread production, advertising, and distribution costs over a larger base. In addition, customers often purchased a "starter bike" in the 250 cc to 400 cc. class and then traded up to larger motorcycles (i.e., larger engine sizes) in a few years. By extending their product lines over a wider range of engine sizes, manufacturers hoped to attract and retain these customers and to provide a base for extending their dealer network as well. Some manufacturers such as Honda used this strategy with considerable success (see Exhibit 4). Others found themselves competing in model categories where they could not offer a high quality product entry. Mr. Wilkie believed that Yamaha's 750 cc. four-stroke "street-bike" was one of these non-competitive products. However, he was not sure to what extent this experience affected Yamaha's overall image.

In 1975, while manufacturers were continuing to expand their production facilities and product lines, industry sales fell by 30 percent. This sharp downturn was attributed to four factors, only one of which was expected to be short-lived:

1. The recession made consumers reluctant to make durable purchases. Major expenditures, such as motorcycles, were postponed.
2. Increasing energy costs, wages and other inflationary pressures were forcing increases in motorcycle prices. According to *Business Week*, list prices of motorcycles increased about 25% between 1973 and 1976.[4]

3. Environmental legislation began to force manufacturers into major expenditures for noise and emission controls. These costs were also ultimately passed on to the consumer.
4. The population mix was changing, with post war baby boom children beginning to enter their 30's. By contrast, about two-thirds of all motorcycle purchasers were under 30.

This combination of elements caught most motorcycle manufacturers off guard. In 1975, the two industry leaders, Honda and Yamaha, lost 30 percent and 40 percent in unit sales, respectively.

By 1976, each manufacturer was scrambling to regain sales volume. Industry advertising budgets were increased 25 percent over 1975 to an estimated $20 million according to *Advertising Age* (Exhibit 5).[5] This factor, coupled with an upturn in the economy, led to an 8 percent increase in total motorcycle sales volume over 1975. While this sales gain represented an improvement, it confirmed that the motorcycle industry had clearly left the rapid growth stage of the late 1960s and early 1970s and had entered the mature stage in its life cycle. This suggested that competition among manufacturers would become more intense in the future as each sought to increase sales by gaining market share points from the other.

Because the change came so rapidly, few manufacturers had made any real effort to reposition themselves or to do anything differently than they had in the past. Honda, the industry leader with a 38 percent market share, was an exception. Also the leader in new product development, Honda introduced a small, relatively inexpensive motorcycle in 1976. Sales results were inconclusive so far. Yamaha, Kawasaki, and Suzuki had all increased their advertising budgets in 1976, but had done little else to change their image or to increase sales. Harley-Davidson, a manufacturer of expensive, heavy, touring and street machines, had weathered the downturn better than other competitors (1975 sales volume fell 12 percent from

---

[4] From *Business Week*, May 3, 1976, p. 80.

[5] From *Advertising Age*, November 15, 1976, p. 30.

1974). Harley was rumored to be shifting advertising emphasis to their lighter weight motorcycles.

In 1976, Yamaha's sales were recovering from their 1975 lows, and Yamaha's market share jumped from 17 percent to 21 percent. (Sales and market share data for Yamaha and its competitors are shown in Exhibit 6.) Still, Yamaha's unit sales volume was 20 percent below its 1974 peak of over 200,000 motorcycles. More importantly, Mr. Wilkie and his staff were at a loss to explain Yamaha's dramatic loss of market share in 1975 or their partial recovery in 1976.

Mr. Wilkie did have a good deal of demographic and psychographic data on motorcycle buyers available to him. A recent *Target Group Index* study showed that in 1975, 7.7 percent of all U.S. households owned at least one motorcycle.[6] Of these, 41 percent had made their purchases within the past year, 40 percent had bought their motorcycles between one and four years ago, and the remaining 9 percent had owned their bikes for five years or more.

Among motorcycle owners, the average number of motorcycles owned was 1.96 percent according to a recent survey of *Cycle World* subscribers.[7] Forty-four percent reported owning one motorcycle, 29 percent owned two, 14 percent had three, and the remaining 13 percent said that they owned four or more motorcycles.

Motorcycle owners tended to be young, with a median age of 26 years (Exhibit 7). Most motorcycle owners were men (81 percent), and about three-quarters were married. Seventy-eight percent had at least a high school degree. About 84 percent were employed, most often as craftsmen and foremen (26 percent) or in professional or managerial positions (24 percent). The median household income for motorcycle owners was about $13,600, with 56 percent of

all owners reporting income between $10,000 and $19,999. Demographic data are detailed in Exhibit 8.

Motorcycle ownership among heads of households was most common in the 18 to 24 year age bracket (11.1 percent owned motorcycles). This figure ranged from 9.6 percent to 10.6 percent for household heads between 25 and 49 years, then dropped off dramatically. The likelihood of motorcycle ownership also increases with household income: 11.2 percent of those with incomes between $20,000 and $24,999 owned motorcycles, versus just 3.0 percent of those with incomes below $5,000 (Exhibit 9).

Motorcycle owners usually became interested in motorcycling through friends (56 percent) and family members (21 percent). Just 8 percent attributed their interest to media advertising, usually through motorcycle magazines (5 percent) and general interest publications (2 percent) (Exhibit 10).

When asked about their buying habits, motorcycle owners were most likely to describe themselves as "planners," "economy-minded," and "cautious." They were least apt to consider themselves "conformists," "style-conscious," "impulsive," or "ecologists" (Exhibit 11). In more general terms, cycle owners regarded themselves as "brave," "trust-worthy," "stubborn," and "dominating," and not as "amicable," "egocentric," or "reserved" (Exhibit 12).

In reviewing a recent survey of *Cycle* magazine subscribers, Mr. Wilkie noted that 44 percent of those responding said they were planning to buy a motorcycle or mini-bike over the next twelve months.[8] Of these, 37 percent intended to buy more than one cycle. About two-thirds of these purchases would be new motorcycles, according to respondents. While this represented considerable sales volume if these plans were realized, Wilkie was concerned that Yamaha's share of these planned

---

[6] From *Target Group Index,* Book No. 161, p. 30, Axiom Market Research Bureau, Inc., 1975, pp. 141–42.

[7] From 1976 Profile of Subscribers—*Cycle World,* conducted by Don Bowdren Associates, p. 7.

[8] From *Cycle Magazine Subscriber Study,* 1977, conducted by Beta Research Corporation, pp. 18–23.

purchases was only 16 percent, considerably lower than Yamaha's share of market in 1976 (Exhibit 13).

In light of these data, Mr. Wilkie had decided on the need for a survey of motorcycle owners. The purpose of the survey was to understand how people make decisions about which brand and type of motorcycle to purchase, what sources of information they use, and what kinds of information were most critical at each stage of the purchase process. By understanding buyers' information needs and interests, he reasoned, Yamaha could tailor its marketing program to the consumer.

A mail questionnaire was developed and pretested, and mailed to a national sample of 5,000 recent motorcycle purchasers. Names and addresses were sampled via a random probability procedure from lists provided by the R. L. Polk Company and from Yamaha's own sales records.[9] A total of 2,245 completed and usable questionnaires were returned (44 percent response rate). Incentives, preletters (telling respondents a questionnaire was coming) and post-letters (follow-up letters asking people to return questionnaires) were used to obtain the excellent response rate. A later survey among nonrespondents was conducted in order to insure that these people were not systematically "different" from respondents in a way which would bias the actual sample. Mr. Wilkie was satisfied that the sample was a reasonably good representation of American motorcycle owners.[10]

The questionnaire, with the results for the total sample typed in, is contained in Appendix A. The organization of the information in it is as follows:

---

[9] This sampling procedure insures that every name has an equal and known probability of being chosen. Stated differently, there was no "bias" toward any segment of names on the lists. This was felt to be an adequate basis for projecting results to the national population of motorcycle buyers who had bought motorcycles during the period represented in Polk's and Yamaha's lists.

[10] A further subsample of 718 has been drawn for analysis purposes of this case.

	Question Number	Computer Variable Numbers
Brand bought	1	2
Model bought	1	3
Engine "cc"	1	5
When cycle bought	2	6–7
Uses and degree of uses	3	8–29
Repeat vs. 1st cycle	4	30
Information about previous cycle (filled in by repeat buyers only)	5	31–41
Knowledge level and desire for knowledge	7	42–73
Helpfulness of information sources at thinking and active stages	8	74–91
Future purchase plans	14	92
Demographics	15	93–98
Reduced variables*		99–123

* See "Note on Reduced Variables."

Mr. Wilkie now turned to decisions about how to analyze the data for maximum usefulness. He faced major decisions concerning market segmentation, product positioning, and promotion, and decisions on which media to use and how much to spend. At the moment, however, he turned to analysis of the data. He recalled the key questions he had asked previously, in specifying problems to be addressed by the research:

What is the profile of the Yamaha buyer?

Do Yamaha buyers differ from other motorcycle buyers in:

> How they use their motorcycles (useful in promotion appeal formulation)?
> Use of different information sources (useful in determining media strategy)?
> Knowledge level and desire for knowledge (useful in determining promotion weights)?
> Models bought and uses of motorcycles?

Do repeat buyers differ from new buyers in their desire for information, and/or usefulness of information from different sources?

In what ways do owners differ regarding helpfulness of information sources at the thinking and active stages of the PDP?

While there were other questions Mr. Wilkie wanted answered, these were indicative of the kinds of questions that he considered important, and they suggested specific analyses. For example, he hypothesized that Yamaha owners might be slightly younger and "downscale" relative to Honda and other motorcycle owners. This would involve cross-tabulating owners' age (Question 15, variable 95) by brand bought (Question 1, variable 2), and family yearly income (Question 15, reduced variable 104)[11] by brand bought. He also thought that Yamaha owners use their bikes more for off-road uses than owners of other brands. Therefore, he wanted to cross-tabulate brand bought (Question 1, variable 2) by primary usage (Question 3, variables 112, 113, 114 and 8).

Mr. Wilkie sketched out a general "model" of the motorcycle purchasing process in order to help him organize the many kinds of data from the survey (Exhibit 14). The model was not intended to represent exactly the steps in buying a motorcycle, but simply to suggest some relationships which might be important. For example, the intensity of a buyer's desire for information might be different at different stages of the PDP, and the relative helpfulness of information sources might also vary by stage. Therefore, Mr. Wilkie reasoned, he might want to cross-tabulate level of desire for knowledge (Question 7) by helpfulness of information sources (Question 8).

Mr. Wilkie did not want to be inundated by data, so he set about the task of specifying the marketing strategy issues in the areas of segmentation, positioning and promotion, and then specifying the most important computer analyses to help him formulate strategy.

---

[11] See "Note on Reduced Variables."

EXHIBIT 1

Retail Motorcycle Prices by Engine Size, 1976

Engine Size (in cc's)	Average Retail Price Range*
150–250	$550– $825
250–400	$825–$1150
500–650	$1225–$1650
750	$1800–$1900
900–1000	$1900–$2700
Over 1000	$2500 and Over

* These prices include a net cost to dealers, a dealer assembly and preparation fee (about $30), and a standard markup.

EXHIBIT 4

Number and Sales Volume of Motorcycle Dealers by Manufacturer, 1974

Company	Number of Dealers	Units Sold per Dealer
Honda	1974	220
Yamaha	1515	135
Kawasaki	1018	127
Suzuki	1103	98

Source: Motorcycle Dealer News.

EXHIBIT 2

Motorcycle Sales by Engine Size and Usage Type, 1974

	Retail Sales (in millions of dollars)			
	Motorcycle Usage Type			
Engine Size (cc's)	Street	Off-Road	Combination	Total
Less than 125	$ 3	$ 64	$ 14	$ 81
125–349	48	72	219	339
350–449	164	15	51	230
450–749	180	6	—	186
750 and over	288	*	—	288
Total Sales	$683	$157	$284	$1124

* Less than $500,000.

Source: Motorcycle Industry Council.

EXHIBIT 5

Media Advertising Budgets of Motorcycle Manufacturers, 1975

Company	1975 Media Advertising (Estimated)
Honda	$ 7,000,000
Kawasaki	3,000,000
Harley-Davidson	2,500,000
Suzuki	1,600,000
Yamaha	1,500,000
Others	600,000
	$16,200,000

Source: Advertising Age, November 11, 1976, pp. 30–33.

EXHIBIT 3

Market Share Differences by Product Class, 1974

Brand	Share of Total Market	Highest Share in Any Product Class*	Lowest Share in Any Product Class
Honda	43%	61%**	34%
Yamaha	20	34	4
Kawasaki	13	19	9
Suzuki	11	16	5

* Product classes are defined by engine size (measured in "cc's"). Classes used here are: under 125 cc.; 125 cc.–349 cc.; 350 cc.–449 cc.; 450 cc.–749 cc.; and 750 cc. and over.

** To be read, "In 1974, Honda held a 61% market share in one of the five product classes listed above. This represents Honda's highest share in any of these product classes."

Source: R. L. Polk and Co., registration data, 1974.

EXHIBIT 6

Sales of Registered Motorcycles by Brand, 1974–1976

	1974		1975		1976 (Projections)	
Brand	Unit Sales (000)	Market Share	Unit Sales (000)	Market Share	Unit Sales (000)	Market Share
Honda	434	43%	294	42%	291	39%
Yamaha	204	20	119	17	157	21
Kawasaki	129	13	123	18	128	17
Suzuki	108	11	81	12	88	12
Harley-Davidson	58	6	51	7	53	7
Others	73	7	28	4	32	4
Total	1,006	100%	696	100%	749	100%

Source: R. L. Polk and Co., registration data 1974.

EXHIBIT 7

Age of Motorcycle Users, 1976 and 1977

	Per Cent of Subscribers*		
Age	Cycle	Cycle World	U.S. Population
Under 18	22%	23%	31.7
18–24	25	22 ⎫	12.7
25–29	18 ⎫ 31	⎭ 29	14.1
29–34	13 ⎰		
35–39	8	19	16.4
40–49	9 ⎫		
50–64	⎬ 5	7 ⎫ 8	14.8 ⎫ 25.1
65 and over	⎭	1 ⎭	10.3 ⎭
Total	100%	100%**	100.0
Median	25.8 years	26.9 years	

* These data are derived from subscriber studies by the two most popular motorcycle-oriented publications. Therefore, they only provide approximations of data from the entire motorcycle user population.

** Data do not sum to 100% because of rounding error.

Sources: Cycle Magazine Subscriber Study, 1977, conducted by Beta Research Corporation, p. 57; and *1976 Profile of Subscribers—Cycle World,* conducted by Don Bowdren Research Associates, p. 1.

EXHIBIT 8

Demographic Profile of Motorcycle Owners

	Per Cent of All Motorcycle Owners	% of U.S. Population
Sex		
Male	81%*	48%
Female	19	52
Total	100%	100%
Marital Status		
Married	73% ⎫	70%
Widowed/divorced/separated	4 ⎬	30
Single	23 ⎭	
Total	100%	100%

EXHIBIT 8 (*cont.*)

	Per Cent of All Motorcycle Owners	% of U.S. Population
Education		
College graduate	12%	14%
Attended college	19	16
High school graduate	47	36
Did not graduate high school	22	34
Total	100%	100%
Employment Status		
Employed full-time	80%	
Employed part-time	4	NA
Not employed, or not in labor force	16	
	100%	

* To be read, "Of those who own motorcycles, 81% are men."

Source: Target Group Index, Book No. 161, p. 30, Axiom Market Research Bureau, Inc., 1975, pp. 441–43.

	Per Cent of All Employed Motorcycle Owners	% U.S. Males
Employment		
Professional and managerial	24%	31%
Clerical and sales	15	13
Craftsmen and foremen	26	21
Other employment	35	35
Total	100%	100%

	Per Cent of All Households Owning Motorcycles	% U.S. Males
Total Household Income		
Less than $5,000	7%	13.7%
$ 5,000–$ 7,999	11	11.2
$ 8,000–$ 9,999	7	10.6
$10,000–$14,999	35	23.0
$15,000–$19,999	21	17.8
$20,000–$24,999	10	10.9
$25,000 and over	9	12.8
Total	100%	100.0%

EXHIBIT 9

Motorcycle Market Penetration, 1975

Age of Head of Household	Per Cent of Population Owning Motorcycles	Total Household Income	Per Cent of Population Owning Motorcycles
18–24	11.1%*	Less than $ 5,000	3.0%
25–34	9.6	$ 5,000–$ 7,999	5.7
35–49	10.6	$ 8,000–$ 9,999	7.0
50–64	4.9	$10,000–$14,999	8.6
65 and over	.7	$15,000–$19,999	10.4
Total	7.7%	$20,000–$24,999	11.2
		$25,000 and over	10.4
		Total	7.7%

* To be read, "11.1% of all heads of households between 18 and 24 owned one or more motorcycles in 1975."

Source: Target Group Index, Book No. 161, p. 30, Axiom Market Research Bureau, Inc., 1975, pp. 441–42.

EXHIBIT 10

Reasons for First Interest in Motorcycling

Which of the following best describes the way in which you first got interested in motorcycling?	Per Cent of Respondents
Friend got me interested	56%
Family member got me interested	21
Went to motorcycle race	5
Saw motorcycles advertised in motorcycling magazine	5
Rode one/previous experience	4
Economical transportation	2
Saw motorcycles advertised in general magazine	2
Saw motorcycles advertised on TV	1
Went to motorcycle club	1
Heard radio advertisement	1
All other	11
No answer	1
Total	100%*

* Data sum to more than 100% because of multiple responses.

Source: Cycle Magazine Subscriber Study, 1977, conducted by Beta Research Corporation, p. 32.

EXHIBIT 11

Motorcycle's Owners' Buying Patterns

Description	Per Cent of Motorcycle Owners Classifying Themselves as:
Planners	40%*
Economy-minded	34
Cautious	32
Brand Loyal	29
Persuasible	26
Experimenter	22
Ecologist	21
Impulsive	20
Style-conscious	18
Conformist	17

* To be read, "40% of all motorcycle owners classify themselves as 'planners' when they buy things."

Source: Target Group Index, Book No. 161, p. 30, Axiom Market Research Bureau, Inc., 1975, p. 443.

EXHIBIT 12

Motorcycle Owners' Self-Concepts

Description	Per Cent of Motorcycle Owners Who Consider Themselves to Be:
Brave	63%*
Trustworthy	59
Stubborn	46
Dominating	46
Kind	41
Tense	37
Broadminded	37
Sociable	35
Reserved	34
Affectionate	33
Frank	31
Awkward	30
Creative	26
Self-assured	25
Efficient	24
Intelligent	20
Funny	20
Reserved	17
Egocentric	16
Amicable	13

* To be read, "63% of all motorcycle owners classify themselves as 'brave.' "

Source: Target Group Index, Book No. 161, p. 30, Axiom Market Research Bureau, Inc., 1975, p. 443.

EXHIBIT 13

Motorcycle Purchasing Plans, 1973 and 1976

	1973	1976
Percent planning to buy a motorcycle in the next 12 months	54%	44%
(N)	(1247)	(1268)
(of those) Purchase plans by brand:		
Honda	26%	27%
Yamaha	22	16
Kawasaki	12	12
Suzuki	10	18
Harley-Davidson	8	7
Other	22	20
Total	100%	100%
(N)	(675)	(555)
(of those) Purchase plans by engine size (in cc's)		
Less than 125	11%	6%
125–349	46	35
350–449	7	11
450–799	25	29
800 and over	11	19
Total	100%	100%
(N)	(675)	(555)

Source: Cycle Magazine Subscriber Studies, 1973 and 1976.

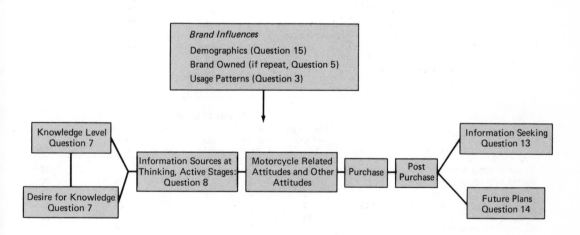

APPENDIX A

Motorcycle Owners Survey

1. Regarding the motorcycle you purchased *most recently*, please indicate below what brand, model type, engine type and "cc" was it?

	Brand (check one)			Model Type (check one)		"CC"
	BMW	2		Street Only	47	
	Harley-Davidson	1		Combination (Street		
	Honda	41	**VAR.**	&Off-Road)	46	
VAR.	Kawasaki	16	**3**	Off-Road Only	5	(Write In)
2	Suzuki	13		Mini-Cycle	1	**VAR.5**
	Yamaha	25		Other _____	1	
	Other _____	1		(Write in)		
	(Write in)					

2. In what month and year did you purchase your *most recent* motorcycle?

Month _____ Year _____

      VAR.6   **VAR.7**

3. Below are listed several ways of using your motorcycle. In the first column check the item which is your primary usage. Then for each item, indicate the extent to which you use your motorcycle for *all* the items.

Usage Item	Primary Usage (Check only one)	VAR.
Cruising along highways & backroads	47	8
Riding over rough trails	14	9
Informal off-road racing	4	10
Exploring places I can't go by foot or car	9	11
Cruising around town	20	12
Riding in an open area or desert	5	13
Improving the performance of my bike	6	14
Going to school or work	37	15
Formal racing	3	16
General maintenance	10	17
Other - what? _____	4	18

	Degree of Usage					
	Almost all of the Time	A lot of the Time	Fairly Often	Once in a While	Hardly ever/ Never	VAR.
Cruising along highways & backroads	24	29	18	11	5	19
Riding over rough trails	6	12	9	23	26	20
Informal off-road racing	2	2	4	18	46	21
Exploring places I can't go by foot or car	3	11	11	29	20	22
Cruising around town	10	19	26	14	10	23
Riding in an open area or desert	2	5	7	24	35	24
Improving the performance of my bike	4	7	12	26	23	25
Going to school or work	26	16	16	10	13	26
Formal racing	2	2	2	4	62	27
General maintenance	10	8	23	16	14	28
Other - what? _____	3	2	2	23	6	29

APPENDIX A *(cont.)*

4. Had you purchased any motorcycle beofre the one you described in question 1 above? (Refers only to motorcycles you purchased for yourself.) **VAR. 30**

   a. No—This was the first motorcycle   34   (Skip over question 5; continue answering with question 6.)
   b. Yes, had owned 1 motorcycle before   29
   c. Yes, had owned 2 or more motorcycles before   35   (Continue with question 5 below.)

5. Regarding the motorcycle you purchased before the one described in question 1, in what month and year did you purchase it?

   Month_____   Year_____
          VAR. 31   **VAR. 32**

5a. What brand, model type and "cc" was it?

	Brand *(Check only one)*			Model Type *(Check only one)*		"CC"
	BMW	1		Street only	28	
	Harley-Davidson	3		Combination (Street & off-road)	28	
	Honda	25	**VAR.**	Off-road only	5	
VAR.	Kawasaki	6	**34**	Mini-cycle	2	(Write in)
33	Suzuki	8		Other_____	1	**VAR. 35**
	Yamaha	13		(Write in)		
	Other_____	10				
	(write in)					

5b. Regarding your previous motorcycle, please indicate for each item below and overall how satisfied you were with it.

	Degree of Satisfaction with Previous Motorcycle					
	1 Extremely Satisfied	2 Very Satisfied	3 Satisfied	4 Somewhat Dissatisfied	5 Extremely Dissatisfied	VAR.
Item						
Performance	21	18	19	5	1	36
Handling	18	19	19	6	1	37
Dependability/reliability	25	17	13	7	2	38
Dealer service	12	10	20	12	9	39
Upkeep costs	19	15	18	8	3	40
Overall brand satisfaction	18	21	17	5	1	41

6. *Instructions:* (Please read carefully)
We would like you to think back to your purchase of your last motorcycle as it relates to *two stages:* (a) A *thinking stage,* when the idea to buy that cycle was in your mind, but you weren't going out of your way to gather information or to learn about what was available; and (b) an *active stage,* when you started thinking pretty seriously about buying and started looking for informaion about different brands and models.

Now, thinking about the motorcycle you purchased most recently, about how long did you spend in the *thinking stage*—from when you first started thinking about buying to when you actively started looking for information?

_____ years   _____ months   _____ weeks

And about how long were you in the *active stage*—from when you first started actively looking and seriously thinking about buying to when you actually bought your cycle?

_____ years   _____ months   _____ weeks

APPENDIX—A (cont.)

7. Below on the left are some things you might have considered during the *thinking stage*. We are interested in knowing *how much you knew* about each of these things during the *thinking stage*—did you know a lot, know some things, or only know a little? And we also would like to find out *how much more you wanted to know*—did you want to know a lot more, a little more, or didn't you want to know any more? For example, if you "knew a lot" about technical features during the *thinking stage*, but you still "wanted to know a little more", then you would answer like this:

	How Much You Knew			How Much More You Wanted to Know		
	Knew a Lot	Knew Some Things	Only Knew a Little	Wanted to Know a Lot More	Wanted to Know a Little More	Did Not Want to Know More
Example Technical Features ***	(✓)	( )	( )	( )	(✓)	( )

Now, for each item listed below, please make one checkmark to indicate "how much you knew" and another checkmark to indicate "how much you wanted to know" about the brand or brands you were considering.

Thinking Stage	How Much You Knew			How Much More You Wanted To Know			VAR.
	1 Knew a Lot	2 Knew Some Things	3 Only Knew a Little	1 Wanted to Know a Lot More	2 Wanted to Know a Little More	3 Did not Want to Know More	
Engine features/mechanical systems	13	52	35	36	40	24	42-43
Model types (street, off-road, combination)	32	44	24	31	40	29	44-45
Performance/handling	28	52	20	50	38	12	46-47
Physical size of bike	58	31	11	28	37	35	48-49
Dealer reputation/service	34	36	30	48	32	20	50-51
Racing wins & capabilities/reputation	16	43	41	50	36	12	52-53
Price offered by dealer	27	32	41	44	35	21	54-55
Brand Comparison	35	41	24	30	48	22	56-57
Uses/things to do with different kinds of bikes	40	45	15	29	49	22	58-59
Dependability/reliability	22	49	29	51	40	9	60-61
New technical features	20	52	28	38	39	23	62-63
Good/bad experiences with brands	17	34	49	25	36	39	64-65
Aspects of owner maintenance	47	38	15	38	36	26	66-67
Styling and sound	25	48	27	33	35	32	68-69
Engine size in "cc"	44	43	13	27	45	28	70-71
Two-stroke/four-stroke engines	19	48	33	58	34	8	72-73

(Check and be sure you have *two* checks for each item listed.)

APPENDIX A (cont.)

8. Instructions: (Please read carefully)

We would like to know how helpful each of the information sources below was to you during the thinking stage and during the active stage, in making your decision about which brand of motorcycle to purchase.

For each information source on the left below, check one space to tell how helpful it was during the thinking stage and one space to tell how helpful it was during the active stage. If an information source was just as helpful during the active stage as it was in the thinking stage, check the same space under both stages.

If, for example, you feel that your mother was "helpful" in the thinking stage, but "not at all helpful" in the active stage, you would answer as in the example below.

	Thinking Stage					Active Stage				
	1 Very Helpful	2 Helpful	3 Not Too Helpful	4 Not at all Helpful	VAR.	1 Very Helpful	2 Helpful	3 Not Too Helpful	4 Not at all Helpful	VAR.
Example: **Your mother**	( )	(✓)	( )	( )		( )	( )	( )	(✓)	
Television/radio advertising	13	17	30	40	74	20	21	21	38	83
Magazine advertising/articles	20	40	22	20	75	28	35	22	15	84
Experience with owning previous bikes	18	41	25	16	76	35	37	18	10	85
Motorcycle specifications brochures	19	40	20	21	77	20	37	24	24	86
Riding other peoples' bikes	13	17	24	46	78	18	18	15	49	87
Motorcycle dealer	38	23	8	31	79	41	23	7	29	88
Dealer mechanic	5	27	35	33	80	6	15	35	44	89
Family member	28	33	17	22	81	30	31	14	25	90
Motorcycle owners	44	37	12	7	82	45	36	12	7	91

(Check to be sure you have one check under thinking stage and one under active stage for each item.)

14. What are your future plans for purchasing another motorcycle for yourself? (Check only one of the four below.)

				VAR.
At present, I have no thought of buying another motorcycle	32	Will consider switching brands	24	92
Will probably buy another of the same brand	38	Will definitely switch brands	5	

APPENDIX A (cont.)

15. Please check the box which applies to yourself or your family under each category below. The purpose of this kind of information is to allow comparisons of the results of the survey between different groups of people. . .those with large families versus those with small families; single versus married, etc.

Sex

Male	92	**VAR.**
Female	6	93

Approximate Yearly Family Income

Under $7,500	14	
$8,000 to $9,999	19	
$10,000 to $14,999	32	**VAR.**
$15,000 to $19,999	18	94
$20,000 to $24,999	9	
$25,000 and over	8	

Your Age

Under 15 years	3	
15 to 19 years	17	
20 to 29 years	49	**VAR.**
30 to 39 years	20	95
40 to 49 years	9	
50 to 59 years	2	
60 years or more	0	

Life Cycle

Which one of the following categories best describes you? (Check only *one*.)

Single, living with parents/relatives	30	
Single, not living with parents/relatives	10	
Young married—no children	16	**VAR.**
Young married—small children	23	96
Married—teenage children	13	
Married—Grown children	5	
Other	3	

Your Occupation (check only one.)

General office/clerical	3	
Labor	17	
Management	11	
Service worker	2	
Sales	4	**VAR.**
Professional	11	97
Technical/skilled/semi-skilled	23	
Junior high school student	1	
High school student	7	
Junior college student	2	
College/university student	3	
Other	16	
(please write in)		

Last School Attended (check only one.)

Grade school	5	
High school	46	**VAR.**
Trade school	10	98
College (1–3 years)	24	
College (4 years or more)	8	
Post graduate	5	

Name _____

Street address _____

City _____ State _____ Zip _____

PLEASE RETURN THIS QUESTIONNAIRE IN THE
ADDRESSED PRE-STAMPED ENVELOPE.

For reduced variables,
see NOTE.

THANK YOU FOR YOUR COOPERATION!

Motorcycle Owners Survey

	Engine Size	Q. 1, **VAR. 5**		Mo. Past Purchase	Q. 5, **VAR. 31**
0	no response		0		.38 did not previously own
1	0–200 cc	.32	1	Jan.	.03
2	201–325	.14	2	Feb.	.05
3	326–400	.22	3	March	.08
4	401–500	.07	4	April	.11
5	> 500	.25	5	May	.08
			6	June	.10
	Month Purchased	Q. 2, **VAR. 6**	7	July	.05
			8	Aug.	.03
1	Jan.	.05	9	Sept.	.03
2	Feb.	.16	10	Oct.	.02
3	March	.45	11	Nov.	.01
4	April	.20	12	Dec.	.03
5	May	.06			
6	June	.02		Yr. Past Purchase	Q. 5, **VAR. 32**
7	July	.01			
8	Aug.	.01	70	1970	.04
9	Sept.	.01	71	1971	.06
10	Oct.	.01	72	1972	.16
11	Nov.	.01	73	1973	.20
12	Dec.	.01	74	1974	.06
	Year Purchased	Q. 2, **VAR. 7**		Last CC's	Q. 5, **VAR. 35**
69	1969	.02	0	no response	
71	1971	.01	1	0–200 cc	.27
72	1972	.02	2	201–325	.09
73	1973	.05	3	326–400	.15
74	1974	.90	4	401–500	.02
			5	> 500	.09

YAMAHA VARIABLE LIST

Following is a copy of a computer print-out of the 123 variables which comprise the Yamaha Data Base. There are a series of numbers corresponding to levels, or values, for each variable. For example, there are 7 values for variable 2, "brand bought," corresponding to the 6 brand names, and "other" listed in that questionnaire item (Question 1). Similarly, there are 5 values for variable 3, "model type" (Question 1).

Variable 5 (engine size) is based on "cc" (Question 1). The values for this variable are on page 320 of the case (as are values from other variables too long to list out in the questionnaire itself). Variable 5 contains 5 values, from 0–200 cc's to over 500 cc's. A "0" response means the proportion of respondents who did not answer the question. Note that variable 5 is also "collapsed" into a reduced variable with fewer values (variable 100). See the Note on Reduced Variables in the Yamaha Data Base for further explanation.

Values for variables 6 and 7 are on page 320 of the case.

Values for variables 8–18 are either a "0" or a "1". A "0" indicates the proportion of respondents who did *not* check the primary usage category indicated by the variable number. A "1" indicates the proportion who *did* check the primary use category.

Variables 19–29 have 5 values, ranging from "almost all of the time" to "hardly ever/never" for each usage. A "0" indicates the proportion not responding.

Variable 30 had 3 levels, corresponding to a, b and c in Question 4. "O" indicates no response.

APPENDIX A (cont.)

Variables 31 and 32 are listed on page 321 of the case. A "0" in this case indicates the proportion of the sample who are NOT previous motorcycle owners. Note that variables in Question 5 all refer to those respondents who had previously owned a motorcycle.

Variables 33–41 (Question 5) are interpretable in terms of the instructions in paragraphs 1–6. Again, "0" indicates the proportion who had not previously owned a motorcycle, in this question only.

Data from Question 6 are reduced to a scale of number of weeks respondents spent in the thinking and active stages. See Note on Reduced Variables in the Yamaha Data Base for further explanation.

The variables pairs in Question 7 refer to the values for each item (engine features, etc.) for "how much you knew" (e.g., variable 42 for engine features/mechanical systems) and for "how much you wanted to know" (variable 43 for engine features (mechanical systems). There are no zeros in this question.

Variables 80–97 (Question 8) all have 4 values for each item, to correspond to the "very helpful"—"not at all helpful" scale. Again, no zeros for this question.

Variables 92–98 (Question 14 and 15) all have values corresponding to the particular question, and "0" indicates no response.

Variables 99–123 are reduced variables, and are explained in the Note on Reduced Variables in the Yamaha Data Base.

NOTE THAT QUESTIONS 9–13 ARE NOT INCLUDED IN THE DATA BASE, OR IN THE QUESTIONNAIRE. ALSO, PLEASE IGNORE VARIABLES 1, 120 AND 121; THERE IS NO VARIABLE 4 IN THE DATA BASE.

Yamaha Variable List

1 ID Number
2 Brand bought
3 Model type
4 Engine type
5 Engine size
6 Month purchased
7 Year purchased
8 Use: cruise hwy
9 Use: trails
10 Use: off-road
11 Use: exploring
12 Use: cruise arnd
13 Use: ride in opn
14 Use: performance
15 Use: school/work
16 Use: frml. race
17 Use: genl maint.
18 Use: other
19 Degree: crus hwy
20 Degree: trails
21 Degree: off-road
22 Degree: explore
23 Degree: crus arn
24 Degree: riding
25 Degree: perform
26 Degree: schl/wrk
27 Degree: racing
28 Degree: maint.

29 Degree: other
30 Prior purchase
31 Mo. past purch
32 Yr. past purch
33 Last brand
34 Last model typ
35 Last cc's
36 Satis: perform
37 Satis: handle
38 Satis: depend
39 Satis: service
40 Satis: upkeep
41 Satis: overall
42 Knew: engine
43 Wanted: engine
44 Knew: model
45 Wanted: model
46 Knew: perform
47 Wanted: perform
48 Knew: size
49 Wanted: size
50 Knew: dealer
51 Wanted: dealer
52 Knew: reputatn
53 Wanted: reputatn
54 Knew: price
55 Wanted: price
56 Knew: brand

57 Wanted: brand
58 Knew: uses
59 Wanted: uses
60 Knew: reliable
61 Wanted: reliable
62 Knew: features
63 Wanted: features
64 Knew: experience
65 Wanted: experience
66 Knew: maintain
67 Wanted: maintain
68 Knew: style
69 Wanted: style
70 Knew: cc's
71 Wanted: cc's
72 Knew: 2/4 stroke
73 Wanted: 2/4 strk
74 Th hlp: TV/rad
75 Th hlp: magazine
76 Th hlp: exprnc
77 Th hlp: brochure
78 Th hlp: riding
79 Th hlp: dealer
80 Th hlp: mchnic
81 Th hlp: family
82 Th hlp: owners
83 Act hlp: TV/rad
84 Act hlp: magzne

85 Act hlp: exprnc	98 Last school	111 Yr past pur R
86 Act hlp: brchre	99 Brand purchased	112 Use: explc
87 Act hlp: riding	100 Size of engine	113 Use: racec
88 Act hlp: dealer	101 Prior cycle	114 Use: transc
89 Act hlp: mchnic	102 Thinking: wks-tg	115 Brandsen2
90 Act hlp: family	103 Active: wks-tg	116 Infosen2
91 Act hlp: owners	104 Yearly income	117 Purpro2
92 Future plans	105 Age	118 Moneysen2
93 Sex	106 Life status	119 Yamaha owner
94 Income/year	107 Education	120 How much knewC
95 Your age	108 Mo purchased R	121 How much wantC
96 Life cycle	109 Yr purchased R	122 How much knew
97 Occupation	110 Mo past pur R	123 How much want

NOTE ON REDUCED VARIABLES IN THE YAMAHA DATA BASE

Some reduction of data was necessary to facilitate Mr. Wilkie's analysis of the data. This data reduction took two forms:

1. Reducing the number of categories within variables with very uneven distributions, in order to make the distributions more even.

2. Reducing the number of categories within variables which contain a great many categories, in order to make analysis more efficient and increase reliability.

3. Summing responses for each respondent across several variables, in order to create a summed scale.

It will be necessary for you to understand each of these data reductions so that you can use the "reduced variables" in the Yamaha data base. These are variables 99–123. Examples of each reduction procedure follows:

1. Reducing the number of categories within varriables with very uneven distributions.

An example of this application is seen in variable 2, "brand bought." The distribution for the total sample is as follows:

BMW	2%
Harley	1
Honda	41
Kawasaki	16
Suzuki	13
Yamaha	25
Other	1

In order to reduce the variable (and because of management's interest) the data was reduced to three instead of 7 categories: Honda, Yamaha, and all other brands. This new reduced variable is #99, "brand purchased," and its distribution is:

Honda	41%
Yamaha	25
Others	34

For cross-tabulations, you would probably use variable 99, unless you were particularly interested in looking at Kawasaki, BMW, etc., respondents. The variables reduced by this method are shown at the top of page 328.

2. Reducing the number of categories within variables which contain a great many categories.

The best example is the data gained from question 6 in the questionnaire, which asked respondents to estimate how long they spent in the "thinking" and "active" stages of the PDP. These data were converted to weeks, and, as you can imagine, the distribution ranged from a very few weeks at each stage, to over 100 weeks. Obviously, the reliability of such a range is suspect, and such a distribution is too cumbersome to analyze by cross-tabulation. Therefore, the distribution was

Reduced Variable Name and Variable Number	Based on Question(s)	New Values
Brand Purchased 99	1 (brand bought)	1 = Honda 2 = Yamaha 3 = Others (including, from Question 1, BMW, Harley-Davidson, Kawasaki, Suzuki, and others)
Size of Engine 100	1 ("CC")	0 = No response 1 = 0–200 cc 2 = 201–400 cc 3 = over 400 cc
Prior Cycle 101	4	1 = First motorcycle 2 = Had owned 1 or more cycles before
Yearly Income 104	15	1 = $9,999 or less 2 = $10,000–14,999 3 = $15,000 and over
Age 105	15	1 = 19 or under 2 = 20–29 3 = over 30
Life Status 106	15	1 = Single, living with parents/relatives 2 = Single, not living with parents/relatives, and young married, no children 3 = Young married, small children, married, grown children
Education 107	15	1 = Grade, high, or trade school 2 = College (1–3 years, and 4 years or more and post. grad.)
Yamaha Owner 119	1	1 = Yamaha owner 2 = Owns any brand other than Yamaha

reduced by collapsing it into a smaller distribution. Cutting points were made, from 1 to 4, to correspond to 0–4 weeks, 5–12 weeks, 13–52 weeks, and over 52 weeks, for Thinking stage. This kind of collapsing not only makes the variable manageable, but greatly increases the reliability of the data.

These reduced variables are #102 for Thinking stage weeks and #103 for Active stage weeks.

The variables reduced by this method are shown at the top of page 329.

3. Summing responses for each respondent across several variables, in order to create a summed scale.

In most market and consumer research involving surveys, the marketer will ask a series of individual questions, about the same topic (e.g., the similar questions asked children in the Parkland case). This is done in order to examine the convergent validity of responses. That is, to what extent do respondents give similar answers to questions tapping the same phenomena? In the Yamaha data base, respondents were asked a series of "attitude and activity" questions (sometimes called "psychographics"). In order to use these data, factor analysis or other multivariate data reduction techniques are employed to distill numerous items down to internally consistent and reliable scales. Because we do not expect familiarity with these advanced multivariate techniques, we have done this work for you on some of the attitude and activity items, and have not included the many items in the questionnaire included as the Appendix to the Yamaha case. (This is simply because we wanted x to reduce the total number of variables you had to work with.)

Reduced Variable Name and Variable Number	Based on Question(s)	New Values
Think: Wks—TG 102	6	1 = 0–4 weeks 2 = 5–12 weeks 3 = 13–52 weeks 4 = over 52 weeks
Active Weeks—TG 103	6	1 = 0–2 weeks 2 = 3–6 weeks 3 = over 6 weeks
How Much Knew 122	7	1–4, quantiles from very high felt knowledge level to very low felt knowledge level
How Much Want 123	7	1–4, quantiles from very high desire for more information to very low desire for information
Mo. Purchased R 108	2	1–12, Jan.–Dec. (0 = no response)
Yr. Purchased R 109	2	71–74, meaning 1971–1974 (0 = no response)
Mo. Past Pur. R 110	5	1–12, Jan.–Dec. (0 = no response)
Yr. Past Pur. R. 111	5	64–74, meaning 1964–1974, year of previous motorcycle purchase (response by previous owners only)

We created four scales from these attitude and activity items by summing across the various items which factor analysis indicated were related. For example, in the "Brand Sensitivity" scale, there were 11 items (individual questions) identified, and since each item required a checkmark or a six-point scale (from strongly agree to strongly disagree), each respondent would have a scale score of from 11 to 66. This extensive distribution was then reduced to quartiles, similar to the procedures reducing the "Thinking" and "Active" stage distribution. The four scales which we have reduced from the data, and created for your use, are as follows:

Scale and Definition	Total # of Items	Representative Items Comprising Scale
		(6-point agree-disagree scales)
Brand Sensitivity: degree of concern with brands of motorcycles over the PDP. Range, from 1 = low br. sen. to 4 = high br. sen.	11	"Most people I talked to about cycles stressed the differences between brands." "When I purchased my last motorcycle, I asked a lot of owners what they thought of their brand."
Information Sensitivity (defined as overall concern with, and potential responsiveness to, information during PDP). Range, from 1 = low info. sen. to 4 = high.	10	"TV advertising was helpful in helping me identify the strong points of the major brands." "I heard or read many different things which made me change my mind about which brand to buy."
Purchase Process (defined as degree of extensiveness of the PDP, or consumer's involvement in the process). Range from 1 = low involve-	8	"I spent a lot of time thinking about owning before I seriously began looking around." "Once I became serious about buying . . . I spent a lot of time collect-

Scale and Definition	Total # of Items	Representative Items Comprising Scale
ment to 4 = high involvement.		ing information and talking to people so as to make the right choice."
Money Sensitive (defined as overall concern with price during PDP). Range from 1 = low money sensitivity to 4 = high sensitivity.	6	"If I could have gotten a better deal on another brand, I would have taken it."

Reduced Variable Name and Variable Number	Based on Question(s)	New Values
Use: Explc 112	3	1 = combines "riding over rough trails" + "exploring places I can't go by foot or car" + "riding in open area or desert" 0 = did not check any of above
Use: Racec 113	3	1 = combines "informal off-road racing" + "formal racing" 0 = did not check any of above
Use: Transc 114	3	1 = combines "cruising around town" + "going to school or work" 0 = did not check any of above
Use: Cruise Hwy 8	3	1 = checked "crusing along highways and back roads" 0 = did not check primary usage "cruising along highways and back roads"
Brandsen 2 115	omitted	1–4, from very low to very high brand sensitivity
Infosen 2 116	omitted	1–4, from very low information sensitivity to very high info. sen.
Purpro 2 117	omitted	1–4, from very low involvement in purchase process to very high invol.
MoneySen 2 118	omitted	1–4, from very low sensitivity to price considerations to very high

13

Modern Volunteer Army

In the spring of 1972, the United States Army was studying how to achieve its goal of converting to an all-volunteer Army by July 1, 1973. Under consideration were various revisions in the compensation structure for enlisted personnel as well as a wide range of alternative recruiting strategies including the expanded use of paid media advertising. Army planners were also examining ways to make the Army's career training programs more attractive to potential recruits. In spite of the Army's attention to the implementation of the Modern

This case was prepared by Ralph G. M. Sultan, Chief Economist, Royal Bank of Canada, and revised by Assistant Professor F. Stewart DeBruicker, The Wharton School, as the basis for class discussion rather than to illustrate either effective or ineffective handling of an administrative situation.

Volunteer Army (MVA) concept, they realized that they would probably face an increasingly difficult problem in filling the combat arms (infantry, artillery and armor) ranks with volunteers.

It was clear that the MVA would require greater marketing effort than was required under the present draft laws, especially if a sufficient force of volunteers was to be obtained. While some planners felt that the recent advertising campaigns were adequate solutions to the problems posed by the MVA concept, others felt that there was still considerable confusion and misunderstanding regarding the definition of the Army's markets, the understanding of the motivations and beliefs of those consumers, and characterization of appropriate revisions in the Army's product policy and communications strategy. The objectives of the MVA recruiting effort were almost deceptively clear, yet concrete means to achieve those objectives had eluded the planners.

The planning staff was currently engaged

in an evaluation of the spring 1971 paid advertising campaign, where the Army had invested $10.6 million in an intensive 13-week broadcast media campaign.

THE PRESIDENT'S COMMISSION ON AN ALL-VOLUNTEER ARMED FORCE

In 1969, opposition to the Vietnam War and to the draft culminated in the appointment by President Nixon of a distinguished committee which took up the task of examining the armed forces manpower requirements, and the feasibility of an all-volunteer military. (See Appendix A for a history of the draft in America, and Appendix B for a review of contemporary foreign approaches to conscription.) The committee, which came to be known as the Gates Commission, included:

Thomas Gates—Chairman; Chairman of the Executive Committee, Morgan Guaranty Trust Company, and former Secretary of Defense.

Thomas Curtis—Vice President and General Counsel, Encyclopedia Britannica.

Frederick Dent—President, Mayfair Mills.

Milton Friedman—Professor, University of Chicago.

Crawford Greenewalt—Chairman, Finance Committee, E. I. du Pont de Nemours.

Alan Greenspan—Chairman of the Board, Townsend-Greenspan & Co.

Alfred Gruenther—Former Supreme Allied Commander, Europe.

Stephen Herbits—Student, Georgetown University Law Center.

Jerome Holland—President, Hampton Institute.

John Kemper—Headmaster, Phillips Academy.

Jean Noble—Professor, New York University.

Lauris Norstad—Chairman of the Board, Owens-Corning Fiberglas.

W. Allen Wallis—President, University of Rochester.

Roy Wilkins—Executive Director, NAACP.

The Commission did not attempt to judge the size of the armed forces the nation re-

quired. Instead, it accepted estimates which anticipated maintaining a total force (Army, Navy and Air Force) somewhere between 2,000,000 and 3,000,000 men. The Commission unanimously concluded that the nation's interests would be better served by an all-volunteer force, supported by an effective stand-by draft than by a mixed force of volunteers and conscripts and that steps should be taken promptly to move in this direction. The Commission defined the size of the recruiting task as follows:[1]

To judge the feasibility of an all-volunteer force, it is important to grasp the dimensions of the recruitment problem in the next decade. If *conscription* is continued, the Commission observed, a stable mid-range force of 2.5 million men (slightly smaller than pre-Vietnam) will require 440,000 new enlisted men per year. To maintain a fully voluntary stable force of the same effective strength, taking into account lower personnel turnover, the Commission estimated that not more than 325,000 men will have to be enlisted annually. In recent years about 500,000 men a year have volunteered for military service. Although some of these volunteered only because of the threat of the draft, the best estimates are that at least half—250,000 men—are "true volunteers." Such men would have volunteered even if there had been no draft, and they did volunteer in spite of an entry pay that is roughly 60 per cent of the amount that men of their age, education, and training could earn in civilian life.

The often ignored fact, therefore, is that the present armed forces are made up predominantly of volunteers. All those men who have more than four years of service—38 per cent of the total—are true volunteers; and so are at least a third of those with fewer than four years of service.

With true volunteers now providing some 250,000 enlisted men annually, a fully volunteer force of 2.5 million men could be achieved, the Commission concluded, by improving pay and conditions of service suffi-

---

[1] Excerpted, with editorial modification from Chapter 13, *President's Commission on an All-Volunteer Armed Force* (Washington, D.C.: Government Printing office, 1970). There is no attempt to summarize the entire mass of data or conclusions of the report; the report will hereafter be referred to as the *Gates Commission Report.*

ciently to induce approximately 75,000 additional young men to enlist each year from the 1.5 million men who would annually turn 19 and who would also meet the physical, moral and mental requirements.

In 1970, the Commission recommended these three steps to implement the concept of the all-volunteer army:

1. Raise the average level of basic pay for military personnel in the first two years of service from $180 a month to $315 a month, effective on July 1, 1970. This involves an increase in total compensation (including the value of food, lodging, clothing and fringe benefits) from $301 a month to $437 a month.

2. Make comprehensive improvements in conditions of military service and in recruiting.

3. Establish a *standby* draft system by June 30, 1971.

MILITARY PERSONNEL REQUIREMENTS

The combined armed services' demands for manpower are indicated by the size of the active duty forces as a percentage of the male population 18–45 years of age shown in the last column of Table 1. The comparatively small force of 2.5 million men in 1960 represented 7.9 per cent of this male population. In light of the projected growth of the male population, all four alternative force levels in 1975 constituted smaller percentages of the projected 18–45-year-old male population.

TABLE 1

Active Duty Force Strength
(Selected Fiscal Years 1950–69 and Projections)

Fiscal Year	Total DOD (millions)	Active Duty as Percent of 18–45 Male Population
1950	1.46	4.8
1953	3.56	11.6
1955	2.94	9.6
1960	2.48	7.9
1965	2.66	8.0
1969	3.49	9.8

TABLE 1 *(cont.)*

Fiscal Year	Total DOD (millions)	Active Duty as Percent of 18–45 Male Population
Alternate Projected Forces		
1975	3.00	7.4
	2.50	6.1
	2.25	5.5
	2.00	4.9

Source: Gates Commission Report.

The required annual inflows of personnel to sustain four assumed mixed force levels in 1975 using a lottery draft are presented in the first and third columns of Table 2. If the draft is abolished and all recruits are true volunteers, the same effective force strength can be maintained by the smaller annual flows of required accessions because true volunteers serve longer. For 1975, the Army is projected to represent 40 per cent of the 2.5 million-man force. The relative size of the Army is important because the projected shortfalls in recruitment are largest for the Army.

TABLE 2

Required Accessions to Enlisted Ranks
(Annual Averages FY 1979–81 in Thousands)

DOD Total Strength (in millions)	Continued Draft			All-Volunteer	
	DOD	Army Draft Calls	Army	DOD	Army
2.0	312	19	138	259	104
2.25	362	46	170	290	118
2.5	440	98	235	332	148
3.0	584	184	340	410	192

Source: Gates Commission Report.

QUALIFICATIONS STANDARDS FOR ENLISTED MEN

While physical and moral standards have remained stable over the past two decades, mental standards have generally risen over time. The mental ability of a recruit is measured by his score on the Armed Forces

Qualification Test (AFQT). Recruits are divided into five mental groups. Men in the lowest mental group, Group V, are exempt by law from military service. The mental group distribution of accessions in the two war years, 1953 and 1969, are shown in Table 3, along with a distribution for a recent peace-time year, 1965.

Another indication of the quality of enlisted personnel is the fraction of voluntary enlistees who are high school graduates. The proportions for 1959 and 1969 are given in Table 4.

because the services must have a large fraction of highly qualified recruits to provide raw material for the noncommissioned officer ranks.

Mental standards were raised significantly between 1957 and 1965. In late 1965, the Department of Defense directed the services to accept 100,000 mental group IV enlistments each year under the New Standards Program (Project 100,000). Experience gained from this program shows that men with lower AFQT scores and less schooling can achieve acceptable levels of performance. Moreover, the new-

TABLE 3

Mental Group Distribution of Enlistments and Inductions: DOD
(In Thousands)

Mental Group	FY 1953		FY 1965		FY 1969	
	Number	Percent	Number	Percent	Number	Percent
I	64	7	22	6	48	6
II	214	24	126	31	247	32
III	279	32	196	49	294	38
IV	283	32	56	14	185	23
Adm acceptee	46	5	2	—	5	1
Total	886	100	402	100	779	100

Source: Gates Commission Report.

TABLE 4

Percentage of Voluntary Enlistments with High School Diplomas

Service	FY 1959	FY 1969
Army	68	69
Navy	60	80
Marine Corps	54	57
Air Force	73	94
Total DOD	65	76

Source: Gates Commission Report.

The services argue that they must have high-quality recruits because of complex technical training, because training costs can be reduced by limiting enlistments to highly qualified individuals, because the disciplinary problems created by men in the lowest mental group detract from force effectiveness, and

standards men have not caused appreciably greater disciplinary problems.

In 1953, 18 per cent of all enlisted men were assigned to ground combat occupations that require comparatively little technical skill. Projections of the force structure in a post-Vietnam environment show that only 11 per cent will be in the ground combat forces. The services' demand for highly skilled men to staff electronics and other technical occupations has climbed over time. Nonetheless, 21 per cent of the distribution of occupations fell in the Ground Combat classification for the Army's 1974 projection (Table 5).

PAY

The history of discrimination in basic pay against first-term enlisted men is striking. During the 1948 to 1965 period the pay of enlisted

TABLE 5

Percentage Distribution of Enlisted Men by Major Occupation
(Selected Fiscal Years, 1945–74)

Occupation	1945	1953	1957	1963	1969*	1974*
Department of Defense:						
Ground combat	23	18	14	14	15	10
Electronics	6	10	13	15	10	11
Other technicians	7	7	8	8	14	17
Adm/clerical	15	20	18	19	18	18
Mechanics	22	23	26	25	24	24
Craftsmen	11	7	8	7	7	7
Services	16	15	13	12	12	13
Army:						
Ground combat	39	35	32	29	26	21
Electronics	4	5	9	9	7	7
Other technicians	7	7	8	9	15	16
Adm/clerical	15	19	16	19	19	22
Mechanics	9	12	14	16	16	17
Craftsmen	7	3	5	4	4	4
Services	19	19	16	14	13	13

* The "Other Technicians" include the three major DOD occupations for communications/intelligence, Medical Corps, and Other Technical. The DOD figures are weighted averages based on enlisted force strengths. The percentages of DOD that were in the Army were respectively 50.4, 43.7, 36.2, 36.7, 44.4, and 39.0 for the 6 years shown in this table.

Source: H. Wool, *The Military Specialist* p. 43 (copyrighted material) and special Service tabulations.

personnel with two or more years of service increased about 45 per cent compared to 4 per cent for those with less than two years of service. The 1970 comparisons with civilian pay in Table 6 also point to the relatively low levels of entry pay. Enlisted pay during the first two years of service is less than 60 per cent of comparable civilian pay. Table 7 shows the Gates Commission's recommended pay profile for enlisted personnel, which reduces the gap between civilian and first-term military enlisted personnel compensation rates.

RECRUITING

The Gates Commission suggested that the armed services devote an increased proportion of their resources to recruiting, especially Army recruiting. Since 1961, as shown in Table 8, the relative proportion of the military's man-

TABLE 6

Enlisted Men's and Comparable Civilian Compensation Profiles by Length of Service
(1970 Pay Rates)

Years of Service	Regular Military Compensation	Total Military Compensation	Total Civilian Compensation	Regular Military Compensation as a Percent of Total Civilian Compensation	Total Military Compensation as a Percent of Total Civilian Compensation
1	$ 2,776	$ 3,251	$ 5,202	53.4	62.5
2	3,357	3,935	5,803	57.8	67.8
3	4,496	5,275	6,370	70.6	82.8

TABLE 6 (cont.)

Years of Service	Regular Military Compensation	Total Military Compensation	Total Civilian Compensation	Regular Military Compensation as a Percent of Total Civilian Compensation	Total Military Compensation as a Percent of Total Civilian Compensation
4	4,909	6,249	6,908	72.2	90.5
5	5,783	8,516	7,409	78.1	114.9
6	6,172	8,151	7,876	78.4	103.5
7	6,636	8,741	8,306	79.9	105.2
8	6,845	9,125	8,691	78.8	105.0
9–10	7,242	9,505	9,065	79.9	104.9
11–12	7,715	9,825	9,327	82.7	105.3
13–16	8,290	10,643	9,956	83.3	106.9
17–20	8,964	11,611	10,298	87.0	112.8
21 +	10,483	14,047	10,723	97.8	131.0

Source: Gates Commission Report. ̄x-8375

TABLE 7

Recommended Pay Profiles for Enlisted Personnel for July 1, 1970

Years of Service	Regular Military Compensation	Total Military Compensation	Regular Military Compensation as a Percent of Total Civilian Compensation	Total Military Compensation as a Percent of Total Civilian Compensation
1	$ 4,498	$ 5,041	86.5	96.9
2	4,917	5,631	84.7	97.0
3	5,311	6,237	83.4	97.9
4	5,735	7,195	83.0	104.2
5	6,143	9,131	82.9	123.2
6	6,530	8,597	82.9	109.2
7	6,880	9,055	82.8	109.0
8	7,203	9,582	82.9	110.3
9–10	7,510	9,838	82.8	108.5
11–12	7,721	9,745	82.8	104.5
13–16	8,296	10,550	83.3	106.0
17–20	8,969	11,616	87.1	112.8
21 +	10,489	14,053	97.8	131.1

Source: Gates Commission Report. ̄x = 8943

TABLE 8

Recruiting Resources, 1961–69

Fiscal Year	Recruiting Expenditure as Percent of Active-Duty Manpower Budget	Total Recruiters All Services
1961	.0064	7,114
1962	.0056	7,219
1963	.0056	7,070

TABLE 8 (cont.)

Fiscal Year	Recruiting Expenditure as Percent of Active-Duty Manpower Budget	Total Recruiters All Services
1964	.0052	6,903
1965	.0057	7,056
1966	.0063	7,241
1967	.0057	7,371
1968	.0054	7,176
1969	.0062	6,987

Source: Gates Commission Report.

power budget devoted to recruiting had remained constant and the number of recruiters had also not increased. This reflects the low priority assigned to recruiting so long as the draft was available to ensure an adequate supply of manpower.

Army planners were not sure what was the relationship between recruiting expenditures and enlistment rates, although preliminary studies had indicated a 10 to 20 per cent rise in enlistment rates could be achieved via a small increase in recruiting expenditures. Whether that relationship would hold in the absence of the draft was the subject of much speculation, as was the entire role of personnel selling under the MVA concept.

Recruiters play an important role in influencing young men to enlist in the armed services. The Gates Commission observed that recruiters should be dedicated career men who are skilled in the art of salesmanship, with a positive attitude toward the military as a profession, some aptitude for public relations role and a genuine desire to undertake recruiting duty.

The Commission advocated elimination of the present system under which each district, city and individual recruiter received an enlistment quota. This eliminated any incentive to seek enlistees in excess of quota. Studies had shown that more recruiters at stations in large cities yielded greater returns than an equal increase in the number of recruiters in one-man offices in small towns.

If instead of drafting 33 men who will serve for a total of 66 years, the Army can recruit 22

men for a total of 66 years, it will need to train 11 less men over that three-year period. Since one trainer (or supporting person) is required for 11 recruits each year, enlisting rather than conscripting 22 men will save one trainer. In fiscal 1965, average enlistments per recruiter were roughly 55. A study conducted that year indicated that additional recruiters easily achieved an annual minimum of 22 enlistments and thus "saved" one trainer.

The Commission also concluded there was need for more indirect selling and advertising in these larger markets: "More advertising in mass media will be both required and rewarding once an all-volunteer force has been instituted, for the elimination of conscription will coincide with improved incentives in the military." The Commission was not specific with respect to the kinds of appeals or messages thought to be effective, nor did it indicate awareness of any fundamental consumer analysis that might guide the formulation of the MVA communications strategy.

ACTION ON THE GATES COMMISSION REPORT

Soon after the 1970 completion of the Gates Commission Report, President Nixon announced that the draft would be switched to a lottery system. Bills were submitted to raise Army first-term pay. Many officials in the Pentagon and in Congress, however, did not perceive that the transition to an all-volunteer Army could be accomplished as readily as the Gates Commission implied.

The Secretary of Defense established a target date of 1 July 1973. Plans for improvement and change in the Army received impetus. The "Modern Volunteer Army" (MVA) Program was initiated. The Program was directed toward "strengthening professionalism, enhancing army life, and developing modernized Accession System."

To support the Program, MVA "Add-on" funds were requested in the proposal presented by the Department of Defense to the Congress.

Within the MVA Program, a small-scale experiment dubbed Project VOLAR was initiated in January 1971 to develop data concerning the cost of a program which would increase the attractiveness of the Army for volunteers. One aspect of the experiment was a program at several Army bases aimed at reducing dissatisfaction with Army life through improvements in the conditions of barracks life, in family housing and in post services. Living conditions were to be improved. There would be reasonable privacy in barracks. Improvements in barracks furniture were envisioned.

Another aspect of the MVA Program was increased professionalism. To the extent feasible, soldiers would be freed from duties that were nonessential. Military skills were to be emphasized. Training measures were to be improved. "Lock step" training was to be eliminated. Unnecessary intrusions on off-duty time were to be avoided.

THE 1971 SPRING RECRUITING OFFENSIVE

Although the complete marketing strategy for the MVA was very much an open subject in the spring of 1971, the Army embarked on a vigorous campaign of paid broadcast advertising as described by the *Wall Street Journal:*

Army Steals a March on Sister Services by Buying TV Ads[2]

_____

[2] *Wall Street Journal,* March 16, 1971. Reproduced by permission.

Longish-Haired Kid is featured in $10.6 Million Campaign: Selling the Army with Soul. By John E. Cooney, Staff Reporter of the *Wall Street Journal.*

"This baby is powered by a 750 horsepower air-cooled, 12-cylinder engine," swears the dark-haired sharpy to a wide-eyed, apple-cheeked youth in a TV ad. As the kid drools, the slick talker purrs: "It can climb on a three-foot-high wall, span an eight-foot ditch and cross water up to four-feet deep."

Yes sir, it can in fact do all that, and the huckster may as well add it's built like a tank. Because that's what it is. What's more, the smoothy is a uniformed U.S. Army recruiter and the fuzzy-faced customer is a potential recruit. By the end of the 60-second spot, the lad has seen the light; he "buys" the Army and rumbles off into the sunset on wide-track treads. Chalk up a sale for Uncle Sam.

The ad is a sample of the Army's extraordinary $10.6 million blitz of television and radio that's making her sister services green (or olive drab) with envy; raising the hackles of Congressmen who disdain the expense as a waste, or worse, a threat to the independence of the airwaves; and giving advertising men Excedrin headache number 1-A. The ad and its problems also could be indications of things to come; the Defense Department may soon become one of the biggest prime-time advertisers on TV.

An Interservice War?

With prospects of an all-volunteer Army looming ever larger and the possibility that the draft won't be extended, the costly four-month recruiting drive was launched to beef up the Army's drawing power. Now the Army wants to spend about $25 million on a follow-up campaign in the fiscal year beginning July 1—about the same amount Ralston Purina spent to push its cereals and dog food last year.

Moreover, other branches of the service, fearful that the Army's campaign will hurt their enlistments, have petitioned Congress for hefty recruiting increases for what may well turn out to be an interservice advertising war. The Marine Corps wants to lift its recruiting budget eightfold, to $7.3 million, and the Air Force wants its current $2 million budget quadrupled. The Navy, however, seeks only an additional $200,000 next year.

Handling the blockbuster Army account is the big Philadelphia ad agency of N. W. Ayer & Son, which has been promoting Army recruiting since 1967. The agency quickly zeroed in on its mission, which it says is to significantly increase accessions (volunteers) for the U.S. Army. To let the staff know what kind of a product it is pushing, two senior vice presidents circulated a memo.

"We have been given an improved and improving product," it said. "A 'changing' United States Army . . . with a new concern for individual expression and preparedness. Specifically, the Army has a program under way to eliminate unnecessary irritants and unattractive features of Army life where they exist. This is not to be construed in any way as a drift toward 'permissiveness.' "

Dad Wouldn't Recognize It

To give the campaign a new look, Ayer replaced familiar recruiting posters with one of a longish-haired, slightly sloppy kid. There's also a new slogan: "Today's Army Wants to Join You." Horace D. Nalle, senior vice president in charge of the account, says enthusiastically, "The slogan says the Army is interested in today's generation. It's an Army the kids' fathers wouldn't recognize."

To meet the broadcasting demands, Ayer has budgeted a little more than $3 million for 30 new TV commercials to be shown on the three major networks; the remainder will go to 100 radio recruiting songs scheduled for some 1,200 stations.

Aside from the "tank sale," however, most of the handful of TV ads produced thus far are pretty routine plugs for the Army as a place where job skills can be learned. It's the radio spots that the ad men feel catch more of the spirit of the "new Army." The songs, which urge kids to "come on and dig" the Army, come in four varieties—rock, soul, country-and-western and a nondescript type Ayer calls "middle of the road."

"My 16-year-old son listened to the recruiting songs," says Ayer's Mr. Nalle, "He told me, 'Dad, you're finally with it.' " One radio spot his son was especially taken with:

". . . went to see the man in Army green. Told him where I'd been, told him bout my dream.
He said he once had the same dream too. So he gave me a pen, and told me what to do.
Good-bye Kentucky (or New York, or Indiana or . . .) Hello Fort Knox."

To get the message to the possible recruits, the Army broke with tradition and began paying for TV and radio commercials. Previously the Army, like the rest of the services, took advantage of public service spots that broadcasters give free to nonpartisan groups or causes, usually at times when few people are watching or listening.

REACTION TO
THE SPRING OFFENSIVE

Between March and June of 1971, the Army experimented with the use of paid broadcast time on radio and television to communicate the facts of the new Army to a national audience. *Advertising Age* reported on the first wave of advertising and a second wave of advertising comtemplated to begin in August 1971, as follows:[3]

The Army has permission to start a second wave of radio and tv ads for military procurement late this summer, but has been temporarily stymied by a dispute over a regional vs. a national approach.

Roughly two weeks ago the office of the Secretary of Defense gave the Army a green light for an interim drive to start about August 1, but specified that it should be confined to a regional effort until there had been a more detailed analysis of the results of this spring's national saturation push. Audits & Surveys' report on that campaign is due in late September.

Convinced that the $10,600,000 campaign just completed is paying off in terms of enlistments, the Army asked Secretary of Defense, Melvin Laird, to okay a second wave of advertising. According to Clay Gompf, an aide to Assistant Army Secretary Hadlai Hull, the Army recommended an interim six-week program to be budgeted at about $3,000,000. The money would go into network tv, spot tv and radio in much the same media pattern as the March-through-June schedule, except for a slight reduction in the frequency of announcements.

The Army's advertising people have been conferring with N. W. Ayer & Son to see if a regional drive seems worth while from the standpoint of cost and efficiency. Obviously the Army's communications experts would prefer another coast-to-coast splash of the kind already tested.

Preliminary results on the first use of paid broadcast time for a branch of the U.S. military are

---

[3] *Advertising Age,* July 15, 1971.

"extremely favorable," Mr. Gompf told *Advertising Age.* Some 47,000 men volunteered for Army services during the months of March through June 1971— 4,000 more than signed up during the same period last year, he pointed out. The Army was particularly encouraged that enlistments for the dangerous combat arms units rose 400 in June of this year for a total of 4,100. Meanwhile, Air Force enlistments have been declining, he said.

These Army gains, Mr. Gompf emphasized, came at a time of great "anti-military pressure."

However, an AP dispatch dated July 13, 1971, reported disagreement within the Pentagon concerning the effectiveness of the first wave of radio and television advertising:[4]

Pentagon Doubts Value of Army's Ad Campaign

Washington, July 13 (AP)—The Army and the Pentagon leadership are at odds over results of the Army's $10.6 million spring advertising drive, which so far has produced only 4,100 new recruits.

That is an average cost of $2,585 a man.

Although the Army calls the results encouraging, sources said today that the Pentagon was not satisfied and had rejected at least for the time being, the Army's proposal to spend an additional $3.1 million in radio and television ads next month.

The sources said Roger T. Kelley, Assistant Secretary of Defense for manpower and reserve affairs, felt that preliminary results of the 13-week ad campaign, which began March 1, did not justify spending more without further evaluation.

Coincidentally with the Army's evaluation of the first wave of advertising, the Pentagon and Columbia Broadcasting System were, in July of 1971, embroiled in a dispute over a CBS documentary television program titled "The Selling of the Pentagon." This documentary was sharply critical of Armed Forces promotional activities, both commercial and noncommercial in nature. Representative Harley O. Staggers even pressed for a contempt citation against CBS President Frank Stanton. One element of the documentary had been clips

from the recent media campaign to gain recruits for the Army.

FALL 1971 REACTION

During 1971, the rate of enlistment in "combat arms" (infantry, artillery, and armor) was still insufficient, according to *Army Times:*[5]

Combat Recruiting Up, but Wavering

Washington—For the fourth straight month, the Army Recruiting Command has enlisted more male civilians for the combat arms that it did for all of calendar year 1970. The 1970 combat arms enlistment total was 3,103.

Figures through August 27 showed 3,147 enlistments for the combat arms. And the expectation is that when final figures are in the total will exceed 3,500 for August.

Overall, recruiters enlisted 14,413 males in August, 913 more than their objective for the month . . .

While the 14,413 male enlistment total for August is impressive, it is well below numbers needed by the Army. The combat arms totals are also well below manpower needs, officials told *Army Times.*

The Army feels it has a "tough road to hoe" to be able to meet manpower needs entirely through volunteers.

Recruiting Command CG Maj. Gen. John Henlon says his organization "must meet the challenge of recruiting 193,000 men with force. The concept of total involvement by each and every member of the Command is the only way we shall achieve success in our mission," Henlon said.

Further analysis revealed the Army's stepped-up promotional campaign might be drawing too many "low quality" recruits, particularly for the combat arms. The *Army Times* reported:[6]

[4] *New York Times,* July 13, 1971.

[5] *Army Times,* September 22, 1971.

[6] *Army Times,* October 6, 1971.

Join Army Drive Hits Quality Hurdle

Washington—the Army's all-out recruiting campaign is drawing too many non-high school graduates and men with low mental aptitudes, particularly in the combat arms.

To improve the caliber of people entering the Army, the Pentagon has set a ceiling of 10 per cent on the number of Category IV people that can be enlisted in any one month under the CONUS unit-of-choice enlistment option. Category IVs are people who score between 10 and 30 on the Armed Forces Qualification Test (AFQT). In April, Stateside combat units recruited 132 people of which 32 per cent were Category IVs and 58 non-high school graduates. In May, 42 per cent of the 211 people joining combat arms units were Category IVs. Sixty-five hadn't finished high school.

In October 1971, Army Secretary Robert Froehlke wrote to the presidents of television networks ABC, NBC, and CBS, and several radio networks, asking them to "substantially increase" the amount of public service announcements they donated to support Army recruiting. He noted that as a result of the 13-week advertising test between March 1 and June 15, 1971, "the response from the target audience was remarkable. Enlistments in the combat arms—infantry, artillery, and armor—increased tenfold." He asserted that "approximately 8,000 enlistments can be attributed to the special advertising campaign."[7]

REVIEW OF THE 1971 PROGRAM

The results of the TV campaign seemed to require re-thinking. The 13-week, $10.6 million television advertising "experiment" by N. W. Ayer in 1971 had been characterized by apparent confusion as to the most desirable copy platform. Some 15 basically different messages could be discerned through viewing 15 different TV spot commercials at random. It furthermore did not seem that systematic measurement of advertising recall or effectiveness had been employed for the campaign.

Nor was there, it seems, any use of control markets in the experiment. Nor does it appear that any special recruiting information was systematically gathered prior to, during, or following the flight of TV advertising. Thus, at the end of the TV experiment, the Army was still not sure what messages had any impact upon the desired prospective recruits.

Given the attitude of the broadcast media, it seemed the Army in the future would have to purchase its advertising time at commercial rates. With budget pressures on the rise, any advertising would have to be efficiently designed for maximum impact on the target group.

A perusal of Army recruiting literature and advertising brochures over the 1965–1971 period revealed several different promotional themes (see Exhibits 1 through 7) had been employed in the past.

Advertising messages varied from the rugged "machismo" appeals favored in 1965, to the "learn a trade" messages increasingly favored in the early 1970s. Apparently the impact of these various types of messages had not been researched.

The Gates Commission had concluded that the major recruiting hurdle was financial: the need to spend more on Army Pay, and allocating more resources to promotion and recruiting. Others were not sure that the problem was so simple and felt that the task had been understated in magnitude.

The Modern Volunteer Army would require at least 200,000 enlistees per year. The estimated 1972 size of the available pool of males in the United States in the non-college, 17 to 21 age bracket inclusive, was approximately:[8]

Size of Pool, Age 17-21, Unmarried Males, in 1972

Enrolled in school below college level:	2.2 million
Not enrolled in school, high school graduate:	0.9 million
Not enrolled in school, not high school graduate:	1.7 million

---

[7] Ibid.

[8] Kim, Farrel and Clagne, *The All-Volunteer Army: An Analysis of Demand and Supply* (New York: Praeger, 1971).

Given the physical, moral, and mental standards of the Army, it appeared that as much as *one-quarter* of the total available unmarried pool would have to be induced to volunteer for the Army.

Alternatively, the Army could increase vastly the number of women in the armed forces (at 2% of the total for over twenty years), or hire more civilians, or lower recruiting standards.

EXHIBIT 1

1965 Print Advertising, "Action Guy" Theme

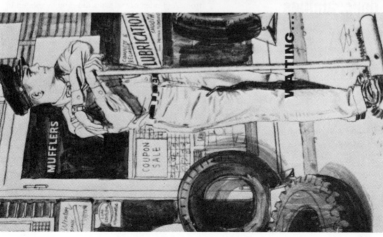

Some young men don't mind killing time. It's easy for them to let day after day roll by. The way they figure it, sooner or later, *something* is bound to happen. Meanwhile...well, they

plugging along just isn't for him. He's too much of a man for that. His mind and his muscles thrive on the challenge of action! To a man like this, living means grabbing adventure by the

can wait. If you're one of these, maybe you'd better stop reading right now!

An *"action guy"* can't just wait for things to happen...he *makes* them happen. Routine

sleeve...before it can pass him by. If you are this kind of man, you can prove it to the world in a way that really counts...as a modern combat soldier. The "action guys" of today's Army.

TAKE THE FIRST STEP NOW...

343

EXHIBIT 2

How do you stack up as an "ACTION GUY"?

Think about these questions. Answer them as fairly as you can:

- Am I man enough to take a new direction and give up the old routine?   YES ☐   NO ☐

- Will I really enjoy the chance of adventure in far-away places?   YES ☐   NO ☐

- Am I in tough physical condition — able to take a rugged, outdoor life?   YES ☐   NO ☐

- Am I able to think for myself in a tight spot?   YES ☐   NO ☐

- Am I a good team player, when teamwork counts most?   YES ☐   NO ☐

- Do I have mechanical aptitude?   YES ☐   NO ☐

- Am I better than average in character and responsibility?   YES ☐   NO ☐

If you can truly answer "yes" to these questions, chances are you can qualify as a combat soldier.

HERE'S WHAT'S WAITING FOR YOU . . .

EXHIBIT 3

today's Action Army offers your son a wide variety of educational and training opportunities

One of the surest roads to success is training and education. If your son faces a military obligation, as 9 out of 10 qualified young men do today, he can continue his education and training for the job he wants in the Army...top training to prepare him for both Army and civilian career fields. There are over 300 training, job, and travel opportunities awaiting him if he qualifies. And his choice is guaranteed to him, in writing, *before he enlists.* But only through enlistment in the *Regular Army* can he be assured of these valuable opportunities.

There are several training programs your son may apply for: — One program offers a choice of over 300 top courses in a wide variety of skills. The requirements are high...and so are the rewards. He must be a high school graduate and pass certain qualification exams in the specialty he chooses. Then, he'll attend the Service School which offers his chosen course or courses. (See the next page for a description of some of the interesting fields and specialties he may choose from.)

Another program offers a wide variety of practical on-the-job training in addition to classroom instruction. There are over 60 areas of technical training to choose from. And most of the skills are directly related to civilian occupations. Although a high school diploma is preferred, it is not an absolute requirement.

Your son may qualify by passing aptitude and physical exams carefully designed to show in what fields his greatest capabilities lie. He then may select from a group of courses falling within his aptitude area. (Page -9 lists some of the major Career Fields from which he may choose specialized training under this system.)

Still another Army training program is designed especially for the action-minded young man. Here, he can apply for training in the Combat Arms; Infantry-Armor, Artillery, Signal Corps, and Engineers, or in Special Forces. If he's the type who likes rugged training, outdoor activity, and an exciting, rewarding job specialty, Tactical Operations is the program for your son. For full details on all Army training programs talk to the local Army Recruiting Sergeant. He can give both you and your son all the information you need. As the Army's needs for various job specialties are continually changing, he can also keep you informed of these changes as they occur.

EXHIBIT 4

1965 Print Advertising, "Division Choice" Theme

JOIN THE "FOREVER FORWARD" BRIGADE.

JOIN "OLD IRONSIDES."

197th Infantry Brigade

1st Armored Division

"All American." The 82nd Airborne Division.

Activated in August 1917, the "All American" Division went to France in 1918, where it participated in three major offensives, claiming Medal of Honor winners Lieutenant Colonel Emory J. Pike and the renowned Sgt. Alvin C. York.

As America's first airborne division in World War II, the "All American" participated in the campaigns of Sicily, Naples-Foggia, Normandy, Ardennes-Alsace, Rhineland and Central Europe. Division members won three Medals of Honor,

79 Distinguished Service Crosses, 32 Legions of Merit, 894 Silver Stars, 2,478 Bronze Stars and numerous foreign decorations.

On February 13, 1968, the Division's 3rd Brigade with attachments deployed to Vietnam. In 1968, a 4th Brigade was activated, bringing the "All American" back to full strength.

Their home is Fort Bragg, North Carolina. And you can serve with the "All American" Division — and be guaranteed a share in its history — with the Army's unit-of-choice enlistment option.

See your Army Recruiter. Tell him you want to serve with the "All American."

EXHIBIT 5

1970–71 Print Advertising, "Career Training" Theme

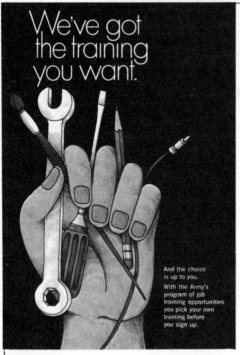

We've got the training you want.

And the choice is up to you.

With the Army's program of job training opportunities you pick your own training before you sign up.

Your Army training will always help you. Because the Army is training men *today* for the kind of jobs you'll find *tomorrow*. The kind of jobs you'll want. To make it on your own. In an Army career. After retirement. Or in civilian life.

On the next pages you'll see many job training opportunities. Look them over. You're bound to find the training you're looking for. The training you qualify for. Check off the ones that interest you. Then go back and mark them 1,2,3, for your first, second and third choice.

Choose the training you want.

First choice_____

Second choice_____

Third choice_____

And show your Army Recruiter. He'll tell you all the details on each kind of training. He'll let you know when your choice is available.

RPI 251. JANUARY 1970. ⋆ U.S. GOVERNMENT PRINTING OFFICE : 1970 O—349-717

- radio and carrier attendant
- drafting and cartography
- chemical
- printing
- missile fire control electronic maintenance
- air defense missiles
- supply
- aircraft components repair
- special intelligence
- prosthetic appliances
- armament maintenance
- fixed plant communications repair
- medical care and treatment
- surveying
- finance
- data processing
- radio code
- electrical and electronic devices maintenance
- laboratory procedures
- preventive medicine specialist
- ballistic missile repair apprentice
- field artillery missiles
- field artillery/missile operations and intelligence assistant
- law enforcement

If you think you'll miss the guys, bring them along.

We know how it is. The good times. The jokes. The horsing around. You'll miss them, right?

So, the Army doesn't want to break it up. In fact, the Army wants to accommodate you. And the guys.

If you and the guys enlist together, you can take basic training together. And we'll guarantee it. In writing.

Not only that, we'll guarantee that you and the guys get a choice of hundreds of job training courses.

Your pal Joey likes wheels? We have more wheels to choose from than GM.

Freddy's an electronic nut? We have circuits that do everything but dance.

Big Mike likes to make noise? We have noisemakers that can be heard ten miles away.

Talk it over with your local Army Representative. Ask about enlisting together, training together. Or send us the coupon.

Talk it over with the guys. Tell them that the gang that enlists together, stays together.

Today's Army wants to join you.

Army Opportunities,
Dept 200, Hampton, Va. 23369

Date _____

2TV 18-9-71

We're interested in enlisting together, training together
Please send us your free book

Name _____ Date of birth _____

Address _____

City _____ County _____

State _____ Zip _____ Phone _____

Education _____

EXHIBIT 7

1971 Print Advertising, "Today's Army Wants to Join You" Theme

Now you can be in Germany just four months after you finish high school. And stay there for at least 16 months. Guaranteed.

Guaranteed by the Army's new European Duty enlistment option.

Here's how it works. When you enlist for Armor, Artillery or Infantry, you can choose to take your first tour of duty in Europe. If you qualify, this is guaranteed in writing before you enlist.

You'll take Basic Training and Advanced Individual Training in the States. That takes four months. After successfully completing this training in the branch you enlisted for, you're off for a minimum of 16 months with the United States Army in Europe. With one of seven crack outfits stationed in Germany.

France, Denmark, Switzerland and Austria are just across the border. All within easy reach of any free weekend. And Italy and the Riviera are just a few hours away. Just waiting for you on some of that 30 days paid vacation you earn every year in the Army.

This is your chance of a lifetime. To get to know places like no tourist ever can. To really get to know the people. Pick up the language.

If you want to live and work where tourists only visit, talk to your Army representative.

Today's Army wants to join you.

Today's Army now offers 16 months in Europe. Guaranteed.

APPENDIX A

The History of Conscription in America[9]

Throughout history, state and federal governments have compelled military service to meet emergencies. Nevertheless, a permanent and comprehensive peacetime draft, such as the United States has known since 1948, is a recent departure in this country.

During the colonial period, hundreds of conscription laws were passed. A militiaman was required to attend drills and was available for call-up to repel Indian attacks or invaders. The maximum term of active service was usually three months. Despite the laws, the militia was primarily made up of volunteers.

The colonists' fear that a large standing army might result in loss of religious and political freedom denied General Washington access to a centralized and compulsory system of procuring men and supplies. The War of Independence was fought almost entirely by volunteers who were attracted by bounties.

The question of conscription next arose during the War of 1812. President Madison and Congress approved creation of a 166,000-man army composed primarily of militiamen. However, three New England states refused to conscript militia forces. In addition, the regular army had difficulty recruiting. The armed forces never reached the desired size and sustained an almost unbroken series of defeats, culminating in the burning of the nation's capital in 1814.

The Civil War was largely fought by volunteers on both sides. When war was declared, the Union Army had fewer than 16,000 officers and men. More than one million men answered the call to arms. Nevertheless, President Lincoln proposed a national draft in early 1863 to ensure that the necessary troops would be forthcoming. When it was enacted in March, the draft immediately aroused widespread resistance, which reached a bloody climax in the New York draft riots. The street fighting left more than 1,000 dead. The Civil War draft was not a "pure" system of conscription. A draftee could provide a substitute or initially purchase an exemption for $300. Only some 46,000 were actually drafted.

In 1917 a comprehensive draft law was passed immediately after the United States entered World War I. All enlistments were *forbidden* so as not to upset the "orderly process of selection" established by the Act, which evaluated the contribution of each registrant to the war effort and made the least "valuable" the most eligible.

During World War I the poor bore a disproportionate share of the burden of service. For example, black persons represented 13 per cent of those inducted, although they accounted for only 9.6 per cent of total registrants. Another unique aspect of the draft was its impact upon military pay. In the past, military pay had risen during a war and had always exceeded comparable manufacturing wages. In World War I, almost total reliance on the draft relieved the U.S. Congress of the necessity for providing pay increases. For the first time, a soldier's pay was less than that of his civilian counterpart. Evasion replaced open resistance. More than 250,000 draftees failed to appear for induction into the armed services.

Prior to the United States' entry into World War II, in September 1940, Congress again passed a draft law. Opposition to this draft virtually disappeared when Pearl Harbor plunged the United States into the war. During World War II the draft was the principal source of military manpower, causing many to enlist "voluntarily," and providing directly more than 10 million or 60 per cent of those who donned uniforms. The draft again enabled the Government to keep military pay low, relative to civilian wage levels.

The Korean War caused Congress to extend the 1948 draft law; and in 1951 it continued the

---

[9] Excerpted, with editorial modification, from Chapter 13,
President's Commission on all All-Volunteer Armed Force
(Washington, D.C.: Government Printing Office, 1970).

draft authority for a four-year period. This completed the evolution of the draft into a permanent part of the military manpower procurement structure, even though the nation was not fighting either a major or a declared war.

During the early 1960s the draft seemed to be generally accepted as a necessary means of military manpower procurement. This is not too surprising. Following the Korean War, the impact of the draft declined. For some years, 95 per cent of those between ages 18 and 35 were excluded from the most-eligible pool (1-A and 1-A-0). The Selective Service found itself faced with an excess of eligible youths. Its solution was to create new deferments. In addition, induction standards were raised and rejection rates increased.

The escalation of the Vietnam War in 1965 once again focused attention on the draft. Monthly calls rose sharply to 20,000–30,000. Deferment criteria were tightened, and the average age of inductees declined to 19. Of the 6 million men who have served in the Armed Forces during the Vietnam War, 25 per cent have been draftees.

APPENDIX B

Recent Foreign Experience[10]

Great Britain, Canada, and, until 1965, Australia have all manned their armed forces on a completely voluntary basis in the recent past.

Britain's decision in 1957 to end conscription coincided with a new defense policy emphasizing nuclear deterrence, withdrawal from positions east of Suez, and a cutback in force levels to 400,000 from 700,000. By 1960 the transition was virtually completed, and all inductions ceased.

The elimination of conscription increased the average length of service per man from less than three years under the draft to roughly eight. Because each man served longer, the percentage of the force which was in training declined from 21 to 14 per cent of the total.

During the past several years the British have experienced a decline in enlistments which is beginning to threaten the achievement of target force levels. There appear to be four reasons for this shortfall. First, more young men are staying in school. Second, new government policies expanding the availability of both apprentice and advanced training have made civilian employment relatively more attractive to youth. The latter factor is especially important in Britain because 15–17 year olds enlist primarily to get training. Third, British youths are less willing to undertake long initial minimum tours of duty ranging from five to twelve years. Fourth, there has been a decline in the number of youths aged 16 to 24 in the population.

Conscription in Australia ceased after World War II. During the Korean War a system of Universal Military Training was introduced requiring every qualified male to complete three months of training and then serve in the Australian reserves. The active duty forces never used these conscripts and only volunteers fought in Korea and Malaya. This system ceased in 1958 and the Australian forces were manned exclusively by volunteers. But, in October of 1964, the Australian government decided to raise force levels from 49,000 to 76,000 by instituting a draft by lottery.

Some have cited the Australian decision to return to a draft as evidence that an all-volunteer force is not feasible for the United States. There are several reasons why this argument by analogy is inappropriate. First, the Australians have not made a concerted effort to attract additional recruits on a voluntary basis. Second, the Australian economy is heavily unionized and apprenticeship programs requiring four or more years deplete the pool of men available for military ser-

---

[10] Gates Commission Report.

vice. Third, Australia has enjoyed a rapid growth in its economy (the unemployment rate is about 1 per cent) which makes civilian jobs relatively more attractive than military service. Finally, civilian earnings significantly exceed military pay rates.

The Canadian Armed Forces have always been entirely voluntary except for the period from 1940 to early 1945. The Canadian forces presently number slightly less than 100,000 men, supported by an annual inflow of about 12,000 men. The quality of the entrants is remarkably high; almost all fall in the upper half of the population as measured by mental aptitude. Military pay more nearly approximates civilian earnings—the monthly pay for privates is $225. Attracting recruits has posed no problem in Canada, and recruiting officers suggest that the number of enlistments could be doubled or tripled with no difficulty.

The recent experiences of the British, Australian, and Canadian Armed Forces suggest that competitive wages will attract an adequate quantity and quality of volunteers. There is no evidence in any of these countries that all-volunteer forces are alienated from the rest of society.

APPENDIX C

Racial Balance and the MVA

The Gates Commission addressed the view that, with an all-volunteer Army, a predominantly Black enlisted force might develop. This would result, according to some, in Blacks bearing a disproportionate share of the burden of defense.

The racial aspects of the relationship between the armed forces and society were given special consideration by the Commission:

We have concluded that the racial composition of the armed forces cannot be fundamentally changed by ending the draft. Even if higher pay appealed only to the "poor," twice as many Whites as Blacks would be attracted. The proportion of Blacks below the poverty line in 1967 was 38 per cent while only 11 per cent of Whites were in the same category. But, in absolute numbers more than twice as many Whites (17.6 million) as Blacks (8.3 million) were below the poverty line.

The relevant comparison is between the racial mix of the all-volunteer force and the racial mix of an alternative force of conscripts and volunteers. We conclude that the similar manpower policies of the two forces will result in similar racial composition in the two forces.

The proportion of Blacks in the armed forces has been slightly less than the proportion in the U.S. male population. In June 1969, two per cent of the officers were Negro as were 10.5 per cent of the total enlisted force as shown in Table 9.

TABLE 9

Negro Participation in the Armed Forces, June 30, 1969 (Percent)

	Officer	Enlisted	Total	In SE Asia
Army	3.2	12.8	11.7	11.4
Navy	0.4	5.3	4.8	4.5
Marine Corps	1.0	11.9	11.0	10.3
Air Force	1.8	10.6	9.2	10.5
DOD total	2.0	10.5	9.5	10.4

Source: Gates Commission Report.

APPENDIX C (cont.)

The racial mix among true volunteers in the first term of service and in the career force gives some insight into the racial composition of the all-volunteer force. Table 10 shows that Blacks constituted only 12.7 per cent of nearly 1.7 million enlisted men serving voluntarily in 1969. Among true volunteers, Blacks are now serving in the armed forces almost exactly in proportion to their numbers in the U.S. population. The same holds for women in the military who, of course, serve free of the compulsion of the draft.

TABLE 10

Blacks as a Percent of Enlisted True Volunteers in the 1969 Armed Forces

	Male			Female
	First Term	Career	Total	Total
Army	16.4	19.2	17.7	15.4
Navy	6.0	7.0	6.5	6.2
Marine Corps	11.8	11.9	11.8	15.1
Air Force	11.4	12.0	11.8	11.1
DOD total	11.6	13.1	12.7	11.0

Source: Gates Commission Report.

The proportion of Blacks in the career force depends on the proportion of re-enlistees who are Black. The data in Table 11 shows Blacks as a per cent of the men flowing into the career force. The percentage of Blacks among those re-enlisting at the end of their first term of service has fallen sharply in recent years. The decline in the percentage of Blacks re-enlisting will eventually lead to a decline in the per cent of Blacks in the Army career force.

TABLE 11

Blacks as a Percent of First-Term Re-enlistments*

	1965	1966	1967	1968	1969
Army	22.3	20.7	19.2	14.3	11.8
Navy	6.8	6.4	7.1	6.5	6.8
Marine Corps	12.5	11.8	13.4	12.0	12.8
Air Force	15.1	10.9	15.1	13.0	14.0
DOD total	16.3	14.7	14.6	11.9	11.4

* Data for 1965 to 1968 is calendar year. Data for 1969 is fiscal year.

Source: Gates Commission Report.

Young men in the 17 to 20 age group are the primary source of initial enlistments. During the 1970s this pool will grow by more than a million men. But, since the White pool will grow at a slower rate than the Black pool, the proportion of Blacks available for military service will increase, as shown in Table 12. This trend makes it likely that the proportion of Blacks in either the all-volunteer force or the mixed force will increase during the 1970s from today's 10.6 per cent.

Various assumptions and estimates yield a variety of estimates of the proportion of Blacks in the future voluntary force. These estimates range from 12.8 per cent to 16.0 per cent. Table 13 gives the best estimate of the proportion of Blacks in an all-volunteer force in 1980.

352

APPENDIX C *(cont.)*

TABLE 12

Trends in the 17–20 Male Population (in Thousands)

Year	Black	White	Total	Percent Nonwhite
1965	782	5,726	6,508	12.0
1970	998	6,456	7,454	13.4
1975	1,159	7,188	8,347	13.9
1980	1,297	7,358	8,655	15.0
1985	1,195	6,388	7,583	15.8

Source: Gates Commission Report.

TABLE 13

Estimated Racial Composition of the Enlisted Male All-Volunteer Force in 1980

	White	Black	Total	Percent Negro
Army	671,250	155,850	827,100	18.8
Navy	476,050	42,550	518,600	8.2
Marine Corps	155,150	29,650	184,800	16.0
Air Force	476,200	82,700	558,900	14.8
DOD total	1,778,650	310,750	2,089,400	14.9

Source: Gates Commission Report.

SPECIAL CONTEXTS
FOR
CONSUMER BEHAVIOR
ANALYSIS

PART  III

CHAPTER 14

Multiple Sclerosis Society: Fund Raising Strategy

"I still don't see that we have the package that's going to motivate people to sit down and write us a check for $3," explained Nick Arnao, Executive Director of the Washington, D.C., Chapter of the National Multiple Sclerosis Society in response to the new family membership concept.

As envisioned, this membership idea was intended to provide the unifying theme for all fund-raising efforts of the Washington Chapter. The family would provide the basic unit of solicitation. In return for each contribu-

This case was prepared by Steven L. Diamond, Management Analysis Center, Scott Ward, The Wharton School, and Thomas S. Robertson, The Wharton School, as a basis for class discussion rather than to illustrate either effective or ineffective handling of an administrative situation.

tion of $3 or more, the family would receive a one-year membership in the Multiple Sclerosis Society. The benefits of membership, in turn, would include a subscription to the Chapter's quarterly newsletter reviewing its activities and progress and an opportunity to vote for the Chapter's Board of Directors.

Nick, along with Tom Bendorf, Director of Commercial and International Programs for Lockheed Aircraft and a member of the Chapter's Board of Trustees, had been in search of a vehicle for increasing the M.S. Society's fund-raising effectiveness in the Washington, D.C., area. "Fund raising is like any other marketing-oriented business," Nick continued, "we have a product to sell—hope, I guess you'd call it—and we must convince our customer, the contributor, that his or her dollar is better spent here than on the Heart Fund, the Cancer Society, or some other product."

Fund raising is, in fact, a very big business. Religious, educational, health, human resource, civil, and cultural causes generated contributions totaling $17.6 billion in 1969. Of this total, $2.9 billion or 16.2 percent was shared by health and hospital agencies, according to the American Association of Fund Raising Council.

HEADQUARTERS OPERATIONS

The National Multiple Sclerosis Society, headquartered in New York, ranked eleventh among the national health agencies, having raised $7.4 million in fiscal 1969. According to the Society's Annual Report, about 9 percent of these funds came from legacies and bequests, while the remainder was generated from the contributing public. In turn, total contributions were divided according to a standard formula whereby approximately 60 percent were shared by the local chapters and the remaining 40 percent were used by the National Headquarters.

A large part of the Multiple Sclerosis Society's budget was committed to research due to the very limited body of medical knowledge about the disease. Neither the cause, prevention nor cure for M.S. had yet been identified. Educational and promotional literature regarding the disease, therefore, took on a symptomatic orientation explaining that "Multiple Sclerosis is a continuing disabling disease of the brain and spinal cord that causes paralysis and other disturbances of nerve impulses which control such bodily functions as walking, talking and seeing." One typical brochure, which was distributed by volunteers during house-to-house fund-raising drives, is illustrated in Exhibit 1.

THE WASHINGTON CHAPTER'S ACTIVITIES

While the headquarters' staff centered its concern on administrative and research-oriented activities, the focus of the local chapters was of a somewhat different nature. The Washington office, exempted from medical research activities by the Society's charter, was very much involved in public education efforts and service programs for M.S. patients.

Working with the support of national headquarters, the Washington staff issued various educationally oriented public relations and advertising materials which were carried by local mass media at no charge. Attention in the public education field was also directed at physicians to encourage early diagnosis of M.S.

Patient services, the other primary thrust of the Chapter's efforts, covered a wide spectrum of activities. Because M.S. is a crippling disease, medical equipment and care cover only part of the services required by the patient. In addition, various peripheral, supportive needs relating to transportation, house design, welfare, child care, social activities and psychiatric family problems were supported by the Washington Chapter.

In 1969 the Chapter allocated $292,000 in disbursements among the following activities.

Washington Chapter—Funds Usage

	Percent of Total Disbursements (1969)	
Program Services	27.8%	
Medical and related patient services		17.1%
Public and professional education and training programs		7.9
Community services		2.8
Supporting Services	72.2	
Headquarters allocation		40.0
Research and development campaign (to headquarters)		3.6
Fund-raising expenditure		17.2
Management and general overhead		11.4
Total	100%	100%

CHAPTER FUND-RAISING EFFORTS

In order to support this vast array of services, fund-raising efforts took on a paramount role in Chapter operations.[1] The Combined

---

[1] The attention of the Washington staff had traditionally been directed at individual givers because corporate con-

Federal Campaign, a coordinated solicitation of federal employees performed by the Washington M.S. office in partnership with other health and service agencies, provided one substantial source of funding, contributing 40 percent of the Chapter's income. Although this combined effort had been judged quite successful by M.S. management, it was determined some time ago that additional partnership arrangements were relatively ineffective. Accordingly, the idea of membership in the local United Fund Drive, for example, was rejected.

Instead, considerable emphasis had been placed on the annual residential house-to-house campaign. Because effective timing was thought to play such an essential role in the giving process, the 12 largest national health agencies had each designated a different month for their bell-ringing campaigns. The Multiple Sclerosis Society appropriately held its annual drive between Mother's Day and Father's Day with the rationale that M.S. attacks people between the ages of 20 and 40—young mothers and fathers. In the Washington metropolitan area, 10,000 volunteers were canvassed by professional telephone solicitors and each was assigned an area in which to solicit donations. This effort generated about 26 percent of the Chapter's total funding.

Special gift solicitation, referring to contributions of $25 or more, was also conducted on an annual basis concurrently with door-to-door efforts. This program was conducted primarily by mail, although Nick Arnao (Executive Director) believed that personal follow-up efforts could raise this source of income above the 4 percent of total contributions level being generated. Similar thinking also applied to legacies and bequests which contributed 6 percent of total income.

Additional funds came from a donor renewal campaign developed by the Washington Chapter. Under this system past contributors were reminded that they had not donated to the Society within the past year and were en-

couraged to write checks. About 2,000 solicitations were mailed monthly out of the Washington office and experience showed approximately a 20 percent return. Interestingly, however, renewal contributions normally double so that the $3 giver of last year becomes the $5 or $6 giver of this year. In this manner, the Chapter has succeeded in raising 14 percent of its total income projecting current figures at an annual rate.

Finally, the Chapter conducted a number of special events which provide 10 percent of its income. An annual fashion show luncheon and a children's Christmas banquet were the most successful and well known of these functions.

This combination of fund-raising efforts had proved reasonably effective in the Washington area. The National Multiple Sclerosis Society generates about three cents per capita on a nationwide basis, whereas the District of Columbia Chapter generates about ten cents per person in the Washington region. While per capita donations in Washington exceeded the national average, M.S. ranked third among health agencies in dollars raised in the Washington area compared with an eleventh ranking nationally. Tom Bendorf and Nick Arnao believed that the critical components in a fund-raising effort included: (1) the leadership, (2) the cause, (3) the volunteers, (4) the contributors, and (5) the dynamics of advertising, public relations and other promotions. "Actually, it's just like any other corporation," Nick explained. "We need leadership to function effectively; we need a good cause which is our product; we need an army of volunteers who are our salesmen; we need contributors, our customers; and we need the dynamics or the marketing package."

MOTIVATIONS FOR GIVING

In attempting to revamp their fund-raising package in search of additional contributions, the M.S. management team reflected on their experiences with people's motivations for giving. They identified four prime motivations which they believed segmented their market.

---

tributions—common in other large cities—were only moderate in the government-dominated Washington area.

The first and most common type of motivation was the *nuisance gift*. In this case, people were thought to donate solely because a volunteer was standing at the door with a canister. The cause really did not matter here for supposedly if contributors were asked what organization they gave money to just an hour after donating they would generally be unable to remember. Gifts in the nuisance category normally range from $1 to $5—a standard contribution which many families would hand over to any volunteer who rang the doorbell.

A second and closely related motivation for giving emanated from the fund-raising precept that people give to people, not to causes. Thus, the degree of need which a given charity could demonstrate really became irrelevant. Rather, the girl on the poster or the volunteer at the door was thought to hold the key to effective solicitation. In order to evoke people's emotions on a personal level, the M.S. Society used as its poster girl a 25-year-old former runner-up for the Miss Kansas title. Her picture, on the cover of its Annual Report (Exhibit 2), showed photographs before and after she was afflicted with M.S. This approach was thought to be effective because people could sympathize with this girl and in turn were led to contribute. Similarly, the giver's relationship to the solicitor was also of vital importance. "When you get a letter from a friend or a visit from a neighbor, it's much more difficult to say 'no' than it is if the letter is printed by a computer or a stranger knocks on your door," Nick Arnao explained.

Unlike the previous two motivations for giving, donors in the third motivational category were thought to be very responsive to the nature of the cause. In this case, the so-called *"captive givers"* contributed because members of the family or friends had been afflicted by a given disease, and they wished to aid in its prevention and cure. Neither Tom Bendorf nor Nick Arnao believed these donors to be especially receptive to particular types of appeals but rather felt that if given the opportunity via personal or mail solicitation, they

would contribute to the cause no matter what the format of the appeal.

The final motivational category according to Bendorf and Arnao was termed *self-interest* giving. In this case, usually found at higher income and higher giving levels, the donor offered his contribution in search of some direct benefit for himself. At the upper levels, the solicitor must usually make a clear demonstration of some return for the giver. The rationale in this case could take any number of forms: political or business benefits, the return of a favor, or the purchase of a ticket for a fashion show or a benefit.

OTHER OPINIONS ON MOTIVATIONS

While Nick Arnao and Tom Bendorf expressed their conception of giving motivations, others had additional ideas regarding the reasons people donated to charities. Dr. Sidney J. Levy of Social Research, Inc., based on research in this area, reached the following conclusions:[2]

When people are asked to donate money to a worthy cause, their reactions are not based solely on whether they understand the need. They are being asked to join in a collective action, to give a sign of recognizing a common bond. Their involvement will grow out of many possible motives. These can be phrased in innumerable ways and at various levels. Being part of the group supporting a particular cause may reflect wishes for:

The feeling of belonging and status

The protection from real or fantasied threat

The enhancement of self-esteem

Internalizing group standards in exchange for love and protection received

Diverting undue aggressiveness onto real evils

---

[2] From Sidney J. Levy, *The Myth of Communication*, talk presented at the National Convention of the United Cerebral Palsy Organizations, Chicago, November 15, 1960. A more complete summary of Dr. Levy's findings is reprinted in Appendix 2.

In more direct and personal terms, this means that people give because of a hierarchy of reasons and goals. The most intense participation and giving usually relate to an emotional awareness due to an afflicted loved one; a wish to be influential in the community; personal anxiety about being sick or deprived; wanting approval in face-to-face relations; and finding it a convenient avenue for demonstrating competence or power-seeking.

Dr. Ernest Dichter of the Institute for Motivational Research relates his interpretation of motivations for giving to action-oriented suggestions:

Practical Uses of Motivations for Giving[3]

NEEDED: TOUGHER THINKING ABOUT "SWEET CHARITY"

Most thinking about raising and dispensing money—be it charity organizations or social welfare operations—is unrealistic. Either too one-sided: "How do we get that guy to make a contribution?" Or too likely to preach conventional axioms about duty. We also assume that recipients of "charity" are sure to be made happy—while actually the unskillfully given contribution can easily backfire and have negative results. Whether the goal is feeding starving children overseas, conquering disease or improving the lot of the slum Negro, policy-makers should consider such human motivations in giving and receiving as these:

The "disease" of poverty. Many people subconsciously fear that poverty will contaminate them. The act of giving (making one's self a little bit poorer) reminds one that, with a little bad luck, one might be as badly off as those to whom the contribution is made. Fund-raising appeals should help to calm this secret fear of involvement—and, if possi-

ble, switch the emphasis from "charity" to "smart business."

Fear of embarrassment also inhibits giving. In everyday life, people are afraid of over- or undertipping. This same fear of not behaving properly also applies to fund-raising: is one acting like too hard or too easy a mark . . . how to decide how much to give and to whom, etc.

"Psychological income taxes." Fund-raisers should point out that giving helps relieve guilt feelings. Tell people they've done some good—and now deserve to go out and enjoy themselves. Or, if they've had some good luck that doesn't seem to have been earned, a contribution will allay that guilt feeling. If you've paid your "taxes."

Giving goes both ways. The donor is dissatisfied if he doesn't receive something too. What the donor really wants is approval—or self-approval, really. If he's not told he's a great guy or given some concrete symbol of his accomplishment in giving, he may not give again. For instance, we found that pictures of happy children ("Win the gift of these children's smiles") more effective in soliciting aid than pictures of starving, miserable ones.

Competitive giving. It's possible that giving could be promoted as a way of competing and earning prestige, just as much as through job titles, buying big houses and boats.

"From a friend." Although a gift is supposed to be a result of love, too often it appears to come from a large, impersonal, nonlove sort of organization. Needed are "personalities" or symbols to establish contact between giver and receiver.

THE IMPORTANCE OF IMAGE AS A MOTIVATOR

As the M.S. management team reflected further, it decided that while the cause may not be a primary determinant of giving behavior among some donors, it remained essential that the charitable organization maintain an attractive image in order to appeal to a broad spectrum of potential donors. In line with this reasoning it reviewed the components which they considered essential to a strong image. The first element mentioned was the product itself—The National Multiple Sclerosis Soci-

---

[3] Excerpted from *Findings,* 4, No. 2 (February 1968), 2 and 3. Dichter is a "founding father" of "motivation research," a term applied to a broad range of qualitative, clinically-oriented research approaches. Typically, a trained interviewer spends one hour or more in individual, "depth interviews," probing product and brand meanings, associations, etc. A review of Dichter's work is in E. Dichter, *Handbook of Consumer Motivation* (New York: McGraw-Hill, 1964).

ety. While they believed that smaller contributions could be generated no matter what the cause, substantial mass efforts and larger gifts programs were thought to require some evidence of the worthiness of the cause.

But merely having a worthwhile objective clearly is not adequate for the development of an effective image. Thus, credibility and a sound reputation constituted the second vital element in image building. Specifically, if people were to be made to feel that their contributions were meaningful, they must first have reason to believe that their donations—however small—would be used wisely and effectively. "Once you give someone reason to believe that his or her money isn't being used as you said it would be, that person will never give you another penny," Nick Arnao explained.

Accordingly, Nick operated his office with a moderate budget and low overhead and made every effort to convey a sense of administrative efficiency to the Washington community. A meal costing only $3 instead of $6 was often served as a $25-a-plate fund-raising dinner. The reasoning behind this "reverse psychology," as Nick called it, was that the appearance of efficiency was more important to many contributors than was the nature of the banquet. Thus, a $6-a-plate dinner might make people feel that their contributions were being squandered, while the lesser meal provided a sense of gratification to many givers.

Finally, Nick explained his belief that even the most selfless giver is in fact selfish:

Our job as fund raisers for Multiple Sclerosis is to sell hope. But we don't just sell hope for the patient; we also offer a motivation for the donor. Namely, we say—although not in so many words— that your contribution of $1, $10, $100 or whatever will indirectly buy you and your family a certain element of *safety*. That is, if you give to M.S., then we in turn will do everything we can through our medical research programs to prevent this disease from striking you. You can call it "hope" or "safety" or "preventability," but whatever you call it—it sells!

GAPS IN THE MARKETING PROGRAM

In reviewing the current status of the Washington Chapter's fund-raising efforts, Nick and Tom recognized that their marketing package suffered two weak links. First, their product, that is, hope for a better understanding of a cause, prevention and cure of Multiple Sclerosis, suffered by comparison with its competitors. Second, they noted that a decidedly imbalanced fund-raising record had developed, showing great strength in the predominantly white metropolitan Washington suburbs and a corresponding weakness in their penetration of the largely black core city.

COMPETITIVE DISADVANTAGES

In comparing the salability of the M.S. cause with that of other charitable organizations, the M.S. Society had these disadvantages:

1. While the M.S. Society was selling hope just as the other national health agencies, medical research efforts had been largely discouraging thus far. Therefore, although M.S. management believed that researchers might be nearing the frontiers of a major breakthrough, it was difficult to bring this message to the public year after year without producing any tangible signs of progress. On the one hand, the Society boasted of its efforts to date, while on the other it was forced to admit, "Many theories as to the cause of M.S. have been advanced over the years. Although some solid clues have been developed, no single fact yet explains why multiple sclerosis behaves as it does."

This lack of research progress had substantial repercussions on the Society's fund-raising efforts. The Heart Fund and the Cancer Society predicated their fund-raising programs on effective public education messages. The Cancer Society, for example, could offer a prospective contributor a printed card listing the Seven Danger Signals of Cancer. This information had meaning to the prospect, and was believed to increase both the number of donors and the size of contributions. The Multiple Sclerosis Society, for lack of definitive research findings, however, could not appeal along similar educational lines.

2. While heart disease affected about 21 million people and cancer strikes over one million each year in the United States, the incidence of multiple sclerosis was substantially lower—approximately 500,000 Americans had been diagnosed as having M.S. or related diseases. This incidence factor in and of itself meant that far fewer people know M.S. victims than cancer or heart victims. In turn, public education and the elicitation of emotional and financial support became relatively more difficult for the M.S. Society than for other agencies.

3. It was well known that children elicited more sympathy on posters and in advertisements than did adults. Multiple sclerosis, however, did not strike until people reached the 20 to 40 age bracket. Although M.S. had come to be known as "the crippler of young adults," this did not evoke as much sympathy as a child in a wheelchair.

4. The emotional appeal of a health-oriented cause was heightened if the disease was a killer. Although people respond to the idea of a young man or woman going through life as a cripple, the message was not as potent as are those which related to terminal afflictions.

For these reasons, Multiple Sclerosis lost some degree of appeal as a fund-raising cause relative to other charities.

WEAK RECORD IN BLACK AREAS

The M.S. Washington, D.C., Chapter faced a second problem—weak penetration among Washington's black population. Studies conducted comparing various segments of the metropolitan Washington population across such lines as contributions per capita, number of M.S. patients per thousand people, and dollars spent on patient services per thousand people indicated that the Washington Chapter had been decidedly less effective in the black communities of the core city than in predominantly white suburban areas.

The reasons for this differential, however, were unclear. "I really don't know what our image is in the black community," Nick Arnao explained. "Our recorded patient population in the central city is off in terms of total population and so is the giving record. Maybe there's a correlation there. We know that blacks do give to charities; just look at their record of giving to churches. But I frankly can't tell you why we've not reaching them."

It was agreed that increased effectiveness among Washington's blacks should be a high priority goal for the local Chapter. First, the low M.S. patient population count in these areas was thought to be the result of poor diagnosis and bad communications. If the organization was to serve as intended, then clearly it would be necessary to identify the multiple sclerosis victims in the area. Providing medical and supportive services would be a second objective—a badly needed though a costly one. Finally, in order to support these added efforts as well as their other functions within the metropolitan area, the Washington Chapter would need to improve substantially its fund-raising effectiveness within the black community.

Because the black population comprised about 70 percent of Washington's total population and approximately one-fourth of the Chapter's market the scope of this task would be a large one. Efforts were underway to determine the image of M.S. organization in the black community by talking to local black leaders. At the same time, a fund-raising strategy was being developed to generate additional funds from blacks, which could then be used in black communities for public education programs and patient services.

THE FAMILY MEMBERSHIP CONCEPT

In attempting to design a program which would overcome the Multiple Sclerosis Society's intrinsic competitive disadvantages as well as its poor fund-raising record in predominantly black areas, M.S. management began by reviewing its past fund-raising efforts.

It was noted that much the same appeal had been used by M.S. and many charitable organizations over the years. Specifically, fund-raising messages had shown M.S.victims in pathetic roles. Possibly a more hopeful message with a greater self-interest appeal would be a welcome relief from the concentration on human suffering.

Arnao and Bendorf also reviewed giving patterns in the Washington metropolitan area. Here they found that although their market consisted of a total population of about 2 million people, only 30 percent or 600,000 were actively contributing to health and welfare organizations. Moreover, while the total fund-raising receipts among these charities approached the $20 million-level annually, about 80 percent of these dollars were generated by a far smaller "givers community" of about 50,000 people or only 2.5 percent of the total metropolitan population. Figures for the Washington Chapter closely followed this pattern. Disposable income statistics, however, indicated a much broader but thus far untapped market for fund-raising efforts.

Based on these observations, Arnao and Bendorf conceived the idea of developing a marketing program geared around a family membership plan. Under this arrangement, all 500,000 families in the metropolitan area would be solicited for $3 contributions in return for which they would be given a one-year membership in the National Multiple Sclerosis Society. This membership concept was not a new one, but it had never before been actively sold to the giving public nor had the approach ever been used on a broad, mass-appeal basis.

A tentative enrollment goal was set for the new program to enlist 100,000 families, a 20 percent market share, over the next two years. Using this plan as the basis for all fund-raising efforts, M.S. management hoped to reach an admittedly high goal of $500,000 in annual contributions by 1973 and $1 million in yearly donations by the late 1970s. While still cautious about the concept, Nick Arnao felt that it held an attractive appeal:

We're no longer emphasizing the sickly and unpleasant aspects of the disease. Instead, we'll talk in terms of supporting research—a preventative approach. And in addition, we're giving something—a membership in our organization. It may not be much, but at least we're developing a two-way giving process where you give and you get at the same time.

Tom Bendorf elaborated further, talking in terms of finding a market niche:

We're offering a good bargain charity opportunity where people can do something for somebody else without pain to themselves. The number of people who will give until it hurts is minimal; there aren't very many really charitable people. At the $3 level you don't have to demonstrate that it's painless. They understand that. Here's where you're really appealing to people's sense of charity and selflessness.

THE MECHANICS OF THE PLAN

Under the new program, members would receive a quarterly publication of the Washington M.S. Society geared specifically to the membership population. In addition, they would be invited to attend the Chapter's annual meeting and would have voting privileges for the Board of Trustees. While Nick did not feel that these benefits in and of themselves would attract givers at the $3 level, he did believe that an appeal to people's sense of belonging could be effective.

The basic fund-raising vehicles—door-to-door solicitation, the Combined Federal Campaign, the annual Fashion Show Luncheon and children's Christmas Festival, the special gifts campaigns—would all be employed as before. In all these cases, however, a theme would be added. That is, all fund-raising efforts emanating from the Washington office would be geared to the membership concept.

In order to reach effectively a greater number of potential contributors, Tom Bendorf envisioned the utilization of one new fund-raising tool for the family membership plan. The chain letter concept, as he referred to it, would be used to compound solicitation results through a process by which givers would also act as solicitors. Under this plan, each member of the Washington Society would send out requests for $3 membership contributions to approximately 100 friends, neighbors, relatives, and business acquaintances. Included in this mailing would be additional materials which recipients would be asked to send to five more families.

The philosophy behind this process would not be one of asking people to give because the M.S. Society needed the money, but because someone they knew had asked them to give. Attractive envelopes, handwritten addresses, postage stamps rather than metered envelopes, and perhaps a card on which the solicitor could write a short note would be used to make the appeal more personal.

To supplement this initial chain letter mailing, additional solicitation letters would also be sent out. Neither Tom nor Nick saw any need to segment their market for these purposes. They felt that, given their objective of a mass appeal, their resources would be better spent in search of quantity than in attempts to appeal to various market segments. "We have all kinds of lists—past givers, social registers, contributions to other charities—but for our purposes here I think the telephone book will probably be our best bet," Nick explained. "On a broad appeal such as this, we don't need to get a contribution from everyone. If we use the phone book it will be much easier to reach a greater number of families."

While door-to-door solicitations would remain an integral part of fund-raising tactics, mail efforts would play an increasingly larger role under the new program. The rationale behind this shift reflected M.S. management's concern that too much of the contributed dollar was being eaten up by fund-raising expenses. Specifically, the Chapter's experience had shown that volunteer campaigns cost 25 cents per dollar raised while the corresponding cost of mail solicitations was only about 20 cents. Thus, from a cost-benefit standpoint, mail solicitations appeared more attractive.

Ultimately, Nick hoped to build a substan-

tial listing of one-time gives and to follow up on each of these families with appeals for repeat gifts. He believed that people could be conditioned to respond to charitable solicitations and, if approached in the proper manner, could be called on annually (or perhaps even more frequently). If in fact such was the case, and if his prior experience with repeat donors who sometimes doubled the size of their original contributions held true, then increasing memberships today could certainly be expected to have attractive repercussions for years to come.

THE DILEMMA

There was some management dissension regarding the proposed membership plan. Tom Bendorf believed that they had developed the essentials of a package which would substantially increase fund-raising results, but Nick Arnao viewed the new plan with some hesitancy. "It's a new idea, something which has never been tried by any M.S. chapter, or any charitable organization at all for that matter. I don't think it's a high risk strategy because we'll still be pursuing the same types of campaigns, they'll just be oriented to a larger market and they'll carry a theme.

"I'm not sure," he continued, "that this mass-market approach is the answer. It looks awfully attractive when you talk in terms of 500,000 families, but when you get down to the costs you run into another problem. It costs us as much to process a $3 contribution as it does to process a $3,000 donation. If we spend an average of $1 on processing, solicitation efforts, pamphlets and on our magazine for members, we come up with only a $2 margin. While this margin should be increased over time, it will take an awful lot of $3 contributions for that to add up to anything significant."

Finally, Nick was concerned with the membership concept as a motivator. He concluded on a note of skepticism: "When we talk about membership, the one part that's missing in the puzzle is the 'grabber.' That is, what's going to motivate the average guy, John Jones, who doesn't know what M.S. is and never knew anyone who had the disease, to sit down and write out a check for three bucks? Tom thinks we have that motivation already, but I don't see it.''

EXHIBIT 1

Multiple Sclerosis Society

"Neurological ailments add up to the leading cause of permanent disability and the third cause of death in the United States."

U.S. Public Health Service

WHAT IS MS?

Multiple sclerosis is a neurological disease—a disease of the central nervous system—the brain and spinal cord. It is not a mental disease, nor is it contagious.

The brain and spinal cord control such important body functions as walking, talking, seeing, hearing, eating, tying a shoe lace, opening a door. These functions are controlled by impulses from the brain and spinal cord. The impulses travel along nerves in the brain and spinal cord, then to other parts of the body. The nerves are coated by a material called myelin. When the disease hits, patches of myelin disintegrate, being replaced by scar tissue. Why this happens, or how, is a medical mystery. But when it does happen, impulses have trouble getting by the scarred spots; there is inteference. And with interference come malfunctions—the danger signals of MS.

WHAT TO WATCH FOR

MS danger signals are many and unpredictable. They are often mistaken for signs of other disorders. Each symptom—by itself—could be a sign of other ailments.

But, warns the Society's Medical Advisory Board, a combination of three or more symptoms such as those listed below, appearing at once, or in succession, *could be* MS danger signals. Never ignore such signals—see your doctor at once. It may very well *not be* MS. But let your doctor tell you—don't guess.

Here are danger signals that could mean MS:

Partial or complete paralysis of parts of the body

Numbness in parts of the body

Double or otherwise defective vision such as involuntary movements of eyeballs

Noticeable dragging of one or both feet

Severe bladder or bowel trouble (loss of control)

Speech difficulties such as slurring

Staggering or loss of balance (MS patients erroneously are thought to be intoxicated)

Extreme weakness or fatigue

Pricking sensation in parts of the body, like pins and needles

Loss of coordination

Tremors of hands

Source: Multiple Sclerosis Facts, March 1969, pp. 1-4.

EXHIBIT 1 *(cont.)*

Of special significance is the unexplained disappearance of one or more of these symptoms either permanently or temporarily. At times symptoms may disappear for periods of several years and occasionally may never return.

WHAT CAN BE DONE?

While no specific treatment exists, the patient can and should be treated. Good general medical care devoted to prevention of upper respiratory and other infections is recommended. Braces may be prescribed at times for stabilizing useable limbs and the physician may consider massage, passive or active exercise, and other physical measures suitable for assuring the greatest effort on the part of the patient to continue active. Nursing needs of wide variation and long duration must be expected. The early establishment of good patterns of care, fullest use of the physical and other resources available and avoidance of fatigue and emotional or physical stress is important.

WHAT HELP IS AVAILABLE?

When MS strikes, families can turn to their local chapter of the National Multiple Sclerosis Society for information, sympathetic help and guidance. Chapters can make available many specific services including aids to daily living, social, recreational and friendly visiting opportunities, professional counseling to alleviate social and psychological pressures and medical guidance through the chapter's medical advisory committee.

The progress made in the Society's programs of basic and clinical research and professional education brings hope and help through the dissemination of accurate, valid, authentic information.

EXHIBIT 2

Multiple Sclerosis Society

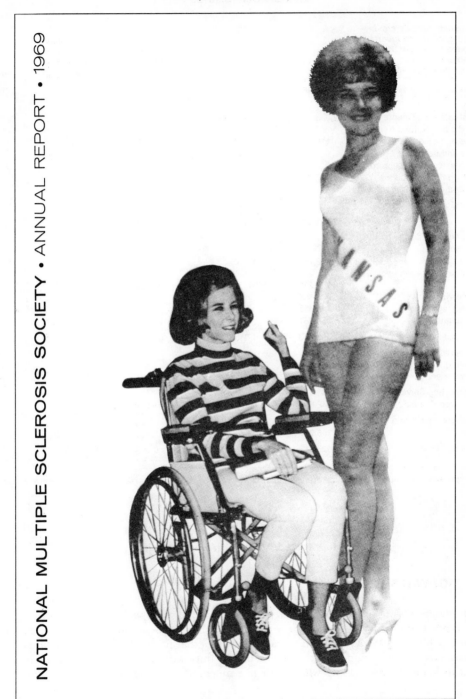

NATIONAL MULTIPLE SCLEROSIS SOCIETY • ANNUAL REPORT • 1969

Multiple Sclerosis Society

National Multiple Sclerosis Society (National Headquarters) Year ended December 31, 1969 Statements of Changes in Fund Balances—Note	General Fund	Research Fund	Fellowship and Scholarship Fund	International Federation of Multiple Sclerosis Societies Fund	Total
Balances at January 1, 1969	$1,020,960	$ 12,574	$ 13,701	$ 37,478	$1,084,713
Receipts:					
Contributions from Chapters	2,083,623	442,368	6,013		2,532,004
Dues and contributions from members and others	119,262	188,405	100	1,415	309,182
Legacies and bequests		208,004			208,004
Federal Services campaign for National Health Agencies	17,979				17,979
Interest and other	39,746				39,746
Total Receipts	2,260,610	838,777	6,113	1,415	3,106,915
	3,281,570	851,351	19,814	38,893	4,191,628
Disbursements and transfers:					
Program services:					
Research	182,760	1,046,653			1,229,413
Professional education and training	180,235		87,625	10,000	277,860
Patient services	288,004			10,000	298,004
Community services	115,437				115,437
Public education	354,367			10,000	364,367
Total Program Services	$1,120,803	1,046,653	$ 87,625	$ 30,000	$2,285,081
Supporting services:					
Fund raising	310,723				310,723
Management and general	275,847				275,847
Total Supporting Services	586,570				586,570
Transfers from (to) fund	548,884	(472,884)	(76,000)		—
Total Disbursements and Transfers	2,256,257	573,769	11,625	30,000	2,871,651
Balances at December 31, 1969	$1,025,313	$ 277,582	$ 8,189	$ 8,893	$1,319,977

Note—Expenses have been allocated to various classifications on the basis of time records and/or estimates made by the Society.

APPENDIX 2

Humanized Appeals in Fund Raising

WHAT MOTIVATES PEOPLE?

An understanding of what motivates people to respond to appeals for money has application to any type of fund drive, whether for a church, a school, a health organization, a community fund or a political party. Motivation research indicates that people—either as individuals or corporations—usually are guided both by a sense of duty and by their own self-interest—often without realizing it—in deciding whether to give much, little, or not at all. And self-interest may

Source: Dr. Sidney J. Levy in Public Relations Journal, July 1965, pp. 17–18.

range from an individual's unconscious (and certainly unexpressed) wish to impress the neighbors all the way to the corporation's conscious wish to affect an entire community favorably.

Other motives for giving: buying a place in heaven; repentance and forgiveness for sins; insurance for good luck; a personal sense of well-being and generosity; to do one's duty; to be kind to the underdog; to achieve membership in desired groups.

All of these motives apply to willingness to participate actively in fund-raising work and should be taken into account when volunteer committees are being organized.

TWO FACTORS TO WATCH

Two corollary factors, in addition to basic motives, are bound up in the entire giving process.

1. People have been taught to give but not *how* to give. They consider charity to be a moral obligation, but find it difficult to decide how much to give and how to allocate their donations among the various causes soliciting their support. The necessity to make these decisions reduces the gratification that otherwise goes with giving. Payroll deduction plans often are welcomed because they relieve the donor of the necessity of deciding how much to give to whom.

   Corporations and upper middle class people are exceptions to the uncertainty factor. They often give consideration to income tax deductions in determining the amount they will give.

2. Patterns of giving are seldom formed on a basis of logical planning but, once established, they are likely to be continued. The majority of people (those in the middle and lower income groups) continue to give to the same five or six charities year after year, usually giving similar amounts each year.

   In an economic recession period, they will be ashamed to reduce their donations and therefore may drop the charity entirely. At such times, public relations men must take care that their appeals do not arouse anxieties that would trigger this reaction. The tendency to give the same amount each year also must be taken into account when attempts must be made to increase donations to meet rising costs of charity operations.

People give most readily to causes that have a personal or emotional meaning to them. They feel obliged to give to other causes, much as they are obliged to pay taxes. These obligatory commitments are made because the project is considered worthy and necessary, not because the donor expects to receive any direct value or even great personal satisfaction.

The hierarchy of loyalties goes like this:

1. The church.
2. Fraternal organizations and other socially purposeful groups, such as schools, with which the donor or his family is associated.
3. Emotionally related organizations such as health groups, orphanages and old people's homes with which the donor can identify present or prospective interests.
4. Obligatory commitments, such as the Red Cross or Community Chest, which the donor feels he has to support regardless of personal considerations.

In each of the first three groups the personal motivation is extremely strong. People recognize the church emotionally. Rationally, they say that individuals are its only means of support and that its existence is essential to the family, the individual and the moral welfare of the community and the world. Socially, the church offers an important in-group, a support that is especially important for minority group members.

Fraternal organizations, schools, colleges, and, to some extent, political parties, provide a "this is mine" incentive. People support groups to which they belong as a matter of prestige, as well as for the opportunity to associate with like-minded people. A college graduate wants his alma mater to be recognized as a leader, whether academically or on the football field. He also wants his children's school to provide the best possible educational facilities.

"PREVENTIVE" GIVING

Health groups receive strong support because a relative or friend has died of heart disease or cancer or polio—or because these are real threats to the individual and the public. Orphanages have a strong emotional appeal to people with many young children. Old people's homes and welfare groups are important to those nearing old age themselves. Supporting such organizations constitutes a kind of "preventive" giving, with anticipation of concrete results that may, conceivably, save one's own life or that of others in the future.

Our studies indicate that the communications should emphasize feelings of individuals, rather than formal needs. The unhappiness of deprived children, their joy in freedom from sordid pressures, the sympathy of helpful adults, the happiness of a reconciled family—all are far more persuasive than a "big picture" approach based on dollar quotes and how money will be divided among agencies.

In money raising, as in vote getting, the doorbell approach is unsurpassed. People find it extremely difficult to say no to a personal request. The same person-to-person effect can be achieved by direct mail, if a solicitation letter is signed by someone known to the recipient. Even when signed by a stranger, a letter forces the recipient to make a conscious decision whether to write a check or throw the letter away. This is a situation he does not face when merely reading about a fund drive in a newspaper, although the right kind of publicity will have aroused his sympathy for the object of the drive.

Whether people are asked to give money or time or both to fund-raising drives, their response is conditioned by their attitudes toward the particular fund-raising group. Attitudes toward charities can be changed or strengthened, just as attitudes toward products can be changed or strengthened by applying the various techniques of public relations.

CHAPTER 15

Campaign Strategies for the Stokes vs. Perk Election

In mid-August, 1969, Dr. Robert C. Sorensen, President of the Sorensen Group, met with Cleveland's Mayor Carl Stokes and a few key members of Stokes' staff to discuss campaign strategies for the upcoming mayoral elections. The Sorensen Group, a relatively young research and consulting organization, had just completed an extensive political public opinion study of the Cleveland electorate which was designed to assist the Mayor in planning for the final months of his campaign. The Sorensen report was generally optimistic, find-

ing that 61.3 percent of Cleveland's 321,000 registered voters were committed or leaning to Stokes while only 35.7 percent favored his Republican opponent, Ralph Perk. Nonetheless, doubt about Stokes' ability to bring Cleveland's black vote to the polls and the memories of some unfortunate racial incidents during Stokes' term in office combined with Perk's proven vote-getting ability to make a Stokes victory far from certain.

STOKES' POLITICAL BACKGROUND

A native of Cleveland, Stokes completed law school in 1957 and was appointed Assistant Prosecutor under City Law Director Ralph Locher a year later. By 1962 he had been elected to the state legislature where he quickly developed a reputation as a hard-working, hard-hitting lawmaker. Running as an in-

This case was prepared by Steven L. Diamond, Management Analysis Center, Scott Ward, The Wharton School, and Thomas S. Robertson, The Wharton School, as a basis for class discussion rather than to illustrate either effective or ineffective handling of an administrative situation.

dependent, Stokes challenged his former boss Locher in the 1965 Cleveland mayoralty election. In a low-key campaign, Stokes stressed a lack of progress in Cleveland and an apathy toward local ghetto problems under Locher's administration. He came within 2,143 votes of election out of the 239,462 cast.

Having come so close to success in 1965, Stokes returned to face Locher again in 1967—this time in the Democratic mayoral primary. Again he played upon ghetto problems, this time armed with the charge that four days of rioting in Hough, a low-income district, were directly attributable to indifference at City Hall. While Locher enjoyed the support of the Democratic Party, Stokes had considerable grassroots support. Gathering 96% of the black and 24% of the white vote, he won the nomination with 110,552 to Locher's 92,321 votes.

Stokes remained unable to gather support from a weak local Democratic Party organization as he faced Republican candidate Seth Taft. He did, however, get the endorsement of Vice President Hubert Humphrey, Democratic National Committee Chairman John M. Bailey, and even Locher himself. The *Cleveland Plain Dealer* came out in favor of Stokes, and most importantly the black population of Cleveland offered its support. There was no violence throughout the Summer and into the Fall, and the slogan "Cool It for Carl" was heard in inner-city areas. And the bulk of the black populace, previously apathetic toward Cleveland politics, began to show a remarkable degree of enthusiasm and cohesion. Ironically, it was Stokes rather than Taft who squarely addressed the racial issue. His campaign theme was embodied in two slogans—"Elect Me as the Best Man for Mayor—Who Just Happens to Be Negro" and "Don't Vote for a Negro for Mayor, Vote for a Man Who Believes in Cleveland, Carl B. Stokes."

Taft, suffering a rather stiff presence and a six-to-one Democratic registration majority, showed himself to be a competent and game campaigner. He stressed the theme that

Cleveland's primary problem was a human relations one resulting from the previous lackluster and unresponsive Democratic Administration. In turn, Taft proposed a number of specific, detailed programs—the establishment of 15 local "city halls" to bring government closer to the people and the revitalization of Cleveland's sluggish urban renewal program—and attacked Stokes' record as a lawmaker. Fundamentally, the Taft strategy was to hold Republican votes while making substantial inroads among Democrats who were discontent with the previous Democratic mayor or who were not yet ready to vote in a black as their next mayor.

Stokes concentrated on this same Democratic bloc, reasoning that his previously strong showings in the predominantly black East Side of Cleveland indicated that he could depend on the vast majority of Cleveland's 120,000 registered nonwhites on Election Day (Exhibits 1 and 2). Because the City population was only about 37 percent black, white support undoubtedly held the key to the election. Thus, Stokes turned his attention to the white West Side where he had managed a mere 3% of the 1965 mayoral vote. Here he attempted to differentiate himself from the do-nothing Democratic Administration of the past and to convince white voters of his intolerance toward crime and riots. He spoke of his three-term record in the Ohio House of Representatives which included sponsorship of gun control and riot control measures. Moreover, Stokes promised to increase Cleveland's police patrol car force by a third in order to limit a rapidly increasing crime rate and vowed to immediately fire Cleveland's Police Chief for being insensitive to the City's racial problems.

The strategy paid off. Because Stokes stood to become the first black mayor of a major American city, the national attention focused on Cleveland. Martin Luther King appeared on Election Day to encourage black voters to go to the polls. As expected Stokes showed overwhelming strength among blacks, receiving 97 percent of that vote. It was the 19 percent of the white vote, however, that gave Stokes a scant but adequate 1,679 vote (.7 percent) plurality necessary to defeat Seth Taft (Exhibit 3).

THE FIRST TERM

Despite the jubilant atmosphere which accompanied Carl Stokes into office, the new mayor inherited a multitude of problems. Under Mayor Locher, Cleveland had embarked on an overly ambitious urban renewal program only to have $10 million in committed federal funds withdrawn. Blocks had been bulldozed, families (mostly black) had been displaced, and needed revenues were lacking. The downtown section of the City was drab and unexciting. Affluent businesses fled to the suburbs leaving high unemployment in Cleveland's ghettos. The City had met little success in attracting new business, while remaining industry continued to pollute the air and the Cuyahoga River which runs through the center of town. Police relations within the community were poor as tension ran high between the heavily ethnic West Side and the predominantly black East Side of the City. Finally, an inadequate tax base offered little opportunity for the alleviation of these problems.

Against this backdrop of difficulties, Stokes made some very real progress during his first term in office. His most substantial accomplishments were embodied in a program called "Cleveland NOW!"—an ambitious and far reaching ten-year plan designed to address many of Cleveland's inner-city ills. Generating considerable enthusiasm from many previously apathetic factors throughout the city, Stokes was able to gather $4.3 million from private businesses, institutions and individuals and another $100 million from Federal sources.

Under the umbrella of Cleveland NOW, the Stokes Administration embarked on many new activities. Promising 5,000 new or rehabilitated housing units by the end of 1969, Stokes managed to keep ahead of schedule

almost from the start. By early 1969, he had found jobs for 5,900 hard core unemployed (more than a quarter of the City's total) and he had disbursed $12,000 from a newly-formed fund of $500,000 to help aid and start small, predominantly black-owned businesses. In addition, Cleveland NOW was engaged in thirty-six projects planned for Cleveland's youth in the Summer of 1969, the opening of four day-care centers, the development of city planning efforts for Federal programs, the support of a Summer arts festival, and the partial sponsorship of a children's camp.

Much of the newly aroused enthusiasm for Stokes' programs came from Cleveland's previously unresponsive business community. Corporate contributions reached $10 million and center city construction began to pick up. Moreover, a number of corporations took on their own community improvement projects— job training for ghetto residents, support of a black-run manufacturing firm, apartment renovation, funding for a neighborhood rehabilitation project and the like.

Stokes' other accomplishments included the passage of a $100 million bond issue to treat the serious water pollution problem in Lake Erie; the solicitation of substantial Federal grants to develop part space in poor neighborhoods; the approval of increased spending on schools and welfare programs; the removal of junked cars and addition of lights along City streets; the opening of a widely acclaimed rapid transit line to Cleveland's airport; and the modernization of police facilities. Finally, less tangible but perhaps more important breakthroughs were made through Stokes' invitation to Cleveland residents to alert City Hall of their problems. For the first time in decades, citizen participation and interest in municipal government became a reality.

Stokes' first term was not without its problems, however, and his greatest (or at least his most emotion-packed) setback came in July of 1968 in Cleveland's black Glenville section. After cooling off a tense black community during the period following Martin Luther King's assassination, Stokes seemed to offer the unify-ing force necessary to keep peace in the City. It was not long afterwards, however, that a group of black militants broke that peace, engaging Cleveland policemen in a four-hour shoot-out. The results: seven dead including three policemen, fourteen others wounded, looting, and arson. In a move destined to evoke criticism for months to come, Stokes removed National Guardsmen and all white policemen from the Glenville area. While this action served to quiet Glenville down, Stokes' already poor relations with the Cleveland police depart-ment worsened.

At the same time, Cleveland's crime rate, especially homicides, increased under the Stokes Administration. In early 1969 a scandal occurred—two Stokes appointees were brought into question and later indicted for passing on information regarding a police promotion test to black candidates. Still further tension developed that Summer as black activists, seek-ing the transferal of four hamburger franchises to black owners at stated prices, engaged in well organized and publicized boycotts.

Having doubled the City income tax from 1/2 to 1 percent, Stokes was also feeling pres-sure to bring about changes rapidly. Serious problems remained, especially in the areas of welfare, crime, pollution, and race relations. His Cleveland NOW program was labelled more style than substance by some, an accusa-tion later to be brought against all facets of his Administration. But this was the record which Carl Stokes had to defend to the people of Cleveland if he was to win re-election in 1969.

THE RE-ELECTION SETTING

As Stokes looked forward to the Fall of 1969, he foresaw formidable opposition from the Republicans' most likely mayoral can-didate, Ralph J. Perk. Perk had been a five-term member of the Cleveland City Council and, as Cuyahoga County Auditor, he was the first Republican to enjoy a county office in twenty-three years. Despite a rather bland

presence, Perk had proven himself in his thirty years of government experience to be a tough and aggressive campaigner and a highly suc-cessful vote-getter.

While Perk could not compete with Stokes' charisma or showmanship, he could certainly be expected to stress a long career as an effec-tive administrator. With the aid of Cleveland's small but strong GOP organization, Perk's ma-jor campaign themes would probably rest with the law and order issue and with charges of ex-cessive spending during the Stokes Administra-tion. Race was not expected to be used as a campaign issue.

As vocalized by his spokesmen, the Perk strategy would be heavily dependent on the ethnic mix of Cleveland's population. While non-whites constituted about 40 percent of the City's population (about 3 percent more than in 1967), a somewhat larger bloc of voters com-prised the "cosmo" (short for cosmopolitan) group. These were primarily the blue-collar workers of first and second generation Eastern European—Rumanian, Czech, Hungarian, Russian, Polish Ukranian, Yugoslav, Greek, German and Italian—descent who offered Stokes only one-fifth of their vote in 1967 (Ex-hibit 4). This potential backlash vote, although registered six-to-one Democratic, constituted the bulk of Czech-descended Perk support. The strength of this ethnic bloc becomes particu-larly apparent in reviewing the national origins of the four Cleveland Mayors preceding Stokes—Slovenian, Irish, Italian and Ruma-nian.

With the exodus of most of Cleveland's upper-middle-class whites (who generally rep-resent a liberal vote) to the suburbs, Stokes would probably have to go beyond the black and hard core Democratic vote if he were to in-sure victory in November. Somehow, it would be necessary to insure a large turnout among these groups while attracting liberal whites and biting into Perk's ethnic oriented support. However, Perk would doubtlessly be focusing on these same groups.

In assessing his position within the white community, Stokes' supporters speculated that the Mayor had broken any association in people's minds with black extremist movements during his first term in office. Yet there was still some reason to believe that whites perceived Stokes as partial to the black community. The indictment of black militant Fred (Ahmed) Evans, who was accused of building an arsenal for the Glenville shoot-out from funds received through one of Stokes' civic action programs, could not help but hurt the Mayor. This incident coupled with the police examination scandal and the boycott was thought to represent a severe threat to Stokes' vote-getting powers in white areas.

Stokes' problems were not limited to the white community, however. While he still received widespread support among blacks, conditions in ghetto sections of Cleveland (especially Hough) had continued to worsen along many fronts in the 1967 to 1969 period. There was also reason to believe that Stokes might have given way to an Uncle Tom image in some black circles.

The major difficulty which he faced among this segment of the population, however, was not so much with changing voters' minds as with insuring a substantial black turnout. The 1969 race would carry with it neither the novelty nor the excitment of the 1967 election, and apathy was thought to pervade much of the black community (Exhibit 5). If Stokes could not succeed in effectively mobilizing what most surely constituted his fundamental base of support, even a relatively strong showing in otherwise hostile white areas would be fruitless.

In assessing his other sources of support, Stokes looked forward to mixed reactions. His carefully cemented alliance with the business community would doubtlessly offer some assistance while an endorsement from organized labor also seemed secure. Cleveland's once alien Democratic Party could be expected to come around, although internal dissension and traditional ineffectiveness made this a mixed blessing at best. Certain Party celebrities such as Maine's Senator Muskie and Detroit's Mayor Cavanaugh had already provided endorsements which could be of some worth and

Cleveland's two major newspapers could probably be counted on for their help. Stokes' trump card, however, would have to come from the vast amounts of manpower which he had depended upon in 1967 to spread his message.

At the other side, there were the Cleveland police and fire departments which would certainly do their best to oust the Mayor. Moreover, Stokes in one way or another had managed to alienate a number of his top assistants from the 1967 campaign whom he could no longer turn to for assistance. Finally, Stokes' poor relations with the Cleveland City Council, a Democratic-dominated body, might ultimately prove to be of significant assistance to Republican Perk.

THE SORENSEN REPORT

In light of the many uncertainties surrounding the upcoming election, Stokes called in Dr. Robert C. Sorensen, President of The Sorensen Group, in June of 1969. After reviewing the situation in Cleveland, Dr. Sorensen decided to embark on an extensive public opinion research study to ascertain the following information from the Cleveland electorate:

1. Voter mayoralty preferences at the time of polling (Exhibits 6 and 7).
2. Voters' knowledge of and attitudes toward the mayoral candidates (Exhibits 8 and 9).
3. The extent to which voters feel activated to support or oppose the candidates for mayor (Exhibit 10).
4. Issues which the Cleveland voters think are of primary importance (Exhibits 11, 12, 13).
5. Demographic descriptions of registered and would-be registered voters who were questioned (Exhibits 14 and 15).

Dr. Sorensen proceeded to design a 46-item questionnaire which required about one hour to administer through personal interviews. While organizing and training interviewers in the Cleveland area, he also developed a master sampling plan to insure that an accurate cross-section of the voting population was reached. Dr. Sorensen described the sampling procedure:

Area probability sampling procedures were used to select specific locations, households, and individuals for the Cleveland Survey. Persons twenty-one or over who were registered to vote in the election for mayor were eligible for the interview.

A total of 175 sample locations was selected for the survey. Locations were first allocated to the 33 Wards in the City of Cleveland in proportion to the number of voters in the 1967 Mayoral election. For example, if 4% of the votes in the 1967 election were in a given Ward, then 4% of the sample locations (or 7 out of 175) were allocated to that Ward.

Within the allocation to Wards, specific blocks or groups of blocks were selected from Census block statistics. Random probability procedures were used for this selection. Blocks with small numbers of housing units were first combined with contiguous blocks to form a segment with a minimum of thirty housing units. Each block or segment was given a probability of selection in proportion to the number of housing units listed in the Census block statistics.

Interviewers were given a map or sketch of the selected block or segment and instructed to list eight consecutive housing units, starting at a designated point. Additional housing units were listed and contacted if the assigned number of interviews (six per location) could not be completed within the first group of eight.

By the beginning of August, Dr. Sorensen's people had completed 1,016 interviews and were able to offer favorable findings to the Mayor. Perhaps the most significant results of the study showed that if the election were held on the day the questionnaires were administered 54.1 percent of the sample would definitely have voted for Stokes while another 7.2 percent leaned toward Stokes. Correspond-

ing figures for Perk were 33.3 and 2.4 percent, respectively, with the remaining 3 percent of the sample undecided or unwilling to vote for either candidate.

Despite Stokes' apparent strength, however, both the Mayor and Dr. Sorensen recognized that the election was far from won. As they reviewed the results of the Sorensen report, they agreed on the need to formulate a strategy for the remaining months of the campaign. As guidelines, they decided that Stokes could not be assured victory unless:

1. Perk's image remained somewhat dull and confined to "good government" issues in contrast to Stokes' charisma.

2. Stokes continued to be thought of as wanting to maintain racial peace in Cleveland despite the mistakes many people felt he had made.

3. Voters concern about public safety saw Stokes as sharing their concern. The issue did not seem to be "law and order," but rather genuine fear of crime in both black and white communities.

4. Voters were assured of Stokes' support of the police. The issue for many voters it appeared was not raw bigotry but concern for the pride of policemen.

5. Stokes watched carefully the strong concern among his supporters and detractors for "spending too much money," despite the popularity of his public housing and urban renewal efforts.

6. Stokes persuaded his black and white supporters to turn out and vote for him in the proportions they promised.

Moreover, even if these six guidelines could be satisfied, maintaining an "August lead" through to November was thought to be no mean task.

With these considerations in mind, Dr. Sorensen and the Mayor set out to translate the research results into actionable campaign strategies.

EXHIBIT 1

City of Cleveland Wards

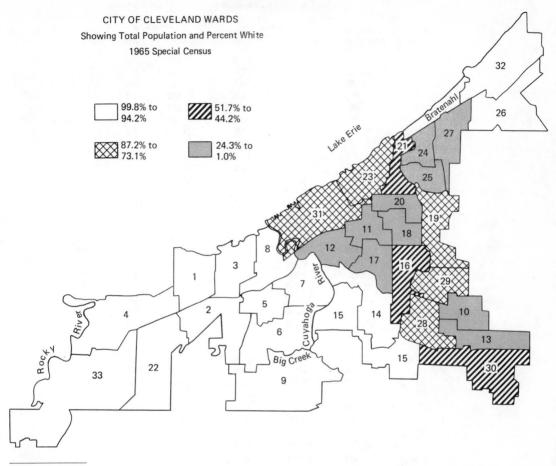

CITY OF CLEVELAND WARDS

Showing Total Population and Percent White

1965 Special Census

Source: Local Government Yearbook—Cuyahoga County, Cleveland, Government Research Institute, 1968.

EXHIBIT 2

**Cleveland's 1965 Population by Wards, Showing White
and Non-White Portions**

Ward Number	Total 1965 Population	White		Non-White	
		Number	Percent	Number	Percent
1	24,410	24,268	99.4%	142	0.6%
2	27,650	27,591	99.8	59	0.2
3	27,662	27,411	.99.1	251	0.9
4	29,404	29,292	99.6	112	0.4
5	21,961	21,830	99.4	131	0.6
6	23,936	23,747	99.2	189	0.8
7	18,295	17,846	97.5	449	2.5
8	23,429	22,701	96.9	728	3.1
9	36,775	36,687	99.8	88	0.2
10	24,150	1,319	5.5	22,831	94.5
11	20,596	1,573	7.6	19,023	92.4
12	12,533	2,383	19.0	10,150	81.0
13	22,106	5,373	24.3	16,733	75.7
14	25,438	25,098	98.7	340	1.3
15	26,332	25,936	98.5	396	1.5
16	20,650	9,556	46.3	11,094	53.7
17	18,304	188	1.0	18,116	99.0
18	25,190	2,277	9.0	22,913	91.0
19	23,750	18,154	76.4	5,596	23.6
20	27,651	2,541	9.2	25,110	90.8
21	23,617	10,428	44.2	13,189	55.8
22	31,805	29,958	94.2	1,847	5.8
23	20,597	17,956	87.2	2,641	12.8
24	25,920	1,080	4.2	24,840	95.8
25	26,470	383	1.4	26,088	98.6
26	27,360	27,040	98.8	320	1.2
27	32,260	4,670	14.5	27,590	85.5
28	23,928	17,484	73.1	6,444	26.9
29	24,608	18,815	76.5	5,793	23.5
30	25,768	13,324	51.7	12,444	48.3
31	13,009	9,983	76.7	3,026	23.3
32	25,001	24,377	97.5	624	2.5
33	30,293	30,238	99.8	55	0.2
Totals	810,858	531,506	65.5%	279,352	34.5%

Source: Local Government Yearbook, 1969.

EXHIBIT 3

Results of Cleveland's 1967 Mayoralty Elections

Democratic Primary, October 3, 1967

Ward	Locher		Stokes		Celeste		Total
	Votes	%	Votes	%	Votes	%	
1	3,479	72.0%	833	17.2%	520	10.8%	4,832
2	5,071	78.1	831	12.8	590	9.1	6,492
3	3,432	79.2	590	13.6	310	7.2	4,332
4	5,432	72.5	1,360	18.2	700	9.3	7,492
5	3,051	79.0	456	11.8	354	9.2	3,861
6	3,813	78.6	607	12.5	431	8.9	4,851
7	2,243	76.6	487	16.6	200	6.8	2,930
8	2,356	68.1	839	24.2	266	7.7	3,461
9	7,251	79.5	1,112	12.2	754	8.3	9,117
10	239	2.4	9,623	97.3	30	0.3	9,892

EXHIBIT 3 *(cont.)*

Democratic Primary, October 3, 1967

Ward	Locher		Stokes		Celeste		Total
	Votes	%	Votes	%	Votes	%	
11	189	3.2	5,620	96.0	46	0.8	5,855
12	263	8.8	2,715	90.4	25	0.8	3,003
13	810	8.8	8,346	90.7	48	0.5	9,204
14	4,523	85.6	413	7.8	349	6.6	5,285
15	4,414	83.3	488	9.2	398	7.5	5,300
16	1,620	27.9	4,054	69.9	130	2.2	5,804
17	68	1.5	4,635	98.1	20	0.4	4,723
18	233	3.3	6,870	96.3	29	0.4	7,132
19	2,609	49.4	2,506	47.5	166	3.1	5,281
20	267	4.3	5,832	95.0	42	0.7	6,141
21	1,913	31.7	4,003	66.3	123	2.0	6,039
22	5,560	68.3	1,831	22.5	744	9.2	8,135
23	3,895	78.5	901	18.1	168	3.4	4,964
24	128	1.5	8,238	98.1	30	0.4	8,396
25	117	1.3	8,942	98.4	25	0.3	9,084
26	4,970	79.2	1,021	16.3	282	4.5	6,273
27	425	4.1	9,975	95.6	31	0.3	10,431
28	3,201	43.0	4,072	54.8	164	2.2	7,437
29	4,355	53.7	3,507	43.2	253	3.1	8,115
30	2,142	23.3	6,891	75.0	153	1.7	9,186
31	1,494	63.7	747	31.8	105	4.5	2,346
32	6,997	86.1	812	10.0	315	3.9	8,124
33	5,761	73.3	1,395	17.7	708	9.0	7,864
Totals	92,321	43.7%	110,552	52.3%	8,509	4.0%	211,382

General Election, November 7, 1967

Ward	Stokes		Taft		Total
	Votes	%	Votes	%	
1	1,478	20.6%	5,710	79.4%	7,188
2	1,536	17.4	7,275	82.6	8,811
3	1,131	20.7	4,332	79.3	5,463
4	2,360	20.9	8,949	79.1	11,309
5	939	17.8	4,326	82.2	5,265
6	1,161	16.8	5,730	83.2	6,891
7	825	23.1	2,746	76.9	3,571
8	1,195	29.5	2,858	70.5	4,053
9	2,153	16.4	10,937	83.6	13,090
10	10,329	96.6	359	3.4	10,688
11	6,105	95.9	263	4.1	6,368
12	3,039	90.5	320	9.5	3,359
13	8,693	88.3	1,151	11.7	9,844
14	893	13.1	5,921	86.9	6,814
15	1,014	14.1	6,155	85.9	7,169
16	4,448	70.1	1,900	29.9	6,348
17	4,987	97.8	113	2.2	5,100
18	7,759	95.5	364	4.5	8,123
19	2,987	39.9	4,500	60.1	7,487
20	6,100	92.6	487	7.4	6,587
21	4,346	67.7	2,071	32.3	6,417
22	2,856	26.2	8,027	73.8	10,883
23	1,265	23.0	4,227	77.0	5,492
24	8,800	97.9	185	2.1	8,985
25	9,621	98.1	185	1.9	9,806
26	1,737	20.0	6,964	80.0	8,701

EXHIBIT 3 *(cont.)*

General Election, November 7, 1967

Ward	Stokes		Taft		Total
	Votes	%	Votes	%	
27	10,429	94.7	579	5.3	11,008
28	4,566	55.9	3,608	44.1	8,174
29	4,227	42.3	5,774	57.7	10,001
30	7,482	71.4	2,995	28.6	10,477
31	1,073	39.0	1,680	61.0	2,753
32	1,532	15.3	8,510	84.7	10,042
33	2,330	21.5	8,516	78.5	10,846
Totals	129,396	50.3%	127,717	49.7%	257,113*

* Does not include 2,461 write-in votes for other candidates.

Source: Local Government Yearbook, 1969.

EXHIBIT 4

Socio-Economic and Ethnic Composition by Wards

Ward #	Predominant Socio-Economic Class	Predominant Ethnic Backgrounds
1	Middle	Irish
2	Middle	Irish, Italian, German, Slovenian
3	Lower Middle	German, Irish, Italian, Rumanian, Puerto Rican, Appalachian Migrant
4	Upper Middle	Irish, German, Bohemian
5	Middle	Italian, Bohemian, Appalachian Migrant
6	Upper Lower	Polish, Slavic, Puerto Rican
7	Lower	Ukranian, Polish, Appalachian Whites, Puerto Rican, Black
8	Upper Lower	Irish, German, Appalachian Migrant, Puerto Rican
9	Upper Middle	Polish, German, Bohemian
10	Lower Middle	Black
11	Lower	Black
12	Lower	Black
13	Middle	Black
14	Middle	Polish, Bohemian, Appalachian Migrant
15	Middle	Polish
16	Lower Middle	Black, Hungarian, Slovenian
17	Lower	Black
18	Lower Middle	Black
19	Upper Middle	Italian, Black
20	Lower	Black
21	Upper Lower	Black, Polish, Slavic
22	Upper Middle	Irish, German, Slovenian
23	Lower Middle	Slovenian, Lithuanian, Black
24	Lower Middle	Black
25	Upper Lower	Black
26	Upper Middle	Italian, Irish, German, Slavic
27	Upper Lower	Black
28	Middle	Black, Irish, Slovenian, Russian
29	Upper Lower	Slavic, Black, Hungarian
30	Upper Middle	Black, Irish, German
31	Middle	Croation, Lithuanian, Black, Slavic
32	Middle	Italian, Slovenian, Irish
33	Middle	Bohemian, Slavic

EXHIBIT 5

Registered Votes Cast By Cleveland Wards—1966, 1967, 1968 Elections

The following table presents the number of voters registered in the city of Cleveland for the 1966, 1967, and 1968 general elections, the number of votes cast in each election by Cleveland ward, and the percentage of those registered who voted in each election.

Ward	1966 State			1967 Municipal			1968 National		
	Voters Reg'd	Votes Cast	Per Cent	Voters Reg'd	Votes Cast	Per Cent	Voters Reg'd	Votes Cast	Per Cent
1	9,766	5,671	58.1%	9,549	7,233	75.7%	9,843	8,227	83.6%
2	10,870	6,944	63.9	10,850	8,902	82.0	11,219	9,719	86.6
3	8,110	4,405	54.3	7,553	5,544	73.4	7,721	6,261	81.1
4	14,240	9,460	66.4	14,202	11,422	80.4	14,356	12,660	88.2
5	6,978	4,054	58.1	6,811	5,320	78.1	7,052	5,958	84.5
6	8,852	5,321	60.1	8,669	6,941	80.1	9,191	7,853	85.4
7	5,051	2,797	55.4	4,860	3,624	74.6	4,850	3,820	78.8
8	6,162	3,159	51.3	5,581	4,185	75.0	5,870	4,446	75.7
9	16,049	10,539	65.7	16,321	13,198	80.9	16,738	14,691	87.8
10	12,127	7,530	62.1	12,881	10,758	83.5	12,001	10,107	84.2
11	8,847	4,776	54.0	8,335	6,450	77.4	7,711	5,807	75.3
12	4,405	2,403	54.6	4,463	3,395	76.1	4,057	3,098	76.4
13	10,863	7,394	68.1	11,562	9,958	86.1	11,226	9,976	88.9
14	8,595	5,519	64.2	8,401	6,886	82.0	8,559	7,355	85.9
15	9,163	5,813	63.4	9,008	7,236	80.3	9,267	7,913	85.4
16	8,028	4,502	56.1	8,266	6,445	78.0	7,760	6,068	78.2
17	7,374	3,756	50.9	6,744	5,175	76.7	5,923	4,542	76.7
18	11,035	5,544	50.2	10,531	8,195	77.8	9,673	7,384	76.3
19	10,217	6,069	59.4	9,886	7,537	76.2	9,730	7,951	81.7
20	9,434	4,500	47.7	8,913	6,662	74.7	7,819	5,979	76.5
21	8,441	4,525	53.6	8,354	6,464	77.4	7,814	6,258	80.1
22	13,287	8,433	63.5	13,477	10,965	81.4	13,761	12,004	87.2
23	7,299	4,478	61.4	7,234	5,579	77.1	7,132	5,845	82.0
24	10,666	6,274	58.8	10,815	9,043	83.6	10,186	8,426	82.7
25	11,890	7,189	60.5	12,030	9,881	82.1	11,154	9,232	82.8
26	11,479	6,807	59.3	11,427	8,784	76.9	12,054	10,108	83.9
27	12,813	7,231	56.4	13,611	11,054	81.2	12,656	10,331	81.6
28	10,109	6,025	59.6	10,492	8,287	79.0	10,006	8,279	82.7
29	12,503	7,998	64.0	12,575	10,081	80.2	12,490	10,600	84.9
30	12,046	7,660	63.6	12,692	10,567	83.3	12,315	10,510	85.3
31	4,156	2,164	52.1	3,922	2,790	71.1	4,033	3,016	74.8
32	12,218	8,098	66.3	12,534	10,110	80.7	12,965	11,248	86.8
33	12,695	8,395	66.1	13,184	10,903	82.7	13,702	12,125	88.5
Cleveland Total	325,768	195,433	60.0%	325,733	259,574	79.7%	320,834	267,797	83.5%

Source: Local Government Yearbook, 1969.

EXHIBIT 6

Voter Preference by Political Affiliation

Prefer/Lean to	Political Affiliation			
	Democrats	Republicans	Independents	All Voters
Stokes	71%	15%	56%	61%
Perk	27	82	38	36
Neither/Not Sure	2	3	6	3
	100%	100%	100%	100%
	(n = 702)	(n = 121)	(n = 196)	(n = 1019)

Source: The Sorensen Group.

EXHIBIT 7

Candidate Preference by Wards

Ward #	Committed To: Stokes	Perk	Neither, Not Sure, or Leaning	% of Total Vote	% of Undecided Vote
*Stokes Dominated (90%)**					
11	100	—	—	2.5%	—
17	99	—	1%	2.1	.2%
24	98	—	2	3.3	.5
25	95	—	5	4.2	1.7
10	94	—	6	3.9	1.9
27	93	1%	6	4.2	2.0
18	93	—	7	3.2	1.8
20	92	6	2	2.7	.4
12	91	1	8	1.4	.9
				27.5	9.4
Stokes Dominated (75–89%)					
30	81%	7%	12%	3.9%	3.7%
13	80	8	12	3.5	3.3
16	77	7	16	2.4	3.0
				9.8	10.0
Stokes Dominated (Under 75%)					
28	65%	30%	5%	3.2%	1.3%
19	58	32	10	3.0	2.4
29	56	26	18	3.8	5.4
23	53	30	17	2.2	3.0
21	50	33	17	2.6	3.5
				14.8	15.6
Tie Wards					
3	37%	37%	26%	2.3%	4.7%
31	46	46	8	1.2	.8
				3.5	5.5
Perk Dominated (Under 60%)					
6	33%	50%	17%	2.7%	3.6%
26	30	53	17	3.5	4.7
1	38	57	5	2.9	1.1
14	17	57	26	2.6	5.4
22	33	58	9	4.1	2.9
4	26	58	16	4.4	5.6
7	18	59	23	1.5	2.7
32	11	59	30	3.8	9.0
				25.5	35.0
Perk Dominated Wards (60 + %)					
15	10%	60%	30%	2.8%	6.7%
5	26	61	13	2.1	2.2
33	26	62	12	4.0	3.8
2	22	63	15	3.3	3.9
8	30	67	3	1.7	.4
9	12	69	19	5.0	7.5
				18.9	24.5
Totals	54.1%	33.3%	12.6%	100.0%	100.0%

(Total *n* = 1019)

* "Stokes Dominated (90 + %) Wards" are those with 90% or more of the respondents committed to Stokes.

Source: The Sorensen Group.

EXHIBIT 8

Voters' Knowledge of Candidates

| | Knowledge of Candidates among Voters Preferring: | | | |
| | Stokes | | Perk | |
	Committed Voters	Leaning Toward	Committed Voters	Leaning Toward
Know a lot	68%	62%	15%	9%
Know a little	29	36	45	45
Know almost nothing	3	2	40	46
	100%	100%	100%	100%
	(n = 552)	(n = 73)	(n = 339)	(n = 24)
	(Total n = 988)			

Source: The Sorensen Group.

EXHIBIT 9

Attitudes toward Stokes' Performance as Mayor

| | Overall Attitudes toward Stokes' Performance as Mayor among Voters Preferring: | | | | |
| | Stokes | | Perk | | |
	Committed Voters	Leaning Toward	Committed Voters	Leaning Toward	Neither/Not Sure
Favorable	96%	89%	15%	25%	37%
Unfavorable	1	1	46	29	25
Neither/Not Sure	3	10	39	46	38
	100%	100%	100%	100%	100%
	(n = 552)	(n = 73)	(n = 339)	(n = 24)	(n = 31)
	(Total n = 1019)				

Source: The Sorensen Group.

EXHIBIT 10

Degree of Candidate Support

| | Candidate Support among Voters Committed To: | |
	Stokes	Perk
Strength of Support		
Very Strong	82%	69%
Somewhat Strong	14	24
Not Strong	4	7
Willing To Talk For		
A Lot	49%	25%
A Little	28	33
Not At All	23	42
Willing To Give Money		
$25 or More	2%	1%
$10 or So	9	4
Few Dollars	65	33
Nothing	24	62
(Total n = 891)	(n = 552)	(n = 339)

Source: The Sorensen Group.

EXHIBIT 11

Most Important Campaign Issues by Ward

Ward #	Most Important Issues* (Combined First%Second Mentions)				
Stokes Dominated (90% +)					
11	C—56%**	H—40%	E—20%	R—19%	P— 5%
17	C—58	H—41	E—23	R—18	P—13
24	C—61	H—40	E—19	R—40	P— 9
25	C—55	H—43	E—25	R—15	P— 6
10	C—58	H—33	E—27	R—20	P— 8
27	C—80	H—45	E—24	R—17	P—15
18	C—69	H—51	E—22	R—21	P— 5
20	C—53	H—22	E—32	R—22	P—12
12	C—66	H—33	E—29	R—17	P— 7
Stokes Dominated (75-90%)					
30	C—83%	H—18%	E—23%	R—24%	P— 9%
13	C—46	H—50	E—34	R—21	P—12
16	C—54	H—13	E—28	R—20	P—16
Stokes Dominated (under 75%)					
28	C—54%	H—30%	E—46%	R—26%	P—16%
19	C—84	H—27	E—31	R—22	P—14
29	C—76	H—29	E—33	R—33	P—19
23	C—58	H—37	E—37	R—26	P—20
21	C—58	H—30	E—28	R—27	P—14
Tie Wards					
3	C—52%	H—24%	E—28%	R—28%	P—22%
31	C—50	H—67	E—27	R—50	P—17
Perk Dominated (Under 60%)					
6	C—84%	H—29%	E—30%	R—34%	P—29%
26	C—61	H—24	E—24	R—32	P—35
1	C—74	H—19	E—26	R—33	P—30
14	C—57	H—30	E—21	R—30	P—17
22	C—39	H—27	E—34	R—34	P—13
4	C—52	H—30	E—34	R—36	P—26
7	C—72	H—34	E—28	R—25	P—16
32	C—48	H—28	E—45	R—29	P—32
Perk Dominated (60% +)					
15	C—47%	H—24%	E—33%	R—26%	P—43%
5	C—39	H—26	E—29	R—26	P—22
33	C—65	H—26	E—30	R—32	P—35
2	C—60	H—22	E—43	R—19	P—17
8	C—45	H—26	E—22	R—34	P—23
9	C—69	H—27	E—36	R—32	P—34
Total (n = 1019)	C—62%	H—31%	E—27%	R—24%	P—17%

* C = crime, H = housing, E = economic, R = race, P = pollution.

** To be read, "56% of the voters in Ward 11 cited 'crime' as one of the two most important issues in the Stokes-Perk campaign."

Source: The Sorensen Group.

EXHIBIT 12

Most Important Campaign Issues

| | Most Important Issue among Voters Preferring: | | | |
| | Stokes | | Perk | |
	Committed Voters	Leaning Toward	Committed Voters	Leaning Toward
Crime	35%	27%	40%	41%
Housing	24	17	3	8
Race	13	8	20	4
Economics	12	9	17	21
Stokes' Record	4	4	6	8
Pollution	4	4	8	4
Public Services	3	2	4	4
Other	5	29	2	10
	100%	100%	100%	100%
	(n = 552)	(n = 73)	(n = 339)	(n = 24)
	(Total n = 988)			

Source: The Sorenson Group.

EXHIBIT 13

Attitude Toward Withdrawal of White Police during Glenville Shootout

| | Attitude toward Withdrawal of White Police during Glenville Shootout among Voters Preferring: | | | | |
| | Stokes | | Perk | | |
	Committed Voters	Leaning Toward	Committed Voters	Leaning Toward	Neither/Not Sure
Approve	78%	62%	18%	21%	24%
Disapprove	11	14	69	54	38
No Opinion	11	24	13	25	38
	100%	100%	100%	100%	100%
	(n = 552)	(n = 73)	(n = 339)	(n = 24)	(n = 31)
	(Total n = 1019)				

Source: The Sorensen Group.

EXHIBIT 14

Demographic Characteristics of Voters Sampled by Candidate Preference

| | | All Respondents-Preferring: | | |
	Total	Stokes	Perk	Neither/Not Sure
Total	100%	61%	36%	3%
Sex				
Male	52%	51%	54%	46%
Female	48	49	46	54
Age				
21–30	19%	19%	20%	13%
31–40	20	21	20	16
41–50	23	27	15	27
51–60	17	16	18	18
61 and over	21	17	27	26

EXHIBIT 14 *(cont.)*

	Total	Stokes	Perk	Neither/Not Sure
		All Respondents-Preferring:		

	Total	Stokes	Perk	Neither/Not Sure
Marital Status				
Married	72%	68%	79%	70%
Single	10	9	11	13
Formerly Married	18	23	10	17
Children				
None	46%	44%	48%	54%
One	14	14	13	16
Two	14	14	14	13
Three	12	13	12	8
Four or more	14	15	13	9
Education				
Grammar School	23%	25%	21%	21%
Some High School	28	28	28	29
High School Graduate	30	30	31	28
Some College	12	11	13	15
College Graduate	4	3	5	5
Other: secretarial, vocational	3	3	5	5
Income				
Under $3M	17%	17%	16%	20%
$3-5M	14	16	12	12
$5-7.5M	23	22	24	24
$7.5-10M	22	24	20	19
$10-15M	18	14	24	19
$15M and over	6	7	4	6
Occupation (Head of Household)				
White Collar	25%	25%	24%	30%
Blue Collar	63	64	63	55
Unemployed	12	11	13	15
Occupation (respondent other				
than head of household)				
White Collar	5%	5%	5%	6%
Blue Collar	7	8	6	8
Unemployed	25	24	26	29
Not in labor force	63	63	63	57
Race				
White	58%	31%	100%	92%
Non-White	42	69	*	8
Religion				
Catholic	34%	19%	59%	48%
Protestant	60	76	36	29
Other	6	5	5	23
Felt National Origin				
African	40%	65%	*	5%
British	8	4	14	11
Czech	2	1	5	2
German	14	8	24	17
Indian	2	2	2	1
Irish	10	6	17	15
Italian	6	4	9	10
Jewish	1	1	—	1
Lithuanian	*	—	1	—
Polish	8	3	15	22
Puerto Rican	1	2	—	—
Slovak	7	3	12	13
Other	1	1	1	3

* Less than 1%.

EXHIBIT 14   *(cont.)*

	All Respondents-Preferring:			
	Total	Stokes	Perk	Neither/Not Sure
Group Membership				
AFL–CIO	20%	20%	20%	18%
PTA	17	19	14	17
NAACP	10	16	—	5
Religious Organizations	10	7	14	15
Fraternal Group	5	3	7	6
Teamsters	5	6	4	3
UAW	5	5	5	4
Veterans Group	4	2	7	4
Urban League	1	2	—	1
CORE	*	1	—	—
John Birch Society	*	*	—	—
League of Women Voters	*	—	1	1

* Less than 1%.

Source: The Sorensen Group.

EXHIBIT 15

Demographic Characteristics of Undecided Voters Sampled

	All Respondents-Leaning To			
	Total	Stokes	Perk	Neither/Not Sure
Total	13%*	7%	2%	3%
Sex				
Male	49%	55%	33%	46%
Female	51	45	67	54
Age				
21–30	12	13	8	13
31–40	22	25	18	16
41–50	24	25	17	27
51–60	17	12	33	18
61 and over	25	25	24	26
Marital Status				
Married	71%	69%	80%	70%
Single	12	13	5	13
Formerly Married	17	18	15	17
Children				
None	51%	46%	63%	54%
One	16	14	21	16
Two	12	13	8	13
Three	9	11	4	8
Four or more	12	16	4	9
Education				
Grammar School	27%	33%	17%	21%
Some High School	25	21	33	29
High School Graduate	27	25	35	28
Some College	15	16	9	15
College Graduate	4	4	2	5
Other: secretarial, vocational	2	1	4	2
Income				
Under $3M	19%	20%	13%	20%
$3–5M	16	18	17	12
$5–7.5M	21	21	17	24
$7.5–10M	21	17	35	19

* Undecided vote does not sum to 13% due to rounding.

EXHIBIT 15 *(cont.)*

| | Total | All Respondents-Leaning To | | Neither/Not Sure |
		Stokes	Perk	
$10–15M	17	16	17	19
$15M and over	6	8	1	6
Occupation (Head of Household)				
White Collar	25%	23%	26%	30%
Blue Collar	50	47	53	55
Unemployed	25	30	21	15
Occupation (respondent other				
than head of household)				
White Collar	6%	6%	8%	6%
Blue Collar	9	11	4	8
Unemployed	30	28	38	29
Not in labor force	55	55	50	57
Race				
White	57%	29%	100%	92%
Non-White	43	71	—	8
Religion				
Catholic	36%	25%	58%	48%
Protestant	51	67	28	29
Other	13	8	14	23
Felt National Origin				
African	24%	39%	**	5%
British	8	5	14	11
Czech	1	1	2	2
German	13	9	20	17
Indian	1	1	1	1
Irish	13	12	13	15
Italian	10	11	7	10
Jewish	1	1	—	1
Lithuanian	1	1	3	—
Polish	14	9	22	22
Puerto Rican	1	1	—	—
Slovak	10	7	16	13
Other	3	3	2	3
Group Membership				
AFL–CIO	18%	18%	17%	18%
PTA	20	18	29	17
NAACP	12	19	—	5
Religious Organizations	10	7	13	15
Fraternal Group	8	7	13	6
Teamsters	4	4	8	3
UAW	5	6	4	4
Veterans Group	2	—	4	4
Urban League	3	4	4	1
CORE	—	—	—	—
John Birch Society	—	—	—	—
League of Women Voters	1	—	4	1

** Less than 1%.

Source: The Sorensen Group.

CHAPTER 16

Parkland Foods Corporation: Marketing in the Midst of a Consumerism Controversy

Dan Wackman, Manager of Public Affairs of the Parkland Foods Corporation, was recently faced with the following problems:

1. He had to appear before a United States Subcommittee investigating advertising practices to children. Parkland was one of several food and toy companies with significant advertising billings ($13 million) on television directed at children (primarily Saturday mornings, with some after-school-hour programming). The Senate Subcommittee wished to know how Parkland designed and evaluated TV ads for children; what safeguards were employed to insure advertising would not be false and/or misleading, whether Parkland Foods Corporation considered what it was now doing in this area adequate, and what

the corporation's strategic posture was for the future regarding advertising to children. The Senate Subcommittee had requested that Mr. Wackman show commercials for Parkland Foods Corporation products to the committee, and comment on them in terms of their objectives, and in terms of their possible capacity to deceive children. The ads he would show were current campaigns for Crunch-O, K-K, and Parkland's Smacks and Moo-Cow, a milk additive. See Appendix A.

2. Mr. Wackman also had to report to Mr. Richard Marks, President and Chairman of the Board of Directors. Mr. Marks wished to know what Mr. Wackman's *strategy* recommendations were regarding the corporation's advertising directed to children. It was agreed that TV advertising could not be eliminated altogether, but the budget could be reduced, if that were a viable alternative. But the marketing department made it quite clear that TV advertising to children must continue, or significant losses in market share would result.[1]

---

[1] Parkland had experimented with reducing and eliminating advertising, but loss of share resulted. Market

The reason why Mr. Wackman's problem was so severe was that there has been a major consumerism controversy surrounding advertising practices to children; moreover, raw materials costs for Parkland Foods Corporation products had all increased dramatically. Even with the recent increase in candy bar retail prices to 15¢, financial considerations were acute, and a decision had been made that further reductions in the size of the bar products would not be made.

THE CHILDREN'S ADVERTISING CONTROVERSY

Recent public opinion polls show Americans disapprove of television advertising to children. Many industry observers feel the roots of these negative attitudes can be traced to the testimony of Robert Choate before a Senate Committee in the Summer of 1970, when he lambasted breakfast cereals as "empty calories," and charged food companies with misleading energy claims in ads to children. Groups such as Action for Children's Television have mounted vigorous public relations campaigns, and have found receptive politicians.

Mr. Wackman believed the major issues were as follows:

1. Whether advertising misleads pre-teenage children, particularly "pre-operational" children (see Appendix B);

2. Whether specific techniques (camera angles, etc.)

---

research had shown that virtually all U.S. children eat candy, and most of them cite chocolate (68%) as the candy most often eaten. Pre-teenage children eat an average of 28 chocolate bars per month, and 20% of children account for 35% of chocolate bar volume. Children eat 3.2 different brands of chocolate bars, and the main chocolate bar competition is between Parkland Foods Corporation, Hershey, Nestle, and M&M Mars. "Chocolate bar" is loosely defined in marketing research, to include products such as bags of Parkland Smacks, Reese's Peanut Butter Cups, etc. These are distinct from hard sucking candies, caramels and toffies and jellied candies.

in ads to children contribute to their being misleading;

3. Whether there is too much advertising to children;

4. Whether children can understand puffery, characteristic of much advertising to adults and children;

5. Whether advertising should be permitted for products which are not "good" for children (Mr. Wackman knew that dental and medical research was not conclusive regarding chocolate candy's role in causing dental cavities and/or digestive and heart ailments, but he knew most people worried about these "effects" of candy consumption, in any case);

6. Whether children irritate their parents by urging them to buy advertised products;

7. Whether advertising has great potency in affecting children's purchase desires, attitudes, etc., and whether effects are particularly strong among disadvantaged children.

The importance of these issues—and the controversy as a whole—was that consumerism pressure might force advertising to children off the air, either an outright ban or a so heavily regulated environment that TV advertising would be a burden instead of a profitable marketing practice. The former Federal Trade Commission Chairman, Lewis Engman, made advertising to children a major theme of the Federal Trade Commission initiatives. At the present time, Mr. Wackman knew that the FTC was seriously considering a trade rule which would require that a substantial portion of every TV commercial be devoted to "nutritional disclosure"—long listings of nutrients in food products. The same proposed rule would ban all TV advertising at times when a significant number of children under 8 years of age were in the audience, and would require "warnings" in commercials for sugared products—including Parkland's candies—directed at older children. There was great industry resistance to this proposal, since it would mandate advertising practices and potentially reduce the effectiveness of commercials, and confuse consumers.

CORPORATE AND INDUSTRY RESPONSES TO THE CONTROVERSY

To date, industry's responses to the controversy on advertising to children had seemingly been to hire good Washington lawyers and lobbyists to forestall congressional or regulatory agency action. However, the controversy was an appetizing one for politicians, for obvious reasons, so normal routes of political pressures were proving ineffective. The primary industry defense mechanism was the Association of National Advertisers, an industry association consisting of major advertisers for national brands. The ANA produced a set of guidelines for advertising practices to be used in appealing to children (see Exhibit 1). The guidelines had been modified by a panel of child development experts, recruited for the task by the National Council of Better Business Bureaus. The political climate was well expressed by the Chairman of the Federal Trade Commission: "If business doesn't regulate itself in this area [advertising to children] we will have to step in and impose regulations." Parkland Foods Corporation also had an advertising philosophy (Exhibit 2), and Mr. Wackman wondered about how the ANA guidelines (which Parkland supported) and the corporate advertising philosophy would be received in the hearing room.

Parkland had taken some action of its own, by employing behavioral scientists to evaluate Parkland Foods Corporation advertising for several of its products (Exhibit 3). Essentially, the research consisted of carefully probing children's reactions to the commercials which they saw in a laboratory test environment. Additionally, these researchers also asked mothers of 4–9-year-olds what their opinions were of the commercials (see Exhibit 4 which are key results).[2] The commercials tested were the same ones Mr. Wackman planned to show to the Senate Subcommittee. Marketing informed Mr. Wackman that the advertising agency only tested ads in terms of their communication effects—recall, attitudes, etc.—and Mr. Wackman felt this communication research data would not be of use, given the Senate Subcommittee's interest.

THE PURCHASE PROCESS AMONG CHILDREN FOR CHOCOLATE CANDY BAR PRODUCTS

Mr. Wackman was discouraged by the lack of hard information about how children make decisions to buy chocolate bar products and brands. There was no time for original research, but Mr. Wackman did find some information in his files, regarding parental attitudes toward children's eating candy (see Exhibit 5) and areas of candy concern among children, teenagers, and adults (Exhibit 6). He was also interested in research which examined how often children ask for various products, including "candy," and how often mothers yield to these requests (Exhibit 7). Finally, he noted some correlations between a number of factors and children's purchase influence attempts and parental yielding (Exhibit 8).

Just before he set about to outline his testimony, Mr. Wackman contacted a team of Boston-area researchers who gave him some preliminary results from a diary study of children's purchase requests (Exhibit 9). He wondered if these data would corroborate the earlier published research (Exhibits 7 and 8). If they did not, should he try to use the diary information? He wondered if the data in the diary study were different, *why* would the data be different?

Mr. Wackman did estimate that about 50% of candy bar volume was attributable to pre-teenage children. Television is obviously the dominant medium for reaching large audiences of children. Recent data showed that

---

[2] Sample size was 500: while not a national, projectible sample, the data were reliable. The purpose was not to generalize results to the national scene, but to gain insight. Marketing research used even smaller samples in some

cases. In any event, Senate staff workers indicated that the data would be accepted, given their purposes, as long as they weren't "oversold," i.e., generalized to *all* children.

children average over three hours per day of television viewing, and that they watch a wide variety of programs (see Exhibit 10). Interestingly, only about 10% of children's viewing occurs on weekend mornings—the prime target of many consumer groups. Rather, most children's viewing takes place during prime time hours (see Exhibit 11).

PREPARING FOR SUBCOMMITTEE APPEARANCE

Mr. Wackman outlined his presentation to the Senate Subcommittee as follows:

1. Brief history of Parkland Foods Corporation;[3]
2. Description of children's decision processes regarding candy buying and consumption;
3. Show commercials;
4. Discuss commercials in light of the behavioral scientist's research findings;
5. Outline Parkland Foods Corporation's strategic plans regarding future advertising to children on television.

A number of things still bothered Mr. Wackman: should he use the corporate advertising philosophy? And how should he use the

ANA code guidelines? How should he address each of the issues surrounding the controversy, and were there any further issues he had not thought about?

Finally, Mr. Wackman realized that, upon his return from Washington, he faced the formidable task of reporting to Mr. Marks and the Board of Directors, and making strategic suggestions to them regarding Parkland Food Corporation's future advertising to children. He knew that Parkland Foods Corporation would continue to advertise, but he also knew that Mr. Marks would insist that the corporation do everything in its power to avoid becoming embroiled in the controversy, i.e., becoming the target of activist groups such as Action for Children's Television or be called before the Federal Trade Commission or the Better Business Bureau's powerful National Advertising Review Board.[4]

Mr. Wackman knew his specific suggestions would be evaluated by Mr. Marks and the Board in terms of (1) how adequately his plan stipulations overcame the controversy issues, and (2) how adequately marketing could still carry on its tasks of effectively promoting Parkland Foods Corporation products to children.

---

[3] He would point out that Parkland had only recently begun mass media advertising, necessitated by eroding market share among pre-teenage children, the Confectionery Division's most important single market segment.

[4] In fact, a candy manufacturer had recently been called before the NARB regarding a ten-second candy bar ad. The ad showed a boy biting into the bar and the sound effects produced a loud sound when biting into the bar. The NARB's complaint charged that the sound when actually eating the bar was not as great as suggested in the ad, hence it may be misleading to children. The company withdrew the ad, at considerable expense, not to mention less tangible "expense" in terms of negative publicity.

EXHIBIT 1

Preamble

Advertising directed to children, for products and services which are used or consumed by children, is appropriate in a society and economy such as ours. Such advertising serves to bring information to children and helps prepare them for maturity. Advertising to children is also the economic base for children's programming with all of its potential for education and entertainment. Without such advertising, continued and improved children's programming would be jeopardized.

At the same time, children are a unique audience as they are in their most formative development period, may be more easily influenced than are adults, and because of their limited experience are not fully equipped to make comparative judgments.

Heretofore, parents, school and church have been the primary guiding forces in shaping values and judgements. However, the amount of time spent with TV today adds it as a fourth major influence. Special responsibilities are therefore placed upon advertisers and broadcasters to deal protectively with children, to help them better understand the world and how to live in it, and to respect and complement the parental role.

These Guidelines, recognizing the uniqueness of children's audience, are designed to assist advertisers in the preparation of advertising that fulfills the special standards that are desirable in advertising to children.

Principles

While the process of communication with children through television must be continually responsive to changing times, four basic principles underlie these Guidelines:

1. Advertisers should always take into consideration the level of knowledge, sophistication and maturity of the audience to which the message is primarily directed. Since younger children have limited capabilities for discerning the credibility of what they watch, they pose a special responsibility for advertisers and broadcasters alike to protect them from their own susceptibilities.

2. Realizing that children are limited in their ability to distinguish between fact and fantasy, advertisers should exercise care not to stimulate (directly or by implication) unreasonable expectations of performance. A child's imagination should be respected rather than exploited.

3. Recognizing that advertising may play an important part in educating a child to become a member of society, product information should be communicated in a truthful and tasteful manner.

4. Advertisers are urged to capitalize on the potential of television to communicate and impart knowledge and understanding by sponsoring children's programs that provide value beyond entertainment alone, and by developing advertising that, where possible, addresses itself to social standards generally regarded as positive and beneficial (such as friendship, equality, kindness, honesty, and generosity).

Interpretation

Advertisers and broadcasters are reminded that the interpretation of these Guidelines should conform to the principles stated above. The intent in all cases should be to deal fairly and honestly with children, and to look at each individual commercial in that context, rather than prescribe rigid or inflexible rules which may deprive children and advertisers of the benefits of innovations and new approaches.

EXHIBIT 1 *(cont.)*

Scope

The clauses in these Guidelines embrace all (whether national or local) commercial messages designed to appeal especially to children under twelve years of age which appear in children's programs or all-family programs in which general audience patterns typically contain more than 50% children.

Social Values

Although many influences affect a child's personal and social development, it remains the prime responsibility of the parents to provide guidance for children, and to exert necessary and proper influences in children's exposure to the world. Advertisers and broadcasters should contribute to this development in a constructive manner in order to facilitate the parental task. Advertising should dwell on the positive aspects of society, and enrich the dignity of human life as opposed to portrayals of violence, appeals to fear, or discrimination of any type. To this end:

a. Advertisements should never suggest practices generally considered unacceptable from the standpoint of social, legal, religious, institutional or family values.

b. Advertisements should not reflect disdain for parents or parental judgment, nor reflect unfavorably on other generally recognized sources of child guidance.

c. Advertisements should never portray undesirable living habits.

d. Advertisements should avoid contending that, through possession of a product, a child betters his peers or, lacking it, will invite their contempt or ridicule.

e. Any material benefits attributed to the product, premium or service should be inherent in the use thereof.

Presentation

Children, especially in their pre-school years, have vivid imaginations. Use of imagination enables a child to project himself beyond his immediate capacities and reach for his future potential. Advertisers should, therefore, always respect a child's imagination.

The use of imaginative situations relevant to the audience concerned is an acceptable and normal communications practice. Implicit in the foregoing is the concept of fantasy, including animation, as an appropriate form of communications to any audience, including the very young. However, the use of special situations and fantasy in advertising directed to children should assure that the advertisement will not suggest unattainable expection of performance.

To this end:

a. Any form of presentation which capitalizes on a child's difficulty in distinguishing between the real and the fanciful should be positively guarded against.

b. In the use of fantasy, advertisers should seek to channel a child's imagination toward healthy and constructive growth and development.

In more specific terms, particular control should be exercised to be sure that:

a. Copy, sound and visual presentation—as well as the commercial in its totality—do not mislead the audience to which it is directed on such performance characteristics as speed, size, color, durability, nutrition, noise, etc.; or on perceived benefits such as the acquisition of strength, popularity, growth, proficiency, intelligence, and the like.

EXHIBIT 1 *(cont.)*

b. The advertisement clearly establishes what is included in the original purchase price of the advertised product, employing where necessary positive disclosure on what items are to be purchased seperately. All advertising for products sold unassembled should indicate that assembly is required.

c. A clearly depicted representation of the advertised product be shown during the advertisement. When appropriate in assisting consumers to identify the product, the package may be depicted, provided that it does not mislead as to product characteristics or content.

d. Advertising demonstrations showing the use of a product or premium can be readily duplicated by the average child for whom the product is intended.

Promotion by Program Character and Personal Endorsements

It is recognized that very young children may not fully recognize differences between commercial messages and program content. Hence, product endorsements by personalities may exert undue influence upon the rationalization process of children. Therefore:

a. Program personalities or program characters (live or animated) on children's programs should not be used to promote products, premiums or services in or adjacent to any program where the personality or character appears.

b. Subject to paragraph A of this section, "product characters"—personalities (real or fanciful) which are closely associated and identified with the product—may be used as presenters for the advertised product or service, provided they do not perform acts, which children might be expected to emulate, which would be misleading as to the attributes of the product or service concerned.

c. Nationally known persons may be used to attribute a characteristic or quality to a product (including a premium) or service when they are generally recognized as qualified to speak to the subject, and their statements represent their good-faith evaluation.

Comparative and Competitive Claims

It is recognized that comparative product information is an important consumer service and will assist children in evaluating product performance and benefits. Therefore, comparative statements may be used when such statements portray a true and significant improvement over prior or existing products, and providing that:

a. All comparative price statements are based upon the usual and customary price paid in a substantial number of sales in the trade area where the advertising is carried.

b. Dangling or open-ended comparative statements are not used.

c. Comparative statements are informational and do not demean other products.

Pressure to Purchase

The purpose of commercial communications is to encourage trial and repeat purchases. Advertisements addressed to children also seek those objectives. Should they fail to do so, their reason for existence would be vitiated, as would the advertiser's motivation for the support, sponsorship and development of improved programming directed to children.

However, children are not as prepared to make independent buying decisions—or contribute to family decisions—as are adults. Accordingly, to avoid undue pressure to purchase:

a. Rather than urging children to pressure their parents to purchase, advertising to children should urge them to seek parental guidance and counsel.

EXHIBIT 1 *(cont.)*

b. Products which by their very nature are not primarily intended for use or consumption by children should not be advertised directly to children; nor should such products be promoted via premiums or other means directly to children. If child-directed premiums are used, they should be advertised to parents.

c. All price representations should be clearly and concisely set forth in a manner so as not to exert undue pressure to purchase, and price minimizations such as "only" or "just" should not be used in any advertising directed to children.

Safety

For the child, imitation, exploration, and experimentation are important facets of the learning process. The various media—and especially television—contribute to this process through programs and commercial messages. Because television is one of the dominant factors in communicating with children, and because many initial exposures to products and services are through this medium, advertising and programming can and should contribute directly and indirectly to sound and safe habits in children.

Children, and occasionally parents, may not be cognizant of hazards that may exist through misuse or abuse of products. Therefore:

a. Advertisements, except specific safety messages, should not portray adults or children in any unsafe acts, situations or conditions.

b. Advertisements should avoid demonstrations or portrayals of any product in a manner that encourages misuse, or is inconsistent with generally accepted standards of safety.

Claim Substantiation

In accordance with the basic principle of "dealing fairly and honestly" with children:

a. Advertising to children shall not claim or imply any product or premium performance characteristics which are not supportable by factual data or research which conforms to sound professional practices. Exceptions are those claims recognized to be generic to products in a category.

b. Puffery (defined as "flattering publicity" or "extravagant commendation") is not acceptable support for an objective product claim. Advertising claims which might be construed as literally true must be literally true. If there is doubt, the burden will be on the advertiser to document the claim.

Adopted May 13, 1972 by the Board of Directors of the Association of National Advertisers, Inc.

EXHIBIT 2

Parkland's Advertising Philosophy

Simply stated, Parkland's advertising philosophy will observe the following guidelines:

1. *Honest*
   Our advertising will maintain the highest standards of integrity and honesty. We will make no false or devious claims.

2. *Ethical*
   We will advertise in good taste. We will not degrade competition. We will not produce advertising whose tone or claims would offend or mislead.

3. *Respectful of Consumers' Intelligence*
   We can entertain and amuse, but never at the expense of truth. We will inform consumers of the merits of our products, but we will not take unfair advantage of the trust or lack of technical expertise of our audience in presenting those merits.

4. *Effective*
   While adhering to the above criteria, Parkland's advertising must effectively contribute to the achievement of the Company's growth and profit goals.

Our intent is not just to be within the law but to be as honest and ethical in our dealings with our unseen audience as we are with our direct customers—and as we would expect others to be with us.

EXHIBIT 3

Sample Characteristics

1. Education

| | Total Sample (n = 500) | | Social Class | | | |
| | | | Lower (n = 250) | | Upper-Middle (n = 250) | |
	Wife	Husband	Wife	Husband	Wife	Husband
9–11 Years	9%	5%	15%	10%	4%	0%
High School Grad.	46	29	75	60	23	4
Some College	15	23	5	30	27	19
Bachelor's Degree	28	21	5	—	39	37
Graduate or Prof. Degree	2	20	—	—	8	31
Other	—	2	—	—	—	10

2. Age

Median Age	
Wife	Husband
37	38

3. Total Family Income

| | Total Sample | Social Class | |
		Lower	Upper-Middle
Under 7,000	7%	5%	0%
7,001–9,000	2	5	0
9,001–11,000	15	25	12
11,001–13,000	20	20	22
13,001–15,000	20	30	15
15,001–20,000	21	15	33
Over 20,000	14	—	17

EXHIBIT 4

Mothers' Responses to Commercials by Child's Age

	Child's Age							
	4 + 5				7 + 9			
		Objectionable				Objectionable		
	Nothing	Little	Somewhat	Very	Nothing	Little	Somewhat	Very
Bits "Curtain"	78%	17%	6%	0%	86%	5%	9%	—%
K–K	56	22	22	0	77	9	5	9
Moo-Cow	61	11	27	0	77	18	5	—
Smacks (Boy)	67	17	11	6	77	18	5	—
Crunch-O	77	12	0	12	64	18	14	5
Smacks (Girl)	67	22	6	6	82	9	9	—
Bits "Dancing"	78	22	0	0	91	5	—	5

Mothers' Responses to Commercials by Social Class

	Social Class							
	Lower				Upper Middle			
		Objectionable				Objectionable		
	Nothing	Little	Somewhat	Very	Nothing	Little	Somewhat	Very
Bits "Curtain"	100%	—	—	—	74%	15%	11%	—
K–K	90	10%	—	—	59	15	19	7%
Moo-Cow	65	20	10%	5%	74	11	15	—
Smacks (Boy)	95	5	—	—	63	22	11	4
Crunch-O	100	—	—	—	54	23	12	12
Smacks (Girl)	95	5	—	—	67	19	11	4
Bits "Dancing"	100	—	—	—	78	15	4	4

Mothers' Responses to Parkland's Commercials

	1	2	3	4	5
Bits Commercials					
Understandable—(1)* not understandable—(5)	72%	13%	11%	2%	2%
Better than most commercials—(1) worse—(5)	28%	19%	32%	13%	9%
Child can fairly evaluate—(1) not fairly evaluate—(5)	62%	11%	23%	4%	—
Enjoyable for child—(1) not enjoyable—(5)	70%	15%	9%	4%	2%
Unlikely child misled—(1) likely child misled—(5)	57%	13%	9%	11%	11%
K–K					
Understandable– not understandable	53%	28%	9%	6%	4%
Better than most commercials–worse	17%	17%	43%	19%	4%

Total Sample (*n* = 500)
(Data from Questionnaire Given to Mothers)

EXHIBIT 4 *(cont.)*

Mothers' Responses to Parkland's Commercials

	1	2	3	4	5
Child can fairly evaluate–not fairly evaluate	49%	26%	15%	9%	2%
Enjoyable for child–not enjoyable	47%	17%	23%	6%	6%
Unlikely child misled–likely child misled	49%	19%	19%	11%	2
Moo-Cow					
Understandable–not understandable	64%	21%	6%	4%	4%
Better than most commercials–worse	32%	17%	32%	9%	11%
Child can fairly evaluate–not fairly evaluate	55%	19%	21%	2%	2%
Enjoyable for child–not enjoyable	70%	6%	19%	2%	2%
Unlikely child misled–likely misled	51%	13%	17%	11%	9%
Smacks (Girl)					
Understandable–not understandable	55%	19%	15%	9%	2%
Better than most commercials–worse	28%	17%	36%	15%	4%
Child can fairly evaluate–not fairly evaluate	45%	21%	19%	13%	2%
Enjoyable for child–not enjoyable	72%	13%	11%	2%	2%
Unlikely child misled–likely child misled	53%	11%	9%	17%	11%
Smacks (Boy)					
Understandable–not understandable	68%	15%	6%	11%	5%
Better than most commercials–worse	30%	19%	30%	13%	9%
Child can fairly evaluate–not fairly evaluate	55%	17%	21%	6%	—
Enjoyable for child–not enjoyable	75%	13%	9%	2%	2%
Unlikely child misled–likely child misled	57%	15%	17%	6%	4%
Crunch-O					
Understandable–not understandable	64%	11%	17%	4%	4%
Better than most commercials–worse	28%	21%	28%	11%	13%
Child can fairly evaluate–not fairly evaluate	47%	21%	17%	13%	2%
Enjoyable for child–not enjoyable	49%	17%	15%	15%	4%
Unlikely child misled–likely misled	68%	9%	19%	2%	2%

* Scale:
1 = "understandable" to 5 = "not understandable"
1 = "better than most commercials" to 5 = "worse than most"
1 = "child can fairly evaluate" to 5 = "not fairly evaluate"
1 = "enjoyable for child" to 5 = "not enjoyable"
1 = "unlikely child misled" to 5 = "likely child misled"

EXHIBIT 4 *(cont.)*

**Summary of Mothers' Responses to Parkland's Commercials:
Average Ratings Across the 5 Scales for Each
Commercial, by Child's Age and by Social Class**

	Child's Age		Social Class	
	4-6	7-9	Lower	Upper-Middle
Bits Commercials	10.89	7.90	7.90	10.37
K-K	11.83	8.95	8.95	11.70
Moo-Cow	10.50	9.55	9.55	9.67
Smacks (Boy)	9.78	7.70	7.70	10.30
Crunch-O	10.44	8.20	8.20	11.44
Smacks (Girl)	10.78	8.50	8.50	11.30

* For each commercial, an overall scale (positive-negative) was constructed by summing the score for each of the five dimensions, for each mother. Thus, a mother could have an average score ranging from 5 (if she rated a "1" for each dimension) to 25 (if she rated a "5" for each dimension). Since there are five dimensions for each commercial, scale values range from 5.00 to 25.00.

**Children's Judgements ("True" or "False") of Statements about
Commercials for Parkland's Products (*n* = 500)**

	Total Sample	
	% True	% False
1. Bits candy bars are a lot bigger than other candy bars.	5%	95%
2. If you gave a real live animal a Parkland's Smack, he would stop chasing you.	9	91
3. If you eat one K-K candy bar, you have to eat a second one, too.	3	97
4. Bits candy bars are about as big as other candy bars.	42	59
5. In the commercial for Parkland Smacks, they are just kidding when they show the kids feeding the animals Smacks—it's not like that in real life.	79	21
6. Milk is just as good for you *without* Parkland's Moo-Cow in it, as it is with Moo-Cow in it.	70	30
7. In the commercial for Moo-Cow the boy puts it in his milk and that makes it more nutritious.	28	72
8. In the commercial for Crunch-O candy bar the boy is real but the chicken is a cartoon.	96	4
9. Milk tastes better if you put Moo-Cow in it.	79	21
10. They want you to think that K-K candy bars are so light you want to eat two, but you can enjoy eating one just as much.	81	19
11. Milk is better for you if you put Moo-Cow in it.	19	81
12. Those were real animals in the Parkland Smack's commercial.	6	94

EXHIBIT 4 (cont.)

Children's Experience with Parkland's Products
(By Total Sample and Social Class)

Question: Have you ever tried (product name)?

Social Class

	Lower			Upper-Middle		
	A Lot	Sometimes	Never	A Lot	Sometimes	Never
Moo-Cow	8%	39%	54%	40%	40%	20%
K-K	7	43	50	13	53	33
Smacks	36	43	21	47	40	13
Crunch-O	21	29	50	7	47	47
Bits	0	21	79	13	40	47

Children's Attitudes toward Parkland's Products
(Total Sample)

Question: How much do you like each of these things?

Social Class

	Lower				Upper-Middle			
	A Lot	Little	Don't Like	Don't Know	A Lot	A Little	Don't Like	Don't Know
Moo-Cow	15%	39%	0%	46%	53%	20%	7%	20%
K-K	39	39	8	15	60	13	7	20
Smacks	62	31	—	7	67	27	7	—
Crunch-O	29	31	—	30	40	20	—	40
Bits	39	8	8	46	40	20	—	40
Choc-Bar	62	23	8	8	87	13	—	—

EXHIBIT 5

Attitudes toward Children's Eating Candy

Perception by:	Children %	Teenagers %	Adults* %
No Limit Set by Parents	11	29	12
Doesn't Mind—Within Reason	66	57	57
Likes Child to Have Only What Parent Gives	14	5	23
Would Not Like Child to Have Any	8	8	6

* Parents only. Based on national sample market research study.

EXHIBIT 6

Areas of Candy Concern
(Mean Values—6 Point Scale)*

	Children		Teenagers		Adults	
	Rank	Mean Score	Rank	Mean Score	Rank	Mean Score
Causes cavities	1	4.70	1	4.34	2	3.85
Sticks to teeth	2	4.09	3	4.07	1	4.07
Upsets stomach	3	4.00		2.81		2.07
Doesn't look good Eating in front of people	4	3.88		3.23		2.45
Messy to eat	5	3.84	4	3.60		3.04
Costs too much		3.72		2.93		2.14
Bad for skin		3.69	2	4.21		3.00
Spoils appetite		3.57		2.86		2.87
Fattening		3.49		3.15	5	3.17
Too sweet		3.41	5	3.54	3	3.30
Too rich		3.39		3.42	4	3.18
Can't stop eating		3.14		2.56		2.15
Artificially flavored		2.79		2.60		2.62
Don't like to be too good to myself		2.73		1.96		1.74
Have to share with others		2.62		2.00		1.49

* Highest rating indicates greatest degree of concern. Based on national sample market research study.

EXHIBIT 7
Frequency of Children's Attempts to Influence Purchases and Percentage of Mothers' "Usually" Yielding

Products	Frequency of Requests*				Percentage of Yielding			
	5–7 Years	8–10 Years	11–12 Years	Total**	5–7 Years	8–10 Years	11–12 Years	Total**
Relevant Foods								
Breakfast Cereal	1.26	1.59	1.97	1.59	88	91	83	87
Snack Foods	1.71	2.00	1.71	1.80	52	62	77	63
Candy	1.60	2.09	2.17	1.93	40	28	57	42
Soft Drinks	2.00	2.03	2.00	2.01	38	47	54	46
Jell-O	2.54	2.94	2.97	2.80	40	41	26	36
Overall Mean	1.82	2.13	2.16	2.03				
Overall Percentage					51.6	53.8	59.4	54.8
Less Relevant Foods								
Bread	3.12	2.91	3.43	3.16	14	28	17	19
Coffee	3.93	3.91	3.97	3.94	2	0	0	1
Pet Food	3.29	3.59	3.24	3.36	7	3	11	7
Overall Mean	3.45	3.47	3.49	3.49				
Overall Percentage					7.6	10.3	9.3	9.0
Durables, for Child's Use								
Game, Toy	1.24	1.63	2.17	1.65	57	59	46	54
Clothing	2.76	2.47	2.29	2.52	21	34	57	37
Bicycle	2.48	2.59	2.77	2.61	7	9	9	8
Hot Wheels	2.43	2.41	3.20	2.67	29	19	17	22
Record Album	3.36	2.63	2.23	2.78	12	16	46	24
Camera	3.91	3.75	3.71	3.80	2	3	0	2
Overall Mean	2.70	2.58	2.73	2.67				
Overall Percentage					25.6	28.0	35.0	29.4
Notions, Toiletries								
Toothpaste	2.29	2.31	2.60	2.39	36	44	40	39
Bath Soap	3.10	2.97	3.46	3.17	9	9	9	9
Shampoo	3.48	3.31	3.03	3.28	17	6	23	16
Aspirin	3.64	3.78	3.97	3.79	5	6	0	4
Overall Mean	3.13	3.09	3.26	3.16				
Overall Percentage					16.8	16.3	18.0	17.0
Other Products								
Automobile	3.55	3.66	3.51	3.57	2	0	0	12
Gasoline Brand	3.64	3.63	3.83	3.70	2	0	3	2
Laundry Soap	3.69	3.75	3.71	3.72	2	0	3	2
Household Cleaner	3.71	3.84	3.74	3.76	2	3	0	2
Overall Mean	3.65	3.72	3.70	3.69				
Overall Percent					2.0	.75	1.50	1.75

(Scale: 1 = "often"—4 = "never")

* On a scale from 1 = often to 4 = never.

** 5–7 years, n = 43; 8–10 years, n = 32; 11–12 years, n = 34; N = 109.

Source: S. Ward and D. B. Wackman. "Children's Purchase Influence Attempts and Parental Yielding," *Journal of Marketing Research,* 9 (August 1972), 316–19.

EXHIBIT 8

**Correlations between Child's Purchase Influence
Attempts, Parental Yielding, and the Independent Variables**

Independent Variables	Child's Purchase Influence Attempts	Parental Yielding
Demographics		
Child's Age	−.13	.20[a]*
Number of Children	−.00	−.00
Social Class	−.01	.00
Interpersonal Variables		
Parent-Child Conflict	.18[b]	−.00
Restrictions on Viewing	−.01	−.24***
Communication Variables		
Mother's Time Spent with Television	.18[b]	−.23
Recall of Commercials	.26[a]	.04
Attitudes toward Advertising	−.00	.16[b]

[a] $p < .01$.

[b] $p < .05$.

* Should be read: the greater the child's age, the greater the incidence of parental yielding to purchase influence attempts (or vice versa), and the correlation coefficient (.20) could only have occurred by chance once in 100 times.

** Should be read: the more parents put restrictions on children's television viewing, the less likely they are to yield to children's purchase influence attempts (or vice versa), and the correlation coefficient (−.24) could only have occurred by chance once in 100 times.

Source: S. Ward and D. B. Wackman. "Children's Purchase Influence Attempts and Parental Yielding," *Journal of Marketing Research,* 9 (August 1972), 316–19.

EXHIBIT 9

**Preliminary Results of Diary Study of
Children's Requests for Products and Services**

In order to assess the frequency and kinds of requests children make in the natural home environment, a team of Boston-area researchers had recently completed a diary study involving 289 mothers of 4–5 and 7–9 year-olds in upper-middle and lower-middle income areas in Boston. The following table presented preliminary results, as their analyses of the data were just beginning.

Each mother was trained to keep diaries of each day for 30 consecutive days (during the months of April and May). Each mother was trained to indicate everything her child asked for each day, which would involve an economic transaction. She also checked appropriate spaces in the diary to indicate her response to the child's request, and her child's subsequent response. Finally, she was asked to give an opinion (or indicate "don't know") concerning where she thought the child got the idea to want to buy the product.

Careful controls were used to maximize reliability: mothers were individually trained to fill out the diaries, a "hot line" was installed for questions, etc.

The total number of requests across all product categories over the 30-day period was 3,632, or an average number of requests per family of about 13. Thirty-nine percent of children recorded 15 or more requests during the month, Mr. Wackman was told. Age and social class differences were not yet analyzed.

EXHIBIT 9 *(cont.)*

Summary of Preliminary Results from Diary Study

Product Categories	% of Requests	Response to Child's Request				
		Yes, Didn't Mind	Yes, Discuss, or Chg.	No, Period	No Discuss	No, Chg: or Stall
Cereal	6.8*	66**	10	3	10	12
Candy	16.7	55	15	10	12	8
Toys	15.2	20	14	10	22	33
Clothing	10.1	46	21	3	9	22
Sporting Goods	5.2	21	17	6	23	34
Snack Foods	23.7	64	13	4	12	8
Other Foods	6.5	70	12	3	8	8
Other (misc., fruits, vegs., fast foods, OTC medicines, toothpaste)		55	15	5	11	14
OTC Medicines	< 1					
Toothpaste	< 1					
Fruits & Vegs.	3.6					
Fast Foods	3.5					
Misc.	6.4					
Average		49.6	14.6	5.5		15.4

Product Categories	Child's Reaction to "No"				Mothers' Perception of "Main Reason" Child Asked					
	Took it OK	Disap- pointed	Argue		Saw in Store	Saw on TV	Brother, Sister, Friend	Saw Ad for It	Don't Know	Other
			Little	Lot						
Cereal	14***	5	4	2	31****	31	9	4	7	33
Candy	13	7	8	2	41	12	17	3	10	23
Toys	35	15	8	7	23	45	26	5	3	10
Clothing	12	11	7	3	26	7	39	2	6	36
Sporting Goods	32	20	7	4	14	9	41	5	4	37
Snack Foods	10	4	4	6	24	8	15	4	12	39
Other Foods	11	3	3	2	21	29	5	3	6	40
Other (Misc., fruits, vegs., fast foods, OTC medicines, toothpaste)	14	10	5	1	22	18	14	4	7	40
OTC Medicines										
Toothpaste										
Fruits & Vegs.										
Fast Foods										
Misc.										
Average	17.5	9.0	4.3							

* Should be read: Of the 3,632 requests in one month, 6.8% were for cereals.

** Should be read: Of all responses to children's requests for cereals, 66% were "Yes, didn't mind."

*** Should be read: Of the 25% of responses to child's requests for cereals which were "No, period," "No, discuss" or "No, change child's request or stall" (see preceeding 3 columns), 14% of responses indicated that child "Took it OK."

**** Should be read: 31% of mothers indicated they felt main reason child asked for cereal was he/she "saw it in store." (Note that responses across this question do not add to 100% because some mothers indicated more than one perceived reason.)

Explanation of Response Categories in Diary Study

1. Response to Child's Request

   Mothers could check one space to indicate their response, from "Yes, didn't mind" (buying what the child asked for) to "No, change or stall" (that is, said no to child's request, but either tried to change child's mind about what was wanted, or stalled). Other categories are "Yes, discuss or change," meaning that the mother agreed to the requested purchase, but discussed it first, and/or tried to change the child's mind about what was wanted. "No, period," means a flat *no*, with no discussion, while "No, discuss," means that the mother said "no," but discussed her reasons with the child.

2. Child's Reaction to "No"

   For each purchase request to which mothers said "no" (any of the three "No" response categories), she also had to check a space to indicate her child's reaction to the "no." The categories under this heading are self-explanatory.

3. Mothers Perception of "Main Reason" Child Asked

   For each purchase request, mothers also were asked to check one of the spaces to indicate *what they think* was the main reason or influence on their child, leading to the purchase request. Some mothers checked more than one influence. The headings under this category are self-explanatory.

EXHIBIT 10

Average Hours per Day Spent Watching
Television, by Age Group

	2–5 Year Olds	6–11 Year Olds
November 1966	3.14	2.59
November–December 1969	4.04	3.22
January–February 1970	4.20	3.38

Source: A. C. Nielsen Company (data are from diaries and are highly consistent with data gathered by others, by other methods).

EXHIBIT 11

Types of Programs Watched by Children*
(1975)

	Total Viewers 2–11 Years Old (millions)
Brady Bunch	12.08
Partridge Family	11.73
Wonderful World of Disney	11.02
All in the Family	8.89
Emergency	8.89
Walters	8.89
Adam 12	7.47
Sonny and Cher	7.11
Sanford and Son	6.75
Room 222	6.40

* All are "prime time" shows, i.e., 7–10 P.M.

APPENDIX A

Ogilvy & Mather

2 East 48th Street, New York 10017

Client: Parkland Foods Corporation
Product: Chocolate Smacks
Title: "Boy" (Hippo)

MUSIC & SOUND EFFECTS
ANNCR. (VO): If a hippo
follows you home from
school . . .

kiss him quick (SFX-KISS)

with a Parkland's smack!

When a crocodile gives you
a smile and says "won't
you wait just a little while . . ."

kiss him quick (SFX-KISS)

with a Parkland's smack!

Parkland's Chocolate
Smacks.

Lots to a bag. So you can
spare one or two.

What do you do when a Kangaroo
puts his foot on the end of
your shoe? . . .

BOYS AND GIRLS (VO): Kiss
him quick (SFX:KISS)

with a Parkland's smack!

ANNCR: Parkland's Chocolate
Smacks.

Ogilvy & Mather

2 East 48th Street, New York 10017

Client: Parkland Foods Corporation
Product: Moo Cow
Title: "Cow in Apartment"

(SFX: MUSIC IN--UNDER & THROUGHOUT)

(SFX)

(SFX)

MOTHER'S VOICE: Finish your milk, George!

LITTLE BOY: There's a cow in the kitchen.
MOTHER'S VOICE: Finish your milk.

LITTLE BOY: Hey, what's that?

SINGERS: Moo Cow.

Gives milk that super Moo Cow taste.

That Moo Cow taste.

LITTLE BOY: A cow brought it!

COW (VO): MOOO!

SINGERS: Moo Cow.
Gives milk that super Moo Cow taste.

Ogilvy & Mather

2 East 48th Street, New York 10017

Client: Parkland Foods Corporation
Product: K-K
Title: "Two Lions"

NATURAL NOISES. BOY: Wherever I go, I always take along a couple of K-K.

What's a K-K?

A chocolate bar.

How come I take along two?

Well, on the outside, a K-K's so delicious and chocolatey. . .

CRUNCH

. . . you want to eat two.

CRUNCH

And on the inside it's so light and crispy and crunchy,

CRUNCH . . . you can eat two.

Chocolatey crispy Kit Kat. It's so light you can eat two?

ROAR, ROAR

Ogilvy & Mather

2 East 48th Street, New York 10017

Client: Parkland Foods Corporation
Product: Bits
Title: "Dancing Bits: 30"

ANNCR: Bits candy brings you.

Lots of chewy Bits in every roll.

JINGLE: There are lots of chewy Bits in a roll for you.

If you're choosey 'bout what you chew . . . Real milk chocolate and caramel too . . .

To chew chew chew . . . chew chew chew!

ANNCR: Choosey chewers can choose and chew

dee-licious chocolate covered caramels . . . Bits!

So choose the chews

choosey chewers choose!

Bits!

Lots of Bits in a roll for you!

Bits!

412

Agency: Ogilvy & Mather Inc.
Product: Crunch-0
Title: "Boy & Chicken Rev. 2"

BOY: Alright, Mildred.

Tell me the name of the
chocolate bar with the
krackelly chocolate taste.
MILDRED: Kaackel!

BOY: No! Here it is. The
chocolate bar with the krackelly
chocolate taste.

Now what is it?
MILDRED: Kaackel!

BOY: No. Crunch-0!

(SFX: BITE) Crunch-0 is full
of little crispies surrounded
by Parkland's milk chocolate.

So what's the chocolate bar
with the krackelly chocolate
taste?

MILDRED: Kaackel!
BOY: Crunch-0!

MILDRED: Kaackel.

BOY: Crunch-0.
MILDRED: Kaackel.

BOY: Crunch-0.
MILDRED: Kaackel.

BOY: Crunch-0.
MILDRED: Kaackel . . .

413

OGILVY & MATHER INC.

2 EAST 48 STREET, NEW YORK 10017
MURRAY HILL 8-8100

Client: Parkland Food Corporation
Product: Bits
Title: "Curtain Going Up-Rev."

1. ANNCR: (VO) Ladies
   and gentlemen: Bits
   candy presents the
   Chewy Bits.

2. (MUSIC UNDER)
   CHORUS: (VO) There
   are lots of chewy
   Bits . . .

3. . . . in a roll
   for you.

4. If you're choosy
   'bout what you chew

5. real milk chocolate
   and caramel too . .

6. . . . to chew, chew,
   chew, chew . . .

7. chew . . . chew
   . . . chew!

8. ANNCR: (VO) Bits.

9. Chewy caramel sur-
   rounded by rich milk
   chocolate.

10. Delicious. And you
    get lots in every
    roll.

11. CHOROUS: (VO) To
    chew, chew, chew,
    chew, chew, chew!

12. ANNCR: (VO) Bits!
    (MUSIC OUT)

APPENDIX B

Child Psychology Concepts*

The term "pre-operational" was coined by the eminent child psychologist, Jean Piaget. Piaget is generally recognized as the leading psychologist studying "cognitive development," i.e., processes by which children form attitudes, behavior patterns, and gain knowledge relevant to their functioning in the world. "Pre-operational children" (roughly ages three through seven) are characterized by their tendency to focus on perceptual aspects of stimuli (what they see is what is real for them), and conversely, lack of ability to abstract from what they see in the immediate environment, relative to older children. Research on responses to advertising has shown that pre-operational children often do not fully understand the concept of advertising—what commercials are, and what they try to do. Moreover, they recall less advertising content, i.e., they focus on a few elements of commercials. Finally, they use fewer dimensions to compare advertised brands for the same product, and these are often perceptual attributes (e.g., "one is bigger than the other").

"Concrete operational" children on the other hand (roughly ages seven or eight to about twelve) can engage in abstract thought, use more dimensions to compare brands, recall more elements in commercials, and are more likely to understand the concept of advertising and its intent, than are younger "pre-operational" children.

As an example of the differences in the abilities of children in these two age groups to process information, research has shown the following typical kinds of responses to questions about how to compare the following objects. Note that pre-operational children are most likely to compare the objects on the basis of perceptual cues, while concrete operational children can abstract, and compare them on the basis of their different furnctions:

	Responses	
Objects Compared	Pre-Operational	Concrete Operational
Car-Truck	"One is small, the other is big." "Trucks go faster."	"Cars carry people; trucks haul a lot of things." "Cars are used by families; trucks are used by businesses."
School-House	"School is a big building; a house is smaller." "Schools are red."	"Schools are where you go to learn; homes are where you live."

* For further information, see E. Zigler and I. L. Child. "Socialization," in *The Handbook of Social Psychology* (2nd. ed.), *The Individual in a Social Context*, II, ed. G. Lindzey and E. Aronson (Reading, Mass.: Addison-Wesley, 1969).